# Lecture Notes in Computer Science 13631

More information about this series at https://link.springer.com/bookseries/558

Sankalp Khanna · Jian Cao · Quan Bai ·
Guandong Xu (Eds.)

# PRICAI 2022: Trends in Artificial Intelligence

19th Pacific Rim International Conference on Artificial Intelligence
PRICAI 2022, Shanghai, China, November 10–13, 2022
Proceedings, Part III

 Springer

*Editors*
Sankalp Khanna 🆔
CSIRO Australian e-Health Research Centre
Brisbane, QLD, Australia

Quan Bai 🆔
University of Tasmania
Hobart, TAS, Australia

Jian Cao 🆔
Shanghai Jiao Tong University
Shanghai, China

Guandong Xu 🆔
University of Technology Sydney
Sydney, NSW, Australia

ISSN 0302-9743                    ISSN 1611-3349  (electronic)
Lecture Notes in Computer Science
ISBN 978-3-031-20867-6          ISBN 978-3-031-20868-3  (eBook)
https://doi.org/10.1007/978-3-031-20868-3

This Springer imprint is published by the registered company Springer Nature Switzerland AG
The registered company address is: Gewerbestrasse 11, 6330 Cham, Switzerland

# Preface

These three-volume proceedings contain the papers presented at the 19th Pacific Rim International Conference on Artificial Intelligence (PRICAI 2022), held as a hybrid conference with both physical and online options during November 10–13, 2022, in Shanghai, China.

PRICAI, which was inaugurated in Tokyo in 1990, started out as a biennial international conference concentrating on artificial intelligence (AI) theories, technologies, and applications in the areas of social and economic importance for Pacific Rim countries. It provides a common forum for researchers and practitioners in various branches of AI to exchange new ideas and share experience and expertise. Since then, the conference has grown, both in participation and scope, to be a premier international AI event for all major Pacific Rim nations as well as countries from all around the world. In 2018, the PRICAI Steering Committee decided to hold PRICAI on an annual basis starting from 2019.

This year, we received an overwhelming number of valid submissions to the main track (403 submissions), the special track (18 submissions), and the industry track (11 submissions). This number was impressive considering the continuing COVID-19 pandemic situation around the globe. All submissions were reviewed and evaluated with the same highest quality standard through a double-blind review process.

Each paper received at least two reviews, with over 90% receiving three or more. During the review process, discussions among the Program Committee (PC) members in charge were carried out before recommendations were made, and, when necessary, additional reviews were sourced. Finally, the conference and program co-chairs read the reviews and comments and made a final calibration for differences among individual reviewer scores in light of the overall decisions. The entire Program Committee (including PC members, external reviewers, and co-chairs) expended tremendous effort to ensure fairness and consistency in the paper selection process.

Eventually, we accepted 91 regular papers and 39 short papers for oral presentation. This gives a regular paper acceptance rate of 21% and an overall acceptance rate of 30%.

The technical program consisted of three workshops and the main conference program. The workshops included the "Principle and practice of data and Knowledge Acquisition Workshop (PKAW 2022)," the "Decoding Models of Human Emotion Using Brain Signals Workshop", and the "The 1st International Workshop on Democracy and AI (DemocrAI2022)". The main program included an industry track and a special track on "Strong and General AI."

All regular and short papers were orally presented over four days in parallel and in topical program sessions. We were honored to have keynote presentations by four distinguished researchers in the field of AI whose contributions have crossed discipline boundaries: Toby Walsh (University of New South Wales, Australia), Qing Li (Hong Kong Polytechnic University, China), Jie Lu (University of Technology Sydney, Australia), and Yu Zheng (JD Technology, China). We were grateful to them for sharing their insights on their latest research with us.

The success of PRICAI 2022 would not be possible without the effort and support of numerous people from all over the world. First, we would like to thank the authors, PC members, and external reviewers for their time and efforts spent in making PRICAI 2022 a successful and enjoyable conference. We are also thankful to various fellow members of the conference committee, without whose support and hard work PRICAI 2021 could not have been successful:

- Advisory Board: Abdul Sattar, Beyong Kang, Takayuki Ito, Zhihua Zhou, Chengqi Zhang, and Fenrong Liu
- Special Track Chairs: Ji Zhang and Biao Wang
- Industry Chair: Hengshu Zhu
- Workshop Chairs: Ryuta Arisaka and Zehong Cao
- Tutorial Chairs: Weiwei Yuan and Rafik Hadfi
- Finance Chair: Shiyou Qian
- Local/Virtual Organizing Chairs: Shiyou Qian and Nengjun Zhu
- Publicity Chairs: Yi Yang and Mukesh Prasad
- Sponsorship Chairs: Dengji Zhao and Xiangfeng Luo
- Webmaster: Shiqing Wu

We gratefully acknowledge the organizational support of several institutions including the University of Tasmania (Australia), the University of Technology Sydney (Australia), Shanghai Jiao Tong University (China), CSIRO (Australia), Griffith University (Australia), Kyoto University (Japan), ShanghaiTech University (China), the University of South Australia (Australia), Nanjing University of Aeronautics and Astronautics (China), Shanghai University (China), Hefei University of Technology (China), the University of Southern Queensland (Australia), and the Shanghai Computer Society (China). Finally, we thank the team at Springer for their assistance in publishing the PRICAI 2022 proceedings as three volumes of its Lecture Notes in Artificial Intelligence series.

November 2022

Sankalp Khanna
Jian Cao
Quan Bai
Guandong Xu

# Organization

## PRICAI Steering Committee

### Steering Committee

| | |
|---|---|
| Hideyuki Nakashima (Chair) | Future University Hakodate, Japan |
| Zhi-Hua Zhou (Vice-chair) | Nanjing University, China |
| Abdul Sattar (Treasurer) | Griffith University, Australia |
| Sankalp Khanna (Secretary) | CSIRO Australian e-Health Research Centre, Australia |
| Quan Bai | University of Tasmania, Australia |
| Tru Hoang Cao | Ho Chi Minh City University of Technology, Vietnam |
| Xin Geng | Southeast University, China |
| Guido Governatori | Singapore Management University, Singapore |
| Takayuki Ito | Kyoto University, Japan |
| Fenrong Liu | Tsinghua University, China |
| Byeong Ho Kang | University of Tasmania, Australia |
| M. G. M. Khan | University of the South Pacific, Fiji |
| Dickson Lukose | Monash University, Australia |
| Abhaya Nayak | Macquarie University, Australia |
| Seong-Bae Park | Kyung Hee University, South Korea |
| Duc Nghia Pham | MIMOS Berhad, Malaysia |
| Alok Sharma | RIKEN, Japan, and University of the South Pacific, Fiji |
| Thanaruk Theeramunkong | Thammasat University, Thailand |

### Honorary Members

| | |
|---|---|
| Randy Goebel | University of Alberta, Canada |
| Tu-Bao Ho | Japan Advanced Institute of Science and Technology, Japan |
| Mitsuru Ishizuka | University of Tokyo, Japan |
| Hiroshi Motoda | Osaka University, Japan |
| Geoff Webb | Monash University, Australia |
| Albert Yeap | Auckland University of Technology, New Zealand |
| Byoung-Tak Zhang | Seoul National University, South Korea |
| Chengqi Zhang | University of Technology Sydney, Australia |

## Conference Organizing Committee

### General Chairs

Guandong Xu                    University of Technology Sydney, Australia
Quan Bai                       University of Tasmania, Australia

### Program Chairs

Sankalp Khanna                 CSIRO Australian e-Health Research Centre,
                                   Australia
Jian Cao                       Shanghai Jiao Tong University, China

### Special Track Chairs

Ji Zhang                       University of Southern Queensland, Australia
Biao Wang                      Zhejiang Lab, China

### Industry Chair

Hengshu Zhu                    Baidu Inc., China

### Workshop Chairs

Ryuta Arisaka                  Kyoto University, Japan
Zehong Cao                     University of South Australia, Australia

### Tutorial Chairs

Weiwei Yuan                    Nanjing University of Aeronautics and
                                   Astronautics, China
Rafik Hadfi                    Kyoto University, Japan

### Local and Virtual Conference Chairs

Shiyou Qian                    Shanghai Jiao Tong University, China
Nengjun Zhu                    Shanghai University, China

### Finance Chair

Shiyou Qian                    Shanghai Jiao Tong University, China

### Sponsorship Chairs

Dengji Zhao                    ShanghaiTech University, China
Xiangfeng Luo                  Shanghai University, China

**Publicity Chairs**

Yi Yang                     Hefei University of Technology, China
Mukesh Prasad               University of Technology Sydney, Australia

**Webmaster**

Shiqing Wu                  University of Tasmania, Australia

**Advisory Board**

Abdul Sattar                Griffith University, Australia
Byeong Kang                 University of Tasmania, Australia
Takayuki Ito                Kyoto University, Japan
Zhihua Zhou                 Nanjing University, China
Chengqi Zhang               University of Technology Sydney, Australia
Fenrong Liu                 Tsinghua University, China

# Program Committee

Eriko Aiba                  University of Electro-Communications, China
Abdullah Alsuhaibani        University of Technology Sydney, Australia
Patricia Anthony            Lincoln University, New Zealand
Mohammad Arshi Saloot       MIMOS Berhad, Malaysia
Mohamed Jaward Bah          Zhejiang Lab, China
Quan Bai                    University of Tasmania, Australia
Chutima Beokhaimook         Rangsit University, Thailand
Ateet Bhalla                Independent Technology Consultant, India
Chih How Bong               Universiti Malaysia Sarawak, Malaysia
Poonpong Boonbrahm          Walailak University, Thailand
Aida Brankovic              CSIRO Australian e-Health Research Centre,
                            Australia
Xiongcai Cai                University of New South Wales, Australia
Jian Cao                    Shanghai Jiao Tong University, China
Jimmy Cao                   University of South Australia, Australia
Tru Cao                     University of Texas Health Science Center at
                            Houston, USA
Hutchatai Chanlekha         Kasetsart University, Thailand
Siqi Chen                   Tianjin University, China
Songcan Chen                Nanjing University of Aeronautics and
                            Astronautics, China
Tony Chen                   University of Adelaide, Australia
Wu Chen                     Southwest University, China
Yakun Chen                  University of Technology Sydney, Australia

| | |
|---|---|
| Van Nam Huynh | Japan Advanced Institute of Science and Technology (JAIST), Japan |
| Masashi Inoue | Tohoku Institute of Technology, Japan |
| Md Rafiqul Islam | University of Technology Sydney, Australia |
| Takayuki Ito | Kyoto University, Japan |
| Sanjay Jain | National University of Singapore, Singapore |
| Guifei Jiang | Nankai University, China |
| Ting Jiang | Zhejiang Lab, China |
| Yichuan Jiang | Southeast University, China |
| Nattagit Jiteurtragool | King Mongkut's University of Technology North Bangkok, Thailand |
| Hideaki Kanai | Japan Advanced Institute of Science and Technology (JAIST), Japan |
| Ryo Kanamori | Nagoya University, Japan |
| Natsuda Kaothanthong | Thammasat University, Thailand |
| Jessada Karnjana | National Electronics and Computer Technology Center, Thailand |
| C. Maria Keet | University of Cape Town, South Africa |
| Gabriele Kern-Isberner | Technische Universitaet Dortmund, Germany |
| Nor Khalid | Auckland University of Technology, New Zealand |
| Sankalp Khanna | CSIRO Australian e-Health Research Centre, Australia |
| Nichnan Kittiphattanabawon | Walailak University, Thailand |
| Sébastien Konieczny | CRIL - CNRS, France |
| Alfred Krzywicki | University of Adelaide, Australia |
| Li Kuang | Central South University, China |
| Young-Bin Kwon | Chung-Ang University, South Korea |
| Ho-Pun Lam | Data61, CSIRO, Australia |
| Nasith Laosen | Phuket Rajabhat University, Thailand |
| Siddique Latif | University of Southern Queensland, Australia |
| Roberto Legaspi | KDDI Research, Inc., Japan |
| Gang Li | Deakin University, Australia |
| Guangliang Li | Ocean University of China, China |
| Qian Li | Chinese Academy of Sciences, China |
| Tianrui Li | Southwest Jiaotong University, China |
| Weihua Li | Auckland University of Technology, New Zealand |
| Yicong Li | University of Technology Sydney, Australia |
| Zihao Li | University of Technology Sydney, Australia |
| Chanjuan Liu | Dalian University of Technology, China |
| Guanfeng Liu | Macquarie University, Australia |
| Hao Liu | HKUST(GZ), China |
| Kangzheng Liu | Huazhong University of Science and Technology, China |

Tun Lu                          Fudan University, China
Dickson Lukose                  GCS Agile Pty. Ltd., Australia
Xiangfeng Luo                   Shanghai University, China
Haiping Ma                      Anhui University, China
Michael Maher                   Reasoning Research Institute, Australia
Xinjun Mao                      National University of Defense Technology,
                                China
Eric Martin                     University of New South Wales, Australia
Sanparith Marukatat             NECTEC, Thailand
Michael Mayo                    University of Waikato, New Zealand
Qingxin Meng                    Nottingham University Business School, China
Nor Liyana Mohd Shuib           Universiti Malaya, Malaysia
M. A. Hakim Newton              University of Newcastle, Australia
Phi Le Nguyen                   Hanoi University of Science and Technology,
                                Vietnam
Kouzou Ohara                    Aoyama Gakuin University, Japan
Mehmet Orgun                    Macquarie University, Australia
Maurice Pagnucco                University of New South Wales, Australia
Songwen Pei                     University of Shanghai for Science and
                                Technology, China
Laurent Perrussel               IRIT, Université de Toulouse, France
Bernhard Pfahringer             University of Waikato, New Zealand
Jantima Polpinij                Mahasarakham University, Thailand
Thadpong Pongthawornkamol       Kasikorn Business-Technology Group, Thailand
Mukesh Prasad                   University of Technology, Sydney, Australia
Shiyou Qian                     Shanghai Jiao Tong University, China
Chuan Qin                       Baidu, China
Joel Quinqueton                 LIRMM, France
Teeradaj Racharak               Japan Advanced Institute of Science and
                                Technology, Japan
Jessica Rahman                  Australian National University, Australia
Farid Razzak                    New York University, USA
Fenghui Ren                     University of Wollongong, Australia
Mark Reynolds                   University of Western Australia, Australia
Vahid Riahi                     CSIRO Australian e-Health Research Centre,
                                Australia
Kazumi Saito                    University of Shizuoka, Japan
Chiaki Sakama                   Wakayama University, Japan
Nicolas Schwind                 National Institute of Advanced Industrial Science
                                and Technology (AIST), Japan
Lin Shang                       Nanjing University, China
Alok Sharma                     RIKEN, Japan

| | |
|---|---|
| Dazhong Shen | University of Science and Technology of China, China |
| Chenwei Shi | Tsinghua University, China |
| Kaize Shi | University of Technology Sydney, Australia |
| Zhenwei Shi | Beihang University, China |
| Soo-Yong Shin | Sungkyunkwan University, South Korea |
| Yanfeng Shu | CSIRO, Australia |
| Chattrakul Sombattheera | Mahasarakham University, Thailand |
| Insu Song | James Cook University, Australia |
| Markus Stumptner | University of South Australia, Australia |
| Xing Su | Beijing University of Technology, China |
| Xin Sun | Catholic University of Lublin, Poland |
| Ying Sun | The Hong Kong University of Science and Technology (Guangzhou), China |
| Boontawee Suntisrivaraporn | DTAC, Thailand |
| Thepchai Supnithi | NECTEC, Thailand |
| David Taniar | Monash University, Australia |
| Xiaohui Tao | University of Southern Queensland, Australia |
| Yanyun Tao | Soochow University, China |
| Mingfei Teng | Rutgers University, USA |
| Michael Thielscher | University of New South Wales, Australia |
| Satoshi Tojo | Japan Advanced Institute of Science and Technology (JAIST), Japan |
| Shikui Tu | Shanghai Jiao Tong University, China |
| Miroslav Velev | Aries Design Automation, USA |
| Muriel Visani | Hanoi University of Science and Technology, Vietnam, and La Rochelle University, France |
| Nhi N. Y. Vo | Royal Melbourne Institute of Technology University, Vietnam |
| Biao Wang | Zhejiang Lab, China |
| Chao Wang | Guangzhou HKUST Fok Ying Tung Research Institute, China |
| Hao Wang | Nanyang Technological University, Singapore |
| Xiangmeng Wang | University of Technology, Sydney, Australia |
| Xinxhi Wang | Shanghai University, China |
| Zhen Wang | Zhejiang Lab, China |
| Xiao Wei | Shanghai University, China |
| Paul Weng | UM-SJTU Joint Institute, China |
| Yang Wenli | University of Tasmania, Australia |
| Wayne Wobcke | University of New South Wales, Australia |
| Sartra Wongthanavasu | Khon Kaen University, Thailand |
| Brendon J. Woodford | University of Otago, New Zealand |

| | |
|---|---|
| Hongyue Wu | Zhejiang University, China |
| Ou Wu | Tianjin University, China |
| Shiqing Wu | University of Technology Sydney, Australia |
| Xing Wu | Shanghai University, China |
| Xiaoyu Xia | University of Southern Queensland, Australia |
| Kaibo Xie | University of Amsterdam, The Netherlands |
| Dawei Xu | University of Technology Sydney, Australia |
| Guandong Xu | University of Technology Sydney, Australia |
| Ming Xu | Xi'an Jiaotong-Liverpool University, China |
| Shuxiang Xu | University of Tasmania, Australia |
| Zenghui Xu | Zhejiang Lab, China |
| Hui Xue | Southeast University, China |
| Kong Yan | Nanjing University of Information, Science and Technology, China |
| Bo Yang | University of Science and Technology of China, China |
| Chao Yang | University of Technology, Sydney, Australia |
| Haoran Yang | University of Technology Sydney, Australia |
| Wencheng Yang | University of Southern Queensland, Australia |
| Yang Yang | Nanjing University of Science and Technology, China |
| Yi Yang | Hefei University of Technology, China |
| Roland Yap | National University of Singapore, Singapore |
| Kenichi Yoshida | University of Tsukuba, Japan |
| Dianer Yu | University of Technology Sydney, Australia |
| Hang Yu | Shanghai University, China |
| Ting Yu | Zhejiang Lab, China |
| Weiwei Yuan | Nanjing University of Aeronautics and Astronautics, China |
| Takaya Yuizono | Japan Advanced Institute of Science and Technology (JAIST), Japan |
| Du Zhang | California State University, USA |
| Haijun Zhang | Harbin Institute of Technology Shenzhen Graduate School, China |
| Ji Zhang | University of Southern Queensland, Australia |
| Le Zhang | University of Science and Technology of China, China |
| Min-Ling Zhang | Southeast University, China |
| Qi Zhang | University of Science and Technology of China, China |
| Shichao Zhang | Guangxi Normal University, China |
| Wen Zhang | Beijing University of Technology, China |
| Xiaobo Zhang | Southwest Jiaotong University, China |

| | |
|---|---|
| Xuyun Zhang | Macquarie University, Australia |
| Yang Zhang | Zhejiang Lab, China |
| Zili Zhang | Deakin University, Australia |
| Dengji Zhao | ShanghaiTech University, China |
| Hongke Zhao | Tianjin University, China |
| Ruilin Zhao | Huazhong University of Science and Technology, China |
| Sirui Zhao | Southwest University of Science and Technology, China |
| Yanchang Zhao | CSIRO, Australia |
| Shuigeng Zhou | Fudan University, China |
| Chen Zhu | Baidu Talent Intelligence Center, China |
| Guohun Zhu | University of Queensland, Australia |
| Hengshu Zhu | Baidu Inc., China |
| Nengjun Zhu | Shanghai University, China |
| Xingquan Zhu | Florida Atlantic University, USA |
| Guobing Zou | Shanghai University, China |

## Additional Reviewers

Agyemang, Brighter
Arisaka, Ryuta
Bea, Khean Thye
Burgess, Doug
Cao, Zehong
Chalothorn, Tawunrat
Chandra, Abel
Chandra, Rohitash
Chen, Siqi
Clifton, Marshall
Colley, Rachael
Dawoud, Ahmed
Delobelle, Jérôme
Dinh, Thi Ha Ly
Duan, Jiaang
Duchatelle, Théo
Effendy, Suhendry
Everaere, Patricia
Feng, Shanshan
Feng, Xuening
Gao, Jianqi
Gao, Shang
Gao, Yi
Geng, Chuanxing

Haiyang, Xia
Han, Aiyang
Hang, Jun-Yi
He, Yifan
He, Zhengqi
Hu, Jianshu
Hu, Liang
Hu, Mengting
Hu, Yuxuan
Ishikawa, Yuichi
Jia, Binbin
Jiang, Shan
Jiang, Yunpeng
Jiang, Zhaohui
Khan, Naimat Ullah
Kliangkhlao, Mallika
Konishi, Tatsuya
Kumar, Shiu
Lai, Zhong Yuan
Le, Van An
Leow, Steven
Li, Jinpeng
Li, Li
Li, Pengbo

Li, Renjie
Li, Ruijun
Li, Shu
Lin, Shuxia
Liu, Xiaxue
Liu, Yuxin
Ma, Zhongchen
Malysiak, Kevin
Mayer, Wolfgang
Meng, Qiang
Mezza, Stefano
Mi, Yuxi
Miao, Ran
Ming, Zuheng
Mittelmann, Munyque
Muhammod, Rafsanjani
Ngo, Courtney
Nguyen, Mau Toan
Nguyen, Minh Hieu
Nguyen, Trong-Tung
Nguyen, Trung Thanh
Niu, Hao
Parker, Timothy
Pereira, Gean

Pho, Ngoc Dang Khoa
Pino Perez, Ramon
Polpinij, Jantima
Qian, Junqi
Raboanary, Toky Hajatiana
Rashid, Mahmood
Ren, Yixin
Riahi, Vahid
Rosenberg, Manou
Sahoh, Bukhoree
Selway, Matt
Sharma, Ronesh
Shi, Jingli
Shi, Kaize
Song, Baobao
Song, Zhihao
Sun, Qisong
Sun, Ruoxi
Takeda, Naoto
Tan, Hongwei
Tang, Huaying

Tang, Wei
Tao, Yanyun
Thao Nguyen, Truong
Tran, Kim Dung
Vo, Chau
Wang, Deng-Bao
Wang, Guodong
Wang, Hui
Wang, Mengyan
Wang, Xinyu
Wang, Zirui
Wanyana, Tezira
Wardah, Wafaa
Wu, Yao
Xia, Dawen
Xia, Yewei
Xiangru, Yu
Xie, Kaibo
Xu, Rongxin
Yang, Bo
Yang, Yang

Yang, Yikun
Yang, Zhichao
Yao, Naimeng
Ye, Tangwei
Yi, Fan
Yin, Ze
Yu, Guanbao
Yu, Yongxin
Yuan, Weiwei
Zang, Hao
Zhang, Chris
Zhang, Jiaqiang
Zhang, Qingyong
Zhang, Sixiao
Zhang, Tianyi
Zhang, Yao
Zhang, Yi-Fan
Zhao, Jianing
Zhou, Wei

# Contents – Part III

# Recommender System

# Mixture of Graph Enhanced Expert Networks for Multi-task Recommendation

Binbin Hu[✉], Bin Shen, Ruize Wu, Zhiqiang Zhang, Yuetian Cao, Yong He,
Liang Zhang, Linjian Mo, and Jun Zhou

Ant Group, Hangzhou, China
{bin.hbb,ringo.sb,kezhui.wrz,lingyao.zzq,yuetian.cyt,
heyong.h,zhuyue.zl,linyi01,jun.zhoujun}@antfin.com

**Abstract.** Multi-task learning (MTL), which jointly tackles multiple tasks through information sharing, has been widely applied to many recommendation applications. Recently, current efforts targeted for recommendation focus on learning task relationships based on the Multi-gate Mixture-of-Experts (MMoE) architecture with shared input features (*i.e.,* subtle feature engineering for user-item interaction). Recent evidences suggest the Graph Neural Network (GNN) as a powerful component in characterizing deep interaction context for recommendation, greatly contributing to easing the data sparseness issue in online advertising services. Hence, we make the first attempt to explore the GNN towards multi-task recommendation, by designing Mixture of Graph enhanced Expert Networks (**MoGENet**). Specifically, we propose a novel multi-channel graph neural network to jointly model high-order information with the user-item bipartite graph as well as derived collaborative similarity graphs for users and items. On the top of the learned deep interaction context, a group of graph enhanced expert networks are introduced for contributing to the multi-task recommendation in a cooperative manner. Experimental results on three real-world datasets show that MoGENet consistently and significantly outperforms state-of-the-art baselines across all target tasks.

**Keywords:** Multi-task learning · Graph learning · Recommender system

## 1 Introduction

The recent integration of multi-task learning into recommender systems (*e.g.,* the Multi-gate Mixture-of-Experts (MMoE) architecture [13] and its variants [12,19]) has demonstrated remarkable strength of comprehensively capturing users' inherent preferences by jointly tackling multiple target behaviors (*e.g.,* click and conversion) [3,8,10,14,25,26]. Unfortunately, its success hinges on the subtle feature engineering and large amounts of labeled data, which are not always easily available (*i.e.,* the undesired data sparseness issue). Although knowledge transfer among multiple tasks (*i.e.,* click and conversion) could be

© The Author(s), under exclusive license to Springer Nature Switzerland AG 2022
S. Khanna et al. (Eds.): PRICAI 2022, LNCS 13631, pp. 3–16, 2022.
https://doi.org/10.1007/978-3-031-20868-3_1

effectively captured by current multi-task recommendation methods, it is still infeasible to obtain enough training data and handcrafted features for long-tailed items in industrial settings. With the increasingly available historical user-item interaction records, characterizing the high-order user-item based connectivity and the user (item) based collaborative similarity sheds some lights on easing the data sparseness issue and facilitating multi-task recommendation.

While it is appealing to distill the connectivity and collaborative similarity from interaction history for the multi-task recommendation, the solution is non-trivial, with several challenges. (1) *How to flexibly extract the most relevant/important information for characterizing interaction?* The high-order user-item connectivity, as well as the collaborative similarity, is complicated. It is imperative to design a unified module to produce expressive representations by exploring and exploiting useful graph structural information in an automatic manner. (2) *How to effectively incorporate learned deep interaction context for contributing to multi-task recommendation?* The learned deep interaction context is composed of different view (*i.e.*, connectivity and similarity) based representations , which drives us to develop a new architecture to incorporate such information for the multi-task recommendation in a cooperative manner.

Recent evidences show that graph neural networks [9,21,28] have the excellent ability in structural feature learning and have been widely adopted in recommender systems for characterizing interaction context [24,31] and side information [2,23]. Inspired by these works, we make the first attempt to investigate the effectiveness of the graph neural network to multi-task recommendation by designing Mixture of Graph enhanced Expert Networks (**MoGENet**) . For simultaneously capturing the high-order user-item based connectivity and the user (item) based collaborative similarity, we propose a novel multi-channel graph neural network (MGNN) module to flexibly learn the most relevant/important information on the bipartite graph as well as derived collaborative similarity graphs for users and items. Based on the learned deep interaction context, we introduce graph enhanced expert networks, which are built upon the architecture of MMoE to flexibly incorporate such context for contributing to the multi-task recommendation. To well guide the learning process of MoGENet, we weigh the loss of each task in an automatic manner and balance multiple parallel expert networks for recommendation in a cooperative way. At last, we conduct extensive experiments on a benchmark and two industrial datasets respectively to show the superiorities of MoGENet.

## 2   The Proposed Method

In this section, we present MoGENet, a novel multi-task recommendation method that leverages the deep interaction context with graph learning. The overall architecture of MoGENet is illustrated in Fig. 1. We start with the construction of the bipartite graph and derived collaborative similarity graphs based on historical user-item interaction records with the user set $\mathcal{U}$ and the item set

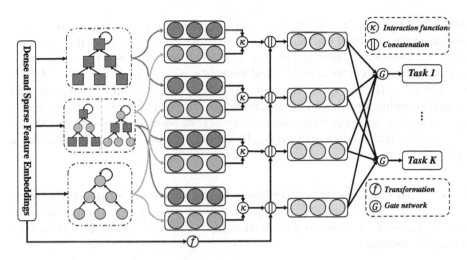

**Fig. 1.** The overall architecture of MoGENet, which consists of multi-channel graph neural network module and graph enhance expert networks.

$\mathcal{I}$. Here, each $\langle u, i \rangle$ is assigned $K$ related labels (*e.g.*, click and conversion in e-commerce scenarios), denoted as $y_{u,i}$. Formally, we define the user-item **Bipartite Graph** as $\mathcal{G} = \{\mathcal{U}, \mathcal{I}, \mathcal{E}\}$ with the user set $\mathcal{U}$ and the item set $\mathcal{I}$. Moreover, $\mathcal{E} \subset \mathcal{U} \times \mathcal{I}$ is the edge set between $\mathcal{U}$ and $\mathcal{I}$ where $e_{u,i} = e_{i,u} = 1$ if and only if $\sum_{k=1}^{K} y_{u,i}^{k} \geq 1$.

In order to effectively exploit deep interaction context for recommendation, we further define collaborative similarity for users (items) with the similar click (clicked) and purchase (purchased) history. Hence, we define the **User based Collaborative Similarity Graph** as $\mathcal{G}^{\mathcal{U}} = \{\mathcal{U}, \mathcal{E}^{\mathcal{U}}\}$ with the user set $\mathcal{U}$ and edge set $\mathcal{E}^{\mathcal{U}} \subset \mathcal{U} \times \mathcal{U}$. Here, $e_{u,v} = e_{v,u} = sim(u,v)$ calculated by the common interaction history of the users [27]. Analogously, we also denote the **Item based Collaborative Similarity Graph** as $\mathcal{G}^{\mathcal{I}}$.

## 2.1 Deep Interaction Context Exploitation with Multi-channel Graph Neural Network

In order to take full advantage of the high-order connectivity in $\mathcal{G}$ and the collaborative similarity in $\mathcal{G}^{\mathcal{U}}$ and $\mathcal{G}^{\mathcal{I}}$, we propose a <u>M</u>ulti-channel <u>G</u>raph <u>N</u>eural <u>N</u>etwork (MGNN) to effectively aggregate most informative neighbors in each channel (*i.e.*, graph). To avoid the over-parameterized issue, the proposed MGNN applies graph learning on each channel with shared initial representations for users and items. Specifically, we encode the feature vector (*i.e.*, $\mathbf{x}_u, \mathbf{x}_i$) of user $u$ and item $i$ into $\boldsymbol{p}_u, \boldsymbol{q}_i \in \mathbb{R}^d$, which are shared in the following propagations and aggregations with bipartite and collaborative similarity graphs.

**MGNN Module.** In general, the underlying reason for the interaction between target user $u$ and item $i$ is fairly complicated, which may be contributed by not only the historical interaction records (*i.e.*, $\mathcal{G}$), but also the deep collaborative similarity between users (*i.e.*, $\mathcal{G}^{\mathcal{U}}$) and items (*i.e.*, $\mathcal{G}^{\mathcal{I}}$). Formally, let $\boldsymbol{h}_u^0 = \boldsymbol{h}_u^{\mathcal{U},0} = \boldsymbol{p}_u$ and $\boldsymbol{h}_i^0 = \boldsymbol{h}_i^{\mathcal{I},0} = \boldsymbol{q}_i$ be the first input layers for the MGNN module with shared encoding for users and items. Subsequently, MGNN layers in each channel can recursively propagate the connectivity or collaborative similarity in different graphs by neighborhood aggregation. Here, we zoom into the detailed process as below.

**MGNN to Capture the User-Item Collaborative Connectivity in $\mathcal{G}$.** Given the $l$-th layer input $\boldsymbol{h}_u^l$ and $\boldsymbol{h}_i^l$ for each user $u$ and item $i$ respectively, we update the user and item representation $\boldsymbol{h}_u^{l+1}$ and $\boldsymbol{h}_i^{l+1}$ at the $(l+1)$-th layer with $\mathcal{G}$ as follows:

$$
\begin{aligned}
\boldsymbol{h}_u^{l+1} &= f(\boldsymbol{h}_u^l, \sigma(\mathbf{W} \sum_{i \in \mathcal{N}(u)} \alpha_{u \leftarrow i} \boldsymbol{h}_i^l)), \\
\boldsymbol{h}_i^{l+1} &= f(\boldsymbol{h}_i^l, \sigma(\mathbf{W} \sum_{u \in \mathcal{N}(i)} \alpha_{i \leftarrow u} \boldsymbol{h}_u^l)),
\end{aligned}
\tag{1}
$$

where $\sigma(\cdot)$ is the LeakyReLU activation function, $\mathbf{W} \in \mathbb{R}^{d \times d}$ is the weight matrix for graph $\mathcal{G}$, $\mathcal{N}(u)$ and $\mathcal{N}(i)$ is the neighbor set of user $u$ and item $i$ in $\mathcal{G}$, respectively. $\alpha_{u \leftarrow i}$ and $\alpha_{i \leftarrow u}$ are implemented by the emerging attention mechanism [20], indicating how much information being propagated through the connectivity $u \leftarrow i$ and $i \leftarrow u$ in $\mathcal{G}$, respectively. $f(\cdot)$ aims to aggregate the messages propagated from corresponding neighbors, which is implemented as the LSTM-like operator, inspired by [29].

**MGNN to Capture the User (item) Based Collaborative Similarity in $\mathcal{G}^U (\mathcal{G}^I)$.** For each user $u$ (item $i$), with its $l$-th layer representation $\boldsymbol{h}_u^{\mathcal{U},l}$ ($\boldsymbol{h}_i^{\mathcal{I},l}$), the updated representation $\boldsymbol{h}_u^{\mathcal{U},l+1}$ ($\boldsymbol{h}_i^{\mathcal{I},l+1}$) in $\mathcal{G}^{\mathcal{U}}$ ($\mathcal{G}^{\mathcal{I}}$) can be calculated as follows:

$$
\begin{aligned}
\boldsymbol{h}_u^{\mathcal{U},l+1} &= f(\boldsymbol{h}_u^{\mathcal{U},l}, \sigma(\mathbf{W}^{\mathcal{U}} \sum_{u \in \mathcal{N}^{\mathcal{U}}(u)} \alpha_{u \leftarrow u} \boldsymbol{h}_u^{\mathcal{U},l})), \\
\boldsymbol{h}_i^{\mathcal{I},l+1} &= f(\boldsymbol{h}_i^{\mathcal{I},l}, \sigma(\mathbf{W}^{\mathcal{I}} \sum_{i \in \mathcal{N}^{\mathcal{I}}(i)} \alpha_{i \leftarrow i} \boldsymbol{h}_i^{\mathcal{I},l})),
\end{aligned}
\tag{2}
$$

where $\mathbf{W}^{\mathcal{U}}, \mathbf{W}^{\mathcal{I}} \in \mathbb{R}^{d \times d}$ is the weight matrix for $\mathcal{G}^{\mathcal{U}}$ and $\mathcal{G}^{\mathcal{I}}$, $\mathcal{N}^{\mathcal{U}}(u)$ and $\mathcal{N}^{\mathcal{I}}(i)$ is the set of collaborative similar neighbors of user $u$ and item $i$ respectively, and $\alpha_{u \leftarrow u}$ and $\alpha_{i \leftarrow i}$ controls the information propagation in $\mathcal{G}^{\mathcal{U}}$ and $\mathcal{G}^{\mathcal{I}}$ respectively.

Through propagation processes, MGNN refines the representations in each channel (*i.e.*, $\boldsymbol{h}_u^{l+1}, \boldsymbol{h}_i^{l+1}, \boldsymbol{h}_u^{\mathcal{U},l+1}, \boldsymbol{h}_i^{\mathcal{I},l+1}$) by aggregating most related information from different graphs at the $l$-th layer.

## 2.2 Graph Enhanced Expert Network

In this part, we investigate into the integration of learned graph representation for multi-task recommendation. As proved in previous works [10,13,17], the design of expert networks guarantees the soft-parameter sharing for modeling task relations and conflicts. Therefore, we build upon the architecture of multi-gate of mixture-of-experts (MMoE) to incorporate graph learning for facilitating multi-task recommendation.

Intuitively, the interactions between users and items are facilitated with not only the bipartite graph, but also corresponding collaborative similarity graphs. Given a user-item pair $\langle u, i \rangle$, after $L$ layers' propagations, we obtain the final graph representation list $\{h_u^L, h_i^L, h_u^{\mathcal{U},L}, h_i^{\mathcal{I},L}\}$, which jointly captures user preferences and item attributes in different graphs. In order to take full advantage of information derived from different graphs, we propose to apply the graph representation interaction between user $u$ and item $i$ in a pair-wise manner.

$$\mathcal{Z} = \{\kappa(h_u^L, h_i^L), \kappa(h_u^L, h_i^{\mathcal{I},L}), \kappa(h_u^{\mathcal{U},L}, h_i^L), \kappa(h_u^{\mathcal{U},L}, h_i^{\mathcal{I},L})\}, \tag{3}$$

where $\kappa(\cdot, \cdot)$ is the interaction function, which can be set as element-wise product, concatenation or multi-layer perceptron, and the corresponding studies are detailed in the experiment part.

In our study, for convenience, we let $|\mathcal{Z}| = N$, which is also the number of expert networks in our model. We denote our expert networks as $\{f^n(\cdot)\}_{n=1}^{N}$, and equip each task $k$ with a separate gating network $g^k(\cdot)$. The output of task $k$ is calculated as follows:

$$o_{u,i}^k = v^T \sum_{n=1}^{N} g^k([\mathbf{x}_u \parallel \mathbf{x}_i])_n [f^n([\mathbf{x}_u \parallel \mathbf{x}_i]) \parallel \mathcal{Z}^n], \tag{4}$$

where "$\parallel$" is the concatenation operator and $v$ is the weight vector for output. Following the common strategies in previous related works [10,13,17], the $n$-th expert network $f^n(\cdot)$ is implemented as the identical multi-layer perceptron with the LeakyReLU activation function, while the $k$-th gating network $g^k(\cdot)$ is implemented as the simple linear transformation of the input with a softmax layer.

## 2.3 Model Learning

We guide the learning process of MoGENet by jointly optimizing multiple related tasks. For the $k$-th task, we adopt the commonly used binary cross entropy as the loss function. Hence, the main loss function can be formulated as follows:

$$\mathcal{L}_{main} = \sum_{k=1}^{K} \mathcal{L}^k = \sum_{k=1}^{K} \sum_{\langle u,i \rangle \in \mathcal{H}} \mathcal{C}(\hat{y}_{u,i}^k, y_{u,i}^k), \tag{5}$$

where $\mathcal{C}(\cdot, \cdot)$ is the cross entropy function. Inspired by the idea of homoscedastic uncertainty [6], we adaptively weigh the loss of each task during model training.

**Algorithm 1.** Model training for MoGENet

**Require:** Bipartite Graph $\mathcal{G} = \{\mathcal{U}, \mathcal{I}, \mathcal{E}\}$, historical user-item interaction records $\mathcal{H} = \{u, i, y_{u,i} | u \in \mathcal{U}, i \in \mathcal{I}, y_{u,i} \in \{0,1\}^K\}$, user features $\{\mathbf{x}_u | u \in \mathcal{U}\}$ and item features $\{\mathbf{x}_i | i \in \mathcal{I}\}$.

1: Obtain $\mathcal{G}^{\mathcal{U}}$ and $\mathcal{G}^{\mathcal{I}}$ from $\mathcal{G}$ through collaborative similarity.
2: Initialize $\{\mathbf{P}, \mathbf{Q}\}$ and other global parameters (*e.g.*, $\mathbf{W}^{\mathcal{U}}$ and $\mathbf{W}^{\mathcal{I}}$) for the MGNN module, and initialize $\{\Theta, \Sigma\}$ for graph enhanced expert networks.
3: **while** Not coverage **do**
4:     Sample a batch of interaction records $\mathcal{H}^{\mathcal{B}}$ from $\mathcal{H}$.
5:     /**MGNN module**/
6:     Collect $L$-hops neighbors for each users (or items) in $\mathcal{H}^{\mathcal{B}}$ over $\mathcal{G}, \mathcal{G}^{\mathcal{U}}$ and $\mathcal{G}^{\mathcal{I}}$, respectively.
7:     Obtain initial representations for users and items in $\mathcal{H}^{\mathcal{B}}$ with shared encoding in Eq. 2.
8:     **for** $l = 0; l < L$ **do**
9:         Perform propagation in each channel (*i.e.*, Eq. 3 ~ 4).
10:     **end for**
11:     /**Graph enhanced expert networks.**/
12:     Apply the graph representation interaction as Eq. 5.
13:     **for** $k = 1; k \leq K$ **do**
14:         Calculate $\hat{y}_{u,i}^k$ according to Eq. 6.
15:     **end for**
16:     Perform back propagation *w.r.t.* $\mathcal{L}$, *i.e.*, Eq. 10.
17: **end while**

Specifically, following [7,22], we learn a relative weight for each task with the task-dependent uncertainty, and thus rewrite the above loss function as follows:

$$
\begin{aligned}
\mathcal{L}_{main}(\Theta, \Sigma) &= \sum_{k=1}^{K} \mathcal{L}^k(\theta^k, \sigma^k) \\
&\approx \sum_{k=1}^{K} \sum_{\langle u,i \rangle \in \mathcal{H}} \left( \frac{1}{\sigma^{k2}} \mathcal{C}(\hat{y}_{u,i}^k, y_{u,i}^k) + \log(\sigma^{k2}) \right),
\end{aligned}
\tag{6}
$$

where $\Theta = \{\theta^k\}_{k=1}^K$, $\Sigma = \{\sigma^k\}_{k=1}^K$ is the parameter set and task uncertainty set of MoGENet, respectively. Noting that $\log(\sigma^{k2})$ serves as a regularizer to avoid overfitting.

As mentioned above, MoGENet contains multiple parallel expert networks, which is hoped to be beneficial to the final prediction in a cooperative manner [5, 16]. Hence, we propose an auxiliary cooperative loss to balance the load of each parallel expert network.

$$
\mathcal{L}_{co} = - \sum_{\langle u,i \rangle \in \mathcal{H}} \sum_{k=1}^{K} \sum_{n=1}^{N} \sum_{m=n+1}^{N} g^k(\hat{\mathbf{x}}_{u,i})_n g^k(\hat{\mathbf{x}}_{u,i})_m.
\tag{7}
$$

By incorporating both of above losses together, the overall loss function for our model is defined as follows:

$$\mathcal{L} = \mathcal{L}_{main} + \beta\mathcal{L}_{co} + \lambda||\Theta||^2, \tag{8}$$

where $\beta, \lambda > 0$ controls the cooperative loss and regularization term, respectively.

## 2.4 Discussion

**Flexibility of MoGENet.** The proposed MoGENet is a flexible framework to leverage graph structure for promoting multi-task recommendation. If we ignore the deep interaction context learned by the MGNN module, MoGENet degrades into the typical MMoE model [13] without graph learning. On the other hand, MoGENet can also naturally degrade into neural graph collaborative filtering model [24] when the collaborative similarity and graph enhanced expert network are overlooked. Moreover, MoGENet is also a general framework which can be easily extended to incorporated more complicated graph structure (*e.g.*, social graphs and item knowledge graphs).

**Efficient Training for Industrial Application.** For efficient numerical computation in the MGNN module, we follow the trick in [11] to perform attention calculation in each channel. Hence, the complexity and storage are both linear with the number of edges in each corresponding graph. In sum, the upper bound of complexity for the MGNN module is $\mathcal{O}(|\mathcal{E}| + |\mathcal{E}^{\mathcal{U}}| + |\mathcal{E}^{\mathcal{I}}|)$. In addition, we follow the similar strategy in [4] to randomly collect multi-hop (*i.e.*, $L$) neighbors for each $\langle u, i \rangle$ pair in batch. Instead of the full graph, we feed the subgraph organized by the sampled multi-hop neighbors into the MGNN module for training, which endows MoGENet with excellent scalability for large-scale data in real-world applications. The pseudocode of the training procedure for MoGENet is detailed in Algorithm 1. *Actually, MoGENet has been deployed in industrial advertising systems to support user-item interaction graphs, consisting of hundreds of millions of nodes and edges.*

## 3 Experiments

In this section, we conduct a series of experiments to evaluate the effectiveness of MoGENet on industrial and public datasets, respectively. To sum up, we aim to answer the following research questions:

- **RQ1**: Does our proposed model outperforms other state-of-the-art methods on both industrial and public datasets.
- **RQ2**: How does our proposed MGNN module improve existing multi-task recommendation methods.
- **RQ3**: How about the impact of key designs of MoGENet (*i.e.*, interaction function, loss function and graph enhanced experts).

**Dataset and Evaluation Metrics.** We evaluate MoGENet on an industrial **Advertising dataset** (extracted as **Adv. A** and **Adv. B**) and a public **IJCAI CUP 2015 dataset**[1]. The detailed descriptions of the three datasets are summarized in Table 1. Following [26,33], we adopt **GAUC** to measure the recommendation performance, which is a more fine-grained metric and proved to be more relevant to online performance. We also report **RelaImpr** [18,30] to measure the relative improvement of MoGENet over the best baseline. It is also worthwhile to note **0.1%** improvement *w.r.t.* GAUC is remarkable in industrial scenarios.

**Table 1.** Statistics of datasets used in experiments.

|  | Adv. A | Adv. B | IJCAI CUP 2015 |
|---|---|---|---|
| #Train | $2.67 \times 10^6$ | $2.18 \times 10^6$ | $3.81 \times 10^6$ |
| #Test | $1.45 \times 10^5$ | $1.72 \times 10^5$ | $9.69 \times 10^5$ |
| #Nodes/#Edges / #Attr. | $3.01 \times 10^6$/$9.31 \times 10^7$/93 | | $1.07 \times 10^6$/$3.94 \times 10^6$/N.A. |
| Tasks | Click/Conversion | | Favorite/Purchase |

**Table 2.** Overall performance comparison *w.r.t.* GAUC (We <u>underline</u> the best performance from the baselines for each comparison. We use "**(or *)" to indicate that improvement of MoGENet over the best performance from the baselines based on paired t-tests at the significance level of 0.01 (or 0.05).). "Conv." is short for "Conversion".

| Dataset | Adv. A | | Adv. B | | IJCAI CUP 2015 | |
|---|---|---|---|---|---|---|
| Task | Click | Conv. | Click | Conv. | Favorite | Purchase |
| MLP | 0.7340 | 0.7818 | 0.7138 | 0.8018 | 0.6049 | 0.7449 |
| NGCF | <u>0.7383</u> | 0.7811 | <u>0.7207</u> | 0.8027 | <u>0.7431</u> | <u>0.7466</u> |
| Shared-Bottom | 0.7288 | 0.7857 | 0.7051 | 0.8015 | 0.6044 | 0.7462 |
| Cross-Stitch | 0.7314 | 0.7857 | 0.7108 | <u>0.8063</u> | 0.6049 | 0.7445 |
| ESMM | 0.7261 | 0.7862 | 0.7009 | 0.7970 | 0.6055 | 0.7448 |
| MMoE | 0.7288 | 0.7860 | 0.7092 | 0.8033 | 0.6013 | 0.7369 |
| SNR-trans | 0.7327 | <u>0.7889</u> | 0.7159 | 0.8059 | 0.6040 | 0.7416 |
| CGC | 0.7307 | 0.7862 | 0.7084 | 0.8012 | 0.6030 | 0.7402 |
| MoGENet | **0.7428**** | **0.8051**** | **0.7232**** | **0.8092*** | **0.7442*** | **0.7477*** |
| **RelaImpr** *v.s.* Best | 1.89% | 5.61% | 1.13% | 0.42% | 0.41% | 0.44% |

**Compared Methods.** We mainly consider two kinds of representative prediction methods and corresponding variants:

– **Single-task methods**, which only contribute to one task with shared features (*i.e.,* **MLP**) or graph structure (*i.e.,* **NGCF**[2] [24]).

---

[1] https://ijcai-15.org/index.php/repeat-buyers-prediction-competition.
[2] https://github.com/xiangwang1223/neural_graph_collaborative_filtering.

– **Multi-task methods**, which learn multiple task relationships (*i.e.*, **Shared-Bottom** [1], **Cross-Stitch**[3] [15], **ESMM**[4] [14], **MMoE**[5] [13], **SNR-trans**[6] [12], **CGC** (see Footnote 6)

**Table 3.** Performance comparison of different methods and their improved variants(*i.e.*, + MGNN) on tree datasets. ↑ means that variants achieve the better performance.

| Dataset | Adv. A | | Adv. B | | IJCAI CUP 2015 | |
|---|---|---|---|---|---|---|
| Task | Click | Conv. | Click | Conv. | Favorite | Purchase |
| Shared-Bottom | 0.7288 | 0.7857 | 0.7051 | 0.8015 | 0.6044 | 0.7462 |
| + MGNN | 0.7333↑ | 0.7872↑ | 0.7189↑ | 0.8079↑ | 0.7439↑ | 0.7351↑ |
| Cross-Stitch | 0.7314 | 0.7857 | 0.7108 | 0.8063 | 0.6049 | 0.7445 |
| + MGNN | 0.7309 | 0.7866↑ | 0.7175↑ | 0.8027 | 0.7378↑ | 0.7457↑ |
| ESMM | 0.7261 | 0.7862 | 0.7009 | 0.7970 | 0.6055 | 0.7448 |
| + MGNN | 0.7363↑ | 0.7879↑ | 0.7177↑ | 0.8067↑ | 0.7417↑ | 0.7438 |
| MMoE | 0.7288 | 0.7860 | 0.7092 | 0.8033 | 0.6013 | 0.7369 |
| + MGNN | 0.7370↑ | 0.7880↑ | 0.7140↑ | 0.8035↑ | 0.7314↑ | 0.7329 |
| SNR-trans | 0.7327 | 0.7889 | 0.7159 | 0.8059 | 0.6040 | 0.7416 |
| + MGNN | 0.7352↑ | 0.7863 | 0.7185↑ | 0.8021 | 0.7366↑ | 0.7385 |
| CGC | 0.7307 | 0.7862 | 0.7084 | 0.8012 | 0.6030 | 0.7402 |
| + MGNN | 0.7342↑ | 0.7862 | 0.7147↑ | 0.8046↑ | 0.7373↑ | 0.7314 |

**Table 4.** Study of the interaction function $\kappa(\cdot, \cdot)$. EP: element-wise product; CON: concatenation; ADD: Addition; MLP: multi-layer perceptron.

| Dataset | Adv. A | | Adv. B | |
|---|---|---|---|---|
| Task | Click | Conversion | Click | Conversion |
| EP | 0.7428 | **0.8051** | 0.7232 | 0.8092 |
| CON | 0.7400 | 0.7961 | 0.7194 | 0.8121 |
| ADD | **0.7436** | 0.7954 | 0.7190 | **0.8126** |
| MLP | 0.7430 | 0.7986 | **0.7250** | 0.8072 |

---

[3] https://github.com/helloyide/Cross-stitch-Networks-for-Multi-task-Learning.
[4] https://github.com/qiaoguan/deep-ctr-prediction/tree/master/ESMM.
[5] https://github.com/drawbridge/keras-mmoe.
[6] https://github.com/tomtang110/Multitask.

**Implementation Details.** We implement all models in our experiments on parameter server based distributed learning systems [32], with the aims of scaling up to large-scale datasets adopted in the paper. For fair comparison, we set learning rate = 1e−4, regularizer = 1e−3, batch size = 256, embedding size = 64 and select Adam as optimizer for all models. Moreover, for MLP and ESMM, we set the architecture as [512, 256, 128]. For NGCF, we follow the optimal architecture reported in the original paper with 2 layers graph neural network. For Shared-Bottom, Cross-stitch, MMoE, SNR-trans and CGC, we set the number of expert networks = 4, and set the architecture of each expert network as [32, 32] and each gate network as [16, 16]. For MoGENet, we follow same architectures of expert networks and gate networks as MMoE, and set $L = 2$, $\beta = 1e-6$, $\lambda = 1e-3$. It is worthwhile to that all parameters for the comparison methods are optimized by using 10% training data as the validation set.

**Table 5.** Study of the loss function. i: the original loss function; ii: the uncertain loss function; iii: the auxiliary cooperative loss.

| Dataset | Adv. A | | Adv. B | |
|---------|--------|------------|--------|------------|
| Task | Click | Conversion | Click | Conversion |
| i | 0.7408 | 0.7940 | 0.7169 | 0.8098 |
| i+ii | 0.7424 | 0.7966 | 0.7180 | **0.8110** |
| i+iii | 0.7381 | 0.7877 | 0.7190 | 0.8084 |
| i+ii+iii | **0.7428** | **0.8051** | **0.7232** | 0.8092 |

## 3.1 Performance Comparison (RQ1)

We show the overall performance of the compared methods on industrial and public datasets in Table 2. Here, we have the following key observations:

– The proposed MoGENet model consistently and significantly achieves the best performance over baselines in all cases. This result validates the effectiveness of MoGENet, benefiting from incorporating the deep interaction context for multi-task recommendation with graph learning.
– Among baselines, multi-task methods outperform single-task methods in most cases, which indicates the usefulness of learning task relations during model training. This phenomenon is fairly obvious in the industrial dataset, since the relation between *Click* and *Conversion* maybe stronger than *Favorite* and *Purchase*.
– It is worthwhile to note that NGCF, as a single-task method, works well among these baselines. It indicates that graph structure plays a vital role in recommendation task, which further inspires the development of MoGENet.

## 3.2   Effect of the MGNN Module

To demonstrate the effectiveness of graph representations learned by our MGNN module, we prepare a series of variants of above multi-task methods, which simply take the output of the MGNN module as input.

As shown in Table 3, the variants of multi-task methods (*i.e.,* + MGNN) yield better performance than the base by a relatively large margin in most cases, which is attributed to the useful graph structure learned by the MGNN module. Nevertheless, our MoGENet provides a more principled mechanism for combining graph learning and multi-task recommendation, and thus still outperforms these variants.

## 3.3   Study of MoGENet

In this section, we conduct a series of ablation studies on MoGENet to investigate the impact and rationality of the interaction function, loss function and graph enhanced experts.

**Ablation Study 1: Interaction Function.** First of all, we investigate the impact of the interaction function $\kappa(\cdot, \cdot)$ in Eq. 3. In particular, we equip our MoGENet model with different interaction functions (*i.e.,* element-wise product (**EP**), concatenation (**CON**), addition (**ADD**) and multi-layer perceptron (**MLP**)) and study the corresponding performance.

As shown in Table. 4, we find that MoGENet yields relatively superior performance when the relatively simple interaction functions (*i.e.,* element-wise product and addition) are applied. A possible reason is that such an interaction function seems enough to capture affinity between users and items, and also increases the model representation ability. This observation is consistent with previous findings in [24].

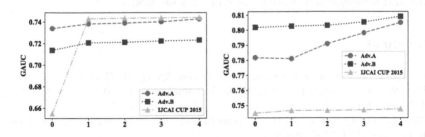

**Fig. 2.** Study of the graph enhanced experts.

**Ablation Study 2: Loss Function.** As mentioned above, we improve the (i) original multi-task loss function (See Eq. 7) by (ii) incorporating task-dependent uncertainty loss (See Eq. 8) and (iii) auxiliary cooperative loss (See Eq. 9), with the aims of effectively learning relatedness and differences across multiple tasks.

As shown in Table 5, we observe that the complete MoGENet (*i.e.*, "i+ii+iii") achieves the best performance in most cases compared with other variants. It demonstrates the rationality and effectiveness of the design of loss function, which provides a more reasonable way to learn knowledge transfer among multiple tasks.

**Ablation Study 3: Graph Enhanced Experts.** Finally, we analysis the impact of graph enhanced experts on the recommendation performance through gradually incorporating them into the proposed model (See Eq. 3).

As illustrated in Fig. 2, we observe that the performance of MoGENet overall improves with the incorporation of graph enhanced experts (as shown in Fig. 1 (b), we add experts from left to right). And the performance will drop a lot without graph enhanced experts in most cases. These observations demonstrate the effectiveness of graph learning for easing the data sparseness issue.

## 4  Conclusion

In this paper, we proposed MoGENet, a novel graph learning enhanced multi-gate mixture-of-experts framework for recommendation. We elaborately developed a MGNN module to jointly model the high-order connectivity and the collaborative similarity. On the top of learned structural information, a group of graph enhanced expert networks was introduced for contributing to multi-task recommendation during end-to-end training. Extensive experimental results have demonstrated the superiority of our model. As for future work, we will investigate into incorporating more complicated graph structures (*e.g.*, knowledge graphs and heterogeneous graphs) into our framework.

## References

1. Caruana, R.: Multitask learning. Mach. Learn. **28**(1), 41–75 (1997)
2. Fan, W., et al.: Graph neural networks for social recommendation. In: WWW, pp. 417–426 (2019)
3. Gao, C., et al.: Neural multi-task recommendation from multi-behavior data. In: ICDE, pp. 1554–1557 (2019)
4. Hamilton, W., Ying, Z., Leskovec, J.: Inductive representation learning on large graphs. In: NIPS, pp. 1024–1034 (2017)
5. Hsu, W.T., Lin, C.K., Lee, M.Y., Min, K., Tang, J., Sun, M.: A unified model for extractive and abstractive summarization using inconsistency loss. In: ACL, pp. 132–141 (2018)
6. Kendall, A., Gal, Y.: What uncertainties do we need in bayesian deep learning for computer vision. In: NIPS, pp. 5574–5584 (2017)

7. Kendall, A., Gal, Y., Cipolla, R.: Multi-task learning using uncertainty to weigh losses for scene geometry and semantics. In: CVPR, pp. 7482–7491 (2018)
8. Kim, S., Ahn, N., Sohn, K.A.: Restoring spatially-heterogeneous distortions using mixture of experts network. In: ACCV (2020)
9. Kipf, T.N., Welling, M.: Semi-supervised classification with graph convolutional networks. In: ICLR (2017)
10. Li, D., Li, X., Wang, J., Li, P.: Video recommendation with multi-gate mixture of experts soft actor critic. In: SIGIR, pp. 1553–1556 (2020)
11. Liu, Z., et al.: GeniePath: graph neural networks with adaptive receptive paths. In: AAAI, pp. 4424–4431 (2019)
12. Ma, J., Zhao, Z., Chen, J., Li, A., Hong, L., Chi, E.H.: SNR: sub-network routing for flexible parameter sharing in multi-task learning. In: AAAI, pp. 216–223 (2019)
13. Ma, J., Zhao, Z., Yi, X., Chen, J., Hong, L., Chi, E.H.: Modeling task relationships in multi-task learning with multi-gate mixture-of-experts. In: SIGKDD, pp. 1930–1939 (2018)
14. Ma, X., et al.: Entire space multi-task model: an effective approach for estimating post-click conversion rate. In: SIGIR, pp. 1137–1140 (2018)
15. Misra, I., Shrivastava, A., Gupta, A., Hebert, M.: Cross-stitch networks for multi-task learning. In: CVPR, pp. 3994–4003 (2016)
16. Niu, X., Li, B., Li, C., Tan, J., Xiao, R., Deng, H.: Heterogeneous graph augmented multi-scenario sharing recommendation with tree-guided expert networks. In: WSDM, pp. 1038–1046 (2021)
17. Qin, Z., Cheng, Y., Zhao, Z., Chen, Z., Metzler, D., Qin, J.: Multitask mixture of sequential experts for user activity streams. In: SIGKDD, pp. 3083–3091 (2020)
18. Shen, Q., Tao, W., Zhang, J., Wen, H., Chen, Z., Lu, Q.: SAR-Net: a scenario-aware ranking network for personalized fair recommendation in hundreds of travel scenarios. In: CIKM, pp. 4094–4103 (2021)
19. Tang, H., Liu, J., Zhao, M., Gong, X.: Progressive layered extraction (PLE): a novel multi-task learning (MTL) model for personalized recommendations. In: Recommender Systems, pp. 269–278 (2020)
20. Vaswani, A., et al.: Attention is all you need. In: NIPS, pp. 5998–6008 (2017)
21. Veličković, P., Cucurull, G., Casanova, A., Romero, A., Lio, P., Bengio, Y.: Graph attention networks. In: ICLR (2018)
22. Wang, M., Lin, Y., Lin, G., Yang, K., Wu, X.M.: M2GRL: a multi-task multi-view graph representation learning framework for web-scale recommender systems. In: SIGKDD, pp. 2349–2358 (2020)
23. Wang, X., He, X., Cao, Y., Liu, M., Chua, T.S.: KGAT: knowledge graph attention network for recommendation. In: SIGKDD, pp. 950–958 (2019)
24. Wang, X., He, X., Wang, M., Feng, F., Chua, T.S.: Neural graph collaborative filtering. In: SIGIR, pp. 165–174 (2019)
25. Wang, X., et al.: Deep mixture of experts via shallow embedding. In: UAI, pp. 552–562 (2020)
26. Wen, H., et al.: Entire space multi-task modeling via post-click behavior decomposition for conversion rate prediction. In: SIGIR, pp. 2377–2386 (2020)
27. Wu, Q., et al.: Dual graph attention networks for deep latent representation of multifaceted social effects in recommender systems. In: WWW, pp. 2091–2102 (2019)
28. Wu, Z., Pan, S., Chen, F., Long, G., Zhang, C., Philip, S.Y.: A comprehensive survey on graph neural networks. IEEE Trans. Neural Netw. Learn. Syst. **32**(1), 4–24 (2020)

29. Xu, K., Li, C., Tian, Y., Sonobe, T., Kawarabayashi, K.i., Jegelka, S.: Representation learning on graphs with jumping knowledge networks. In: ICML, pp. 5449–5458 (2018)
30. Yan, L., Li, W.J., Xue, G.R., Han, D.: Coupled group lasso for web-scale CTR prediction in display advertising. In: ICML, pp. 802–810 (2014)
31. Ying, R., He, R., Chen, K., Eksombatchai, P., Hamilton, W.L., Leskovec, J.: Graph convolutional neural networks for web-scale recommender systems. In: SIGKDD, pp. 974–983 (2018)
32. Zhou, J., et al.: KunPeng: parameter server based distributed learning systems and its applications in Alibaba and ant financial. In: SIGKDD, pp. 1693–1702 (2017)
33. Zhu, H., et al.: Optimized cost per click in taobao display advertising. In: SIGKDD, pp. 2191–2200 (2017)

# MF-TagRec: Multi-feature Fused Tag Recommendation for GitHub

Liu Yang[1], Ruo Yang[1], Tingxuan Chen[1(✉)], Hongxiao Fei[1], and Jiuqi Tang[2]

[1] School of Computer Science and Engineering, Central South University,
Changsha, China
{yangliu,yangruo,chentingxuan,hxfei}@csu.edu.cn
[2] Viterbi School of Engineering, University of Southern California,
Los Angeles, USA
jiuqitan@usc.edu

**Abstract.** GitHub is one of the most popular hosting platforms for open-source projects, where tags are widely used to facilitate software organization and retrieval. However, the existences of inadequate and low-quality tags on GitHub hinder users from searching and retrieving their desired projects. In this paper, we propose MF-TagRec, an automatic tag recommendation method for projects by extracting multiple features from Readme documents, programming languages and dependency package tags of projects. We capture topics and global semantics of Readme documents as text features, along with programming languages and dependency package tags as word vector features. We construct a convolutional neural network and feed text and word vector features to predict the most relevant tags for untagged or few tag-assigned projects. We evaluate our proposed MF-TagRec on a real dataset GitHubDep-DataSet compared with five baselines. The results show that MF-TagRec achieves *Recall@5* and *Recall@10* to 0.756 and 0.864 respectively, which outperforms the previous baselines.

**Keywords:** Github · Open-source projects · Tag recommendation · Convolutional neural network

## 1 Introduction

With the continuous development of open-source movement, an increasing number of teams host their projects in open-source communities. As the largest project hosting platform, GitHub [1] has attracted more than 60 million newly created projects, 56 million registered users and 1.9 million repository contributions from October 2019 to September 2020.

To help developers identify tags when creating projects, GitHub presented a tag suggestion tool *re-po-topix* in 2017 [2]. However, only 5% of public projects in GitHub had at least one tag till to February 2020 [3]. We also discovered over 32% of projects are untaged in the dataset GitHubDepDataSet [4]. In fact, these tags are especially useful to browse and filter projects. Consequently, inadequate tags

S. Khanna et al. (Eds.): PRICAI 2022, LNCS 13631, pp. 17–31, 2022.
https://doi.org/10.1007/978-3-031-20868-3_2

**Fig. 1.** An open-source project react on GitHub.

make users hard to retrieve open-source projects accurately on GitHub. Against this background, tag recommendation for open-source communities have been widely studied.

Recently, most researchers only utilize description documents for tag recommendation [5,6]. In fact, programming languages and dependency package tags also imply the features of an open-source project, as well as its Readme document. Figure 1 shows the open-source project *facebook/react* on Github, and it contains a Readme document, dependency packages, as well as six example tags *react, javascript, library, ui, frontend* and *declarative*.

Besides Readme documents, we further discover the existence of co-occurrences between actual tags of projects and programming languages, along with dependency package tags. The open-source project *TryGhost/Ghost* shown in Fig. 2, its actual tags of *ghost* and *blogging* are relative to its Readme document, containing with *ghost* and *blog*. Besides, *javascript* is relative to its programming languages, containing with *JavaScript*. Likewise, *web-application* and *ghost* are also relative to its dependency package tags, containing with *web* and *ghost*.

Motivated by the above observations, we propose a tag recommendation method MF-TagRec, which takes into account the following features, namely, Readme documents, Programming languages and dependency packages tags. In view of Readme documents with abundant topical and semantic sentences, we use LDA [7] and Word2vec [8] to extract topics and global semantics as text features. In terms of multi-programming languages in one project, we transform programming languages into word vector features by the ratios of different programming languages. As for dependency package tags, we transform them into word vector features by one-hot encoding. Finally, we use a fully connected projection to output top-$k$ tags of projects. The main contributions of this paper are as follows:

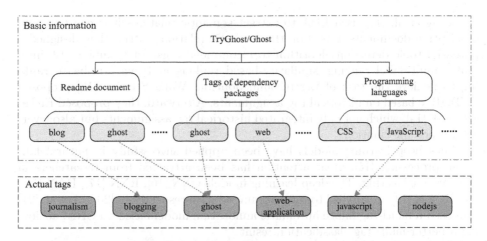

**Fig. 2.** Co-occurrences between project tags and Readme document, programming languages, along with dependency package tags.

- We investigate that tags are relative to not only topics but also global semantics of Readme documents. Therefore, We extract topics from Readme documents by LDA, and learn global semantics by Word2vec. Afterwards, we combine topics and global semantics as text features of projects.
- We incorporate dependency package tags in projects as side information for tag recommendation. We combine dependency package tags and programming languages as word vector features of projects.
- We introduce a novel tag recommendation method MF-TagRec, designed to integrate multi-features containing text and word vector features of projects.
- We evaluate our method with a set of well-defined metrics(namely *Recall@k*, *Precision@k*, and *F1-score@k*) on a real dataset GitHubDepDataSet.

The rest of this paper is organized as follows: Sect. 2 introduces related work on tag recommendation. Section 3 presents our method MF-TagRec in detail. Section 4 discusses our experiments and results. Finally, we conclude the future work in Sect. 5.

## 2   Related Work

In this section, we firstly review the previous works on tag recommendation, and then present kinds of literature concerning tagging in open-source communities.

### 2.1   Tag Recommendation

In the era of Web 2.0, tags have been used to organize and index Web resources efficiently [9]. Thus, many researchers focus on tag recommendation methods [10], such as traditional approaches and deep learning models.

Wang et al. [11] used LDA to extract semantic relations between tags and description documents. Based on the semantic relation matrix, they designed a potential topic detection algorithm to recommend tags. TagCombine [12] integrates multi-label ranking, similarity-based ranking and tag-term-based ranking to achieve the task of tag recommendation. Wang S et al. [13] proposed EnTagRec based on historical tag assignments. Afterward, they proposed EnTagRec++ [14], which not only integrated historical tag assignments but also leveraged users' information.

Since deep learning models have been applied successfully in natural language processing [15], great attention has been attracted from researchers in software engineering. The deep learning models CNN [16], RNN [17], HAN [18], and RCNN [19] are applied to tag recommendation respectively [20]. Li et al. [21] proposed a multi-tag image automatic annotation model based on CNN, achieving a better multi-tag classification result.

Traditional tag recommendation methods always encounter problems of "tag disorder" and "tag redundancy". On the contrary, deep learning models have good recommendation performance with enough training tags, even if the training tags contain noise or even errors.

## 2.2  Tag Recommendation in Open-Source Communities

Some recent researches on tag recommendation are associated with open-source communities. TagMulRec [22] calculates semantic similarity between tags and software descriptions for recommending tags. Liu et al. proposed FastTagRec [23], using neural network-based classification.

In addition, considerable effort has been made in the domain of tag recommendation for GitHub. Jing Jiang et al. proposed FNNRec [24] to analyze titles, descriptions, file paths and contributors based on a feed-forward neural network for tag recommendation. TopFilter [25] was proposed to build a project-topic matrix and apply a syntactic-based similarity function to recommend missing topics.

As previously mentioned, most tag recommendation methods only take into account topics or global semantics while encoding project descriptions. Different from these works, our method MF-TagRec considers both topics and global semantics of Readme documents, programming languages, and dependency package tags in tag recommendation task.

## 3    Method

In this section, we first formally present tag recommendation problem and introduce our tag recommendation method MF-TagRec for projects. We then discuss how to encode features for open-source projects and predict tags based on a Convolutional Neural Network (CNN).

## 3.1  Problem Formulation

The open-source Community GitHub is a set $C = \{pr_1, ..., pr_\omega\}$, where $pr_i (1 \ll i \ll \omega)$ denotes a project. For project $pr_i$, its features consist of a few associated tags, a Readme document, programming languages and dependency package tags. Let a Readme document be $pr_i.Readme$ containing topics $pr_i.P$ and global semantics $pr_i.V$, programming languages be $pr_i.Lang$ along with dependency package tags be $pr_i.DepTag$. The research question in tag recommendation task is the following: given project $pr_i$ with above-mentioned features, how to automatically recommend a set of appropriate tags for project $pr_i$.

## 3.2  Overview of MF-TagRec

Figure 3 illustrates our method MF-TagRec. It is designed to integrates text and word vector features of projects, capturing semantic information of Readme documents, and high-quality representations for programming languages and dependency package tags. More precisely, MF-TagRec consists of two parts: (1) data preparation, and (2) CNN for tag prediction.

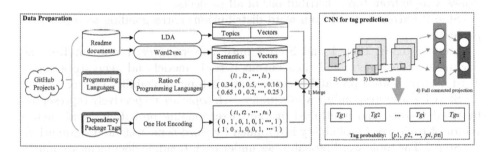

**Fig. 3.** Overview of our proposed method MF-TagRec.

In the phrase of data preparation, the goal is to learn from Readme documents, programming languages and dependency package tags. As for Readme documents with abundant texts, we utilize LDA and Word2vec to extract topic as well as global semantic features. In addition, we transform programming languages into word vectors according to the ratios of programming languages, and encode dependency package tags into word vectors by one-hot encoding. In the phrase of tag prediction, we construct a CNN to model the intrinsic interactions between three kinds of project information, namely, Readme documents, programming languages and dependency package tags, capturing hidden word-tag correlations. Afterward, we merge related feature vectors obtained in the previous phrase, and use a fully connected projection to output top-$k$ tags of projects.

**Text Features Representation.** As mentioned previously, actual tags of a project are relative to not only topics but also global semantics of its Readme document. However, text features extracted from description documents in current researches only consider their topic features, resulting in singularity of text features. Therefore, we use LDA and Word2vec to learn both topic features and global semantic features from Readme documents.

*Topic Features.* LDA is capable of identifying implicit topics in a document. In this paper, we utilize LDA to extract topics from Readme documents, and it treats Readme document of each project as a probability distribution composed of different topics, and each topic as a probability distribution consisting of many words. The definition is as

$$P(W_{i,m}|W) = P(W_{i,m}|K_m) * P(K_m|W) \tag{1}$$

where $W_{i,m}$ represents the $m$th word in a Readme document $W$ and $K_m$ represents the topic corresponding to the $m$th word. Thus, the steps of generating topic vectors of Readme documents are described as the following steps:

Step 1 Input all Readme documents $Y_i$, and for each Readme document, $Y_i$ draws a topic from topic distributions of all projects.

Step 2 Extract a word from word distributions corresponding to topics of a project.

Step 3 Repeat Step 1 and Step 2 until traversing each word in Readme document of a project, and then output a topic model and generate a topic-word matrix, a word probability matrix, and a topic probability matrix.

Step 4 The corresponding words under each topic are respectively represented by word vectors, and multiplied by the corresponding probability, and then a vector of topic-word probability is obtained by word-topic weighted summation.

Step 5 The topic-word probabilities under each Readme document are multiplied with a topic word vector, and then the topic vector of a Readme document is obtained by topic-document weighted summation.

Step 6 Output the latent topic vector as $P$, which is topic probability distributions for each Readme document.

*Global Semantic Features.* LDA learn topics from Readme documents, but it is uncapable to learn contextual information. Hence, we also use Word2vec to mine global semantics from Readme documents. Word2vec considers word contexts and trains each word by mapping it to a K-dimensional vector. Generally, it includes two training models, namely CBOW and skip-gram. In this paper, we utilize CBOW to construct word vectors. Firstly, we conduct word segmentation on a Readme document $W = [w_1, \cdots, w_i, \cdots w_\delta]$, where $w_i$ is the $i$th word in a Readme document. According to word vector library of Word2vec, we replace the segmented text with a low-dimensional vector $V = [V_{W_1}, \cdots, V_{W_i}, \cdots V_{w_\delta}]$, where $V_{W_1}$ represents the word vector of $w_i$. Afterward, each Readme document is converted into a continuous and dense matrix data representation similar to an image.

**Word Features Representation.** In the introduction section, we observe that programming languages and dependency package tags have a close correspondence with the actual tags of projects. Therefore, programming languages of all projects on GitHub are represented numerically, $Lang = \{\, l_1, l_2, \ldots, l_\sigma \}$, where $l_i$ represents the percentage of the $i$th programming language in the current project among all of $\sigma$ programming languages. For example, a project with a vector of $[0.957, 0.019, 0.01, 0.014]$ indicates that the probability of this project written by the first programming language is 0.975. For dependency package tags, we use one-hot encoding to vectorize them as $DepTag = [t_1, t_2, \ldots, t_\theta]$, where each item represents a tag. The value of these elements is either 0 or 1, depending on whether the current dependency package is assigned with the target tag.

### 3.3   CNN for Tag Prediction

We construct a CNN consisting four parts, to propose more suitable tags for projects. For a project $pr_i$ containing multi features, namely, $pr_i.Readme$, $pr_i.Lang$ and $pr_i.DepTag$, CNN 1) merges these multi-feature vectors, generating features $G$ with length $n$, and 2) mines feature correlations among those multi features of projects, generating a new feature $c_i$ associated potential correlations, and 3) learns from each feature $c_i$, generating a downsampling feature *map*. Afterward, it 4) constructs a fully connected projection to generate a final prediction score for the input multi features of projects.

**Merging Relatedness Feature Vectors.** Given a project $pr_i$, we have converted its multiple features into word representations in the above. Let $x_i \epsilon \mathbb{R}^{dim}$ be a *dim*-dimensional word vector corresponding to the $i$th word in these features, we concatenate these word vectors as features $G$. The multiple features $G$ of project $pr_i$ are represented as

$$G_{1:n} = pr_i.P \oplus pr_i.V \oplus pr_i.Lang \oplus pr_i.DepTag = x_1 \oplus \cdots \oplus x_n \qquad (2)$$

where $pr_i.P$ and $pr_i.V$ denotes topic features and semantics features of a Readme document, respectively. *Lang* represents programming languages, and *DepTag* represents dependency package tags. In addition, $\oplus$ is a connector used to connect various features in order.

**Mining Correlations Between Relatedness Feature Vectors.** A convolution operation involves a filter $w \in R^{hk}$, which is mainly capture interactions between each words in multiple features $G$. In order to generate a new feature $c_i$ associated with potential correlations, we resort to convolution layer to model intrinsic interactions between $h$ words in multiple features $G$. A new feature $c_i$ is generated from a region of words $G_{i\ :\ i+h}$ by

$$c_i = f\left(w \cdot G_{i\ :\ i+h} + b\right) \qquad (3)$$

where function $f(\ \cdot\ )$ is a ReLU activation function, $G_{i\ :\ i+h}$ is a sequence of word vectors of $h$ words, and $b \in R$ is a bias term.

**Learning from Downsampling Features.** We obtain feature vectors $c_i$ associated potential correlations from multiple features of projects, then we conduct the maximum pooling operation on $c_i$ to obtain downsampling feature $map$, which is mathematically expressed as

$$map = max\,\{0, c_i\} \tag{4}$$

**Constructing Fully Connected Projection For Prediction.** We construct a fully connected projection and input the obtained $map$, where it will be multiplied with the weight $w_f$. In addition, a drop-out strategy is added to randomly discard the features of projects. The function of tag prediction obtained by the weighted sum is as

$$\hat{y} = f\,(w_f \times map + b_f) \tag{5}$$

where softmax is used as the activation function $f$, $\hat{y}$ is tag prediction of project $pr_i$, $w_f$ is weight matrix, and $b_f$ is bias of the fully connected layer.

### 3.4   Network Training Process

The goal of our proposed MF-TagRec is to recommend tags for projects, hence,we use the mean squared error function MSE (Mean Squared Error) as loss function. Following suggestions from relevant works, our loss function is defined as

$$L = \sum_{(pr_i,\ \ tag)\in D} (\hat{y} - y)^2 \tag{6}$$

where $pr_i$ represents a project, $tag$ is a certain tag of project $pr_i$, $D$ represents the set of training samples, $y$ are actual tags of project $pr_i$, and $\hat{y}$ are all the tags recommended to project $pr_i$. In the process of model training, we adopt Adam in the loss function to cope with sparse gradient and noise problems.

## 4   Experiments

We perform extensive experiments to evaluate our proposed MF-TagRec on the dataset GitHubDepDataSet. In the following, we present our experimental setup, followed by our results and discussions.

### 4.1   Experimental Dataset

We conduct experiments on the dataset GitHubDepDataSet [4]. Table 1 shows the main statistics of GitHubDepDataSet classified by programming languages.

In total, we collect 43,593 projects with 24,590 tags, which reflects the existence of tag missing on Github. We first filter out 25467 projects with the highest number of stars and filter out 100 tags with the highest occurrences. Javascript

**Table 1.** Statistics of GitHubDepDataSet.

| Programming languages | # projects | # tags |
|---|---|---|
| Python | 13159 | 10834 |
| JavaScript | 23746 | 12657 |
| PHP | 6688 | 7090 |
| Total | 43593 | 24590 |

projects and Python projects shown in Table 1 are almost four times and twice of PHP projects, respectively. Regarding class imbalance of those projects, we select 80, 60, 40 dependency package tags from different websites of package registries (*i.e.*, https://npmjs.com, https://pypi.python.org and https://packagist.org).

## 4.2  Evaluation Metrics

We use three evaluation metrics of *Recall@k*, *Precision@k* and *F1-score@k*, which are widely used in recommendation systems.

$$Recall@k = \frac{\sum_{p \in Test} \left| Tag_k^{predict} \bigcap Tag^{actual} \right|}{\sum_{p \in Test} \left| Tag^{actual} \right|} \tag{7}$$

$$precision@k = \frac{\sum_{p \in Test} \left| Tag_k^{predict} \bigcap Tag^{actual} \right|}{\sum_{p \in Test} \left| Tag_k^{predict} \right|} \tag{8}$$

$$F1 - score@k = 2 \times \frac{Recall@k \times Precision@k}{Recall@k + Precision@k} \tag{9}$$

where *Test* represents testing set, $Tag_k^{predict}$ refers to the top-$k$ tags recommended, and $Tag_k^{actual}$ refers to actual tags of projects. Since the major goal of tag recommendation is to recommend more correct labels and *Recall@k* takes into account the number of actual project tags, it pays more attention to the performance of *Recall*. The closer *Recall@k* is to 1, the more correct tags are successfully recommended for projects. Based on the above factors, We consider *Recall@k* as the most important indicator in the tag recommendation task.

## 4.3  Experimental Settings

*Baselines:* We compare the tag recommendation performance of MF-TagRec against five baselines, including TopFilter, TagRNN, DepTagRec, GRU and BiGRU.

TopFilter [25] builds a project-topic matrix and applies a syntactic-based similarity function to recommend missing topics.

TagRNN is based on Recurrent Reural Networks [20], which aims to put more weight on recent information.

DepTagRec is based on a fully connected neural network [4], which only considers topics of Readme documents in projects. Additionally, it selects the equal quantity of dependency package tags from different packages registries for tag recommendation, neglecting various proportions of programming languages.

GRU [26] introduces gating mechanisms of reset gate and update gate, where it can not only capture the semantic association of long sequences, but also suppress the disappearance or explosion of gradients.

BiGRU is a two way structure similar to GRU, but it takes into account information both in the preceding and the following [27].

Table 2. Hyperparameters used in our experiments.

| Hyperparameter | Default value |
| --- | --- |
| embedding_size | 100 |
| learing_rate | 0.001 |
| batch_size | 64 |
| num_epoch | 100 |
| dropout_rate | 0.5 |
| filter_size | 2, 3, 4, 5 |

*Hyperparameter Setting:* We study the impact of several key parameters in MF-TagRec, *i.e.*, the embedding size, the learning rate, the batch size, etc. We vary dimension values from 50 to 200 step by 20, and choose a relatively appropriate dimension value 100 to obtain acceptable results. The learning rate also significantly affects model training process. Therefore, we utilize Adam optimization algorithm with the learning rate 0.001. In addition, a dropout strategy is added to MF-TagRec to randomly discard the features. By default, we set the size of batch as 64, the region sizes to (2, 3, 4, 5) with 25 filters for each region size, and the dropout rate with 0.5. The details of the hyperparameters are listed in Table 2.

## 4.4   Experimental Results

We conduct several experiments on GitHubDepDataSet. Firstly, we test recommendation performance using different encoding methods for Readme documents. Secondly, we analyze the impacts of the number of dependency package tags from various package registries on tag recommendation. Finally, we compare the experimental results of our MF-TagRec and the baselines.

**Different Encoding Methods for Readme Documents.** Readme documents are the most important features in tag recommendation, since they describe use precautions of projects. In order to demonstrate how various encoding methods for Readme documents improve tag recommendation performance, we design three variant models:

Readme_Word2vec utilizes Word2vec to obtain global semantics on tag recommendation task.

Readme_LDA utilizes LDA to obtain topics of Readme documents on tag recommendation task.

Readme_all combines Word2vec and LDA to encode Readme documents, obtaining not noly global semantics but also topics.

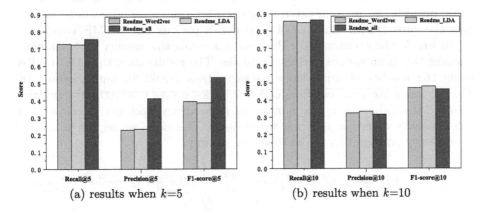

(a) results when $k=5$      (b) results when $k=10$

**Fig. 4.** Impacts of different encoding methods for Readme documents.

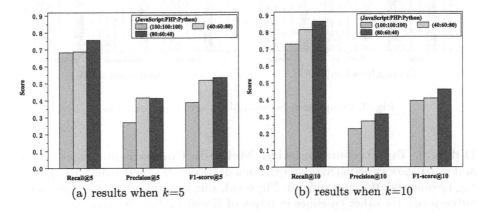

(a) results when $k=5$      (b) results when $k=10$

**Fig. 5.** Impacts of the number of dependency package tags.

We compare performance based on different encoding methods for Readme documents in Figs. 4 (a) and 4 (b). It is observed that the performance of tag recommendation combining two encoding methods outperforms a single encoding method. In Fig. 4 (a), Readme_all achieves *Recall@5* as 0.756, *Precision@5* as 0.412 and *F1-score@5* as 0.533, which are higher than those of two single encoding methods. Furthermore, the best *Recall@10* showed in Fig. 4 (b) is achieved as 0.864 in terms of Readme_all. This can be explained by the fact that Readme_all obtains not only global semantics and topics from Readme documents.

**Different Numbers of Dependency Package Tags.** As previously mentioned in Sect. 4.1, GitHubDepDataSet contains 23746 *JavaScript* projects, 13159 *Python* projects and 6688 *PHP* projects. Regarding class imbalance of those projects, we perform extensive parameter tuning experiments to investigate the impacts of the number of dependency package tags on MF-TagRec.

In Fig. 5, (JavaScript: PHP: Python) represents the number of dependency package tags from various package registries. The results show that MF-TagRec using the number of dependency packages tags (80:60:40) outperforms MF-TagRec using the number of dependency package tags (100:100:100). In other words, MF-TagRec using the number of dependency packages (80:60:40) can recommend a wider range of tags for projects. Therefore, we set the number of dependency package tags as (80:60:40) by default.

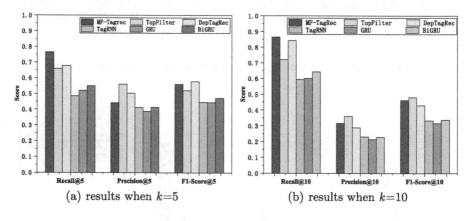

(a) results when $k=5$        (b) results when $k=10$

**Fig. 6.** Comparison between MF-TagRec and baselines.

**Different Tag Recommendation Methods Comparison.** Figures 6 (a) and 6 (b) show experimental comparisons between MF-TagRec and five general tag recommendation methods. In Fig. 6 (a), our method MF-TagRec generally outperforms the other baselines in terms of *Recall@5*, but *Precision@5* and *F1-score@5* of MF-TagRec are lower than DepTagRec. *Precision@5* of MF-TagRec is also lower than TopFilter. We know the main task of tag recommendation is to recommend more correct tags, hence *Recall* is the most important indicator. In other words, our method MF-TagRec exhibits good performance at $k=5$.

In addition, we also find out that each method shows a progressive trend of performance in *Recall*, with the increase of number of recommending tags. More specifically, these tag recommendation methods achieve 0.756, 0.66, 0.679, 0.485, 0.52, 0.55 in terms of *Recall@5*, and 0.864, 0.72, 0.842, 0.594, 0.601, 0.643 in terms of *Recall@10*. Furthermore, compared to other baselines, the improvements of MF-TagRec on *Recall@5* are 14.5%, 11.34%, 55.8%, 45.4%, 37.5%, while the improvements on *Recall@10* are 20%, 2.6%, 45.4%, 43.7%, 32.8%, respectively. Obviouslly, MF-TagRec improves *Recall@5* more than *Recall@10*. In actual applications, an improvement on *Recall@5* is more important than that on *Recall@10*, since users would be more focused on top 5 rather than top 10 for practical purposes.

We also use some sample projects to demonstrate the effectiveness of our method MF-TagRec. Table 3 presents recommended tags of MF-TagRec for a few sample projects.

**Table 3.** Recommendations for sample projects.

| Projects | Actual tags | Recommended tags |
|---|---|---|
| **mybatis/spring** | – | java, spring, MyBatis, framework, adapter |
| **pypa/pip** | python, packaging, pip | python, pip, package, dependency-management, yaml |
| **springprojects/spring-boot** | java, framework, spring, spring-boot | java, framework, spring-boot, spring development, spring application |

*Mybatis/spring* is a *java* project without any tags on Github. Therefore, MF-TagRec can be applied to recommend 5 tags such as *java, spring, MyBatis, framework* and *adapter* for *mybatis/spring*. As for a project *spring-projects/spring-boot* with special tags, MF-TagRec is also capable of recommending functionality-related tags such as *spring development* and *spring application* for it. In other words, our method MF-TagRec can recommend a wider range of tags for GitHub projects.

## 5   Conclusions and Future Work

In this paper, we propose a tag recommendation method MF-TagRec. We consider Readme documents, programming languages and dependency package tags for tag recommending. We compare MF-TagRec with the five baselines on a real dataset GitHubDepDataSet. The experimental results show that our MF-TagRec has significantly improved the accuracy of tag recommendation, verifying the effectiveness of MF-TagRec in tag recommendation task. In the future, we plan to investigate tag recommendation associated with users' preferences in GitHub, such as their historical logs of tag-assigned.

**Acknowledgements.** This work is being supported by the National Natural Science Foundation of China under the Grant No. 62172451, and supported by Scientific and Technological Innovation 2030-Major Project of New Generation Artificial Intelligence under the Grant No. 2020AAA0109601, by Open Research Projects of Zhejiang Lab under the Grant No.2022KG0AB01, and in part by the Natural Science Foundation of Hunan under the Grant No. 2020JJ4754 and 2020JJ5775.

# References

1. GitHub.: The state of the octoverse the state of the octoverse celebrates a year of building across teams, time zones, and millions of merged pull requests (2021). https://octoverse.github.com
2. Kavita, G.: Topic suggestions for millions of repositories the github blog (2017)
3. Izadi, M., Heydarnoori, A., Gousios, G.: Topic recommendation for software repositories using multi-label classification algorithms. Empir. Softw. Eng. **26**(5), 1–33 (2021)
4. Liu, Y., Li, W., Zhigang, H., Yanwen, W., Jun, L.: Automatic tagging for open source software by utilizing package dependency information. In: 2020 International Symposium on Theoretical Aspects of Software Engineering (TASE), pp. 137–144. IEEE (2020)
5. Stefanie, B., Martin, P.: Synonym suggestion for tags on stack overflow. In: 2015 IEEE 23rd International Conference on Program Comprehension, pp. 94–103. IEEE (2015)
6. Xinhao, Z., Lin, L., Dong, Z.: An attentive deep supervision based semantic matching framework for tag recommendation in software information sites. In: 2020 27th Asia-Pacific Software Engineering Conference (APSEC), pp. 490–494. IEEE (2020)
7. David, M.B., Andrew, Y.Ng., Michael, I.J.: Latent dirichlet allocation. J. Mach. Learn. Res. **3**, 993–1022 (2003)
8. Tomas, M., Kai, C., Greg, C., Jeffrey, D.: Efficient estimation of word representations in vector space. arXiv preprint arXiv:1301.3781, 2013
9. Tim o'Reilly.: What is web 2.0. O'Reilly Media, Inc (2009)
10. Fabiano, M.B., Jussara, M.A., Marcos, A.G.: A survey on tag recommendation methods. J. Assoc. Inform. Sci. Technol. **68**(4), 830–844 (2017)
11. Tao, W., Gang, Y., Xiang, L., Huaimin, W.: Labeled topic detection of open source software from mining mass textual project profiles. In: Proceedings of the First International Workshop on Software Mining, pp. 17–24 (2012)
12. Wang, X.-Y., Xia, X., Lo, D.: Tagcombine: recommending tags to contents in software information sites. J. Comput. Sci. Technol. **30**(5), 1017–1035 (2015)
13. Wang, S., Lo, D., Vasilescu, B., Serebrenik, A.: EnTagRec: an enhanced tag recommendation system for software information sites. IEEE (2014)
14. Wang, S., Lo, D., Vasilescu, B., Serebrenik, A.: Entagrec++: an enhanced tag recommendation system for software information sites. Empir. Softw. Eng. **23**(2), 800–832 (2018)
15. Otter, D.W., Medina, J.R., Kalita, J.K.: A survey of the usages of deep learning for natural language processing. IEEE Trans. Neural Netw. Learn. Syst. **32**(2), 604–624 (2021)
16. Nal, K., Edward, G., Phil, B.: A convolutional neural network for modelling sentences. arXiv preprint arXiv:1404.2188 (2014)
17. Pengfei, L., Xipeng, Q., Xuanjing, H.: Recurrent neural network for text classification with multi-task learning. arXiv preprint arXiv:1605.05101 (2016)

18. Zichao, Y., Diyi, Y., Chris, D., Xiaodong, H., Alex, S., Eduard, H.: Hierarchical attention networks for document classification. In Proceedings of the 2016 Conference of The North American Chapter of The Association for Computational Linguistics: Human Language Technologies, pp. 1480–1489 (2016)
19. Siwei, L., Liheng, X., Kang, L., Jun, Z.: Recurrent convolutional neural networks for text classification. In Twenty-Ninth AAAI Conference on Artificial Intelligence (2015)
20. Zhou, P., Liu, J., Liu, X., Yang, Z., Grundy, J.: Is deep learning better than traditional approaches in tag recommendation for software information sites? Inf. Softw. Technol. **109**, 1–13 (2019)
21. Li, J.C., Yuan, C., Song, Y.: Multi-label image annotation based on convolutional neural network. Comput. Sci. **43**(7), 41–45 (2016)
22. Pingyi, Z., Jin, L., Zijiang, Y., Guangyou, Z.: Scalable tag recommendation for software information sites. In: 2017 IEEE 24th International Conference on Software Analysis, Evolution and Reengineering (SANER), pp. 272–282. IEEE (2017)
23. Liu, J., Zhou, P., Yang, Z., Liu, X., Grundy, J.: FastTagRec: fast tag recommendation for software information sites. Autom. Softw. Eng. **25**(4), 675–701 (2018)
24. Jiang, J., Qiudi, W., Cao, J., Xia, X., Zhang, L.: Recommending tags for pull requests in github. Inf. Softw. Technol. **129**, 106394 (2021)
25. Juri, D.R., Davide, D.R., Claudio, D.S., Phuong, N., Riccardo, R.: TopFilter: an approach to recommend relevant github topics. In Proceedings of the 14th ACM/IEEE International Symposium on Empirical Software Engineering and Measurement (ESEM), pp. 1–11 (2020)
26. Junyoung, C., Caglar, G., KyungHyun, C., Yoshua, B.: Empirical evaluation of gated recurrent neural networks on sequence modeling. arXiv preprint arXiv:1412.3555 (2014)
27. Jin, L., Yihe, Y., Shiqi, L., Jin, W., Hui, C.: Attention-based BiGRU-CNN for Chinese question classification. J. Ambient Intell. Human. Comput. 1–12 (2019)

# Co-contrastive Learning
# for Multi-behavior Recommendation

Qingfeng Li[1], Huifang Ma[1(✉)], Ruoyi Zhang[1], Wangyu Jin[1],
and Zhixin Li[2]

[1] Northwest Normal University, Lanzhou 730070, Gansu, China
mahuifang@yeah.net
[2] Guangxi Normal University, Guilin 541001, Guangxi, China

**Abstract.** Multi-behavior recommender system (MBR) typically utilizes multi-typed user interactive behaviors (e.g., view, add-to-cart and
purchase) in learning user preference on target behavior (i.e., purchase).
Existing MBR models suffer from sparse supervised signals, which may
degrade recommendation performance to some extent. Inspired by contrastive learning's recent success in mining additional supervision signals from raw data itself, in this work, we propose a non-sampling
**C**o-**C**ontrastive **L**earning (CCL) to enhance MBR. Technically, we first
exploit the multi-behavior interaction graph to augment two views (interactive view and fold view) that capture both local and high-order structures simultaneously, and then two asymmetric graph encoders are performed over the two views, which recursively leverage the different
structural information to generate ground-truth samples to collaboratively supervise each other by contrastive learning and finally high-level
node embeddings are learned. Moreover, divergence constraint further
improves co-contrastive learning performance. Extensive experiments on
two real-world benchmark datasets demonstrate that CCL significantly
outperforms the state-of-the-art methods of existing MBR.

**Keywords:** Contrastive learning · Multi-behavior recommendation ·
Graph neural network · Collaborative filtering

## 1 Introduction

With the rapid development of online platforms and the dramatic increase of
online user behavior types, an emerging multi-behavior recommendation (MBR)
scenario has played a vital role in improving user experience [1]. Unlike traditional recommendation methods, MBR typically utilizes auxiliary behaviors
(e.g., view, add-to-cart and click) to enhance user preference learning on the
target behavior (i.e., purchase). Multiple types of behaviors are interdepen-
dent and complementary to each other, and reveal user preferences in different
intention dimensions. Therefore, modeling hidden dependencies between multiple behaviors is essential for better learning of user preference. Recently, some

S. Khanna et al. (Eds.): PRICAI 2022, LNCS 13631, pp. 32–45, 2022.
https://doi.org/10.1007/978-3-031-20868-3_3

studies seek to explicitly model multi-behavior inter-dependencies by introducing prior behavior correlations. For example, Neural Multi-Task Recommendation (NMTR) [2] assumes that there is a total order to the behavior types, and then sorts them according to prior knowledge. Analogously, Efficient Heterogeneous Collaborative Filtering (EHCF) [3] is based on a transfer learning paradigm to correlate multiple behaviors and optimize the model by using a non-sampling method based on the whole data. Another line of research models behavior dependency by generating specific types of embeddings. For example, MBGCN [4] develops a behavior-aware embedding propagation layer to capture the collaborative signals transmitted by high-hop neighbors under different behaviors, thus enhancing preference learning in target behaviors. Criterion-based Heterogeneous Collaborative Filtering (CHCF) [5] introduces selection criteria learning to fine-grained modeling of different user preference strengths for different items. Despite their achievements, these models based on a supervised learning paradigm are still hampered by the same problem (i.e., sparse supervised signals), for the sparsity of observed interactions. Therefore, we are unable to infer a precise user preference, resulting in degraded recommendation performance.

Excitingly, contrastive learning, as a typical self-supervised learning technique, can mine auxiliary supervision signals from the raw data itself to complement the classical supervision signals derived only from observed interactions [6]. This novel technique is regarded to be an antidote to the sparse supervised signals problem and gradually attracts more and more attention. A common way of applying contrastive learning to recommendation is to perform stochastic data augmentations by randomly dropping some nodes from the raw user-item interaction graph to create supervision signals [7], which has achieved promising results. For example, SGL [8] summarizes three types of stochastic augmentations on graphs including node dropout, edge dropout and random walk, and then integrate them into a general self-supervised learning framework for recommendation. CML [7] utilizes meta-learning to preserve multi-behavior contextual information and refines the user representation by maximizing multi-behavior view consistency. MMCLR [9] considers the commonalities and differences between different behaviors and views by performing contrastive learning on three different views. However, neither conducting dropout on the user-item interaction graph nor simply considering different user behavior characteristics is unfit for improving recommendation performance.

To address the above problems, we propose a non-sampling Co-Contrastive Learning (CCL) to generate more informative self-supervision signals to enhance multi-behavior recommendation. Specifically, two distinct graph encoders are built over these two views (interactive view and fold view) so as to capture both local and high-order structures simultaneously. Then a co-contrastive objective function is optimized towards refining the view encoders and user representations. Meanwhile, to make the co-contrastive learning of these two views more complex, divergence constraint are exploited to encourage divergence between the two view encoders. Finally, we adopt an efficient non-sampling learning strategy to optimize our model parameters, and integrate the above modules into a unified framework.

In summary, the contributions of our work are as follows:

- We propose a novel non-sampling co-contrastive learning framework for multi-behavior recommendation which can exploit both local and high-order structural information of multi-behavior interaction graph, and then generate more informative and practicable supervised signals.
- In our CCL, two independent but also complementary views learn from each other with co-contrastive learning, thus capturing user preference in two aspects and finally learning high-level user embeddings. Furthermore, divergence constraint makes the two encoders differ, so as to improve co-contrastive leaning performance.
- Extensive experiments on two benchmark datasets show that our proposed framework CCL consistently outperforms the state-of-the-art baselines and achieves significant improvements, especially for cold-start users.

The rest of this paper is organized as follows. Some preliminary information of our CCL is provided in Sect. 2. Then, we present our CCL in Sect. 3. The experimental results and analysis are reported in Sect. 4. Finally, we conclude this paper in Sect. 5.

## 2 Preliminaries

We denote the user and item sets as $U = \{u_1, u_2, \ldots, u_m\}$ and $V = \{v_1, v_2, \ldots, v_n\}$, where $m$ and $n$ represent the number of users and items, respectively. We use $u$ and $v$ to denote a user and an item respectively. The user-item interaction matrices with $K$ types of behavior are denoted as $\{\mathbf{Y}_{(1)}, \mathbf{Y}_{(2)}, \ldots, \mathbf{Y}_{(K)}\}$, where a value of 1 for each entry of $\mathbf{Y}_{(k)}$ indicates that the user has interacted with the item under $k$-th behavior, otherwise the value is 0. Generally, in multi-behavior recommendation scenarios, we regard the last $K$-th behavior as the target behavior to be optimized, and the first $K - 1$ behaviors as auxiliary behaviors. The relevant concepts of the view are further defined as follows:

**Interactive View.** $G^I$. Based on multiple types of interactions between users and items, the interactive view with behavior multiplicity is defined as: $G^I = \{G_k^I = (U, V, \mathbf{Y}_{(k)})\}_{k=1}^{k=K}$. Interactive view is used to describe the direct connections between users and items, which contains local structural information and can capture direct interactive messages.

**Fold View.** $G^F$. To exploit high-order relationships, we define $G_u^F = \{G_{u,k}^F = (U, \mathbf{Y}_{(k)}^F)\}_{k=1}^{k=K}$ to characterize the common interaction of multiple behaviors between users. In $G_u^F$, $y_{(k)u,u'}^F = 1$, $\{(u, k, u') \mid u, u' \in U, k \in K\}$ indicates that both $u$ and $u'$ have interacted with the same item under $k$-th behavior. Such as $u$

and $u'$ purchased the same items, viewed the same items, or have the same items in the shopping cart. Otherwise, $y^F_{(k)u,u'} = 0$. Analogously, we can get the definition of the items as $G^F_v$. Finally, we obtain the full definition $G^F = (G^F_u, G^F_v)$.

**Problem Statement:** Given the target user $u$, the target item $v$, the interactive view $G^I$ and fold view $G^F$. The task of our model is to predict the interaction probability between user $u$ and item $v$ under the target behavior.

# 3   Methodology

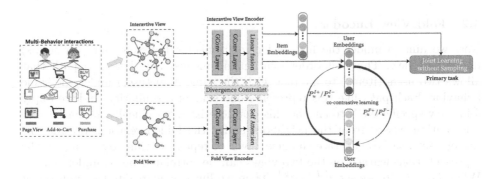

**Fig. 1.** The overall architecture of our proposed CCL.

In this section, we propose CCL, a novel non-sampling dual-view co-contrastive learning model. The overall architecture is shown in Fig. 1, which has three important components: (1). Two asymmetric view encoders, which respectively encode users and items from interactive view and fold view so as to exploit both local and high-order heterogeneous user-item interactions simultaneously. (sections 3.1 and 3.2); (2). Divergence constraint in training, which utilizes adversarial samples to encourage divergence between the two view encoders. With the two view-specific embeddings, we employ a co-contrastive learning to exploit two different aspects of structural information across these two views. (sections 3.3 and 3.4); (3). Efficient non-sampling learning module is introduced to achieve effective and stable model optimization (Sect. 3.5).

## 3.1   Interactive View Encoder

Here we follow LightGCN [10] to capture the CF signals along with the graph structure of user-item heterogeneous interactions. LightGCN discards redundant nonlinear activation and feature transformation, making it more adaptable to recommendation scenarios. In our model, the embedding of a user (or item) is modeled by accumulating the incoming messages from all the heterogeneous interacted items (or users). Given user $u$, after performing $L$ layers of embedding propagation under $k$-th behavior, we get multiple representations of user $u$, i.e., $\{\mathbf{q}_u^{k,1}, \mathbf{q}_u^{k,2}, \ldots, \mathbf{q}_u^{k,L}\}$, where $\mathbf{q}_u^{k,l}$ denotes the embedding of user $u$ at the $l$-th layer under $k$-th behavior, and $\mathbf{q}_u^{k,0}$ is generated from ID embedding layer which is trainable parameters. Noted that the embeddings at 0-th layer do not distinguish between types of behavior. To obtain final embedding of each layer, then we introduce the behavior coefficient parameter $\lambda_k$ to fuse embeddings of user $u$ under $K$ types of behaviors. It can be calculated as follows: $\mathbf{q}_u^l = \sum_{k=1}^K \lambda_k \mathbf{q}_u^{k,l}$. Note that we additionally require that $\sum_{k=1}^K \lambda_k = 1$ to make tweaking these hyper-parameters easier. The embeddings obtained from different layers emphasize the information conveyed from different hops. Therefore, we further average them to be the final learned embeddings: $\mathbf{q}_u = \frac{1}{L+1} \sum_{l=0}^L \mathbf{q}_u^l$.

## 3.2 Fold View Encoder

Now we aim to model the high-order relationships between users (or items) under fold view. This high-order relationship means that there is a path that allows two users (items) to interact with the same item (user) under the same behavior. Each path like this represents one semantic similarity, and we apply fold view specific GCN to encode this characteristic. Specifically, we gather the information passed from the neighbors under the folded relationship and the target user itself to generate the next layer of representation. By doing so, the representations learned on the two views can be correlated but complementary. When layer $l = 0$, we set $\mathbf{z}_u^{k,l} = \mathbf{q}_u^{k,l}$. Then we linearly aggregate the multi-layer representations. With $K$ behaviors, we can get $K$ embeddings $\{\mathbf{z}_u^1, \mathbf{z}_u^2, \ldots, \mathbf{z}_u^K\}$ for user $u$. Then we utilize behavior-level attention to fuse them into the final embedding $\mathbf{z}_u$ under the fold view:

$$\mathbf{z}_u = \sum_{k=1}^K \beta_u^k \mathbf{z}_u^k \qquad (1)$$

where $\beta_u^k$ weighs the importance of behavior $k$, and it can be calculated as follows:

$$w_u^k = \mathbf{h}_f^T \cdot tanh(\mathbf{W}_f \mathbf{z}_u^k + \mathbf{b}_f)$$
$$\beta_u^k = \frac{exp\left(w_u^k\right)}{\sum_{k=1}^K exp\left(w_u^k\right)} \qquad (2)$$

where $\mathbf{W}_f \in \mathbb{R}^{d \times d}$ and $\mathbf{b}_f \in \mathbb{R}^d$ are the learnable parameters, and $\mathbf{h}_f \in \mathbb{R}^d$ denotes the behavior-level attention vector. Note that item embeddings in both the interactive view and fold view are generated similarly to the user embeddings, so we omit these process for brevity.

## 3.3 Divergence Constraint

In our CCL, the two views for contrastive learning are constructed from the same data source by exploiting different structural information, which may cause mode collapse problems. Inspired by [11], we integrate adversarial samples into training to impose divergence constraint on the co-contrastive learning mechanism so that the two view encoders become different to some extent. In theory, the adversarial samples against one encoder can mislead it to generate incorrect predictions. However, if two encoders are trained to resist each other's adversarial samples while still output correct predictions, we can achieve the aim of keeping them different. The divergence constraint is defined as follows:

$$
\begin{aligned}
\mathcal{L}_{dc} = KL(P_I(\mathbf{Q}_v), P_F(\mathbf{Z}_v + \Delta_a^I)) \\
+ KL(P_F(\mathbf{Z}_v), P_I(\mathbf{Q}_v + \Delta_a^F))
\end{aligned}
\tag{3}
$$

where $\mathbf{Q}_v \in \mathbb{R}^{n \times d}$ and $\mathbf{Z}_v \in \mathbb{R}^{n \times d}$ are the representations of items in the interactive view and fold view, respectively. $P_I(\cdot)$ and $P_F(\cdot)$ represent the likelihood of each item to be recommended to a given user $u$, which are calculated by two view encoders: $P_I = Softmax(\mathbf{Q}_v \mathbf{q}_u)$, and $P_F = Softmax(\mathbf{Z}_v \mathbf{z}_u)$. The adversarial perturbations on the item embeddings with respect to interactive view and fold view are represented by $\Delta_a^I$ and $\Delta_a^F$, and $KL(\cdot)$ represent KL divergence. Specifically, $P_F(\mathbf{Z}_v + \Delta_a^I)$ is the likelihood distribution generated by the fold view encoder when $\mathbf{Z}_v$ is perturbed by $\Delta_a^I$. If the fold view encoder is immune to $\Delta_a^I$ that is harmful to the interactive view encoder, it will output a likelihood distribution similar to $P_I(\mathbf{Q}_v)$, and then leading to a smaller loss, otherwise not. Inspired by the FGSM method [12], we add adversarial perturbations $\Delta_a^I$ and $\Delta_a^F$ on item embedding under two views through fast gradient calculation.

### 3.4  Co-contrastive Learning

In this section, we show how co-contrastive learning mines informative supervised signals to enhance multi-behavior recommendation.

**Mining Supervision Signals.** Recall that in the previous four subsections, we design two distinct view encoders over two different views that can supply complementary information to each other. As a result, it is natural to refine each view encoder by using the information from the other view. This can be accomplished by following the co-contrastive learning regimen. First of all, we design a novel sample selection strategy with the core idea that those users who are similar to the target user on one view are also similar to the target user on another view. To be specific, given a user $u$ in the interactive view, we predict its positive and negative samples by using its representation learned across the fold view:

$$
\mathbf{s}_u^F = Softmax(\mathbf{score}_u^F), \mathbf{score}_u^F = \mathbf{Z}_u \mathbf{z}_u
\tag{4}
$$

where $\mathbf{Z}_u \in \mathbb{R}^{m \times d}$ is the representations of users in the fold view, $\mathbf{z}_u \in \mathbb{R}^d$ is the representation of user $u$ in the fold view, and $\mathbf{s}_u^F \in \mathbb{R}^m$ denotes the similarity scores of the target user $u$ with all other users in fold view. $\mathbf{z}_u$ can be regard as a linear classifier, and $\mathbf{Z}_u$ can be considered as the original unlabeled sample set. With the computed similarity scores under fold view, we can select users with the top-$N$ highest similarity scores as the positive samples, which operate as the augmented ground-truths to supervise the interactive view encoder. The positive sample selection is formalized as follows:

$$P_u^{I+} = \text{top-}N(\mathbf{s}_u^F). \tag{5}$$

As for the strategy of selecting negative samples, a simple idea is to take the items with the lowest similarity scores as negative samples. However, this method can only choose simple samples that contribute little. Instead, we first exclude positive samples from the top 10% of user rankings $\mathbf{s}_u^F$, and then randomly select $N$ samples as our negative samples to construct $P_u^{I-}$. These users can be considered as hard negatives that provide sufficient information while also being less likely to fall into the set of false negatives that would mislead the learning. Analogously, we select informative samples for the fold view encoder in a similar manner and then obtain user's positive and negative samples denoted as $P_u^{F+}$ and $P_u^{F-}$. For the sake of brevity, this part is omitted. The positive and negative pseudo-labels for each user in each view are iteratively reconstructed in each training batch, and then are supplied to the other view as the positive and negative samples for refining user representations.

**Co-contrastive Learning.** With the generated positive and negative samples, the task for refining view encoders can be performed through a co-contrastive objective function. Formally, we work as the previous studies [8,13] to follow InfoNCE [14], which is effective in mutual information estimation, as our learning objective to maximize the agreement between positive pairs and minimize that of negative pairs. With the positive set $P_u^{I+}$ and negative set $P_u^{I-}$, we have the following contrastive loss under interactive view:

$$\mathcal{L}_u^I = -log \frac{\sum_{i \in P_u^{I+}} exp\left(g\left(\mathbf{q}_u, \mathbf{q}_i\right)/\tau\right)}{\sum_{i \in P_u^{I+}} exp\left(g\left(\mathbf{q}_u, \mathbf{q}_i\right)/\tau\right) + \sum_{j \in P_u^{I-}} exp\left(g\left(\mathbf{q}_u, \mathbf{q}_j\right)/\tau\right)} \tag{6}$$

where $\tau$ is the temperature parameter to amplify the effect of discrimination, and $g\left(\cdot\right)$ is the cosine similarity function. The contrastive loss $\mathcal{L}_u^F$ is similar as $\mathcal{L}_u^I$, but the difference is that the target user embedding is from the fold view, while the positive and negative samples are generated from the interactive view. The overall co-contrastive loss is defined as follows:

$$\mathcal{L}_{ccl} = \frac{1}{|U|} \sum_{u \in U} \left[\rho \cdot \mathcal{L}_u^I + (1 - \rho) \cdot \mathcal{L}_u^F\right] \tag{7}$$

where $\rho$ is a hyper-parameter that balances the effects of the two views. Two views can continuously exchange information through co-contrastive learning between positive and negative pairs, thus merging the local collaborative signals from the interactive view and the high-order semantic information from the fold view, and finally obtaining a high-level user representation.

## 3.5  Efficient Joint Learning Without Sampling

With the dense vector representations of users and items, we predict user preference by projecting the user representations and item representations under interactive view to the predict layer, which can be written as follows: $\hat{y}_{uv} = \alpha_r^T(\mathbf{q}_u \odot \mathbf{q}_v) = \sum_{i=1}^d \alpha_{r,i} q_{u,i} q_{v,i}$. To train model in a more effective and stable manner, we follow [5] to introduce criterion-based learning. Specifically, we introduce user idiosyncrasies matrix $\mathbf{H} \in \mathbb{R}^{|U| \times K}$ and item properties matrix $\mathbf{G} \in \mathbb{R}^{|V| \times K}$ to approximate bound matrices: $\mathbf{T}^{(k)} = \mathbf{H}_k \mathbf{G}_k^T, \mathbf{B}^{(k)} = \mu \mathbf{T}^{(k)}$. where $0 \leq \mu \leq 1$ is a hyper-parameter that can be used to alter the ratio of two bounds. Note that $\mathbf{T}^{(k)} \in \mathbb{R}^{|U| \times |V|}$ and $\mathbf{B}^{(k)} \in \mathbb{R}^{|U| \times |V|}$ are upper and lower bound matrices under the $k$-th behavior, respectively. After obtaining the user-item likelihood and bound matrices, the non-sampling learning loss of the $k$-th behavior is given as follows:

$$
\mathcal{L}_{main}^{(k)} = \sum_{u \in U} \left( \sum_{v \in V_u^{(k)+}} \phi\left(f\left(T_{uv}^{(k)} - \hat{y}_{uv}\right)\right) + c \sum_{v' \in V_u^{(k)-}} \phi\left(f\left(\hat{y}_{uv'} - B_{uv'}^{(k)}\right)\right) \right)
$$

(8)

where $V_u^{(k)+}(V_u^{(k)-})$ denotes the set of observed (unobserved) items for user $u$ under the $k$-th behavior, $f(\cdot)$ denotes $max(\cdot, 0)$, $c$ represents the weight of negative entry. Here $\phi(x) = x^2$ is used to describes the distance between the scores and bounds.

To learn model parameters more effectively from all of the heterogeneous data, we leverage a multi-task learning strategy (MTL) [15] to jointly train the models of distinct but related tasks, and the final main recommendation loss is defined as:

$$
\mathcal{L}_{main} = \sum_{k=1}^K \lambda_k \mathcal{L}_{main}^{(k)}
$$

(9)

where $\lambda_k$ is the same as in the interactive view encoder, and the final target behavior prediction score $\hat{y}_{uv}^{(K)}$ is computed by $\hat{y}_{uv}/T_{uv}^{(K)}$. The overall objective of the joint learning is defined as:

$$
\mathcal{L}_{all} = \mathcal{L}_{main} + \zeta \mathcal{L}_{ccl} + \eta \mathcal{L}_{dc} + \gamma \|\Theta\|_2^2
$$

(10)

where $\zeta$, $\eta$ and $\gamma$ are hyper-parameters used to control the magnitude of the co-contrastive learning, divergence constraint and $L_2$ regularization, $\Theta$ is the set of learnable parameters. Note that we jointly optimize the three tasks throughout the training.

# 4    Experiments

## 4.1    Datasets

Table 1. Statistical details of the two evaluation datasets.

| Dataset | #User | #Item | #View | #Add-to-cart | #Purchase |
|---|---|---|---|---|---|
| Beibei | 21,716 | 7,977 | 2,412,586 | 642,622 | 304,576 |
| Taobao | 48,749 | 39,493 | 1,548,126 | 193,747 | 259,747 |

We perform extensive experiments on two real-world benchmark datasets : Beibei[1] and Taobao[2] which contain three types of user behaviors including view, add-to-cart, purchase. We present the statistical details of two datasets in Table 1. The datasets performed in the experiments are the same as previous works [3, 5, 18][3] for fair comparison.

## 4.2    Compared Models

To demonstrate the effectiveness of our proposed CCL, we compare it with various representative and state-of-the-art methods: (1). Single-behavior methods including NCF [16], ENMF [17] and LightGCN [10]; (2). Multi-behavior methods including NMTR [2], EHCF [3], MBGCN [4], GHCF [18] and CHCF [5].

## 4.3    Experimental Settings

**Parameter Settings.** After the tuning process, the number of layers $l$ is set to 1, and c is set to 0.1 for Beibei and 0.01 for Taobao. The coefficient parameter $\lambda_k$ is set to 1/6, 5/6 and 0 for Beibei and 2/6, 4/6 and 0 for Taobao for view, cart and purchase behaviors, respectively. The number of positive and negative samples is set to 10. The introduced hyper-parameter, such as bound ratio $\mu$ is set to 0.1 for Beibei and 0.5 for Taobao by validation. For space reasons, we only show the analyses of the coefficient parameter $\lambda_k$.

**Evaluation Metrics.** Following [3, 5, 18], we adopt the leave-one-out evaluation strategy, and then investigate the ranking performance by using two widely used ranking-based metrics: HR@N and NDCG@N. For each method, we run it five times and report the average results.

---

[1] https://www.beibei.com/.
[2] https://tianchi.aliyun.com/dataset/dataDetail?dataId=649/.
[3] http://github.com/chenchongthu/EHCF.

## 4.4  Performance Comparison

To more clearly demonstrate the great potential of contrastive learning in alleviating the issue of sparse supervised signals, we choose the Taobao dataset with more sparse interactions to present the experimental results in Table 2. And similar observations are made on the Beibei dataset. In order to evaluate the impact of different recommendation lengths on Top-N performance, we set the value of N to {10, 50, 100} following [3, 5, 18]. From these results, the following key observations can be made: (1). Multi-behavior methods generally perform better than single-behavior methods; (2). Non-sampling methods (EHCF, GHCF, CHCF, CCL) generally perform better than sampling-based methods (NMTR, MBGCN); (3). Co-contrastive learning can effectively alleviate the problem of sparse supervision signals. Compare with the state-of-the-art baseline method CHCF, our proposed method CCL has a greater improvement on the Taobao dataset; (4). Our proposed method CCL consistently outperforms other baseline methods on Taobao dataset. The substantial improvements can be attributed to two reasons: 1). The dual-view mechanism captures both local and high-order structural information; 2). The proposed co-contrastive learning, which explicitly distill richer supervised signals from two views. Divergence constraint further improve the performance of co-contrastive learning.

**Table 2.** The performance of all compared methods on Taobao. All results have the statistical significance for $p < 0.01$ compared with the best baseline.

| Taobao | HR | | | NDCG | | |
|---|---|---|---|---|---|---|
| | 10 | 50 | 100 | 10 | 50 | 100 |
| **NCF** | 0.0391 | 0.0728 | 0.0897 | 0.0233 | 0.0281 | 0.0321 |
| **ENMF** | 0.0398 | 0.0743 | 0.0936 | 0.0244 | 0.0298 | 0.0339 |
| **LightGCN** | 0.0415 | 0.0814 | 0.1025 | 0.0237 | 0.0325 | 0.0359 |
| **NMTR** | 0.0585 | 0.0942 | 0.1368 | 0.0278 | 0.0334 | 0.0394 |
| **MBGCN** | 0.0701 | 0.1522 | 0.2169 | 0.0390 | 0.0571 | 0.0653 |
| **EHCF** | 0.0717 | 0.1618 | 0.2211 | 0.0403 | 0.0594 | 0.0690 |
| **GHCF** | 0.0807 | 0.1892 | 0.2599 | 0.0442 | 0.0678 | 0.0792 |
| **CHCF** | <u>0.1465</u> | <u>0.2416</u> | <u>0.2829</u> | <u>0.0891</u> | <u>0.1102</u> | <u>0.1169</u> |
| **CCL** | **0.1817** | **0.2883** | **0.3400** | **0.1154** | **0.1390** | **0.1473** |

## 4.5  Effectiveness Analysis on Data Sparsity Issue

The issue of data sparsity is a key challenge for recommender system. Although the introduction of multi-behavior information can expand the interaction data, there is still a lack of data self-driven methods (i.e., contrastive learning) to alleviate this problem. Therefore, we further investigate how CCL alleviates the issue of users with few records of target behavior. From Fig. 2, we can find that compared with the best baseline method CHCF, our method CCL consistently outperforms more than 7% in both metrics HR @100 and NDCG @100 on two datasets. Since CCL models heterogeneous behavior relations from different aspects and utilizes a co-contrastive learning mechanism to adaptively extract supervision signals, it can achieve good performance for users with sparse interactions.

### 4.6   Ablation Study

To understand the effectiveness of dual-view learning, co-contrastive learning and divergence constraint, we design several variants of CCL as follows: (1). CCL-I only uses interactive view to learn user/item embeddings; (2). CCL-F only uses fold view to learn user/item embeddings; (3). CCL-S removes co-contrastive learning mechanism and then only uses simple summing of user/item embeddings on two views to get the final embedding; (4). CCL-D removes divergence constraint in co-training.

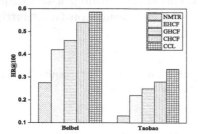 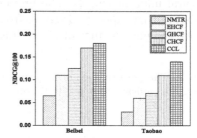

**Fig. 2.** The performance comparison of NMTR, EHCF, GHCF, CHCF and our CCL on users with $5 \sim 8$ purchase records.

**Table 3.** The performance of variants of CCL on two datasets.

| Variants | Beibei | | Taobao | |
|---|---|---|---|---|
| | HR@100 | NDCG@100 | HR@100 | NDCG@100 |
| **CCL-I** | 0.5645 | 0.1677 | 0.3025 | 0.1210 |
| **CCL-F** | 0.4208 | 0.1531 | 0.2480 | 0.1013 |
| **CCL-S** | 0.5520 | 0.1799 | 0.2711 | 0.1149 |
| **CCL-D** | 0.5886 | 0.1814 | 0.3297 | 0.1438 |
| **CCL** | **0.5942** | **0.1851** | **0.3400** | **0.1473** |

From Table 3, the following observations can be made: (1). From the comparison of CCL-I with CCL-F, we find that the information delivered by directly connected neighbors is even more important in modeling user behavior preferences. Therefore, we choose the interactive view encoder as main encoder; (2).

CCL using co-contrastive mechanism is consistently superior to CCL-S, which validates that co-contrastive learning can extract high-level factors from both two views to guide user preference learning; (3). CCL consistently outperforms CCL-D, which validates that utilizing divergence constraint in co-contrastive learning can further improve recommendation performance. The reasons are that divergence constraint is effective to prevent mode collapse and further make the co-contrastive learning of these two views more complex by differentiating the two view encoders.

### 4.7  Parameter Sensitivity Analysis

As the parameter of behavior coefficient $\lambda_k$ in the multi-task loss function plays a critical role in CCL, we also investigate its influences on the performance. Since there are three types of behavior on Beibei and Taobao (i.e., view, add-to-cart, and purchase), which indicates that there are three behavior coefficient parameters $\lambda_1$, $\lambda_2$ and $\lambda_3$, respectively. From Fig. 3, we can find that a relatively large coefficient parameter of cart behavior achieves better performance on both two datasets, which may be due to the inference that purchase interactions are too sparse to provide sufficient supervision signals and the view interactions contain too much noise. The best performance of CCL is achieved at $\{1/6, 5/6, 0\}$ on Beibei and $\{2/6, 4/6, 0\}$ on Taobao. It should be noted that the purchase behavior coefficient value of 0 does not mean that we do not use purchase behavior data, we adaptively learn behavior-related information for prediction by using co-contrastive learning.

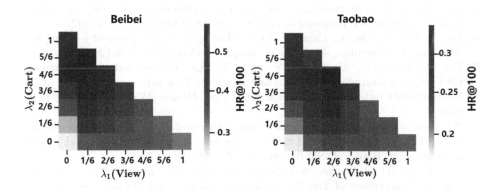

**Fig. 3.** The performance of CCL on Beibei and Taobao with different $\lambda_1$ and $\lambda_2$.

## 5  Conclusion

In this paper, we investigate the problem of enhancing multi-behavior recommendation with contrastive learning. Two independent but also complementary views are mutually supervised by co-contrastive learning, divergence constraint are introduced to further improve the contrastive learning performance, and finally the model is optimized using joint learning. Extensive experiments on two real-world benchmark datasets indicate that our method CCL consistently and significantly outperforms the state-of-the-art recommendation methods.

**Acknowledgment.** This study is supported by the National Natural Science Foundation of China (61762078, 61363058, 61966004), Natural Science Foundation of Gansu Province (21JR7RA114), Northwest Normal University Young Teachers Research Capacity Promotion plan (NWNU-LKQN2019-2), Industrial Support Project of Gansu Colleges (No. 2022CYZC-11).

# References

1. Wei, Y., Ma, H., Wang, Y., Li, Z., Chang, L.: Multi-behavior recommendation with two-level graph attentional networks. In: Proceedings of the 27th International Conference on Database Systems for Advanced Applications (DASFAA), pp. 248–255 (2022)
2. Gao, C., et al.: Neural multi-task recommendation from multi-behavior data. In: Proceedings of the 35th International Conference on Data Engineering (ICDE), pp. 1554–1557 (2019)
3. Chen, C., Zhang, M., Zhang, Y., Ma, W., Liu, Y., Ma, S.: Efficient heterogeneous collaborative filtering without negative sampling for recommendation. In: Proceedings of the AAAI Conference on Artificial Intelligence, vol. 34, pp. 19–26 (2020)
4. Jin, B., Gao, C., He, X., Jin, D., Li, Y.: Multi-behavior recommendation with graph convolutional networks. In: Proceedings of the 43rd International ACM SIGIR Conference on Research and Development in Information Retrieval (SIGIR), pp. 659–668 (2020)
5. Luo, X., et al.: Criterion-based heterogeneous collaborative filtering for multi-behavior implicit recommendation. arXiv preprint arXiv:2105.11876 (2021)
6. Yu, J., Yin, H., Xia, X., Chen, T., Li, J., Huang, Z.: Self-supervised learning for recommender systems: a survey. arXiv preprint arXiv:2203.15876 (2022)
7. Wei, W., Huang, C., Xia, L., Xu, Y., Zhao, J., Yin, D.: Contrastive meta learning with behavior multiplicity for recommendation. In: Proceedings of the 15nth ACM International Conference on Web Search and Data Mining (WSDM), pp. 1120–1128 (2022)
8. Wu, J., et al.: Self-supervised graph learning for recommendation. In: Proceedings of the 44th International ACM SIGIR Conference on Research and Development in Information Retrieval (SIGIR), pp. 726–735 (2021)
9. Wu, Y., et al.: Multi-view multi-behavior contrastive learning in recommendation. In: Proceedings of 27th International Conference on Database Systems for Advanced Applications (DASFAA), pp. 166–182 (2022)
10. He, X., Deng, K., Wang, X., Li, Y., Zhang, Y., Wang, M.: LightGCN: simplifying and powering graph convolution network for recommendation. In: Proceedings of the 43rd International ACM SIGIR Conference on Research and Development in Information Retrieval (SIGIR), pp. 639–648 (2020)
11. Qiao, S., Shen, W., Zhang, Z., Wang, B., Yuille, A.: Deep co-training for semi-supervised image recognition. In: Ferrari, V., Hebert, M., Sminchisescu, C., Weiss, Y. (eds.) ECCV 2018. LNCS, vol. 11219, pp. 142–159. Springer, Cham (2018). https://doi.org/10.1007/978-3-030-01267-0_9

12. Goodfellow, I.J., Shlens, J., Szegedy, C.: Explaining and harnessing adversarial examples. In: Proceedings of the 3rd International Conference on Learning Representations (ICLR) (2015)
13. Wang, X., Liu, N., Han, H., Shi, C.: Self-supervised heterogeneous graph neural network with co-contrastive learning. In: Proceedings of the 27th ACM SIGKDD International Conference on Knowledge Discovery & Data Mining, pp. 1726–1736 (2021)
14. Van den Oord, A., Li, Y., Vinyals, O.: Representation learning with contrastive predictive coding. arXiv e-prints pp. arXiv-1807 (2018)
15. Argyriou, A., Evgeniou, T., Pontil, M.: Multi-task feature learning. In: Proceedings of the International Conference on Neural Information Processing Systems (NeurIPS), pp. 41–48 (2006)
16. He, X., Liao, L., Zhang, H., Nie, L., Hu, X., Chua, T.S.: Neural collaborative filtering. In: Proceedings of the 26th International Conference on World Wide Web (WWW), pp. 173–182 (2017)
17. Chen, C., Zhang, M., Zhang, Y., Liu, Y., Ma, S.: Efficient neural matrix factorization without sampling for recommendation. ACM Trans. Inform. Syst. (TOIS) **38**(2), 1–28 (2020)
18. Chen, C., et al.: Graph heterogeneous multi-relational recommendation. In: Proceedings of the AAAI Conference on Artificial Intelligence, vol. 35, pp. 3958–3966 (2021)

# Pattern Matching and Information-Aware Between Reviews and Ratings for Recommendation

Wei Yang[1,2($\boxtimes$)], Tengfei Huo[3,4], Yiqun Chen[1,2], and Zhiqiang Liu[4]

[1] University of Chinese Academy of Sciences, Beijing, China
[2] Institute of Automation, Chinese Academy of Sciences, Beijing, China
`weiyangvia@gmail.com, chenyiqun2020@ia.ac.cn`
[3] Institute of Computing Technology, Chinese Academy of Sciences, Beijing, China
`huotengfei19s@ict.ac.cn`
[4] WeChat AI, Tencent Inc., Beijing, China

**Abstract.** Real recommendation scenarios have diverse and multi-modal features, which are often high-dimensional, sparse, and heterogeneous, making it difficult to learn. To improve model performance, many studies jointly model the semantic information of user and item reviews. However, due to the inherent changes in natural language processing, it has become a challenge to more accurately model the semantic interaction and matching relationship between user and item reviews. In addition, most of the previous work directly connects text representations and numerical features without considering their natural gap. In view of this, we propose a novel Pattern Matching and Information-aware Network (MIAN). Specifically, we design a matching network composed of global matching and specific matching, which is used to model the matching information between user and item reviews. The specific matching module uses the item description as a bridge to assist in modeling more fine-grained matching relationships. In addition, we construct an information perception layer to align the information between reviews and numerical features. Furthermore, we adopt a joint learning manner for better model training by employing a matching task fusion, which benefits from the prior matching knowledge. Comprehensive experiments on five real-world datasets show that MIAN outperforms the state-of-the-art methods.

**Keywords:** Pattern matching · Information perception · Attention mechanism · Review-based recommendation

## 1 Introduction

Recommendation systems are widely used in advertising, e-commerce, media and other scenarios because they can effectively solve the problem of information overload [2]. There are rich feature data in real recommendation scenarios, including attribute features, context features, and historical features [4]. The

© The Author(s), under exclusive license to Springer Nature Switzerland AG 2022
S. Khanna et al. (Eds.): PRICAI 2022, LNCS 13631, pp. 46–59, 2022.
https://doi.org/10.1007/978-3-031-20868-3_4

rich features of users reflect personalized preference information [25]. How to effectively learn feature information from different modal data so as to improve recommendation performance is an important research direction [10,12]. The text data of the language modality is often generated in the form of item descriptions and user reviews. Since it directly covers the description information of the item, user reviews are of great value to assist in improving the recommendation effect [15,27]. User reviews contain the user's personal preference information, such as preferences for product styles and colors, while item reviews contain the feature description information of the item. Therefore, many researchers have begun to combine text review data to assist in recommendation [20,24].

However, the previous work has overlooked some problems. First, the simple connection of text representation and numerical features will introduce a lot of noise, making it difficult for the model to effectively learn important feature information [11]. Second, most of the work mainly learns text representation vectors for feature interaction, without in-depth consideration of the matching relationship between user and item reviews [21]. Third, although many works design joint modeling of user and item reviews to learn the semantic interaction information, user reviews and item reviews are obtained through the fusion of multiple reviews, which contain a lot of noisy information, such as the case where the same entity may have multiple emotional polarities [10]. If there is no solution designed to solve these problems, it will seriously affect the accuracy of the model [22,23].

Considering the above problems, we propose a new solution. First, we design a matching network for modeling the matching relationship between user and item reviews, so as to introduce matching information between reviews to assist recommendation. Specifically, we design a global matching module to learn the overall semantic matching degree between user and item reviews. Then we design a specific matching module to model the matching relationship between users and item reviews in a finer-grained manner by introducing product description information as a bridge. Second, we design an information perception layer to achieve information alignment between review features and numerical features. Third, we combine the text features and numerical features after information perception to learn high-level feature interactions through the interaction model. Finally, we design a model learning method for the joint optimization of matching task-assisted loss and rating prediction loss.

The main contributions of this paper can be summarized as follows:

- We first propose to introduce item description as a bridge to assist in modeling the matching relationship between user and item review, so that the model can learn more fine-grained matching information.
- We propose a novel and effective model named Pattern Matching and Information-aware Network (MIAN). MIAN can learn the matching information between user and item reviews, and provide more accurate recommendations based on the textual representation of information perception.
- We conduct comprehensive experiments on five real data sets, and our proposed MIAN model outperforms the state-of-the-art methods. Further experi-

ments verify that our proposed matching network and information perception are of real significance.

## 2  Related Work

Text reviews are used as incidental information to the ratings, expressing users' personal preferences for different product features [17]. Therefore, its rich information can learn useful features for the model to help improve the model's effect [28]. Some previous work is based on Latent Dirichlet Allocation (LDA) [1] and other topic models to learn review information. Obtaining the implicit vector representation of the topic information improves the model's ability to understand the text topic to a certain extent. However, the topic model is based on the bag-of-words model, which cannot effectively learn the semantic information of the text [21]. In addition, some researchers have proposed to learn more detailed review features from the perspective of aspect. Explicit Factor Model (EFM) [28] extracts user preferences for specific product features through aspect-level sentiment analysis, and then integrates the results into the Matrix Factorization (MF) [13] framework. Attentive Aspect-based Recommendation Model (AARM) [6] models the interaction between synonyms and similar aspects, and introduces an attention module to learn the importance of user features, and aspect information. However, these methods rely highly on the accuracy of external tools.

Due to its powerful learning and representation ability, neural networks can learn the semantic information of text more accurately than traditional methods [18]. Many methods start to learn implicit vector representation of reviews based on Convolutional Neural Network (CNN). Convolutional MF (ConvMF) [8] is based on CNN to learn text representation and integrates with the probabilistic matrix factorization model. Deep Cooperative Neural Network (DeepCoNN) [29] consists of two parallel neural networks, which are then coupled in the last layer. One network learns user preferences from user reviews, and the other network learns item attributes from item reviews. D-attn [16] designs the attention module to learn local and global text semantic information, thereby enhancing the model's semantic representation ability for reviews. Context-aware Representation Learning (CARL) [21] learns the semantic representation of user review documents and item review documents based on CNN, and designs an attention network to model the importance of different information.

There are also many works that use the attention mechanism to learn text features. D-attn [16] designs local and global attention networks to learn text features. Local attention focuses on user preferences or item attributes, and global attention can help learn the semantics of the entire review text. Neural Attentional Regression model with Review-level Explanations (NARRE) [3] introduces an attention mechanism to explore the usefulness of reviews to provide interpretable recommendations. Hierarchical User and Item Representation with Three-Tier Attention (HUITA) [20] designs a hierarchical representation network composed of three layers of attention networks, which are used to learn word-level, sentence-level, and article-level text semantic representations. Dual Attention Mutual Learning (DAML) [10] uses a convolutional neural network to learn reviews information, and designs a local attention layer and a mutual attention layer to learn important semantic information from the text.

# 3    The Proposed MIAN Model

In this section, we introduce the proposed MIAN model in detail, which is mainly composed of four parts. The overall architecture is shown in Fig. 1.

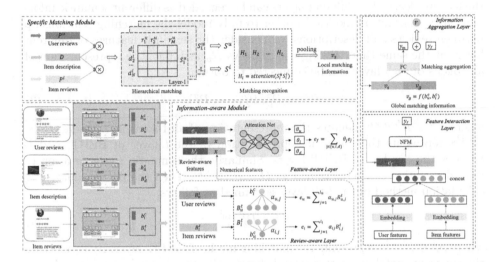

**Fig. 1.** The components and architecture of the proposed MIAN model.

## 3.1    Global Matching Module

User reviews contain the user's personal preference information, including purchase preferences, product type preferences, etc. Item reviews contain item attribute information, including item color, material, style, etc. Different from some previous work, we use BERT [5] to construct the semantic representation of the text. User reviews are denoted as $R_u$, which consists of $l_u$ words. We take $R_u$ as input and get the text representation through BERT as:

$$b_u^c, B_u^t = BERT(R_u) \tag{1}$$

where $b_u^c \in R^k$ represents the vector representation of [CLS] token, which contains the information of the entire text. $B_u^t \in R^{l_u \times k}$ denotes the vector representation of each token in the text. $k$ is the internal hidden size of BERT. Similarly, through BERT we can get the vector representations $b_i^c \in R^k$ and $B_i^t \in R^{l_i \times k}$

of item reviews. We calculate the global matching degree between user and item reviews based on the global representation of reviews:

$$v_g = f_g(W_g^T([b_u^c; b_i^c; b_u^c \odot b_i^c; b_u^c - b_i^c]) + \eta_g) \tag{2}$$

where $v_g \in R^d$ denotes the global matching vector, $\odot$ denotes the multiplication of the vector dimensions, and $f_g$ represents the activation function.

### 3.2 Specific Matching Module

**Hierarchical Matching Layer.** By modeling text information through BERT, the features learned at different layers can be regarded as different semantic information representation modes. In order to fully model the matching relationship between reviews and descriptions, we consider the semantic features of different layers at the same time. Taking user reviews $R_u$ as input, the representation of all tokens of each layer can be connected to obtain:

$$P^u = [P_1^u, P_2^u, \cdots, P_L^u] \tag{3}$$

where $P^u \in R^{L \times k \times l_u}$ denotes the representation of all tokens in $L$ layers, $P_l^u \in R^{k \times l_u}$ represents the semantic representation of the $l$ layer of BERT, and L denotes the number of BERT layers. Similarly, the semantic representation of item description can be obtained as $D \in R^{L \times k \times l_d}$. Then the pattern matching calculation method of the $l$-th layer is defined as follows:

$$S_l^u = D_l^T P_l^u \tag{4}$$

where $S_l^u \in R^{l_d \times l_u}$ represents the matching mode of the $l$-th layer. By connecting the different matching patterns of $L$ layers, the hierarchical matching of user reviews and item descriptions can be obtained as follows:

$$S^u = [S_1^u, S_2^u, \cdots, S_L^u] \tag{5}$$

where $S^u \in R^{L \times l_d \times l_u}$ represents a hierarchical matching matrix based on user reviews and item descriptions. In the same way, we can get the matrix $S^i \in R^{L \times l_d \times l_i}$ based on item reviews and item description.

**Matching Recognition Layer.** Through the hierarchical matching layer, two hierarchical matching matrices representing the matching relationship with the item description can be obtained. Further, the hierarchical matching information needs to be identified to determine the degree of matching between user and item reviews, which can be regarded as a secondary matching. We use the inner product to measure the similarity of two vectors as follows:

$$S^{ui} = S^{uT} S^i \tag{6}$$

where $S^{ui} \in R^{L \times l_u \times l_i}$ represents the similarity between user and item reviews in L semantic modes. Considering that the importance of different levels of semantic similarity is not the same, we introduce a self-attention mechanism to learn the importance of similarity, which is defined as:

$$H_l = softmax(\frac{Q_s K_s^T}{\sqrt{d_k}})V_s \tag{7}$$

where $H_l \in R^{l_u \times d_k}$ represents the matching matrix, $d_k$ denotes the dimension of the parameter matrix. $Q_s$, $K_s$ and $V_s$ are calculated as follows:

$$Q_s = S_l^{ui}W^Q, K_s = S_l^{ui}W^K, V_s = S_l^{ui}W^V \tag{8}$$

where $W^Q, W^K, W^V \in R^{l_i \times d_k}$ refer to the attention parameter matrix. Further, considering different levels of semantic matching information, we can obtain the multi-level attention perception matching matrix as follows:

$$A_s = Concat([H_1, H_2, \cdots, H_L])W_o \tag{9}$$

where $A \in R^{l_u \times d_k}$ represents the similarity information of multi-head attention perception. $W_o \in R^{Ld_k \times d_k}$ denotes the parameter matrix. In order to extract the most critical specific matching information, we use average pooling and max pooling for the first dimension of $A_s$ as follows:

$$
\begin{aligned}
v_s &= [a_{avg}; a_{max}] \\
a_{avg} &= average\_pooling(A_s) \\
a_{max} &= max\_pooling(A_s)
\end{aligned}
\tag{10}
$$

where $v_s \in R^{2d_k}$ represents specific matching information after hierarchical matching and matching recognition. $a_{avg} \in R^{l_u}$ represents the average similarity, and $a_{max} \in R^{l_u}$ represents the maximum similarity in each dimension.

### 3.3    Information-Aware Layer

**Review-Aware Feature Extraction.** User reviews reflect the user's preference information, and item reviews reflect the feature information of the item, so we achieve the alignment of information by establishing the feature perception between the two. First, we use item reviews information to perceive user reviews information, which is defined as follows:

$$\alpha_{u,j} = \frac{exp(b_i^c B_{u,j}^t)}{\sum_{j=1}^{l_u} exp(b_i^c B_{u,j}^t)} \tag{11}$$

where $\alpha_{u,j}$ represents the attention weight of the $j$-th token of the user perceived by the item's reviews. $b_i^c$ represents the overall semantic information representation of item reviews learned through BERT, and $B_{u,j}^t$ denotes the representation of the $j$-th token of user reviews. Therefore, we can get the user reviews representation based on item reviews perception as:

$$e_u = \sum_{j=1}^{l_u} \alpha_{u,j} B_{u,j}^t \tag{12}$$

where $e_u \in R^k$ represents the user reviews representation aligned with the item reviews. In the same way, we can get the item reviews representation $e_i \in R^k$. We mark the global semantic representation of item description as $e_d \in R^k$.

**Features-Aware Feature Extraction.** Although $e_u$ and $e_i$ represent the semantic interactions between user and item reviews, they are not connected with numerical features that have strong relevance. Therefore, we take all the numerical features of the $n$ fields of users and items as input, and learn the implicit representation of the features through the embedding layer as follows:

$$x = embedding([c_1, c_2, \cdots, c_n]) \tag{13}$$

where $x$ refers to the implicit vector representation of the numerical features, and $c_j \in R^{d_j}$ represents the $j$-th field feature of the input. Learning the importance of text features by perceiving numerical features is defined as follows:

$$\gamma = q^T tanh(W_1^a e + W_2^a x) \tag{14}$$

where $\gamma$ represents the attention score perceived by numerical features. $e$ denotes the text representation, represented by $e_u$, $e_i$ and $e_d$ respectively. $e_d$ represents the global semantic representation of item description. $W_1^a \in R^k$ and $W_2^a \in R^d$ represent the attention network parameters. For user reviews representation $e_u$, we can get the corresponding attention score $\gamma_u$. Similarly, item reviews attention score $\gamma_i$ and item description attention score $\gamma_d$ can be obtained. Further, we fuse the text features of the numerical feature perception to obtain:

$$e_f = \theta_u e_u + \theta_i e_i + \theta_d e_d \tag{15}$$

where $e_f \in R^k$ represents the fusion text representation. $\theta_u$, $\theta_i$ and $\theta_d \in [0, 1]$ represent the weights obtained by normalizing $\gamma_u$, $\gamma_i$ and $\gamma_d$.

### 3.4   Interaction Aggregation Layer

**Feature Interaction Layer.** Since rich feature interactions can significantly improve the learning ability of the model [26], we use the NFM [7] to construct feature interactions between text features and numerical features. We connect text features and numerical features together as input, and learn feature interactions through the NFM model as:

$$z = NFM([e_f; x]) \tag{16}$$

where $z \in R^d$ denotes the learned high-order feature interaction information, which represents the comprehensive interaction between text feature information and numerical features. Further, considering the importance of low-order information, we simultaneously fuse low-order and high-order features to obtain:

$$y_f = w_f^T z + \sum_{j=1}^{|x|} \delta_j x_j + \delta_0 \tag{17}$$

where $y_f \in R$ represents the predicted score based on feature interaction.

**Information Aggregation Layer.** Matching information reflects the degree of matching between user and item reviews, and feature interaction information represents the interaction between text features and numerical features. We fuse text matching information and feature interaction information as follows:

$$r_{u,i} = y_f + ReLU(w_m^T[v_g; v_s] + b_m) \tag{18}$$

where $r_{u,i} \in R$ represents the final prediction score. $y_f$ represents the predicted score based on the comprehensive feature interaction. $w_m \in R^{d+2d_k}$ and $b_m \in R$ are the parameters used to learn the matching score. $v_g$ denotes the learned global matching vector, and $v_s$ represents the learned specific matching vector.

### 3.5 Joint Learning of Review Matching and Rating Prediction

In the matching network, we use item descriptions as a bridge to build the matching relationship between user and item reviews. In general, item reviews tend to be more similar to item description than user reviews, because item reviews contain the user's description of the characteristics of an item, while user reviews contain the user's subjective comments on multiple items. Therefore, we design review matching loss auxiliary model training, which is defined as follows:

$$L_m = \frac{1}{N} \sum_{(u,i) \in D} (b_i^{c^T} b_d^c - b_u^{c^T} b_d^c)^{y_p} (-b_i^{c^T} b_d^c + b_u^{c^T} b_d^c)^{1-y_p} \tag{19}$$

where $L_m$ represents auxiliary matching loss, which means minimizing the gap between the user and item reviews of the positive sample, and maximizing the gap between the user and item reviews of the negative sample. $y_p \in \{0,1\}$ denotes the polarity label corresponding to the true rating $y_{u,i}$, which represents the positive and negative polarity of the rating. In this paper, we mainly study the problem of rating prediction, which can be regarded as a regression problem. We define the square loss as follows:

$$L_c = \frac{1}{N} \sum_{(u,i) \in D(u,i)} (y_{u,i} - r_{u,i})^2 \tag{20}$$

Further, we construct joint training to minimize joint loss as follows:

$$L = \varphi L_c + (1 - \varphi)L_m \tag{21}$$

where $\varphi$ represents a hyperparameter, which is used to balance the importance of rating prediction loss and review matching loss.

## 4    Experiments

In this section, we conduct experiments to answer the following questions:

- **RQ1** How does our MIAN model perform compared to the state-of-the-art methods?
- **RQ2** How do different designs (e.g., matching network, auxiliary task, information-aware layer) affect the performance of the MIAN model?
- **RQ3** What is the specific effect of MIAN modeling reviews semantic information?

### 4.1 Experimental Settings

**Datasets.** We select five datasets[1] from the Amazon product dataset [9], including Video Games, Grocery and Gourmet Food, Sports and Outdoors, Office Products, Music Instruments. These datasets include users' explicit ratings of items ranging from 1 to 5, as well as rich meta information about users and items, such as item descriptions. In addition, the dataset includes user reviews on items. Following [3], we use the same preprocessing method for reviews. We connected user reviews together as a review document, and removed all stop words from it, and then controlled the length of the review document to 300 words. The statistical results of the datasets after preprocessing are shown in Table 1.

Table 1. Statistics of the five datasets.

| Dataset | #users | #items | #ratings | Word per item | density |
| --- | --- | --- | --- | --- | --- |
| Video Games | 24,303 | 10,672 | 231,577 | 135 | 0.089% |
| Grocery and Gourmet Food | 14,681 | 8,713 | 151,254 | 155 | 0.118% |
| Sports and Outdoors | 35,598 | 18,357 | 296,337 | 154 | 0.045% |
| Office Products | 4,905 | 2,420 | 53,228 | 172 | 0.448% |
| Musical Instruments | 1,429 | 900 | 10,261 | 163 | 0.798% |

**Baselines.** To evaluate the performance, we compared the proposed MIAN with the following baselines:

- **NeuMF** [7] combines generalized matrix factorization and MLP for learning nonlinear feature interactions.
- **ConvMF** [8] combines the text representation learned by CNN with the probabilistic matrix factorization model.
- **CDL** [19] combines the click-through rate estimation model and deep learning model to form a bayesian model that can extract the features of content.
- **D-Attn** [16] designs local and global attention networks to learn text features. Local attention focuses on user preferences or item attributes, and global attention can help learn the semantics of the entire review text.

---

[1] http://jmcauley.ucsd.edu/data/amazon/.

- **DeepCoNN** [29] consists of two parallel neural networks. One network learns user preferences from user reviews, and the other network learns item attributes from item reviews.
- **NARRE** [3] introduces an attention mechanism to explore the usefulness of reviews to provide interpretable recommendations.
- **CARL** [21] learns the semantic representation of user review documents and item review documents based on convolutional neural networks, and designs an attention network to model the importance of different information.
- **DAML** [10] uses a convolutional neural network to learn reviews information, and designs a local attention layer and a mutual attention layer to learn important semantic information from the text.
- **MSAR** [14] designs a review encoder based on mutual self attention to extract the semantic features of users and items from their reviews. Another encoder is utilized to learn representations from the rating patterns.

**Evaluation Metrics and Parameter Settings.** In this paper, we mainly focus on the problem of rating prediction, which is to predict the user's rating of items based on reviews and numerical features. Therefore, in order to measure the performance of the model, we use the Mean Square Error (MSE) as evaluation metric [10]. we randomly split each dataset into training set (80%), validation set (10%) and test set (10%). The validation set is used to select model hyperparameters, and the test set is used to evaluate the effect of the model. Considering the training time and convergence speed, batch size is set to 256, and the learning rate is adjusted from [0.00001, 0.00005, 0.0001, 0.001]. The dimension of the hidden vector is selected from [32, 64, 128]. The hyperparameter $\varphi$ is searched in [0, 0.1, 0.2, 0.3, 0.4, 0.5]. To avoid over-fitting, we apply dropout to all neural network-based models, and the dropout rate is searched

**Table 2.** Overall performance comparison on the five datasets.

| Model | Musical | Office | Food | Games | Sports |
|---|---|---|---|---|---|
| NeuMF | 0.8932 | 0.8225 | 1.0353 | 1.1630 | 0.8904 |
| ConvMF | 0.9113 | 0.8427 | 1.0568 | 1.1992 | 0.9629 |
| CDL | 0.9762 | 0.9796 | 1.1278 | 1.2545 | 1.0182 |
| DeepCoNN | 0.8863 | 0.8093 | 1.0169 | 1.1410 | 0.9312 |
| D-Attn | 0.8730 | 0.8078 | 0.9962 | 1.1330 | 0.8675 |
| NARRE | 0.8360 | 0.7842 | 0.9368 | 1.0916 | 0.8279 |
| CARL | 0.8175 | 0.7403 | 0.9463 | 1.0930 | 0.8304 |
| DAML | 0.8012 | 0.7037 | 0.9372 | 1.0761 | 0.8083 |
| MSAR | 0.7710 | 0.6843 | 0.9051 | 1.0679 | 0.7911 |
| MIAN | **0.7057** | **0.6355** | **0.8613** | **1.0225** | **0.7522** |
| Improvement | 8.47% | 7.13% | 4.84% | 4.25% | 4.92% |

from [0, 0.1, 0.2, 0.3, 0.4, 0.5]. The pre-training language model BERT used in our MIAN model is the standard bert-base model [5].

## 4.2 Overall Performance (RQ1)

To verify the effectiveness of our proposed MIAN model, we conducted comprehensive experiments on five datasets, and the experimental results are shown in Table 2. Analyzing the experimental results, we have the following observations:

- The MIAN model outperforms all state-of-the-art methods on five data sets and has a significant improvement. The experimental results fully verify the effectiveness of our model. Multi-level matching information helps the model improve the accuracy of prediction.
- Whether it is a dense data set or a sparse data set such as Video Games and Sports and Outdoors, the improvement brought by the MIAN model is the same. There is no difference in model effect due to data sparsity. The rich feature interactions further enhance the learning and representation ability of the model.

## 4.3 Ablation Experimental Study (RQ2)

**Effect of Matching Network.** To study the impact of our proposed matching network on the performance of the model, we removed different components and performed the following four ablation experiments. The experimental results are shown in Table 3. After we remove the global matching module, the model effect on all datasets is reduced, which directly shows that the global matching information is helpful to the improvement of the model effect. Without considering the matching information between user and item reviews, the model effect is significantly reduced.

**Table 3.** The impact of Matching Network. Without GM: we remove the global matching module. Without SM: we remove the specific matching module. Without IAM: we remove the information-aware module.

| Model | Musical | Office | Food | Games | Sports |
|---|---|---|---|---|---|
| MIAN | **0.7057** | **0.6355** | **0.8613** | **1.0225** | **0.7522** |
| -without GM | 0.7389 | 0.6614 | 0.8904 | 1.0465 | 0.7690 |
| -without SM | 0.7525 | 0.6847 | 0.9097 | 1.0626 | 0.8027 |
| -without GM & SM | 0.7491 | 0.6968 | 0.9245 | 1.0761 | 0.8114 |
| -without IAM | 0.7135 | 0.6468 | 0.8694 | 1.0361 | 0.7594 |

**Effect of Auxiliary Task.** In order to explore whether the matching loss is helpful to improve the model effect, we remove the matching loss and perform ablation experiments on all data sets. The experimental results are shown in Fig. 2. From the experimental results, we can see that after removing the matching loss, the performance of the model on all data sets has a certain degree of decline, which directly verifies the effectiveness of the joint learning of the matching loss.

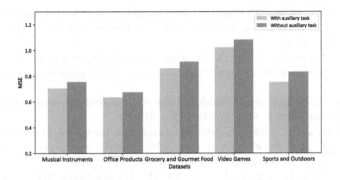

**Fig. 2.** Effect of auxiliary task.

## 4.4  Case Study (RQ3)

To specifically explore the effect of our MIAN model in modeling user and item reviews, we conduct case studies. We randomly select some positive samples from the five datasets, and extract the attention weights of user reviews and item reviews of each sample. We find that the important semantic information part of reviews is recognized by the model. Specifically, "work well", "good option" and "cheap" are mentioned in user reviews, expressing the user's preference for product quality, ease of use, and affordable prices. Item reviews mentioned "good quality", "save space" and "convenient", indicating that the product is affordable and has good quality. We find that the key semantic information that reflects user preferences extracted from user reviews closely matches the item-specific semantic information extracted from item reviews, which directly illustrates the reliability and effectiveness of matching based on reviews.

## 5  Conclusion

In this paper, we focus on exploring more effective use of text review data for recommendation. We propose a novel model MIAN, which consists of a matching network and an information perception layer. Comprehensive experiments on five real datasets demonstrate that MIAN outperforms the state-of-the-art methods. In the future, we will introduce more data from different modalities, such as image data and video data, to further explore multimodal fusion recommendation.

# References

1. Blei, D.M., Ng, A.Y., Jordan, M.I.: Latent dirichlet allocation. J. Mach. Learn. Res. **3**, 993–1022 (2003)
2. Bobadilla, J., Ortega, F., Hernando, A., Gutiérrez, A.: Recommender systems survey. Knowl. -Based Syst. **46**, 109–132 (2013)
3. Chen, C., Zhang, M., Liu, Y., Ma, S.: Neural attentional rating regression with review-level explanations. In: Proceedings of the 2018 World Wide Web Conference, pp. 1583–1592 (2018)
4. Covington, P., Adams, J., Sargin, E.: Deep neural networks for Youtube recommendations. In: Proceedings of the 10th ACM Conference on Recommender Systems, pp. 191–198 (2016)
5. Devlin, J., Chang, M.W., Lee, K., Toutanova, K.: Bert: pre-training of deep bidirectional transformers for language understanding. arXiv preprint arXiv:1810.04805 (2018)
6. Guan, X.: Attentive aspect modeling for review-aware recommendation. ACM Trans. Inform. Syst. (TOIS) **37**(3), 1–27 (2019)
7. He, X., Chua, T.S.: Neural factorization machines for sparse predictive analytics. In: Proceedings of the 40th International ACM SIGIR conference on Research and Development in Information Retrieval, pp. 355–364 (2017)
8. Kim, D., Park, C., Oh, J., Lee, S., Yu, H.: Convolutional matrix factorization for document context-aware recommendation. In: Proceedings of the 10th ACM Conference on Recommender Systems, pp. 233–240 (2016)
9. Lakkaraju, H., McAuley, J., Leskovec, J.: What's in a name? Understanding the interplay between titles, content, and communities in social media. In: Proceedings of the International AAAI Conference on Web and Social Media, vol. 7, pp. 311–320 (2013)
10. Liu, D., Li, J., Du, B., Chang, J., Gao, R.: DAML: dual attention mutual learning between ratings and reviews for item recommendation. In: Proceedings of the 25th ACM SIGKDD International Conference on Knowledge Discovery & Data Mining, pp. 344–352 (2019)
11. Liu, P., Zhang, L., Gulla, J.A.: Multilingual review-aware deep recommender system via aspect-based sentiment analysis. ACM Trans. Inform. Syst. (TOIS) **39**(2), 1–33 (2021)
12. Liu, Y., Yang, S., Zhang, Y., Miao, C., Nie, Z., Zhang, J.: Learning hierarchical review graph representations for recommendation. IEEE Trans. Knowl. Data Eng. (2021)
13. Mnih, A., Salakhutdinov, R.R.: Probabilistic matrix factorization. In: Advances Neural Information Processing Systems, vol. 20, pp. 1257–1264 (2007)
14. Peng, Q., Liu, H., Yu, Y., Xu, H., Dai, W., Jiao, P.: Mutual self attention recommendation with gated fusion between ratings and reviews. In: Nah, Y., Cui, B., Lee, S.-W., Yu, J.X., Moon, Y.-S., Whang, S.E. (eds.) DASFAA 2020. LNCS, vol. 12114, pp. 540–556. Springer, Cham (2020). https://doi.org/10.1007/978-3-030-59419-0_33
15. Qiu, Z., Wu, X., Gao, J., Fan, W.: U-BERT: pre-training user representations for improved recommendation. In: Proceedings of the AAAI Conference on Artificial Intelligence, vol. 35, pp. 4320–4327 (2021)
16. Seo, S., Huang, J., Yang, H., Liu, Y.: Interpretable convolutional neural networks with dual local and global attention for review rating prediction. In: Proceedings of the Eleventh ACM Conference on Recommender Systems, pp. 297–305 (2017)

17. Sun, P., Wu, L., Zhang, K., Fu, Y., Hong, R., Wang, M.: Dual learning for explainable recommendation: towards unifying user preference prediction and review generation. In: Proceedings of The Web Conference 2020, pp. 837–847 (2020)

18. Vaswani, A., et al.: Attention is all you need. arXiv preprint arXiv:1706.03762 (2017)

19. Wang, H., Wang, N., Yeung, D.Y.: Collaborative deep learning for recommender systems. In: Proceedings of the 21th ACM SIGKDD International Conference on Knowledge Discovery and Data Mining, pp. 1235–1244 (2015)

20. Wu, C., Wu, F., Liu, J., Huang, Y.: Hierarchical user and item representation with three-tier attention for recommendation. In: Proceedings of the 2019 Conference of the North American Chapter of the Association for Computational Linguistics: Human Language Technologies, vol. 1 (Long and Short Papers), pp. 1818–1826 (2019)

21. Wu, L., Quan, C., Li, C., Wang, Q., Zheng, B., Luo, X.: A context-aware user-item representation learning for item recommendation. ACM Trans. Inform. Syst. (TOIS) 37(2), 1–29 (2019)

22. Wu, S., Zhang, Y., Zhang, W., Bian, K., Cui, B.: Enhanced review-based rating prediction by exploiting aside information and user influence. Knowl. -Based Syst. 222, 107015 (2021)

23. Xie, F., Zheng, A., Chen, L., Zheng, Z.: Attentive meta-graph embedding for item recommendation in heterogeneous information networks. Knowl.-Based Syst. 211, 106524 (2021)

24. Xiong, K., et al.: Counterfactual review-based recommendation. In: Proceedings of the 30th ACM International Conference on Information & Knowledge Management, pp. 2231–2240 (2021)

25. Yang, W., Fan, X., Chen, Y., Li, F., Chang, H.: An effective implicit multi-interest interaction network for recommendation. In: Mantoro, T., Lee, M., Ayu, M.A., Wong, K.W., Hidayanto, A.N. (eds.) ICONIP 2021. LNCS, vol. 13111, pp. 680–691. Springer, Cham (2021). https://doi.org/10.1007/978-3-030-92273-3_56

26. Yang, W., Hu, T.: DFCN: an effective feature interactions learning model for recommender systems. In: Jensen, C.S., et al. (eds.) DASFAA 2021. LNCS, vol. 12683, pp. 195–210. Springer, Cham (2021). https://doi.org/10.1007/978-3-030-73200-4_13

27. Yang, Z.: Generating knowledge-based explanation for recommendation from review. In: Proceedings of the 45th International ACM SIGIR Conference on Research and Development in Information Retrieval, p. 3494 (2022)

28. Zhang, Y., Lai, G., Zhang, M., Zhang, Y., Liu, Y., Ma, S.: Explicit factor models for explainable recommendation based on phrase-level sentiment analysis. In: Proceedings of the 37th International ACM SIGIR Conference on Research & Development in Information Retrieval, pp. 83–92 (2014)

29. Zheng, L., Noroozi, V., Yu, P.S.: Joint deep modeling of users and items using reviews for recommendation. In: Proceedings of the tenth ACM International Conference on Web Search and Data Mining, pp. 425–434 (2017)

# Cross-View Contrastive Learning for Knowledge-Aware Session-Based Recommendation

Xiaohui Zhang[1], Huifang Ma[1,2,3](✉), Fanyi Yang[1], Zhixin Li[2],
and Liang Chang[3]

[1] Northwest Normal University, Lanzhou, Gansu 730070, China
[2] Guangxi Normal University, Guilin, Guangxi 541004, China
[3] Guilin University of ElectronicTechnology, Guilin, Guangxi 541004, China
mahuifang@yeah.net

**Abstract.** Session-based Recommendation (SBR) methods play a crucial role in modern recommender systems owing to their ability to capture
an anonymous user's dynamic preference from his/her short-term historical interactions. Despite previous success, we argue that existing models generally suffer from the sparsity problem of user-item interactions,
which may make their actual performance drop to some extent. To tackle
this, inspired by the recent success of contrastive learning in mining
supervised signals from data itself, we propose a novel Cross-view Contrastive learning mechanism for Knowledge-aware Session-based Recommendation, named CCKSR. Our model comprehensively considers two
different graph views, i.e., subjectively structural view and objectively
semantic view. Specifically, we take cross-session graph as the structural
view, and the item-attribute hypergraph is regarded as the semantic
view. Then, a query-aware graph attention network and a hypergraph
convolutional network are designed to learn node representations from
two views, so as to capture comprehensive sequential structure information and item-item attribute semantic relation in a contrastive self-
supervised manner. Extensive experiments on three benchmark datasets
show the superiority performance of our proposed method over the state-
of-the-art baselines.

**Keywords:** Session-based recommendation · Contrastive learning ·
Hypergraph · Cross-session · Graph attention network

## 1 Introduction

Session-based Recommendation (SBR) aims to capture short-term and dynamic
user preferences according to user behaviors (e.g., clicked items) within anonymous users [1–3]. Conventional SBR approaches (e.g., Markov Chain (MC) [4])

© The Author(s), under exclusive license to Springer Nature Switzerland AG 2022
S. Khanna et al. (Eds.): PRICAI 2022, LNCS 13631, pp. 60–73, 2022.
https://doi.org/10.1007/978-3-031-20868-3_5

rely on the previous behavior of the user in the session sequence to predict the next behavior. However, MC-based methods usually only model first-order transitions and cannot capture more complex sequential patterns. A widely-adopted solution is to leverage Recurrent Neural Networks (RNNs), such as GRU4REC [5], NARM [6], and STAMP [7], which summarizes the behavioral sequences, to learn high-quality user and item representations for SBR. However, treating data as simply linear sequential is not expressive enough to represent and model the complex non-sequential dependencies between items. Sequentially, SBR is further enhanced by the recent powerful Graph Neural Networks (GNNs), which models session data as directed graph and then applies GNNs to capture complex item transitions, such as SR-GNN [1], FGNN [8] and CKSR [9]. Despite effectiveness, current GNN-based SBR models greatly suffer from data sparsity problem, owing to the extreme sparsity of interactions [10–13].

However, alleviating the data sparsity problem faces a significant challenge, that is, the inadequacy of training labels, as labels are usually scarce in real SBR applications. Recently, contrastive learning [14–17], one of the classical Self-Supervised Learning (SSL) methods, has shown its magic in SBR, as its powerful capability in learning discriminative embeddings from unlabeled sample data [18,19]. Consequently, it is non-trivial to design a proper contrastive learning framework for SBR, which requires us to address the following challenges: 1) **How to construct proper views for contrastive learning?** A straightforward way is that, we can construct the input session sequence as the structural view (cross-session graph), analogous to [20,21]. Nevertheless, it is far from enough to solely consider structural view for SBR, because it is incapable of fully leveraging the rich semantic information of items. 2) **How to design proper node representation learning mechanisms?** Due to different views (structural/semantics), the designed encoders are naturally required to simultaneously handle two types of views and capture different relations among items.

To address the abrove challenges, we propose a novel model based on the SSL paradigm, named Cross-view Contrastive learning for Knowledge-aware Session-based Recommender (CCKSR), to fully leverage the rich structure and semantic information over session sequence. Specifically, a cross-session graph (structural view) and an item attribute hypergraph (semantic view) are first constructed from session sequences and item attributes. Then a novel cross-view contrastive learning mechanism is proposed to collaboratively supervise the two graph views. In particular, in the structural view, an effective query-aware attention mechanism is proposed for explicitly capturing the sequential relations between items; in the semantic view, a hypergraph convolutional network is designed for considering item-item semantic similarity from item knowledge. Moreover, adaptive attention aggregation mechanism is designed for two graph views, stressing different parts of graph information according to the views' features. Empirically, CCKSR outperforms the state-of-the-art models on three benchmark datasets. Our contributions of this work can be summarized as follows:

- We construct two independent and complementary views, i.e., structural view and semantic view, to capture both subjective interaction and objective properties, which assists session graph contrastive learning tasks.
- We propose query-aware graph attention networks and hypergraph convolutional networks with co-contrastive learning for SBR, which can capture the pairwise relations and beyond pairwise relations among items.
- Extensive experiments on three public datasets show that our proposed model outperforms the state-of-the-art and even semi-supervised method, which demonstrates the effectiveness of CCKSR from various aspects.

## 2    Notations and Problem Statement

Let $\mathcal{S} = \{S_1, S_2, \cdots, S_{|\mathcal{S}|}\}$ denote a set of sessions over an item set $\mathcal{V} = \{v_1, v_2, \cdots, v_N\}$, $\mathcal{A} = \{m_1, m_2, \cdots, m_M\}$ is a set of item attributes. An anonymous session $s_t = [v_{t,1}, v_{t,2}, \cdots, v_{t,n}] \in \mathcal{S}$ is a sequence of items ordered by timestamps, where $v_{t,j} \in \mathcal{V}$ is the $j$-th clicked item in $s_t$ and $n$ is the length of session $s_t$, which may contain duplicated items. For learning node representations, we embed each item $v_i \in \mathcal{V}$ into the same space and let $\mathbf{X}^{(l)}[i] \in \mathbb{R}^d$ denote the representation of item $v_i$ of dimension $d$ in the $l$-th layer of a deep neural network. The final representation of the whole item set is denoted as $\mathbf{X} \in \mathbb{R}^{N \times d}$, and $\mathbf{X}^{(0)}$ is randomly initialized with uniform distribution. Each session $s_t$ is represented by a vector $\mathbf{s}_t$.

The goal of our model is to take all session sequences $\mathcal{S}$ and item attribute $\mathcal{A}$ as input, given a target session $s_t = [v_{t,1}, v_{t,2}, \cdots, v_{t,n}] \in \mathcal{S}$, returns a list of top-$K$ candidate items to be consumed as the next one $v_{t,n+1}$.

## 3    Method

The proposed CCKSR is comprised three main components: 1) **View generation.** It generates two different views from session sequences and item attributes, including structural view (cross-session graph) and semantic view (item attribute hypergraph). 2) **Dual-channel graph view encoder.** It encodes two views with a query-aware graph attention networks and a hypergraph convolutional networks for capturing pairwise relations and beyond pairwise relations among items respectively. 3) **Contrastive learning and recommendation.** It first performs cross-view contrastive learning between two views for supervising two views to learn discriminative item and session embeddings, and then utilizes an attention mechanism to aggregate the embeddings learned through two views and predicts the probability of target item that will appear to be the next-click one for target session.

We now present the proposed CCKSR. CCKSR aims to incorporate cross-view contrastive learning into knowledge-aware SBR for improving node representation learning. Figure 1 displays the working flow of CCKSR.

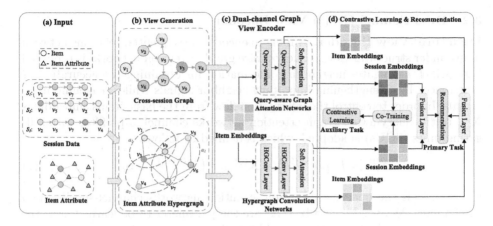

**Fig. 1.** The overall framework of our proposed CCKSR.

## 3.1   View Generation

To conduct contrastive learning, we construct two independent and complementary views by jointly considering structural-level and semantic-level view, i.e., a cross-session graph and an item attribute hypergraph.

**Cross-session Graph Construction.** To capture the pairwise item transitions between items, we construct the cross-session graph, which describes the temporal relations between items in all sessions. The cross-session graph, defined as $\mathcal{G}_C = (\mathcal{V}, \mathcal{E}_C)$, is viewed as structural view, where node set $\mathcal{V}$ represents all items in $\mathcal{S}$, and edge set $\mathcal{E}_C$ represents all weighted directed edges $(v_i, v_j, w_{i,j})$, where $v_j$ is the click of item after $v_i$ in any sessions, and $w_{i,j}$ is the weight of the edge. The weight of the edge is counted how many times they are adjacent in different sessions in the form of $[v_i, v_j]$. Notably, the purpose of cross-session graph construction is to incorporate cross-session information into the individual session representation learning procedure.

**Item Attribute Hypergraph Construction.** To capture the beyond pairwise relations among items, we propose to construct an item attribute hypergraph based on session data and internal item knowledge, which helps to explore the semantic attribute similarity among items. Specifically, the item attribute hypergraph , denoted as $\mathcal{G}_H = (\mathcal{V}, \mathcal{E}_H)$, is deemed to semantic view, in which the node set $\mathcal{V}$ consists of all the unique items appearing in $\mathcal{S}$, the hyperedges set $\mathcal{E}_H = \{\epsilon_1, \epsilon_2, \cdots \epsilon_M\}$ is guided by $M$ attributes in $\mathcal{A}$. We denote each attribute hyperedge as $\epsilon_i = [v_{i,1}, v_{i,2}, \cdots, v_{i,m}] \in \mathcal{E}_H$ and each item $v_{i,m} \in \mathcal{V}$, where $\epsilon_i \in \mathcal{E}_H$ contains any number of items and is assigned a positive weight $W_{\epsilon\epsilon}$, and all the weights formulate a diagonal matrix $\mathbf{W} \in \mathbb{R}^{M \times M}$. In this paper, for $W_{\epsilon\epsilon}$, we assign each hyperedge the same weight value of 1.

## 3.2 Dual-channel Graph View Encoder

**Structural View Encoder.** Aiming to encode the sequential relations between items under structural view, a query-aware graph attention networks is proposed here, which aggregates neighboring information for obtaining the accurate user preferences by strengthening important neighbor signals while weakening noise signals. In order to control the information flow from the basic items embeddings $\mathbf{X}^{(0)}$ to the query-aware graph attention networks channel, a prefilter with self-gating units (SGUs) is adopted, which is defined as follows:

$$\mathbf{X}_c^{(0)} = f_{gate}\left(\mathbf{X}^{(0)}\right) = \mathbf{X}^{(0)} \odot \sigma\left(\mathbf{X}^{(0)}\mathbf{W}_c + \mathbf{b}_c\right) \tag{1}$$

where $\mathbf{X}_c^{(0)}$ is the query-aware graph attention networks channel-specific item embeddings, $\mathbf{W}_c \in \mathbb{R}^{d\times d}$ and $\mathbf{b}_c \in \mathbb{R}^d$ are the parameter to be learned, $\odot$ is the element-wise product, $\sigma$ is the sigmoid function.

Specifically, the query-aware graph attention networks consider the following two aspects: Firstly, for the weighted and directed cross-session graph, we use an attention coefficient related to edge weight to effectively convey information carried by the weighted directed edges between items. In particular, we compute the importance score $\alpha_{i,j}^{(l)}$ for every node $v_i$ from its neighboring nodes $v_j \in N(v_i)$, which is defined as the nodes with edges toward the node $v_i$ (may contain $v_i$ itself if there is a self-loop edge):

$$\alpha_{i,j}^{(l)} = \left(\mathbf{q}^{(l)}\right)^T \sigma\left(\mathbf{W}_e^{(l)}\left(\mathbf{X}_c^{(l-1)}[i]||\mathbf{X}_c^{(l-1)}[j]\right) + \mathbf{w}_{i,j}^{(l)}\right), \tag{2}$$

where $\mathbf{q}^{(l)} \in \mathbb{R}^d$ and $\mathbf{W}_e^{(l)} \in \mathbb{R}^{d\times 2d}$ are learnable parameters, $\sigma$ denotes the sigmoid activation function, $\mathbf{X}_c^{(l-1)}[i]$ represent the embedding of item $v_i$ in the structural view at $(l-1)$-th layer and $||$ is the concatenation operator. Here, for each layer $l$, we embed the weight $w_{i,j}$ of edge $(v_i, v_j)$ into a dense vector as the feature vector $\mathbf{w}_{i,j}^{(l)}$ of this edge.

Secondly, we consider the correlation between the neighborhood node $v_j$ and the query item $v_k$. If the neighborhood node $v_j$ is more correlated with the query item $v_k$, its weight in the aggregation towards the target node $v_i$ will be more significant, and vice versa. Since only relevant behaviors can play a role in the final prediction, we only keep relevant information, and irrelevant information will be discarded during aggregation,

$$\beta_j^{(l)} = MLP\left(\mathbf{W}_q^{(l)}\mathbf{X}_c^{(l-1)}[j]||\mathbf{X}_c^{(l-1)}[k]\right), \tag{3}$$

where $\mathbf{W}_q^{(l)}$ is a transformation matrix, and $MLP(\cdot)$ is a two-layers feedforward neural network applying the LeakyReLU nonlinearity.

To consider both neighbor node's edge score and neighbor node's query score, we apply an additive attention mechanism [22] to update weight of the neighbor node $v_j$. The attention coefficients $E_{ij}$ is computed as:

$$E_{ij}^{(l)} = softmax_j\left(\alpha_{ij}^{(l)} + \beta_j^{(l)}\right) = \frac{\exp(\alpha_{ij}^{(l)} + \beta_j^{(l)})}{\sum_{v_m \in N(v_i)} \exp(\alpha_{im}^{(l)} + \beta_m^{(l)})}, \tag{4}$$

where neighborhood $v_m \in N(v_i)$ of node $v_i$ includes node $v_i$ itself, $\alpha_{ij}$ controls how much information the neighbor node $v_j$ to $v_i$ along the edge $e = (v_i, v_j)$, and $\beta_j$ controls how much information the neighbor node can send.

Once obtained alignment score $E_{ij}^{(l)}$, the normalized attention coefficients are used to perform a weighted combination of the embeddings corresponding to them, to serve as the refined output embeddings for each node:

$$\mathbf{X}_c^{(l)}[i] = \mathbf{W}_1^{(l)}\mathbf{X}_c^{(l-1)}[i] + \sum_{v_j \in N(v_i)} E_{ij}^{(l)}\mathbf{W}_2^{(l)}\mathbf{X}_c^{(l-1)}[j], \tag{5}$$

where $\mathbf{W}_1^{(l)}, \mathbf{W}_2^{(l)} \in \mathbb{R}^{d \times d}$ are matrices of learning parameters. After passing $\mathbf{X}_c^{(0)}$ through $L$ layer, we average the items embeddings obtained at each layer to get the final items embeddings: $\mathbf{X}_c[i] = \frac{1}{L+1}\sum_{l=0}^{L}\mathbf{X}_c^{(l)}[i]$.

Finally, the embedding of a specific session $s_t$ is represented by aggregating item embeddings of the session through a soft-attention mechanism [1]:

$$\gamma_i = \delta\left(\mathbf{f}^T\sigma\left(\mathbf{W}_3\mathbf{X}_c[n] + \mathbf{W}_4\mathbf{X}_c[i] + \mathbf{b}\right)\right), \mathbf{s}_t^c = \sum_{i=1}^{n}\gamma_i\mathbf{X}_c[i]. \tag{6}$$

where $\mathbf{f} \in \mathbb{R}^d$ is a linear projection vector for generating the weight scalar $\gamma_i$, $\mathbf{W}_3, \mathbf{W}_4 \in \mathbb{R}^{d \times d}$ and $\mathbf{b} \in \mathbb{R}^d$ are the parameter to be learned, $\mathbf{s}_t^c$ is the representation of session $s_t$ in structural view, $\sigma(\cdot)$ and $\delta(\cdot)$ denotes the sigmoid and softmax function, respectively.

**Semantic View Encoder.** The semantic view focuses on semantic attribute similarity among items, which has been confirmed to be important but ignored by previous work. Now we aim to learn item representations and capture the high-order attribute relations among items by a hypergraph convolution network encoder over the semantic view. Analogously, we first pass $\mathbf{X}^{(0)}$ through the SGU to obtain the item attribute hypergraph channel-specific item embeddings $\mathbf{X}_h^{(0)}$.

The biggest difficulty in defining convolution on hypergraph is how to propagate items embedding. Referring to the spectral hypergraph convolution proposed in [23,24], an incidence matrix for item attribute hypergraph $\mathcal{G}_H$ is defined as $\mathbf{H} \in \mathbb{R}^{N \times M}$, where $H_{i\epsilon} = 1$ if hyperedge $\epsilon \in \mathcal{E}$ contains the vertex $v_i \in \mathcal{V}$, otherwise 0. We define hypergraph convolution as:

$$\mathbf{X}_h^{(l+1)}[i] = \sum_{j=1}^{N}\sum_{\epsilon=1}^{M} H_{i\epsilon}H_{j\epsilon}W_{\epsilon\epsilon}\mathbf{X}_h^{(l)}[j]\mathbf{P}^{(l)}, \tag{7}$$

where $\mathbf{P}^{(l)} \in \mathbb{R}^{d \times d}$ is the learnable parameter matrix.

Hypergraph convolution can be regarded as a two-stage refinement of 'items - attribute - items' feature transformation of item attribute hypergraph structure. After passing $\mathbf{X}_h^{(0)}$ through $L$ hypergraph convolutional layer, we average the items embeddings obtained at each layer to get the final items embeddings: $\mathbf{X}_h[i] = \frac{1}{L+1}\sum_{l=0}^{L}\mathbf{X}_h^{(l)}[i]$.

After obtaining the items representations under semantic view, similar structural view, the session embedding learning under semantic view is adopted as:

$$\eta_i = \mathbf{g}^T \sigma \left( \mathbf{W}_5 \mathbf{X}_h[n] + \mathbf{W}_6 \mathbf{X}_h[i] + \mathbf{c} \right), \mathbf{s}_t^h = \sum_{i=1}^{n} \eta_i \mathbf{X}_h[i]. \qquad (8)$$

where $\mathbf{g} \in \mathbb{R}^d$ is a linear projection vector for generating the weight scalar $\eta_i$, $\mathbf{W}_5, \mathbf{W}_6 \in \mathbb{R}^{d \times d}$ and $\mathbf{c} \in \mathbb{R}^d$ are the parameter to be learned, $\mathbf{s}_t^h$ is the representation of session $s_t$ in semantic view.

### 3.3   Contrastive Learning and Recommendation

**Co-contrastive Learning.** After getting two different embeddings of session and item from the above two views, we need to define positive and negative samples to calculate contrastive loss. Inspired by [19], for any session in one view, if the predicted probability of each item being recommended to it have the top-$K$ highest confidence in other view, they are positive samples, and we randomly select $K$ negative samples from the predicted probability in top 10% excluding the positive. Given a session $s_t$ and the positive sample set $f_c^{t^+}$ and $f_h^{t^+}$, the negative sample set $f_c^{t^-}$ and $f_h^{t^-}$ over two views, we follow InfoNCE [25], which can maximize the lower bound of mutual information between the session and item pairs, as our contrastive learning objective:

$$\mathcal{L}_{ssl} = -\log \frac{\sum\limits_{i \in f_c^{t^+}} \exp\left(sim(\mathbf{s}_t^c, \mathbf{X}_c[i])/\tau\right)}{\sum\limits_{i \in f_c^{t^+}} \exp\left(sim(\mathbf{s}_t^c, \mathbf{X}_c[i])/\tau\right) + \sum\limits_{j \in f_c^{t^-}} \exp\left(sim(\mathbf{s}_t^c, \mathbf{X}_c[j])/\tau\right)}$$

$$-\log \frac{\sum\limits_{i \in f_h^{t^+}} \exp\left(sim(\mathbf{s}_t^h, \mathbf{X}_h[i])/\tau\right)}{\sum\limits_{i \in f_h^{t^+}} \exp\left(sim(\mathbf{s}_t^h, \mathbf{X}_h[i])/\tau\right) + \sum\limits_{j \in f_h^{t^-}} \exp\left(sim(\mathbf{s}_t^h, \mathbf{X}_h[j])/\tau\right)} \qquad (9)$$

where $sim(\mathbf{u}, \mathbf{v})$ denotes the cosine similarity between two vectors $\mathbf{u}$ and $\mathbf{v}$, and $\tau$ denotes a temperature parameter (we empirically use 0.2 in our experiments). By minimizing $\mathcal{L}_{ssl}$, the denoising item can be leveraged to guide the session and item representation and alleviate the sparsity of supervision signals.

**Model Optimization and Recommendation Generation.** We exert an attention strategy to create more expressive item and session embeddings by capturing both user's interaction sequence and item attribute knowledge. For the item $v_k$, its final embedding $\mathbf{v}_k$ can be aggregated as:

$$\mathbf{v}_k = \sum_{r \in \{c,h\}} \alpha(r, v_k) \mathbf{X}_r[k], \alpha(r, v_k) = \frac{\exp(w_{r,v_k})}{\sum_{r' \in \{c,h\}} \exp(w_{r',v_k})}, \qquad (10)$$

where $\mathbf{X}_r[k]$ is the $r$-th view-specific embedding of item $v_k$, which is assigned with an attention score $\alpha(r, v_k)$ to quantify its importance, $w_{r,v_k}$ is a trainable weight. Similarly, for session $s_t$, its final embedding $\mathbf{s}_t$ can be aggregated as:

$$\mathbf{s}_t = \sum_{r \in \{c,h\}} \beta(r, s_t)\mathbf{s}_t^r, \beta(r, s_t) = \frac{\exp(q_{r,s_t})}{\sum_{r' \in \{c,h\}} \exp(q_{r',s_t})}, \quad (11)$$

Based on the final session and item embedding, the score of each candidate item $v_k \in \mathcal{V}$ to be recommended for a session $s_t$ is computed as:

$$\hat{y}_{v_k} = softmax_k \left(\mathbf{s}_t^{\mathrm{T}} \mathbf{v}_k\right), \quad (12)$$

As for the session recommendation loss function, we take a widely used end-to-end training approach, Cross Entropy Loss, and it is formulated as:

$$\mathcal{L}_S = - \sum_{v_k \in \mathcal{V}} y_{v_k} \log(\hat{y}_{v_k}) + (1 - y_{v_k}) \log(1 - \hat{y}_{v_k}), \quad (13)$$

where $\mathbf{y}$ is the one-hot encoding vector of the ground truth. Finally, we unify the SBR task with the auxiliary SSL task. The total loss $\mathcal{L}$ is defined as:

$$\mathcal{L} = \mathcal{L}_S + \lambda_1 \mathcal{L}_{ssl} + \lambda_2 ||\Theta||_2^2. \quad (14)$$

where $\lambda_1$ is a hyperparameter to control the scale of the self-supervised graph co-training, $\Theta$ is the set of model parameters, and $||\Theta||_2^2$ is the L2-regularization that parameterized by $\lambda_2$ to prevent over-fitting.

## 4  Experiments

### 4.1  Experimental Settings

**Datasets.** To evaluate the effectiveness of our model, we conduct experiments on three benchmark datasets: TMALL[1], Retailrocket[2] and JDATA[3]. For the fairness and the convenience of comparison, we follow [1,18,19] to filter out sessions whose length is 1 and items appearing less than 5 times in each dataset respectively. We augment and label the datasets by using a sequence splitting method. The latest data is set to be test set and previous data is used as training set. The data statistics are presented in Table 1.

**Methods for Comparison.** To comprehensively evaluate the performance, we compare our CCKSR against various baselines from different research lines: 1) RNN-based method including GRU4REC [5]. 2) Attention-based methods

---

[1] https://tianchi.aliyun.com/dataset/dataDetail?dataId=45.
[2] https://www.kaggle.com/retailrocket/ecommerce-dataset.
[3] https://jdata.jd.com/html/detail.html?id=8.

**Table 1.** Dataset statistics.

| Dataset | #Train sessions | #Test sessions | #Items | Average lengths |
|---|---|---|---|---|
| Tmall | 351,268 | 25,898 | 40,728 | 6.69 |
| RetailRocket | 43,643 | 15,132 | 36,968 | 5.43 |
| JDATA | 439,214 | 16,267 | 1,134,548 | 18.186 |

**Table 2.** The performance of different methods on three datasets. All our results have the statistical significance for $p < 0.01$ compared to the best baseline.

| Dataset | Tmall | | RetailRocket | | JDATA | |
|---|---|---|---|---|---|---|
| | P@20 | MRR@20 | P@20 | MRR@20 | P@20 | MRR@20 |
| GRU4REC | 10.92 | 5.89 | 44.22 | 23.59 | 35.22 | 13.85 |
| NARM | 23.34 | 10.72 | 50.08 | 24.38 | 36.61 | 16.93 |
| STAMP | 26.44 | 13.37 | 50.97 | 25.38 | 35.73 | 12.85 |
| SR-GNN | 27.58 | 13.69 | 51.34 | 26.56 | 40.47 | 15.86 |
| FGNN | 33.32 | 15.51 | 52.67 | 26.91 | 44.77 | 18.15 |
| $S^2$-DHCN | 31.43 | 15.02 | 53.67 | 27.32 | 43.48 | 17.83 |
| COTREC | <u>36.33</u> | <u>17.93</u> | <u>56.09</u> | <u>29.85</u> | <u>48.46</u> | <u>18.42</u> |
| **CCKSR** | **38.41** | **18.47** | **57.98** | **30.51** | **49.58** | **18.75** |
| improv.(%) | 5.73 | 3.01 | 3.37 | 2.21 | 2.31 | 1.79 |
| p-value | 3.23e−3 | 4.27e−5 | 2.52e−3 | 2.32e−3 | 5.48e−3 | 3.18e−3 |

including NARM [6] and STAMP [7]. 3) GNN-based methods including SR-GNN [1] and FGNN [8]. 4)SSL-based methods including $S^2$-DHCN [18] and COTREC [19]. For performance evaluations, we use two representative metrics: P@K (Precision) and MRR@K (Mean Reciprocal Rank) which have been widely adopted in SBR tasks [26]. We investigate the Top-$K$ performance with $K = 20$ following [18,19].

## 4.2   Over Performance

We first compare the performance of our CCKSR with state-of-the-art methods. Table 2 summarizes the best results of all models on three datasets. Note that the improvement columns are the performance of CCKSR relative to the second-best baselines. Based on the experiment results, we have following observations:

1) Our CCKSR achieves the best performance compared with all baselines across all the datasets by four metrics. Our proposed CCKSR method effectively exploits the cross-session information and item attribute information in the SSL of SBR tasks. 2) GRU4REC is the first session-based model that uses a recurrent structure to capture sequential information. But a big issue of the RNN-based methods is that there is a catastrophic forgetting of the early information. For the attention-based baselines, NARM and STAMP, they are better

than linearly rolling out as RNN structure by outperforming the GRU4REC. 3) Graph-based baseline methods all outperform RNN-based methods, showing the great capacity of GNNs in modeling session data. These methods use a session graph to represent the session sequence by linking the interactions according to their chronological order. Among them, FGNN obtains higher accuracy than SR-GNN. This proves that capturing cross-session information helps accurately predict user intent in SBR. 4) Most of the SSL-based baseline methods perform better than general GNN-based methods, suggesting the importance of utilizing SSL for SBR. The truth inspires us that learning session/item representations with a proper contrastive learning mechanism could improve the model performance.

### 4.3  Model Ablation Study

To evaluate the rationality of design sub-modules in our CCKSR framework, we consider four model variants. 1) CCKSR-Cross: We only use the semantic view to model session data, removing the cross-session graph and the self-supervised graph co-training. 2) CCKSR-HG: We only use the structural view to model session data, removing the item attribute hypergraph and the self-supervised graph co-training. 3) CCKSR-QA: We remove the query-aware graph attention networks and replace it with general graph convolution network. 4)CCKSR-Soft: we remove the soft-attention mechanism and replace it with averaging item representations as the representation of each session.

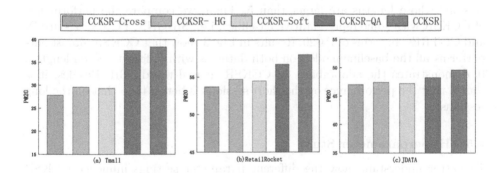

**Fig. 2.** Ablation study on key components of CCKSR.

The ablation study results are shown in Fig. 2. From the evaluation results, we can observe that each component consistently contributes on three datasets. The self-supervised co-training improves the base model the most, serving as the driving force of the performance improvement. Besides, the query-aware graph attention network is effective to improve the model performance. According to the results of CCKSR -Soft, it is shown that learning different item importance across sessions is better than directly averaging representations of contained items for learning session representations in SBR.

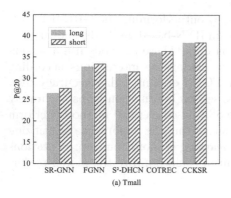 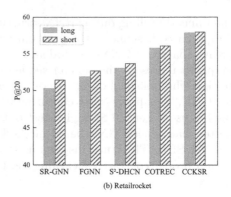

(a) Tmall                    (b) Retailrocket

**Fig. 3.** The performance of different methods with different session lengths evaluated in terms of P@20 on Tmall and Retailrocket. The blue bars stand for short sessions and the green ones for long sessions. (Color figure online)

### 4.4 Handling Different Session Lengths

In real-world situations, sessions with various lengths are common, so it is interesting to know how stable our CCKSR as well as the baseline models are when dealing with them, and it is also a critical indicator for production environments. To evaluate this, we follow [19] to split the sessions of Tmall and RetailRocket into two groups with different lengths and name them as short and long. Short contains sessions whose lengths are less than or equal to 5, while long contains sessions whose lengths are larger than 5. Then, we compare the performance of CCKSR with some representative baselines, i.e., SR-GNN, FGNN, $S^2$-DHCN and COTREC in terms of P@20. Results in Fig. 3 show that CCKSR almost outperforms all the baseline models on both datasets with different session lengths. It demonstrates the adaptability of CCKSR in real-world SBR. Besides, it is shown that the performance on the short sessions is better than that on the long sessions.

### 4.5 Hyperparameter Study

To better understand how the different parameter settings influence CCKSR framework performance, we check model sensitivity to two key hyperparameters, namely, the hidden state dimensionality $d$, and the depth $L$ of our graph convolution network. We report the sensitivity analysis results (using P@20) in Fig. 4. The discussions are summarized as follows.

**Hidden State Dimensionality:** $d$. For our model, the embedding dimensionality $d = 100$ resolves with the best performance. Smaller embedding dimensionality is insufficient for representing node information, while large dimensionality does not always bring stronger model representation ability in learning associations between items for SBR. This is caused by the model over-fitting.

**Depth of Graph convolution Paradigm:** $L$. By stacking three graph convolution layers, CCKSR-3 performs better than CCKSR-1, which suggests the

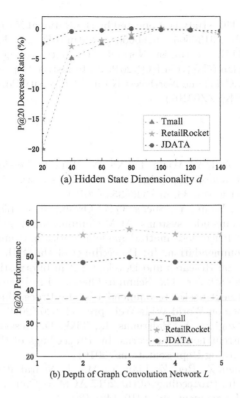

**Fig. 4.** Hyper-parameter study of CCKSR.

positive effect of high-order connectivity injection. However, with the increasing of depth of graph model, the performance starts to deteriorate. This is because stacking more embedding propagation layers may involve noise signals for modeling associations between items, which leads to the over-smoothing.

## 5  Conclusion

In this paper, we propose a novel model called Cross-view Contrastive learning mechanism for Knowledge-aware Session-based Recommendation (CCKSR), which can improve the quality of session/item representation learning in a self-supervised manner from two dimensions: 1) CCKSR captures pair-wise relations between items and high-order relations among items from two views, including structural view and semantic view. 2) CCKSR leverages query-aware graph attention networks and hypergraph convolution networks to learn node embeddings and further performs cross-view contrastive learning between two views to learn discriminative representations. Extensive experimental results verify the effectiveness of our CCKSR model. As an ongoing work, we tend to deepen the application of SSL in SBR models and design more general auxiliary tasks for the SBR to improve the recommendation performance.

**Acknowledgment.** This study is supported by the National Natural Science Foundation of China (61762078, 61363058, 61966004), Natural Science Foundation of Gansu Province (21JR7RA114), Northwest Normal University Young Teachers Research Capacity Promotion plan (NWNU-LKQN2019-2), Industrial Support Project of Gansu Colleges(No. 2022CYZC-11) and Northwest Normal University Post-graduate Research Funding Project (2021KYZZ02107).

# References

1. Wu, S., Tang, Y., Zhu, Y., Wang, L., Xie, X., Tan, T.: Session-based recommendation with graph neural networks. In: Proceedings of the AAAI Conference on Artificial Intelligence, vol. 33, pp. 346–353 (2019)
2. Wang, S., Cao, L., Wang, Y., Sheng, Q.Z., Orgun, M.A., Lian, D.: A survey on session-based recommender systems. ACM Comput. Surv. **54**(7), 1–38 (2021)
3. Zhang, X., et al.: Price does matter! modeling price and interest preferences in session-based recommendation. In: Proceedings of the 45th International ACM SIGIR Conference on Research and Development in Information Retrieval (2022)
4. Rendle, S., Freudenthaler, C., Schmidt-Thieme, L.: Factorizing personalized markov chains for next-basket recommendation. In: Proceedings of the 19th International Conference on World Wide Web, pp. 811–820 (2010)
5. Hidasi, B., Karatzoglou, A., Baltrunas, L., Tikk, D.: Session-based recommendations with recurrent neural networks. In: Proceedings of the 4th International Conference on Learning Representations (2016)
6. Li, J., Ren, P., Chen, Z., Ren, Z., Lian, T., Ma, J.: Neural attentive session-based recommendation. In: Proceedings of the 2017 ACM on Conference on Information and Knowledge Management, pp. 1419–1428 (2017)
7. Liu, Q., Zeng, Y., Mokhosi, R., Zhang, H.: Stamp: short-term attention/memory priority model for session-based recommendation. In: Proceedings of the 24th ACM SIGKDD International Conference on Knowledge Discovery & Data Mining, pp. 1831–1839 (2018)
8. Qiu, R., Huang, Z., Li, J., Yin, H.: Exploiting cross-session information for session-based recommendation with graph neural networks. ACM Trans. Inf. Syst. (TOIS) **38**(3), 1–23 (2020)
9. Zhang, X., Ma, H., Gao, Z., Li, Z., Chang, L.: Exploiting cross-session information for knowledge-aware session-based recommendation via graph attention networks. Int. J. Intell. Syst. **37**, 7614–7637 (2022)
10. Meng, W., Yang, D., Xiao, Y.: Incorporating user micro-behaviors and item knowledge into multi-task learning for session-based recommendation. In: Proceedings of the 43rd International ACM SIGIR Conference on Research and Development in Information Retrieval, pp. 1091–1100 (2020)
11. Yuan, J., Song, Z., Sun, M., Wang, X., Zhao, W.X.: Dual sparse attention network for session-based recommendation. In: Proceedings of the AAAI Conference on Artificial Intelligence, vol. 35, pp. 4635–4643 (2021)
12. Zhang, X., Ma, H., Gao, Z., Li, Z., Chang, L.: Enhancing session-based recommendation with global context information and knowledge graph. In: International Conference on Database Systems for Advanced Applications, pp. 281–288. Springer (2022). https://doi.org/10.1007/978-3-031-00126-0_20
13. Yuan, J., Ji, W., Zhang, D., Pan, J., Wang, X.: Micro-behavior encoding for session-based recommendation. In: Proceedings of the 45th International ACM SIGIR Conference on Research and Development in Information Retrieval (2022)

14. Velickovic, P., Fedus, W., Hamilton, W.L., Liò, P., Bengio, Y., Hjelm, R.D.: Deep graph infomax. **2**, 4 (2019)
15. Liu, X., et al.: Self-supervised learning: Generative or contrastive. IEEE Trans. Knowl. Data Eng. **33**, 1–24 (2021)
16. Xu, D., Cheng, W., Luo, D., Chen, H., Zhang, X.: InfoGCL: information-aware graph contrastive learning. In: Advances in Neural Information Processing Systems, vol. 34 (2021)
17. Zou, D., et al.: Multi-level cross-view contrastive learning for knowledge-aware recommender system. In: Proceedings of the 45th International ACM SIGIR Conference on Research and Development in Information Retrieval (2022)
18. Xia, X., Yin, H., Yu, J., Wang, Q., Cui, L., Zhang, X.: Self-supervised hypergraph convolutional networks for session-based recommendation. In: Proceedings of the AAAI Conference on Artificial Intelligence, vol. 35, pp. 4503–4511 (2021)
19. Xia, X., Yin, H., Yu, J., Shao, Y., Cui, L.: Self-supervised graph co-training for session-based recommendation. In: Proceedings of the 30th ACM International Conference on Information & Knowledge Management, pp. 2180–2190 (2021)
20. Wang, Z., Wei, W., Cong, G., Li, X.L., Mao, X.L., Qiu, M.: Global context enhanced graph neural networks for session-based recommendation. In: Proceedings of the 43rd International ACM SIGIR Conference on Research and Development in Information Retrieval, pp. 169–178 (2020)
21. Huang, C., et al.: Graph-enhanced multi-task learning of multi-level transition dynamics for session-based recommendation. In: Proceedings of the AAAI Conference on Artificial Intelligence, vol. 35, pp. 4123–4130 (2021)
22. Bahdanau, D., Cho, K., Bengio, Y.: Neural machine translation by jointly learning to align and translate. In: Proceedings of the 3rd International Conference on Learning Representations (2014)
23. Feng, Y., You, H., Zhang, Z., Ji, R., Gao, Y.: Hypergraph neural networks. In: Proceedings of the AAAI Conference on Artificial Intelligence, vol. 33, pp. 3558–3565 (2019)
24. Wu, F., Souza, A., Zhang, T., Fifty, C., Yu, T., Weinberger, K.: Simplifying graph convolutional networks. In: International Conference on Machine Learning. PMLR, pp. 6861–6871 (2019)
25. Van den Oord, A., Li, Y., Vinyals, O.: Representation learning with contrastive predictive coding. arXiv e-prints (2018)
26. Hou, Y., Hu, B., Zhang, Z., Zhao, W.X.: Core: simple and effective session-based recommendation within consistent representation space. In: Proceedings of the 45th International ACM SIGIR Conference on Research and Development in Information Retrieval (2022)

# Reinforcement Learning

# HiSA: Facilitating Efficient Multi-Agent Coordination and Cooperation by Hierarchical Policy with Shared Attention

Zixuan Chen[1], Zhirui Zhu[1], Guang Yang[1], and Yang Gao[1,2]([✉])

[1] National Key Laboratory for Novel Software Technology, Nanjing University, Nanjing, China
chenzx@nju.edu.cn
[2] Shenzhen Research Institute of Nanjing University, Shenzhen 518057, China
gaoy@nju.edu.cn

**Abstract.** While numbers of partially observable agents improve their policies throughout decentralized training, the performance of multi-agent systems under this setting suffers from severe non-cooperation and non-stationary. Most previous works attempt to introduce communication into the training and optimization to facilitate cooperation between agents, but the noise message brought by communication may lead to misunderstandings during complex tasks and even lead to catastrophic failure of long-term training. To alleviate the above dilemma, in this paper, we propose the Hierarchical Structure with Shared Attention Mechanism (HiSA), a novel communication-based approach, to facilitate the efficiency and robustness of coordination and cooperation in multi-agent reinforcement learning (MARL). HiSA can not only resist the negative impact of noise in communication, but also effectively utilize attention as communication tool to build efficient cooperative hierarchical policies. Experimental results demonstrate that HiSA significantly outperforms existing communication-based MARL methods especially in the long-term complex cooperation scenarios with isomorphic agents.

**Keywords:** Multi-agent · Communication · Reinforcement-learning

---

Supported by Science and Technology Innovation 2030 New Generation Artificial Intelligence Major Project (No.2018AAA0100905), the National Natural Science Foundation of China (No. 62192783), Primary Research & Developement Plan of Jiangsu Province (No. BE2021028), Shenzhen Fundamental Research Program (No. 2021Szvup056).
Z. Chen and Z. Zhu—Contribute equally to this work.

S. Khanna et al. (Eds.): PRICAI 2022, LNCS 13631, pp. 77–90, 2022.
https://doi.org/10.1007/978-3-031-20868-3_6

# 1   Introduction

The cooperative multi-agent reinforcement learning (MARL) algorithm is currently one of the most popular mainstream methods that can be used to solve learning problems in multi-agent system (MAS) [3,14]. Despite the efficiency of cooperative MARL, its performance is limited to a certain extent by the shortcomings brought about by cooperation. There are mainly the following two challenges. First, the joint action space that increases exponentially with the number of agents leads to scalability issues [21]. Second, partial observability leads to cognitive errors between cooperative agents in the joint optimization process.

To alleviate the negative impact of the above challenges, the current mainstream works regard **communication** as one of the basic paradigms of cooperative MARL tasks, in which agents can always share information with others. The communication mechanism provides the necessary additional information for message receivers, which can help agents clarify the overall situation of the partially observable environment. It also brings clues to the intentions of others to provide opportunities for pre-interaction before the agent takes actual action in the shared-information environment. By constructing communication channels on a single-agent deep neural network, the latest communication framework algorithms can provide information as joint learning methods and can be extended as independent learning ways [5,16].

Shared knowledge is a widely adapted communication trick in cooperative MARL, which works by sharing the same environment and the same set of network parameters, providing opportunities for agents to learn to communicate and ultimately lead to policy improvement. Related works mainly focus on using more primitive information, i.e. currently available information, to facilitate interactions between agents [5,16]. However, agents communicating without any prior knowledge of the environment or language logic may make communicating information very noisy, which makes the convergence of collaborative MARL more difficult. Recent works attempt to reduce the noise by combining the importance information of neighbor agents [10], but to a certain extent, the basic principle of solving noise problems in MAS has not been fully discussed: *Considering how the material of message is defined and the way in which it affects policy is critical to improving the efficiency and performance of cooperation.*

This insufficiency motivates our research, inspiring us to take advantages of the shared attention mechanism [17] to infer and transfer the implicit intention between agents, and further establish a novel communication mechanism in MAS. From a biological point of view, shared attention mechanism is a silent and instinctive way of communication that is very common in human daily life. For example, once your friend shows interest in the kettle in front of you, naturally, you will notice the kettle and infer his/her intention to be thirsty, so you bring your friend a cup of tea. Generally speaking, shared attention in MAS can be divided into two steps. First, agents should inform each other what they are focusing on now. Then, they can infer implicit intentions based on the content of their concerns and adjust their policies accordingly.

Consequently, in this work, we propose the Hierarchical Structure with Shared Attention Mechanism (HiSA) for MARL, which artfully combines the shared attention mechanism with a hierarchical structure to achieve the above-mentioned purpose of efficient communication. It is worth mentioning that in this hierarchical structure, sub-policies that embody the agents' implicit intention can in turn be queried by the agents, this enables a single-agent to integrate the corresponding sub-policies into its high-level policy according to the relevance between some specific agents and itself, that is, to flexibly adjust the agent's policy according to the shared attention. To reflect this relevance, we further introduce a shared attention map to achieve this assumption in HiSA, this shared attention map can be expediently drawn from all local attentions and is of great importance for developing cooperation among individuals. In this way, HiSA bridges the gap between shared knowledge and cooperative behaviors, and ultimately facilitates efficient cooperation and coordination among agents.

The main contributions of this paper can be summarized as follows:

- We propose a novel communication-based Hierarchical Structure with Shared Attention Mechanism (HiSA) for MARL. HiSA is a synchronous communication framework that is built and learned levelwise.
- We further propose a new communication-driven solution to reflect the widely adopted relevance assumption in HiSA.
- Experimental studies evaluate HiSA with four baselines from five perspectives in two domains. The results show that, comparing to the baselines, HiSA achieves the following advantages: (i) HiSA can discover useful implicit intentions more effectively, (ii) HiSA can infer better intertask-transferable sub-policies, and (iv) HiSA has a good ability to facilitate multi-agent communication and cooperation.

## 2    Preliminaries and Related Work

### 2.1    Communicative Decentralized Partially Observable Markov Decision Process

Agents could receive essential global information, negotiate actions, and boost specific coordination in behavior with proper communication. Recently, by the springing up of deep neural network, more and more works put forward to exploiting different communicative methods in an end-to-end model. Here, to better illustrate our work, we give a novel mathematical definition of *Communicative Decentralized Partially Observable Markov Decision Process* (CD-POMDP), based on the classic *Decentralized Partially Observable Markov Decision Process* (Dec-POMDP).

**Definition 1.** *CD-POMDP is defined as a tuple* $\langle \mathcal{N}, \mathcal{S}, \{\mathcal{O}^i\}_{i \in \mathcal{N}}, \{\mathcal{A}^i\}_{i \in \mathcal{N}}, P,$ $\{R^i\}_{i \in \mathcal{N}}, \{\mathcal{M}^i\}_{i \in \mathcal{N}}, \gamma\rangle$, *where* $\mathcal{N}$ *denotes the set of* $N > 1$ *agents,* $\mathcal{S}$ *denotes the global state space,* $\mathcal{O}^i$ *denotes the local observation space of agent i,* $\mathcal{A}^i$ *denotes the action space of agent i. Let* $\mathcal{A} := \mathcal{A}^1 \times \cdots \times \mathcal{A}^N$, *then* $\mathcal{P} : \mathcal{S} \times \mathcal{A} \to \Delta(\mathcal{S})$ *is the* *transition function, $R^i : \mathcal{S} \times \mathcal{A} \times \mathcal{S} \to \mathbb{R}$ is the reward function of agent $i$, $\mathcal{M}^i$ is the message space of agent $i$ that is sent out by itself, and $\overline{\mathcal{M}}^i$ is the message space of agent $i$ that is received by it, $\gamma$ is the discount factor for long term reward.*

At time-step $t$ of the CD-POMDP, each agent $i \in \mathcal{N}$ observes the environment locally, and then sends messages to other agents, eventually makes decision upon its action space according to its local observation and messages received. After that, the MAS executes the joint action, and turns to the next state. Each agent $i$ is aim to find a policy $\pi^i : \mathcal{O}^i \times \overline{\mathcal{M}}^i \to \Delta\left(\mathcal{A}^i\right)$ to optimize its long term rewards.

## 2.2  Communicative Methods in MAS

Generally, the communication mechanism in MAS is implemented by discrete-channel or mix channel, and such methods are most commonly used in MARL. Typical discrete-channel methods allocate independent communication channel for each agent. [5] sends differentiable messages by discrete communication channels. [13] utilizes messages of last step and on time both. [8] learns a robust communication by the dropped-out manner. Discrete communication channel is efficient in small-scale agent group, but has poor behavior when its communicative scale increases by number of agents. Mix channel usually aggregates multiple messages with an additive manner. [16] takes hidden states as messages and computes the mean value. [2,7] clean message by weight and agent-wise weight instead of mean respectively. While such public communication channels face severe decay of information, [10] designs a specific communication protocol to limit information flow, so that refrain from the dirty messages problem somehow. In summary, most current communicative methods suffer from a dilemma between the communication efficiency and information quality. To avoid this dilemma, our work introduces the attention mechanism into MAS and applies a communication-driven attention map to further promote cooperation between agents.

## 2.3  Attention Mechanism

Attention mechanism is widely adopted in Computer Vision and Neural Machine Translation to extract important local information [4,18]. In high-dimensional RL tasks, it is proved to be effective as well [12]. Using different attention model as message filter, recent communication methods partly remove redundant parts of the received information. Besides, Multi-Actor-Attention-Critic (MAAC) [6] outperforms in mix-cooperative-competitive tasks by attention to local observations of agents in its critic. As attention working as weighted average over sources, it needs score function to estimate correlation between source and task, which has been implemented by learning differential parameters,multi-layer perceptrons, dot-production and defined features of source etc. We adopt the wildly used dot-production of query and key as the score function: $\text{score}(source_i, task) = <\text{query}(task), \text{key}(source_i)>$, where

$< \cdot >$ is a inner-product, query($task$) is about the feature of a target task, and key($source_i$) is about the feature of a specific source. After normalization by the softmax function, the the attention weight $w_i$ of source $i$ is then defined as $w_i = \frac{\exp(\text{score}(source_i, task)))}{\sum_j \exp(\text{score}(source_j, task)))}$. The attention mechanism has advantages in selectively processing complex information through importance weights. To further exploit the advantages of attention for MARL, we introduce a hierarchical structure in our framework.

## 2.4   Hierarchical Policy with Attention

Hierarchical Reinforcement Learning (HRL) is proposed to deal with the complex RL tasks by decomposing them into a series of sub-tasks. Considering automatically sub-task partition by time-scale, Hierarchical-DQN (H-DQN) [9] introduces goal-conditioned Q-value, while the Option-Critic architecture [1] derives policy gradient theorems for options. Diversity-Driven Extensible HRL (DEHRL) [15] encourages the diversity of sub-policies by using intrinsic reward, which improves the exploration and speeds up learning. Specially, MAS attaches more importance to cooperation-competence of sub-policies besides heterogeneity. Role-Oriented MARL Framework (ROMA) [20] studies on the map from role to policy-net. Deep Cognitive Hierarchies From the perspective of a MAS, the HRL framework most similar to our work is the Attention Multi-Agent Deep Deterministic Policy Gradient (ATT-MADDPG) [11], while it trains "critics" with hard attention mechanism.

# 3   Method

In this paper we propose to facilitate flexible and robust cooperation among agents in long-term complex tasks by a hierarchical structure with shared attention.

## 3.1   Shared Attention Map for Communication

Shared attention is considered as an instinct ability to human beings and develops throughout the life [17], which usually results in joint intention to cooperate. In order to make full use of the information processing ability of shared attention, we propose the concept of **heads**, and regard it as the refined and abstract information that agents should learn to pay attention to. The design details and theoretical description of heads will be described in Subsect. 3.2. Besides, in the communication, we take the self attention $W_{Self}$ as the communication material that a single-agent sends, and the shared attention $W_{Shared}$ as messages received, so that under the Definition 1 of CD-POMDP, these two types of messages for agent $i$ are defined by $\mathcal{M}^i \Longleftrightarrow W_{Self}^i$ and $\overline{\mathcal{M}}^i \Longleftrightarrow W_{Shared}$. To further tap the potential of shared attention as communication material, we put forward three implementation forms of shared attention map based on Mean, Entropy and Similarity.

**Mean.** One of effective approaches to define the message and further construct the shared attention map is to process the mean of all attention weights. According to the messages that agent $i$ receives, each value of shared attention map based on mean can be defined by:

$$\overline{\mathcal{M}}^i_{mean} = \frac{1}{N} \sum_{j \in \mathcal{N}} \mathcal{M}^j. \tag{1}$$

Mean value could unify the intention of all the agents, which is effective for large-scale MAS tasks such as concentrated firepower in StarCraft II.

**Entropy.** In the perspective of information entropy, the importance of an attention weight could be evaluated by its distribution, which is inversely proportional to entropy $\mathrm{H}(\mathcal{M}^i) = -\sum_{x \in \mathcal{H}^i} \mathcal{M}^i_x \log(\mathcal{M}^i_x)$, where $\mathcal{H}^i$ is the head set of agent $i$ and $x \in \mathcal{H}^i$ is a head for agent $i$. Now that an agent has no preference for any of its sub-policy, it may be better to listen to the "opinions" of other agents. Then, each value of shared attention map based on entropy is defined as:

$$\overline{\mathcal{M}}^i_{entropy} = \sum_{j \in \mathcal{N}} \frac{\exp(\mathrm{H}(\mathcal{M}^j))}{\sum_{k \in \mathcal{N}} \exp(\mathrm{H}(\mathcal{M}^k))} \mathcal{M}^j. \tag{2}$$

**Similarity.** In order to deal with the complex relationship between agents, we try to consider the distance between them. The measurement of neighbors could be relevant to the cosine similarity $d_{i,j}$ between queries $q^i$ and $q^j$ of agent $i$ and agent $j$, that is $d(i,j) = \frac{(q^i)^\top \cdot q^j}{||q^i|| \times ||q^j||}$. Then, after weighted summation by softmax normalization, each value of shared attention map based on similarity is defined as:

$$\overline{\mathcal{M}}^i_{similarity} = \sum_{j \in \mathcal{N}} \frac{\exp(d(i,j))}{\sum_{k \in \mathcal{N}} \exp(d(i,k))} \mathcal{M}^j. \tag{3}$$

## 3.2 Hierarchical Structure with Shared Attention Mechanism

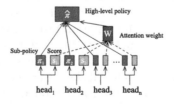

**Fig. 1.** Hierarchical Policy Structure with Shared Attention.

In this subsection, we first introduce a novel hierarchical policy structure for MARL, which lays the foundation of key communication phrase in our work.

We then introduce the core HiSA in this work and illustrate how it combines shared attention with a hierarchical policy structure to generate policies. As shown in Fig. 1, the hierarchical structure constructs diversified sub-policy space with fixed number of heads, and each head computes an vector of Q-value as sub-policy $\pi$, then it computes weighted average of sub-policies as high-level policy $\hat{\pi}$. More specifically, to improve the efficiency of communication, we apply the shared attention to simplify the hierarchical policy structure, where each agent has a $|\mathcal{A}|^{n-1}$-heads critic to activate corresponding Q-value heads by specific joint action.

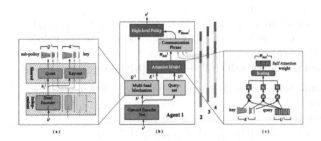

**Fig. 2.** Communication Mechanism between Agents. (a) Multi-head Mechanism; (b) High-level Policy Structure; (c) Attention Model.

Figure 2 shows the communication mechanism between agents and the roadmap of entire policy generation process of a certain agent, other agents are presented in the form of colorized clubs. Specifically, our framework first derives diversified sub-policy space through multi-head mechanism, and compute attentions for sub-policies. Through the communication phrase, attention is shared among all agents, and the policy generated by weighting sub-policies would be regarded as the high-level policy of each agent. We further elaborate the above three key implementations as follows.

**Multi-head Mechanism.** In Fig. 2(a), we present the key realization of the multi-head mechanism, in which the multi-heads would learn and make decisions based on their own diversified representations. To diversify the perspective of heads and still benefit from consistent model, we built Q-net and Key-net, and separate head-encoder but share the Q-net and Key-net for multi-heads. For each head $x$, the Q-net outputs Q-value function of sub-policy $Q_x(o^i) = [Q_x(o^i, a_0), Q_x(o^i, a_1), \ldots, Q_x(o^i, a_{|\mathcal{A}|-1})]^{\top}$, where $|\mathcal{A}|$ is the number of actions. The Key-net outputs key-value of self-attention $k_x(o^i)$. The reason for this setting is that it could be consistent in the computational logic of the Q-net and Key-net although the diversified representation of each head stresses different parts of the environment. In addition, shared key function helps to shuffle the feature of each head in a unified form, which avoids over-estimating of a particular head when accessing score of multi-heads.

**Algorithm 1.** Hierarchical Structure with Shared Attention Mechanism for MARL

---

1: **Initialize:** exploration probability $\epsilon$, ending exploration probability $\epsilon_e$, decay rate $\eta$, discount rate $\gamma$, learning rate $\alpha$.
2: **Initialize:** experience replay buffer $\mathcal{D}$
3: **Initialize:** main network parameters $\theta = \{\theta_{GENET}, \theta_{MHNET}, \theta_{QNET}\}$ for the Ground Encoder Net GENET, Multi-head Mechanism MHNET and Query Net QNET, target network $\theta^- = \theta$
4: **for** episode $m = 1$ **to** $M$ **do**
5:     Initialize environment $\boldsymbol{o}_0 = [o_0^1, o_0^2, \ldots, o_0^N]$
6:     **for** step $t = 0$ **to** terminal $T$ **do**
7:         **for** each agent $i$ **do**
8:             Compute hidden variables $h_t^i \leftarrow \text{GENET}(o_t^i; \theta_{GENET,m})$
9:             Compute sub-policy Q-value and key value, $Q_t^i, K_t^i \leftarrow$ MHNET$(h_t^i; \theta_{MHNET,m})$
10:            Compute query value $U_t^i \leftarrow \text{QNET}(h_t^i; \theta_{QNET,m})$
11:            Compute self-attention weights $W_{self,t}^i \leftarrow \text{softmax}\left(\frac{U_t^i K_t^{i\top}}{\sqrt{\xi}}\right)$
12:        **end for**
13:        Share attention by communication phrase
           $W_{shared,t} \leftarrow \text{COM}(W_{self,t}^1, W_{self,t}^2, \ldots, W_{self,t}^N)$     ▷ COM is an
           implementation form of shared attention
14:        **for** each agent $i$ **do**
15:            Compute high-level policy $\hat{Q}_t^i \leftarrow Q_t^i \cdot W_{shared,t}^\top$
16:            Sample action $a_t^i \sim \epsilon-$greedy policy $\hat{\pi}_t^i$
17:        **end for**
18:        Execute joint action $\boldsymbol{a}_t = [a_t^1, a_t^2, \ldots, a_t^N]$ and observe reward $\boldsymbol{r}_{t+1} = [r_{t+1}^1, r_{t+1}^2, \ldots, r_{t+1}^N]$ and next observation $\boldsymbol{o}_{t+1} = [o_{t+1}^1, o_{t+1}^2, \ldots, o_{t+1}^N]$
19:    **end for**
20:    Store trajectory $\langle \boldsymbol{o}_0, \boldsymbol{a}_0, \boldsymbol{r}_1, \boldsymbol{o}_1, \ldots, \boldsymbol{r}_T, \boldsymbol{o}_T \rangle$ into $\mathcal{D}$
21:    Update parameters $\theta_{m+1}, \theta_{m+1}^- \leftarrow \text{OP}(\theta_m, \theta_m^-, \mathcal{D}, \alpha)$     ▷ OP is a standard DQN optimization method
22:    Update exploration probability $\epsilon \leftarrow \max\{\epsilon_e, \epsilon - \eta\}$
23: **end for**

---

**Attention Model.** [18] introduced Multi-Head Attention (MHA) based on several scaled dot-product attention heads for Neural Machine Translation (NMT). For agent $i$, it stacks key from different heads into corresponding matrix $K^i$, which is $K^i = \|_{x \in \mathcal{H}^i} k_x(o^i)$, where $\|$ represents concatenation, $\mathcal{H}^i$ is the head set of agent $i$ and $x \in \mathcal{H}^i$ is a head for agent $i$. For the query, it is quite different between tasks of NMT and tasks of MARL. Specifically, we introduce the way of query by agent instead of head, as shown in Fig. 2(c), self-attention weight can be computes by $W_{self}^i = \text{softmax}\left(\frac{U^i K^{i\top}}{\sqrt{\xi}}\right)$, where $U^i$ is the query matrix for agent $i$ and $\xi$ is number of heads. It should be noticed that $W_{self}^i$ is a vector of dimension $\xi$. As mentioned in Subsect. 3.1, we share attention of each agent by communication phrase to further highlight the cooperative behavior, which also paves a way for high-level policy representation.

**Representation of High-level Policy.** In this work, we adopt the value-based algorithm framework, and the sub-policy will use a vector of Q-values as its representation. Based on the multi-head mechanism and attention model described above, the Q-value of a high-level policy for agent $i$ is naturally defined by $\hat{Q}(o^i, a) = \sum_{x \in \mathcal{H}^i} w_x \cdot Q_x(o^i, a)$, where $w_x \in W_{Shared}$ is an element of shared attention. Then, a greedy high-level policy is naturally defined by $\hat{\pi}_{greedy} = \arg\max_a \hat{Q}(o^i, a)$. High-level policy integrates sub-policies effectively through shared attention mechanism, which could abstract the similarity preferences between agents and promote cooperative behavior.

### 3.3 HiSA for Multi-agent Reinforcement Learning

Based on the above two subsections, now we present the combined HiSA framework for agent communication, and further demonstrate the overall algorithm when it is used in the training and optimization process of MARL. The specific algorithm process of our HiSA-MARL can be seen in Algorithm 1. The loss in HiSA-MARL is agent-independent, which is then defined by $\mathcal{L}(\theta) = \mathbb{E}_{\mathcal{T} \subset \mathcal{D}}\left[\left(y - \hat{Q}(o, a; \theta)\right)^2\right]$, where $\mathcal{T}$ is the batch transitions sampled from the replay buffer $\mathcal{D}$, a transition $\langle o, a, r, o' \rangle \sim \mathcal{T}$, $y = r + \gamma \max_{a'} \hat{Q}(o', a'; \theta^-)$ and $\theta^-$ are the parameters of a target network. it is worth noting that HiSA is a generalized training framework for all agents, and it is a synchronous communication framework rather than the traditional MARL framework of the Centralized Training Decentralized Execution (CTDE) mechanism. The proposed HiSA algorithm separates the sample collection and optimization process in each episode. For the sample collection, we adopt the $\epsilon-$greedy policy with decay factor $\eta$, this greedy policy has been presented in previous Subsect. 3.2. In addition, we use a ground encoder network GENET to process the primitive local observation, which outputs hidden representations $h^i$. It is implemented by a full connected layer and a Gated Recurrent Unit (GRU) layer that bridges present observation with past states. In the optimization process, HiSA is a fully differentiable framework, so that it could be trained end-to-end to minimize a standard deep q-learning network (DQN) loss. Particularly, HiSA shares network parameters among agents, which has been proved that it could speed up learning and even reach better score in many cooperative tasks [8, 16].

## 4   Experiments

We evaluate our method on two classic cooperative MARL benchmarks, that is the StarCraft Multi-Agent Challenge (SMAC) [14] and the Overcooked [3].

### 4.1   Experimental Setup

To better illustrate the advantages of HiSA, the following three classical frameworks are selected as the baselines in the experiments.

**DIAL** [5] is the founder of learning by discrete communication channels. The DIAL agent processes messages by the discretise/regularise unit, which delivers the messages to others in the next time step.

**CommNet** [16] exchanges information about hidden state when an agent selects an action, the information computes the mean of hidden states of all agents. Then, agents could update their hidden states by their previous own hidden states and the mean value.

**GA-Comm** [10] puts forward a communication method based on the CommNet, while it filters irrelevant messages by graph abstraction.

Besides, to conduct ablation experiments, we perform a hierarchical structure method without communication based on HiSA, named the Self-Att. In SMAC experiments, HiSA calculates the value of shared attention map in the form of mean during communication phrase as Equation (1). In Overcooked, this value is calculated as Equation (3).

## 4.2 Experiments on the StarCraft Multi-Agent Challenge

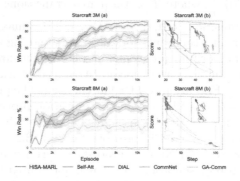

**Fig. 3.** Results on the SMAC.

Originated from the StarCraft II [19], the StarCraft Multi-Agent Challenge (SMAC) consists of a set of StarCraft II micro scenarios which aim to evaluate the micro-management of a team. Each round starts from fixed formation on a plain landform, while it ends when all units of one side are killed, or the time limit is exceeded. After each round, SMAC will feedback a non-zero reward, which will be adjusted according to the casualties of both parties. Each agent, corresponding to a particular single unit, locally observes and acts at every time step. To dominate the fighting between two groups, agents should acquire several necessary team strategies, including focusing fire, avoiding overkill and so on. We have drawn Episode-WinRate curve and Step-Score curve to show the performance of MARL methods, as shown in Fig. 3. The Episode-WinRate curve is the progress of win rate and convergence by episode, at the same time, we also designed the Step-Score curve to indicate the efficiency of the fights which distinguishes the outcome of latter episode from former by richer ink.

**StarCraft II 3M Scenario (3 Marines vs 3 Marines).** As shown in Fig. 3(3M-a), the win rate of the proposed method reaches 90% after $7k$ episodes, then it converges to 98% after $10k$, while the Self-Att also performs well, DIAL and GA-Comm wave only ranging from 60% to 80%, this is most likely because they are still learning how to deliver information accurately. In Fig. 3(3M-b), trajectory of HiSA ends about point $(19.9, 19.8)$ which means that it can win the fight in 20 steps in most case (the victory bonus scales to 20 in the setting).

**StarCraft II 8M Scenario (8 Marines vs 8 Marines).** As shown in Fig. 3(8M-a), although more units in the case poses challenges to coordination and cooperation, the win rate of HiSA also rapidly achieves an average higher than 50%, and end at 90% eventually. The DIAL agents wave around 85% in this scenario, for its discrete communication channel deliveries valuable message. The above two also perform well on the Step-Score curve. However, CommNet suffers from large information blur in its communication phrase. Although GA-Comm solves this problem through graphic abstraction, it stagnates in the early stages, as shown in Fig. 3(8M-b).

### 4.3 Experiments on the Overcooked

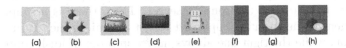

(a)      (b)      (c)      (d)      (e)      (f)      (g)      (h)

**Fig. 4.** Objects in Overcooked environment.

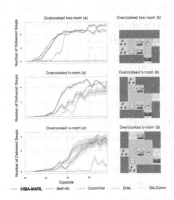

**Fig. 5.** Results on the Overcooked.

To show the ability of HiSA of facilitating communication, we further apply above MARL methods in a more complicated cooperation environment, the

Overcooked, where agents rely on a series of combined policies. In the cooking tasks, agents should travel through specific terrains, prepare food material, cook, and serve the orders. For maximum return, they should process as many orders as possible within the time limit. At each time step, an agent observes its position and relative positions of other objects. Then, it chooses an action from {move[direction], turn[direction], interaction and no-option}. Fig. 4 vividly shows the related objects in the cooking tasks: (a) is a cupboard of dishes and (b) is a bunch of onions. Agent could acquire a dish/onion by interacting with it. (c) is a pot, which starts a 5-timestep-cooking to produce soup once players put 2 onions into it. (d) is a server where the completed soup should be delivered to. (e) is an agent who walk on the road. Two sides of (f) are the road and the obstacle, respectively. (g) and (h) show obstacles where objects (dish/onion) are placed. If the agent has an object in its hand, it can interact with the empty obstacle and place the object on it. Conversely, the agent without an object in its hand can interact with the obstacle where the object is placed and obtain the object. The number of soups served by the agent is applied as the experimental performance indicator, because this value directly determines the "cumulative rewards" of all agents in the game.

**Two-Room.** As in Fig. 5 (two-room-b), this layout separates units in the two apart rooms. The left agent only accesses to onion and pot, while the right one should learn how to send the soup to server. Then, there is a simplest policy that left agent turns to onion cupboard to get an onion, then turns to pot to put an onion, while the right one always moves in order of [dish cupboard, pot, server]. Furthermore, two agents should learn how to schedule their cooking tasks on the two pots, to enhance efficiency. As shown in Fig. 5(two-room-a), both paying attention to its own (Self-Att) and learning with communication could settle the matter, while our HiSA can even deliver up to 9 orders at the end of the training. **h-Room.** As in Fig. 5 (h-room-b), 'h' represents the shape of the room. This scenario shares similarity with the last one, so that the simplest policy pointed in the two-room still works in this case. The challenge is that agents should explore more position, but they may become an obstacle to each other on such one-way street. Using the two pot in parallel becomes a little bit harder, which calls for deeper cooperation. HiSA and DIAL win higher scores, while Self-Att could manage the game though its agents can not communicate with each other. **o-Room.** As in Fig. 5 (o-room-b), when road unblocked, an agent can visit any gray position and do any thing, so that it might be possible to solve the order on its own, which actually implies a more complex long-term policy. Still, cooperation is the key to improve efficiency. The hierarchical policy structure with multi-head mechanism and shared attention model, which was equipped by the HiSA and Self-Att, significantly makes great advantages.

Exploration leads to a lot of noise which might drag down the performance in early training period of the DIAL, so that DIAL has to be trained longer to warm up. Because complex tasks require better ability to understand the situation, both CommNet and GA-Comm use the hidden state of each agent as communication material, weakening their awareness of their own environment, thus useless in an overcooked environment. Compared with the above methods, HiSA can exhibit great robustness through complex tasks, further illustrating that the superior performance of HiSA comes from a shared attention mechanism and a communication-driven solution.

## 5  Summary and Outlook

As we demonstrated in this paper, by combining this shared attention with a multi-head hierarchical structure, we innovatively propose a novel communicative framework, HiSA, to infer and transfer the implicit intention and common preferences among agents, and ultimately promote the cooperative behavior of MARL. In the future, we would like to explore the relationship between communication and credit assignment based on HiSA, and try to use imitation learning to speed up the communication between agents, both of which are important issues in MARL.

**Acknowledgements.** Thanks to Science,Technology and Innovation Commission of Shenzhen Municipality. This work is supported by Science and Technology Innovation 2030 New Generation Artificial Intelligence Major Project (No. 2018AAA0100905), the National Natural Science Foundation of China (No. 62192783), Primary Research & Developement Plan of Jiangsu Province (No. BE2021028), Shenzhen Fundamental Research Program (No. 2021Szvup056).

## References

1. Bacon, P., Harb, J., Precup, D.: The option-critic architecture. In: Proceedings of the Thirty-first AAAI Conference on Artificial Intelligence, San Francisco, California, pp. 1726–1734. AAAI Press (2017)
2. Bengio, S., et al.: Learning Attentional Communication for Multi-Agent Cooperation. In: Proceedings of the Thirty-second International Conference on Neural Information Processing Systems, Montréal, Canada, pp. 7265–7275 (2018)
3. Carroll, M., et al.: On the utility of learning about humans for human-AI coordination. In: Proceedings of the Thirty-Third International Conference on Neural Information Processing Systems, Vancouver, BC, pp. 5175–5186 (2019)
4. Chen, L., Zhang, H., Xiao, J., et al.: SCA-CNN: spatial and channel-wise attention in convolutional networks for image captioning. In: Proceedings of the IEEE Conference on Computer Vision and Pattern Recognition, Honolulu, HI, pp. 6298–6306. IEEE Computer Society (2017)
5. Foerster, J.N., Assael, Y.M., de Freitas, N., Whiteson, S.: Learning to communicate with deep multi-agent reinforcement learning. In: Proceedings of the Thirtieth International Conference on Neural Information Processing Systems, Barcelona, Spain, pp. 2137–2145 (2016)
6. Iqbal, S., Sha, F.: Actor-attention-critic for multi-agent reinforcement learning. In: Proceedings of the Thirty-sixth International Conference on Machine Learning. PMLR, Long Beach, California, pp. 2961–2970 (2019)

7. Kim, D., Moon, S., Hostallero, D., et al.: Learning to schedule communication in multi-agent reinforcement learning. In: Proceedings of the Seventh International Conference on Learning Representations, New Orleans, LA (2019)
8. Kim, W., Cho, M., Sung, Y.: Message-dropout: an efficient training method for multi-agent deep reinforcement learning. In: Proceedings of the Thirty-Third AAAI Conference on Artificial Intelligence, Honolulu, Hawaii, pp. 6079–6086. AAAI Press (2019)
9. Kulkarni, T.D., Narasimhan, K., Saeedi, A., Tenenbaum, J.: Hierarchical deep reinforcement learning: integrating temporal abstraction and intrinsic motivation. In: Proceedings of the Thirtieth International Conference on Neural Information Processing Systems. Barcelona, Spain, pp. 3675–3683 (2016)
10. Liu, Y., Wang, W., Hu, Y., et al.: Multi-agent game abstraction via graph attention neural network. In: Proceedings of the Thirty-Fourth AAAI Conference on Artificial Intelligence, New York, NY, pp. 7211–7218. AAAI Press (2020)
11. Mao, H., Zhang, Z., Xiao, Z., Gong, Z.: Modelling the dynamic joint policy of teammates with attention multi-agent DDPG. In: Proceedings of the Eighteenth International Conference on Autonomous Agents and MultiAgent Systems. IFAAMAS, Montreal, QC, pp. 1108–1116 (2019)
12. Niv, Y., Daniel, R., Geana, A., et al.: Reinforcement learning in multidimensional environments relies on attention mechanisms. J. Neurosci. **35**(21), 8145–8157 (2015)
13. Pesce, E., Montana, G.: Improving coordination in small-scale multi-agent deep reinforcement learning through memory-driven communication. Mach. Learn. **109**(9–10), 1727–1747 (2020)
14. Samvelyan, M., Rashid, T., de Witt, C.S., et al.: The StarCraft multi-agent challenge. In: Proceedings of the Eighteenth International Conference on Autonomous Agents and MultiAgent Systems. IFAAMAS, Montreal, QC, pp. 2186–2188(2019)
15. Song, Y., Wang, J., Lukasiewicz, T., et al.: Diversity-driven extensible hierarchical reinforcement learning. In: Proceedings of the Thirty-Third AAAI Conference on Artificial Intelligence, Honolulu, Hawaii. AAAI Press, pp. 4992–4999 (2019)
16. Sukhbaatar, S., Szlam, A., Fergus, R.: Learning multiagent communication with backpropagation. In: Proceedings of the Thirtieth International Conference on Neural Information Processing Systems, Barcelona, Spain, pp. 2244–2252 (2016)
17. Tomasello, M. (ed.): Origins of Human Communication. MIT Press, USA (2010)
18. Vaswani, A., Shazeer, N., Parmar, N., et al.: Attention is all you need. In: Proceedings of the Thirty-first International Conference on Neural Information Processing Systems, Long Beach, CA pp. 5998–6008 (2017)
19. Vinyals, O., Ewalds, T., Bartunov, S., et al.: StarCraft II: a new challenge for reinforcement learning (2017)
20. Wang, T., Dong, H., Lesser, V.R., Zhang, C.: ROMA: multi-agent reinforcement learning with emergent roles. In: Proceedings of the Thirty-seventh International Conference on Machine Learning. PMLR, Virtual Event, pp. 9876–9886 (2020)
21. Wang, W., Yang, T., Liu, Y., et al.: Action semantics network: considering the effects of actions in multiagent systems. In: Proceedings of the Eighth International Conference on Learning Representations. OpenReview.net, Addis Ababa, Ethiopia (2020)

# DDMA: Discrepancy-Driven Multi-agent Reinforcement Learning

Chao Li[1,4], Yujing Hu[2], Pinzhuo Tian[1,3], Shaokang Dong[1,4],
and Yang Gao[1,4(✉)]

[1] State Key Laboratory for Novel Software Technology,
Nanjing University, Nanjing, China
chaoli1996@smail.nju.edu.cn, gaoy@nju.edu.cn
[2] NetEase Fuxi AI Lab, Hangzhou, China
[3] School of Computer Engineering and Science, Shanghai University, Shanghai, China
[4] Shenzhen Research Institute, Nanjing University, Shenzhen, China

**Abstract.** Multi-agent reinforcement learning algorithms depend on quantities of interactions with the environment and other agents to derive an approximately optimal policy. However, these algorithms may struggle in the complex interactive relationships between agents and tend to explore the whole observation space aimlessly, which results in high learning complexity. Motivated by the occasional and local interactions between multiple agents in most real-world scenarios, in this paper, we propose a general framework named Discrepancy-Driven Multi-Agent reinforcement learning (DDMA) to help overcome this limitation. In this framework, we first parse the semantic components of each agent's observation and introduce a proliferative network to directly initialize the multi-agent policy with the corresponding single-agent optimal policy, which bypasses the misalignment of observation spaces in different scenarios. Then we model the occasional interactions among agents based on the discrepancy between these two policies, and conduct more focused exploration on these areas where agents interact frequently. With the direct initialization and the focused multi-agent policy learning, our framework can help accelerate the learning process and promote the asymptotic performance significantly. Experimental results on a toy example and several classic benchmarks demonstrate that our framework can obtain superior performance compared to baseline methods.

**Keywords:** Multi agent · Reinforcement learning · Exploration

## 1 Introduction

Multi-Agent Reinforcement Learning (MARL) has shown great potential in solving many real-world problems such as coordination of robot swarm [10] and autonomous car [1]. However, learning effective policies in such multi-agent systems remains challenging owing to the complex interactions among agents. These

© The Author(s), under exclusive license to Springer Nature Switzerland AG 2022
S. Khanna et al. (Eds.): PRICAI 2022, LNCS 13631, pp. 91–105, 2022.
https://doi.org/10.1007/978-3-031-20868-3_7

dynamical interactions result in two major issues that prevent us from directly extending classic single-agent reinforcement learning algorithms to the multi-agent scenarios. One is the scalability problem, which means that the size of the joint observation-action space grows exponentially with the number of agents. The other is the non-stationarity problem, which means that the environment changes dynamically from the individual perspective of each agent owing to the simultaneous updates of all agents' policies.

Hence, existing MARL algorithms aim to solve these two problems to learn an optimal multi-agent policy. Recently the paradigm of Centralized Training with Decentralized Execution (CTDE) alleviates these two problems by accessing the global information during training and outputting the decentralized policies conditioned on the agents' local observation-action histories during execution. Such design strides a balance between the full centralization and the full decentralization. Specially, the multi-agent policy-based algorithms such as MADDPG [15], COMA [7], MAAC [11] train a centralized critic that takes as inputs the actions of all agents including the state information and then guide the optimization of decentralized policies with an actor-critic framework. Value-decomposition algorithms under this paradigm such as VDN [22], QMIX [19], QTRAN [21], QPLEX [25] learn a centralized state-action value function that can be factorized into the individual utility value functions conditioned on the local observation-action history of each agent, which needs to satisfy the IGM [21] constraint.

While the CTDE-based algorithms have achieved significant performance in some challenging scenarios such as StarCraft [20], their drawbacks are also apparent in the complex tasks. They usually require substantial interactions and trials in the tasks where agents are tightly coupled, which usually results in high learning complexity. In fact, the interactions between agents usually happen locally and occasionally in many real-world multi-agent systems, which means that each agent only needs to take some other agents into consideration and coordinates with them in some certain observations. In such situation, the algorithm should focus more on these interactive areas, instead of searching for the whole observation space aimlessly. Exploiting such properties existing in the interactions between agents can dramatically promote the learning efficiency of the CTDE-based algorithms.

However, modeling the interactions among agents accurately still remains intractable owing to the simultaneous updates of all agents' policies. Recent works [4,12] learn the reward dynamics of the multi-agent environment and distinguish the interactions through detecting the changes in the received immediate or long-term rewards. But these methods may fail owing to the inaccurate approximated reward model, which usually needs sufficient prior knowledge or complete search of the environment. In addition, some works [11,13] implicitly characterize the interactions between agents in real time through the attention mechanism. But such redundant networks and tedious optimizations may further increase the learning complexity of the algorithms. In this paper, we solve this problem by proposing several structural and learning novelties.

To simplify the multi-agent policy learning and reduce the high learning complexity of CTDE-based algorithms, we propose a general framework named Discrepancy-Driven Multi-Agent reinforcement learning (DDMA). In this framework, we first (1) initialize the multi-agent policy directly with a pre-learned single-agent optimal policy derived from an auxiliary single-agent scenario as previous works [4,12], then (2) recognize the dynamical interactions between agents through measuring the discrepancy between the updating multi-agent policy and the single-agent optimal policy. In detail, we propose an interaction detector to quantify this discrepancy. This detector can be used to recognize the interactive areas where current agent is more likely to be influenced by other agents. Accordingly, as shown in Fig. 1, we conduct more focused multi-agent policy learning in these interactive areas, instead of exploring and learning in the whole observation space aimlessly and costly. In addition, we parse the semantic components of the agents' observations and further introduce a proliferative network to achieve the direct initialization from the pre-learned single-agent optimal policy to the multi-agent policy, which can solve the terrible misalignment of observation spaces in different scenarios. Under the direct initialization and the focused multi-agent policy learning, DDMA can help accelerate the learning process and promote the asymptotic performance significantly.

In order to demonstrate the effectiveness of DDMA, we evaluate it in a toy example and three classic multi-agent scenarios under Multi-agent Particle Environment (MPE) [16]. Experimental results demonstrate that DDMA can achieve faster learning and better asymptotic performance compared to baseline methods. In addition, by ablation studies, we confirm that DDMA indeed promotes the learning efficiency with the direct initialization and the focused multi-agent policy learning.

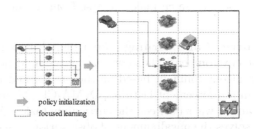

**Fig. 1.** Under the multi-agent policy initialized by the corresponding single-agent optimal policy, the agent (the red car) should conduct more focused multi-agent policy learning in the collision area (the red rectangle with dashed line).

In summary, the primary contributions of this paper are listed as follows: (1) Inspired by the pre-training mechanism, we introduce a proliferative network to directly initialize the multi-agent policy with the pre-learned single-agent optimal policy, which solves the misalignment of observation spaces in different scenarios. (2) In order to further improve the learning efficiency, we introduce an interaction detector to characterize the interactions between agents, and conduct more focused multi-agent policy learning in these interactive areas. (3) Experimental results highlight that DDMA can achieve superior performance compared to other algorithms. Ablation study further verifies the effectiveness of our algorithm.

## 2    Related Work

There exist many works devoting to reducing the high learning complexity rooted in MARL, such as transfer learning [3–5,12,24], curriculum learning [6,17,27] and game abstraction [13,26,29]. In this section, we briefly describe these methods and detail some related algorithms.

**Transfer Learning.** Transfer learning tries to improve the algorithm's learning efficiency through extracting and reusing some task-relevant knowledge. In MARL problem, some works focus on the knowledge transfer between agents, such as LeCTR [18], SEAC [2] and MAPTF [28]. Other works about the sparse-interaction problem learn to transfer knowledge from the corresponding single-agent scenario to the multi-agent scenario, where CQ-Learning [4] identifies the interactive areas through detecting changes in the received immediate rewards and conducts the multi-agent policy learning only in these areas selectively, as well as expanding the state representations. Then NSR [12] extends it to more difficult scenarios through detecting the changes in the long-term rewards. In this paper, we don't try to let agents choose whether to utilize the pre-learned knowledge or learn. Instead, our proliferative network structure shown in Sect. 4.1 can directly initialize the multi-agent policy with the pre-learned single-agent optimal policy, which makes us free from the negative transfer during learning.

**Curriculum Learning.** Curriculum learning considers first learning in the simple environments then conducting the final policy learning in the original multi-agent environment based on the pre-learned knowledge. In multi-agent curriculum reinforcement learning, DyMA-CL [27] introduces three kinds of knowledge transfer ways between the curriculum tasks with different number of agents. And it solves the misalignment of observation spaces in different tasks through aggregating information about others by GNN, which promises the direct initialization from pre-learned policy to the current policy. Although GAS [6] can implicitly create curriculum tasks through restricting available action space of each agent in different stages, the choices of action spaces in each curriculum stage matters and the final policy learned may be sub-optimal. Usually, curriculum learning and transfer learning are tightly coupled and are combined implicitly in related researches.

**Game Abstraction.** Game abstraction mainly attempts to reduce the scale of Markov Game, such as Mean Field MARL [29], G2ANet [13] and RODE [26]. Mean-field theory averages effects from neighboring agents to reduce the learning complexity of each agent, which enables efficient multi-agent policy learning in the large-scale scenarios. G2ANet models the interactive relationships between agents through a two-stage attention network structure. Such combination of hard and soft attention network can indicate the interactive strengths between all pair-wise agents and remove some humble correlations. RODE pre-defines several roles based on the action-effect-based clustering, then conducts the hierarchical multi-agent policy learning.

## 3  Preliminary

In this section, we formalize the multi-agent task in our work and briefly review some concepts of reinforcement learning.

### 3.1  Partially Observable Stochastic Game

In this paper, we focus on Partially Observable Stochastic Game $< N, S, \boldsymbol{A}, R, P,$ $O, \boldsymbol{Z}, \gamma >$, where $S$ is the state space and $\boldsymbol{A} = \{A^1 \times A^2 \times \ldots \times A^n\}$ represents the joint action space of all agents. At each time step $t$, each agent $i \in N$ receives its partial observation $o_t^i \in Z^i$ according to the observation function $O(s_t, i)$ and selects action $a_t^i \in A^i$, forming a joint action $\boldsymbol{a}_t$. Then the environment will transit to the next state $s_{t+1}$ according to the transition function $P(s_{t+1}|s_t, \boldsymbol{a}_t)$, and provide each agent with its reward $r_{t+1}^i$ according to the reward function $R(s_t, \boldsymbol{a}_t, i)$. Each agent $i$ conditions its policy $\pi^i$ on its own observation-action history $\tau^i$. The value function of all agents' joint policy $\boldsymbol{\pi} = (\pi^1, \pi^2, ..., \pi^n)$ to agent $i$ at state $s$ is defined as: $V_{\boldsymbol{\pi}}^i(s) = E_{\boldsymbol{\pi}}[\sum_{k=0}^{\infty} \gamma^k r_{t+k+1}^i | s_t = s]$, where $\gamma$ is the discount factor and each agent aims to maximize its own value function.

### 3.2  Reinforcement Learning

In single-agent RL, value-based algorithms define the state-action value function $Q(s, a) = E_{\pi}[\sum_{k=0}^{\infty} \gamma^k r_{t+k+1} | s_t = s, a_t = a]$ and state value function $V(s) = E_{\pi}[\sum_{k=0}^{\infty} \gamma^k r_{t+k+1} | s_t = s]$, which both can be updated according to the bellman equation. Then the optimal action can be derived by the greedy policy $a^* = argmax_a Q(s, a)$. In contrast, policy-based algorithms directly optimize the policy instead of evaluating the value function. Furthermore, actor-critic algorithms combine the former two, which guide the update of the actor according to the critic. In multi-agent RL, agents can utilize a MARL algorithm to learn approximately optimal policies to adapt to the multi-agent scenarios.

## 4  Method

In this section, we introduce our framework DDMA to promote the multi-agent policy learning. We first describe how our method efficiently transfer the pre-learned knowledge. Then how we model the interactions among agents and conduct the focused multi-agent policy learning will be stated.

## 4.1  Initialization of the Multi-agent Policy

In contrast to the prior works that decide when transfer should occur [4,12], we propose to directly initialize the multi-agent policy with the corresponding single-agent optimal policy. The intuition behind this is that there exist similar situations between the single-agent scenario and the multi-agent scenario, as well as strong correlations between the policies in them. For example, when one company wants to train a group of UAV transport formations, it first put only one UAV into the target environment to learn some basic skills such as takeoff, landing and so on, which corresponds to the single-agent version of the target multi-agent scenario. After mastering these primary skills, each UAV can learn to coordinate with others and adapt to the multi-agent scenario more efficiently.

However, the misalignment of observation spaces in the single-agent scenario and the multi-agent scenario obstructs this direct initialization (we assume the same action space in these two scenarios). To overcome this limitation, we parse the semantic components of the agent's observation in the multi-agent scenario and accordingly introduce a novel proliferative policy network, which can simplify the structure of the multi-agent policy compared to GNN, attention networks [14,27] and avoid the tricky trade-off between the original policy learning and the extra policy distillation [12].

As shown in Fig. 2, the only difference between the multi-agent scenario and the single-agent scenario lies in the emergence of other agents. Accordingly, we parse the agent $i$'s observation $o^i$ in the multi-agent scenario into three semantic components: the agent's individual information $o^i_{self}$, the agent's cognition towards the environment such as the entities $o^i_{env}$ and the cognition to all other agents

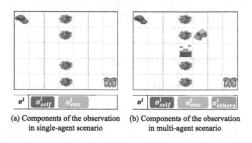

(a) Components of the observation in single-agent scenario    (b) Components of the observation in multi-agent scenario

**Fig. 2.** The semantic components of the agent's observation in the single-agent scenario and the multi-agent scenario.

$o^i_{others}$ such as the relative distances. The former two components make up the agent's observation in the corresponding single-agent scenario. Here we assume the same action space in these two scenarios. As for the inconsistency of action spaces, we can also parse the semantic actions through mapping them to a latent space, and new actions can be approximated according to their neighboring latent representations.

Based on this parse, we introduce the proliferative policy network, as shown in Fig. 3 4. Considering that the agent's observation $o^i$ only contains $[o^i_{self}, o^i_{env}]$ in the single-agent scenario, the single-agent optimal policy takes as inputs these two parts. When the other agents emerge in the multi-agent scenario, $o^i_{others}$ also emerges in the agent's observation, besides the $[o^i_{self}, o^i_{env}]$ existing in the single-agent scenario. Therefore, we decompose the actor in the multi-agent policy into two parts: (1) the main network that deals with $[o^i_{self}, o^i_{env}]$ and (2) the prolifer-

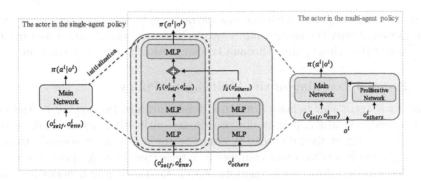

**Fig. 3.** The structure of the actor network. In the actor of the multi-agent policy, the main network deals with $[o_{self}^i, o_{env}^i]$ and the proliferative network embeds $[o_{others}^i]$. The main network can be initialized directly with the actor of the pre-learned single-agent optimal policy.

ative network that embeds $[o_{others}^i]$. Similarly, we also decompose the centralized critic into: (1) the main network that deals with $[o_{self}^i, o_{env}^i, a^i]$ and (2) the proliferative network that embeds $[o_{self}^{-i}, o_{env}^{-i}, a^{-i}]$, where $-i$ represents the other agents except agent $i$. Note that we remove $o_{others}^i$ and $o_{others}^{-i}$ from the centralized critic's inputs $o^i, o^{-i}$ to derive a more compact global state representation.

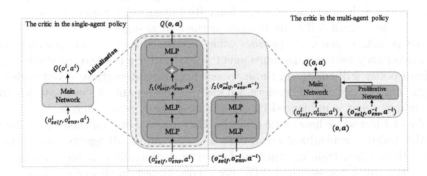

**Fig. 4.** The structure of the critic network. In the centralized critic of the multi-agent policy, the main network deals with $[o_{self}^i, o_{env}^i, a^i]$ and the proliferative network embeds $[o_{self}^{-i}, o_{env}^{-i}, a^{-i}]$. Similarly, the main network can be initialized directly with the critic of the pre-learned single-agent optimal policy.

Furthermore, we connect the proliferative network to the final layer of the main network. Specially, we use the element-wise summation of the outputs of the proliferative network and the outputs of the penultimate layer of the main network as the inputs of the final layer in the main network. Through such combination of these two networks, we can directly initialize the main network in the multi-agent policy with the pre-learned single-agent optimal policy that is composed of only the same main network. Then the proliferative network can help update the whole policy through tracking other agents' information.

## 4.2   Focused Learning of the Multi-agent Policy

While each agent can benefit from this direct initialization owing to the lossless knowledge transfer, it may not coordinate with other agents well. In such situation, the agent should gradually adapt to the multi-agent scenario through updating its policy with a large number of interactive data. And current MARL algorithms usually force each agent to search for the whole observation space aimlessly and costly, which will result in high learning complexity.

Motivated by the occasional and local interactions between multiple agents in most real-world scenarios, we propose to model the interactions between agents and conduct more focused multi-agent policy learning in these interactive areas but a little in the other areas. Through focusing more on these interactive areas where rewards explicitly differ from the ones in the single-agent scenario, each agent can conduct steeper policy update in the corresponding observations to adapt to the multi-agent scenario, but only deviate slightly from the initialization of its policy in other areas that have similar rewards. Therefore, we can promote the learning efficiency through such adaptive and focused learning.

Specially, we characterize the dynamical interactions between agents through measuring the discrepancy between the multi-agent policy and the pre-learned single-agent optimal policy. The intuition behind this is that the initialized multi-agent policy will gradually diverge from its initialized version in some observations where agent following the pre-learned single-agent optimal policy may receive penalties owing to ignoring other agents. Based on this phenomenon, the discrepancy between the multi-agent policy and the pre-learned single-agent optimal policy will emerge in those areas where the interactions occur under all agents' current policies. Therefore, we use this discrepancy to evaluate whether the current agent is influenced by others under the current policies.

We first introduce how to measure the discrepancy between these two policies. DDMA trains a centralized critic that takes as inputs all agents' observations and actions when training, then updates the decentralized actor according to this critic, which follows the CTDE paradigm. Based on this centralized critic, the discrepancy between the multi-agent policy and the pre-learned single-agent optimal policy for agent $i$ in observation $o^i$ can be obtained according to:

$$D^i(o^i) = D_{KL}[\pi^i_{multi}(a^i|o^i, o^{-i}, a^{-i})||\pi^i_{single}(a^i|o^i)], \tag{1}$$

where:

$$\pi^i_{multi}(a^i|o^i, o^{-i}, a^{-i}) = \frac{e^{kQ^i_{multi}(o^i_{self}, o^i_{env}, a^i, o^{-i}_{self}, o^{-i}_{env}, a^{-i})}}{\sum_{a' \in A^i} e^{kQ^i_{multi}(o^i_{self}, o^i_{env}, a', o^{-i}_{self}, o^{-i}_{env}, a^{-i})}}, \tag{2}$$

$$\pi^i_{single}(a^i|o^i) = \frac{e^{kQ^i_{single}(o^i_{self}, o^i_{env}, a^i)}}{\sum_{a' \in A^i} e^{kQ^i_{single}(o^i_{self}, o^i_{env}, a')}}. \tag{3}$$

Note that we derive the Boltzmann policy according to the centralized Q-values instead of directly using the output of the actor network. This is because that the critic can characterize the long-term influence induced by the environmental rewards through bellman update compared to the actor which is updated under the supervision of the critic.

In order to achieve better generalization over the whole observation space, we then introduce an interaction detector for each agent to model this discrepancy, which takes each agent's observation as inputs and predicts whether the agent is influenced by other agents in the current observation. This detector is trained in the form of a binary classifier, whose loss can be written as:

$$\mathcal{L}_{detec} = CrossEntropy(p^i_{detec}(o^i), label(o^i)), \tag{4}$$

where $label(o^i)$ is set to 0 when $D^i(o^i) < \tau^i$ else 1, and $p^i_{detec}(o^i)$ refers to the output of this interaction detector. We set the threshold $\tau^i$ as some certain percentile of all $D^i(o^i)$ in the buffer (sixty in the code).

Finally, based on this detector model, we conduct more focused multi-agent policy learning in the interactive areas, instead of searching for the whole observation space aimlessly and costly. In detail, we equip each agent $i$ with two exploration policies for environments with discrete and continuous action spaces respectively, which can induce the focused exploration in the areas with high interactive strengths, based on the predictions $p^i_{detec}(o^i)$.

The exploration policy for environments with continuous action spaces is defined as:

$$u^i_e(\tau^i) = u^i(\tau^i|\theta^i) + \alpha * |\max(0, p^i_{detec}(o^i) - 0.5)| * \mathcal{N}(0,1), \tag{5}$$

where $\alpha$ is the decay rate, $u^i$ is the actor with parameters $\theta^i$ and $\mathcal{N}(0,1)$ represents the noise sampled from a standard normal distribution. We approximately calculate $\pi^i_{single}, \pi^i_{multi}$ through sampling several actions from the continuous action space. With this exploration policy, we add adaptive noise to the outputs of the actor to achieve more focused policy learning.

The exploration policy for environments with discrete action spaces is defined as:

$$\pi(u^i_e|\tau^i) = \begin{cases} 1 - \min(\epsilon + \frac{\max(0, p^i_{detec}(o^i) - 0.5)}{\sqrt{T}}, 1) & if \ u^i_e = u^{i,*} \\ \min(\epsilon + \frac{\max(0, p^i_{detec}(o^i) - 0.5)}{\sqrt{T}}, 1) & if \ u^i_e \neq u^{i,*}, \end{cases} \tag{6}$$

where $T$ is the environment step, $u^{i,*}$ is the optimal action under the current policy and $\epsilon$ is the random probability.

Finally, DDMA drives agents to explore more in these interactive areas through these two exploration policies. Under this motivation, agents can conduct steeper policy update in the corresponding observations and adapt to the dynamical multi-agent scenario quickly.

## 4.3 Training

Now we briefly state the alternate updates of the interaction detector and the multi-agent policy. When learning the multi-agent policy, we freeze the detector and add extra exploration to the current action selection according to the exploration policies above. Similarly, when the detector is updated, the multi-agent policy learning is paused. Such optimization can guarantee stability and behaves like a Generative Adversarial Network (GAN) [9]. Interestingly, the interaction detector acts like a discriminator, which aims to find out the current most-likely interactive areas under all agents' current multi-agent policies. On the contrary, the multi-agent policy plays the role of the generator, which updates itself to change the interactive probabilities in all areas and misleads the delayed-updated detector. Owing to such adversarial relationship between these two components, DDMA can achieve the adaptive policy update in different areas according to the interaction detector and agents can adapt to the multi-agent scenario quickly based on such focused policy learning process.

## 5 Experiments

For the environment with discrete action space, We design Collision Corridor to illustrate our method comprehensively. As for the environment with continuous action space, we evaluate our method in three classic multi-agent scenarios under Multi-agent Particle Environment: Cooperative Navigation, Predator and Prey, and Individual Defense, where Individual Defense is constructed ourselves.

Below we will describe these environments briefly and show the superior performance of our method compared to other baselines. In addition, we also conduct some ablation studies to decide the effectiveness of each component.

### 5.1 Collision Corridor

We start with Collision Corridor to answer the following two questions: (1) Whether this algorithm can conduct more focused policy learning? (2) Can the interaction detector characterize the interactions between agents approximately?

**Environments.** As shown in Fig. 6 (a), each autonomous car starts in a corner and the goal is to arrive at the diagonal corner. A dangerous collision will occur when both cars try to pass through the corridor hidden in the obstacles, resulting in −10 penalty. Both cars will receive +30 reward if they all succeed in arriving at their target corners.

**Baselines.** In such situation with discrete actions, We compare DDMA with the state-of-the-art VDN and QMIX, as well as MAPG. We regard the original policy gradient algorithm [23] with a centralized critic as MAPG, and we achieve DDMA based on it.

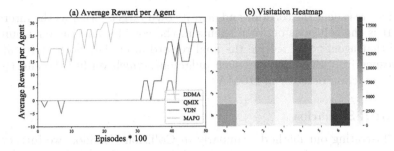

**Fig. 5.** (a) The experimental result in Collision Corridor. The result is averaged over four random seeds and we only show the average owing to the discrete reward setting. (b) The visitation heatmap shows the total visitation number of both cars in all areas during training.

**Results.** Figure 5 (a) exhibits the average rewards per agent of all algorithms. It's obvious that DDMA outperforms other baselines and converges faster, owing to the direct initialization and the focused multi-agent policy learning (owing to the less effort in pre-training the single-agent optimal policy, we don't consider it here). On the contrary, VDN and QMIX struggle to learn the policy through quantities of aimless trials. Even MAPG fails to solve this task, which further demonstrates the effectiveness of DDMA. Also, we present a heatmap to show the visitation number of both agents in all areas during training, which is shown in Fig. 5 (b). We observe that the agents always wander around the corridor to learn to coordinate with each other to avoid the collision, which demonstrates that the interaction detector indeed encourages the focused multi-agent policy learning in these interactive areas.

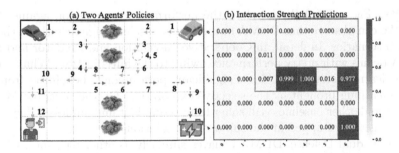

**Fig. 6.** (a) The final learned policies of two cars. The red line is the policy of car 1 and the green line is the policy of car 2. (b) The interaction strength predictions of car 1, where red lines represent the routes of car 1. (Color figure online)

In addition, we further analyze the effect of the interaction detector in some areas from the viewpoint of the upper left agent in Fig. 6 (b). Considering all agents' current policies shown in Fig. 6 (a), we notice that this agent tends to recognize areas near the corridor and near its own target corner as the interactive areas. It is the collisions between agents in the corridor and the environmental setting that agents only receive the final reward after they both arrive at their goals respectively that produces such judgment, which verifies the effectiveness of the interaction detector in DDMA.

## 5.2   MPE Scenarios

After illustrating our method granularly in Collision Corridor, we further evaluate it in more complex scenarios under Multi-Agent Particle Environment.

**Environments.** Here we choose Cooperative Navigation, Predator and Prey and Individual Defense as the test scenarios.[1]

**Baselines.** In the situations with continuous action spaces, we choose MAD-DPG [15], MAAC [11], G2ANet [13] and Noisy-MADDPG [8] as the baselines.

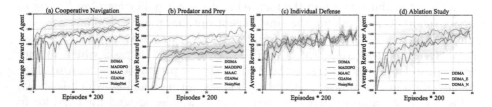

**Fig. 7.** (a), (b), (c) are the experimental results in Cooperative Navigation, Predator and Prey and Individual Defense respectively. (d) is the ablation experimental results in Cooperative Navigation. All results are averaged over four random seeds.

**Results.** Figure 7 (a) (b) (c) show the performance comparison against baselines. We can observe that DDMA outperforms baselines significantly in the former two scenarios. In detail, in Cooperative Navigation and Predator and Prey, DDMA begins with pretty performance owing to the initialization. What's more, DDMA learns faster and achieves significant performance, benefiting from the focused learning brought by the selective exploration. On the contrary, MAAC, G2ANet and other baselines still suffer from redundant and aimless policy learning, even getting trapped in the sub-optimal solutions.

In Individual Defense, DDMA behaves similarly as other baselines, which is owing to little interactions existing between agents. In this situation, each good agent pays more attention to approaching its own target landmark itself, ignoring the little collisions with other good agents owing to the low probabilities. Even the independent learner will adapt to this scenario well. What's more, this experimental results verify that DDMA essentially produces the interaction-driven multi-agent policy learning, and it will degrade into an independent learner when there is little interactions between agents.

---

[1] Please refer to https://github.com/chaobiubiu/DDMA for more details.

## 5.3 Ablation Study

To further demonstrate the effectiveness of each component in our method, we compare DDMA with extra baselines: (1) DDMA-E. We derive this baseline by removing the interaction detector's learning from vanilla DDMA, which can test the influence brought by this discriminator-like detector. (2) DDMA-N. This baseline only considers conducting the focused multi-agent policy learning through the interaction detector, regardless of the direct initialization from the single-agent optimal policy to the multi-agent policy, which can highlight the contribution from this fine initialization.

As shown in Fig. 7 (d), although the interaction detector drives much exploration, DDMA-N converges slowly owing to the lack of transferred knowledge. Similarly, benefiting from the superior initialization, DDMA-E can converge quickly but to a sub-optimal policy, which may result from the confused and aimless multi-agent policy learning. On the contrary, the vanilla DDMA can converge faster and achieve better performance due to the advantages existing in its all components.

In summary, these experiments demonstrate that DDMA indeed promotes the learning efficiency through the direct initialization and the focused policy learning. Drawing supports from these two factors mostly, DDMA can achieve superior performance in complex multi-agent tasks compared to other algorithms.

## 6  Conclusion

In this paper, we propose DDMA to alleviate the high learning complexity inherent in the multi-agent policy learning, through the direct initialization and the focused policy learning. Our approach has several benefits. It is simple and does not introduce any complex network structures. It is natural to extend the pre-learned single-agent optimal policy to further conduct the focused multi-agent policy learning instead of only initialization. Lastly, DDMA can be applied to any multi-agent situations with discrete or continuous action spaces.

Simplifying the tedious multi-agent policy learning matters mostly in MARL. We make a simple attempt to achieve it. We believe that MARL can be applied to some real scenarios by such way and we will continue to reduce the high learning complexity of MARL in future works.

**Acknowledgements.** This work is supported by Shenzhen Fundamental Research Program (No.2021Szvup056), Primary Research & Development Plan of Jiangsu Province (No. BE2021028), National Natural Science Foundation of China (No. 62192783), and Science and Technology Innovation 2030 New Generation Artificial Intelligence Major Project (No.2018AAA0100905).

# References

1. Cao, Y., Yu, W., Ren, W., Chen, G.: An overview of recent progress in the study of distributed multi-agent coordination. IEEE Trans. Industr. Inf. **9**(1), 427–438 (2012)
2. Christianos, F., Schäfer, L., Albrecht, S.: Shared experience actor-critic for multi-agent reinforcement learning, vol. 33, pp. 10707–10717 (2020)
3. Da Silva, F.L., Costa, A.H.R.: A survey on transfer learning for multiagent reinforcement learning systems. J. Artif. Intell. Res. **64**, 645–703 (2019)
4. De Hauwere, Y.M., Vrancx, P., Nowé, A.: Learning multi-agent state space representations. In: Proceedings of the 9th International Conference on Autonomous Agents and Multiagent Systems, vol. 1, pp. 715–722 (2010)
5. Diuk, C., Cohen, A., Littman, M.L.: An object-oriented representation for efficient reinforcement learning. In: Proceedings of the 25th International Conference on Machine Learning, pp. 240–247 (2008)
6. Farquhar, G., Gustafson, L., Lin, Z., Whiteson, S., Usunier, N., Synnaeve, G.: Growing action spaces. In: International Conference on Machine Learning. PMLR, pp. 3040–3051 (2020)
7. Foerster, J., Farquhar, G., Afouras, T., Nardelli, N., Whiteson, S.: Counterfactual multi-agent policy gradients. In: Proceedings of the AAAI Conference on Artificial Intelligence, vol. 32 (2018)
8. Fortunato, M., et al.: Noisy networks for exploration. arXiv preprint arXiv:1706.10295 (2017)
9. Goodfellow, I.J., et al.: Generative adversarial nets. In: Proceedings of the 27th International Conference on Neural Information Processing Systems, vol. 2, pp. 2672–2680 (2014)
10. Huang, Y., Wu, S., Mu, Z., Long, X., Chu, S., Zhao, G.: A multi-agent reinforcement learning method for swarm robots in space collaborative exploration. In: 2020 6th International Conference on Control, Automation and Robotics (ICCAR), pp. 139–144. IEEE (2020)
11. Iqbal, S., Sha, F.: Actor-attention-critic for multi-agent reinforcement learning. In: International Conference on Machine Learning. PMLR, pp. 2961–2970 (2019)
12. Liu, Y., Hu, Y., Gao, Y., Chen, Y., Fan, C.: Value function transfer for deep multi-agent reinforcement learning based on n-step returns. In: IJCAI, pp. 457–463 (2019)
13. Liu, Y., Wang, W., Hu, Y., Hao, J., Chen, X., Gao, Y.: Multi-agent game abstraction via graph attention neural network. In: Proceedings of the AAAI Conference on Artificial Intelligence, vol. 34, pp. 7211–7218 (2020)
14. Long, Q., Zhou, Z., Gupta, A., Fang, F., Wu, Y., Wang, X.: Evolutionary population curriculum for scaling multi-agent reinforcement learning. arXiv preprint arXiv:2003.10423 (2020)
15. Lowe, R., Wu, Y., Tamar, A., Harb, J., Abbeel, P., Mordatch, I.: Multi-agent actor-critic for mixed cooperative-competitive environments. arXiv preprint arXiv:1706.02275 (2017)
16. Mordatch, I., Abbeel, P.: Emergence of grounded compositional language in multi-agent populations. In: Thirty-Second AAAI Conference on Artificial Intelligence (2018)
17. Narvekar, S., Peng, B., Leonetti, M., Sinapov, J., Taylor, M.E., Stone, P.: Curriculum learning for reinforcement learning domains: a framework and survey. J. Mach. Learn. Res. **21**, 1–50 (2020)

18. Omidshafiei, S., et al.: Learning to teach in cooperative multiagent reinforcement learning. In: Proceedings of the AAAI Conference on Artificial Intelligence, vol. 33, pp. 6128–6136 (2019)
19. Rashid, T., Samvelyan, M., Schroeder, C., Farquhar, G., Foerster, J., Whiteson, S.: QMIX: monotonic value function factorisation for deep multi-agent reinforcement learning. In: International Conference on Machine Learning. PMLR, pp. 4295–4304 (2018)
20. Samvelyan, M., et al.: The starcraft multi-agent challenge. In: Proceedings of the 18th International Conference on Autonomous Agents and MultiAgent Systems, pp. 2186–2188 (2019)
21. Son, K., Kim, D., Kang, W.J., Hostallero, D.E., Yi, Y.: QTRAN: learning to factorize with transformation for cooperative multi-agent reinforcement learning. In: International Conference on Machine Learning. PMLR, pp. 5887–5896 (2019)
22. Sunehag, P., et al.: Value-decomposition networks for cooperative multi-agent learning. arXiv preprint arXiv:1706.05296 (2017)
23. Sutton, R.S., McAllester, D.A., Singh, S.P., Mansour, Y.: Policy gradient methods for reinforcement learning with function approximation. In: Advances in Neural Information Processing Systems, pp. 1057–1063 (2000)
24. Vezhnevets, A., Wu, Y., Eckstein, M., Leblond, R., Leibo, J.Z.: Options as responses: grounding behavioural hierarchies in multi-agent reinforcement learning. In: International Conference on Machine Learning. PMLR, pp. 9733–9742 (2020)
25. Wang, J., Ren, Z., Liu, T., Yu, Y., Zhang, C.: QPLEX: duplex dueling multi-agent Q-learning. arXiv preprint arXiv:2008.01062 (2020)
26. Wang, T., Gupta, T., Mahajan, A., Peng, B., Whiteson, S., Zhang, C.: RODE: learning roles to decompose multi-agent tasks. arXiv preprint arXiv:2010.01523 (2020)
27. Wang, W., et al.: From few to more: large-scale dynamic multiagent curriculum learning. In: Proceedings of the AAAI Conference on Artificial Intelligence, vol. 34, pp. 7293–7300 (2020)
28. Yang, T., et al.: An efficient transfer learning framework for multiagent reinforcement learning, vol. 34 (2021)
29. Yang, Y., Luo, R., Li, M., Zhou, M., Zhang, W., Wang, J.: Mean field multi-agent reinforcement learning. In: International Conference on Machine Learning. PMLR, pp. 5571–5580 (2018)

# PRAG: Periodic Regularized Action Gradient for Efficient Continuous Control

Xihui Li[1], Zhongjian Qiao[1], Aicheng Gong[2], Jiafei Lyu[1], Chenghui Yu[1], Jiangpeng Yan[3], and Xiu Li[1(✉)]

[1] Tsinghua Shenzhen International Graduate School, Tsinghua University, Shenzhen, China
{xh-li21,qzj22,lvjf20,ych20}@mails.tsinghua.edu.cn,
li.xiu@sz.tsinghua.edu.cn
[2] China Nuclear Power Engineering Company Ltd., Shenzhen, China
gongaicheng@cgnpc.com.cn
[3] Department of Automation, Tsinghua Unversity, Beijing, China
yanjp17@mails.tsinghua.edu.cn

**Abstract.** For actor-critic methods in reinforcement learning, it is vital to learn a useful critic such that the actor can be guided efficiently and properly. Previous methods mainly seek to estimate more accurate Q-values. However, in continuous control scenario where the actor is updated via deterministic policy gradient, only the action gradient (AG) is useful for updating the actor. It is thus a promising way to achieve higher sample efficiency by leveraging the action gradient of Q functions for policy guidance. Nevertheless, we empirically find that directly incorporating action gradient into the critics downgrades the performance of the agent, as it can be easily trapped in the local maxima. To fully utilize the benefits of action gradient and escape from the local optima, we propose Periodic Regularized Action Gradient (PRAG), which periodically involves action gradient for critic learning and additionally maximizes the target value. On a set of MuJoCo continuous control tasks, we show that PRAG can achieve higher sample efficiency and better final performance without much extra training cost, comparing to common model-free baselines. Our code is available at: https://github.com/Galaxy-Li/PRAG.

**Keywords:** Actor-critic · Action gradient · Continuous control

## 1 Introduction

In recent years, Reinforcement Learning (RL) [21,24] has achieved great success in artificial intelligence [11,13], such as AlphaGo. One of the most popular classes of RL methods is actor-critic [9] which involves both value function estimation [1] and policy gradients [19]. In actor-critic scheme, there is an actor for action execution, and a critic that evaluates how good the policy is. Since the actor uses the value function that the critic provides to improve the policy, the actor's

---

X. Li and Z. Qiao—Equal contribution.

behavior highly depends on how good the critic is. Therefore, it is crucial to train a better critic to guide policy improvement.

Then a natural problem arises: how to train a good and useful critic? In most actor-critic methods, the critic is parameterized as a neural network and trained by temporal difference [25]. Many prior methods [10,14,15,17] set their focus on alleviating estimation bias in critic learning by leveraging softmax operator, double actors, distributional RL, etc. They aim at learning an accurate Q function that approximates the true Q function as much as possible. However, in the continuous-control scenario where deterministic policy gradient [22] is employed, Q-value itself does not contribute to policy gradient. Instead, only the **action gradient** (AG) of Q-value is useful for improving the policy (see Eq. 3). Hence, a better critic for policy improvement should provide a more accurate approximation of the action gradient of Q-value instead of an accurate estimation of Q-value itself.

We begin by theoretically finding that minimizing the TD-error can make the learned performance function close to the true performance function. Meanwhile, the difference in policy gradients is bounded by the action gradient of the TD- error. Motivated by this, we propose using the action gradient of Q-values as a regularizer in this paper so that a better action gradient estimation can be ensured. We expect better empirical performance by incorporating action gradient into the critic loss, which is different from prior methods. However, in the course of the empirical experiment, we find that directly injecting the action gradient of TD-error into the vanilla bellman error often results in a performance drop, i.e., the actor is stuck in local optima and fails to learn a useful policy (see evidence in Fig. 1 where TD3+AG underperforms vanilla TD3). This paper aims at alleviating this problem and fully utilizing the benefits of the action gradient. Our contributions can be summarized as follows:

- To the best of our knowledge, we firstly incorporate action gradient into the model-free online RL learning fashion;
- We propose to periodically integrate the action gradient term into the critic loss for better efficiency and utilization of the action gradient;
- We additionally propose to maximize the logsumexp of the target value to help the agent escape from the local optima, which leads to Periodic Regularized Action Gradient (PRAG) algorithm;
- On a set of challenging MuJoCo continuous control tasks [3,26], PRAG shows significant superiority in both sample efficiency and overall performance compared against popular baseline methods.

## 2   Background

We consider a Markov Decision Process (MDP) [20] which is defined by the tuple $(\mathcal{S}, \mathcal{A}, p, r, \gamma, \mu)$. $\mathcal{S}$ and $\mathcal{A}$ are the state and action spaces. $p(s'|s, a)$ is the transition probability. $r(s, a)$ is the reward function. $\gamma \in [0, 1)$ is the discount factor. $\mu(s)$ is the initial state distribution. $\pi_\theta(\cdot|s) : \mathcal{S} \mapsto \mathbb{R}$ is the deterministic policy parameterized by $\theta$ that the agent follows. Under the given policy $\pi_\theta(\cdot|s)$, $\gamma$-discounted state distribution is defined as $d_\mu^\pi(s) = (1-\gamma)\sum_{t=0}^\infty \gamma^t Pr(s_t = s|\pi, \mu)$. The goal of reinforcement learning is to find a policy $\pi^*$ that maximizes the expected discounted return:

$$\pi^* = \arg\max_\pi \mathbb{E}\left[\sum_{t=0}^\infty \gamma^t r(s_t, a_t)|s_0 \sim \mu, a_t = \pi(s_t)\right]. \tag{1}$$

The state-action value function is defined:

$$Q^\pi(s, a) = \mathbb{E}_\pi\left[\sum_{t=0}^\infty \gamma^t r(s_t, a_t)|s_0, a_0\right], \tag{2}$$

which measures the expected discounted return starting from state $s$ and action $a$, and following policy $\pi$. With function approximation, we aim at finding $\hat{Q}(s, a)$ to approximate the true Q-value $Q^\pi(s, a)$. The performance function can be represented as $J(\theta) = \mathbb{E}_{s\sim\mu}[Q^\pi(s, \pi_\theta(s))]$. The policy is then improved by conducting gradient ascending with respect to $J(\theta)$. We consider deterministic policy in this work, and therefore the policy gradient can be evaluated according to the deterministic policy gradient (DPG) [22] theorem.

$$\nabla_\theta J(\theta) = \mathbb{E}_s\left[\nabla_a Q_\phi(s, a)|_{a=\pi_\theta(s)}\nabla_\theta \pi_\theta(s)\right]. \tag{3}$$

## 3    From TD-Error to Action Gradient Error

### 3.1    TD-Error and TD-Learning

Typical actor-critic algorithms that involve deterministic policy gradient, such as DDPG [12] and TD3 [6], are trained by utilizing the critics for value function estimation and the actor for policy improvement. Ideally, the goal of the critic is to find a $\widetilde{Q}(s, a)$ that minimizes the error between the approximated Q-value $\widetilde{Q}$ and the true Q-value $Q^\pi$:

$$\widetilde{Q} \leftarrow \arg\min_{\hat{Q}} \mathbb{E}_{s\sim d_\mu^\pi}\left|\delta^{\pi,\hat{Q}}(s, \pi(s))\right|, \tag{4}$$

where $\delta^{\pi,\hat{Q}}(s, \pi(s)) = Q^\pi(s, \pi(s)) - \hat{Q}(s, \pi(s))$ is the error between the approximated Q-value and the true Q-value. The rationality and intuition of Eq. 4 can be validated by the following proposition.

**Proposition 1.** (Performance difference is bounded by TD-error). *Let $\mathcal{Q}$ be a space of approximate value function, then given $\hat{Q} \in \mathcal{Q}$, and $\|\cdot\|_p$ be any p-norm, then the difference between true $J(\theta)$ and its approximation $\hat{J}(\theta)$ is bounded:*

$$\left\|J(\theta) - \hat{J}(\theta)\right\|_p \leq \frac{1}{1-\gamma}\mathbb{E}_{s\sim d_\mu^\pi}\left\|\delta^{\pi,\hat{Q}}(s, a)\right\|_p. \tag{5}$$

*Proof.* It is easy to find that,

$$\left\|J(\theta) - \hat{J}(\theta)\right\|_p = \frac{1}{1-\gamma}\left\|\int_{\mathcal{S}} d_\mu^\pi(s)\left(Q^\pi(s,a) - \hat{Q}(s,a)\right)ds\right\|_p$$

$$= \frac{1}{1-\gamma}\left\|\int_{\mathcal{S}} d_\mu^\pi(s)\delta^{\pi,\hat{Q}}(s,a)ds\right\|_p$$

$$\leq \frac{1}{1-\gamma}\mathbb{E}_{s\sim d_\mu^\pi}\left\|\delta^{\pi,\hat{Q}}(s,a)\right\|_p.$$

Proposition 1 shows that by minimizing the error term $\delta^{\pi,\hat{Q}}(s,a)$, we can make the approximated performance function $\hat{J}(\theta)$ to be as close as possible to the true performance function $J(\theta)$. However, unfortunately, we usually do not have much knowledge about the true Q-value $Q^\pi$. It is worth noting that it is hard for us to get the true Q-value, especially in complex continuous control tasks. Therefore, in practice, temporal difference error (TD-error) $\hat{\delta}^{\pi,\tilde{Q}}(s,a,s')$ is usually used to approximate $\delta^{\pi,\hat{Q}}(s,a)$, where

$$\hat{\delta}^{\pi,\hat{Q}}(s,a,s') = r(s,a) + \gamma\hat{Q}(s',\pi(s')) - \hat{Q}(s,a). \tag{6}$$

Then the critic just needs to find a $\tilde{Q}$ to minimize TD error:

$$\tilde{Q} \in \arg\min_{\hat{Q}}\mathbb{E}_{s\sim d_\mu^\pi,s'\sim p(\cdot|s,\pi(s))}\left|\hat{\delta}^{\pi,\hat{Q}}(s,a,s')\right|. \tag{7}$$

With function approximation, we can follow the traditional TD-learning, which is widely used in standard off-policy reinforcement learning algorithms [6,22], by substituting $\delta^{\pi,\hat{Q}}(s,a)$ with TD-error $\hat{\delta}^{\pi,\hat{Q}}(s,a)$. After the critic is trained, the actor can find the optimal policy by maximizing the performance function $J(\theta) = \mathbb{E}_{s\sim\mu}\left[\hat{Q}^\pi(s,\pi_\theta(s))\right]$ through gradient ascending.

## 3.2 Action Gradient Error and Action Gradient Regularizer

As mentioned above, the actor merely relies on the action gradient for improvement, which can be shown by the Deterministic Policy Gradient Theorem [22]:

$$\nabla_\theta J(\theta) = \frac{1}{1-\gamma}\int_{\mathcal{S}} d_\mu^\pi(s)\nabla_a Q^\pi(s,a)|_{a=\pi_\theta(s)}\nabla_\theta\pi_\theta(s)ds. \tag{8}$$

Given this, MAGE [4] proposes to directly minimizes the action gradient error so as to approximate the gradient of the true return (see proposition 2).

**Proposition 2** (Policy gradient difference is bounded by the gradient of TD-error). *Let $\Pi$ be a parametric space of $L_\pi$ − Lipschitz continuous differentiable deterministic policies, then given $\pi \in \Pi$ and $\hat{Q} \in \mathcal{Q}$, the norm of the difference between true policy gradient $\nabla_\theta J(\theta)$ and its approximation $\nabla_\theta \hat{J}(\theta)$ is bounded:*

$$\left\|\nabla_\theta J(\theta) - \nabla_\theta\hat{J}(\theta)\right\|_p \leq \frac{L_\pi}{1-\gamma}\mathbb{E}_{s\sim d_\mu^\pi}\left\|\nabla_a\delta^{\pi,\hat{Q}}(s,a)|_{a=\pi(s)}\right\|_p. \tag{9}$$

*Proof.* By using deterministic policy gradient theorem, we have

$$
\begin{aligned}
\left\| \nabla_\theta J(\theta) - \nabla_\theta \hat{J}(\theta) \right\|_p &= \frac{1}{1-\gamma} \left\| \int_S d_\mu^\pi(s) \nabla_a \left( Q^\pi(s,a) - \hat{Q}(s,a) \right) |_{a=\pi(s)} \nabla_\theta \pi(s) ds \right\|_p \\
&= \frac{1}{1-\gamma} \left\| \int_S d_\mu^\pi(s) \nabla_a \delta^{\pi,\hat{Q}}(s,a)|_{a=\pi(s)} \nabla_\theta \pi(s) ds \right\|_p \\
&\leq \frac{1}{1-\gamma} \int_S d_\mu^\pi(s) \left\|_p \nabla_a \delta^{\pi,\hat{Q}}(s,a)|_{a=\pi(s)} \right\| \cdot \|\nabla_\theta \pi(s)\|_p \, ds \\
&\leq \frac{L_\pi}{1-\gamma} \int_S d_\mu^\pi(s) \left\| \nabla_a \delta^{\pi,\hat{Q}}(s,a)|_{a=\pi(s)} \right\|_p \, ds \\
&= \frac{L_\pi}{1-\gamma} \mathbb{E}_{s \sim d_\mu^\pi} \left\| \nabla_a \delta^{\pi,\hat{Q}}(s,a)|_{a=\pi(s)} \right\|_p.
\end{aligned}
$$

Proposition 2 shows that we can control the error between $\nabla_\theta J(\theta)$ and $\nabla_\theta \hat{J}(\theta)$ by bounding the action gradient error. Intuitively, since the actor is more affected by the action gradient, we can optimize the action gradient of the TD-error directly. Similarly, however, we cannot get the true gradient of the performance function. We hence substitute $\delta^{\pi,\hat{Q}}(s,a)$ with TD-error $\hat{\delta}^{\pi,\hat{Q}}(s,a)$. A natural solution for training useful and effective critics is to regularize TD-error while simultaneously constraining the action gradient of the TD-error in a valid scale. That is,

$$
\min_{\theta \in \Theta} \mathbb{E}_{s \sim d_\mu^\pi, s' \sim p(\cdot|s,a)} \left\| \hat{\delta}^{\pi,Q_\phi}(s,a,s') \right\|_p
$$

$$
\text{s.t.} \quad \mathbb{E}_{s \sim d_\mu^\pi, s' \sim p(\cdot|s,a)} \left\| \nabla_a \hat{\delta}^{\pi,Q_\phi}(s,a,s')|_{a=\pi(s)} \right\|_p \leq \eta \tag{10}
$$

By doing so, we ensure that the estimated performance function approximates the true performance function in both zero-order and first-order manner. It is beneficial as the learned performance function will better approximate the true performance function. In practice, we resort to penalty function methods [23] by regularizing the original TD-error with action gradient error to avoid the complex and expensive cost of nonlinear programming. However, we observe that directly optimization Eq. (10) will result in a sub-optimal policy, i.e., the actor is stuck in a local optimum and fails to learn a useful policy, which is also reported in MAGE [4]. As shown in Fig. 1, a direct application of the action gradient on TD3 results in a performance drop, which validates the above concern.

### 3.3   Periodic Regularized Action Gradient Algorithm

It is not reliable to directly use action gradient estimation as a regularizer to guide the improvement of policy network as the actor may fall into a local optimum which impedes it from further improvement. Since the target value in DRL does not convey the gradient, the action gradient of the TD-error is

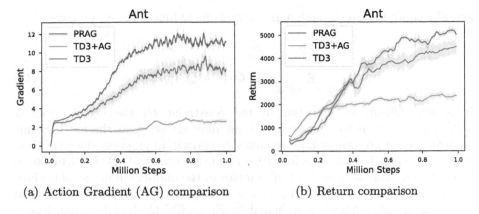

(a) Action Gradient (AG) comparison      (b) Return comparison

**Fig. 1.** Action gradient (AG) and return comparison between PRAG, TD3 and TD3+AG on Ant-v2 task. TD3+AG involves action gradient in critic loss, while PRAG additionally maximizes the target Q-value. The experiments are run over 5 random seeds and the shaded region denotes the standard deviation. (a) The action gradient is larger and faster-increasing in PRAG compared to TD3 and TD3+AG, indicating that PRAG is less likely to be stuck in a local optimum. TD3 has a higher action gradient than TD3+AG. (b) PRAG achieves higher performance than TD3 and TD3+AG.

---

**Algorithm 1.** Periodic Regularized Action Gradient (PRAG)

---

1: Initialize actor network $\pi_\theta$, critic network $Q_{\phi_1}, Q_{\phi_2}$ with random parameters
2: Initialize target networks $\theta' \leftarrow \theta, \phi_1' \leftarrow \phi_1, \phi_2' \leftarrow \phi_2$
3: Initialize empty replay buffer $\mathcal{B} \leftarrow \emptyset$, period parameter $k$
4: **for** $t = 1$ to $T$ **do**
5:     Select action $a$ with Gaussian exploration noise $\epsilon$ based on $\pi_\theta$, $\epsilon \sim \mathcal{N}(0, \sigma)$, and observe next state $s'$ and scalar reward signal $r$
6:     Store $(s, a, r, s')$ tuple in the replay buffer $\mathcal{B}$, $\mathcal{B} \leftarrow \mathcal{B} \cup (s, a, r, s')$
7:     Sample $N$ transitions $(s, a, r, s')$ from $\mathcal{B}$
8:     Calculate target value $y = r(s, a) + \gamma \min_{i=1,2} Q_{\phi_i'}(s', \pi_{\theta'}(s'))$
9:     **if** $t \bmod k$ **then**
10:         Calculate $\hat{\delta}_1(s, a, s'; \phi) \leftarrow r(s, a) + \gamma \min_{i=1,2} Q_{\phi_i}(s', \pi_\theta(s')) - Q_{\phi_1}(s, a)$
11:         Calculate $\hat{\delta}_2(s, a, s'; \phi) \leftarrow r(s, a) + \gamma \min_{i=1,2} Q_{\phi_i}(s', \pi_\theta(s')) - Q_{\phi_2}(s, a)$
12:         Update critics $\phi_i \leftarrow \arg\min_{\phi_i} \frac{1}{N} \sum \left[ (Q_{\phi_i}(s, a) - y)^2 - \alpha Q_t + \lambda \left( \nabla_a \hat{\delta}_i(s, a, s'; \phi) \right)^2 \right]$,
          where $Q_t = \log \left( \frac{1}{N} \sum_{s,a,s'} \left( \exp(r(s, a) + \gamma Q_{\phi_i}(s', \pi_{\theta'}(s'))) \right) \right), i = 1, 2$
13:     **else**
14:         Update critics $\phi_i \leftarrow \arg\min_{\phi_i} \frac{1}{N} \sum \left[ (Q_{\phi_i}(s, a) - y)^2 \right], i = 1, 2$
15:     **end if**
16:     **if** $t \bmod 2$ **then**
17:         Update actor parameter $\theta$ by: $\nabla_\theta \hat{J}(\theta) = \frac{1}{N} \sum \nabla_a Q_{\phi_1}(s, a)|_{a=\pi_\theta(s)} \nabla_\theta \pi_\theta(s)$
18:     **end if**
19:     Update target networks: $\theta' \leftarrow \tau\theta + (1 - \tau)\theta', \phi_i' \leftarrow \tau\phi_i + (1 - \tau)\phi_i', i = 1, 2$
20: **end for**

---

actually equivalent to the action gradient of the $Q$ function, i.e., we have:

$$\min_{\phi \in \Phi} \mathop{\mathbb{E}}_{s \sim d_\mu^\pi, s' \sim p(\cdot|s,a)} \left\| \hat{\delta}^{\pi, Q_\phi}(s, a, s') \right\|_p$$

$$\text{s.t.} \quad \mathop{\mathbb{E}}_{s \sim d_\mu^\pi, s' \sim p(\cdot|s,a)} \left\| \nabla_a Q_\phi(s, a)|_{a=\pi(s)} \right\|_p \leq \eta. \tag{11}$$

It is not difficult to find that if the constraint on the action gradient $\nabla_a Q_\phi(s,a)|_{a=\pi(s)}$ is too strong, the agent may get stuck in the local optima since the action gradient will be penalized towards 0. In practice, since (1) there exists errors in neural network for fitting and prediction, and (2) the algorithm is trained on a mini-batch and not all samples in the mini-batch are local optima, the action gradient $\nabla_a Q_\phi(s,a)|_{a=\pi(s)}$ is usually not 0 (as shown in Fig. 1(a) where the action gradient is evaluated by $\mathbb{E}_{i=1,2}\mathbb{E}[\nabla_a Q_{\phi_i}(s,a)|_{a=\pi(s)}]$). Nevertheless, we find that the action gradient of TD3+AG is smaller than that of vanilla TD3, indicating that directly employing action gradient on TD3 results in much conservative and pessimistic update.

To fully utilize the advantages of the action gradient and to enjoy better sample efficiency, we propose Periodic Regularized Action Gradient(PRAG) algorithm. PRAG has two main components that make it efficient: periodic injection of action gradient, and maximizing the target Q-value to escape from the local optimum.

**First, Periodically Using Action Gradient for Guiding Critics.** With action gradient regularizer, the actor can learn useful policy faster while it is not a good option to always follow the action gradient guidance. The reason lies in the fact that (1) always adopting action gradient may negatively affect the policy improvement, as the agent is easily trapped in the local optima; (2) since the process of computing action gradient takes much time and computing resource, it would be time-inefficient to always involve action gradient in critic loss function. Thereby, we choose to plug action gradient constraint into the critics periodically, i.e., we split the training process into three steps:

STEP 1: using random policy for exploration to gather initial experience;
STEP 2: integrating action gradient constraint into the critics for guiding the agent to learn better and faster;
STEP 3: adopting standard TD-error to guide the agent for further improvement for the rest of the interactions.

By alternating between STEP 2 and STEP 3 with a proper frequency, we can ensure that useful policy can be learned faster (see Fig. 1(b)), while meanwhile the actor would not be stuck in a local optimum. Also, the training cost is tolerable with this scheme since the action gradient is calculated periodically. It is beneficial since in the latter stage of training, high return states expect little change in action gradient. While if this state is a local optimum, frequently involving action gradient constraint makes it hard for the agent to escape from local optima. By periodical action gradient guidance, the agent is capable of escaping from it.

**Second, Maximizing the Target Q-value While Constraining Action Gradient.** To further alleviate the issue of being trapped in the local optima, we propose to constrain the action gradient while **maximizing the instant target Q-value** to encourage further improvement in value estimation. That is, if the agent is stuck in the local optima, it is hard to escape as the action gradient on the optima is 0, which results in no change in the actor (according to the DPG theorem). While as we maximize the target Q-value at the same time, the value estimate would not fall into a local sub-optimum as the estimated Q-value and its corresponding action gradient can still be maximized and become larger instead of remaining unchanged. To be specific, we regularize TD-error with action gradient estimation and meanwhile maximizing the target Q-value:

$$\min_{\phi} \mathbb{E}_{s \sim d_{\mu}^{\pi}, s' \sim p(\cdot|s,a)} \left| \hat{\delta}^{\pi, Q_{\phi}}(s, a, s') \right| - \alpha \cdot Q_t$$

$$\text{s.t.} \quad \mathbb{E}_{s \sim d_{\mu}^{\pi}, s' \sim p(\cdot|s,a)} \left\| \nabla_a \hat{\delta}^{\pi, Q_{\phi}}(s, a, s')|_{a=\pi(s)} \right\| \leq \eta \tag{12}$$

where $Q_t = \log \left( \frac{1}{|\mathcal{B}|} \sum_{s,a,s' \sim \mathcal{B}} \left( \exp(r(s,a) + \gamma Q_{\phi}(s', \pi_{\theta'}(s'))) \right) \right)$ is the extra *logsumexp* term that is correlated to the target Q-value, i.e., maximizing $Q_t$ is equivalent to maximizing the target Q-value. $\phi'$ is the parameter of the target network. We do not stop gradient on $Q_t$ here and hence it can contribute to the critic update. This term is added to improve the estimated Q-value if the actor is stuck in a local optimum, thus forcing them to escape from the local optimum. $\alpha$ is an additional coefficient hyperparameter to control how much we maximize the Q-value target term.

**In summary**, the critic loss function for PRAG can be written as follows:

$$\mathcal{L}(\phi) = \mathbb{E}_{(s,a,s') \sim \rho} \left[ \left( \hat{\delta}^{\pi, Q_{\phi}}(s, a, s') \right)^2 - \alpha \cdot Q_t + \lambda \left\| \nabla_a \hat{\delta}^{\pi, Q_{\phi}}(s, a, s')|_{a=\pi(s)} \right\|_2^2 \right],$$
$$\tag{13}$$

where $\rho$ is the sample distribution in the replay buffer. Either $\lambda$ and $\alpha$ ought not to be too large. We present the detailed PRAG algorithm in Algorithm 1.

## 4  Experiment

In this section, we evaluate our method and conduct experiments on six continuous control tasks. We compare our PRAG algorithm against the previous common baseline methods including DDPG [12], TD3 [6] and SAC [7]. Note that we use the fine-tuned version of DDPG proposed in TD3 and temperature auto-tuned SAC [7] in this work, as they perform better than their vanilla versions. We then conduct a detailed ablation study to investigate which component contributes most to the performance improvements of PRAG. Moreover, we present a detailed parameter sensitivity experiment on selected MuJoCo tasks to show that our algorithm has good robustness.

To evaluate our algorithm, we measure its performance on the suite of MuJoCo [26] continuous control tasks, we don't make any change to the environment and reward. Each task is run for 1 million gradient steps over 5 independent seeds and evaluated for 10 episodes every 5000 gradient steps. PRAG shares the identical network configuration with TD3. We set the action gradient regularization coefficient $\lambda = 0.001$ and the period parameter $k = 2$ by default as we experimentally find that they work well for all of the tasks. The target maximization coefficient $\alpha$ is mainly selected from $\{0.05, 0.1, 0.2, 0.3, 0.4, 0.5\}$. We use the same hyperparameters in PRAG as the default setting for TD3 on all of the tasks. Detailed hyperparameter setup can be found below.

**Table 1.** Hyperparameters setup for PRAG

| Hyperparameter | Value |
|---|---|
| Shared | |
| Actor network | $(400, 300)$ |
| Critic network | $(400, 300)$ |
| Batch size | 100 |
| Learning rate | $10^{-3}$ |
| Optimizer | Adam [8] |
| Discount factor | 0.99 |
| Replay buffer size | $10^{6}$ |
| Warmup steps | $10^{4}$ |
| PRAG | |
| Exploration noise | $\mathcal{N}(0, 0.1)$ |
| Noise clip | 0.5 |
| Target update rate | $5 \times 10^{-3}$ |
| Action gradient regularization parameter $\lambda$ | 0.001 |
| Period parameter $k$ | 2 |
| SAC | |
| Reward scale | 1 |
| Entropy weight | 0.2 |
| Maximum log std | 2 |
| Minimum log std | $-20z$ |

## 4.1 Overall Performance

We evaluate PRAG on six Mujoco tasks: HalfCheetah-v2, Hopper-v2, Ant-v2, Walker2d-v2, Swimmer-v2 and InvertedPendulum-v2. The overall performance comparison is presented in Fig. 2 where the solid line represents the averaged return and the shaded region denotes the standard deviation. PRAG matches or outperforms all other algorithms in both final performance and sample efficiency

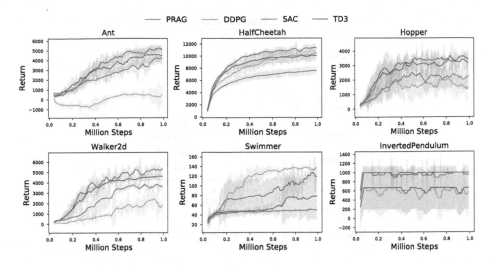

**Fig. 2.** Performance in terms of average return of PRAG against common baselines on six MuJoCo continuous control tasks (5 runs, mean $\pm$ standard deviation). $\lambda = 0.001$ and $k = 2$ are adopted for all of the tasks, and we use $\alpha = 0.05$ for Ant-v2, 0.5 for HalfCheetah-v2, and 0.1 for the rest.

across most of the tasks. PRAG learns faster and behaves better compared with previous baselines. Furthermore, TD3 consumes 12.59 s for 1000 gradient steps on HalfCheetah-v2, while our PRAG consumes 19.04 s. Our method significantly boosts the performance of TD3 with tolerable training costs.

## 4.2   Ablation Study

We perform ablation studies on HalfCheetah-v2 to understand the contribution of each individual component in PRAG: action gradient(AG) and maximizing target Q-value $(Q_t)$. The results are shown in Fig. 3 where we compare the performance of PRAG, TD3+AG, TD3+$Q_t$, and TD3 with the identical hyperparameter setup as PRAG. It can be found that leaving out any component would lead to a decrease in the performance on the environment. We find that maximizing the Q target contributes to the performance improvement on TD3 while pure action gradient can guide the actor to learn a bad policy (the performance drops with pure action gradient).

## 4.3   Parameter Study

PRAG generally contains two key hyperparameters action gradient constraint coefficient $\lambda$ and target maximization coefficient $\alpha$. We conduct the parameter study on one typical MuJoCo environment HalfCheetah-v2 to show the influence of different parameters, and to better under PRAG algorithm.

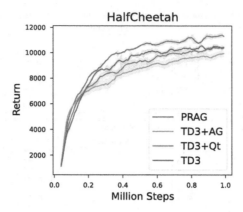

**Fig. 3.** Ablation study on HalfCheetah-v2.

**The Action Gradient Regularization Parameter** $\lambda$. $\lambda$ balances the influence of action gradient in two critic networks. Large $\lambda$ may force the critic to be trapped in the local optima and impede the agent from learning a good policy. While small $\lambda$ may induce a slow and conservative update, which weakens the effect of action gradient regularization. Luckily, we observe that there exists an intermediate value that could achieve a trade-off as is shown in Fig. 4(a). We set $\lambda = 0.001$ by default and empirically find it works well on all of the tasks.

**The Target Maximization Coefficient** $\alpha$. For the weighting coefficient $\alpha$, it balances how much we want the estimated Q-value to escape from the local optima. Large $\alpha$ may induce severe overestimation bias (as estimated values are consistently required to become larger) and too small $\alpha$ will result in a longer time for the agent to escape from the local optimum. By tuning this parameter, we can take a balance between conservatism and overestimation. On some tasks, overestimation is better (e.g., swimmer-v2, as shown in Fig. 2, PRAG can match the performance of DDPG, outperforming TD3 and SAC). We show in Fig. 4(b) that there exists a suitable $\alpha$ that could offer the best trade-off. The target maximization coefficient $\alpha$ is diverse for different tasks (see Sect. 4.1).

**The Period Parameter** $k$. $k$ controls the frequency that action gradient is used to update the critic. Large $k$ leads to slow learning for the actor and small $k$ incurs a strict restriction. We show how different $k$ influences the performance on HalfCheetah-v2 in Fig. 4(c). It can be found that $k$ is not a sensitive parameter except it equals 1. In all experiments we set $k$ as 2.

## 5    Related Work

Actor-critic methods [9] are a popular class of reinforcement learning methods. In such methods, the key is to learn as accurate a critic as possible. Approximation error in critic learning and its effect on policy learning have been studied in prior works [16,18]. These works show that reducing critic approximation error is of great importance. Most present methods [10,14,15,17] focus on reducing Q-value approximation error. Our work builds on the Deterministic Policy Gradient theorem [12,22], where the action gradient of Q-value instead of Q-value itself explicitly contributes to policy improvement. Our work sets a different focus on reducing action gradient approximation error.

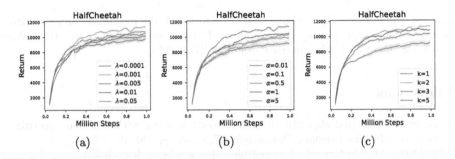

**Fig. 4.** Parameters sensitivity test on HalfCheetah-v2.

A significant point in our work is to bound action gradient error while minimizing TD-error. As far as we know, GProp [2] is the only model-free method that explicitly optimizes the accuracy of action gradient. GProp is based on gradient estimation via noisy perturbations together with an additional deviator network, which is different from PRAG. MAGE [4] is a model-based actor-critic algorithm that explicitly learns the action gradient of the Q function. Different from PRAG, MAGE leverages a trained dynamics model as a proxy for a differentiable environment and techniques reminiscent of double backpropagation [5]. Our method is not only simpler to implement compared with MAGE, but also more time-effective due to the model-free scheme.

Local optima [8,27] is a general and challenging problem inside and outside reinforcement learning. We show that directly using action gradient estimation as regularizer will lead to local-optima, which results in degenerated solutions. It suggests the existence of a trade-off between the easier minimization of the TD error and the more theoretically grounded minimization of its action gradient. Our work regularizes the critic periodically and adds an additional Q-target term to mitigate the problem.

## 6    Conclusion

Different from prior work that aims at learning an accurate Q-function, we leverage the action gradient of TD-error for learning the critic. Nevertheless, we empirically find that directly injecting the action gradient into the critic incurs a performance drop. To alleviate the phenomenon and better utilize the action gradient, we propose Periodic Regularized Action Gradient (PRAG) in this paper, which periodically involves action gradient for guidance while simultaneously maximizing the target value to escape from the local optima. The empirical evaluation of PRAG shows its superiority over common model-free baselines on a set of challenging Gym MuJoCo continuous-control tasks.

The major limitation of our work is the need to tune the target maximization coefficient $\alpha$. We leave the automatic tuning of hyperparameters we introduced in PRAG as future work.

**Acknowledgement.** The authors would like to thank the insightful comments from anonymous reviewers. This work was supported in part by the Science and Technology Innovation 2030-Key Project under Grant 2021ZD0201404.

# References

1. Baird, L.: Residual algorithms: reinforcement learning with function approximation. In: Machine Learning Proceedings. Elsevier, pp. 30–37 (1995)
2. Balduzzi, D., Ghifary, M.: Compatible value gradients for reinforcement learning of continuous deep policies. arXiv preprint arXiv:1509.03005 (2015)
3. Brockman, G., et al.: OpenAI Gym. arXiv preprint arXiv:1606.01540 (2016)
4. D'Oro, P., Jaśkowski, W.: How to learn a useful critic? Model-based action-gradient-estimator policy optimization. Adv. Neural. Inf. Process. Syst. **33**, 313–324 (2020)
5. Drucker, H., LeCun, Y.: Improving generalization performance using double back-propagation. IEEE Trans. Neural Netw. **36**, 991–997 (1992)
6. Fujimoto, S., Hoof, H., Meger, D.: Addressing function approximation error in actor-critic methods. In: International conference on machine learning. PMLR, pp. 1587–1596 (2018)
7. Haarnoja, T., et al.: Soft actor-critic algorithms and applications. arXiv: Learning (2018)
8. Kingma, D.P., Ba, J.: Adam: a method for stochastic optimization. CoRR abs/1412.6980 (2015)
9. Konda, V., Tsitsiklis, J.: Actor-critic algorithms. In: Advances in Neural Information Processing Systems, p. 12 (1999)
10. Kuznetsov, A., Shvechikov, P., Grishin, A., Vetrov, D.P.: Controlling overestimation bias with truncated mixture of continuous distributional quantile critics. arXiv preprint arXiv:2005.04269 (2020)
11. Li, G., Gomez, R., Nakamura, K., He, B.: Human-centered reinforcement learning: a survey. IEEE Trans. Human-Mach. Syst. **49**(4), 337–349 (2019)
12. Lillicrap, T.P., et al.: Continuous control with deep reinforcement learning. arXiv preprint arXiv:1509.02971 (2015)
13. Liu, Y., Zeng, Y., Chen, Y., Tang, J., Pan, Y.: Self-improving generative adversarial reinforcement learning. In: Proceedings of the 18th International Conference on Autonomous Agents and MultiAgent Systems, pp. 52–60 (2019)
14. Lyu, J., Ma, X., Yan, J., Li, X.: Efficient continuous control with double actors and regularized critics. In: Thirty-sixth AAAI Conference on Artificial Intelligence (2022)

15. Lyu, J., Yang, Y., Yan, J., Li, X.: Value activation for bias alleviation: generalized-activated deep double deterministic policy gradients. arXiv preprint arXiv:2112.11216 (2021)
16. Mannor, S., Simester, D., Sun, P., Tsitsiklis, J.N.: Bias and variance approximation in value function estimates. Manage. Sci. **53**(2), 308–322 (2007)
17. Pan, L., Cai, Q., Huang, L.: Softmax deep double deterministic policy gradients. arXiv preprint arXiv:2010.09177 (2020)
18. Pendrith, M.D., Ryan, M.R., et al.: Estimator Variance in Reinforcement Learning: Theoretical Problems and Practical Solutions. University of New South Wales, School of Computer Science and Engineering (1997)
19. Peters, J., Bagnell, J.A.: Policy gradient methods. Scholarpedia **5**(11), 3698 (2010)
20. Puterman, M.L.: Markov decision processes. In: Handbooks in Operations Research and Management Science, vol. 2, pp. 331–434 (1990)
21. Puterman, M.L.: Markov Decision Processes: Discrete Stochastic Dynamic Programming. Wiley (2014)
22. Silver, D., Lever, G., Heess, N., Degris, T., Wierstra, D., Riedmiller, M.: Deterministic policy gradient algorithms. In: International Conference on Machine Learning. PMLR, pp. 387–395 (2014)
23. Smith, A.E., Coit, D.W., Baeck, T., Fogel, D., Michalewicz, Z.: Penalty functions. In: Handbook of Evolutionary Computation, vol. 97, no. 1, p. C5 (1997)
24. Sutton, R.S., Barto, A.G.: Reinforcement Learning: An Introduction. MIT Press (2018)
25. Tesauro, G., et al.: Temporal difference learning and TD-Gammon. Commun. ACM **38**(3), 58–68 (1995)
26. Todorov, E., Erez, T., Tassa, Y.: MuJoCo: a physics engine for model-based control. In: 2012 IEEE/RSJ International Conference on Intelligent Robots and Systems, pp. 5026–5033. IEEE (2012)
27. Zeiler, M.: ADADELTA: an adaptive learning rate method. Computer Science (2012)

# Identifying Multiple Influential Nodes for Complex Networks Based on Multi-agent Deep Reinforcement Learning

Shengzhou Kong[1], Langzhou He[2], Guilian Zhang[1], Li Tao[1(✉)], and Zili Zhang[1]

[1] College of Hanhong, Southwest University, Chongqing 400715, China
shengzhoukong@gmail.com, guilianzhang1998@163.com,
{tli,zhangzl}@swu.edu.cn
[2] College of Computer and Information Science, Southwest University,
Chongqing 400715, China
leolouis@foxmail.com

**Abstract.** The identification of multiple influential nodes that influence the structure or function of a complex network has attracted much attention in recent years. Distinguished from individual significant nodes, the problem of overlapping spheres of influence among influential nodes becomes a key factor that hinders their identification. Most approaches artificially specify the spacing distance between selected nodes through graph coloring and greedy selection. However, these approaches either fail to find the best combination accurately or have high complexity. Therefore, we propose a novel identification framework, namely *multi-agent identification framework* (MAIF), which selects multiple influential nodes in a distributed and simultaneous manner. Based on multi-agent deep reinforcement learning, the framework introduce several optimization models and extend to complex networks to solve distributed problems. With sufficient training, MAIF can be applied to real-world problems quickly and effectively, and perform well in large-scale networks. Based on SIR model-based simulations, the effectiveness of MAIF is evaluated and compared with three baseline methods. The experimental results show that MAIF outperforms the baselines on all four real-world networks. This implies using multiple agents to find multiple influential nodes in a distributed manner is an efficient and accurate new way to differentiate from the greedy methods.

**Keywords:** Multiple influential nodes · Multi-agent deep reinforcement learning · Multi-agent identification framework · Complex networks

## 1 Introduction

Propagation is an inherent feature of complex systems, which describes the dynamics of endogenous activity in various scenarios [21,23,34]. By representing the complex systems as complex networks following the propagation, existing

S. Khanna et al. (Eds.): PRICAI 2022, LNCS 13631, pp. 120–133, 2022.
https://doi.org/10.1007/978-3-031-20868-3_9

researchers have solved a great number of real-world problems. Based on the scenario of the Covid-19 epidemic, the identification of multiple influential nodes is one of the most important problems, which helps to understand the maximization of the infection propagation in complex networks [16]. This problem is often referred to as the *influence maximization problem* (IMP) in the literature [22].

Existing researches indicate that different nodes do not have the same potential to promote the spread of epidemic [16,27]. Thus, most studies focus on the node influence in impacting others and describe this problem as identifying the top-k central nodes using greedy algorithms [3,8,35]. However, these methods always obtain an inaccurate solution with high complexity, due to the network community [31] which leads to the aggregation of selected nodes, and is not suitable for real-world problems.

By analyzing the best combination of influential nodes, existing studies point out that the distances between nodes are the key parameter determining the combined spread influence [15]. To realize the dispersion between nodes, researchers transform the maximization into an optimization problem using heuristics methods [11,28,29]. However, existing heuristic or approximation algorithms either have high complexity or deteriorated performances [4] and it is difficult to achieve an impressive trade-off state between accuracy and efficiency. In addition, these methods are always applied to specific problems and fail to solve general cases.

Inspired by recent research on multi-agent deep reinforcement learning for solving the multi-objective combinatorial optimization [2,9,25,33], in this paper, we propose a novel *multi-agent identification framework* (MAIF) to identify multiple influential nodes in complex networks. The proposed framework utilizes multiple well-trained agents for distributed identification of influential nodes and is more general and scalable for networks of different sizes. Using the actor-critic model, MAIF can train various policy networks for different agents online based on a central controller. Specifically, MAIF introduces GRU network [7] for controlling the complete action history and the COMA [6] to solve the multi-agent credit assignment problem [19].

To assess the effectiveness of MAIF, we apply the *susceptible-infected-recovered* (SIR) model [13] to approximate the influence of identified multiple influential nodes. After extensive training in multiple agents, the results of MAIF on four complex networks show that the proposed framework outperforms the baseline methods in terms of effectiveness and accuracy.

The rest of this paper is organized as follows. Section 2 gives the problem formulation. The proposed MAIF is introduced and described in Sect. 3. Section 4 describes the preliminary setup of experiments. Section 5 compares our framework with several baseline methods. The conclusion is given in Sect. 6.

## 2   Problem Formulation

The scenario of this paper is to identify multiple influential nodes in an epidemic spread. The complex network for spread can be described as a tuple $G = \{V, E\}$, where $V = \{v_1, v_2, \ldots, v_n\}$ and $E = \{e_1, e_2, \ldots e_m\}$. It is worth noting that all edges are undirected and weightless.

In this paper, we utilize the expected outbreak size $\Omega$ by the SIR model-based simulations to represent the influence of selected influential nodes in the spread process. Thus, the goal of this problem is formally defined as detecting $k$ influential nodes which maximum $\Omega$, where the size $k$ is determined by the total number of nodes. The research objective is thus defined as [14] Eq. 1:

$$\underset{\mathbf{v}^* \in V}{argmax}\, \Omega = \underset{\mathbf{v}^* \in V}{argmax} \left\langle \frac{N_I + N_R}{N} \right\rangle \tag{1}$$

where $\mathbf{v}^* = \{v_1^*, v_2^*, \ldots, v_k^*\}$ denotes the $k$ identified influential nodes, $N_I$ and $N_R$ denote the number of infected and recovered nodes after the stabilized outbreak, respectively, and $N$ represents the total number of nodes in the complex network.

# 3   Multi-agent Identification Framework

In this section, we introduce the *multi-agent identification framework* (MAIF) in Sect. 3.1 and illustrate how the specific elements work within the framework to achieve effective training and application of multiple agents in Sect. 3.2. After that, we describe various additional methods, including independent actor-critic model in Sect. 3.3, *counterfactual multi-agent* (COMA) policy gradients and *gate recurrent unit* (GRU) network in Sect. 3.4, to improve the integrity of MAIF.

## 3.1   General Framework of MAIF

We design MAIF to identify multiple influential nodes based on multi-agent deep reinforcement learning. As shown in Fig. 1, MAIF consists of multiple agents [9] and a central controller. By real-time interaction with the environment, it realizes the mutual collaboration between the controller and each agent. Moreover, the actor-critic model is applied in our method, where each distributed agent works as the actor and the central controller as the critic.

Different from traditional methods, MAIF takes a purely data-driven approach without using any problem-specific heuristics. As shown in Fig. 1 (left part), MAIF is trained online using feature matrixes generated by embedding networks, where the embedding method refers to FINDER [4]. For each set of agents' actions, MAIF uses the controller to evaluate the trajectory of actions as a Markov decision process: interacting with the environment through states, joint actions, and global rewards. In this process, the environment is the target complex network, the states (observation states and global state) are subsets of the feature matrix, the joint actions are the set of independent actions of agents, and the global rewards are the increase of influence value after the actions are executed. It should be noted that using a central critic there is no need for the agents to communicate with one another. Meanwhile, the central controller updates the parameters of the deep Q network based on the joint actions and global rewards, and each agent updates its respective policy network parameters based on the independent advantage function value fed by the controller.

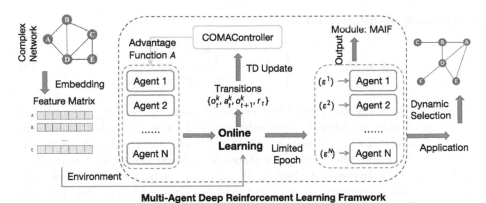

**Multi-Agent Deep Reinforcement Learning Framwork**

**Fig. 1.** The general framework of MAIF, including: (1) the inputed complex network which is embedded and used as environment; (2) the central framework presented in the red part; (3) the application of well-trained agents for new complex networks.

Through extensive training, MAIF becomes intelligent enough to solve the identification task of multiple influential nodes, as shown in Fig. 1 (red part in the middle).

Having completed the actor-critic online learning, the well-trained MAIF can provide 15 agents which are capable of interacting with the environment and acting independently to identify multiple influential nodes in complex networks with an approximate maximum reward. It's worth mentioning that the number of agents during the training phase is a fixed value, due to limited computing resources. When applied to a new network, MAIF randomly selects $k$ agents depending on the network size to realize the dynamic application without upper limit. Moreover, MAIF does not require the participation of the central controller in the application phase. In detail, MAIF can return the best combination of $k$ influential nodes $\mathbf{v}^*$ by distributing multiple agents to different nodes and waiting for each agent to finish the search process, which has a total complex $O(k * n \log n)$, as shown in Fig. 1 (right part).

## 3.2  Framework Elements

Similar to the traditional deep reinforcement learning [24], MAIF also contains the following main elements, including states (observation state and global state), action, and reward. We design and refine specific definitions of these elements for practical problems in Fig. 1.

In our framework, the states are divided into observation state and global state, which are attributed to the agent and the central controller, respectively. Each agent interacts with the environment to obtain its observation state according to its location and predefined observable distance, which can be defined as a subset of the feature matrix. The observation state of agent $a$ located at node

$v_i$ is formally described as Eq. 2:

$$\tau_i^a = \mathbf{O}_{v_i \to \Gamma_{v_i}^l} = \begin{cases} e_{v_j} & \& v_j \in \Gamma_{v_i}^l \\ -1 & \& v_j \in \Gamma_{v_i}^l \& A \ agent \ in \ v_j \\ 0 & \& other \end{cases} \tag{2}$$

where $e_{v_j}$ represents the embedding vector of node $v_j$, and $\Gamma_{v_i}^l$ denotes the neighbors of node $v_i$ within the observable range ($l$-level). Note that when there are other agents in $\Gamma_{v_i}^l$, the features of located nodes need to be all set to $-1$. Thus, we can denote the observation states of multiple agents as $\tau = \{\tau_i^a | v_i \in V; A \ agent \ in \ v_i\}$. In contrast, the central controller can obtain the entire feature matrix of network from the environment, which is denoted by the global state $\mathbf{S}$ in MAIF. Moreover, for the central controller, the observation states are equally important as the global states, and we note the states as $s = (\tau, \mathbf{S})$.

We define the action space of an agent in MAIF as how to move the current agent. In this paper, agent $a$ acts the following three actions depending on its independent policy network with observation states. We denote the probabilities of different actions as $\pi^a (u^a | \tau^a)$, where $u^a$ represents the specific action of agent $a$. And we define the joint actions of multiple agents as $\mathbf{u}$. Specifically, the first action is to stay in the original place, indicating that the movement of this agent will decrease the maximum reward. The second action is to move to another node that is least similar to the current structure within the observable range where other agents are not presented, expecting to increase the maximum reward. In contrast to the second, in the third action, the agent looks for the node that is most similar to the current structure within the observation, also requiring the environment to ensure none conflict between agents. The purpose of this action is to try to find other nodes with similar structures and better propagation capabilities, given that the current agent has great structural features. When changing the current locations of the agents, MAIF selects the best or randomly selects another node while several nodes match the situation. However, for non-connected complex networks, the agent's action space limits its range of activity, i.e., it cannot escape the currently connected network. This causes the distribution of identified influential nodes by MAIF to be limited by the initial distribution of multiple agents when applied to a non-connected network.

The role of reward is to provide feedback to MAIF about previous joint actions, and it is necessary to define rewards appropriately. Through the evaluation of joint actions, the training process can be correctly guided, to help the agent take the best action strategy based on current observation states. In MAIF, our goal is to train multiple agents to effectively identify influential nodes in a distributed manner while collaborating to achieve the best combination of nodes. We define the reward $r(\tau)$ under joint actions as the global influence of agents on the spread of an epidemic in given states, formally described as Eq. 3:

$$r\left(\tau\right) = \sum_{v_i \in \{v_1, v_2, \ldots, v_k\}} \Omega_{v_i}$$

$$\Omega_{v_i} = \mathbf{I}_{v_i \to v_j} = \begin{cases} 1 & v_j \text{ is } v_i \\ \left(\frac{\beta - \beta\gamma}{\gamma + \beta - \beta\gamma}\right)^{L_{v_i, v_j}} & other \end{cases} \tag{3}$$

where $\Omega_{v_i}$ denotes the influence of node $v_i$ on other nodes in the network, also known as $\mathbf{I}_{v_i \to v_j}$. $L_{v_i, v_j}$ denotes the ground distance between node $v_i$ and $v_j$ which shows that nodes that are further away from $v_i$ are less affected by the infection and converge to 0. Considering that the reward is always positive, our goal is to maximize the reward and thus identify the best combination of influential nodes.

### 3.3  Independent Actor-Critic Model

For multi-agent frameworks, the simplest training way is to assign policy networks to each agent and uses independent Q-learning method [9] to train themselves by policy gradients. Instead of this way, using the actor-critic model for each agent has been a commonly used learning method at present, named the *independent actor-critic* (IAC) model.

As shown in Fig. 2, in our implementation of IAC, we set the central controller as the sole critic and different agents as their actors to train the private parameters. As the training method, the actions of actors are computed and executed in real-time using online learning, and the critic continuously feeds back the action-based values to train the actors' policy networks. Specifically, the central controller as a critic follows the gradient update of reward $r(s)$ as temporal difference (TD) error [30] and calculates the value of joint actions $Q(s, \mathbf{u})$ which is distributed to each equivalently. The TD gradient is formally defined as Eq. 4:

$$g_\theta = \nabla_\theta \left(r\left(s_t\right) + \lambda \cdot max_{\mathbf{u}'} Q\left(s_{t+1}, \mathbf{u}'\right) - Q\left(s_t, \mathbf{u}\right)\right) \tag{4}$$

where $s_t$ and $\mathbf{u}$ represent the states and joint actions at the current moment, respectively, while $s_{t+1}$ and $\mathbf{u}'$ represent the corresponding parameter information at the next moment. $\lambda$ represents the update rate of TD.

Then, agents follow the feedback action-based values $Q(s, \mathbf{u})$ to update the parameters of their policy networks. However, the IAC model is always independent and straightforward, due to the lack of information sharing during training. It is difficult to learn joint strategies that depend on interactions between multiple agents and difficult to estimate the contribution of individual agent's action to the global reward, named *confidence assignment problem* [19].

### 3.4  *Counterfactual Multi-agent* (COMA) Policy Gradients and *Gate Recurrent Unit* (GRU) Network

The above difficulties arise due to the uniqueness of the critic's feedback for joint actions. IAC fails to take advantage of the fact that agents learn to be distributed

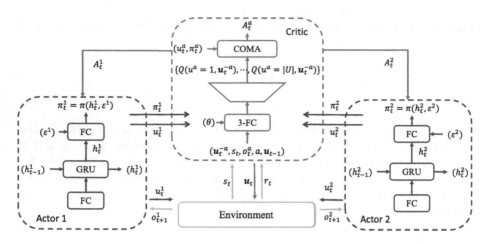

**Fig. 2.** The implementation details of MAIF, including: (1) multiple agents presented in blue part which is utilized as actors; (2) a central controller presented in orange part which is utilized as a critic; (3) the environment presented in green part which is generated by the input network.

in the environment which leads to the inconsistent confidence assignment. In MAIF, we introduced *counterfactual multi-agent* (COMA) policy gradients [6] to overcome this limitation. The most important innovation of COMA is the use of a counterfactual baseline.

In IAC, an agent $a$ follows gradient update $g_{\varepsilon^a}$ by the same action-based values $Q(s, \mathbf{u})$ from a central critic's feedback, as Eq. 5:

$$g_{\varepsilon^a} = \nabla_{\varepsilon^a} \log \left( \pi^a \left( u^a | \tau^a \right) \right) Q\left( s, \mathbf{u} \right) \tag{5}$$

However, when there are too many agents, the impact of other agents on $Q(s, \mathbf{u})$ while exploring is very significant. It is very noisy to only consider the joint action-based values for gradient update. Therefore, COMA proposes a counterfactual baseline [6], as shown in Fig. 2 (orange part), which is inspired by differential rewards. Each agent learns from a mutual reward $D^a = r\left( s, \mathbf{u} \right) - r\left( s, \left( \mathbf{u}^{-a}, c^a \right) \right)$, which compares the global reward with the reward obtained when replacing the action of agent $a$ with the default action $c^a$. $\mathbf{u}^{-a}$ denotes the joint actions of other agents except for $a$. Thus, since $r\left( s, \left( \mathbf{u}^{-a}, c^a \right) \right)$ does not depend on the actual action executed by agent $a$, any optimizations of $D^a$ will turn to optimize the global reward $r\left( s, \mathbf{u} \right)$.

Differential rewards are a powerful way to overcome the confidence assignment problem. However, a concrete implementation usually requires building an additional simulator to estimate $r\left( s, \left( \mathbf{u}^{-a}, c^a \right) \right)$. When introducing the necessary simulator, differential rewards for different agents significantly increase the computational consumption and it is hard to be conclusive about the choice of default action $c^a$. Thus, COMA proposes to approximate the differential reward by the central critic to avoid these limitations. It is known that the controller estimates $Q$-values in terms of states $s$ and joint actions $\mathbf{u}$. Then, we can compute an advantage function that compares the $Q$-value of the current action $u^a$ with a counterfactual baseline of a marginalized $u'^a$ [6], while fixing the joint actions $\mathbf{u}^{-a}$ of others. The formula of the advantage function is defined as Eq. 6:

$$A^a(s, \mathbf{u}) = Q(s, \mathbf{u}) - \sum_{u'^a} \pi^a \left( u'^a \mid \tau^a \right) Q \left( s, \left( \mathbf{u}^{-a}, u'^a \right) \right) \tag{6}$$

Thus, $A^a(s, \mathbf{u})$ can compute a separate counterfactual baseline for each agent and reason from the central critic. The gradient update of agent $a$ is formally described as Eq. 7:

$$g_{\varepsilon^a} = \nabla_{\varepsilon^a} \log \left( \pi^a \left( u^a | \tau^a \right) \right) A^a \left( s, \mathbf{u} \right) \tag{7}$$

It is worth noting that the selection of agent actions $u^a$ is learned directly from the policy network, rather than relying on additional simulators or user-set default action $c^a$. Thus, COMA has no self-consistency problem and converges to a locally optimal policy [6].

In addition, referring to previous works [5,6,9,17], the trainings of multiple agents always need to rely on the local observation history of actions during execution, while the central controller is trained with global state information. To limit the complete history, each agent can be implemented using a recurrent neural network [12]. Thus, in this paper, MAIF introduces *Gate Recurrent Unit* (GRU) network [7] for each independent policy network, as shown in Fig. 2 (blue part), which utilizes the agent's observation history of actions to enhance local temporal correlation when following the policy gradients.

## 4  Experimental Preliminaries

In this section, we illustrate the experimental preliminaries, including (1) the complex networks used for evaluation, (2) the baseline identification methods used for comparison, (3) the SIR model used for simulation, and (4) multiple evaluation metrics used to assess the effectiveness of our proposed framework.

### 4.1  Dataset

We chose four real-world networks with different scales and domains to compare MAIF with three baseline methods. Specifically, the networks are:

- **Crime** [4,18], a crimial network projected from a bipartite network of persons and crimes, which contains 829 nodes (person) and 1473 undirected edges which represent they are involved in the same crime.
- **Digg** [4,18], a reply network of the social news website Digg, which contains 29652 nodes (users) and 84781 undirected edges which denote the replies.
- **Enron** [4,20], the Enron email network that covers all the email communications within a dataset of around half a million emails, which contains 33696 nodes (address) and 180811 undirected edges (communications).
- **College** [26], a college network that records the social connections among students at the University of California, which contains 60810 nodes (students) and 73487 undirected edges which represent they are socializing.

## 4.2  Comparison Method

We utilize three baseline identification methods to compare with the performance of our proposed framework, which include top-k degree centrality [1], independent set [32], and FINDER [4].

Specifically, top-k degree centrality (TDC) [1] ranks the degree centrality calculated by the number of paths within a fixed-length $l(l \in N^+)$ rooted from a given node to select the top-k. The most common equation to describe the degree centrality $Deg(v)$ of node $v$ is $Deg(v) = \frac{|\{\tau_v^l\}|}{|N+1|}$.

Independent set (IS) [32], as a heuristic method, considers the impact of overlapping and divides the complex networks into multiple independent sets in which every two nodes are non-adjacent. After that, in the largest set, this method selects the top-k influential nodes based on any centrality index.

Based on deep reinforcement learning, the FINDER framework [4] achieves superior performance in finding key nodes. The framework can be effectively applied in real-world networks using well-trained agents based on small synthetic graphs for offline self-training. It should be noted that FINDER is typically used to find a single key node but can greedily select multiple influential nodes.

## 4.3  *Susceptible-Infected-Recovered* (SIR) Model

To evaluate the effectiveness of the selected influential nodes by different methods, we employ the SIR model to simulate epidemic outbreaks. The infection mechanism of the model is shown as Eq. 8:

$$\begin{cases} S(v_i) + I(v_j) \xrightarrow{\beta} I(v_i) + I(v_j) \\ I(v_i) \xrightarrow{\gamma} R(v_i) \end{cases} \tag{8}$$

where susceptible node $S(v_i)$ can be infected with probability $\beta$ by infected one $I(v_i)$ which will recover itself to $R(v_i)$ with probability $\gamma$.

We use the proportion of infected and recovered nodes after the stabilized outbreak to approximate the propagation influence. To eliminate the randomness of the simulations, the influences of different combinations will be averaged over 2000 episodes.

## 5  Experimental Results

In this section, we demonstrate the experimental results based on the SIR model. We also present the effectiveness of the proposed framework with three state-of-the-art methods, i.e., top-K degree centrality, independent set and FINDER. The sensitivity of key parameters in MAIF is finally discussed in this section.

As an evaluation metric, we utilize the SIR model-based simulation results $\Omega$ an epidemic to estimate the accuracy of selected influential nodes. The experimental results based on the SIR model on four real-world complex networks are shown in Fig. 3. It represents the simulation results of four identification methods

(MAIF, TDC, IS and FINDER), where the abscissa is different methods and the ordinate is the outbreak size $\Omega$. For the sake of illustration, we set the infection rate and recovery rate in Fig. 3 as fixed values, $\beta = \frac{\langle k \rangle}{\langle k^2 \rangle - \langle k \rangle}$ and $\gamma = 1.5 * \beta$ [10], respectively. Figure 3 shows that MAIF in four networks outperforms the baseline methods with higher accuracy in identifying multiple influential nodes.

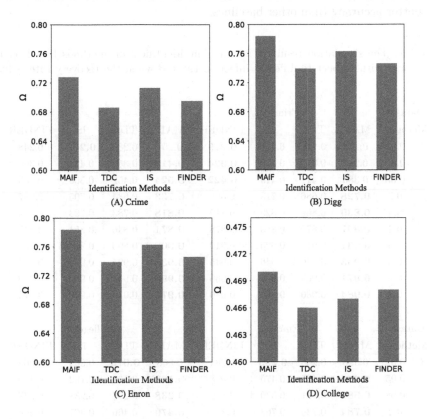

**Fig. 3.** The SIR model-based simulation results $\Omega$ of different identification methods, where the larger outbreak size means a higher effectiveness of identified influential nodes.

In addition, as the influence of identified influential nodes may be varied with respect to different infection rates $\beta$ and recovery rates $\gamma$, and thus affect the effectiveness of MAIF, we investigate the performance of MAIF and the other baselines with respect to different settings of the two key parameters. The relevant results are shown in Tables 1 and 2, which represent the simulation results of different methods (including MAIF,TDC, IS and FINDER) based on the SIR model. In which, the highest values of different methods in various key rates are bolded. For the sake of illustration, we assume a fixed recovery rate $\gamma = 0.3$ [1] for experiments in Table 1, and a fixed infection rate $\beta = 0.2$ [1] for experiments in Table 2, respectively.

The comparison results show that the simulation results of our MAIF are always higher than the other three baselines on four complex networks with a large infection rate and a small recovery rate, which indicate the higher effectiveness. In a word, the proposed framework MAIF has strong robustness and is capable of adapting to different environments, i.e., when the two key parameters (infection rate and recovery rate) of the SIR model are changed, MAIF always has better accuracy than other baselines.

**Table 1.** The simulation results $\Omega$ of different identification methods based on the SIR model with respect to different infection rates $\beta$ when the recovery rate is fixed $\gamma = 0.3$.

| Dataset | | Crime | | | | Digg | | | |
|---------|------|--------|-------|-------|--------|--------|-------|-------|--------|
| Methods | | MAIF | TDC | IS | FINDER | MAIF | TDC | IS | FINDER |
| $\beta$ | 0.02 | 0.178 | 0.216 | 0.208 | **0.219** | 0.251 | 0.239 | **0.272** | 0.248 |
| | 0.05 | 0.262 | 0.315 | 0.310 | **0.324** | **0.418** | 0.355 | 0.414 | 0.369 |
| | 0.08 | 0.380 | 0.411 | 0.419 | **0.422** | **0.524** | 0.452 | 0.506 | 0.463 |
| | 0.2 | **0.728** | 0.686 | 0.713 | 0.695 | **0.733** | 0.684 | 0.705 | 0.687 |
| | 0.3 | **0.839** | 0.809 | 0.820 | 0.812 | **0.818** | 0.783 | 0.793 | 0.784 |
| | 0.4 | **0.897** | 0.875 | 0.880 | 0.878 | **0.871** | 0.846 | 0.851 | 0.847 |
| | 0.5 | **0.931** | 0.917 | 0.920 | 0.919 | **0.908** | 0.890 | 0.893 | 0.891 |
| | 0.6 | **0.953** | 0.946 | 0.946 | 0.945 | **0.936** | 0.924 | 0.925 | 0.924 |
| | 0.7 | **0.971** | 0.965 | 0.967 | 0.965 | **0.958** | 0.949 | 0.950 | 0.949 |
| | 0.8 | **0.984** | 0.980 | 0.980 | 0.980 | **0.975** | 0.970 | 0.970 | 0.970 |

| Dataset | | Enron | | | | College | | | |
|---------|------|--------|-------|-------|--------|--------|--------|-------|--------|
| Methods | | MAIF | TDC | IS | FINDER | MAIF | TDC | IS | FINDER |
| $\beta$ | 0.02 | 0.326 | 0.265 | **0.333** | 0.284 | 0.068 | **0.070** | 0.069 | 0.068 |
| | 0.05 | **0.484** | 0.405 | 0.476 | 0.428 | **0.162** | 0.160 | 0.162 | 0.159 |
| | 0.08 | **0.586** | 0.511 | 0.570 | 0.532 | **0.238** | 0.236 | 0.238 | 0.237 |
| | 0.2 | **0.784** | 0.739 | 0.763 | 0.746 | **0.470** | 0.466 | 0.467 | 0.468 |
| | 0.3 | **0.857** | 0.828 | 0.839 | 0.831 | **0.602** | 0.599 | 0.601 | 0.599 |
| | 0.4 | **0.902** | 0.881 | 0.888 | 0.883 | **0.701** | 0.698 | 0.698 | 0.697 |
| | 0.5 | **0.931** | 0.917 | 0.922 | 0.919 | 0.776 | 0.776 | **0.777** | 0.775 |
| | 0.6 | **0.952** | 0.942 | 0.946 | 0.944 | 0.839 | 0.839 | 0.839 | **0.840** |
| | 0.7 | **0.969** | 0.962 | 0.964 | 0.963 | **0.891** | 0.889 | 0.889 | 0.891 |
| | 0.8 | **0.981** | 0.977 | 0.979 | 0.978 | **0.933** | 0.932 | 0.932 | 0.932 |

**Table 2.** The simulation results $\Omega$ of different identification methods based on the SIR model with respect to different recovery rates $\gamma$ when the infection rate is fixed $\beta = 0.2$.

| Dataset | Methods | Recovery rate $\gamma$ | | | |
|---|---|---|---|---|---|
| | | 0.1 | 0.3 | 0.5 | 0.7 |
| Crime | MAIF | **0.909** | **0.728** | 0.571 | 0.450 |
| | TDC | 0.891 | 0.686 | 0.548 | 0.459 |
| | IS | 0.895 | 0.713 | **0.574** | **0.479** |
| | FINDER | 0.892 | 0.695 | 0.561 | 0.469 |
| Digg | MAIF | **0.883** | **0.733** | **0.638** | **0.568** |
| | TDC | 0.861 | 0.684 | 0.572 | 0.497 |
| | IS | 0.865 | 0.705 | 0.609 | 0.545 |
| | FINDER | 0.861 | 0.687 | 0.580 | 0.507 |
| Enron | MAIF | **0.909** | **0.784** | **0.697** | **0.631** |
| | TDC | 0.888 | 0.739 | 0.635 | 0.560 |
| | IS | 0.897 | 0.763 | 0.677 | 0.613 |
| | FINDER | 0.891 | 0.746 | 0.649 | 0.579 |
| College | MAIF | 0.721 | **0.470** | **0.349** | **0.278** |
| | TDC | **0.724** | 0.466 | 0.348 | 0.277 |
| | IS | 0.723 | 0.467 | 0.348 | 0.277 |
| | FINDER | 0.722 | 0.468 | 0.347 | 0.277 |

# 6  Conclusion

In this paper, we introduce multi-agent deep reinforcement learning to propose a novel identification framework named *multi-agent identification framework* (MAIF) and utilize the SIR model to verify the effectiveness of the proposed model in selecting multiple influential nodes. Experimental results on four real-world networks of various sizes show that MAIF outperforms the baseline methods in terms of effectiveness and accuracy, and can effectively apply well-trained agents in large-scale networks in a distributed manner. Moreover, due to the high flexibility of MAIF, we only need to change the reward mechanism to suit different application scenarios, such as the IMP problem addressed in this paper. Finally, MAIF opens a new research direction of using multi-agent deep learning techniques to uncover the dynamics behind complex networks, which allows us to design more distributed executions to cope with larger-scale networks. Subsequent research will extend the proposed framework to dynamic and multi-layer networks for solving more practical problems.

# References

1. Chen, D.B., Lü, L.Y., Shang, M.S., Zhang, Y.C., Zhou, T.: Identifying influential nodes in complex networks. Phys. A: Stat. Mech. Its Appl. **391**(4), 1777–1787 (2012)
2. Du, W., Ding, S.F.: A survey on multi-agent deep reinforcement learning: from the perspective of challenges and applications. Artif. Intell. Rev. **54**(5), 3215–3238 (2021)
3. Dudkina, E., Bin, M., Breen, J., Crisostomi, E., Ferraro, P., Kirkland, S., Marecek, J., Murray Smith, R., Parisini, T., Stone, L.: On node ranking in graphs (2021). arXiv:2107.09487
4. Fan, C.J., Zeng, L., Sun, Y.Z., Liu, Y.Y.: Finding key players in complex networks through deep reinforcement learning. Nat. Mach. Intell. **2**(6), 317–324 (2020)
5. Foerster, J., Assael, I.A., De Freitas, N., Whiteson, S.: Learning to communicate with deep multi-agent reinforcement learning. In: Advances in Neural Information Processing Systems, vol. 29 (2016)
6. Foerster, J., Farquhar, G., Afouras, T., Nardelli, N., Whiteson, S.: Counterfactual multi-agent policy gradients. In: Proceedings of the AAAI Conference on Artificial Intelligence. pp. 2974–2982. AAAI Press (2018)
7. Gao, Y., Glowacka, D.: Deep gate recurrent neural network. In: Asian Conference on Machine Learning, pp. 350–365. PMLR (2016)
8. Gómez, S.: Centrality in networks: finding the most important nodes. In: Business and Consumer Analytics: New Ideas, p. 401 (2019)
9. Gronauer, S., Diepold, K.: Multi-agent deep reinforcement learning: a survey. Artif. Intell. Rev. **55**(2), 895–943 (2022)
10. Guo, C.G., Yang, L.W., Chen, X., Chen, D.B., Gao, H., Ma, J.: Influential nodes identification in complex networks via information entropy. Entropy **22**(2), 242 (2020)
11. Guo, L., Lin, J.H., Guo, Q., Liu, J.G.: Identifying multiple influential spreaders in term of the distance-based coloring. Phys. Lett. A **380**(7–8), 837–842 (2016)
12. Hausknecht, M., Stone, P.: Deep recurrent Q-learning for partially observable MDPs. In: 2015 AAAI Fall Symposium Series (2015)
13. Holme, P.: Epidemiologically optimal static networks from temporal network data. PLoS Comput. Biol. **9**(7), e1003142 (2013)
14. Holme, P.: Temporal network structures controlling disease spreading. Phys. Rev. E **94**(2), 022305 (2016)
15. Hu, Z.L., Liu, J.G., Yang, G.Y., Ren, Z.M.: Effects of the distance among multiple spreaders on the spreading. EPL **106**(1), 18002 (2014)
16. Kitsak, M., Gallos, L.K., Havlin, S., Liljeros, F., Muchnik, L., Stanley, H.E., Makse, H.A.: Identification of influential spreaders in complex networks. Nat. Phys. **6**(11), 888–893 (2010)
17. Kraemer, L., Banerjee, B.: Multi-agent reinforcement learning as a rehearsal for decentralized planning. Neurocomputing **190**, 82–94 (2016)
18. Kunegis, J.: Konect: the koblenz network collection. In: WWW. pp. 1343–1350 (2013)
19. Lansdell, B.J., Prakash, P.R., Kording, K.P.: Learning to solve the credit assignment problem. In: International Conference on Learning Representations (2019)
20. Leskovec, J., Lang, K.J., Dasgupta, A., Mahoney, M.W.: Community structure in large networks: natural cluster sizes and the absence of large well-defined clusters. Internet Math. **6**(1), 29–123 (2009)

21. Li, L.X., Yang, Z.H., Dang, Z.K., Meng, C., Huang, J.Z., Meng, H.T., Wang, D.Y., Chen, G.H., Zhang, J.X., Peng, H.P.: Propagation analysis and prediction of the COVID-19. Infect. Dis. Model. **5**, 282–292 (2020)
22. Lü, L.Y., Chen, D.B., Ren, X.L., Zhang, Q.M., Zhang, Y.C., Zhou, T.: Vital nodes identification in complex networks. Phys. Rep. **650**, 1–63 (2016)
23. Montavon, G., Binder, A., Lapuschkin, S., Samek, W., Müller, K.R.: Layer-wise relevance propagation: an overview. In: Explainable AI: Interpreting, Explaining and Visualizing Deep Learning, pp. 193–209 (2019)
24. Mousavi, S.S., Schukat, M., Howley, E.: Deep reinforcement learning: an overview. In: Proceedings of SAI Intelligent Systems Conference. pp. 426–440. Springer, Berlin (2016)
25. OroojlooyJadid, A., Hajinezhad, D.: A review of cooperative multi-agent deep reinforcement learning (2019). arXiv:1908.03963
26. Panzarasa, P., Opsahl, T., Carley, K.M.: Patterns and dynamics of users' behavior and interaction: network analysis of an online community. J. Am. Soc. Inform. Sci. Technol. **60**(5), 911–932 (2009)
27. Peng, L.R., Yang, W.Y., Zhang, D.Y., Zhuge, C.J., Hong, L.: Epidemic analysis of COVID-19 in China by dynamical modeling (2020). arXiv:2002.06563
28. Ren, X.L., Gleinig, N., Helbing, D., Antulov Fantulin, N.: Generalized network dismantling. Proc. Natl. Acad. Sci. **116**(14), 6554–6559 (2019)
29. Srinivas, S., Rajendran, C.: Community detection and influential node identification in complex networks using mathematical programming. Expert Syst. Appl. **135**, 296–312 (2019)
30. Wang, L.M., Tong, Z., Ji, B., Wu, G.S.: TDN: Temporal difference networks for efficient action recognition. In: Proceedings of the IEEE/CVF Conference on Computer Vision and Pattern Recognition. pp. 1895–1904 (2021)
31. Wellman, B.: The network community: an introduction. In: Networks in the Global Village, pp. 1–47. Routledge (2018)
32. Zhao, X.Y., Huang, B., Tang, M., Zhang, H.F., Chen, D.B.: Identifying effective multiple spreaders by coloring complex networks. EPL **108**(6), 68005 (2015)
33. Zheng, Y., Meng, Z.P., Hao, J.Y., Zhang, Z.Z.: Weighted double deep multi-agent reinforcement learning in stochastic cooperative environments. In: Pacific Rim International Conference on Artificial Intelligence, pp. 421–429. Springer, Berlin (2018)
34. Zhong, L.F., Shang, M.S., Chen, X.L., Cai, S.M.: Identifying the influential nodes via eigen-centrality from the differences and similarities of structure. Phys. A **510**, 77–82 (2018)
35. Zhou, C., Zhang, P., Zang, W.Y., Guo, L.: Maximizing the long-term integral influence in social networks under the voter model. ACM, pp. 423–424 (2014)

# Online Learning in Iterated Prisoner's Dilemma to Mimic Human Behavior

Baihan Lin[1(⊠)], Djallel Bouneffouf[2], and Guillermo Cecchi[2]

[1] Columbia University, New York, USA
baihan.lin@columbia.edu
[2] IBM Research, Yorktown Heights, NY, USA
djallel.bouneffouf@ibm.com, gcecchi@us.ibm.com

**Abstract.** As an important psychological and social experiment, the Iterated Prisoner's Dilemma (IPD) treats the choice to cooperate or defect as an atomic action. We propose to study the behaviors of online learning algorithms in the Iterated Prisoner's Dilemma (IPD) game, where we investigate the full spectrum of reinforcement learning agents: multi-armed bandits, contextual bandits and reinforcement learning. We evaluate them based on a tournament of iterated prisoner's dilemma where multiple agents can compete in a sequential fashion. This allows us to analyze the dynamics of policies learned by multiple self-interested independent reward-driven agents, and also allows us study the capacity of these algorithms to fit the human behaviors. Results suggest that considering the current situation to make decision is the worst in this kind of social dilemma game. Multiples discoveries on online learning behaviors and clinical validations are stated, as an effort to connect artificial intelligence algorithms with human behaviors and their abnormal states in neuropsychiatric conditions.

**Keywords:** Online learning · Bandits · Contextual bandits · Reinforcement learning · Iterated Prisoner's Dilemma · Behavioral modeling

## 1 Introduction

Social dilemmas expose tensions between cooperation and defection. Understanding the best way of playing the iterated prisoner's dilemma (IPD) has been of interest to the scientific community since the formulation of the game seventy years ago [5]. To evaluate the algorithm a round robin computer tournament was proposed, where algorithms competed against each others [2]. The winner was decided on the average score a strategy achieved. Using this framework, we propose here to focus on studying reward driven online learning algorithm with different type of attentions mechanism, where we define attention "as the

---

The data and codes to reproduce all the empirical results can be accessed at https://github.com/doerlbh/dilemmaRL.

© The Author(s), under exclusive license to Springer Nature Switzerland AG 2022
S. Khanna et al. (Eds.): PRICAI 2022, LNCS 13631, pp. 134–147, 2022.
https://doi.org/10.1007/978-3-031-20868-3_10

behavioral and cognitive process of selectively concentrating on a discrete stimulus while ignoring other perceivable stimuli" [21]. Following this definition, we analyze three algorithms classes: the no-attention-to-the-context online learning agent (the multi armed bandit algorithms) outputs an action but does not use any information about the state of the environment (context); the contextual bandit algorithm extends the model by making the decision conditional on the current state of the environment, and finally reinforcement learning as an extension of contextual bandits which makes decision conditional on the current state of the environment and the next state of the unknown environments. This paper mainly focuses on an answer to two questions:

- Does attending to the context for an online learning algorithm helps on the task of maximizing the rewards in an IPD tournament, and how do different attention biases shape behavior?
- Does attending to the context for an online learning algorithm helps to mimic human behavior?

To answer these questions, we have performed two experimenters: (1) The first one where we have run a tournament of the iterated prisoner's dilemma: Since the seminal tournament in 1980 [5], a number of IPD tournaments have been undertaken [2,10,12]. In this work, we adopt a similar tournament setting, but also extended it to cases with more than two players. Empirically, we evaluated the algorithms in four settings of the Iterated Prisoner's Dilemma: pairwise-agent tournament, three-agent tournament, "mental"-agent tournament. (2) Behavioral cloning prediction task: where we train the the three types of algorithm to mimic the human behavior on some training set and then test them in a test set. Our main results are the following:

- We observe that contextual bandits are not performing well in the tournament, which means that considering the current situation to make decision is the worst in this kind of social dilemma game. Basically we should either do not care about the current situation or caring about more situations, but not just the current one.
- We observe that bandit algorithms (without context) is the best in term of fitting the human data, which implies that humans may not consider the context when they play the iterated prisoner's dilemma.

This paper is organized as follows. We first review related works and introduces some background concepts. Then we explain the two experiments we have performed. Experimental evaluation highlights the empirical results we have got. Finally, the last section concludes the paper and points out possible directions for future works.

As far as we are aware, this is the first work that evaluated the online learning algorithms in social gaming settings. Although the agents that we evaluated here are not newly proposed by us, we believe that given this understudied information asymmetry problem setting, our work helps the community understand how the inductive bias of different methods yield different behaviors in social agent settings (e.g. iterated prisoners' dilemma), and thus provides a nontrivial contribution to the fields, both in understanding machine learning algorithms, and in studying mechanistic models of human behaviors in social settings.

## 2   Related Work

There is much computational work focused on non understanding the strategy space and finding winning strategies in the iterated prisoner's dilemma; Authors in [22] present and discuss several improvements to the Q-Learning algorithm, allowing for an easy numerical measure of the exploitability of a given strategy. [18] propose a mechanism for achieving cooperation and communication in Multi-Agent Reinforcement Learning settings by intrinsically rewarding agents for obeying the commands of other agents. We are interested in investigating how algorithms are behaving and also how they are modeling the human decisions in the IPD, with the larger goal of understanding human decision-making. For-instance, In [39] authors have proposed an active modeling technique to predict the behavior of IPD players. The proposed method can model the opponent player's behavior while taking advantage of interactive game environments. The data showed that the observer was able to build, through direct actions, a more accurate model of an opponent's behavior than when the data were collected through random actions. [15] they propose the first predictive model of human cooperation able to organize a number of different experimental findings that are not explained by the standard model and they show also that the model makes satisfactorily accurate quantitative predictions of population average behavior in one-shot social dilemmas. To the best of our knowledge no study has been exploring the full spectrum of reinforcement learning agents: multi-armed bandits, contextual bandits and reinforcement learning in social dilemma.

## 3   Background

**Multi-armed Bandit (MAB):** The multi-armed bandit (MAB) algorithm models a sequential decision-making process, where at each time point a the algorithm selects an action from a given finite set of possible actions, attempting to maximize the cumulative reward over time [3,23].

**Contextual Bandit Algorithm (CB).** Following [24], this problem is defined as follows. At each time point (iteration) $t \in \{1, ..., T\}$, an agent is presented with a *context (feature vector)* $\mathbf{x}_t \in \mathbf{R}^N$ before choosing an arm $k \in A = \{1, ..., K\}$. We will denote by $X = \{X_1, ..., X_N\}$ the set of features (variables) defining the context. Let $\mathbf{r}_t = (r_t^1, ..., r_t^K)$ denote a reward vector, where $r_t^k \in [0, 1]$ is a reward at time $t$ associated with the arm $k \in A$. Herein, we will primarily focus on the Bernoulli bandit with binary reward, i.e. $r_t^k \in \{0, 1\}$. Let $\pi : X \to A$ denote a policy. Also, $D_{c,r}$ denotes a joint distribution over $(\mathbf{x}, \mathbf{r})$. We will assume that the expected reward is a linear function of the context, i.e. $E[r_t^k | \mathbf{x}_t] = \mu_k^T \mathbf{x}_t$, where $\mu_k$ is an unknown weight vector associated with arm $k$.

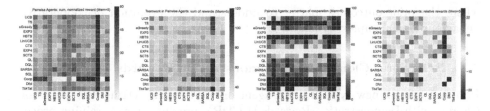

**Fig. 1.** Success, Teamwork, Cooperation & Competition in two-agent tournament.

**Table 1.** IPD Payoff

|   | C | D |
|---|---|---|
| C | R,R | S,T |
| D | T,S | P,P |

**Reinforcement Learning (RL).** Reinforcement learning defines a class of algorithms for solving problems modeled as Markov decision processes (MDP) [46]. An MDP is defined by the tuple $(\mathcal{S}, \mathcal{A}, \mathcal{T}, \mathcal{R}, \gamma)$, where $\mathcal{S}$ is a set of possible states, $\mathcal{A}$ is a set of actions, $\mathcal{T}$ is a transition function defined as $\mathcal{T}(s, a, s') = \Pr(s'|s, a)$, where $s, s' \in \mathcal{S}$ and $a \in \mathcal{A}$, and $\mathcal{R} : \mathcal{S} \times \mathcal{A} \times \mathcal{S} \mapsto \mathbb{R}$ is a reward function, $\gamma$ is a discount factor that decreases the impact of the past reward on current action choice. Typically, the objective is to maximize the discounted long-term reward, assuming an infinite-horizon decision process, i.e. to find a policy function $\pi : \mathcal{S} \mapsto \mathcal{A}$ which specifies the action to take in a given state, so that the cumulative reward is maximized: $\max_{\pi} \sum_{t=0}^{\infty} \gamma^t \mathcal{R}(s_t, a_t, s_{t+1})$.

## 4 Experimental Setup

Here, we describe the two main experiments we run, Iterated Prisoner's Dilemma (IPD) and Behavioral Cloning with Demonstration Rewards (BCDR).

### 4.1 Iterated Prisoner's Dilemma (IPD)

The Iterated Prisoner's Dilemma (IPD) can be defined as a matrix game $G = [N, \{A_i\}_{i \in N}, \{R_i\}_{i \in N}]$, where $N$ is the set of agents, $A_i$ is the set of actions available to agent $i$ with $\mathcal{A}$ being the joint action space $A_1 \times \cdots \times A_n$, and $R_i$ is the reward function for agent $i$. A special case of this generic multi-agent IPD is the classical two-agent case (Table 1). In this game, each agent has two actions: cooperate (C) and defect (D), and can receive one of the four possible rewards: R (Reward), P (Penalty), S (Sucker), and T (Temptation). In the multi-agent setting, if all agents Cooperates (C), they all receive Reward (R); if all agents defects (D), they all receive Penalty (P); if some agents Cooperate (C) and some Defect (D), cooperators receive Sucker (S) and defector receive Temptation (T). The four payoffs satisfy the following inequalities: $T > R > P > S$ and $2R > T + S$. The PD is a one round game, but is commonly studied in a manner where the prior outcomes matter to understand the evolution of cooperative behaviour from complex dynamics [6].

## 4.2   Behavioral Cloning with Demonstration Rewards

Here we define a new type of multi-agent online learning setting, the Behavior Cloning with Demonstration Rewards (BCDR), present a novel training procedure and agent for solving this problem. In this setting, and similar to [7,8,37] the agent first goes through a constraint learning phase where it is allowed to query the actions and receive feedback $r_k^e(t) \in [0,1]$ about whether or not the chosen decision matches the teacher's action (from demonstration). During the deployment (testing) phase, the goal of the agent is to maximize both $r_k(t) \in [0,1]$, the reward of the action $k$ at time $t$, and the (unobserved) $r_k^e(t) \in [0,1]$, which models whether or not the taking action $k$ matches which action the teacher would have taken. During the deployment phase, the agent receives no feedback on the value of $r_k^e(t)$, where we would like to observe how the behavior captures the teacher's policy profile. In our specific problem, the human data plays the role of the teacher, and the behavioral cloning aims to train our agents to mimic the human behaviors.

## 4.3   Online Learning Agents

We briefly outlined the different types of online learning algorithms we have used:

**Multi-armed Bandit (MAB):** The multi-armed bandit algorithm models a sequential decision-making process, where at each time point a the algorithm selects an action from a given finite set of possible actions, attempting to maximize the cumulative reward over time [3,13,23]. In the multi-armed bandit agent pool, we have Thompson Sampling (TS) [48], Upper Confidence Bound (UCB) [3], epsilon Greedy (eGreedy) [46], EXP3 [4] and the Human Based Thompson Sampling (HBTS) [14].

**Contextual Bandit (CB).** Following [24], this problem is defined as follows. At each time point (iteration), an agent is presented with a *context* (*feature vector*) before choosing an arm. In the contextual bandit agent pool, we have Contextual Thompson Sampling (CTS) [1], LinUCB [26], EXP4 [11] and Split Contextual Thompson Sampling (SCTS) [29,33].

**Reinforcement Learning (RL).** Reinforcement learning defines a class of algorithms for solving problems modeled as Markov decision processes (MDP) [46]. An MDP is defined by the tuple with a set of possible states, a set of actions and a transition function. In the reinforcement learning agent pool, we have Q-Learning (QL), Double Q-Learning (DQL) [19], State-action-reward-state-action (SARSA) [44] and Split Q-Learning (SQL) [28,32]. We also selected three most popular handcrafted policy for Iterated Prisoner's Dilemma: "Coop" stands for always cooperating, "Dfct" stands for always defecting and "Tit4Tat" stands for following what the opponent chose for the last time (which was the winner approach in the 1980 IPD tournament [5]).

The choices of the agents evaluated in this work are the most common online learning agents in bandits, contextual bandits and reinforcement learning (the three online learning classes). We thought that competing them against one another, and competing the three online learning classes against one another might be an interesting experiment to study how the inductive bias of different methods yield different behaviors in social agent settings (e.g. IPD).

## 5   Results: Algorithms' Tournament

**Game settings.** The payoffs are set as the classical IPD game: $T = 5, R = 3, P = 1, S = 0$. Following [42], we create create standardized payoff measures from the R, S, T, P values using two differences between payoffs associate with important game outcomes, both normalized by the difference between the temptation to defect and being a sucker when cooperating as the other defects.

**State Representations.** In most IPD literature, the state is defined the pair of previous actions of self and opponent. Studies suggest that only one single previous state is needed to define any prisoner's dilemma strategy [41]. However, as we are interested in understanding the role of three levels of information (no

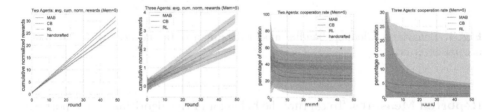

**Fig. 2.** Cumulative reward and cooperation rate averaged by class in two- and three-player setting.

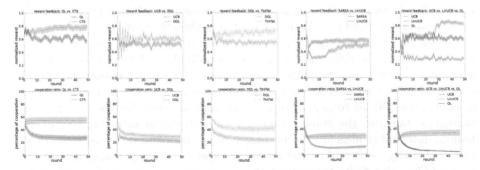

**Fig. 3.** Reward feedbacks and cooperation rates in some two-player and the three-player settings.

information, with context but without state, and with both context and state), we expand the state representation to account for the past $n$ pairs of actions as the history (or memory) for the agents. For CB algorithms, this history is their context. For RL algorithms, this history is their state representation. In the following sections, we will present the results in which the memory is set to be the past 5 action pairs.

**Learning Settings.** In all experiments, the discount factor $\gamma$ was set to be 0.95. The exploration is included with $\epsilon$-greedy algorithm with $\epsilon$ set to be 0.05 (except for the algorithms that already have an exploration mechanism). The learning rate was polynomial $\alpha_t(s, a) = 1/n_t(s, a)^{0.8}$, which was shown in previous work to be better in theory and in practice [16]. All experiments were performed and averaged for at least 100 runs, and over 50 steps of dueling actions from the initial state.

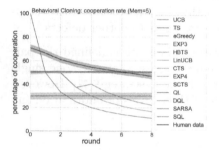 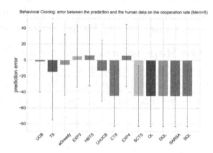

**Fig. 4.** Behavioral Cloning: bandits modeled human data the best with the lowest prediction error.

**Reported Measures.** To capture the behavior of the algorithms, we report five measures: individual normalized rewards, collective normalized rewards, difference of normalized rewards, the cooperation rate and normalized reward feedback at each round. We are interested in the individual rewards since that is what online learning agents should effectively maximize their expected cumulative discounted reward for. We are interested in the collective rewards because it might offer important insights on the teamwork of the participating agents. We are interested in the difference between each individual player's reward and the average reward of all participating players because it might capture the internal competition within a team. We record the cooperation rate as the percentage of cooperating in all rounds since it is not only a probe for the emergence of strategies, but also the standard measure in behavioral modeling to compare human data and models [30,31,36]. Lastly, we provided reward feedback at each round as a diagnostic tool to understand the specific strategy emerged from each game. (The color codes throughout this paper are set constant for each of the 14 agents, such that all handcrafted agents have green-ish colors, MAB agents red-ish, CB agents blue-ish and RL agents purple-ish).

## 5.1   Multi-agent Tournament

**Results for Two-agent Tournament.** We record the behaviors of the agents playing against each other (and with themselves). Figure 1 summarizes the reward and behavior patterns of the tournament. We first notice that MAB and RL algorithms learn to cooperate when their opponent is *Coop*, yielding a high mutual reward, while CB algorithms mostly decide to defect on *Coop* to exploit its trust. From the cooperation heatmap, we also observe that RL algorithms appear to be more defective when facing an MAB or CB algorithm than facing another RL algorithm. MAB algorithms are more defective when facing a CB algorithm than facing an RL or another MAB algorithm. Adversarial algorithms EXP3 and EXP4 fail to learn any distinctive policy. We also note interesting teamwork and competition behaviors in the heatmaps of collective rewards and relative rewards: CB algorithms are the best team players, yielding an overall highest collective rewards, followed by RL; RL are the most competitive opponents, yielding an overall highest relative rewards, followed by MAB.

Figure 2 summarizes the averaged reward and cooperation for each of the three classes, where we observe handcrafted algorithms the best, followed by RL algorithms and then MAB algorithms. CB algorithms receive the lowest final rewards among the four agent classes. Surprisingly, it also suggests that a lower cooperation rate don't imply a higher reward. The most cooperative learning algorithm class is CB, followed by RL. MAB, the most defective agents, don't score the highest. Detailed probing into specific games (Fig 3) uncovers more diverse strategies than these revealed by the cooperation rates. For instance, in the game of QL vs. CTS, we observe that CTS converges to a fixed cooperation rate within the first few rounds and stayed constant since then, while the QL gradually decays its cooperation rate. In the game of UCB1 vs. DQL, UCB1 seemed to oscillate between a high and low cooperation rate within the first few rounds (because it is built to explore all actions first), while DQL gradually decays its cooperation rate. In DQL vs. Tit4Tat, we observe a seemingly mimicking effect of DQL to a tit-for-tat-like behaviors. In the game of SARSA vs. LinUCB, LinUCB converges to a fixed cooperation rate with the first few rounds and stays constant since then, while SARSA slowly decays its cooperation rate. There seems to be a universality of the three classes within the first few rounds.

**Cognitive Interpretations of These Learning Systems.** The main distinctions between the three classes of algorithms are the complexity of the learning mechanism and the cognitive system they adopt. In MAB setting, there is no attention to any contexts, and the agents aim to most efficiently allocate a fixed limited set of cognitive resources between competing (alternative) choices in a way that maximizes their expected gain. In CB setting, the agents apply an attention mechanism to the current context, and aim to collect enough information about how the context vectors and rewards relate to each other, so that they can predict the next best action to play by looking at the feature vectors. In RL setting, the agents not only pay attention to the current context, but also apply the attention mechanism to multiple contexts relate to different states, and aim to use the past experience to find out which actions lead to higher cumulative rewards. Our results suggest that in the Iterate Prisoner's Dilemma of two learning systems, an optimal learning policy should hold memory for different state representations and allocate attention to different contexts across the states, which explained the overall best performance by RL algorithms. This further suggests that in zero-sum games like the IPD, participating learning systems tend to undergo multiple states. The overall underperformance of CB suggests that the attention to only the current context was not sufficient without the state representation, because the learning system might mix the context-dependent reward mappings of multiple states, which can oversimplify the policy and potentially mislead the learning as an interfering effect. On the other hand, MAB ignores the context information entirely, so they are not susceptible to the interfering effect from the representations of different contexts. Their learned policies, however, don't exhibit any interesting flexibility to account for any major change in the state (e.g., the opponent may just finish a major learning episode and switch strategies).

**Results for Three-agent Tournament.** Here we wish to understand how all three classes of algorithms interact in the same arena. For each game, we pick one algorithm from each class (one from MAB, one from CB and one from RL) to make our player pool. We observe in Fig. 2 a very similar pattern as the two-player case: RL agents demonstrate the best performance (highest final rewards) followed by MAB, and CB performed the worst. However, in three-agent setting, although CB is still the most cooperative, and RL became the most defective. More detailed probing into the specific games (Fig. 3) demonstrate more diverse strategies than these revealed by the cooperation rates. Take the game UCB1 vs. LinUCB vs. QL as an example, MAB algorithms start off as the most defective but later start to cooperate more in following rounds, while RL algorithms became more and more defective. CB in both cases stays cooperative at a relatively high rate.

# 6   Behavioral Cloning with Human Data

We collate the human data comprising 168,386 individual decisions from many human subjects experiments [2,10,12] that used real financial incentives and transparently conveyed the rules of the game to the subjects. As a standard procedure in experimental economics, subjects anonymously interact with each other and their decisions to cooperate or defect at each time period of each interaction are recorded. They receive payoffs proportional to the outcomes in the same or similar payoff as the one we use in Table 1. Following the similar preprocessing steps as [30,31,36], we can construct the comprehensive collection of game structures and individual decisions from the description of the experiments in the published papers and the publicly available data sets. This comprehensive dataset consists of behavioral trajectories of different time horizons, ranging from 2 to 30 rounds, but most of these experimental data only host full historical information of at most past 9 actions. We further select only those trajectories with these full historical information, which comprise 8,257 behavioral trajectories. We randomly select 8,000 of them as training set and the other 257 as test set.

In the training phase, all agents are trained with the demonstration rewards as feedback sequentially for the trajectories in the training set. In the testing phase, we paused all the learning, and tested on 257 trajectories independently, recorded their cooperation rate. In each test trajectory, we compared their evolution of cooperation rate to that of the human data and compute a prediction error.

Figure 4 summarizes the testing results of all the agents in predicting the actions and their cooperation rates from human data. From the heatmap of the cooperation rates, we observe that the behavioral policy that each agent cloned from the data varies by class. RL algorithms all seem to learn to defect at all costs ("tragedy of the commons"). CB algorithms mostly converge to a policy that adopted a fixed cooperation rate. Comparing with the other two, MAB algorithms learn a more diverse cooperation rates across test cases. The line plot on the right confirms our understanding. The cooperation rate by the real humans (the black curve) tends to decline slowly from around 70% to around 40%. UCB1 and epsilon Greedy both captured the decaying properties, mimicking the strategy of the human actions. The prediction error analysis matches this intuition. The UCB1 and epsilon greedy (or MAB algorithms in general), appear to be best capturing human cooperation.

# 7    Clinical Evidences and Implications

Evidence has linked dopamine function to reinforcement learning via midbrain neurons and connections to the basal ganglia, limbic regions, and cortex. Neuron firing rates computationally represent reward magnitude, expectancy, and violations (prediction error) and other value-based signals [45], allowing an animal to update and maintain value expectations associated with particular states and actions. When functioning properly, this helps an animal develop a policy to maximize outcomes by approaching/choosing cues with higher expected value and avoiding cues associated with loss or punishment. This is similar to reinforcement learning widely used in computing and robotics [46], suggesting mechanistic overlap in humans and AI. Evidence of Q-learning and actor-critic models have been observed in spiking activity in midbrain dopamine neurons in primates [9] and in human striatum by blood-oxygen-level-dependent imaging (BOLD) [38].

The literature on the reward processing abnormalities in particular neurological and psychiatric disorders is quite extensive; below we summarize some of the recent developments in this fast-growing field. It is well-known that the neuromodulator dopamine plays a key role in reinforcement learning processes. Parkinson's disease (PD) patients, who have depleted dopamine in the basal ganglia, tend to have impaired performance on tasks that require learning from trial and error. For example, [17] demonstrate that off-medication PD patients are better at learning to avoid choices that lead to negative outcomes than they are at learning from positive outcomes, while dopamine medication typically used to treat PD symptoms reverses this bias. Alzheimer's disease (AD) is the most common cause of dementia in the elderly and, besides memory impairment, it is associated with a variable degree of executive function impairment and visuospatial impairment. As discussed in [40], AD patients have decreased pursuit of rewarding behaviors, including loss of appetite; these changes are often secondary to apathy, associated with diminished reward system activity. Moveover, poor performance on certain tasks is associated with memory impairments. Frontotemporal dementia (bvFTD) usually involves a progressive change in personality and behavior including disinhibition, apathy, eating changes, repetitive or compulsive behaviors, and loss of empathy [40], and it is hypothesized that those changes are associated with abnormalities in reward processing. For instance, alterations in eating habits with a preference for carbohydrate sweet rich foods and overeating in bvFTD patients can be associated with abnormally increased reward representation for food, or impairment in the negative (punishment) signal associated with fullness. Authors in [34] suggest that the strength of the association between a stimulus and the corresponding response is more susceptible to degradation in Attention-deficit/hyperactivity disorder (ADHD) patients, which suggests problems with storing the stimulus-response associations. Among other functions, storing the associations requires working memory capacity, which is often impaired in ADHD patients. [43] demonstrated that patients suffering from addictive behavior have heightened stimulus-response associations, resulting in enhanced reward-seeking behavior for the stimulus which generated such association. [47] suggested that chronic pain can elicit in a hypodopaminergic (low dopamine) state that impairs motivated behavior, resulting into a reduced drive in chronic pain patients to pursue the rewards. Reduced reward response may underlie a key system mediating the anhedonia and depression, which are common in chronic pain.

## 8   Discussion

The broader motivation of this work is to increase the two-way traffic between artificial intelligence and neuropsychiatry, in the hope that a deeper understanding of brain mechanisms revealed by how they function ("neuro") and dysfunction ("psychiatry") can provide for better AI models, and conversely AI can help to conceptualize the otherwise bewildering complexity of the brain.

The behavioral cloning results suggest that bandit algorithms (without context) are the best in term of fitting the human data, which open the hypothesis that human are not considering the context when they are playing the iterated prisoner's dilemma. This discovery proposes new modeling effort on human study in the bandit framework, and points to future experimental designs which incorporate these new parametric settings and control conditions. In particular, we propose that our approach may be relevant to study reward processing in different mental disorders, for which some mechanistic insights are available.

A body of recent literature has demonstrated that a spectrum of neurological and psychiatric disease symptoms are related to biases in learning from positive and negative feedback [35]. Studies in humans have shown that when reward signaling in the direct pathway is over-expressed, this may enhance state value and incur pathological reward-seeking behavior, like gambling or substance use. Conversely, enhanced aversive error signals result in dampened reward experience thereby causing symptoms like apathy, social withdrawal, fatigue, and depression. Both genetic predispositions and experiences during critical periods of development can predispose an individual to learn from positive or negative outcomes, making them more or less at risk for brain-based illnesses [20]. This highlight our need to understand how intelligent systems learn from rewards and punishments, and how experience sampling may impact reinforcement learning during influential training periods. Simulation results of the mental variants matches many of the clinical implications presented here, but also points to other complications from the social setting that deserve future investigation.

The approach proposed in the present manuscript, we hope, will contribute to expand and deepen the dialogue between AI and neuropsychiatry.

# 9    Conclusion

In this work, we explore the full spectrum of online learning agents: multi-armed bandits, contextual bandits and reinforcement learning. To quantitatively study their behaviors, we evaluate them based on a series of tournaments of iterated prisoner's dilemma. This allows us to analyze the dynamics of policies learned by multiple self-interested independent reward driven agents, where we observe that the contextual bandit is not performing well in the tournament, which means that considering the current situation to make decision is the worst in this kind of game. Basically we should either not care about the current situation or caring about more situations, but not just the current one. We have also studied the capacity of these algorithms to fit the human behavior. We observed that bandit algorithms (without context) are the best in term of fitting the human data, which opens the hypothesis that human are not considering the context when they are playing the IPD. Next steps include extending our evaluations to other sequential social dilemma environments with more complicated and mixed incentive structure, such as fruit Gathering game and Wolfpack hunting game [25,49], comparing these mechanistic decision making models with predictive modeling surrogate models [30,31], and building reinforcement learning-based recommendation systems that model properties of human decision making [27].

# References

1. Agrawal, S., Goyal, N.: Thompson sampling for contextual bandits with linear payoffs. In: ICML (3), pp. 127–135 (2013)
2. Andreoni, J., Miller, J..H.: Rational cooperation in the finitely repeated prisoner's dilemma: experimental evidence. Econ. J. **103**, 570–585 (1993)

3. Auer, P., Cesa-Bianchi, N., Fischer, P.: Finite-time analysis of the multiarmed bandit problem. Mach. Learn. **47**(2–3), 235–256 (2002)
4. Auer, P., Cesa-Bianchi, N., Freund, Y., Schapire, R..E.: The nonstochastic multi-armed bandit problem. SIAM J. Comput. **32**(1), 48–77 (2002)
5. Axelrod, R.: Effective choice in the prisoner's dilemma. J. Conflict Resolut. **24**, 3–25 (1980)
6. Axelrod, R., Hamilton, W..D.: The evolution of cooperation. Science **211**(4489), 1390–1396 (1981)
7. Balakrishnan, A., Bouneffouf, D., Mattei, N., Rossi, F.: Incorporating behavioral constraints in online AI systems. In: Proceedings of AAAI (2019)
8. Balakrishnan, A., Bouneffouf, D., Mattei, N., Rossi, F.: Using multi-armed bandits to learn ethical priorities for online ai systems. IBM Journal of Research and Development 63 (2019)
9. Bayer, H..M., Glimcher, P..W.: Midbrain dopamine neurons encode a quantitative reward prediction error signal. Neuron **47**(1), 129–141 (2005)
10. Bereby-Meyer, Y., Roth, A.E.: The speed of learning in noisy games: partial reinforcement and the sustainability of cooperation. Am. Econ. Rev. **96**(4), 1029–1042 (2006)
11. Beygelzimer, A., Langford, J., Li, L., Reyzin, L., Schapire, R.: Contextual bandit algorithms with supervised learning guarantees. In: AISTATS (2011)
12. Bó, P..D..: Cooperation under the shadow of the future: experimental evidence from infinitely repeated games. Am. Econ. Rev. **95**(5), 1591–1604 (2005)
13. Bouneffouf, D., Rish, I.: A survey on practical applications of multi-armed and contextual bandits. (2019). CoRR abs/ arXiv: 1904.10040
14. Bouneffouf, D., Rish, I., Cecchi, G.A.: Bandit models of human behavior: Reward processing in mental disorders. In: AGI. Springer (2017)
15. Capraro, V.: A model of human cooperation in social dilemmas. PloS one **8**(8), e72427 (2013)
16. Even-Dar, E., Mansour, Y.: Learning rates for q-learning. JMLR (2003)
17. Frank, M.J., Seeberger, L.C., O'reilly, R.C.: By carrot or by stick: cognitive reinforcement learning in parkinsonism. Science **306**(5703), 1940–1943 (2004)
18. Gupta, G.: Obedience-based multi-agent cooperation for sequential social dilemmas (2020)
19. Hasselt, H.V.: Double q-learning. In: NIPS (2010)
20. Holmes, A..J., Patrick, L..M.: The myth of optimality in clinical neuroscience. Trends Cognit. Sci. **22**(3), 241–257 (2018)
21. Johnson, A., Proctor, R.W.: Attention: Theory and Practice. Sage (2004)
22. Kies, M.: Finding best answers for the iterated prisoner's dilemma using improved q-learning. Available at SSRN 3556714 (2020)
23. Lai, T.L., Robbins, H.: Asymptotically efficient adaptive allocation rules. Adv. Appl. Math. **6**(1), 4–22 (1985)
24. Langford, J., Zhang, T.: The epoch-greedy algorithm for multi-armed bandits with side information. In: NIPS (2008)
25. Leibo, J.Z., Zambaldi, V., Lanctot, M., Marecki, J., Graepel, T.: Multi-agent reinforcement learning in sequential social dilemmas. arXiv preprint (2017)
26. Li, L., Chu, W., Langford, J., Wang, X.: Unbiased offline evaluation of contextual-bandit-based news article recommendation algorithms. In: WSDM (2011)
27. Lin, B.: Supervisorbot: Nlp-annotated real-time recommendations of psychotherapy treatment strategies with deep reinforcement learning. arXiv preprint (2022)
28. Lin, B., Bouneffouf, D., Cecchi, G.: Split q learning: reinforcement learning with two-stream rewards. In: Proceedings of the 28th IJCAI (2019)

29. Lin, B., Bouneffouf, D., Cecchi, G.: Unified models of human behavioral agents in bandits, contextual bandits, and RL. arXiv preprint arXiv:2005.04544 (2020)
30. Lin, B., Bouneffouf, D., Cecchi, G.: Predicting human decision making in psychological tasks with recurrent neural networks. PLoS ONE **17**(5), e0267907 (2022)
31. Lin, B., Bouneffouf, D., Cecchi, G.: Predicting human decision making with LSTM. In: 2022 International Joint Conference on Neural Networks (IJCNN) (2022)
32. Lin, B., Bouneffouf, D., Reinen, J., Rish, I., Cecchi, G.: A story of two streams: Reinforcement learning models from human behavior and neuropsychiatry. In: Proceedings of the 19th AAMAS, pp. 744–752 (2020)
33. Lin, B., Cecchi, G., Bouneffouf, D., Reinen, J., Rish, I.: Models of human behavioral agents in bandits, contextual bandits and RL. In: International Workshop on Human Brain and Artificial Intelligence, pp. 14–33. Springer (2021)
34. Luman, M., Van Meel, C..S., Oosterlaan, J., Sergeant, J..A., Geurts, H..M.: Does reward frequency or magnitude drive reinforcement-learning in attention-deficit/hyperactivity disorder? Psych. Res. **168**(3), 222–229 (2009)
35. Maia, T.V., Frank, M.J.: From reinforcement learning models to psychiatric and neurological disorders. Nat. Neurosci. **14**(2), 154–162 (2011)
36. Nay, J.J., Vorobeychik, Y.: Predicting human cooperation. PloS one **11**(5), e0155656 (2016)
37. Noothigattu, R., Bouneffouf, D., Mattei, N., Chandra, R., Madan, P., Varshney, K.R., Campbell, M., Singh, M., Rossi, F.: Teaching AI agents ethical values using reinforcement learning and policy orchestration. In: IJCAI, pp. 6377–6381 (2019)
38. O'Doherty, J., Dayan, P., Schultz, J., Deichmann, R., Friston, K., Dolan, R.J.: Dissociable roles of ventral and dorsal striatum in instrumental. Science **304**(5569), 452–454 (2004)
39. Park, H., Kim, K.J.: Active player modeling in the iterated prisoner's dilemma. Computational intelligence and neuroscience 2016 (2016)
40. Perry, D.C., Kramer, J.H.: Reward processing in neurodegenerative disease. Neurocase **21**(1), 120–133 (2015)
41. Press, W.H., Dyson, F.J.: Iterated prisoner's dilemma contains strategies that dominate any evolutionary opponent. PNAS **109**(26), 10409–10413 (2012)
42. Rapoport, A., Chammah, A.M., Orwant, C.J.: Prisoner's Dilemma: A Study in Conflict and Cooperation, vol. 165. University of Michigan Press, Ann Arbor (1965)
43. Redish, A.D., Jensen, S., Johnson, A., Kurth-Nelson, Z.: Reconciling reinforcement learning models with behavioral extinction and renewal: implications for addiction, relapse, and problem gambling. Psychol. Rev. **114**(3), 784 (2007)
44. Rummery, G.A., Niranjan, M.: On-line Q-learning Using Connectionist Systems, vol. 37. University of Cambridge, Cambridge, England (1994)
45. Schultz, W., Dayan, P., Montague, P.R.: A neural substrate of prediction and reward. Science **275**(5306), 1593–1599 (1997)
46. Sutton, R.S., Barto, A.G., et al.: Introduction to Reinforcement Learning. MIT Press, Cambridge (1998)
47. Taylor, A.M., Becker, S., Schweinhardt, P., Cahill, C.: Mesolimbic dopamine signaling in acute and chronic pain: implications for motivation, analgesia, and addiction. Pain **157**(6), 1194 (2016)
48. Thompson, W.: On the likelihood that one unknown probability exceeds another in view of the evidence of two samples. Biometrika **25**(3–4), 285–294 (1933)
49. Wang, W., Hao, J., Wang, Y., Taylor, M.: Towards cooperation in sequential prisoner's dilemmas: a deep multiagent reinforcement learning approach. arXiv preprint (2018)

# Optimizing Exploration-Exploitation Trade-off in Continuous Action Spaces via Q-ensemble

Wei Xue, Haihong Zhang, Xueyu Wei, Tao Tao$^{(\boxtimes)}$, and Xue Li

School of Computer Science and Technology, Anhui University of Technology,
Maanshan 243032, China
{xuewei,taotao}@ahut.edu.cn, {haihong.zhang,xueyu.wei}@foxmail.com,
lixue_angel@163.com

**Abstract.** Ensemble-based reinforcement learning methods that combine multiple models of Q-function (i.e., value function) or policy have recently achieved excellent performance on continuous action space benchmarks. However, many ensemble methods only focus on one of exploration or exploitation for improvement, and the computational efficiency and ensemble diversity are also ignored. To mitigate these issues, in this paper, we propose a Q-ensemble-based exploration-exploitation trade-off method (QE3). Specifically, QE3 integrates two key ingredients based on Q-ensemble. Firstly, to improve exploration as well as ensemble diversity, we use an upper-confidence bound and a diversity regularizer in continuous action space, which encourages the agent to visit novel state-action pairs and enforces the diversity between Q-functions. Secondly, to improve exploitation for balancing exploration, we propose the selective repeat update, which improves the sample efficiency and mitigates the error propagation caused by high variance data. Empirical results show that QE3 has better performance than other baselines, and also show that our reuse data trick and the small ensemble of Q-functions make QE3 more computationally efficient than similar methods. Ablation study further shows its ability to balance the exploration and exploitation in continuous action space.

**Keywords:** Reinforcement learning · Continuous action spaces · Exploration-exploitation trade-off · Ensemble method

## 1 Introduction

Model-free reinforcement learning (RL) has been applied to many decision problems with high-dimensional state and action spaces, such as video game benchmarks [15], robotic manipulation [12], etc. But the performance gains of traditional model-free RL methods usually come at the cost of sample efficiency [11]. RL methods generally require millions of training samples to solve a task [8,14], the poor sample efficiency seriously limits the applicability of RL methods. Recently, some of the off-policy methods have been proposed to improve

© The Author(s), under exclusive license to Springer Nature Switzerland AG 2022
S. Khanna et al. (Eds.): PRICAI 2022, LNCS 13631, pp. 148–160, 2022.
https://doi.org/10.1007/978-3-031-20868-3_11

sample efficiency by reusing past transitions [3,7]. However, these algorithms have a few shortcomings:

- The maximization of value estimation leads to an estimation bias and will be further exaggerated [7].
- Difficult balance between exploration and exploitation causes convergence to the sub-optimal policy [5,17].

To mitigate these issues, many ensemble-based methods have been proposed, which combine multiple models of the Q-functions to achieve excellent performance. In [6], Chen et al. proposed a randomized ensembled double Q-learning (REDQ) method. REDQ achieves high sample efficiency by using high update-to-data (UTD) ratio, and uses a large ensemble of Q-functions to suppress the estimation bias induced by using of high UTD ratio. In [16], Osband et al. proposed Bootstrapped DQN, which leverages an ensemble of Q-functions for more effective exploration. Bootstrapped DQN selects a Q-function uniformly at random at the beginning of an episode and follows the same exploration policy for the whole episode, which enables the agent to conduct temporally-extended exploration. However, many ensemble methods are solely focused on improving one of the exploration or exploitation. Besides, the reuse of past transitions and the use of large ensembles cause computational inefficiencies, and the consistent update way leads to a lack of diversity among ensembles. Namely, if the Q-functions in the ensembles converge to a common representation, the performance of these approaches significantly degrades [19].

Motivated by these issues, we propose an exploration-exploitation trade-off method based on Q-ensemble. Firstly, we define an upper-confidence bound as the loss of actor (i.e., policy network) based on the estimates of Q-functions, and then define a diversity regularizer consisting of Q-functions parameters similar to Hassam et al. [19], finally maximize them using gradient ascent, which encourages the agent to visit novel state-action pairs and enforces the diversity between Q-functions. Secondly, for effective exploitation, we update the parameters multiple times using the same batch of data. In addition, we also reduce the usage priority of high variance data in subsequent updates after the first round.

The main contributions of this paper are summarized as follows:

- We propose an ensemble-based exploration strategy. Based on ensemble method, we extend the upper-confidence bound method applied in traditional RL to continuous control tasks. In addition, we use a diversity regularizer to enforce the diversity between Q-functions. We show that exploration is thus improved.
- We propose an exploitation strategy called selective repeat update. Based on uncertainty estimates from ensembles (i.e., variance), we reduce the priority of high variance data and then repeatedly update the parameters to improve sample efficiency. We show that exploitation is thus improved.
- Experiments on the continuous control tasks show that our proposed method promotes sufficiently training Q-ensemble within a few interactions, which achieves better performance than other baselines. Additionally, ablation study shows the effectiveness of the trade-off between exploration and exploitation.

## 2  Related Work

**Exploration Strategy in RL.** To balance exploration and exploitation, SAC [8] based on the maximum entropy framework is proposed, which avoids policies from falling into local optimums prematurely and to encourage agents to explore the state space more sufficiently. Further, Kumar et al. proposed DisCor [13], which substantially improves SAC by reweighting the bellman backup based on estimated cumulative bellman errors, especially in challenging settings, such as multi-task RL and learning from noisy rewards. In ensemble methods, because the aleatoric uncertainty can be measured through distributional value functions [2,16], Chen et al. [5] successfully invokes upper-confidence bound, a traditional RL method used for exploration, into DRL. However, Chen's method is only applicable to the discrete action space, our method extends this strategy to continuous action spaces.

**Sample Efficiency in RL.** For effective exploitation, one way is to improve the sample efficiency. The off-policy algorithms (e.g., TD3) that provide sample efficient learning by reusing past experience [1,7,8]. The model-based method MBPO [10] uses a high UTD ratio to achieve significantly higher sample efficiency, the UTD ratio is defined as the number of updates taken by the Q-function compared to the number of actual interactions with the environment. REDQ [6] introduces high UTD ratios to model-free RL. However, high UTD ratio methods leave room for improvement in terms of computational efficiency. Our method reuses data similar to the high UTD ratio method, but with better computational efficiency.

## 3  Preliminaries

In this section, we first introduce RL basics. Additionally, since we use the twin delayed deep deterministic policy gradient algorithm (TD3) to demonstrate the effectiveness of our proposed method, we also introduce TD3-related knowledge afterwards.

**RL** considers an agent as a infinite-horizon Markov Decision Process (MDP) defined as a five element tuple $(S, A, P, R, \gamma)$, where the state space $S$ and the action space $A$ are continuous, $P : S \times A \times S \rightarrow R$ are the state-action transition probabilities, $R : S \times A \rightarrow R$ denotes the reward function, and $\gamma \in [0, 1]$ is the discount factor. At each time-step $t$ the agent observes the state of the environment $s_t \in S$ and selects an action $a_t \in A$ based on its policy $\pi$. The environment returns a reward $r_t$ and the agent transitions to the next state $s_{t+1}$ according to the transition probabilities $P$. The return $R_t = r_{t+1} + \gamma r_{t+2} + \cdots + \gamma^n r_{t+n}$ is the expectation of the discounted sum of future rewards. The goal of the agent is to learn a policy $\pi$ that maximizes the expected return.

**TD3** [7] is an improvement of the DDPG (Deep Deterministic Policy Gradient algorithm) [20], in which three key improvements are used: (a) clipped double Q-learning, which allows the TD3 algorithm learns two Q-functions independently and uses the smaller of the two Q-values to construct the td-target for critic learning to alleviate critic's overestimation; (b) delayed policy updates, which delays policy updates until the value error is small enough so that the variance can be reduced; (c) target policy smoothing, which add noise to the actions when constructing the td-target, will have the benefit of smoothing the value estimate. The critic network updates its parameters by minimizing the following objective:

$$\mathcal{L}_{\text{critic}}(\tau_t, \theta) = \mathbb{E}_{\tau_t \sim \mathcal{B}} \left[ \mathcal{L}_Q (\tau_t, \theta) \right], \tag{1}$$

$$\mathcal{L}_Q (\tau_t, \theta_i) = (y_t - Q_{\theta_i}(s_t, a_t))^2, \tag{2}$$

where $\tau = (s_t, a_t, r_t, s_{t+1})$ is a transition, $\mathcal{B}$ is a replay buffer, $\phi$ and $\theta_i$ are the parameters of the actor and critic, and $\phi'$ and $\theta_i'$ are the parameters of the actor target network and critic target network, with $i = 1, 2$. Actor is updated by maximizing the following objective:

$$\mathcal{L}_{\text{actor}}(\tau_t, \phi) = \mathbb{E}_{\tau_t \sim \mathcal{B}} \left[ Q_{\theta_1} (s_t, \pi_\phi (s_t)) \right] \tag{3}$$

The three target network parameters are updated as follows:

$$\begin{cases} \theta_i' \leftarrow \rho\theta_i + (1 - \rho)\theta_i' \\ \phi' \leftarrow \rho\phi + (1 - \rho)\phi' \\ \rho \leqslant 1 \end{cases}$$

## 4   Proposed Method

In this section, we introduce the proposed algorithm QE3, which is generic and can be used in conjunction with most off-policy algorithms. QE3 integrates two key ingredients based on estimates from Q-ensemble: we first propose an ensemble-based exploration strategy in Sect. 4.1 (see Fig. 1); we then propose the selective repeat update method in Sect. 4.2 (see Fig. 2).

### 4.1   Ensemble-Based Exploration Strategy

To explore effectively, Chen et al. [5] proposes an upper-confidence bound exploration strategy using Q-ensemble. In this strategy, agents are optimistic and take actions with high uncertainty (i.e., standard deviation). Specifically, by first defining an ensemble of $N$ Q-functions, i.e., $\{Q_{\theta_i}\}_{i=1}^N$, where $\theta_i$ denote the parameters of the $i$-th Q-function. Then construct a upper-confidence bound by adding the empirical standard deviation $Q_{std} (s_t, a)$ of $Q_{\theta_i}(s_t, a)_{i=1}^N$ to the empirical mean $Q_{mean} (s_t, a)$ of $Q_{\theta_i}(s_t, a)_{i=1}^N$. Finally, the agent chooses the action that maximizes this upper-confidence bound:

$$a_t = \max_a \{Q_{\text{mean}} (s_t, a) + \lambda Q_{std} (s_t, a)\}, \tag{4}$$

where $\lambda \in \mathbb{R}^+$ is a hyper-parameter, and $Q_{mean} (s_t, a)$ reflect to whether the Q-functions overestimate or underestimate that state-action pairs, and $Q_{std} (s_t, a)$

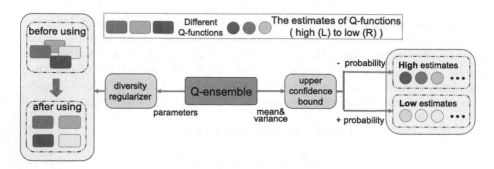

**Fig. 1.** Overview of ensemble-based exploration strategy. The diversity regularizer (left part) keeps a degree of diversity between Q-functions. The upper-confidence bound (right part) encourages exploration by visiting non-optimal but high-uncertainty samples.

reflect to whether the Q-functions estimate that unseen state-action pairs uniformly (i.e., uncertainty).

Chen et al. extends the intuition of upper-confidence bound method to the RL setting. However, their method requires traversing all actions to find the one with the highest upper-confidence bound value, so it is not straightforward to apply upper-confidence bound method to continuous action spaces. To solve this problem, we propose an approximate framework, which first uses the upper-confidence bound as the loss of actor, and then uses gradient ascent to maximize it. In addition, to prevent ensembles from falling back to a single network, we add a diversity regularizer to the loss of the critic, as a way to maximize representation diversity between the networks of the ensemble.

Specifically, first we construct a upper-confidence bound using the estimates from Q-ensemble:

$$Q_{\mathrm{mean}}\left(s_t, a\right) + \lambda Q_{std}\left(s_t, a\right), with\ a = \pi_\phi\left(s_t\right), \tag{5}$$

Secondly, we construct a diversity regularizer using the parameters of Q-ensemble:

$$\sigma\left(\bar{\theta} \cdot \theta_i\right) = \sum_i^n \left\|\bar{\theta} - \theta_i\right\|^2 \tag{6}$$

where $\theta_i$ is the $i$-th neural network's parameters, $\bar{\theta}$ is the mean of all the parameters. Next, substituting Eq. 5 into Eq. 3 and adding Eq. 6 to Eq. 1, we obtain two loss functions as follows:

$$\mathcal{L}_{actor}\left(\tau_t, \phi\right) = \mathbb{E}_{\tau_t \sim \mathcal{B}}\left[Q_{\mathrm{mean}}\left(s_t, \pi_\phi\left(s_t\right)\right) + \lambda Q_{std}\left(s_t, \pi_\phi\left(s_t\right)\right)\right], \tag{7}$$

$$\mathcal{L}_{\mathrm{critic}}(\tau_t, \theta) = \mathbb{E}_{\tau_t \sim \mathcal{B}}\left[\left(y_t - Q_{\theta_i}\left(s_t, a_t\right)\right)^2 - \delta\sigma\left(\bar{\theta} \cdot \theta_i\right)\right], \tag{8}$$

where $\phi$ denote the parameters of the policy, $\delta$ is the regularization weight. Finally, the actor generates deterministic action samples after maximizing Eqs. 5 and 6 by gradient ascent. In this way, our approach not only extends the upper-confidence bound method to continuous control, but also maintains sufficient diversity between the Q-functions in the ensembles.

## 4.2   Selective Repeat Update

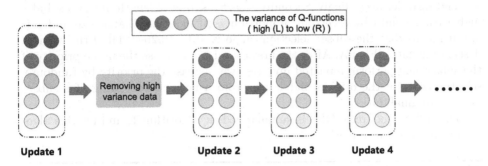

**Fig. 2.** Overview of selective repeat update. After the first round of updates, we lowered the priority of high variance data in subsequent updates.

For effective exploitation, one way is to improve the sample efficiency. REDQ [6] uses a high UTD ratio to achieve significantly higher sample efficiency. A high UTD ratio means sampling $T$ batches of data in single time-step and subsequently updating the parameters $T$ times. However, the use of a high UTD ratio promotes estimation bias in value estimation. Due to estimation bias, this accumulated error can cause arbitrarily bad states to be estimated as high value, resulting in suboptimal policy updates and divergent behavior [7,13]. So REDQ uses a large Q-function ensemble to suppress the estimation bias. Since the high UTD ratio and the large ensemble, REDQ is less computationally efficient than other model-free algorithms [9]. However, the computational efficiency is important in the application of RL algorithms to lightweight devices.

To mitigate these issues, we propose an exploitation strategy called selective repeat update, which improves the sample efficiency and also takes into account the computational efficiency. Unlike the high UTD method, in our method, sampling one batch of data in single time-step and subsequently updating the parameters $T$ times. This way of reusing data can provide significant runtime savings compared to high UTD ratio methods. Similar to the high UTD ratio methods, reusing data can cause estimation bias. To handle this issue, we propose to reduce the priority of high variance data in subsequent updates after the first update. In addition, in practical implementations we also reduce the priority of low variance data that have been adequately trained before.

The main reason why estimation bias can be harmful to the algorithm comes from the non-uniform estimation of high variance data. As mentioned in Sect. 4.1, $Q_{std}(s_t, a)$ can reflect whether the Q-functions estimate that unseen data uniformly, so we use the value of $Q_{std}(s_t, a)$ to label each data and reduce the priority of high variance data from the training samples that subsequently participate in the update. Thus, error propagation is mitigated by reducing the effect of high variance data in the repeated update process. So we do not need to use a large Q-function ensemble to suppress the estimation bias as REDQ does. To summarize the above, due to our reuse data trick and the small ensemble of Q-functions make QE3 more computationally efficient than high UTD ratio methods while achieving comparable performance.

The implementation details of selective repeat update are as follows: We first sample a batch of data, calculate their variances (i.e., $Q_{std}$) and sort them in descending order accordingly. Secondly, select a subset of length $m$ that excludes high variance data by a certain proportion $p$ (if $m$ is 0.25*batch-size and $p$ is 0.1, it means that the subset selection range is [0.1 - (0.25+0.1)] of the original descending data). Finally, After the first round, we increase the usage priority of the subset and perform repeated updates (we increase the priority by randomly selecting data of the original batch size from a new set consisting of a subset and the original data).

The full procedure of QE3 is summarized in Algorithm 1, and for this algorithm, we have two remarks.

---

**Algorithm 1 : QE3**

---

1: Initialize policy parameters $\phi$, $N$ Q-function parameters $\theta_i$, $i{=}1,...,N$, empty replay buffer $\mathcal{D}$. Set target parameters $\theta'_i \leftarrow \theta_i$, for $i{=}1,2,...,N$
2: **repeat**
3:     Take one action $a_t \sim \pi_\theta (\cdot \mid s_t)$. Observe reward $r_t$, new state $s_{t+1}$.
4:     Add data to buffer: $\mathcal{D} \leftarrow \mathcal{D} \cup \{(s_t, a_t, r_t, s_{t+1})\}$
5:     Sample a mini-batch: $\mathcal{B} = \{(s, a, r, s')\}$ from $\mathcal{B}$
6:     **for** $i = 1, 2, ... , T$ **do**
7:         Compute the Q target $y$ (same for all of the $N$ Q-functions)

$$y = r + \gamma \min_{i=1,2} Q_{\theta'_i} (s', \tilde{a}_t), \quad \tilde{a}_t = \pi_{\phi'} (s') + \varepsilon'$$

8:         Compute the diversity regularizer

$$\sigma (\bar{\theta} \cdot \theta_i) = \sum_i^n \left\| \bar{\theta} - \theta_i \right\|^2$$

9:         Update $\theta_i$ ($i = 1,...,N$) with gradient descent using

$$\nabla_\theta \frac{1}{|\mathcal{B}|} \sum_{(s,a,r,s')\in\mathcal{B}} ((Q_{\theta i}(s,a) - y)^2 - \delta\sigma (\bar{\theta} \cdot \theta_i)))$$

10:         Update target networks $\theta'_i$ ($i = 1,...,N$)
11:         Update $\phi$ with gradient ascent using

$$\nabla_\theta \frac{1}{|\mathcal{B}|} \sum_{s\in\mathcal{B}} (Q_{\text{mean}} (s, \pi_\phi (s)) + \lambda Q_{std} (s, \pi_\phi (s)))$$

12:         **if** $i = 1$ **then**
13:             Select a subset $\mathcal{B}'$ of mini-batch $\mathcal{B}$ that excludes high variance data.
14:             Increase the usage priority of subset $\mathcal{B}'$ in subsequent parameter updates.
15:         **end if**
16:     **end for**
17: **until** max time step

---

**Remark 1.** The ensemble-based exploration strategy is in lines 8 to 9 and 11. The selective repeat update includes the filtered data performed in lines 12–15 and the repeated update in lines 6–16.

**Remark 2.** Both the subset length $m$ and the screening high variance proportion $p$ in selective repeated updates are hyper-parameters, more details are in the parameter settings.

# 5 Experiments

We empirically examine the performance of QE3 on seven locomotion tasks from the OpenAI Gym library [4,21]: HalfCheetah, Ant, Hopper, Humanoid, Walker2d, LunarLanderContinuous, and BipedalWalker. In seven challenging tasks, we apply our method to TD3 [7] and compare the existing excellent model-free deep RL algorithms, including two state-of-the-art model-free RL methods, TD3 and SAC [8]; PPO [18], a popular on-policy deep RL algorithms; DisCor [13], which improves SAC by reweighting the bellman backup based on estimated cumulative bellman errors; Dr.Q [9], which is a variant of REDQ that uses a small ensemble of dropout Q-functions. To make fair comparisons on each algorithm, we repeat the experiment five times for each algorithm in all tasks to exclude the effect of randomness on the comparison results.

## 5.1 Parameter Settings

All baselines used for the comparison experiments using the publicly released implementation repository without any modifications on hyper-parameters and architectures. For our method, the max time step is chosen from $[3 \cdot 10^5, 4 \cdot 10^5, 8 \cdot 10^5]$, the hyper-parameter $\lambda$ controls the degrees of exploration is chosen from $[0.1, 0.5, 1]$, the regularization weight $\delta$ is chosen from $[10^{-5}, 10^{-6}, 10^{-7}]$, the hyper-parameter $T$ is the number of repeated updates of the parameter chosen from $[2,3,5]$, the subset length $m$ is chosen from $[0.25*\text{batch-size}, 0.5*\text{batch-size}]$, the proportion $p$ of excluded high variance data is chosen from $[0.125, 0.25]$. Figure 3 shows that continuing to increase the ensemble size after $N{=}6$ does not significantly improve performance, so we choose $N{=}6$ for all experiments.

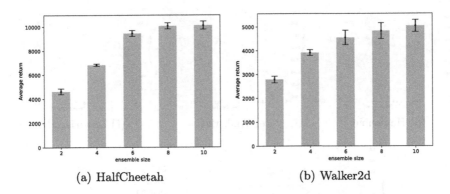

      (a) HalfCheetah              (b) Walker2d

**Fig. 3.** Comparison of the average returns of QE3 with varying values of ensemble size on the mujoco environment.

## 5.2 Comparative Evaluation

Figure 4 demonstrates the training curves of QE3, Dr.Q, DisCor, SAC, TD3 and PPO. We can observe that QE3 consistently improves the performance of TD3 across all tasks and outperforms other methods. Table 1 records the max

average returns over five trials for all six algorithms on each task, showing that
QE3 is still the best. We can observe that QE3 is more sample efficient than
other methods, because of using the same number of limited samples, our agents
are more sufficiently trained.

**Table 1.** Max Average Return over five trials. The second column indicates the
employed timesteps of the algorithms on each task.

| Environment | Timesteps | QE3 | Dr.Q | Discor | SAC | TD3 | PPO |
|---|---|---|---|---|---|---|---|
| HalfCheetah | $4 \cdot 10^5$ | **9479** | 6633 | 6766 | 5609 | 5068 | 406 |
| Ant | $3 \cdot 10^5$ | **4015** | 2544 | 1975 | 2157 | 841 | 48 |
| Hopper | $3 \cdot 10^5$ | **3655** | 3279 | 3399 | 3173 | 3007 | 3116 |
| Humanoid | $1 \cdot 10^5$ | **5360** | 5077 | 4877 | 5103 | 4833 | 5078 |
| Walker2d | $3 \cdot 10^5$ | **4086** | 2663 | 2964 | 3119 | 1830 | 2113 |
| LunarLander | $3 \cdot 10^5$ | **592** | 244 | 177 | 113 | $-122$ | 55 |
| BipedalWalker | $3 \cdot 10^5$ | **509** | 110 | 165 | $-25$ | $-111$ | 142 |

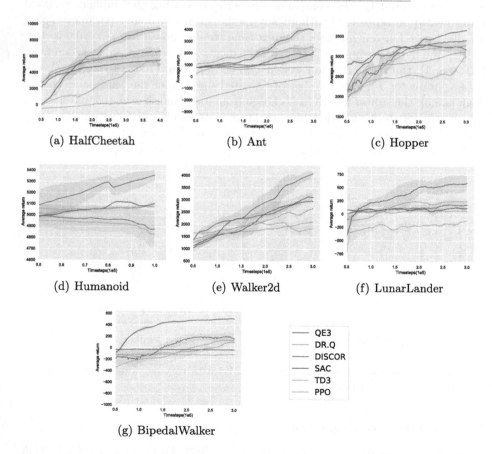

(a) HalfCheetah          (b) Ant          (c) Hopper

(d) Humanoid          (e) Walker2d          (f) LunarLander

(g) BipedalWalker

**Fig. 4.** Comparison of the training curves averaged over five trials for QE3, Dr.Q,
DisCor, SAC, TD3, and PPO on seven locomotion tasks.

**Table 2.** Average running times (in seconds) required for executing overall loop (e.g., lines 2–16 in Algorithm 1).

| Method | Cheetah | Ant | Hopper | Humanoid | Walker | LunarLander | BipedalWalker |
|--------|---------|-----|--------|----------|--------|-------------|---------------|
| **QE3** | **17.43** | **18.33** | **17.23** | **19.07** | **33.67** | **43.8** | **42.4** |
| Dr.Q | 68.15 | 68.85 | 50.9 | 41.9 | 57.6 | 104 | 97.9 |

Moreover, Fig. 4 and Table 2 show that QE3 is more computationally efficient than the similar method Dr.Q. QE3 and Dr.Q have a common feature that increases the frequency of parameter updates in single time-step. Dr.Q increases the frequency by a high UTD ratio, while we use selective repeat update. For fair comparisons, we use the same update frequency as Dr.Q and the same ensemble size, the results show that QE3 outperforms Dr.Q across all the tasks, as observed in Fig. 4. Table 2 records the running times of QE3 and Dr.Q at a single time-step. As expected, Dr.Q are much slower than our method.

## 5.3 Ablation Study

**Effects of Ensemble-Based Exploration Strategy.** For our proposed ensemble based exploration strategy, briefly called EES. We examine the effectiveness of EES by comparing QE3 with QE3 without EES on four locomotion tasks. We

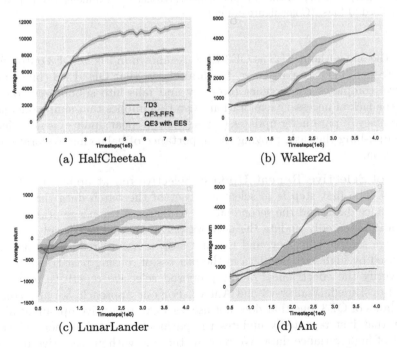

(a) HalfCheetah

(b) Walker2d

(c) LunarLander

(d) Ant

**Fig. 5.** Learning curves of QE3 with EES (red color) and without EES (QE3-EES, blue color) on four mujoco tasks. (Color figure online)

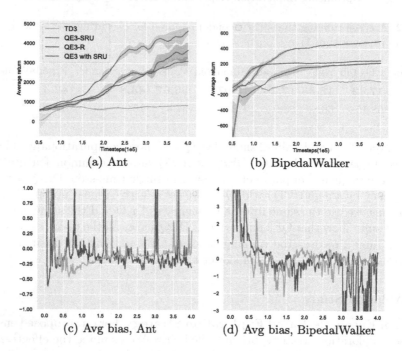

**Fig. 6.** (a), (b) Learning curves of QE3 with SRU (red color), QE3-R (blue color) and QE3-SRU (purple color) on the Ant and BipedalWalker environment. (c), (d) Average of normalized Q bias. (Color figure online)

refer to the one without EES as QE3-EES. As shown in Fig. 5, QE3 outperforms QE3-EES and TD3. In particular, Fig. 5(a) shows that QE3-EES (blue curve), the curve completes convergence too early and falls into suboptimal solutions due to the lack of necessary exploration. Also this implies that simply increasing the frequency of parameter updates (e.g. selective repeat update) is not effective in accomplishing the task, proving the importance of balancing exploration and exploitation.

**Effects of Selective Repeat Update.** Selective repeat update involves two key steps. The first step is to select a subset of the batch data that excludes high variance data, and the second step is to increase the usage priority of this subset and repeatedly update the network parameters. The second step serves to improve sample efficiency, and the first step serves to reduce the impact of bias caused by high variance data in the process of reusing past transitions.

To verify the effectiveness of the proposed selective repetitive update, we evaluate on BipedalWalker-v3 and Ant-v2. For our approach, we also consider two variants of QE3, one that does not use selective repetitive update at all and another that just repeatedly updates the parameters but does not reduce the priority of high variance data. We refer to the one without selective repetitive update as QE3-SRU, which just repeats updates as QE3-R. Finally, the original TD3 is then added for comparison.

Figure 6(a) and Fig. 6(b) show the learning curves of all methods on two tasks over 3 trials. QE3-R (blue curve) obviously outperforms QE3-SRU (purple curve) and the original TD3 (yellow curve), which illustrates that increased reuse of past data on top of off-policy can continue to improve sample efficiency. Additionally, we can observe that the QE3 with SRU (red curve) works better than QE3-R (blue curve), which indicates that high variance data has a negative impact on the algorithm performance.

Further, to explain why QE3 can perform better than QE3-R, we introduce average of the normalized estimation bias of Q-functions for comparison, which represents the difference between the estimation and the actual return. Figure 6(c) and Fig. 6(d) shows the average bias for QE3 and QE3-R. We observe in Fig. 6(c) that at the beginning the curve of QE3-R is closer to zero compared to QE3, and after 150k time steps the opposite happens. This explains very well the situation in Fig. 6(a), it can be observed that the curves of QE3 and QE3-R are overlapped at the beginning, after 150k time steps, the gap gradually becomes obvious, which disclosing the effectiveness of selective repeat update.

# 6  Conclusion

In this paper, we proposed a new ensemble RL method called QE3, which utilizes uncertain estimates of Q-ensemble to achieve a trade-off between exploration and exploitation. We first extended the upper-confidence bound method applied in traditional RL to continuous control tasks to improve exploration, and enlarged the gap between parameters to increase ensemble diversity. And then we reduced the priority of high variance data in the data reuse process to increase exploitation. Empirical results show the effectiveness of the proposed method to balance the exploration and exploitation in continuous action space. In the future, we will try to implement automatic tuning of hyper-parameters in QE3, and hope that QE3 can be applied to other relevant fields, such as offline RL and model-based methods.

**Acknowledgements.** This work was supported in part by the National Natural Science Foundation of China (Grant Nos. 61806004, 12071104 and 62172003), the Anhui Provincial Natural Science Foundation (Grant Nos. 2208085MF168 and 2008085QF305), and the Natural Science Foundation of Zhejiang Province, China (Grant No. LD19A010002).

# References

1. Amos, B., Stanton, S., Yarats, D., Wilson, A.G.: On the model-based stochastic value gradient for continuous reinforcement learning. In: Learning for Dynamics and Control, pp. 6–20 (2021)
2. Bai, C., et al.: Principled exploration via optimistic bootstrapping and backward induction. In: International Conference on Machine Learning, pp. 577–587 (2021)
3. Barth-Maron, G., et al.: Distributed distributional deterministic policy gradients. arXiv preprint arXiv:1804.08617 (2018)

4. Brockman, G., et al.: Openai gym. arXiv preprint arXiv:1606.01540 (2016)
5. Chen, R.Y., Sidor, S., Abbeel, P., Schulman, J.: Ucb exploration via q-ensembles. arXiv preprint arXiv:1706.01502 (2017)
6. Chen, X., Wang, C., Zhou, Z., Ross, K.: Randomized ensembled double q-learning: Learning fast without a model. In: International Conference on Learning Representations (2021)
7. Fujimoto, S., Hoof, H., Meger, D.: Addressing function approximation error in actor-critic methods. In: International Conference on Machine Learning, pp. 1582–1591 (2018)
8. Haarnoja, T., Zhou, A., Abbeel, P., Levine, S.: Soft actor-critic: off-policy maximum entropy deep reinforcement learning with a stochastic actor. In: International Conference on Machine Learning, pp. 1856–1865 (2018)
9. Hiraoka, T., Imagawa, T., Hashimoto, T., Onishi, T., Tsuruoka, Y.: Dropout q-functions for doubly efficient reinforcement learning. arXiv preprint arXiv:2110.02034 (2021)
10. Janner, M., Fu, J., Zhang, M., Levine, S.: When to trust your model: Model-based policy optimization. In: Advances in Neural Information Processing Systems, pp. 12498–12509 (2019)
11. Kaiser, L., et al.: Model-based reinforcement learning for atari. arXiv preprint arXiv:1903.00374 (2019)
12. Kober, J., Bagnell, J.A., Peters, J.: Reinforcement learning in robotics: a survey. Int. J. Robot. Res. **32**(11), 1238–1274 (2013)
13. Kumar, A., Gupta, A., Levine, S.: Discor: corrective feedback in reinforcement learning via distribution correction. Adv. Neural. Inf. Process. Syst. **33**, 18560–18572 (2020)
14. Mendonca, R., Gupta, A., Kralev, R., Abbeel, P., Levine, S., Finn, C.: Guided meta-policy search. In: Advances in Neural Information Processing Systems, pp. 9653–9664 (2019)
15. Mnih, V., et al.: Playing atari with deep reinforcement learning. arXiv preprint arXiv:1312.5602 (2013)
16. Osband, I., Blundell, C., Pritzel, A., Van Roy, B.: Deep exploration via bootstrapped dqn. In: Advances in Neural Information Processing Systems, pp. 4026–4034 (2016)
17. Osband, I., Van Roy, B., Wen, Z.: Generalization and exploration via randomized value functions. In: International Conference on Machine Learning, pp. 2377–2386 (2016)
18. Schulman, J., Wolski, F., Dhariwal, P., Radford, A., Klimov, O.: Proximal policy optimization algorithms. arXiv preprint arXiv:1707.06347 (2017)
19. Sheikh, H.U., Phielipp, M., Bölöni, L.: Maximizing ensemble diversity in deep q-learning. arXiv preprint arXiv:2006.13823 (2020)
20. Silver, D., Lever, G., Heess, N., Degris, T., Wierstra, D., Riedmiller, M.: Deterministic policy gradient algorithms. In: International Conference on Machine Learning, pp. 387–395 (2014)
21. Todorov, E., Erez, T., Tassa, Y.: Mujoco: a physics engine for model-based control. In: 2012 IEEE/RSJ International Conference on Intelligent Robots and Systems, pp. 5026–5033 (2012)

# Hidden Information General Game Playing with Deep Learning and Search

Zachary Partridge[ID] and Michael Thielscher[✉][ID]

UNSW Australia, Sydney, Australia
{z.partridge,mit}@unsw.edu.au

**Abstract.** General Game Playing agents are capable of learning to play games they have never seen before, merely by looking at a formal description of the rules of a game. Recent developments in deep learning have influenced the way state-of-the-art AI systems can learn to play games with perfect information like Chess and Go. This development is popularised by the success of AlphaZero and was subsequently generalised to arbitrary games describable in the general Game Description Language, GDL. Many real-world problems, however, are non-deterministic and involve actors with concealed information, or events with probabilistic outcomes. We describe a framework and system for General Game Playing with self-play reinforcement learning and search for hidden-information games, which can be applied to any game describable in the extended Game Description Language for imperfect-information games, GDL-II.

**Keywords:** General game playing · Reinforcement learning · Imperfect information

## 1 Introduction

The field of Artificial Intelligence has been around almost as long as computers have existed, and the development of algorithms to play games has been central to AI development. Games provide a great testbed for developing and measuring the success of an algorithm which could eventually be deployed into the real world as they can possess the same core challenges without the noise [19]. As technology has been improving, humans are surpassed in more and more games: AlphaGo in the game of Go [19], Pluribus in six player poker [3], and AlphaStar in Starcraft 2 [22].

These are very impressive achievements for AI, but the algorithms are specialised: they cannot play any of the other games at even a beginner level. Whilst most AI algorithms are built for a singular purpose, the field of general game playing (GGP) attempts to broaden this concept. In the general game playing setting, an agent should be able to solve any problem (play any game) that is given to it in a formal game description language (GDL). Such an agent may not be as strong as an agent that was specifically designed for a single game but makes up for it in its generalisability. AlphaZero (a successor to AlphaGo) was able to achieve state of the art performance across multiple games (Go, Chess

© The Author(s), under exclusive license to Springer Nature Switzerland AG 2022
S. Khanna et al. (Eds.): PRICAI 2022, LNCS 13631, pp. 161–172, 2022.
https://doi.org/10.1007/978-3-031-20868-3_12

and Shogi) [20] indicating its potential for GGP. Consequently, AlphaZero has recently been further generalised to learn to play any game described by GDL, not just the two-player, turn-based games that AlphaZero could play [11]. However, GDL only describes deterministic games with perfect information, meaning that there are still a large class of hidden information games that cannot be solved with the current methods.

A successor to GDL (GDL-II) was developed to describe a larger, more general class of games that include hidden information and stochastic events [21]. Some real world problems such as auctions, network traffic, cybersecurity, pricing, negotiations and politics are all part of this wider class of imperfect information scenarios, and such games and are quite difficult to solve for traditional algorithms. There has been little research done into applying deep reinforcement learning to hidden information games and just one recent work Player of Games [16] that applies this to a range of games. Player of Games incorporates some game specific knowledge, e.g. poker bet size abstractions and game specific network architectural designs. Also, all information states per public state must be enumerated, limiting the approach to games with small action space.

In this paper, we address these limitations and generalise the approach further by developing a method and system that can successfully learn to play hidden information games described in GDL-II with the help of the recently developed technique of recursive belief-based learning (ReBeL) [2]. A first experimental evaluation shows that our system can even outperform handcrafted algorithms in some games.

## 2   Background

### 2.1   General Game Playing

State of the art in General Game Playing is revealed by the International General Game Playing competition, which was run from 2005 to 2016, where teams submitted algorithms that would compete in a set of unseen games. For each game, the rules are described to the players in the standard Game Description Language, and players are given a fixed amount of time to prepare for the game (in the order of minutes). At each step of the game, the game manager sends a play message to each of the players describing how everyone has played on the last turn. The players then have a fixed time limit to respond with their moves for the next turn. This is continued until the end of the game and the players are rewarded for how well they performed [9].

Multiple approaches can be used for GGP. Over time they improve as would be expected, and as more research is put into a new technique, it can start to dominate the leaderboard. Initially, the prevailing technique was Minimax with a heuristic function for evaluating leaf nodes [6], then Upper Confidence Bounds on Trees (UCT) dominated the field for the majority of the competition [8] until it was surpassed by a Constraint Satisfaction Programming (CSP) algorithm in 2016 [12].

**GDL-II.**  GDL-II (Game Description Language with Incomplete Information) provides a fundamental extension of the existing game description language to describe truly general games [21]. The addition of just two keywords to the language can achieve this effect: In addition to the normal players, games are allowed to have a `random` player who can choose the outcome of stochastic events like the roll of a die. The other keyword is `sees`, which is used to control which, and how, players have access to hidden information. This simple and elegant modification fundamentally changes the way agents must play the game. Games can no longer be fully described by the information available to a player, who now must reason about what other players know about each other and themselves [17].

## 2.2  Generalised AlphaZero

In 2017 DeepMind released a system that the system could learn to play Go without any human knowledge, it learnt everything purely from self play. By just using Monte Carlo Tree Search and reinforcement learning, it was then also deployed to other games as well. As a result, AlphaZero learnt to play Go, Chess and Shogi and surpassed the previous state of the art in all three games [20]. But while AlphaZero may be able to play multiple games, it is still a long way from being able to play *all* games, so it was further generalised to a system that can read in any game rules in GDL and can learn to play via reinforcement learning using MCTS and a neural network similar to AlphaZero but with many of the restrictions removed [11]. The Generalised AlphaZero system is no longer restricted to only two-player, zero-sum, turn-based, and player-symmetric games [11]. However, it still cannot play hidden information games.

## 2.3  Recursive Belief-Based Learning

Recursive Belief-based Learning (ReBeL) is a recent (2020) general RL and search algorithm applied to play the hidden information game of poker [2]. Fundamentally this algorithm can translate any imperfect information game into a perfect information game. This is done through removing any information that is local (only seen by a subset of players), and instead of stating what actions to take, an agent states their policy (what is the probability they would make an action for all possible states they could currently be in). This process unfortunately will take a game from being discrete to having a continuous state and action space—the policy probabilities. It would theoretically be possible to train an AlphaZero or MCTS type algorithm on a discretised version of this now, but the high dimensionality of it would cause it to take an impractical amount of time. Instead this continuous perfect information game can be solved better with fictitious play (FP) [1] or counterfactual regret minimisation (CFR) [23], because the problem is a convex optimisation problem. While both FP and CFR can be used, it has been shown that CFR achieves superior performance [2].

For both training and inference the same procedure is used to find an optimal policy: sample many of the possible perfect information states from the current imperfect information state, run a depth limited version of CFR (CFR-D) and evaluate leaf nodes with the learnt value network. This procedure is then iterated many times as the yielded policy is dependent on the original policy. The average policy will converge to a Nash equilibrium for two-player zero-sum games and is expected to also perform well outside of that domain [2]. The starting policy can just be uniform random, but faster convergence can be achieved by initialising it with a learnt policy network. At inference time the only limitation is that the policies of the other players are not known, so instead CFR-D is run for a random number of iterations and it is assumed that the players are following that policy. By stopping CFR-D at a random iteration it reduces exploitation even if the opponents have access to the algorithms being used.

## 3   Method

### 3.1   Propositional Networks for GDL-II

Adapting the aproach takein by Generalised AlphaZero for general GDL-games, GDL-II game descriptions can be converted into a propositional network (prop-net) as this provides a simpler interface for interacting with the game and a well defined state to input to the neural network [15]. This can be done based on freely available code from ggp-base [18], but needs to be extended to account for the additional sees keyword in GDL-II to feed into the neural network the state-dependent observations that players make according to the game rules. Once the game is in propnet format, we can build on previous work done on generalised AlphaZero [11] and again expand to include processing of the additional sees information.

For each game that the agent is asked to play, the propnet that is generated can be queried for: extracting the game input state from the current game data—this is used for input to the neural network; the valid moves for a given role and game state; updating the game data to the next step when provided with a valid action for all players (for non-simultaneous games some agents will make a no-op action); specific to GDL-II and imperfect-information games, a list of all that is visible for a given role and game state. In a large number of games tested, the computational bottleneck is in transitioning from one state to the next. In [11], the whole propnet framework was optimised in Cython, which provided a 6x speedup. Here we note that the process of running CFR requires going back and forth between the same states many times over, and hence a least recently used cache (LRU) can be used to store these state transitions. We implemented an LRU in our system and found that it can provide up to a further 10x speedup.

### 3.2   Sampling GDL-II States

In order to estimate the optimal policy when there is hidden information, an agent samples plausible states based on all information it has gathered through-out the game. For each state, an optimal policy is found. The final policy is a weighted average of these policies, based on how likely it is in each state.

**Naïve Sampling.** A naïve method for sampling possible states in general GDL-II games is to:

1. Start a new game
2. Select the first action recorded for the agent and for all other agents, randomly select a valid move.
3. Repeat 2. until the recorded history is exhausted.
4. If the sampled state ever does not match the recorded observations, restart.

Unfortunately, this approach cannot be realistically scaled up to larger games. When searching for a state later in the game, there can be a vast number of possible states to choose from but there may only be a small handful of those states that match the recorded history. Finding this handful of valid states can be particularly difficult if the states are only found to be invalid deep into the search.

**Training Method.** We improve upon the naïve method in two ways. Firstly, in order to reduce the computational limitations, we introduce a cache for all states that are invalid each game. If all the states a step deeper into the game are invalid, then the parent state is also added to the invalid state cache. This means that invalid states won't be investigated more than once and whole segments of the game tree will no longer need to be searched. Secondly, we introduce a bias into this sampling distribution. The neural network (NN) that is used for policy approximation for the output of CFR-D is also used here to bias the sampler towards choosing actions for the other players that the NN predicts are more likely to be played. Formally, the probability of choosing action $a$ in state $s$ for player $i$ is given by $P(s, i, a) = f(s, i, a) + \frac{1}{|Actions(s,i)|}$, where the function $f$ represents the output of the policy neural network. This bias is not required, but we found that it drastically decreases the training time needed to reach convergence. Introducing this bias during training ensures that the true state is sampled with higher frequency and areas of the game tree that the NN views as more interesting get explored more.

**Evaluation Method.** The method used for training is sufficiently fast and leads to efficient game exploration during training but does not translate optimally to play against unknown other agents, which may play via a vastly different policy. An additional problem with the caching method as used for training (without the bias) is that it eventually leads to all valid leaf nodes being sampled with equal frequency even when this should not be the case. As an example, in the Monty Hall problem [17] the agent would view the two possible valid states equally (similar to many humans) and would hence adopt a policy of switching only 50% of the time. In order to maintain the same leaf node selection distribution as the naïve method whilst caching, the probabilities of reaching each node need to be stored on the node and updated every time it is accessed. The first time that a state node is accessed, all possible combinations of moves are listed, shuffled randomly and the first child set of moves is chosen to act as the transition to

166 Z. Partridge and M. Thielscher

the first child node. Also, the probability of reaching this node from the root is stored for future use. Upon subsequent access to the node, the next child set of moves $c$ is returned until the list is exhausted. Once every child node has been explored exactly once, the probability of reaching this node from the root is updated on each access, as is the probability of reaching each child node conditional on having already reached the current node.

## 3.3 CFR Search

Systems for playing perfect information games, such as AlphaZero, use Monte Carlo Tree Search to explore future possible game states [20]. This does not translate well to the hidden information games as it does not depend on the policies of other agents. Instead, a form of Counterfactual Regret Minimisation (CFR) can be used to search for the optimal policies. The most suitable specific form of CFR is depth-limited deep CFR as is described by [2,4]. CFR is a self-play algorithm, meaning that it learns by playing repeatedly against itself. Our version of CFR-D can be run in any grounded sub-tree of the complete game. Once a state is sampled at the correct depth, we run the algorithm down the tree until the maximum depth or terminal leaf nodes are reached. The value of depth limited leaf nodes are approximated via a neural network whereas the known values are used for terminal states.

---

**Algorithm 1.** High level training loop

---
  **while** Time left to train **do**
     Reinitialise game state
     **while** Game not finished **do**
        Perform CFR on current game state
        Add triple of (state, $\pi$, q) to the replay buffer     ▷ $\pi$ and q represent the policies and values for all agents
        **for each** agent **do**
           Perform CFR on states sampled with this agent's history
           Make moves proportionally to new policy probabilities
        **end for**
        Sample and train neural network on 20 mini-batches from replay buffer
     **end while**
  **end while**

---

CFR typically starts with uniform random policies, but to speed up convergence, all policies can be initialised using the neural network as an estimation of the final policies. Then it simulates playing the game against itself and after every game, it revisits each decision and finds ways to improve the policy. This process can be iterated indefinitely and it is the average policy that eventually approximates the game's optimal policy or Nash equilibrium. The final policy used for move selection is the weighted average of policies at all sampled states, weighted by how frequently each state is sampled.

## 3.4   Reinforcement Learning

Large scale reinforcement learning projects often use a separate process dedicated to evaluating positions, one for training on new data and many for generating games [5]. On more modest hardware, for efficiency and simplicity, it has been implemented by running a game, adding the recorded data to the replay buffer, training on a small number, say 20, of mini-batches from the replay buffer and repeating as indicated in Algorithm 1.

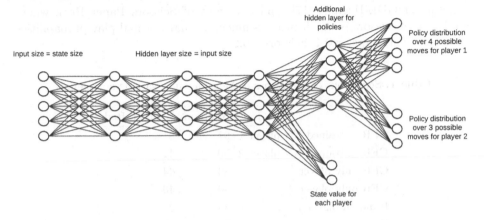

**Fig. 1.** Sample Neural Network Architecture

The neural network takes in a single grounded game state, and outputs the value and policy for all agents. For each agent, the value of the state is the expected final reward and the policy is the estimated optimal policy in this current state. It is possible to have separate models for each player's values and each player's policies, but it should be noted that all of these models would learn to extract the same features. For this reason, it is possible to combine the early layers into a shared model head to extract the useful game features as shown in Fig. 1. From this shared internal representation a single linear layer is used to estimate the values for all players, and an additional hidden layer is added before estimating the policies separately for each player. Figure 1 represents only a small toy game for simplicity. This simple game only has a state size of 5 and two players, one with 4 possible actions and the other with 3. In a larger and more interesting game like, for example, Blind Tic Tac Toe [10], the input and hidden layers would be of size 199 and the output policy size for each player would be of 9.

## 4   Experiments

### 4.1   Evaluation Methodology

We have tested our solution on several GDL-II games known from the literature [7,17]. The easy games can be compared with known optimal solutions and harder games were tested against both random play and handcrafted solutions. The following results tables for the harder games show the final scores over 100 games achieved by the agents listed on the left. Column names correspond to the opponents that each of these agents were playing against; these opponents will be playing the opposing role to that listed next to the agent. The agents iteratively increase CFR search depth until the time expires and between 60 and 100 states have been generated with replacement at each depth. Explicitly, they search until maximum game depth or for a minimum of 1 s, and a maximum of 15 s.

The two easy games that we tested on were the Monty Hall Problem (a game of probability that most people find very counterintuitive [14], formalised as a single-player GDL-II game [17]) and a variant of Scissors–Paper–Rock where winning with scissors is worth twice as much, so that optimal play probabilities are: Rock = 0.4, Paper = 0.4, Scissors = 0.2.

**Table 1.** Scores out of 100 games of Meier against various opponents

|  | Random | Hand crafted |
|---|---|---|
| CFR + trained NN player 1 | 97 | 81 |
| CFR + trained NN player 2 | 80 | 41 |
| CFR only player 1 | 83 | 64 |
| CFR only player 2 | 80 | 40 |
| Random player 1 | 33 | 21 |
| Random player 2 | 72 | 35 |

The three harder games were Meier, Blind Tic Tac Toe and Biased Blind Tic Tac Toe. Meier, otherwise known as liar's dice [13], is an asymmetric dice game requiring the ability to deceive and to detect an opponent's deception. The game involves rolling two dice and announcing the outcome to the other player or bluffing that it was a better roll. Unlike Meier, Blind Tic Tac Toe is a symmetrical and simultaneous game. The difference from the traditional Tic Tac Toe is that agents play simultaneously and cannot see where their opponents have played. They only get told if their last move was successful or not. If both players attempt to play in the same cell at the same time, one of them is chosen randomly to be successful [10]. Biased Blind Tic Tac Toe is very similar, but in cases where both agents choose the same cell at the same time, the "X" player is given the cell every time.

## 4.2   Results and Discussion

Due to the small total number of states in the easy games, they can be completely searched to terminal states at inference time with CFR. In the Scissors–Paper–Rock variant, the optimal solution of Rock = 0.4, Paper = 0.4, Scissors = 0.2 is found quickly at inference time even without any training time. For the Monty Hall Problem, the interesting feature of this game is how often the candidate switches—where it is optimal to always switch. There are two possible states that the agent could be in at this stage, and if the state sampling is done correctly, we should see the agent sample the "switch" state twice as often as the state that already has the car. Therefore the weighted average policy that the agent plays by is to switch with $p = \frac{2}{3}$. While this is not optimal play, it is still superior to random or standard human play, and an extension is discussed in Sect. 5 in which it will switch with $p = 1$.

As Table 1 shows, our agent playing Meier easily beats a random player selecting valid moves from a uniform distribution and even the CFR only agent (using an untrained neural network) wins at least 80% of games. We also supplied a handcrafted opponent that will bluff in proportion to the value of its own roll and will call the opponent's bluff in proportion to their claim. Our untrained agent managed to play on a similar level to the handcrafted solution. After the neural network has finished training, performance is significantly improved against both the random and handcrafted agents.

**Table 2.** Scores out of 100 games of Blind Tic Tac Toe against various opponents

|                      | Random | Hand crafted |
|----------------------|--------|--------------|
| CFR + trained NN x   | 79.5   | 48           |
| CFR + trained NN o   | 79.5   | 55           |
| CFR only x           | 54     | 25           |
| CFR only o           | 60     | 20           |
| Random x             | 48     | 23.5         |
| Random o             | 52     | 21.5         |

As Blind Tic Tac Toe is symmetrical, the small differences for X and O players in Table 2 must be attributed to random chance. By applying CFR with the untrained NN, performance is slightly improved over random but is still very weak in comparison to the handcrafted algorithm. After training, performance is improved significantly against both a random opponent and the handcrafted solution. Our method is designed to approximate a non-exploitable policy but does not attempt to exploit other players. The handcrafted solution it played against was strong but could be easily exploited by an adversary that knows its policy, but it also does not attempt to exploit other players.

As can be expected from the removal of player symmetry, the results are in the favour of "X". Table 3 shows that the trained defensive "O" players only win around 25% of games against the other trained players, but against the handcrafted player they can win almost half the games while playing at a significant disadvantage.

Both seeds eventually settle into very similar strategies and consequently very similar performance against all opponents. This is not the case all the way through training however, for example if we evaluate a snapshot of the networks from halfway through the training process against a handcrafted "O" player,

**Table 3.** Scores out of 100 games of Very Biased Blind Tic Tac Toe against various opponents

|  | Random | Hand crafted | Trained (seed 1) | Trained (seed 2) |
|---|---|---|---|---|
| CFR + trained NN x (seed1) | 89.5 | 79.5 | 66 | 75.5 |
| CFR + trained NN o (seed1) | 46 | 44 | 34 | 26 |
| CFR + trained NN x (seed2) | 91.5 | 80.5 | 74 | 73 |
| CFR + trained NN o (seed2) | 52 | 45 | 24.5 | 27 |
| CFR only x | 84 | 40.5 | | |
| CFR only o | 36 | 14.5 | | |
| Random x | 80.5 | 35 | | |
| Random o | 18 | 11 | | |

seed 1 wins 100% of games and seed 2 only wins 23%. These non-converged players are both quite exploitable at this stage in training, even seed 1 which won 100% of games against the handcrafted player just can be seen as lucky with its match-up because when it plays against the final version of seed 1, it only scores a very modest 54.5.

## 5    Conclusion and Future Work

Our work has successfully demonstrated that hidden information games can be played at a high standard by using a combination of CFR search, state sampling and reinforcement learning. This approach can, in principle, be applied to any GDL-II game and is not limited to zero-sum, a set number of players, turn-based or symmetrical games.

An evaluation of the system shows that small games can be played optimally even without training or with only minimal training. Larger, more complex games can be learnt in the order of 24 h on a single CPU to such a degree that it outperforms even handcrafted algorithms specifically designed for the individual games.

The current time spent in training is much longer than a conventional 10 min start clock used in GGP competitions, however with parallelised training and further optimisations mentioned below, many games could still be played very well within the reduced time limitations.

### Future Work

**Optimisation.** The proposed algorithm has the potential to be massively parallelised. During training, almost the entire time is spent on playing out many self-play games and these games can efficiently be played in parallel without any need for communication during the game as described in [5]. Even within a single game at training or inference time, there are many independent components that can be run in parallel. At inference time and sometimes during training as well, sampling the states is the bottleneck, but every state could be sampled on a separate processor. During training, the bottleneck normally is in running CFR for longer on the true current state to use as the training target. There is no reason that this needs to be done at the same time as the practice game is being played. Instead only the states need to be stored and the optimal policy for each state could be calculated in parallel separately.

**Larger Games.** Once sufficient optimisations have been made, our approach could be extended to larger, more difficult games. Eventually, real-world problems could be cast into GDL-II or the algorithm could be exported to other domains such that it could be used to make a positive impact on society.

**Exploiting Opponents.** Our approach aims to approximate a policy that is non-exploitable, but does not yet attempt to exploit other players. Future work on exploitation could model the policies of other players, estimate their weaknesses and slowly deviate from the existing policy to capitalise on any biases they may have.

# References

1. Brown, G.W.: Iterative solution of games by fictitious play. In: Koopmans, T. (ed.) Activity Analysis of Production and Allocation. Wiley (1951)
2. Brown, N., Bakhtin, A., Lerer, A., Gong, Q.: Combining deep reinforcement learning and search for imperfect-information games. CoRR abs/2007.13544 (2020). arXiv:2007.13544
3. Brown, N., Sandholm, T.: Superhuman AI for multiplayer poker. Science **365**(6456), 885–890 (2019). https://doi.org/10.1126/science.aay2400
4. Brown, N., Sandholm, T., Amos, B.: Depth-limited solving for imperfect-information games. In: Proceedings of NeurIPS, pp. 7674–7685 (2018). arXiv:1805.08195
5. Clemente, A.V., Martínez, H.N.C., Chandra, A.: Efficient parallel methods for deep reinforcement learning. CoRR abs/1705.04862 (2017). arXiv:1705.04862
6. Clune, J.: Heuristic evaluation functions for general game playing. In: Proceedings of AAAI, pp. 1134–1139 (2007)
7. Edelkamp, S., Federholzner, T., Kissmann, P.: Searching with partial belief states in general games with incomplete information. In: Glimm, B., Krüger, A. (eds.) KI 2012. LNCS (LNAI), vol. 7526, pp. 25–36. Springer, Heidelberg (2012). https://doi.org/10.1007/978-3-642-33347-7_3
8. Finnsson, H., Björnsson, Y.: Simulation-based approach to general game playing. In: Proceedings of AAAI, pp. 259–264 (2008)
9. Genesereth, M., Björnsson, Y.: The international general game playing competition. AI Mag. **34**(2), 107–111 (2013)
10. Genesereth, M., Thielscher, M.: General Game Playing. Morgan & Claypool Publishers (2014)
11. Goldwaser, A., Thielscher, M.: Deep reinforcement learning for general game playing. In: Proceedings of AAAI, pp. 1701–1708, April 2020. https://doi.org/10.1609/aaai.v34i02.5533, https://ojs.aaai.org/index.php/AAAI/article/view/5533

12. Koriche, F., Piette, S.L.É., Tabary, S.: General game playing with stochastic CSP. Constraints **21**(1), 95–114 (2016)
13. Liar's dice: Liar's dice – Wikipedia, the free encyclopedia (2021). https://en.wikipedia.org/wiki/Liar%27s_dice. Accessed Nov 2021
14. Rosenhouse, J.: The Monty Hall Problem. Oxford University Press, Oxford (2009)
15. Schkufza, E., Love, N., Genesereth, M.: Propositional automata and cell automata: representational frameworks for discrete dynamic systems. In: Proceedings of the Australasian Joint Conference on AI. LNCS, vol. 5360, pp. 56–66 (2008)
16. Schmid, M., et al.: Player of games. CoRR abs/2112.03178 (2021). arXiv:2112.03178
17. Schofield, M., Thielscher, M.: General game playing with imperfect information. J. Artif. Intell. Res. **66**, 901–935 (2019)
18. Schreiber, S., et al.: GGP-base. https://github.com/ggp-org/ggp-base (2010). Accessed June 2021
19. Silver, D., et al.: Mastering the game of Go with deep neural networks and tree search. Nature **529**, 484–489 (2016). https://doi.org/10.1038/nature16961
20. Silver, D., et al.: A general reinforcement learning algorithm that masters chess, shogi, and Go through self-play. Science **362**, 1140–1144 (2018). https://doi.org/10.1126/science.aar6404
21. Thielscher, M.: A general game description language for incomplete information games. In: Proceedings of AAAI, pp. 994–999, January 2010
22. Vinyals, O., et al.: Grandmaster level in StarCraft II using multi-agent reinforcement learning. Nature **575** (2019). https://doi.org/10.1038/s41586-019-1724-z
23. Zinkevich, M., Johanson, M., Bowling, M., Piccione, C.: Regret minimization in games with incomplete information. In: Proceedings of NeurIPS, pp. 1729–1736 (2007)

# Sequential Decision Making with "Sequential Information" in Deep Reinforcement Learning

Aimin Xu, Linghui Yuan, and Yunlong Liu[✉] [iD]

Department of Automation, Xiamen University, Xiamen, China
ylliu@xmu.edu.cn

**Abstract.** By learning policy directly from high-dimensional visual inputs, e.g., video frames, Deep Reinforcement Learning (DRL) has achieved great successes for solving sequential decision-making problems, where 2D convolutional network is usually adopted for extracting the underlying spatial features. However, such spatial feature extraction methods do not consider the temporal information existed in the input frames. To address this issue, Transformer, 3D convolutional network and Long Short-Term Memory (LSTM) have been used in DRL, but often result in excessive increase of model parameters and computation cost. Furthermore, multiple down-sampling of images will lead to the loss of sequential information. In this paper, we propose a novel model for extracting sequential information, namely temporal aggregation network (TAN). Comparing with existing methods, TAN can extract the sequential information without the needs of multiple downsampling of consecutive images. Moreover, by decoupling the computation between spatial and channel dimensions, a lightweight model is built in TAN. Experiments in classic Atari 2600 games show that our method can improve the efficiency of decision-making of DRL algorithms compared with baselines.

**Keywords:** Deep reinforcement learning · Temporal aggregation network · Sequential decision-making · Lightweight model

## 1 Introduction

For agents sequentially interacting and learning from a stochastic environment, e.g., video games [27], aircraft control [10] and weather prediction [26], at each time step, the agent receives an observation of the environment and takes an action that is executed in the environment [29]. In this process, the goal of the agent is to maximize the rewards received by making rational decisions, which is also called the problem of sequential decision making [21].

Deep Reinforcement Learning (DRL) has achieved great success in sequential decision making problems [19,27]. In recent years, images or video frames are usually used as the input for the agent, but only one frame used as the current observation is not enough to contain necessary information for the decision, which will lead to the partially observable problem [17]. To address this issue,

© The Author(s), under exclusive license to Springer Nature Switzerland AG 2022
S. Khanna et al. (Eds.): PRICAI 2022, LNCS 13631, pp. 173–184, 2022.
https://doi.org/10.1007/978-3-031-20868-3_13

one commonly used technique is to use a sequence of frames as the inputs, and then multi-layer 2D convolutional neural network [18] is adopted to extract the state representation.

However, the feature extraction network built by 2D convolutional network doped all the channel information of the input images together from the first level of convolution, and the temporal features of continuous frames are ignored as in Deep Q-Learning (DQN) [25] and Deep Deterministic Policy Gradient (DDPG) [20] etc. Some relevant studies have realized the extraction of temporal features in the sequence of frames by using recurrent neural network (RNN) [8], which is then used to assist the decision-making of the agent. In [12], Hausknecht et al. proposed the Deep Recurrent Q-Learning (DRQN) for Partially Observable MDPs by adding the Long Short-Term Memory (LSTM) [14]. A natural way to learn sequential features of continuous images is to use 3D convolutional neural network, which can learn spatial-temporal feature.

Besides, The successful applications of the recent proposed framework Transformer [7,32,35] in the fields of natural language processing and computer vision also show strong abilities of sequential information extraction. However, in order to extract the sequential information existed in the input frames, these mentioned methods have to perform many dimensionality reduction operations on the image, which inevitably result in the loss of sequential information contained in pixels. Moreover, the complex layer structure contained in LSTM and Transformer, and the additional deep channel introduced by 3D convolution also lead to expensive computation and memory requirements.

To alleviate theses problems, in this paper, a novel temporal aggregation network (TAN) is proposed. TAN uses the concept of a depthwise separable convolution [5], which decouples the joint mapping relationship between the spatial and temporal dimensions, then greatly reduces the parameters and computation of the model. At the same time, in order to avoid multiple downsampling of consecutive images, TAN uses 3D temporal convolution to ensure that convolution is performed in the channel dimension to extract sequential features. To demonstrate the performance of the proposed TAN, it is directly extended to one of the DRL algorithms, namely Advantage Actor-Critic (A2C) [24], and then is executed in the classic Atari 2600 game tasks. Comparing with other spatial-temporal feature extraction models, TAN has the advantages of less computation, fewer parameters and strong decision-making ability.

## 2   Related Work

With the development of deep neural network, especially convolutional neural network (CNN), which is then combined with the sequential decision of RL. In 2013, Mnih et al. proposed DQN which firstly uses 2D convolution to extract features from video frames and then trains agents in Atari games [25]. In 2016, by using 2D convolution as the feature extraction method, AlphaGo is the first computer to defeat a professional human Go player [27]. In [36], 2D convolution was used to build an autoencoder model to restore the native continuous game images, thus enhance the representation learning ability. Taking video frames as inputs for decision making usually requires not only the spatial information, but also the temporal information contained in the sequence, however such sequential information is not considered in the mentioned 2D convolution.

Long Short-Term Memory (LSTM) was proposed in 1997 and is widely used in sequential decision problems. In 2016, LSTM was used in Deep Recurrent Q-Network (DRQN) to extract statistical historical information [12]. In the next year, Alahi et al. treated people's historical location information as sequential data and used LSTM to extract the temporal information to realize the prediction of human's trajectory [2]. As a variant of LSTM, Gate Recurrent Unit (GRU) [4] is more computation efficient compared with LSTM and is also usually used as the method for dealing with the sequential information.

3D convolutional neural network, which can convolve simultaneously from both spatial and temporal dimensions. Tran et al. [31] said that temporal information would completely disappear after the first-layer 2D convolutional neural network, so 3D convolutional kernels were used to extract spatio-temporal features. Most of the excellent spatio-temporal feature extraction networks are based on two-stream [28] feature fusion, e.g., TSN [33], I3D [3] and Slowfast network [9]. Relevant studies have applied 3D convolution to DRL, in [22], 3D convolution is used to extract robustness features of points in the eye window to localize and segment. However, large amount of computational resources is required due to the increased number of parameters in the 3D framework.

Recently, based on self-attention mechanisms, Vaswani et al. proposed a powerful model, namely Transformer, which dispenses with recurrence and convolutions entirely [32]. Transformer also effectively extract sequential information between images, such as vision Transformer [7], Vanilla Transformer [1] and swin Transformer [23]. In [37], Chen et al. reconstructs RL into a sequential problem suitable for Transformer to solve, and then Transformer is trained based on the collected experience to make decisions directly. However, it is easy to find Transformer will lead to a large number of calculations and parameters.

While the introduction of ResNet [13] has improved the accuracy of the deep neural network model by the adding of more layers of deep network, the number of network parameters and computation cost are also increase significantly. To address this issue and under the assumption that the space and channel dimension of the feature map in convolutional neural network can be decoupled, the depthwise separable convolution is proposed in 2017. Conceptually, it can reduce the number of weight coefficients while retaining the representation learning ability of the convolution kernel. The weight number of the depthwise separable convolution is about 10% to 25% of the standard 2D convolution [5], it also achieves joint mapping of spatial and channel features [15].

## 3   Background

### 3.1   Deep Reinforcement Learning

Model-free reinforcement learning algorithms [6] can be divided into two types, namely policy-based and value-based [16]. In order to speed up the learning process, the advantages of the two algorithms are utilized to result in the Actor-Critic algorithm [30]. Assume the parameters of Actor network and Critic network are denoted as $\theta$ and $\omega$. In the environment, the agent obtains the first state $s$ as the input of the Actor, and executes the action $a$. Subsequently, the next state $s'$ and a reward $R$ are obtained, where $s$ and $s'$ are input to the Critic to get the state value $V(s)$ and $V(s')$. The $TD - error$ is computed as follows [34]:

$$\delta = R + \gamma V(s') - V(s) \tag{1}$$

Critic uses the following loss function to update network parameters:

$$L(\omega) = \sum R + \gamma V(s', \omega) - V(s, \omega) \tag{2}$$

$\gamma$ is discounting factor, the learning rate $\alpha$ is used to update Actor:

$$\theta = \theta + \alpha \nabla_\theta log \pi_\theta(S_t, A)\delta \tag{3}$$

Based on Actor-Critic, asynchronous advantage actor-critic (A3C) [24], soft actor-critic (SAC) [11] and other related algorithms have also been proposed.

## 3.2  Depthwise Separable Convolution

Depthwise separable convolution mainly includes depthwise convolution and pointwise convolution. Depthwise separable convolution is usually used to build models, such as Mobilenet [15]. In depthwise convolution, one channel is convolved by only one convolution kernel, as shown in Fig. 1.

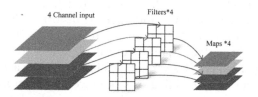

**Fig. 1.** Depthwise convolution

Pointwise convolution is used to combine these feature maps in different channels, as shown in Fig. 2. When the stride is set to 1 and the padding is the same, $N(5)$ 2D convolution kernels with a size of $D_f \times D_f$ are used to operate the data with a channel depth of $M(4)$ and with a size of $D_k \times D_k$. The required computation and model parameters as follows:

$$FLOPs_{2d} = D_k \cdot D_k \cdot M \cdot N \cdot D_f \cdot D_f \tag{4}$$

$$PARAMS_{2d} = M \cdot N \cdot D_f \cdot D_f \tag{5}$$

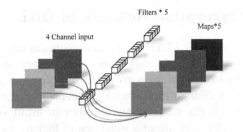

**Fig. 2.** Pointwise convolution

If the size of depthwise convolution kernel is set as $D_f \times D_f$ and the number of pointwise convolution kernel is set as $N$, the depthwise separable convolution can get same output as 2D convolution. At this point, the calculation amount and model parameters as follows:

$$FLOPs_{dw+pw} = D_k \cdot D_k \cdot M \cdot D_f \cdot D_f + M \cdot N \cdot D_f \cdot D_f \tag{6}$$

$$PARAMS_{dw+pw} = M \cdot D_f \cdot D_f + M \cdot N \tag{7}$$

It can be seen that the computation cost and model parameters of the Depthwise separable convolution are $1/N + 1/D_f{}^2$ and $1/N + 1/D_k{}^2$ of the standard 2D convolution.

### 3.3   3D Temporal Convolution

3D temporal convolution is a specific type of ordinary 3D convolution, and the spatial size of its convolution kernel is always maintained at $1 \times 1$, which is shown in Fig. 3.

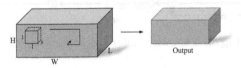

**Fig. 3.** 3D temporal convolution

For sequential frames, the 3D temporal convolution can perform convolution only in the temporal dimension, which can address the problems existed in the ordinary 3D convolution that along with the extraction of the temporal features of the sequential images, the down-sampling of the spatial dimension of the sequential images should be also executed. In this way, more specific and sufficient temporal features can be extracted.

## 4    Temporal Aggregation Network in DRL

Temporal aggregation network (TAN) attempts to obtain more specific temporal information with less computation and model parameters. According to Fig. 4, TAN first uses depthwise convolution to perform convolutional downsampling operations separately on $N$ high-dimensional sequential images, and the number of output feature maps is the same as the number of input sequences with the same sequence order. After obtaining a sequence of feature maps with a smaller size, 3D temporal convolutions is used to perform multiple aggregations of temporal features in the temporal dimension, while the size of the space dimension remains unchanged. When the moving step of 3D temporal convolutions are greater than 1, each convolution operation will reduce the channel depth of outputs. Therefore, it can be seen from Fig. 4 that with the increasing of the number of temporal feature aggregations, the number of feature maps after the convolution operation decreases. Each feature map obtained in the beginning contains the temporal feature of the adjacent frames, and gradually the temporal features of longer sequence of the continuous frames are contained in each feature map. Subsequently, pointwise convolution is used to raise the feature maps of different depths to a uniform depth, and a fusion operation on these feature maps is performed to contain the temporal information. This process not only makes up for the lost channel correlation due to the depthwise convolution operation, but also increases the learning ability of the model.

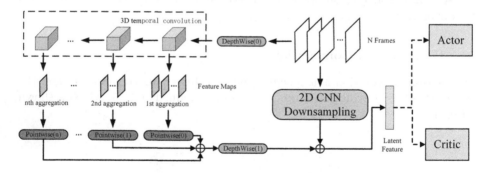

**Fig. 4.** TAN with Actor-Critic framework

In reality, the speed and moving direction of objects may unpredictable and difficult to calculate, where in some cases, the temporal information can only play an auxiliary role in the perception of the environment. To integrate both the temporal and spatial information, we then put the sequence of video frames into the TAN and 2D convolutional network respectively to obtain temporal features and spatial features, and finally fuse them for agent's decision-making. As shown in Algorithm 1, the update process of the whole algorithm includes TAN and Actor-Critic algorithm, which are respectively explained in this section and the relevant work of this paper.

---

**Algorithm 1:** Actor-Critic with TAN

---

**Input**: continuous frames $x$, dimension of depthwise convolutional, $3d$ temporal convolution, pointwise convolution kernel $d$, $t$, $p$, the same layers of $3d$ temporal convolution and pointwise convolution $l$, training steps $T$, learning rate $\alpha$, discount factor $\gamma$;

**Output**: Actor, Critic parameters $\theta$ and $\omega$;

Initialize randomly;

**for** $i$ *in range(T)* **do**

    Calculate the depthwise convolution layer $D(x) = dwconv(x, d)$;

    **for** $k = 1, 2, ..., l$ **do**

        Calculate the k-th $3d$ temporal convolution layer $T_k$;

        **if** *k=1* **then**

            |   $T_k = 3dconv(D(x), t)$;

        **else**

            |   $T_k = 3dconv(T_{k-1}(x), t)$;

    **for** $k = 1, 2, ..., l$ **do**

        | Calculate the k-th pointwise convolution layer $P_k = pwconv(T_k(x), t)$;

    Merge the feature maps of all layers get $M = [P_1, P_2, ..., P_k]$;

    Obtain temporal feature vector $u = RELU(FC(x))$;

    Get spatial feature vector $v = Conv(x)$;

    Decision vector $\phi(s) = u + v$;

    Input $\phi(s)$ to Actor, execute action $a$, next state $s'$ and reward $r$;

    Update Critic $\omega$, Actor $\theta$.

---

## 5 Experiments

In this section, for comparisons, TAN, 3D convolution, Gate Recurrent Unit (GRU) and Transformer are adopted to extract the temporal features among sequential images with the combination of the A2C algorithm to assist the agent in decision-making. Source code is available at https://github.com/DMU-XMU/temporal-aggregation-network.

### 5.1 Experimental Setup

To verify the performances of different methods, our proposed approach and other baselines are tested in Atari 2600 games, they generate continuous game images that contain rich sequential information. A version of the game without the word ram indicates the observations are from a $210 \times 160$ image, e.g., StarGunnerNoFrameskip-v0, which is shown in Fig. 5.

First, as usually adopted in the literature, the size of the original image was reduced from $210 \times 160$ to $84 \times 84$ and the color image is also grayscaled. 4 consecutive frames of gray game images are used as the input of the network. When TAN is combined with the A2C algorithm, the kernel size of dw0 and dw1 are $8 \times 8$, the stride of all 3D temporal convolutions are 2. The convolutional network is built by a 3-layer standard 2D convolutional network, and the size of

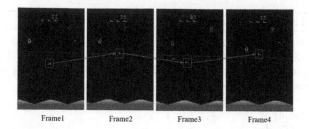

Frame1          Frame2          Frame3          Frame4

**Fig. 5.** Four continuous game frames from StarGunner game

the convolution kernel is $8 \times 8$, $4 \times 4$, and $3 \times 3$ respectively. As mentioned, in the case where GRU or Transformer is used as the sequential feature extractor, each frame in consecutive images must be down-sampled and flattened into a one-dimensional vector to extract the sequential information. In the process of using the 3D convolution with a consistent spatial downsampling process of $8 \times 8$, $4 \times 4$, and $3 \times 3$ and three convolutional operations in the temporal dimension are also added, and the stride size is set to 2, 2 and 1 respectively. All models are deployed on the Nvidia GeForce RTX 2080 TI device for training and the learning rate is set to 0.0007. The total number of training steps in the game environment is 10 million. In order to address the problem that some iterative gradients are too large and the adaptive gradient cannot be changed, the RMSProp optimizer was used to update the network weights.

## 5.2   Results Analysis

According to the curve trends shown in Fig. 6, it can be found that the A2C_3D algorithm performs better than the standard A2C algorithm in most games, such as Alien, DemonAttack, Seaquest, etc., which demonstrates that the incorporation of the temporal information with A2C has better performances than the A2C algorithm with only the spatial information of the continuous 4 frames extracted by the 2D convolution.

The A2C_GRU algorithm, which tries to use the GRU to reserve temporal information, can actually only extract the temporal information between the one-dimensional vectors. Compared with the original two-dimensional image, the one-dimensional vector is more abstract and uncertain, which ignores the movement trajectory between pixels. As a result, the performance of the A2C_GRU and the A2C_Transformer is poor and unstable. But due to the effective self-attention mechanism, the overall performance of A2C_Transformer is better than A2C_GRU. On the whole, the results show that A2C_TAN can extract the temporal information between sequences of higher-dimensional images and retains the correlation between pixels, which helps the agents to obtain higher game scores and accelerate the convergence speed of training. Besides, the extracted temporal information may have little effect on decision-making. For examples, in shooting games such as Demon Attack and Seaquest, the extracted temporal

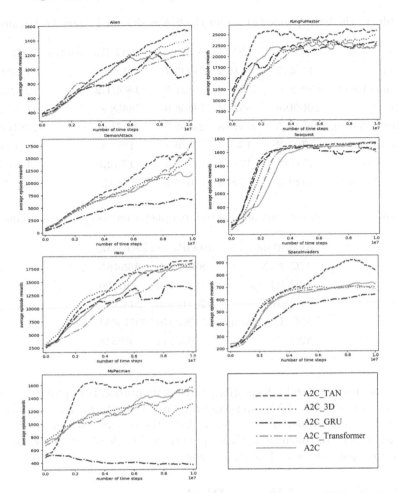

**Fig. 6.** Average reward curves for the five models on 7 Atari 2600 games

information is of great help, but it is of little help in action games like Hero. Table 1 shows the best rewards from multiple random experiments.

Table 2 shows the amount of calculation and model parameters of different methods, where FlOPs represents the amount of calculation consumed by the feature extraction network, and PARAMS represents the total number of parameters of the feature extraction network. The above statistics are the calculation results obtained by inputting 4 continuous game images with a size of 84 × 84 into the network. As mentioned, the standard A2C algorithm uses a three-layer 2D convolutional neural network to build a network to extract the continuous frame spatial information.

**Table 1.** The best episode reward for the five models on 7 Atari 2600 games.

| Game tasks | A2C_TAN | A2C_3D | A2C_GRU | A2C_Transformer | A2C |
|---|---|---|---|---|---|
| Alien | **1545.2** | 1415.9 | 1233.7 | 1199.9 | 1289.6 |
| DemonAttack | 15989.6 | 15056.8 | 6821.5 | **18021.2** | 12152.2 |
| Hero | **19050.6** | 18528.3 | 14366.9 | 18458.2 | 17801.2 |
| KungFuMaster | **26214.8** | 24843.3 | 23655.2 | 23774.0 | 22841.5 |
| MsPacman | **1701.2** | 1335.6 | 526.5 | 1567.8 | 1514.6 |
| Seaquest | 1737.0 | 1722.3 | 1701.8 | **1742.9** | 1721.7 |
| SpaceInvaders | **920.3** | 706.6 | 638.1 | 713.3 | 735.2 |

**Table 2.** The computation amount and parameter number of 5 algorithms.

| Algorithms | FLOPs | PARAMS |
|---|---|---|
| A2C_TAN | **8991520** | **865485** |
| A2C_3D | 10323552 | 891520 |
| A2C_GRU | 27113856 | 2432640 |
| A2C_Transformer | 154260576 | 60776464 |
| A2C | 7656544 | 862848 |

After adding temporal information, extra computation is required. But compared to other baselines, TAN can successfully reduce both calculation and model parameters. Even compared to standard A2C, the cost of our approach is only increased slightly. In conclusion, TAN can extract the effective temporal features in the sequential images with a smaller cost.

# 6    Conclusion and Future Work

In this paper, we propose a lightweight temporal aggregation network (TAN) for extracting sequential information of consecutive frames, then this framework is integrated with A2C. Compared with other sequential information extraction models, TAN requires less model parameters and computation. Moreover, the sequential information extracted by TAN is effective and can better assist the agent in learning appropriate strategies. Our proposed approach is evaluated in Atari 2600 Games, which shows the TAN networks can help agents to achieve higher game scores and improve convergence speed. Future work includes the application of our proposed model to more complex sequential decision tasks, e.g., robotics, healthcare and aircraft control.

**Acknowledgements.** This work was supported by the National Natural Science Foundation of China (No. 61772438 and No. 61375077). This work was also supported by the Innovation Strategy Research Program of Fujian Province, China (No. 2021R0012).

# References

1. Al-Rfou, R., Choe, D., Constant, N., Guo, M., Jones, L.: Character-level language modeling with deeper self-attention. In: Proceedings of the AAAI Conference on Artificial Intelligence, vol. 33, No. 01, pp. 3159–3166. AAAI Press, Hawaii (2019)
2. Alahi, A., Goel, K., Ramanathan, V., et al.: Social LSTM: human trajectory prediction in crowded spaces. In: Proceedings of the IEEE Conference on Computer Vision and Pattern Recognition, pp. 961–971. IEEE Press, Las Vegas (2016)
3. Carreira, J., Zisserman, A.: Quo vadis, action recognition? A new model and the kinetics dataset. In: Proceedings of the IEEE Conference on Computer Vision and Pattern Recognition, pp. 6299–6308. IEEE Press, Hawaii (2017)
4. Cho, K., et al.: Learning phrase representations using RNN encoder-decoder for statistical machine translation. arXiv preprint arXiv:1406.1078 (2014)
5. Chollet, F.: Xception: deep learning with depthwise separable convolutions. In: Proceedings of the IEEE Conference on Computer Vision and Pattern Recognition, pp. 1251–1258. IEEE Press, Hawaii (2017)
6. Degris, T., Pilarski, P.M., Sutton R.S.: Model-free reinforcement learning with continuous action in practice. In: 2012 American Control Conference (ACC), pp. 2177–2182. IEEE Press, Montreal (2012)
7. Dosovitskiy, A., Beyer, L., Kolesnikov, A., et al.: An image is worth $16 \times 16$ words: transformers for image recognition at scale. arXiv preprint arXiv:2010.11929 (2020)
8. Elman, J.L.: Finding structure in time. Cogn. Sci. **14**(2), 179–211 (1990)
9. Feichtenhofer, C., Fan, H., Malik, J., He, K.: SlowFast networks for video recognition. In: Proceedings of the IEEE/CVF International Conference on Computer Vision, pp. 6202–6211. IEEE Press, Seoul (2019)
10. Grefenstette, J.J., Ramsey, C.L., Schultz, A.C.: Learning sequential decision rules using simulation models and competition. Mach. Learn. **5**(4), 355–381 (1990)
11. Haarnoja, T., Zhou, A., Abbeel, P., Levine, S.: Soft Actor-Critic: off-policy maximum entropy deep reinforcement learning with a stochastic actor. In: International Conference on Machine Learning, pp. 1861–1870. PMLR, Stockholm (2018)
12. Hausknecht, M., Stone, P.: Deep recurrent Q-learning for partially observable MDPs. In: 2015 AAAI fall symposium series (2015)
13. He, K., Zhang, X., Ren, S., Sun, J.: Deep residual learning for image recognition. In: Proceedings of the IEEE Conference on Computer Vision and Pattern Recognition, pp. 770–778. IEEE Press, Las Vegas (2016)
14. Graves, A.: Long short-term memory. Supervised sequence labelling with recurrent neural networks, pp. 37–45 (2012)
15. Howard, A.G., et al. : MobileNets: efficient convolutional neural networks for mobile vision applications. arXiv preprint arXiv:1704.04861 (2017)
16. Howard, R.A.: Dynamic programming and Markov processes (1960)
17. Kaelbling, L.P., Littman, M.L., Cassandra, A.R.: Planning and acting in partially observable stochastic domains. Artif. Intell. **101**(1–2), 99–134 (1998)
18. LeCun, Y., Bottou, L., Bengio, Y., Haffner, P.: Gradient-based learning applied to document recognition. Proc. IEEE **86**(11), 2278–2324 (1998)
19. Li, Y.: Deep reinforcement learning: an overview. arXiv preprint arXiv:1701.07274 (2017)
20. Lillicrap, T.P., et al.: Continuous control with deep reinforcement learning. arXiv preprint arXiv:1509.02971 (2015)
21. Littman, M.L.: Algorithms for Sequential Decision-Making. Brown University (1996)

22. Liu, F., et al.: 3DCNN-DQN-RNN: a deep reinforcement learning framework for semantic parsing of large-scale 3D point clouds. In: Proceedings of the IEEE Conference on Computer Vision, pp. 5678–5687. IEEE Press, Venice (2017)
23. Liu, Z., et al.: Swin transformer: hierarchical vision transformer using shifted windows. In: Proceedings of the IEEE/CVF International Conference on Computer Vision, pp. 10012–10022. IEEE Press, Montreal (2021)
24. Mnih, V., et al.: Asynchronous methods for deep reinforcement learning. In: International Conference on Machine Learning, pp. 1928–1937. PMLR, New York (2016)
25. Mnih, V., et al.: Playing Atari with deep reinforcement learning. arXiv:1312.5602 (2013)
26. Read, P., Lermit, J.: Bio-energy with carbon storage (BECS): a sequential decision approach to the threat of abrupt climate change. Energy **30**(14), 2654–2671 (2005)
27. Silver, D., et al.: Mastering the game of Go with deep neural networks and tree search. Nature **529**(7587), 484–489 (2016)
28. Simonyan, K., Zisserman, A.: Two-stream convolutional networks for action recognition in videos. Adv. Neural Inf. Process. Syst. **27** (2014)
29. Sutton, R.S., Barto, A.G.: Reinforcement Learning: An Introduction. MIT press, Cambridge (2018)
30. Sutton, R.S., McAllester, D., Singh, S., Mansour, Y.: Policy gradient methods for reinforcement learning with function approximation. Adv. Neural Inf. Process. Syst. **12** (1999)
31. Tran, D., et al.: Learning spatiotemporal features with 3d convolutional networks. In: Proceedings of the IEEE International Conference on Computer Vision, pp. 4489–4497. IEEE Press, Washington (2015)
32. Vaswani, A., et al.: Attention is all you need. Adv. Neural Inf. Process. Syst. **30**, 30 (2017)
33. Wang, L., et al.: Temporal segment networks: towards good practices for deep action recognition. In: European Conference on Computer Vision, pp. 20–36. Springer, Amsterdam (2016). https://doi.org/10.1007/978-3-319-46484-8_2
34. Watkins, C.J.C.H.: Learning from delayed rewards (1989)
35. Yang, J., et al.: Focal self-attention for local-global interactions in vision transformers. arXiv preprint arXiv:2107.00641 (2021)
36. Yarats, D., et al.: Improving sample efficiency in model-free reinforcement learning from images. In: Proceedings of the AAAI Conference on Artificial Intelligence, vol. 35(12), pp. 10674–10681 (2021)
37. Chen, L., et al.: Decision transformer: reinforcement learning via sequence modeling. Adv. Neural Inf. Process. Syst. **34**, 15084–15097 (2021)

# Two-Stream Communication-Efficient Federated Pruning Network

Shiqiao Gu, Liu Yang$^{(\boxtimes)}$, Siqi Deng, and Zhengyi Xu

College of Intelligence and Computing, Tianjin University, Tianjin, China
{gushiqiao,yangliuyl}@tju.edu.cn

**Abstract.** Federated learning is a distributed machine learning framework which enables different parties to collaboratively train a model while protecting data privacy and security. This form of privacy-preserving collaborative learning comes at the cost of a significant communication overhead during training. Another key challenge in federated learning is to handle the heterogeneity of local data distribution across parties. To solve these problems, we proposed a novel two-stream communication-efficient federated pruning network (FedPrune), which consists of two parts: in the downstream stage, deep reinforcement learning is used to adaptively prune each layer of global model to reduce downstream communication costs; in the upstream stage, a pruning method based on the proximal operator is proposed to reduce the upstream communication costs as well as limit the drift of the local update, which is robust to non-IID client data. FedPrune is tested on three DNN models and publicly available datasets. The results demonstrate that it can well control the training overhead while still guaranteeing the learning performance.

## 1 Introduction

The recent advancements in deep neural networks lay huge potential in harnessing the rich data provided by IoT devices to improve learning effectiveness and model performance. At the same time, data privacy has become a growing concern for many users. This leaves us facing the following dilemma: How are we going to make use of the rich combined data of IoT devices for training deep learning models if this data cannot be stored at a centralized location? Federated learning (FL) resolves this issue as it allows multiple parties to jointly train a collaborative learning model, while each participant conducts the training process only using their own data without the need of data sharing to a centralized server [21, 22].

One important issue in federated learning is the massive communication overhead that arises from sending around and receiving the model updates. In general, a large number of parameters have to be uploaded and downloaded between the server and clients during every training iteration [19]. Consequently, if the bandwidth is limited or communication is expensive, federated learning will become unproductive or even completely unfeasible [23]. In order to achieve

S. Khanna et al. (Eds.): PRICAI 2022, LNCS 13631, pp. 185–196, 2022.
https://doi.org/10.1007/978-3-031-20868-3_14

communication efficient federated learning, some gradient/model compression techniques [1,9,18,20,25,26,30,33] were proposed for reducing the cost of communication. While they did not consider the compression the server-to-client. Some methods [6,13,24] were proposed to reduce both the downstream and upstream communication costs. However, due to the different parameter distribution of each layer, it is not appropriate to use a fixed pruning strategy (fixed pruning threshold/ratio) to compress each layer of the global model. Recently, AutoML pruning methods based on deep reinforcement learning (DRL) [2–4,32] obtain better results with higher versatility. Inspired by these methods, we propose to take deep Q-networks (DQN) agent [29] as a pruning policy for federated learning.

Another key challenge is the heterogeneity of data distribution on different parties [5,7,15]. Several studies have shown that multiple local updates in the clients with non-IID data would lead to client-drift, diverging updates in the individual clients. Such a phenomenon introduces high variance associated with the averaging step of FedAvg [21] for the global update, which hampers the convergence to the optimal average loss over all clients. Thus, the averaged global model is away from the global optimal solution. Recent methods for non-IID data [8,14,16,17,28] mainly focus on learning efficiency, i.e., improving training stability and using the minimum training rounds to get the target accuracy. However, these solutions often incur extra communication costs.

In this paper, in order to address the two key issues jointly, we proposed a two-stream compression federated pruning framework named FedPrune, which can not only compress both upstream and downstream communications, but also robust to non-IID user data. The main contributions of this work can be summarized as follows:

- In order to reduce the downstream communication costs, deep reinforcement learning is used to guide the adaptive pruning of the global model on the server through deep Q-networks agent.
- A local update pruning method based on the proximal operator is proposed to reduce the upstream communication costs. Moreover, it limits the drift of local updates, so it is robust to non-IID setting.
- The experimental results on benchmark real-world datasets are reported to demonstrate that it can well reduce the communication cost without affecting the learning performance.

## 2    Proposed Method

In this section, this paper first establishes preliminaries of our proposed method FedPrune, and then presents the details which consist of three parts, downstream compression via DRL agent and upstream compression based on proximal operator.

## 2.1  Preliminary

We first formally introduce the symbols and notations used in this paper and then give the framework of FedPrune. In the $t$-th round of the federated learning, the server maintains a global model with $l$ layers $\bar{w}_t = \{\bar{w}_t^{(1)}, \bar{w}_t^{(2)}, \cdots, \bar{w}_t^{(l)}\}$. The goal of downstream compression is to prune $\bar{w}_t$ and get the sub-model $\bar{w}_t' = \{\bar{w}_t'^{(1)}, \bar{w}_t'^{(2)}, \cdots, \bar{w}_t'^{(l)}\}$. And then the compressed model $\bar{w}_t'$ will be sent to all clients.

For the $k$-th client, local SGD is performed on its private dataset $\mathcal{D}_k$ to get the local model $w_{k,t}$. And then the difference between its local model and the global model is obtained, i.e. $h_{k,t} := w_{k,t} - \bar{w}_t'$. The purpose of upstream pruning is to compress $h_{k,t}$ into $h_{k,t}'$, and send $h_{k,t}'$ back to the server. Finally, all local compressed updates are aggregated to generate a new global model $\bar{w}_{t+1}$. The overall framework of our approach is shown in Fig. 1.

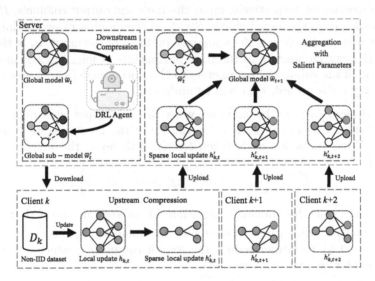

**Fig. 1.** Overall framework of FedPrune for two-stream communication-efficient federated learning.

## 2.2  Downstream Compression via DRL Agent

In this subsection, we focus on pruning the global model $\bar{w}_t$ to reduce downstream communication costs. The $\bar{w}_t$ is compressed into $\bar{w}_t'$ with the objective function:

$$\min_{\bar{w}'} \frac{1}{2} \|\bar{w}' - \bar{w}_t\|_2^2 \quad \text{s.t.} \quad \|\bar{w}'\|_0 \leq \kappa \tag{1}$$

where $\kappa \geq 0$ is a parameter to control the sparsity. $\|\cdot\|_2$ and $\|\cdot\|_0$ are the $L_2$-norm and $L_0$-norm respectively. Equation (1) is equivalent to the following constrained problem,

$$\bar{w}_t' := \arg\min_{\bar{w}'} \frac{1}{2} \|\bar{w}' - \bar{w}_t\|_2^2 + \alpha \|\bar{w}'\|_0 \tag{2}$$

where $\alpha \geq 0$ is a hyperparameter. Solving Eq. (2) is difficult because the $L_0$-norm is not differentiable. In addition, as the layers in $\bar{w}_t$ are correlated in an unknown way, determining the compression policy is highly non-trivial. To this end, DRL is used to efficiently sample the design space and improve the compression quality of the model. The task of pruning the global model $\bar{w}_t$ is regarded as a Markov decision problem (MDP). We formulate and construct each element of the MDP tuple to enable us to use DRL for pruning. In the below subsections, we elaborate on each of the tuple elements.

**State Space.** In order to discriminate each layer in the global model at different rounds, a 10-dimensional vector space is used to model a continuous state space:

$$s_j = [t, j, C, N, H, W, Stride, Padding, u_j, v_j] \qquad (3)$$

where $t$ represents the $t$-th global round, $j$ is the index of the layer, $C$ and $N$ are the dimension of, respectively, input channels and output channels, $H$ is the kernel height, $W$ is the kernel width, $Stride$ is the number of pixels shifts over the input matrix, $Padding$ is the boundary padding of the input, $u_j$ is the ratio of the $j$-th layer parameters to the total parameters of initial global model, $v_j$ is the ratio of the sub-model parameters to the initial model parameters at this time. As layer $j$ is pruned, $v_{j+1}$ will be updated.

**Action Space.** Inspired by previous work [3], this paper uses a magnitude threshold derived from the standard deviation of the layer weights as pruning criterion. When an action $a_j$ is taken for the $j$-th layer, the weight set after pruning is

$$\bar{w}_t^{\prime(j)} = \left\{ \bar{w}_t^{(j)}(u) \,\middle|\, |\bar{w}_t^{(j)}(u)| > a_j \sigma \left( \bar{w}_t^{(j)} \right) \right\}, \qquad (4)$$

where $\sigma \left( \bar{w}_t^{(j)} \right)$ is the standard deviation of weights in the $j$-th layer. In the experiments, this paper discretizes the value of $a_j$ i.e. $a_j \in \mathcal{A} = \{0.1, 0.2, \cdots, 1.5\}$ to further reduce the search complexity, which is relatively fine-grained for accurate compression.

**Reward Function.** By the reasonable reward function, DRL agent can find the compression limit without losing the performance of the model. According to Eq. (2), the reward function is designed as follows:

$$r_j = - \|\bar{w}_t^{\prime} - \bar{w}_t\|_2 \cdot \log(\|\bar{w}_t^{\prime}\|_0) \qquad (5)$$

where $\bar{w}_t^{\prime} = \{\bar{w}_t^{\prime(1)}, \bar{w}_t^{\prime(2)}, \cdots, \bar{w}_t^{\prime(j)}, \bar{w}_t^{(j+1)}, \cdots, \bar{w}_t^{(l)}\}$ is the global sub-model obtained by pruning the $j$-th layer of the global model $\bar{w}_t$. The performance degradation of $\bar{w}_t^{\prime}$ compared with $\bar{w}_t$ is approximately measured by the Euclidean distance of these two models. In each episode, as the number of layers pruned by DRL agent increases, the Euclidean distance of the two models will gradually increase, but the size of the sub-model will gradually decrease. Because of the game relationship between the two terms in the reward function, the DRL agent can learn the optimal sparsification policy based on the objective of maximization of total reward per episode.

**Training the Pruning Agent with DRL Algorithm.** To solve the MDP, this paper chooses amongst various available DRL algorithms. Value-based DRL algorithms formally uses an action-value function $Q(s_j, a)$ to estimate an expected return starting from state $s_j$. Typically, a deep neural network $Q(s_j, a; \theta)$ is used to represent the function approximator with the parameters $\theta$. In this paper, Dueling DQN [29] algorithm is used to train the pruning agent. The Dueling DQN learning problem becomes minimizing the MSE loss between the target and the approximator, which is defined as:

$$l_j(\theta) = (r_j + \gamma Q(s_{j+1}, \text{argmax}_{a'} Q(s_{j+1}, a'; \theta')) - Q(s_j, a_j; \theta))^2 \tag{6}$$

where $\theta$ is the online parameters updated per time step, and the $\theta'$ is the frozen parameters to add stability to action value estimation, and $\gamma$ is the discount factor.

## 2.3 Upstream Compression Based on Proximal Operator

**Local Training with Proximal Regularization.** Non-IID data has a significant impact on FedAvg [21]'s performance. Because the distribution of each local dataset is very different from the global distribution, the local objective of each party is inconsistent with the global optimal value [16]. FedProx improved the local target based on FedAvg [21]. As shown in Eq. (7), the $L_2$ proximal term is added to the local objective function to limit the distance between the local model and the global model.

$$f_k(w_{k,t}) = \mathbb{E}_{\xi_k}[L_k(w_{k,t}; \xi_k)] + \frac{\mu}{2}\|w_{k,t} - \bar{w}'_t\|_2^2 \tag{7}$$

where $\xi_k$ is a random data sample drawn according to the distribution of $\mathcal{D}_k$, and $L_k(w_{k,t}; \xi_k)$ is a loss function corresponding to this sample and local model $w_{k,t}$. The hyperparameter $\mu$ is introduced to control the weight of $L_2$ regularization.

Equation (7) is also used as the client optimization objective by FedPrune, which can bring two benefits. Firstly, it can make local update $h_{k,t}$ more suitable for sparse compression, because the parameters of local update $h_{k,t}$ will be closer to zero after training via Eq. (7). Secondly, it is a direct way to limit the drift of local update $h_{k,t}$ so that the averaged model does not deviate too far from the global optimum.

**Optimal Compressed Local Update.** Because the edge devices are often resource-constrained, it is not practical to use DRL to guide compression of local updates on the client side. Thus $L_1$-norm is used as the optimal convex approximation for $L_0$-norm in Eq.(1):

$$h'_{k,t} := \arg\min_h \frac{1}{2}\|h - h_{k,t}\|_2^2 + \lambda_t\|h\|_1 \tag{8}$$

where $\lambda_t$ is a parameter decays with $t$. The optimal solution of Eq. (8) is defined as follows:

$$h'_{k,t} = \text{sign}(h_{k,t}) \cdot \text{relu}(\|h_{k,t}\|_1 - \lambda_t) \tag{9}$$

After all participating federated learning clients completing this step, their sparse local updates are sent to the server for aggregating $\bar{w}_{t+1}$.

# 3    Experimental Setup and Results

## 3.1    Compared Methods

We compare FedPrune with two methods in two-steam communication compression, i.e., FedAvg [21] and LotteryFL [13]. For the downstream compression, MCFL [24] is compared with the proposed FedPrune. For the upstream compression, federated average masked pruning and random mask [9] are compared with the proposed FedPrune. In the heterogeneous data environment, this paper compares FedPrune with three state-of-the-art approaches FedNova [28], FedProx [16], and SCAFFOLD [8].

## 3.2    Datasets and Simulation Settings

This paper conducts experiments on three datasets MNIST, FashionMNIST [31] and CIFAR-10 [10]. For FashionMNIST dataset, we use the 2-CNN model: a CNN with two $5 \times 5$ convolution layers (the first with 20 channels, the second with 50, each followed by $2 \times 2$ maxpooling). The 2 FC layers have 500 and 10 nodes respectively. All of them are followed by ReLU activation. For the CIFAR-10 and MNIST datasets, we use the AlexNet [11] and LeNet-5 [12]. For all three datasets, we conduct experiments on IID and non-IID settings respectively. Like previous study [27], this paper uses Dirichlet distribution $\mathrm{Dir}(\beta)$ ($\beta{=}0.5$ by default) to generate non-IID data partition between parties. For LotteryFL [13], we vary the target pruning rate $r_{target} \in \{0.1, 0.3, 0.5\}$ as in its original paper.

## 3.3    Experiment Results

**Performance of Two-stream Compression.** In this term, we use the FedAvg [21] as the baseline, and report the test accuracies and the transmission parameters of LotteryFL [13] and our method FedPrune. The communication costs for total 100 rounds on MNIST, 100 rounds on CIFAR-10 and 200 rounds on FashionMNIST are summarized in Table 1. From the table, we have the following observation: FedPrune can achieve considerable performance with the lowest communication costs on all three datasets, especially in non-IID settings. For example, it can achieve 97.65%, 87.13% and 72.20% accuracies on MNIST, FashionMNIST and CIFAR-10 non-IID dataset, which is 0.50%,1.40% and 3.94% higher than that of LotteryFL(0.5) [13]. Moreover, LotteryFL [13] and FedAvg [21] respectively consume more communication costs compared to FedPrune. The reason is that FedPrune automatically finds the compression policy for global network to achieve even better performance than human strategy. Moreover, it can limit the client drift and accelerate the convergence of FL in the non-IID environment.

**Table 1.** Results on MNIST, FashionMNIST and CIFAR-10 datasets.

| Dataset | Method | IID | | Non-IID ($\beta = 0.5$) | |
|---|---|---|---|---|---|
| | | Acc. (%, ↑) | #Params (↓) | Acc. (%, ↑) | #Params (↓) |
| MNIST | FedAvg [21] | 98.97 | 123.41M | 98.64 | 123.41M |
| | LotteryFL (0.1) [13] | 97.89 | 43.77M | 96.31 | 44.16M |
| | LotteryFL (0.3) [13] | 97.95 | 50.24M | 96.38 | 50.24M |
| | LotteryFL (0.5) [13] | 98.19 | 60.20M | 97.15 | 60.20M |
| | **FedPrune(Ours)** | 98.11 | **27.59M** | 97.65 | **30.39M** |
| FashionMNIST | FedAvg [21] | 89.98 | 1724.32M | 88.74 | 1724.32M |
| | LotteryFL (0.1) [13] | 86.66 | 944.31M | 85.02 | 945.21M |
| | LotteryFL (0.3) [13] | 88.32 | 945.21M | 85.07 | 945.21M |
| | LotteryFL (0.5) [13] | 88.01 | 945.21M | 85.73 | 948.36M |
| | **FedPrune(Ours)** | 88.09 | **412.83M** | 87.13 | **513.19M** |
| CIFAR-10 | FedAvg [21] | 79.17 | 48686.23M | 73.71 | 48686.23M |
| | LotteryFL (0.1) [13] | 74.04 | 36555.91M | 69.81 | 37715.99M |
| | LotteryFL (0.5) [13] | 73.64 | 38957.74M | 68.26 | 37715.99M |
| | **FedPrune (Ours)** | 77.23 | **24590.71M** | 72.20 | **26570.10M** |

### 3.4 Ablation Study

In this section, we use the compression rate of communication costs to measure communication efficiency. Let $N$ and $P$ be the number of total transmission parameters and the sparse ratio respectively. After model compression, the number of parameters are compressed from $N$ to $N \times (1 - P)$, then the compressed rate is $1/(1 - P)$.

**Effect of Dueling DQN Agent.** In this part, we compare several different pruning strategies for the AlexNet model (75.28% accuracy) at the 50-th round of FedAvg. Specifically, we use the action space $\mathcal{A} = \{0.1, 0.2, \cdots, 1.5\}$ to train the Dueling DQN agent and specify the last layer as the end state, i.e., do not prune this layer. The pruning results of global model is shown in Fig. 2(a) and the total number of parameters is reduced by 75.01%. The parameter distribution of each layer in the global model is shown in Fig. 2(b). It can been seen that FedPrune adaptively prunes global model based on the parameter distribution of each layer. For example, the first layer has a large absolute value distribution range, so the DRL agent conservatively prunes this layer. While the absolute values of the 7-th layer parameters are mostly concentrated near zero, so the DRL agent progressively prunes this layer. Moreover, as shown in Fig. 3, the test accuracies of uniform pruning, MCFL [24] and FedPrune are 25.71%, 10.00% and 74.48% under the same total pruning ratio, respectively. Various colors represent the activation vectors for different classes. It can be seen that FedPrune's pruning strategy outperforms to the other two strategies. Since our method FedPrune can adaptively prune the global model according to the redundancy of each layer, both feature extraction ability and classification performance of pruned model are almost the same as the original model.

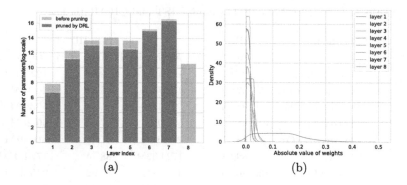

(a)                                      (b)

**Fig. 2.** (a): Adaptive pruning via Dueling DQN agent. (b) The parameter distribution of each layer in the global model.

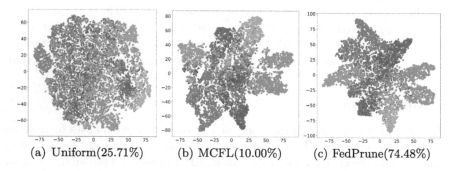

(a) Uniform(25.71%)    (b) MCFL(10.00%)    (c) FedPrune(74.48%)

**Fig. 3.** T-SNE visualization of hidden vectors with 75.01% pruning rate on the CIFAR-10 dataset, and the test accuracy is in parenthesis.

**Downstream Communication Efficiency.** For FedPrune and MCFL [24], we run 100 and 200 rounds respectively on CIFAR-10 and FashionMNIST datasets. From Table 2, it is obvious that our method outperforms MCFL [24] under both IID and non-IID settings. Specifically, on the FashionMNIST dataset, our Dueling DQN agent can compress downstream communications by 6.32× and 7.62× at IID and non-IID settings, respectively. And the test accuracies are almost as same as that of uncompressed FedAvg. But MCFL [24] achieves smaller compression rates (5.74×,6.58×) with little loss of accuracy. For the AlexNet model trained on the CIFAR-10 dataset, our method still outperforms MCFL [24]. It can be seen from these results that our Dueling DQN agent can play a good role in both deep and shallow neural networks, but the defects of MCFL [24] will be magnified in deep networks.

**Robustness to Non-IID.** We study the effect of data heterogeneity by varying the concentration parameter $\beta$ of Dirichlet distribution on FashionMNIST during 200 rounds. For a smaller $\beta$, the partition will be more unbalanced. The results are shown in Table 3. Our method can achieve similar performance to

**Table 2.** Comparison of downstream compression performance between FedPrune and MCFL($\lambda = 10^{-3}$).

| Dataset | Method | IID/Non-IID ($\beta = 0.5$) | | |
|---|---|---|---|---|
| | | Test Acc. (%, ↑) | #Params ($\times 10^{10}$, ↓) | Down.Compr. (↑) |
| FashionMNIST | FedAvg [21] | 89.98/88.74 | 0.086 | 1× |
| | MCFL [24] | 89.59/87.88 | 0.015/0.013 | 5.74×/6.58× |
| | **FedPrune(Ours)** | **90.04/89.40** | **0.014/0.011** | **6.32×/7.62×** |
| CIFAR-10 | FedAvg [21] | 79.17/73.71 | 2.430 | 1× |
| | MCFL [24] | 69.17/65.46 | 1.410/1.650 | 1.72×/1.47× |
| | **FedPrune(Ours)** | 78.79/72.79 | **1.090/1.030** | **2.22×/2.36×** |

**Table 3.** The accuracy with 50 parties and 100 parties (sample fraction=0.1) on FashionMNIST.

| #Parties | Method | $\beta = 0.3/0.1$ | | |
|---|---|---|---|---|
| | | Test Acc. (%, ↑) | #Params ($\times 10^9$, ↓) | Upstream Compr. (↑) |
| 50 | FedAvg [21] | 88.64/87.34 | 0.431 | 1× |
| | SCAFFOLD [8] | 86.73/87.28 | 0.862 | 0.5× |
| | FedNova [28] | 89.83/87.76 | 0.862 | 0.5× |
| | FedProx [16] | 88.67/88.04 | 0.431 | 1× |
| | **FedPrune(Ours)** | 88.97/87.42 | **0.063/0.064** | **6.83×/6.78×** |
| 100 | FedAvg [21] | 87.39/86.69 | 0.862 | 1× |
| | SCAFFOLD [8] | 88.26/85.63 | 1.720 | 0.5× |
| | FedNova [28] | 89.29/87.96 | 1.720 | 0.5× |
| | FedProx [16] | 88.06/87.14 | 0.862 | 1× |
| | **FedPrune(Ours)** | 88.18/86.38 | **0.127/0.152** | **6.77×/5.67×** |

other methods regardless of whether there are 50 or 100 participants. More importantly, FedPrune is far more communication-efficient than other methods.

**Upstream Communication Efficiency.** In this part, we first compare two methods of upstream compression on FashionMNIST and CIFAR-10. Like previous work [18], the first method for FedPrune to compare is federated average masked pruning, which prunes local update weights based on magnitude before sending them to the server. The second is the random mask [9], which randomly generates a mask matrix for the local model update to sparse its parameters. Model compression is challenging in early training process because the parameters of neural networks change rapidly. Therefore, in order to further demonstrate the efficiency of our method, we compare FedPrune with the other two upstream compression methods in the first 30 rounds. Figure 4(a)–(d) show the relationship between the number of transmission parameters and performance of global model. Figure 4(e)–(f) show the communications required for each method to achieve the same target accuracy. From these figures, we find that the overall

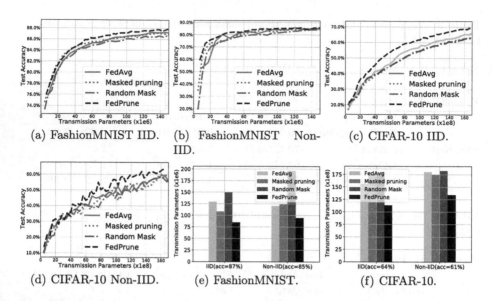

Fig. 4. (a)–(d): Accuracy v.s. transmission parameters. (e)–(f): Communication costs of different methods to achieve target accuracy on FashionMNIST and CIFAR-10 datasets.

performance of FedPrune is better than the other two methods in both IID and non-IID conditions. This is because a direct mask for client updates is lacking in regularization of the structure, which cannot be used effectively in each round. Therefore, it is hard to achieve extremely high compression rate with reasonable accuracy and fast coverage speed by this way.

## 4    Conclusion

In this paper, the proposed FedPrune model is a two-stream federated learning network pruning framework and can reduce both the upstream communication costs and the downstream communication costs. FedPrune includes a DRL-based adaptive pruning method for efficient FL, which finds a desired model size to achieve a good accuracy-communication trade-off. The experiments show that FedPrune not only can reduce data transmission effectively. Moreover, it is robust to user non-IID data due to the drift limitation of the local update. In the future, we will investigate combining FedPrune with other compression methods, such as quantization, to further reduce the communication overhead.

**Acknowledgments.** This work was supported in part by the National Natural Science Foundation of China under Grant 62076179, in part by the Beijing Natural Science Foundation under Grant Z180006.

# References

1. Alistarh, D., Grubic, D., Li, J., Tomioka, R., Vojnovic, M.: QSGD: communication-efficient SGD via gradient quantization and encoding. In: Advances in Neural Information Processing Systems, pp. 1709–1720 (2017)
2. Ashok, A., Rhinehart, N., Beainy, F., Kitani, K.M.: N2N learning: network to network compression via policy gradient reinforcement learning. In: ICLR, pp. 1–20 (2017)
3. Gupta, M., Aravindan, S., Kalisz, A., Chandrasekhar, V., Jie, L.: Learning to prune deep neural networks via reinforcement learning. arXiv preprint arXiv:2007.04756, pp. 1–11 (2020)
4. He, Y., Lin, J., Liu, Z., Wang, H., Li, L.-J., Han, S.: AMC: AutoML for model compression and acceleration on mobile devices. In: Ferrari, V., Hebert, M., Sminchisescu, C., Weiss, Y. (eds.) ECCV 2018. LNCS, vol. 11211, pp. 815–832. Springer, Cham (2018). https://doi.org/10.1007/978-3-030-01234-2_48
5. Hsu, T.M.H., Qi, H., Brown, M.: Measuring the effects of non-identical data distribution for federated visual classification. arXiv preprint arXiv:1909.06335, pp. 1–5 (2019)
6. Jiang, Y., et al.: Model pruning enables efficient federated learning on edge devices. arXiv preprint arXiv:1909.12326, pp. 1–26 (2019)
7. Kairouz, P., et al.: Advances and open problems in federated learning. In: FTML, pp. 1–210 (2021)
8. Karimireddy, S.P., Kale, S., Mohri, M., Reddi, S.J., Stich, S.U., Suresh, A.T.: Scaffold: stochastic controlled averaging for on-device federated learning, pp. 1–41 (2019)
9. Konečnỳ, J., McMahan, H.B., Yu, F.X., Richtárik, P., Suresh, A.T., Bacon, D.: Federated learning: strategies for improving communication efficiency. arXiv preprint arXiv:1610.05492, pp. 1–10 (2016)
10. Krizhevsky, A., Hinton, G., et al.: Learning multiple layers of features from tiny images. Technical report (2009)
11. Krizhevsky, A., Sutskever, I., Hinton, G.E.: Imagenet classification with deep convolutional neural networks. In: NIPS, pp. 1097–1105 (2012)
12. LeCun, Y., et al.: Lenet-5, convolutional neural networks, p. 14 (2015). http://yann.lecun.com/exdb/lenet
13. Li, A., et al.: LotteryFL: empower edge intelligence with personalized and communication-efficient federated learning. In: 2021 IEEE/ACM Symposium on Edge Computing (SEC), pp. 68–79. IEEE (2021)
14. Li, Q., Diao, Y., Chen, Q., He, B.: Federated learning on non-IID data silos: an experimental study. arXiv preprint arXiv:2102.02079, pp. 1–20 (2021)
15. Li, Q., et al.: A survey on federated learning systems: vision, hype and reality for data privacy and protection. In: TKDE, pp. 1–44 (2021)
16. Li, T., Sahu, A.K., Zaheer, M., Sanjabi, M., Talwalkar, A., Smith, V.: Federated optimization in heterogeneous networks. In: MLSYS, pp. 429–450 (2020)
17. Li, X., Huang, K., Yang, W., Wang, S., Zhang, Z.: On the convergence of FedaVG on non-IID data. arXiv preprint arXiv:1907.02189, pp. 1–26 (2019)
18. Lin, S., Wang, C., Li, H., Deng, J., Wang, Y., Ding, C.: ESMFL: efficient and secure models for federated learning. In: NIPS, pp. 1–7 (2020)
19. Liu, J., et al.: From distributed machine learning to federated learning: a survey. In: KAIS, pp. 1–33 (2022)

20. Luping, W., Wei, W., Bo, L.: CMFL: mitigating communication overhead for federated learning. In: ICDCS, pp. 954–964 (2019)
21. McMahan, B., Moore, E., Ramage, D., Hampson, S., Arcas, B.A.: Communication-efficient learning of deep networks from decentralized data. In: AISTATS, pp. 1273–1282 (2017)
22. Nguyen, D.C., et al.: Federated learning for smart healthcare: a survey. In: CSUR, pp. 1–37 (2022)
23. Sattler, F., Wiedemann, S., Müller, K.R., Samek, W.: Robust and communication-efficient federated learning from non-IID data. In: TNNLS, pp. 3400–3413 (2019)
24. Shah, S.M., Lau, V.K.: Model compression for communication efficient federated learning. In: TNNLS, pp. 1–15 (2021)
25. Tao, Z., Li, Q.: Esgd: Communication efficient distributed deep learningon the edge. In: USENIX Workshop on HotEdge, pp. 1–6 (2018)
26. Wang, H., Sievert, S., Liu, S., Charles, Z., Papailiopoulos, D., Wright, S.: Atomo: communication-efficient learning via atomic sparsification. In: NIPS pp. 1–12 (2018)
27. Wang, H., Yurochkin, M., Sun, Y., Papailiopoulos, D., Khazaeni, Y.: Federated learning with matched averaging. In: ICLR, pp. 1–16 (2020)
28. Wang, J., Liu, Q., Liang, H., Joshi, G., Poor, H.V.: Tackling the objective inconsistency problem in heterogeneous federated optimization. In: NIPS, pp. 7611–7623 (2020)
29. Wang, Z., Schaul, T., Hessel, M., Hasselt, H., Lanctot, M., Freitas, N.: Dueling network architectures for deep reinforcement learning. In: ICML, pp. 1995–2003 (2016)
30. Wen, W., et al.: TernGrad: ternary gradients to reduce communication in distributed deep learning. In: NIPS, pp. 1–11 (2017)
31. Xiao, H., Rasul, K., Vollgraf, R.: Fashion-MNIST: a novel image dataset for benchmarking machine learning algorithms. arXiv preprint arXiv:1708.07747, pp. 1–6 (2017)
32. Yu, S., Mazaheri, A., Jannesari, A.: GNN-RL compression: topology-aware network pruning using multi-stage graph embedding and reinforcement learning. arXiv preprint arXiv:2102.03214, pp. 1–10 (2021)
33. Yu, S., Nguyen, P., Anwar, A., Jannesari, A.: Adaptive dynamic pruning for non-IID federated learning. arXiv preprint arXiv:2106.06921, pp. 1–7 (2021)

# Strong General AI

# Multi-scale Lightweight Neural Network for Real-Time Object Detection

Yuan Li[1], Qiaojun Wu[2], Song Chen[1,2,3], and Yi Kang[1,2,3(✉)]

[1] School of Microelectronics, University of Science and Technology of China,
Hefei, China
`ly549826@mail.ustc.edu.cn`, {`songch,ykang`}`@ustc.edu.cn`
[2] Institute of Advanced Technology, University of Science and Technology of China,
Hefei, China
`qjwu@mail.ustc.edu.cn`
[3] Institute of Artificial Intelligence, Hefei Comprehensive National Science Center,
Hefei, China

**Abstract.** Deep learning-based object detection methods have been widely used in computer vision recently. Many previous works on object detection improve performance by utilizing complex algorithms and architectures or involving expensive calculations. But they often ignore the real-time requirement of applications such as autonomous driving. Our work is to design a lightweight network for real-time inference on edge devices. Considering the inference speed of one-stage object detection is significantly faster than that of two-stage object detection, we propose a one-stage Multi-scale Lightweight Neural Network (MLNet), which integrates various classification and detection features on multiple scales. The proposed neural network contains parallel multi branches, and each branch has different output feature mapping sizes. We also propose lightweight feature extraction blocks used in the network branches to improve performance and reduce computations. A lightweight detection head is used to reduce the inference time further. Experimental results on COCO datasets demonstrate that MLNet achieves 28.7% AP on COCO with only about 2.1M parameters and shows its superiority compared to the five widely used state-of-the-art object detection methods.

**Keywords:** One-stage · Object detection · Lightweight network · Multi-scale features

## 1 Introduction

The object detection neural network is used to identify and locate objects in an image accurately and has made good progress with the development of the Convolution Neural Network (CNN) in recent years. Many innovative CNN works have achieved excellent accuracies when they are used in object detection.

However, in terms of real-time processing, many algorithms have a large number of computations. Some complex neural networks, such as Depth Residual Network (ResNet) [6], Dense Convolution Network (DenseNet) [9], Dual Path

S. Khanna et al. (Eds.): PRICAI 2022, LNCS 13631, pp. 199–211, 2022.
https://doi.org/10.1007/978-3-031-20868-3_15

Network (DPN) [2] and YOLOv3 [23], can run fast on cloud servers with intensive computing resources, but they are stretched on edge devices with limited computing resources, such as mobile phones. Therefore, researchers have designed some small and efficient lightweight neural networks, such as MobileNetV1 [8], MobileNetV2 [24], ShuffleNetV1 [30], ThunderNet [21], YOLO-LITE [10] and YOLO-Tiny series [22,23,31], which have less intensive computing requirements and can be more easily deployed in edge devices.

Inspired by these previous works, we propose a one-stage multi-scale lightweight neural network, which improves inference speed and the accuracy of object location and classification through a multi-scale branch structure with lightweight convolution filter groups in branches and detection head. For downsampling modules, we propose a fast method using dilated convolution groups which can expand receptive fields while taking only a tiny extra amount of computations and parameters. For the feature extraction part, special blocks composed of convolution filter banks and channel shuffling blocks similar to ShuffleNetV1 [30] are designed to reduce the computations in each branch. Based on the concept of Trident Network [12], convolution kernels of different sizes are sensitive to objects of various sizes. It inspires us to set different dilation coefficients to obtain multi-scale convolution kernels to extract the features of different scales while the amount of computations is unchanged. Because the operations in different network branches are carried out in parallel, the network inference time can be reduced. From reference [13], too many straight convolution operations lead to the loss of detailed feature information, affecting the prediction of boundary areas. To avoid the disappearance of object location information extracted from the shallow layer, we design a detection part that is improved from FPN [13] to fuse the features of different branches to improve the accuracy of object location and classification.

Our proposed one-stage object detection network can properly extract and combine features with different resolutions generated from three branches, which can speed up network inference and improve accuracy. Our main contributions are summarised as follows:

We propose a Fast Down-sampling Module (FDM) and use dilation convolution groups to form convolution kernels, which can increase the receptive field and reduce computations. Based on this module, feature extraction is improved, and the network inference time can be shorter.

We propose a three-branch structure with multi-scale convolution kernels called Reduced Computational Block (RCB) to extract features with reduced computational overhead, and each branch consists of several RCBs. The three-branch structure can perform computing in parallel, so our method is more suitable for real-time processing.

We have established a practical, lightweight detection part, called E-FPN, fully fusing and utilizing features of different resolutions to achieve high accuracy by the Enhanced Connection Module (ECM). Compared with state-of-the-art mainstream model results, our network achieves the highest accuracy at the low level of parameters (2.1M).

## 2   Related Works

This section introduces previous works on the three aspects: multi-scale branch design, convolution filter with reduced computation, and detection.

**Multi-branch.** Multi-branch network is a variant of a deep convolution network, which is widely used in multi-input fields such as binocular vision. This structure has a strong ability to combine different kinds of features. In 2017, Chen et al. [2] proposed a Dual Path Network for image classification, presenting a new topology of connection paths internally. Recently, many network models have adopted multi-branch structures to obtain multi-scale features and efficient combinations. Li et al. [12] proposed a Scale-aware Trident Network for object detection. Different branches share the same convolution filter and have scale-aware dilation sensitive to objects of different sizes. Goyal et al. [4] designed a series of Non-deep Networks with three branches using convolution filters of the same size but not sharing weights. Although these models take advantage of the multi-branch structure, they still have some limitations. For example, the branch of the Non-deep Network [4] is composed of VGG blocks, which have extremely high computational costs.

**Computation Based.** Computation is one of the most important performance indexes of neural networks. In recent years, researchers have designed many high-performance models with reduced computation. Convolution groups are a variant of convolution in which the channels of the input feature maps are grouped, and convolution operations are independently performed for each grouped channel. Mamalet et al. [19] put forward the concept of depthwise separable convolution in 2012. And the depthwise convolution significantly reduces the computational cost by omitting the convolution in the channel domain. MobileNetV1 is an efficient CNN model consisting of depthwise convolution modules and pointwise convolution modules. Because the kernel size is 1×1, the computational cost is reduced by 1/9 compared with conv3x3. Channel shuffling is an operation (layer) to change the order of channels used in ShuffleNet [30]. This operation is implemented by tensor shaping and transposition. If there is no channel shuffling, the outputs of grouped convolutions are never exploited among groups, resulting in the degradation of accuracy. Dilation convolution was first proposed by Yu et al. [27] in 2015 and applied to context aggregation. Based on dilation convolution, Liu et al. [16] proposed a Receptive Field Block Net in object recognition to realize accurate and fast object recognition. These methods can improve the performance of the model and reduce computational costs. Based on these methods, we design the module suitable for our network.

**Detection Based.** Lin et al. [13] proposed Feature Pyramid Networks (FPN) in 2017. They exploit deep convolution networks' inherent multi-scale and pyramidal hierarchy to construct feature pyramids at additional marginal cost. To make features of different scales contain rich semantic information while not making the computation cost too high, the author adopts the top-down architecture with lateral connections so that the low-level features with high resolution and low semantics and the high-level features with low resolution and high

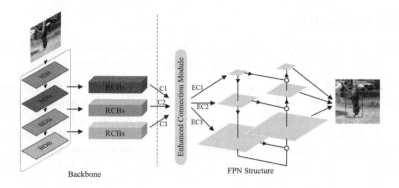

**Fig. 1.** The overview of the whole architecture

semantics can be fused so that the final feature maps of different scales have rich semantic information. Based on FPN, PANet [26] was proposed in 2019. The greatest contribution of PANet is to put forward a top-down and bottom-up bidirectional fusion backbone and add a shortcut between the bottom layer and the top layer to shorten the path between layers. PANet also proposed two modules: the Full-connected Fusion module and the Adaptive Features Pooling module. Specifically, the Adaptive Features Pooling module can aggregate features between different layers to ensure the integrity and diversity of features, and a more accurate prediction mask can be obtained through the Full-connected Fusion module. These methods are innovative in feature extraction and fusion, but we can explore more possibilities based on their works.

## 3   Methodology

In this section, we discuss our proposed model in detail. Firstly, we explain the overall network architecture. And then, we introduce the Fast Down-sampling Module (FDM) and the Reduced Computational Module (RCM) design in the network model. Finally, we describe the details of the E-FPN with the Enhanced Connection Module (ECM).

### 3.1   Network Architecture

The overall network architecture is shown in Fig. 1, including the backbone and the detection part. The FDM processes the input image, then three kinds of feature map information with different scales are obtained and handed over to three branches, respectively. To improve inference speed, the three branches extract varying information with different resolutions by multi-scale BDBs in parallel to get feature maps (C1, C2, C3). The high-performance detection part aims at the feature information of different scales and enriches the semantic information of features in different scales by ECM to get feature maps (EC1, EC2, EC3). Finally, the optimized FPN detection network is used to obtain the final prediction.

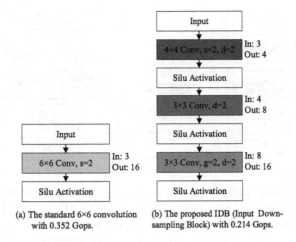

(a) The standard 6×6 convolution with 0.352 Gops.

(b) The proposed IDB (Input Down-sampling Block) with 0.214 Gops.

**Fig. 2.** The description of two different versions of the initial layer of the network (s is the stride, d is the number of dilations, g is the number of groups, and we use 1 for group, stride, and dilation if not mentioned). The input is an image with a size of $3 \times 640 \times 640$. Compared with the module in (a), the module in (b) can reduce the computing cost by about 39.2% and improve the network performance.

## 3.2 Fast Down-Sampling Module

Multi-scale feature representations of CNNs are of great importance for object detection [1,5,18,28]. Inspired by these works, we design a Fast Down-sampling Module (FDM) to get feature maps of different scales, including an Input feature map Down-sampling Block (IDB) and Branch Down-sampling Blocks (BDB). Lightweight is the focus of our design. Previous works usually adopt convolution kernels with large sizes (such as $6 \times 6$) to extract features from the input feature map. Still, instead, we use one conv4 × 4 (dilation = 2) kernel and two conv3 × 3 kernels (dilation = 2) to reduce the computational cost and expand the receptive field of convolution operation to maintain network performance. The structure of the down-sampling module is shown in Fig. 2.

References [15–17] demonstrate that the CNNs can only capture the information inside the receptive field, and a sizeable receptive field is very effective in semantic segmentation and object detection. Therefore, we adopt dilation convolutions with different dilation rates to adapt to varying sizes of feature maps and use Group Convolution [19] to reduce floating-point operations and model parameters in down-sampling operations. The structure of the BDBs is shown in Fig. 3. The design of BDB is referred to from the design method of the down-sampling module of ThunderNet [21]. The conv5×5 kernel replaces the conv3×3 kernel, and the number of groups is doubled, so the receptive field is more extensive, and the computations are increased slightly. At the beginning of the BDB, the input features are processed by parallel down-sampling convolution operations. A pointwise convolution operation and a conv5×5 operation with four groups on the feature map are performed, and average pooling and a pointwise

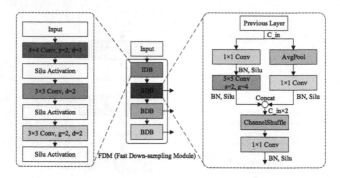

**Fig. 3.** The structure of FDM (Fast Down-sampling Module) and BDB (Branch Down-sampling Block). The input is an image with a size of $3 \times 640 \times 640$. C_in is the number of input feature map channels. Other terms are the same as Fig. 2.

convolution operation on the feature map are also carried out. Then the two groups of features are concatenated and shuffled [24]. Finally, a pointwise convolution is performed. The dilation rate of the conv5×5 kernel is set according to the size of the input feature map. For example, if the input feature map is large enough, such as $160 \times 160$, the dilation rate of BDB is set to (dilation $= 2$).

### 3.3  Reduced Computational Block

Reduced Computational Block (RCB) extracts features from branches of different scales. Meanwhile, it is of great importance for us to reduce the computation cost. RCB can keep the convolution performance while using fewer computations and parameters. Figure 4 shows an overview of RCBs. The group convolution kernel size of RCB is $5 \times 5$. In RCB, feature map computations perform two parallel convolutions first. The process path on the left is a pointwise convolutional operation, a dilated group convolutional operation, and an addition operation. The group convolution describes the information exchange between adjacent feature maps and the spatial features of each channel. The process path on the right is a pointwise convolution, representing each point's features and the information exchange between channels. After two parallel convolution operations, the channel shuffling operation is used, which enables the feature maps between different groups to communicate and improves the feature extraction capability of the network. Finally, an extra pointwise convolution is carried out to extract features and exchange information across channels. The network performance degradation could be caused by setting the same dilation rate in multiple consecutive multi-scale convolution blocks. So the dilation rate should be adjusted dynamically. For example, if the input feature map is large enough, such as $160 \times 160$, the dilation rate of 4 RCBs is set to (dilation $= 2,1,2,1$).

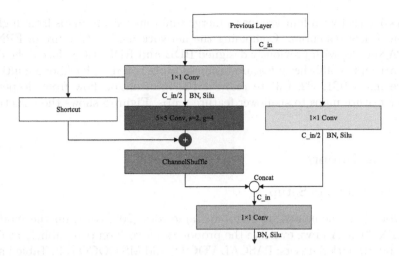

**Fig. 4.** The structure of RCB (Reduced Computational Block). C_in is the number of input feature map channels. Other terms are the same as Fig. 2.

### 3.4 Detection Part

Previous studies [7,13,26] indicate that large-scale feature maps have more object details, such as edges, corners, or textures, while small feature maps have comprehensive semantic understanding. So that the final feature maps of different scales have rich semantic information. A more accurate prediction can be achieved by fusing the features of these different layers. Because of the multi-scale branch design, the resolution and semantic information of features in different scales lack fusion and enhancement. GiraffeDet [25] proposed a concept that FPN structure plays a more critical role in detection networks than traditional backbones. This inspires us to design an Enhanced Connection Module (ECM) at the front end of the detector, which performs fusion operations on multi-scale features to narrow the semantic gap between them. A fusion block contains a

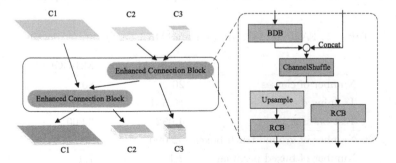

**Fig. 5.** The structure of the Enhanced Connection Module

conv5×5 kernel with four groups to merge different feature maps from high resolution to low resolution. Combining the network model structure of FPN [13] and PANet [26] with previously designed BDB and RDB, ECM forms the detection part and establishes a feature fusion module based on backbone multi-scale feature maps (C1, C2, C3) to redirect the information flow from deeper and smaller feature maps to shallower feature maps. Figure 5 shows the structure of ECM.

## 4 Experiments

### 4.1 Experiments Setup

Our work is implemented on Pytorch framework [20]. We train the model on one RTX 3090. And we evaluate the proposed network on two publicly available image benchmark datasets: PASCAL VOC [3] and MS COCO [14]. Table 1 shows the details of the PASCAL VOC and MS COCO datasets.

**PASCAL VOC Dataset.** The VOC2007 contains 9,963 annotated images with a total of 24,640 objects. The VOC2012 dataset is an updated version of the VOC2007 dataset with 11,530 images. For the detection task, the VOC2012's datasets contain all corresponding images for the years 08–11. And the training datasets and validation datasets have 11,540 images for a total of 27,450 objects. The VOC2012 dataset is divided into 20 categories, including 21 categories for backgrounds. The networks are trained on the union set of VOC2007 and VOC2012, and we report model results on the set of the VOC2007 Test. We use the Adam optimizer [11]. The base learning rate is set to 1e−3 and dropped to 1e−4 and 1e−5 at the 120th and 240th epochs, respectively. We train the model for a total of 300 epochs.

**COCO Dataset.** The COCO dataset consists of over 200,000 images and 250,000 people instances labeled with 17 key points. We train our model on COCO train2017 dataset, including 57,000 images and 150,000 person instances, and evaluate our method on the val2017 set containing 5,000 images. We apply the basic augmentation methods such as flip, rotate, and mix-up [29] instead of

**Table 1.** PASCAL VOC dataset and MS COCO dataset details.

|  | PASCAL VOC | MS COCO |
|---|---|---|
| Number of classes | 20 | 80 |
| Training dataset | 16,551 | 117,264 |
| Test dataset | 4,952 | 5,000 |
| Number of ground-truth boxes | 52,090 | 866,678 |
| Number of boxed per image | 2.1 | 7.4 |

**Table 2.** Performance comparison on PASCAL VOC dataset.

| Model | Backbone | Input Size | MFLOPs | Params | mAP (%) |
|---|---|---|---|---|---|
| YOLOv2 | Darknet-19 | 416 × 416 | 17,400 | 50.5M | 76.8 |
| MobileNet-SSD | MobileNet | 300×300 | 1,150 | 4.7M | 68.0 |
| SqYOLOv3-tiny | Tiny-Darknet | 416×416 | 2,780 | 8.7M | 62.5 |
| YOLOv4-tiny | Tiny-CSPDarknet | 416×416 | 3,450 | 5.9M | 72.3 |
| MLNet (*ours*) | Tri-bone | 320 × 320 | 1,420 | 2.0M | 71.2 |
| | | 416×416 | 2,390 | 2.0M | 78.4 |

the fancy methods. We set the batch size as 128 and chose SGD as the optimizer with a weight decay of 1e-4 and a momentum of 0.9. The learning rate starts from 1e-2 and drops as a cosine curve to 1e-3 in 300 epochs.

## 4.2   Results

**Results on PASCAL VOC.** Table 2 lists the mAP accuracy results, the number of model parameters, and the FLOPs for our network and other state-of-the-art networks. It can be seen from Table 2 that our proposed model surpasses prior state-of-the-art lightweight one-stage detectors by having much fewer parameters and the cost of much fewer computations while keeping comparable mAP accuracy. Specifically, MLNet with input size 416×416 outperforms YOLOv4-tiny with merely 31% of its computation overhead; MLNet with input size 320 × 320 surpasses MobileNet-SSD by 3.2% mAP score with a similar amount of computations and about 57% fewer number of parameters. Overall, MLNet achieves significantly better detection accuracy under comparable computational costs. As shown in Table 2, MLNet surpasses other one-stage counterparts by at least 1.6% mAP score.

**Results on COCO.** Table 3 shows the accuracy, the number of model parameters, and the computation overhead in MFLOPs for our network and referenced state-of-the-art networks on the validation set of MS COCO. From Table 3, we can see that MLNet, with the input size 640 × 640, achieves a 46.8% AP50 score and outperforms other methods in other input sizes. Compared to YOLOv4-tiny, MLNet has about 66% fewer model sizes and 42% fewer computations, achieving a 4.3% AP score gain with input size 416 × 416. Compared to YOLOv5n, though our network has higher total computations and a similar number of parameters, the performance of our network achieves 0.7%, AP score gain. Based on the analysis of Table 4, our optimized parallel processing architecture can process three branches in the network's backbone in parallel. In MLNet architecture, the critical path is the third branch with the most computations. However, it has much lower computations compared to YOLOv5n. Therefore, MLNet can have less inference latency compared to YOLOv5n.

**Table 3.** Performance comparison on MS COCO dataset.

| Model | Backbone | Input size | MFLOPs | Params | AP (%) | AP50 (%) |
|---|---|---|---|---|---|---|
| YOLOv2 | Darknet-19 | 416×416 | 17,500 | 50.5M | 21.6 | 44.0 |
| MobileNet-SSDLite | MobileNet | 320×300 | **1,300** | 4.7M | 22.2 | – |
| YOLOv3-tiny | Tiny-Darknet | 416×416 | 2,780 | 8.7M | 16.0 | 33.1 |
| YOLOv4-tiny | Tiny-CSPDarknet | 416×416 | 3,450 | 5.9M | 21.7 | 40.2 |
| YOLOv5n | Darknet | 640×640 | **4,450** | **1.9M** | 28.0 | 46.3 |
| MLNet(*ours*) | Tri-bone | 320×320 | 1,480 | **2.1M** | **22.6** | **37.9** |
| | | 416×416 | **2,500** | 2.1M | **26.0** | **43.5** |
| | | 640×640 | 5,930 | 2.1M | **28.7** | **46.8** |

**Table 4.** Further FLOPs comparison with YOLOv5n on MS COCO dataset.

| Model | Backbone | Backbone MFLOPs | Detection MFLOPs | Total MFLOPs |
|---|---|---|---|---|
| YOLOv5n | Darknet | 2,620 | 1,830 | 4,450 |
| MLNet(*ours*) | Tri-bone | 1,390 | 2,300 | 3,690 |
| | | 1,480 | | 3,780 |
| | | 1,490 | | 3,790 |

### 4.3   Ablation Study

We perform some ablation studies to investigate the effectiveness of the design of MLNet on the COCO2017 validation set. Table 5 compares AP accuracy results under different improvement factors.

**BL (Baseline).** We choose the multi-branch network with a standard convolution kernel as the baseline. We use a conv6×6 kernel to replace the IDB, a conv3×3 kernel group (groups = 2) to replace the BDB, RCB, and the blocks of ECM are all replaced by the conv3×3 kernel group (groups = 2), too. This model requires 6,140 MFLOPs and achieves 25.3% AP (Table 5(a)).

**IDB.** We test IDB's effect, consisting of one conv4×4 layer and two conv3×3 layers with dilation and convolution. The contrast method is the standard conv6×6 layer. It can be seen from Fig. 2 that the number of input channels is three, and the number of output channels is set to 16. As shown in Table 5, compared to the conv6×6 operation, IDB achieves a 0.4 AP score gain with slightly fewer parameters and significantly fewer FLOPs. The plausible reason is that the conv6×6 operation is redundant, and IDB can extract enough feature maps in a lightweight network.

**BDB.** We use the BDB to replace the conv3×3 kernel group (groups = 2). The number of output channels remains unchanged. This design increases the computational cost while improving the accuracy (Table 5(c)). Because the amount of BDBs is not many in the network, we believe such a trade-off is reasonable.

**Table 5.** Ablation studies on the proposed block on MS COCO dataset.

|     | BL | IDB | BDB | RCB | ECM | AP (%) | AP50 (%) | MFLOPs |
|-----|----|-----|-----|-----|-----|--------|----------|--------|
| (a) | ✓  |     |     |     |     | 25.3   | 39.6     | 6,140  |
| (b) |    | ✓   |     |     |     | 25.7   | 40.5     | 6,000  |
| (c) |    | ✓   | ✓   |     |     | 26.6   | 41.8     | 6,230  |
| (d) |    | ✓   | ✓   | ✓   |     | 28.2   | 45.7     | 5,920  |
| (e) |    | ✓   | ✓   |     | ✓   | 27.7   | 44.6     | 6,240  |
| (f) |    | ✓   | ✓   | ✓   | ✓   | 28.7   | 46.8     | 5,930  |

These results demonstrate that heavy down-sampling modules introduce great redundancy for a lightweight network.

**RCB.** We use the RCB to replace the conv3×3 kernel group (groups = 2). This design reduces the computational cost by 10% and improves the accuracy (Table 5(d)). Because the RCB is the main component of the network, the total FLOPs are reduced by about 5%. Compared to standard convolution groups, we can see that channel shuffle improves the performance, showing that information exchange between the groups can bring gain.

**ECM.** We test the effect of ECM, which consists of two ECBs. The contrast method is ECM structure with conv3×3 kernel group (groups = 2). As is shown in Table 5, compared to standard convolution operations, ECM achieves 0.5% AP score gain with similar FLOPs.

## 5   Conclusion

This paper proposes a novel one-stage lightweight object detection network (MLNet). To reduce the consuming time of object detection, we adopt a multi-branch structure to perform network inference in parallel and propose two components, FDM and RCB, which achieve better performance with fewer FLOPs. In the detection part, the Enhanced Connection Module is designed to improve the feature representation by merging the global and local features of the detection object. We verify the effectiveness of the invented blocks through extensive ablation studies. We compare MLNet to state-of-the-art lightweight detectors such as MobileNet-SSD, YOLO-tiny (v3, v4), and YOLOv5n on two object detection benchmarks (PASCAL VOC, COCO). It shows that MLNet achieves the highest accuracy by reasonable FLOPs and parameter size.

**Acknowledgement.** This work was partly supported by the National Key R&D Program of China under grant No. 2019YFB2204800.

# References

1. Cai, Z., Fan, Q., Feris, R.S., Vasconcelos, N.: A unified multi-scale deep convolutional neural network for fast object detection. In: Leibe, B., Matas, J., Sebe, N., Welling, M. (eds.) ECCV 2016. LNCS, vol. 9908, pp. 354–370. Springer, Cham (2016). https://doi.org/10.1007/978-3-319-46493-0_22
2. Chen, Y., Li, J., Xiao, H., Jin, X., Yan, S., Feng, J.: Dual path networks. In: Advances in Neural Information Processing Systems, vol. 30 (2017)
3. Everingham, M., Van Gool, L., Williams, C.K., Winn, J., Zisserman, A.: The pascal visual object classes (VOC) challenge. Int. J. Comput. Vision **88**(2), 303–338 (2010)
4. Goyal, A., Bochkovskiy, A., Deng, J., Koltun, V.: Non-deep networks. arXiv preprint arXiv:2110.07641 (2021)
5. Guo, C., Fan, B., Zhang, Q., Xiang, S., Pan, C.: AugFPN: improving multi-scale feature learning for object detection. In: Proceedings of the IEEE/CVF Conference on Computer Vision and Pattern Recognition, pp. 12595–12604 (2020)
6. He, K., Zhang, X., Ren, S., Sun, J.: Deep residual learning for image recognition. In: Proceedings of the IEEE Conference on Computer Vision and Pattern Recognition, pp. 770–778 (2016)
7. He, L., Ray, N., Guan, Y., Zhang, H.: Fast large-scale spectral clustering via explicit feature mapping. IEEE Trans. Cybern. **49**(3), 1058–1071 (2018)
8. Howard, A.G., et al.: MobileNets: efficient convolutional neural networks for mobile vision applications. arXiv preprint arXiv:1704.04861 (2017)
9. Huang, G., Liu, Z., Van Der Maaten, L., Weinberger, K.Q.: Densely connected convolutional networks. In: Proceedings of the IEEE Conference on Computer Vision and Pattern Recognition, pp. 4700–4708 (2017)
10. Huang, R., Pedoeem, J., Chen, C.: Yolo-lite: a real-time object detection algorithm optimized for non-GPU computers. In: 2018 IEEE International Conference on Big Data (Big Data), pp. 2503–2510. IEEE (2018)
11. Kingma, D.P., Ba, J.: Adam: a method for stochastic optimization. arXiv preprint arXiv:1412.6980 (2014)
12. Li, Y., Chen, Y., Wang, N., Zhang, Z.: Scale-aware trident networks for object detection. In: Proceedings of the IEEE/CVF International Conference on Computer Vision, pp. 6054–6063 (2019)
13. Lin, T.Y., Dollár, P., Girshick, R., He, K., Hariharan, B., Belongie, S.: Feature pyramid networks for object detection. In: Proceedings of the IEEE Conference on Computer Vision and Pattern Recognition, pp. 2117–2125 (2017)
14. Lin, T.-Y., et al.: Microsoft COCO: common objects in context. In: Fleet, D., Pajdla, T., Schiele, B., Tuytelaars, T. (eds.) ECCV 2014. LNCS, vol. 8693, pp. 740–755. Springer, Cham (2014). https://doi.org/10.1007/978-3-319-10602-1_48
15. Liu, L., Wu, F.X., Wang, Y.P., Wang, J.: Multi-receptive-field CNN for semantic segmentation of medical images. IEEE J. Biomed. Health Inform. **24**(11), 3215–3225 (2020)
16. Liu, S., Huang, D., Wang, Y.: Receptive field block net for accurate and fast object detection. In: Ferrari, V., Hebert, M., Sminchisescu, C., Weiss, Y. (eds.) ECCV 2018. LNCS, vol. 11215, pp. 404–419. Springer, Cham (2018). https://doi.org/10.1007/978-3-030-01252-6_24
17. Luo, W., Li, Y., Urtasun, R., Zemel, R.: Understanding the effective receptive field in deep convolutional neural networks. In: Advances in Neural Information Processing Systems, vol. 29 (2016)

18. Ma, W., Wu, Y., Cen, F., Wang, G.: MDFN: multi-scale deep feature learning network for object detection. Pattern Recogn. **100**, 107149 (2020)
19. Mamalet, F., Garcia, C.: Simplifying ConvNets for fast learning. In: Villa, A.E.P., Duch, W., Érdi, P., Masulli, F., Palm, G. (eds.) ICANN 2012. LNCS, vol. 7553, pp. 58–65. Springer, Heidelberg (2012). https://doi.org/10.1007/978-3-642-33266-1_8
20. Paszke, A., et al.: PyTorch: an imperative style, high-performance deep learning library. In: Advances in Neural Information Processing Systems, vol. 32 (2019)
21. Qin, Z., et al.: ThunderNet: towards real-time generic object detection on mobile devices. In: Proceedings of the IEEE/CVF International Conference on Computer Vision, pp. 6718–6727 (2019)
22. Redmon, J., Farhadi, A.: Yolo9000: better, faster, stronger. In: Proceedings of the IEEE Conference on Computer Vision and Pattern Recognition, pp. 7263–7271 (2017)
23. Redmon, J., Farhadi, A.: Yolov3: an incremental improvement. arXiv preprint arXiv:1804.02767 (2018)
24. Sandler, M., Howard, A., Zhu, M., Zhmoginov, A., Chen, L.C.: Mobilenetv 2: inverted residuals and linear bottlenecks. In: Proceedings of the IEEE Conference on Computer Vision and Pattern Recognition, pp. 4510–4520 (2018)
25. Tan, Z., Wang, J., Sun, X., Lin, M., Li, H., et al.: Giraffedet: a heavy-neck paradigm for object detection. In: International Conference on Learning Representations (2021)
26. Wang, K., Liew, J.H., Zou, Y., Zhou, D., Feng, J.: Panet: few-shot image semantic segmentation with prototype alignment. In: Proceedings of the IEEE/CVF International Conference on Computer Vision, pp. 9197–9206 (2019)
27. Yu, F., Koltun, V.: Multi-scale context aggregation by dilated convolutions. arXiv preprint arXiv:1511.07122 (2015)
28. Yuan, J., et al.: Gated CNN: integrating multi-scale feature layers for object detection. Pattern Recogn. **105**, 107131 (2020)
29. Zhang, H., Cisse, M., Dauphin, Y.N., Lopez-Paz, D.: mixup: Beyond empirical risk minimization. arXiv preprint arXiv:1710.09412 (2017)
30. Zhang, X., Zhou, X., Lin, M., Sun, J.: ShuffleNet: an extremely efficient convolutional neural network for mobile devices. In: Proceedings of the IEEE Conference on Computer Vision and Pattern Recognition, pp. 6848–6856 (2018)
31. Ultralytics/yolov5. https://github.com/ultralytics/yolov5. Accessed 4 June 2022

# Hyperspectral Image Classification Based on Transformer and Generative Adversarial Network

Yajie Wang[1], Zhonghui Shi[2(✉)], Shengyu Han[2], and Zhihao Wei[2]

[1] Engineering Training Center, Shenyang Aerospace University, Shenyang, China
wangyajie@sina.com
[2] School of Computer, Shenyang Aerospace University, Shenyang, China
szh13463337193@163.com

**Abstract.** In recent years, hyperspectral image (HSI) classification methods based on generative adversarial networks (GANs) have been proposed and have made great progress, which can alleviate the dilemma of limited training samples. However, GAN-based HSI classification methods are heavily affected by the problem of imbalanced training data. The discriminator always tries to associate false labels with a few samples, which will reduce the classification accuracy. Another problem is the mode collapse based on the GAN network, which hinders the classification performance of HSI. A combined Transformer and GAN (TransGAN) model for HSI classification is proposed in this paper. First, in order to solve the problem of reduced classification accuracy caused by imbalanced training data, the discriminator is adjusted to a classifier with only one output. Second, the generator is constructed by using the Transformer, and the discriminator is added with a multi-scale pooling module (MSPM) to alleviate the problem of GAN model collapse. Experimental results on two HSI datasets show that the proposed TransGAN achieves better performance.

**Keywords:** Multi-scale pooling module · Transformer · Generative adversarial network · Hyperspectral image classification

## 1 Introduction

Hyperspectral image (HSI) is a high-dimensional image with hundreds of continuous spectral bands, so it contains both spatial information and rich spectral information. HSI has the advantages of identifying weak information and quantitative detection. With the continuous development of high resolution imaging technology, hyperspectral remote sensing has become one of the important research directions in the field of remote sensing in the 21st century. At present, hyperspectral remote sensing has been used in the fields of environment and disaster detection, precision agriculture, geological exploration, and earth resources survey [1].

S. Khanna et al. (Eds.): PRICAI 2022, LNCS 13631, pp. 212–225, 2022.
https://doi.org/10.1007/978-3-031-20868-3_16

The classification of HSIs is an important technology for ground object observation. The classification of HSIs faces great challenges due to high-dimensional characteristics, high correlation between bands, and spectral mixing. The purpose of HSI classification is to distinguish different types of objects according to the different characteristics reflected by the image information. The spectral information was focused on by researchers because it can reflect the characteristics of different substances. Many traditional methods identify the classification maps in a pixel-wise way, which can be divided into two steps, the first is feature engineering, such as principal component analysis (PCA) [16] and bands selection [3], the second is classifier development, such as support vector machine (SVM) [24] and random forest [22].

With the breakthrough of deep learning in computer vision tasks, deep learning is also been introduced into HSI classification and achieved good results. Compared with traditional methods, deep learning can extract more information features [18], and it is considered an effective feature extraction method in HSI classification. Different networks can extract the feature of different types. Many methods [2,19] based on Convolutional Neural Networks (CNNs) have received a lot of attention and have achieved success in vision tasks. The CNN can perform feature extraction on HSI of different dimensions. The one-dimensional CNN (1DCNN) directly uses 1D spectral vectors for classification networks, and the relationship between the spectral features and the information contained in each HSI pixel is learned through the network. The 2D-CNN reduces the dimensionality of hyperspectral data through PCA and learns the spatial features of the data through the network. The 3D-CNN is used to explore the HSI Spectral-spatial features for classification, such as He et al. [7] proposed multiscale 3D deep CNN, Liu et al. [13] proposed 3D CNN.

Goodfellow et al. [5] designed the generative adversarial network (GAN), which is comprised of a generator $G$ and a discriminator $D$. GAN was first used to classify HSIs in the semi-supervised HS-GAN proposed by Zhan et al. [23]. Zhu et al. [26] proposed 3D-GAN as a spectral-spatial classifier for HSI classification. A multi-class spatial spectral GAN (MSGAN) method is proposed by Feng et al. [4], which consists of two generators to generate samples containing spatial and spectral information, respectively, and a discriminator to extract joint spatial and spectral features and output multi-class probabilities. Zhong et al. [25] integrated GAN and conditional random field (CRF), and softmax prediction is seen as HSI conditional probability to improve the classification map. Wang et al. [21] proposed an adaptive dropblock-enhanced GAN (ADGAN) for HSI classification. The adaptive dropblock part is used to increase the stability of the model. Vaswani et al. [20] first proposed the Transformer model. The Transformer model has become the mainstream model in the field of natural language processing, and it has also begun to attract attention in the field of vision. Hong et al. [8] applied the Transformer model to the HSI classification task for the first time.

Although the GAN-based model in HSI classification has achieved certain results, there are still problems to be solved. The first problem is unbalanced training data. The classification accuracy will be greatly affected when the training samples of different classes are unevenly distributed. The second problem is the mode collapse of GANs. To tackle the aforementioned limitations of GAN-based classification methods, the SPCA-TransGAN model for HSI classification is proposed. The Transformer is used to build the generator and the CNN is used to build the discriminator. To validate the effectiveness of the proposed method, experiments on the proposed method and several other methods are performed on two datasets, respectively. The contributions of this paper are as follows:

1) We propose a SPCA-TransGAN model for hyperspectral image classification. The generator is constructed by using the Transformer to alleviate the problem of GAN model collapse.
2) To make better use of local and global information, the discriminator is added with a multi-scale pooling module (MSPM).
3) Superpixelwise PCA (SPCA) extracts more efficient features instead of PCA to improve the performance of HSI classification.

The rest of this paper is organized as follows. In Sect. 2, the basic concepts of ACGAN and SuperPCA are briefly reviewed. The scheme of the proposed method and its components are introduced in Sect. 3 Experimental results and analysis are presented in Sect. 4 Finally, conclusions are drawn in Sect. 5.

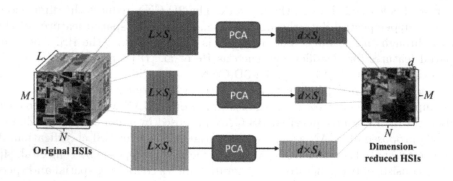

**Fig. 1.** The architecture of SuperPCA-based dimensionality reduction for HSIs

## 2   Related Works

### 2.1   Superpixelwise PCA

The high dimensionality of HSI data brings the problems of dimensional disaster and the burden of data transmission and storage. At the same time, many continuous spectral bands are highly correlated due to spectral reflectance, and some features cannot be extracted with useful information [12]. Dimensionality reduction is widely used in HSI preprocessing steps to alleviate these problems and preserve essential information in low-dimensional spaces. PCA is one of the most widely used dimensionality reduction techniques in HSI. Different regions in HSI correspond to different objects and have different spectral features. To allow different regions to learn different projection matrices. Jiang et al. [10] proposed an unsupervised feature extraction method based on superpixel PCA. The architecture of SuperPCA-based dimensionality reduction for HSIs is illustrated in Fig. 1.

## 2.2   Auxiliary Classifier GANs

In the GAN proposed by Goodfellow et al. [5], the task of the discriminator is only to judge the authenticity of the sample. In order that GAN can be applied to multi-class image classification, Odena et al. [14] proposed ACGAN, the discriminator can output multi-class labels. Zhu et al. [26] applied ACGAN to HSI classification, the structure of ACGAN is shown in Fig. 2. The generator $G$ accepts a class label $c$ and noise as input. The real data with the corresponding label and the data generated by $G$ are regarded as the input of $D$. The discriminator $D$ has two outputs, one is used to distinguish real data from fake data, and one another is used to classify the input. The loss function of ACGAN is comprised of two parts, the log-likelihood of the right source of input $L_S$ and the log-likelihood of the right class labels $L_C$. The $L_S$ and $L_C$ are computed as follows:

$$L_S = E[log P(S = real|X_{real})] + E[log P(S = fake|X_{fake})] \qquad (1)$$

$$L_C = E[log P(C = c|X_{real})] + E[log P(C = c|X_{fake})] \qquad (2)$$

During training, the generator $G$ is optimized to maximize $L_C$ - $L_S$, and the discriminator $D$ is optimized to maximize $L_S+L_C$.

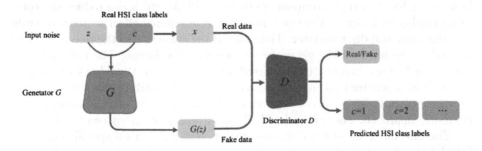

**Fig. 2.** The architecture of ACGAN for HSI classification

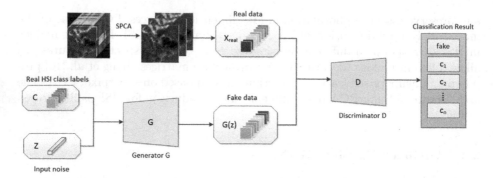

**Fig. 3.** The Framework of SPCA-TransGAN for HSI classification.

## 3 Proposed Method

### 3.1 The Framework of the Proposed SPCA-TransGAN

Traditional HSI classification methods cannot make full use of the spectrum of HSI spatial characteristics, resulting in low classification accuracy. The classification method based on deep learning can mine the hidden information in the data and extract the features that are more favorable for image classification. How to use the rich characteristics of limited data samples to improve classification accuracy is a hot spot in HSI classification. To better utilize the rich features, a combined Transformer and GAN (TransGAN) model for HSI classification is proposed. The proposed SPCA-TransGAN framework is shown in Fig. 3. It includes a generator $G$ and a discriminator $D$.

Since HSI contains hundreds of bands and there is a lot of redundancy between the bands, it is difficult for the generator to simulate real data and a robust generator cannot be obtained. So the number of input HSI spectral bands is reduced to three components by SuperPCA, which can reduce the computational complexity and extract more low-dimensional effective data to train the generator and discriminator. The noise of the same size as the real data label is used as the input of the generator to generate the image. The discriminator continuously discriminates the generated images and feeds them back to the generator. The generator continues to generate the image until the discriminator can no longer distinguish it. At the same time, the ability of the discriminator is continuously improved. Then, the ideal HSI classification accuracy can be obtained.

The discriminator $D$ has only one output, which returns a specific class $c$ or fake label. After that, the generator $G$ is trained to generate image patches that match the desired class label. The discriminator $D$ is trained to maximize the log-likelihood and the generator $G$ is trained to maximize the log-likelihood as follows:

$$L_D = E[logP(C = c|X_{real})] + E[logP(C = fake|X_{fake})])] \tag{3}$$

$$L_G = E[logP(C = c|X_{fake})] \tag{4}$$

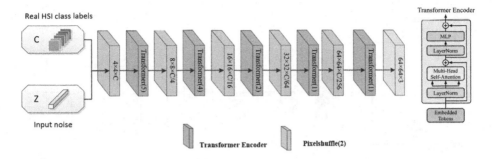

**Fig. 4.** The Framework of Generator for HSI classification.

The first term of $L_D$ encourages the discriminator $D$ assigns real labels to real samples, the second term expects to assign a fake label to the generated samples. On the contrary, the generator $G$ expects to draw a sample of the desired class. Through adversarial learning, the generator $G$ captures the real data distribution of the desired class.

## 3.2 The Network Framework of Generator

Transformer is a network structure composed of a self-attention module. It has been widely concerned for its advantages of strong scalability and learning long-distance dependencies, and has achieved good results in natural language processing (NLP). It is gradually being applied in the field of images [15]. The proposed Visual Transformer (ViT) expands the application of Transformer in images. The Transformer Encoder consists of two parts, a multi-head self-attention module and a feed-forward Multilayer Perceptron (MLP) with GELU nonlinearity. Layer normalization is applied before each part and residual connections are used. Stacking Transformer encoders to generate images on a pixel-by-pixel basis has an exploding cost. So the adopted strategy is to gradually increase the input sequence and reduce the embedding dimension [11].

The framework of the generator in this paper is shown in Fig. 4, which consists of 5 layers of upsampling modules consisting of 5, 4, 2, 1, and 1 stacked Transformer Encoder modules and 5 layers of pixelshuffle,respectively. Random noise of the same size as the label data is used as the input, the linear layer passes it to a vector of length $H \times W \times C$, which is shaped into a feature map of $H \times W$ (H=W=4). Each point is a one-dimensional embedding. This "feature map" is treated as a sequence of C-dimensional representations of length 1024, which is combined with a learnable positional encoding. Transformer encoders take the embedding tokens as input and recursively compute the correspondence between each token to synthesize a higher resolution image. The upsampling module shapes the 1D sequence of the token embedding back to a 2D feature map $X_0 \in R^{H \times W \times C}$. The pixelshuffle module is used to upsample its resolution and downsample the embedding dimension to obtain the output. $X_0 \in R^{2H \times 2W \times 2C}$. The 2D feature map $X_0$ is again reshaped into a 1D sequence of embedding tokens, where the number of tokens

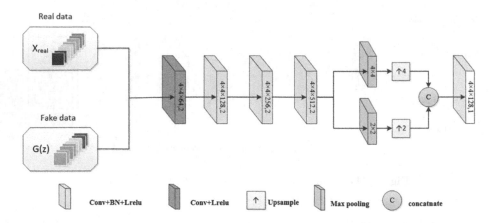

**Fig. 5.** The Framework of discriminator for HSI classification.

becomes $4 \times H \times W$ and the embedding dimension is $C/4$. Thus, at each stage, the resolution $(H,W)$ becomes two times larger, while the embedding dimension $C$ is reduced to a quarter of the input dimension. This process is repeated until the resolution reaches $64 \times 64$, at which point we project the embedding dimension to 3 to obtain the desired image $X_{gan} \in R^{64 \times 64 \times 3}$.

## 3.3 The Network Framework of Multi-scale Discriminator

The framework of the discriminator is shown in Fig. 5. A 5-layer convolutional neural network is used as the underlying network to form the discriminator, and the filter size of each layer is $4 \times 4$. The extracted features for each layer are 64, 128, 256, 512 and 128. Leaky Relu is used as activation function except for the last layer. To enable the discriminator to better utilize global and local information for discrimination and classification, a multi-scale pooling module (MSPM) is stacked in the discriminator, which can extract features at two different scales, and the filter sizes are $4 \times 4$ and $2 \times 2$, respectively. The output of the discriminator is the classification result.

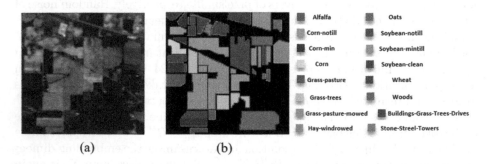

**Fig. 6.** Indian Pines dataset. (a) False-color composite. (b) Ground-truth labels.

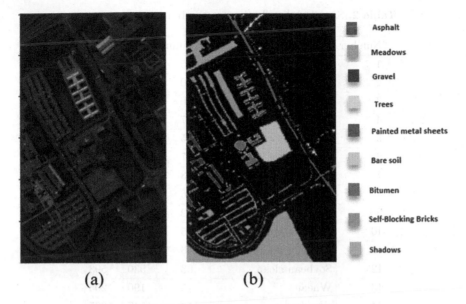

(a)                              (b)

**Fig. 7.** Pavia University dataset. (a) False-color composite. (b) Ground-truth labels.

**Table 1.** Samples' distribution for the Pavia university dataset

| Number | Class | Training | Test | Total |
|--------|-------|----------|------|-------|
| 1 | Asphalt | 676 | 5955 | 6631 |
| 2 | Meadows | 1858 | 16791 | 18649 |
| 3 | Gravel | 216 | 1883 | 2099 |
| 4 | Trees | 320 | 2726 | 3046 |
| 5 | Painted metal sheets | 130 | 1215 | 1345 |
| 6 | Bare Soil | 512 | 4517 | 5029 |
| 7 | Bitumen | 122 | 1208 | 1330 |
| 8 | Self-Blocking Bricks | 348 | 3334 | 3682 |
| 9 | Shadows | 94 | 853 | 947 |
| | Total | 4276 | 38341 | 42617 |

# 4  Experimental Results and Analysis

In this section, the datasets are first introduced. Then, the experimental results of the method proposed in this paper and the other five methods are analyzed according to the classification result and classification evaluation index.

**Table 2.** Samples' distribution for the Indian pines dataset

| Number | Class | Training | Test | Total |
|---|---|---|---|---|
| 1 | Alfalfa | 5 | 41 | 46 |
| 2 | Corn-notill | 150 | 1278 | 1428 |
| 3 | Corn-min | 86 | 716 | 802 |
| 4 | Corn | 27 | 210 | 237 |
| 5 | Grass-pasture | 45 | 438 | 483 |
| 6 | Grass-trees | 67 | 663 | 730 |
| 7 | Grass-pasture-moved | 3 | 25 | 28 |
| 8 | Hay-windrowed | 56 | 422 | 478 |
| 9 | Oats | 2 | 18 | 20 |
| 10 | Soybean-notill | 85 | 887 | 972 |
| 11 | Soybean-mintill | 256 | 2178 | 2434 |
| 12 | Soybean-clean | 63 | 530 | 593 |
| 13 | Wheat | 15 | 190 | 205 |
| 14 | Woods | 118 | 1147 | 1265 |
| 15 | Buildings-Grass-Trees | 38 | 324 | 362 |
| 16 | Stone-Steel-Towers | 8 | 85 | 93 |
| | Total | 1024 | 9152 | 10176 |

## 4.1 DataSets

To evaluate the performance of the SPCA-TransGAN on HSI classification, two representative HSI datasets are used, including the Indian Pines dataset and Pavia University dataset.

1)The Indian Pines dataset is a mixed vegetation site in Northwestern Indiana, and it was collected by the AVIRIS sensor. The size of the data set is 145 × 145 pixels. It is comprised of 220 spectral bands in the wavelength range of 0.4–2.5 µm. The false-color composite image and the ground reference map are shown in Fig. 6.

2)The Pavia University dataset was acquired by the Reflective Optics System Imaging Spectrometer (ROSIS) in Northern Italy in 2001. The data set converts nine urban land-cover types. The size of the data set is 610 × 340 pixels, and the resolution of the image is 1.3 m per pixel. The data set is comprised of 103 spectral bands in the wavelength range from 430 to 860 nm. The false-color composite image and the ground reference map are shown in Fig. 7.

For all two datasets, the labeled samples are divided into training sets and test sets. After numerous experiments, we found that the classification results obtained by randomly selecting 10% of the training samples on the Indian Pines dataset and the Pavia University dataset are relatively stable. The number of training and testing samples for each category in the two datasets are shown in Table 1 and Table 2, respectively. The parameters are adjusted by the training set during training by testing the classification accuracy and the loss of the resulting ephemeral model. The network with the lowest loss is selected for testing. All test samples in the dataset are used to estimate the capability of the trained network. Three evaluation criteria, including overall accuracy (OA), average accuracy (AA), and Kappa coefficient (K), are presented for all test samples.

## 4.2  Classification Results on Two Data Sets

The proposed model is implemented with Pytorch 1.10 with CUDA 10.2 and trained on an RTX 2028TI. We use the Adaptive moment estimation (Adam) method to optimize the weights of networks. The initial learning rate is 0.0001, the decay rate is 0.99, and the batch size is 5.

The effectiveness of the proposed SPCA-TransGAN is verified compared with five methods. The other five methods include 1D-CNN [9], 3D-CNN [6], HybridSN [17], Multiscale 3D-CNN [7], and ADGAN [21]. To ensure a fair comparison, all the methods use default parameters and the same proportion of training sets. All the experimental results are obtained by running ten times independently with a random division for training and testing.

1)*Result of the Indian pines dataset* The statistical classification results on the Indian Pines dataset are summarized in Table 3. The classification results of five different methods are displayed in Fig. 8. As can be observed from Table 3. ADGAN, SPCA-TransGAN with additionally generated training samples with better classification performance than 1D-CNN, 3D-CNN, HybridSN, and multiscale 3D-CNN. For minority classes, such as Alfalfa, Grass-pasture-mowed, Oats the classification performance of the proposed SPCA-TransGAN is better than

**Table 3.** Classification results of different models in Indian Pines dataset

| Class | 1D-CNN | 3D-CNN | Multiscale 3D-CNN | HybridSN | ADGAN | SPCA-TransGAN |
|---|---|---|---|---|---|---|
| Alfalfa | $83.70 \pm 10.16$ | $93.26 \pm 4.06$ | $78.91 \pm 9.89$ | $97.42 \pm 1.62$ | $100 \pm 0.00$ | $100 \pm 0.00$ |
| Corn-notill | $81.95 \pm 5.58$ | $92.49 \pm 4.06$ | $90.76 \pm 3.33$ | $95.67 \pm 0.84$ | $98.96 \pm 0.85$ | $98.46 \pm 0.62$ |
| Corn-min | $80.92 \pm 10.49$ | $87.19 \pm 1.33$ | $82.82 \pm 3.59$ | $94.25 \pm 0.65$ | $95.38 \pm 1.20$ | $96.88 \pm 1.21$ |
| Corn | $75.49 \pm 7.54$ | $96.29 \pm 3.29$ | $91.73 \pm 3.56$ | $96.23 \pm 0.54$ | $94.17 \pm 1.32$ | $99.58 \pm 0.45$ |
| Grass-Pasture | $92.46 \pm 2.12$ | $95.45 \pm 0.83$ | $87.74 \pm 3.62$ | $98.51 \pm 0.65$ | $94.33 \pm 1.75$ | $96.56 \pm 0.72$ |
| Grass-trees | $96.68 \pm 1.55$ | $99.12 \pm 0.28$ | $73.21 \pm 1.20$ | $96.75 \pm 0.45$ | $92.87 \pm 2.65$ | $98.90 \pm 0.64$ |
| Grass-pasture-moved | $82.50 \pm 7.73$ | $98.57 \pm 3.27$ | $73.21 \pm 1.20$ | $94.52 \pm 1.24$ | $89.71 \pm 1.87$ | $96.43 \pm 0.72$ |
| Hay-windrowed | $98.54 \pm 2.05$ | $99.64 \pm 0.28$ | $99.71 \pm 0.35$ | $98.75 \pm 0.27$ | $99.58 \pm 0.42$ | $100 \pm 0.00$ |
| Oats | $78.00 \pm 14.7$ | $98.50 \pm 4.50$ | $79.00 \pm 10.98$ | $79.25 \pm 3.75$ | $80.00 \pm 5.00$ | $100 \pm 0.00$ |
| Soybean-notill | $82.91 \pm 8.44$ | $90.13 \pm 1.43$ | $88.49 \pm 1.99$ | $98.23 \pm 0.43$ | $92.28 \pm 2.64$ | $96.81 \pm 0.94$ |
| Soybean-mintill | $86.79 \pm 4.15$ | $93.83 \pm 0.52$ | $92.35 \pm 2.67$ | $98.25 \pm 0.52$ | $98.50 \pm 0.95$ | $99.84 \pm 0.16$ |
| Soybean-clean | $84.42 \pm 7.02$ | $90.05 \pm .54$ | $91.10 \pm 4.71$ | $96.52 \pm 0.72$ | $90.72 \pm 0.88$ | $96.60 \pm 1.24$ |
| Wheat | $99.02 \pm 0.49$ | $99.80 \pm 0.45$ | $99.22 \pm 1.00$ | $96.53 \pm 0.87$ | $99.51 \pm 0.5$ | $98.54 \pm 0.90$ |
| Woods | $96.75 \pm 1.64$ | $99.50 \pm 0.27$ | $97.72 \pm 1.29$ | $98.83 \pm 0.27$ | $99.60 \pm 0.41$ | $99.92 \pm 0.16$ |
| Buildings-grass-trees | $66.67 \pm 10.14$ | $83.29 \pm 1.92$ | $67.88 \pm 5.28$ | $96.23 \pm 0.52$ | $99.71 \pm 0.92$ | $98.90 \pm 0.89$ |
| Stone-steel-towers | $92.37 \pm 4.84$ | $96.77 \pm 1.80$ | $98.28 \pm 1.46$ | $88.57 \pm 1.23$ | $97.84 \pm 0.64$ | $85.24 \pm 2.43$ |
| OA (%) | $95.78 \pm 0.12$ | $93.79 \pm 0.24$ | $91.32 \pm 1.21$ | $96.90 \pm 0.81$ | $96.98 \pm 0.58$ | $98.27 \pm 0.22$ |
| AA (%) | $95.80 \pm 0.12$ | $92.63 \pm 0.28$ | $88.65 \pm 1.25$ | $96.44 \pm 1.24$ | $94.75 \pm 0.81$ | $96.85 \pm 0.40$ |
| k×100 | $95.21 \pm 0.13$ | $92.93 \pm 0.28$ | $90.14 \pm 1.38$ | $96.80 \pm 0.57$ | $96.55 \pm 0.87$ | $97.81 \pm 0.42$ |

**Table 4.** Classification results of different models in Pavia university dataset

| Class | 1D-CNN | 3D-CNN | Multiscale3D-CNN | HybridSN | ADGAN | SPCA-TransGAN |
|---|---|---|---|---|---|---|
| Asphalt | 94.54 ± 0.63 | 97.24 ± 0.17 | 96.74 ± 0.19 | 97.47 ± 0.50 | 98.83 ± 0.51 | **98.52 ± 0.72** |
| Meadows | 96.49 ± 1.06 | 94.41 ± 0.03 | 92.29 ± 0.21 | 99.64 ± 0.12 | 97.83 ± 0.62 | **99.30 ± 0.52** |
| Gravel | 83.09 ± 3.81 | 94.61 ± 0.63 | 91.74 ± 1.10 | 91.19 ± 1.35 | 99.80 ± 0.20 | **99.13 ± 0.63** |
| Trees | 91.90 ± 2.32 | 97.93 ± 0.39 | 96.95 ± 0.70 | 98.63 ± 0.21 | **96.28 ± 0.47** | 93.21 ± 1.21 |
| Painted metal Sheets | 99.63 ± 0.14 | 99.81 ± 0.17 | 100 ± 0.00 | 99.26 ± 0.23 | 99.80 ± 0.20 | **99.85 ± 0.15** |
| Bare Soil | 88.95 ± 4.40 | 99.22 ± 0.28 | 99.24 ± 0.71 | 99.23 ± 0.45 | 97.85 ± 1.23 | **99.88 ± 0.12** |
| Bitumen | 88.00 ± 1.59 | 98.04 ± 0.35 | 97.17 ± 0.88 | 87.03 ± 0.23 | 99.32 ± 0.65 | **99.62 ± 0.32** |
| self-Blocking Bricks | 90.00 ± 2.24 | 98.13 ± 0.43 | 99.15 ± 0.33 | 97.16 ± 0.27 | 98.64 ± 0.64 | **98.52 ± 0.82** |
| Shadows | 99.86 ± 0.08 | 99.62 ± 0.20 | 99.61 ± 0.45 | 89.90 ± 4.11 | 94.47 ± 0.83 | **95.47 ± 0.62** |
| OA (%) | 93.66 ± 0.29 | 96.40 ± 0.07 | 95.25 ± 0.13 | 98.07 ± 0.20 | 97.29 ± 0.62 | **98.52 ± 0.34** |
| AA (%) | 92.50 ± 0.51 | 97.68 ± 0.11 | 96.99 ± 0.19 | 95.71 ± 0.09 | 97.61 ± 0.62 | **97.75 ± 0.37** |
| k×100 | 91.60 ± 0.40 | 95.30 ± 0.09 | 93.83 ± 0.17 | 97.42 ± 0.07 | 96.68 ± 0.82 | **97.92 ± 0.41** |

ADGAN. It is demonstrat that it has better classification when handling minority class samples on this dataset. Among all these methods, SPCA-TransGAN obtains the best classification results in terms of the OA, AA, and Kappa.

2)*Result of the Pavia Unversity dataset* The statistical classification results on the Pavia Unversity dataset are summarized in Table 4. The classification results of five different methods are displayed in Fig. 9. As can be observed from

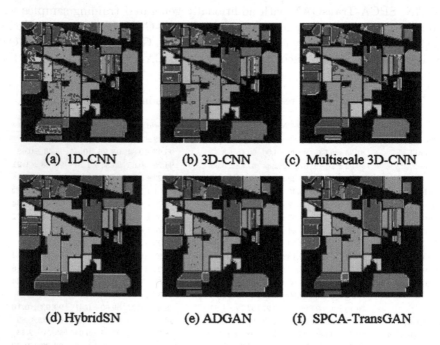

(a) 1D-CNN          (b) 3D-CNN          (c) Multiscale 3D-CNN

(d) HybridSN          (e) ADGAN          (f) SPCA-TransGAN

**Fig. 8.** Visualized results of different classification methods on the Indian Pines data set. (a) 1D-CNN. (b) 3D-CNN. (c) Multiscale 3D-CNN. (d) HybridSN. (e) ADGAN. (f) SPCA-TransGAN.

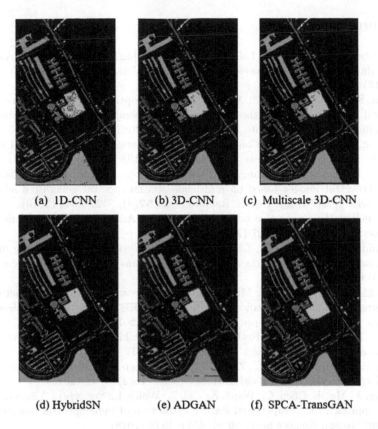

(a) 1D-CNN        (b) 3D-CNN        (c) Multiscale 3D-CNN

(d) HybridSN        (e) ADGAN        (f) SPCA-TransGAN

**Fig. 9.** Visualized results of different classification methods on the Pavia University dataset. (a) 1D-CNN. (b) 3D-CNN. (c) Multiscale 3D-CNN. (d) HybridSN. (e) ADGAN. (f) SPCA-TransGAN.

Table 4. Among all these methods, SPCA-TransGAN obtains the best classification results in terms of the OA, AA, and Kappa.

## 5    Conclusion

In this paper, a combined Transformer and GAN (TransGAN) model for HSI classification is proposed. This model can alleviate the problem of imbalanced training data and improve classification accuracy. The multi-scale pooling module can enable the discriminator to better utilize global and local information for discrimination. To evaluate the proposed method, experiments were conducted on two hyperspectral datasets. The results showed that the proposed SPCA-TransGAN has better classification accuracy. In the future, we will continue to study models with higher classification accuracy.

# References

1. Audebert, N., Le Saux, B., Lefèvre, S.: Deep learning for classification of hyperspectral data: A comparative review. IEEE Geosci. Remote Sens. Mag. **7**(2), 159–173 (2019)
2. Bera, S., Shrivastava, V.K.: Analysis of various optimizers on deep convolutional neural network model in the application of hyperspectral remote sensing image classification. Int. J. Remote Sens. **41**(7), 2664–2683 (2020)
3. Chang, C.-I., Wang, S.: Constrained band selection for hyperspectral imagery. IEEE Trans. Geosci. Remote Sens. **44**(6), 1575–1585 (2006)
4. Feng, J., Haipeng, Y., Wang, L., Cao, X., Zhang, X., Jiao, L.: Classification of hyperspectral images based on multiclass spatial-spectral generative adversarial networks. IEEE Trans. Geosci. Remote Sens. **57**(8), 5329–5343 (2019)
5. Goodfellow, I.: Generative adversarial nets. In: Advances in Neural Information Processing Systems, vol. 27 (2014)
6. Hamida, A.B., Benoit, A., Lambert, P., Amar, C.B.: 3-d deep learning approach for remote sensing image classification. IEEE Trans. Geosci. Remote Sens. **56**(8), 4420–4434 (2018)
7. He, M., Li, B., Chen, H.: Multi-scale 3d deep convolutional neural network for hyperspectral image classification. In: 2017 IEEE International Conference on Image Processing (ICIP), pp. 3904–3908. IEEE (2017)
8. Hong, D.: Spectralformer: Rethinking hyperspectral image classification with transformers. IEEE Trans. Geosci. Remote Sens. (2021)
9. Wei, H., Huang, Y., Wei, L., Zhang, F., Li, H.: Deep convolutional neural networks for hyperspectral image classification. J. Sens. **15**(2), 1–12 (2015)
10. Jiang, J., Ma, J., Chen, C., Wang, Z., Cai, Z., Wang, L.: Superpca: A superpixelwise pca approach for unsupervised feature extraction of hyperspectral imagery. IEEE Trans. Geosci. Remote Sens. **56**(8), 4581–4593 (2018)
11. Jiang, Y., Chang, S., Wang, Z.: Transgan: Two pure transformers can make one strong gan, and that can scale up. In Ranzato, M., Beygelzimer, A., Dauphin, Y., Liang, P.S., Wortman Vaughan, J., (eds.) Advances in Neural Information Processing Systems, vol. 34, pp. 14745–14758. Curran Associates Inc. (2021)
12. Kumar, B., Dikshit, O., Gupta, A., Singh, M.K.: Feature extraction for hyperspectral image classification: A review. Int. J. Remote Sens. **41**(16), 6248–6287 (2020)
13. Liu, B., Xuchu, Y., Zhang, P., Tan, X., Wang, R., Zhi, L.: Spectral-spatial classification of hyperspectral image using three-dimensional convolution network. J. Appl. Remote Sens. **12**(1), 016005 (2018)
14. Odena, A., Olah, Shlens, J.: Conditional image synthesis with auxiliary classifier gans. In: International Conference on Machine Learning, pp. 2642–2651. PMLR (2017)
15. Parmar, N., et al.: Image transformer. In: International Conference on Machine Learning, pp. 4055–4064. PMLR (2018)
16. Plaza, A., Martínez, P., Plaza, J., Pérez, R.: Dimensionality reduction and classification of hyperspectral image data using sequences of extended morphological transformations. IEEE Trans. Geosci. Remote Sens. **43**(3), 466–479 (2005)
17. Roy, S.K., Krishna, G., Dubey, S.R., Chaudhuri, B.B.: Hybridsn: Exploring 3-d-2-d cnn feature hierarchy for hyperspectral image classification. IEEE Geosci. Remote Sens. Lett. **17**(2), 277–281 (2019)

18. Song, H., Kim, M., Park, D., Shin, Y., Lee, J.-G.: A survey. IEEE Trans. Neural Netw. Learn. Syst. Learn. Noisy Labels Deep Neural Netw. (2022)

19. Tun, N.L., et al.: Hyperspectral remote sensing images classification using fully convolutional neural network. In: 2021 IEEE Conference of Russian Young Researchers in Electrical and Electronic Engineering (ElConRus), pp. 2166–2170. IEEE (2021)

20. Vaswani, A., et al.: Attention is all you need. In: Advances in Neural Information Processing Systems, vol. 30 (2017)

21. Wang, J., Gao, F., Dong, J., Qian, D.: Adaptive dropblock-enhanced generative adversarial networks for hyperspectral image classification. IEEE Trans. Geosci. Remote Sens. **59**(6), 5040–5053 (2020)

22. Xia, J., Ghamisi, P., Yokoya, N., Iwasaki, A.: Random forest ensembles and extended multiextinction profiles for hyperspectral image classification. IEEE Trans. Geosci. Remote Sens. **56**(1), 202–216 (2017)

23. Zhan, Y., Dan, H., Wang, Y., Xianchuan, Y.: Semisupervised hyperspectral image classification based on generative adversarial networks. IEEE Geosci. Remote Sens. Lett. **15**(2), 212–216 (2017)

24. Zhang, L., Zhang, L., Tao, D., Huang, X.: On combining multiple features for hyperspectral remote sensing image classification. IEEE Trans. Geosci. Remote Sens. **50**(3), 879–893 (2011)

25. Zhong, Z., Li, J., Clausi, D.A., Wong, A.: Generative adversarial networks and conditional random fields for hyperspectral image classification. IEEE Trans. Cybern. **50**(7), 3318–3329 (2019)

26. Zhu, L., Chen, Y., Ghamisi, P., Benediktsson, J.: Generative adversarial networks for hyperspectral image classification. IEEE Trans. Geosci. Remote Sens. **56**(9), 5046–5063 (2018)

# Deliberation Selector for Knowledge-Grounded Conversation Generation

Huan Zhao[✉], Yiqing Wang, Bo Li, Song Wang, Zixing Zhang, and Xupeng Zha

College of Computer Science and Electronic Engineering, Hunan University, Changsha, China
{hzhao,wangyiqing,blee,swang17,zixingzhang,zhaxupeng}@hnu.edu.cn

**Abstract.** The integration of external knowledge is an important aspect for developing multi-turn conversation generation. However, most existing knowledge-background conversation generation models ignore the characteristics of the human brain to select knowledge, which often results in the generation of inappropriate responses. To tackle this issue, we propose a novel Deliberation Knowledge Selector (DKS) for neural conversation generation. It comprises two-pass attention knowledge selector to select appropriate knowledge and generates high-quality responses in the multi-turn conversation, further improving the performance of utterance generation. In addition, the DKS model achieves competitive results in simulating the human cognitive process for knowledge selection. Experimental studies on Wizard of Wikipedia and Holl-E show that the DKS delivers better predictive performance than several state-of-the-art methods in knowledge selection.

**Keywords:** Conversation generation · Knowledge background · Human-computer interaction

## 1 Introduction

The conversation generation system is one of the quite important cross-disciplines for human-computer interaction, which can be applied to customer service, smart home robots, and smart speakers. Conversation generation systems have achieved impressive success based on the sequence-to-sequence (SEQ2SEQ) [16] framework. SEQ2SEQ contains an encoder for mapping sequence into latent space, and a decoder for refactoring sequence. However,

Supported by National Natural Science Foundation of China under Grant 62076092, Special Project of Foshan Science and Technology Innovation Team under Grant FS0AA-KJ919-4402-0069.

traditional conversation generation systems often generate meaningless security responses and cannot well handle multiple turns of conversation. To handle this, knowledge-grounded conversation generation (KCG) has been proposed and received much attention.

Generally, KCG selects the appropriate knowledge from external knowledge datasets and responds according to the context, as illustrated in Fig. 1. From the perspective of knowledge selection, the related algorithms [6, 8, 22] can be separated into two categories: non-sequential models and sequential models. The non-sequential models select knowledge in different turns independently. The sequential models select knowledge with the help of selected knowledge in the past turns. Research shows that sequential models have achieved better accuracy in knowledge selection than non-sequential models due to the good use of the knowledge information between different turns. Therefore, we focus on the sequential-based KCG methods in this paper. In recent years, varieties of sequential methods have been designed to handle the KCG tasks. Concretely, these approaches pay attention to the relationship of previously selected knowledge, contexts, and the response of the current turn, or focus on the differences between selected knowledge of different turns to promote knowledge selection. For example, sequential knowledge transformer (SKT) [6] adopts the former idea, which employs the overall situation of the conversation. And difference-aware knowledge selection (DiffKS) [22] is a typical model of the second method, which focuses on the differences between knowledge. Sequential models take into

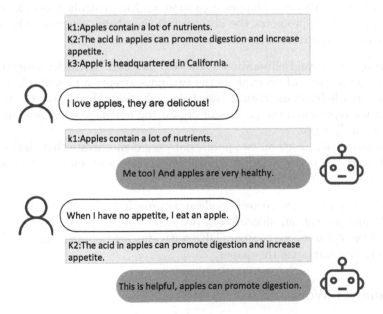

**Fig. 1.** An example conversation. In multiple turns of conversation, the robot selects appropriate knowledge from the candidate knowledge sentences and generates a response.

account the overall situation of the previous conversation turns, which is suitable for multiple turns of conversation. Thus, more and more researchers have proposed sequential-based KCG models, which have achieved good performance and have been widely used in conversation systems.

Although achieving great progress, the existing sequential-based KCG methods have still a major limitation. Most of the existing methods cannot well select appropriate external knowledge, causing the low quality response. For instance, SKT [6] employs the prior and posterior distribution of knowledge to finish the KCG tasks. However, this technique ignores the interrelationship between currently and previously selected knowledge, which chooses repetitive or irrelevant knowledge and follows the decreased accuracy of the KCG tasks. Apart from this, DiffKS [22] leverages a attention to picks up knowledge with a moderate difference from the selected knowledge in the previous turns. However, this strategy does not conform to the process of human organization language, resulting in insufficient use of context, and consequently a decrease in accuracy. In summary, such methods select repetitive or low-relevant knowledge or are inconsistent with the cognitive process of the human brain, which cannot well select knowledge.

In this paper, we propose a novel **D**eliberation **K**nowledge **S**elector (DKS) for knowledge-grounded conversation generation. The theme of our model not only chooses the appropriate knowledge for the current post, but also generates a diverse and meaningful response in conversation. DKS employs deliberation attention to select the appropriate knowledge including knowledge and context attention which encodes the difference and contexts. Besides, deliberation attention simulates the process of human cognition: multiple calculations of knowledge and context, which promotes the accuracy of knowledge selection. Our contributions are summarized as follows:

- We propose a novel Deliberation Knowledge Selector (DKS) for neural conversation generation, which exploits the two-pass attention to well select appropriate knowledge in multi-turn knowledge selection. Meanwhile, the two-pass attention reproduces the process of organizing language when human beings engage in dialogue.
- Adequate experiments on two public datasets demonstrate that the proposed DKS produces better accurate knowledge choices and informative responses than several state-of-the-art methods.

In the following, we review modern approaches to conversation systems (Sect. 2), and present our algorithm in two sub-blocks (Sect. 3). Through experiments on two datasets, we compare DKS with state-of-the-art methods (Sect. 4). Moreover, we summarize this paper.

## 2   Related Work

There are two main methods for a non-task-oriented conversation system. (1) Search methods: using search and sorting algorithms to pick response among the candidate responses [19,25,26]. (2) Generation methods: generating response based on SEQ2SEQ method [5,11,18]. Generally, the generation topics have changeable topics, rich semantics, and results that fit the topic of the question sentence.

The purpose of the generation method is to create more human-like robots, where the robot's response should be diverse and meaningful. Therefore, researchers usually improve the ability of the response through the following three aspects: emotion [24], theme or personality consistency [10] and external knowledge [3,6,7,22]. Especially, the generation method based on KCG can add new information, which is the best way to improve response quality. Thus, we aim to study a KCG system, which can introduce external knowledge to improve the diversity of response. And there are many related corpora which greatly promotes research.

The task of the generation method based on KCG requires the use of specific knowledge and multi-turns of context. However, there are two research directions in the research of applying knowledge to conversation generation systems.

**Knowledge use:** using knowledge to generate meaningful responses [7,15,23]. Incremental transformer with deliberation decoder (ITE+DD) [7] adds corresponding knowledge in the process of encoding context to improve context consistency. Commonsense knowledge aware conversational model (CCM) [23] uses a graph attention mechanism to encode knowledge, thereby enhancing the model's ability to inject large-scale knowledge. Conversation with on-demand Machine Reading (CMR) [15] encodes contexts as a question, and encodes knowledge as the context in QA. CMR uses the MRC framework to achieve conversation generation.

**Knowledge Selection:** selecting appropriate knowledge now based on the context of the conversation and the previously selected knowledge [6,12,21,22]. DiffKS [22] exploits the difference between the knowledge selected in different turns to promote knowledge selection. Based on BERT, pre-trained knowledge selector [21] uses pre-training technology to predict knowledge sequences based on context. Dual Knowledge Interaction Network (DukeNet) [12] has two tasks for mutual learning: knowledge tracking (connect the selected knowledge with the context) and knowledge selection. Dual learning enhances the performance of each other. Moreover, the process of selecting appropriate knowledge also promotes the use of knowledge. As a result, we focus on knowledge selection.

Motivated by the above methods, especially DiffKS [22], we propose a DKS which focuses on knowledge selection. DKS adopts DiffKS's knowledge difference-aware module. Additionally, DKS employs a deliberation attention structure to simulate the process of human cognition.

## 3 Approach

In this section, we introduce the framework of the proposed DKS method and describe the details of our model.

## 3.1  Problem Statement

In the multi-turn conversations, our goal is to give an appropriate response based on the context and knowledge of each turn. Besides, we select the appropriate knowledge to accomplish a response.

Formally, let $U = \{u^1, ..., u^t, ..., u^T\}$ be a whole conversation composed of $T$ turns posts. We take $u^t = \{u_1^t, ..., u_m^t, ..., u_M^t\}$ as the $t$-th post containing $M$ words, where $u_m^t$ denotes the $m$-th word in the $t$-th post. Similarly, we use $a^t = \{a_1^t, ..., a_l^t, ..., a_L^t\}$ and $k^t = \{k_1^t, ..., k_{|k^t|}^t\}$ to denote the response at $t$-th turn and the background knowledge sentences, respectively.

In the multi-turn conversations, the contexts are represented by the posts and responses of the previous turns as well as the post of the current turn. Therefore, in the $t$-th turn, we concatenate all posts and responses into $c^t = [u^{t-1}; a^{t-1}; u^t]$ as the context for the $t$-th turn.

## 3.2  Model Description

Given the candidate knowledge sentences and the context, the purpose of the DKS model is to afford a superb response. To this end, we leverage two encoders to encode knowledge sentences and context, deliberation attention selects the appropriate knowledge and encodes the selected knowledge with context, and decoder outputs the response. Figure 2 displays the workflow of the proposed DKS, which consists of two encoders, deliberation attention, and a decoder.

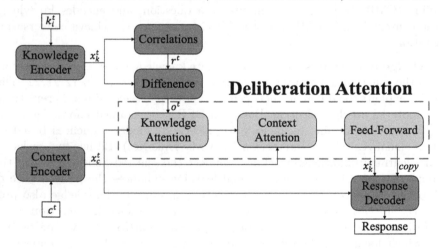

**Fig. 2.** The framework of the Deliberation Knowledge Selector (DKS) model.

**Encoder.** In the conversation, the knowledge is usually a paragraph or a document. And in the multi-turn conversations, the knowledge sentences in the previous turns also need to be used. To capture dependencies in long sequences, we develop two variants of the encoder (a.k.a. knowledge encoder and context encoder) based on the bidirectional gating recurrent unit (BiGRU) [1]. The knowledge encoder and context encoder are constructed as follows:

$$x_k^t = BiGRU_k(k^t), \tag{1}$$

$$x_c^t = BiGRU_c(c^t). \tag{2}$$

By calculating the correlation between candidate knowledge sentences, our model is capable of obtaining relevant and dependency information for calculating $o^t$ in the candidate knowledge sentences. Therefore, we compare candidate knowledge sentences in the same turn:

$$r^t = BiGRU(x_k^t). \tag{3}$$

To select the appropriate knowledge sentence from the candidate sentences, we perform the $Diff$ function [17] to compute the difference between each candidate knowledge sentence and selected knowledge in the previous N turns:

$$o^t = \sum_{n=1}^{N} \lambda_n Diff(x_k^{t-n}, r^t), \tag{4}$$

$$\sum_{n=1}^{N} \lambda_n = 1, \forall n, \lambda_n \geq 0, \tag{5}$$

$$Diff(x, r) = F(|x - r; x \odot r|), \tag{6}$$

where $F(\cdot)$ is a fully connected layer, using $tanh$ as the activation function. And $o^1$ is initialized to a zero vector. Consequently, the model selects the knowledge sentence, which has the largest relevance to the knowledge in the previous turns.

**Deliberation Attention.** In the real world, humans first choose the response topic (a.k.a. knowledge) in the communication process, such as extracting keywords, then deciding which background knowledge to use based on what the interlocutor says. Inspired by the above reason, we introduce deliberation attention [20] based on DiffKS, which consists of two attention passes to enhance the coherence as well as relevance between knowledge and context.

The first-pass attention is knowledge attention for presenting the candidate knowledge, which is a simulation of the first stage of human conversation cognition. The knowledge attention takes in the concatenation of difference $o^t$ and knowledge $x_k^t$ as the key and value of the input. We make context $x_c^t$ as query:

$$\beta_k^t = \mathbf{W}_{val}[x_k^t; o^t]tanh(\mathbf{W}_{que}[x_c^t] + \mathbf{W}_{key}[x_k^t; o^t]), \tag{7}$$

where $\mathbf{W}_{val}^k$, $\mathbf{W}_{que}^k$ and $\mathbf{W}_{key}^k$ are trainable parameters.

The second-pass attention is context attention which takes in the representation of the first-pass attention results and context sentences as input. This pass attention focuses on increasing context usage for enhancing coherence. Similarly, the context $x_c^t$ is used as the key and value of the input of the context attention, and it uses the knowledge attention results in $\beta_k^t$ as query:

$$\beta_c^t = \mathbf{W}_{val}^c[x_c^t]tanh(\mathbf{W}_{que}^c[\beta_k^t] + \mathbf{W}_{key}^c x_c^t). \tag{8}$$

To sum up, the DKS selects the most appropriate knowledge coding, which has the highest attention score. The corresponding softmax function is defined as:

$$\beta_i^t = softmax(\beta_{c,i}^t), \tag{9}$$

$$\hat{i} = argmax_i \beta_i^t, x^t = x_{k,\hat{i}}^t, \tag{10}$$

where $x^t$ is the selected knowledge sentence.

**Decoder.** Response's words decoding is computed by GRU:

$$s_j = GRU(s_j - 1, [\mathbf{e}(a_{j-1}); x]), \tag{11}$$

$$s_0 = \mathbf{W}_D[x_c; x_k] + \mathbf{b}_D, \tag{12}$$

where $\mathbf{W}_D$ and $\mathbf{b}_D$ are trainable parameters, $\mathbf{e}(\cdot)$ is an embedding method and $a_{j-1}$ denotes the response's word generated in the last time step. Then the decoder computes the probability of generating words based on the vocabulary:

$$p^G(y_j = w) = \mathbf{w}^T(\mathbf{W}_G s_j + \mathbf{b}_G), \tag{13}$$

where $w$ is a word and $\mathbf{w}$ is the one-hot vector of $w$. And in the real world, humans tend to repeat phrases and entity names in the conversation, such as location phrase, school name, and person's name. Thus, we use a copy network [4] to compute the probability of the copy words in the knowledge $k_i$:

$$p^C(a_j = w) = \sum_{q:k_{\hat{i},q}=w} (s_j)^T H(x_{k,\hat{i},q}), \tag{14}$$

where $H(\cdot)$ is a fully connected layer activated by $tanh$. We add the generation probability and the copy probability to calculate the probability distribution:

$$P(a_j = w) = \frac{1}{Z}(e^{p^G(a_j=w)} + e^{p^C(a_j=w)}), \tag{15}$$

where $Z$ is the normalization term. DKS selects the word with the highest probability:

$$k_j = argmax P(a_j = w). \tag{16}$$

**Training.** We compute the loss by using the final knowledge selection:

$$L_{KS} = -\sum_{t=1}^{T} log\beta_{i^{t*}}^t, \tag{17}$$

where $i^{t*}$ is the index of the final selected knowledge after passing the deliberation attention selector at the $t$-th turn. And we minimize the following negative log-likelihood loss:

$$L_{NLL} = -\sum_{t=1}^{T}\sum_{j=1}^{|a^t|} log P(a_j^{j*}), \tag{18}$$

where $a_j^{j*}$ denotes the $j$-th word in the response generated at the $t$-th turn. According to the effects of $L_{KS}$ and $L_{NLL}$, we integrate the final loss:

$$L = L_{KS} + L_{NLL}. \tag{19}$$

## 4  Experiments

In the following, we first introduce two public datasets, evaluation metrics, the baselines, and the parameter settings. Then, we show and analyze the results of the accuracy experiments and the case examples in detail.

### 4.1  Datasets

We evaluate our model on two frequently-used datasets: Wizard of Wikipedia (WoW) [2], and Holl-E [13].

WoW [2] is a typical dataset of human-human conversations, which contains multi-turn knowledge-grounded conversations. This dataset is divided into 166,787/17,715/17,497 for train/validation/test. And the test set is split into Test Seen and Test Unseen subsets, where Test Seen contains 533 topics. And Test Unseen contains 58 topics without being appeared in train or validation.

Holl-E [13] is a dataset containing multi-turn conversations, where the knowledge is selected from review, plot, and comments. The number of turns and candidate knowledge sentences in the conversation are 5 and 60.

### 4.2  Evaluation Metrics

We adopt **ACC, BLEU-2/4** [14] and **ROUGE-2** [9] to automatically evaluate the response generation performance.

Thereinto, ACC is the accuracy of candidate knowledge selection on the test dataset. BLEU evaluates generated sentences in machine translation tasks. BLEU evaluates the difference between the sentence generated by the model and the actual sentence. Its value range is between 0.0 and 1.0. And ROUGE is a set of indicators for evaluating automatic abstracts and machine translation, which calculates the recall rate on N-gram. Moreover, the higher values of these three metrics indicate the better performance of the models.

### 4.3  Baselines

For fair comparison, we select several advanced methods [3,6,8,22] as the baselines to compare our proposed model.

**MemNet** [3]: A model stores selected knowledge sentences in memory units, and the sum of selected knowledge and conversation encodings is input to the decoder. We make its candidate knowledge selection constrained by $L_{KS}$ as our model does.

**PostKS** [8]: A knowledge selection method uses prior and posterior distributions over background knowledge. We add a copy mechanism and use $L_{KS}$ as our model does.

**SKT** [6]: An improvement method based on the PostKS model. It uses two GRU to update the status of the context and previously selected knowledge respectively. And we replaced the BERT encoder with BiGRU as our model does. In the meanwhile, we add a copy mechanism as our model does.

**DiffKS** [22]: A difference-aware selection method for selecting appropriate external knowledge sentence for conversation. Knowledge selection calculates the differences between the current candidates and knowledge sentences that are selected previously.

### 4.4  Supplementary Details

Specifically, our model uses two BiGRU encoders and a GRU decoder. Meanwhile, DKS uses difference-aware and deliberation attention to select appropriate knowledge provided. And DKS tokenizes the sentences with NLTK. Our word embeddings are 300 dimensional. We perform PyTorch experiments on the GPU of NVIDIA-SMI 430.40 and CUDA Version 10.1.

Other additional parameter settings are given below: first, the dropout rate for word embeddings is set to 0.5. Second, the encoder and decoder take 200 and 400 as the hidden size, respectively. Finally, the batch size is set to 8, and all models are trained for 20 epochs.

### 4.5  Experimental Results

Table 1 shows the comparison results of all methods in terms of accuracy, BLEU-2/4 and ROUGE-2 on the WoW and Holl-E datasets. Our method performs better than all baselines on three test sets. Compared with DiffKS, DKS with deliberation structure increases the use of context, resulting in better results. And DKS has the highest accuracy of knowledge selection, which indicates our selector can more accurately select suitable knowledge from candidate knowledge sentences. And compared with DiffKS, the most competitive model, the performance of DKS improves 5% and 4% for both BLEU-4 and ROUGE-2 on WoW Seen, respectively. DKS not only selects more accurate knowledge but also uses knowledge better.

Especially, the experimental results of DKS have greater improvement in Holl-E. It may be because Holl-E's one speaker is instructed by copying sentences from knowledge, which makes context and knowledge have a strong correlation. Thus, deliberation attention can easily select the appropriate knowledge. Compared with DiffKS, DKS adds a deliberation attention module to simulate the human cognitive process to select knowledge, which increases a small number of computing resources. As we analyzed, compared with DiffKS, the speedup ratio of DKS is increased by 1.05%. The above contents can demonstrate the superiority of the proposed DKS.

**Table 1.** Automatic evaluation results. Automatic evaluation for baselines and our proposed model. The best results are in bold.

| Models | ACC | BLEU-2/4 | | ROUGE-2 |
|---|---|---|---|---|
| *WoW Seen* | | | | |
| MemNet+$L_{KS}$ | 18.8 | 7.4 | 2.1 | 3.6 |
| PostKS+$L_{KS}$ | 22.8 | 10.5 | 5.1 | 6.1 |
| SKT | 23.3 | 11.4 | 5.4 | 6.5 |
| DiffKS | 25.5 | 11.5 | 5.7 | 6.8 |
| **DKS (ours)** | **25.8** | **11.9** | **6.0** | **7.1** |
| *WoW Unseen* | | | | |
| MemNet+$L_{KS}$ | 16.7 | 6.3 | 1.4 | 2.4 |
| PostKS+$L_{KS}$ | 15.2 | 9.0 | 3.9 | 4.5 |
| SKT | 15.0 | 8.9 | 3.8 | 4.8 |
| DiffKS | 20.7 | 10.2 | 4.9 | 5.8 |
| **DKS (ours)** | **21.0** | **10.5** | **5.1** | **6.0** |
| *Holl-E* | | | | |
| MemNet+$L_{KS}$ | 11.5 | 9.1 | 4.9 | 8.9 |
| PostKS+$L_{KS}$ | 30.6 | 30.1 | 26.1 | 26.0 |
| SKT | 28.5 | 29.4 | 25.4 | 24.9 |
| DiffKS | 32.9 | 30.0 | 25.9 | 25.8 |
| **DKS (ours)** | **33.2** | **30.5** | **26.5** | **26.4** |

## 4.6  Ablation Test

To verify the effectiveness of the deliberation attention in multi-turn dialogue knowledge selection, we design an ablation test (DKS-A), as shown in Fig. 3. Concretely, DKS-A removes the second-pass attention and uses a self-attention to encode context sentences before being input the decoder.

The comparison results of the DKS-A and DKS are shown in Table 2. Without deliberation attention, DKS' performance is significantly worse in all the metrics. And Fig. 4 shows the difference between DKS-A and DKS in the real case. In

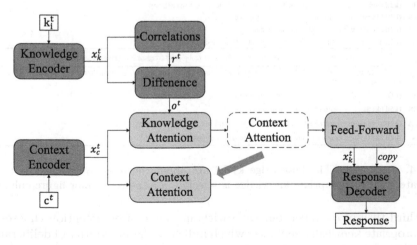

**Fig. 3.** The ablation model of the proposed DKS-A. We changed the position of context attention to compare with DKS.

**Table 2.** Ablation test. We compared the differences between DKS-A and DKS in automatic metrics.

| Models | ACC | BLEU-2/4 | | ROUGE-2 |
|---|---|---|---|---|
| *WoW Seen* | | | | |
| DKS | **25.8** | **11.9** | **6.0** | **7.1** |
| DKS-A | 25.3 | 11.5 | 5.7 | 6.7 |
| *WoW Unseen* | | | | |
| DKS | **21.0** | **10.5** | **5.1** | **6.0** |
| DKS-A | 20.1 | 10.3 | 4.9 | 5.7 |
| *Holl-E* | | | | |
| DKS | **33.2** | **30.5** | **26.5** | **26.4** |
| DKS-A | 32.2 | 30.0 | 26.0 | 25.8 |

| **Topic: Rapping** |
|---|
| **K1**: Rapping (or rhyming, spitting, emceeing, mcing) is a musical form of vocal delivery that incorporates" rhyme, rhythmic speech, and street vernacular", which is performed or chanted in a variety of ways. <br> **K2**: The components of rap include "content"(what is being said), "flow"(rhythm, rhyme), and "delivery"(cadence, tone ). <br> **K3**: Rap is often associated with , and is a primary ingredient of hip-hop music , but the origins of the phenomenon predate hip-hop culture. <br> **K4**: Rap differs from spoken-word poetry in that rap is usually performed in time to an instrumental track. <br> **K5**: Rap is often associated with , and is a primary ingredient of hip-hop music, but the origins of the phenomenon predate hip-hop culture. <br> **K6**: Illmatic is the debut studio album by american rapper nas. |

| | **Post 1:** Do you like rap music ? Meek mill is my favorite rapper by far. |
|---|---|
| **PostKS+** | **(k1)**Rapping is a musical form of vocal delivery that incorporates "rhyme, rhythmic, rhythmic speech, and street vernacular", which is a musical form of vocal delivery that incorporates "rhyme, rhythmic speech, and street. |
| **SKT** | **(k1)**I like rapping too. I like to listen to the musical form of vocal delivery that incorporates rhyme, rhythmic, and street vernacular |
| **DiffKS** | **(k1)**I love rapping, I like rapping, rapping, and street vernacular . |
| **DKS-A** | **(k1)**I love rapping, I like to sing. I like to play a musical form of vocal delivery that incorporates rhyme , rhythmic speech , and street vernacular . |
| **DKS** | **(k1)**I love rapping, rhyming, mcing, and street vernacular . |

| | **Post 2:** Sometimes it is really catchy , other times it is impressive how techinical someone gets or how fast they rap. |
|---|---|
| **PostKS+** | **(k2)**The components of rap include "content"(what is being said), "flow" and "delivery"(rhythm, rhyme, and "delivery" (rhythm, rhyme, and "delivery". |
| **SKT** | **(k2)**I think it' s a great idea. The components of rap include content and delivery . |
| **DiffKS** | **(k5)**I like rap music. I like rap music. It' s a hip-hop music . ✗ |
| **DKS-A** | **(k2)**I like to play with content, flow and rhythm . |
| **DKS** | **(k2)**I think it is very popular. It includes "content", "flow", and"delivery". |

| | **Post 3:** Yeah, all of those things make for some really great songs, it is my favorite genre. |
|---|---|
| **PostKS+** | **(k2)**The components of rap include "content"(what is being said), "flow" and "delivery"(rhythm, rhyme, and "delivery" (rhythm, rhyme, and "delivery". ✗ |
| **SKT** | **(k1)**I like to listen to the music of rap, but I' m not sure . ✗ |
| **DiffKS** | **(k6)**I like nas. It' s the debut album by american rapper nas. ✗ |
| **DKS-A** | **(k3)**Rap is a primary ingredient of hip hop music but I think it's a primary ingredient of hip hop music. ✗ |
| **DKS** | **(k4)**I like to listen to spoken-word poetry in time to an instrumental track. |

**Fig. 4.** Case study. The knowledge k1-k6 are about the topic *Rapping*. The red × indicates that inappropriate knowledge is selected in response. (Color figure online)

the third turn of conversation, DKS without deliberation attention chooses an inappropriate knowledge sentence, which indicates the superiority of deliberation attention.

## 4.7  Case Study

In this subsection, we represent a case to demonstrate the difference between DKS and baseline models. DKS selects the most appropriate knowledge in each turn of conversation, and the generated responses are natural and coherent. In detail, we see the following. At the first turn, the knowledge of all model choices is the same. However, at the second turn, the response of the PostKS+ is unnatural, and the DiffKS selects the inappropriate knowledge. At the following third turn, the PostKS+ chooses the repeated knowledge, and the SKT's response is a "safe answer" with poor diversity. In multiple turns of conversation, the responses generated by DKS are all rich and natural, which is no "safe answer" and reflects its improvement in diversity.

## 5  Conclusion

In this paper, we propose a Deliberation Knowledge Selector (DKS) for the task of knowledge-grounded response generation in multi-turn conversations. DKS adopts the two-pass attention to select appropriate knowledge used in response generation. Experimental results demonstrate the superiority of DKS against several state-of-the-art methods in selecting knowledge and injecting knowledge. In the future, we plan to integrate selected knowledge with the multi-turn context to generate more informative responses.

## References

1. Cho, K., et al., F.B.: Learning phrase representations using RNN encoder-decoder for statistical machine translation. In: Proc. Empirical Methods in Natural Language Processing (EMNLP), pp. 1724–1734 (2014)
2. Dinan, E., et al.: Wizard of wikipedia: Knowledge-powered conversational agents. In: Proceedings of the International Conference on Learning Representations (ICLR), pp. 1–18 (2019)
3. Ghazvininejad, M., et al.: A knowledge-grounded neural conversation model. In: Proceedings of the Association for the Advance of Artificial Intelligence (AAAI), pp. 5110–5117 (2018)
4. Gu, J., Lu, Z., Li, H., Li, V.O.K.: Incorporating copying mechanism in sequence-to-sequence learning. In: Proceedings of the Association for Computational Linguistics (ACL), pp. 1631–1640 (2016)
5. He, W., et al.: Multi-goal multi-agent learning for task-oriented dialogue with bidirectional teacher-student learning. Knowl. Based Syst. **213**, 106667 (2021)
6. Kim, B., Ahn, J., Kim, G.: Sequential latent knowledge selection for knowledge-grounded dialogue. In: Proceedings of the International Conference on Learning Representations (ICLR), pp. 1–14 (2020)
7. Li, Z., et al.: Incremental transformer with deliberation decoder for document grounded conversations. In: Proceedings of the Association for Computational Linguistics (ACL), pp. 12–21 (2019)

8. Lian, R., Xie, M., Wang, F., Peng, J., Wu, H.: Learning to select knowledge for response generation in dialog systems. In: Proceedings of the International Joint Conference on Artificial Intelligence (IJCAI), pp. 5081–5087 (2019)

9. Lin, C.Y.: Rouge: A package for automatic evaluation of summaries. In: Proceedings of the Text Summarization Branches Out, pp. 74–81 (2004)

10. Liu, Q., et al.: You impress me: Dialogue generation via mutual persona perception. In: Proceedings of the Association for Computational Linguistics (ACL), pp. 1417–1427 (2020)

11. Liu, Q., et al.: Heterogeneous relational graph neural networks with adaptive objective for end-to-end task-oriented dialogue. Knowl. Based Syst. **227**, 107186 (2021)

12. Meng, C., et al.: Dukenet: A dual knowledge interaction network for knowledge-grounded conversation. In: Proceedings of the Special Interest Group on Information Retrieval (SIGIR), pp. 1151–1160 (2020)

13. Moghe, N., Arora, S., Banerjee, S., Khapra, M.M.: Towards exploiting background knowledge for building conversation systems. In: Proceedings of the Empirical Methods in Natural Language Processing (EMNLP), pp. 2322–2332 (2018)

14. Papineni, K., Roukos, S., Ward, T., Zhu, W.: Bleu: a method for automatic evaluation of machine translation. In: Proceedings of the Association for Computational Linguistics (ACL), pp. 311–318 (2002)

15. Qin, L., et al.: Conversing by reading: Contentful neural conversation with on-demand machine reading. In: Proceedings of the Association for Computational Linguistics (ACL), pp. 5427–5436 (2019)

16. Sutskever, I., Vinyals, O., Le, Q.V.: Sequence to sequence learning with neural networks. In: Ghahramani, Z., Welling, M., Cortes, C., Lawrence, N.D., Weinberger, K.Q. (eds.) Proceedings of the Neural Information Processing Systems (NIPS), pp. 3104–3112 (2014)

17. Wang, S., Yu, M., Jiang, J., Chang, S.: A co-matching model for multi-choice reading comprehension. In: Proceedings of the Association for Computational Linguistics (ACL), pp. 746–751 (2018)

18. Wang, W., Feng, S., Chen, L., Wang, D., Zhang, Y.: Learning to improve persona consistency in conversation generation with information augmentation. Knowl.-Based Syst. **228**, 107246 (2021)

19. Wu, Y., Wu, W., Xing, C., Zhou, M., Li, Z.: Sequential matching network: A new architecture for multi-turn response selection in retrieval-based chatbots. In: Proceedings of the Association for Computational Linguistics (ACL), pp. 496–505 (2017)

20. Xia, Y., et al.: Deliberation networks: Sequence generation beyond one-pass decoding. In: Proceedings of the Neural Information Processing Systems (NIPS), pp. 1784–1794 (2017)

21. Zhao, X., et al.: Knowledge-grounded dialogue generation with pre-trained language models. In: Proceedings of the Empirical Methods in Natural Language Processing (EMNLP), pp. 3377–3390 (2020)

22. Zheng, C., Cao, Y., Jiang, D., Huang, M.: Difference-aware knowledge selection for knowledge-grounded conversation generation. In: Proceedings of the Empirical Methods in Natural Language Processing (EMNLP), pp. 115–125 (2020)

23. Zhou, H., et al.: Commonsense knowledge aware conversation generation with graph attention. In: Proceedings of the International Joint Conference on Artificial Intelligence (IJCAI), pp. 4623–4629 (2018)

24. Zhou, X., Wang, W.Y.: Mojitalk: Generating emotional responses at scale. In: Proceedings of the Association for Computational Linguistics (ACL), pp. 1128–1137 (2018)

25. Zhou, X., et al.: Multi-view response selection for human-computer conversation. In: Proceedings of the Empirical Methods in Natural Language Processing (EMNLP), pp. 372–381 (2016)
26. Zhou, X., et al.: Multi-turn response selection for chatbots with deep attention matching network. In: Proceedings of the Association for Computational Linguistics (ACL), pp. 1118–1127 (2018)

# Training a Lightweight ViT Network for Image Retrieval

Hanqi Zhang[1](✉), Yunlong Yu[2], Yingming Li[2], and Zhongfei Zhang[3]

[1] School of Software Technology, Zhejiang University, Hangzhou, China
`zhanghanqi@zju.edu.cn`
[2] College of Information Science and Electronic Engineering, Zhejiang University, Hangzhou, China
`{yuyunlong,yingming}@zju.edu.cn`
[3] Computer Science Department, Binghamton University, Binghamton, USA
`zhongfei@cs.binghamton.edu`

**Abstract.** Recently, Vision Transformer (ViT) networks have achieved promising advancements on many computer vision tasks. However, a ViT network has a large number of parameters, which is not conducive to deploy of the models in the edge devices. In this paper, we focus on learning lightweight ViT models and formulate both the quantization and distillation strategies into the multi-exit framework to compress the size of the model as much as possible. Specifically, we use the quantized heterogeneous distillation strategy based on the relaxed contrastive loss that incorporates pairwise similarities in the convolutional teacher network into the training process of a student network based on ViT whose weights are quantized to a limited set of levels. Then, we deploy the quantized heterogeneous distillation strategy on the multi-exit framework to further compress the model and explore five types of early exits for the ViT-based models. This paper establishes the latest technical level on four popular image retrieval benchmarks, and achieves the leading Recall@1 results **78.5%**, **84.5%**, **90.3%** and **95.2%** respectively on CUB-200–2011, SOP, Cars196, In-Shop, while reducing the size of the model by 50%, ensuring that the ViT-based models run in a resource-constrained environment but without much performance loss.

**Keywords:** Heterogeneous knowledge distillation · Quantization · Lightweight · Image retrieval

## 1 Introduction

Recently, Vision Transformer (ViT) [5] has shown promising performances in the field of computer vision, ranging from feature-based object retrieval [2,6], image classification [1,3,14], image detection [27,28], to semantic segmentation [22,25,29]. Touvron et al. [25] propose Data-efficient image Transformers (DeiT) to achieve competitive results on image classification tasks. El-Nouby et al. [6] apply the ViT on the image retrieval task and show consistent improvements of transformers over convolution-based approaches. Liu et al. [14] propose a hierarchical Transformer called Swin Transformer (Swin) that achieves the leading

© The Author(s), under exclusive license to Springer Nature Switzerland AG 2022
S. Khanna et al. (Eds.): PRICAI 2022, LNCS 13631, pp. 240–250, 2022.
https://doi.org/10.1007/978-3-031-20868-3_18

results on both object detection and semantic segmentation tasks. Mehta et al. [18] propose a light-weight ViT for mobile devices and present a different perspective for the global processing of information with transformers, i.e., transformers as convolutions. However, the existing ViT architectures have a large number of parameters, which are not conducive to deploy of the models in the edge devices. Thus, designing a lightweight and effective ViT model is more favored and is the main challenge to be addressed in this paper.

In order to reduce the size of ViT, several methods have been proposed to quantize ViT. For example, [15] first applies the post-training quantization algorithm for ViT. [13] applies the quantization-aware training algorithm and designs a fully differentiable quantization method for ViT named Q-ViT, in which both of the quantization scales and bit-widths are learnable parameters. Though the quantization strategy could significantly reduce the size of the model, it inevitably reduces the performance. How to reduce the model size of ViT while maintaining the performance is still under-explored.

In this paper, we combine quantization, multi-exit architecture, and distillation into a united framework to compress the ViT model as much as possible, ensuring that the ViT-based models run in a resource-constrained environment but without much performance loss. First, we use a heterogeneous distillation method based on the relaxed contrastive loss [11] to achieve the knowledge transfer. The relaxed contrastive loss incorporates pairwise similarities in the convolutional teacher network into the training process of a ViT student network. Then, we combine the heterogeneous distillation with quantization. The distillation loss is computed with respect to the predictions made by the quantized model, but the gradient updates (i.e. the backward pass) is applied to the full precision parameters. Finally, we deploy the quantized heterogeneous distillation strategy on the multi-exit framework to further compress the model and explore five types of early exits for the ViT-based models. We evaluate our framework on the image retrieval tasks and validate the framework could achieve the leading results **78.5%**/**78.5%**/76.1% on CUB-200–2011, **84.5%**/**84.5%**/**82.0%** on SOP, **90.3%**/90.2%/89.7% on Cars196 and **95.2%**/95.1%/95.0% on In-Shop, while reducing the size of the model by 50%/75%/88%.

In a nutshell, our highlights include:

- We combine quantization, multi-exit architecture, and distillation into a united framework to compress the ViT model size while maintaining the performances. Though each single model compression method and the combination of the two have been explored in the existing literature, the combination of the three methods is the first attempt as far as we know.
- The proposed framework achieves leading results on four image retrieval benchmarks and obtains significant performance improvements compared to the state-of-the-art methods. The framework could still maintain the advantage even if the model size is reduced by 88%.

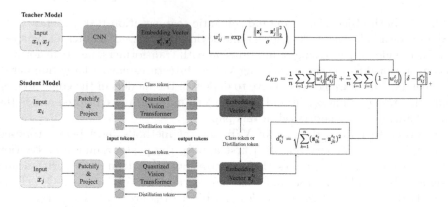

**Fig. 1.** The framework of the heterogeneous distillation quantization method based on the relaxed contrastive loss. A CNN model is used for teacher to produce the pair-wise relations as the knowledge for the ViT student.

## 2    Methodology

In this section, we introduce a heterogeneous distillation method based on the relaxed contrastive loss and discuss how to combine distillation and quantization. Then, we extend the quantized distillation strategy for multi-exit architectures.

### 2.1    Knowledge Distillation with Relaxed Contrastive Loss

Under the knowledge distillation framework, we assume that we have access to a teacher network in advance that performs as a feature extractor or a classifier. It could be either a convnet or a transformer. We tackle the problem of how to train a lightweight transformer with the assistance of the teacher network. It is called heterogeneous distillation when the teacher network and the student network share different architectures. In this section, we introduce a heterogeneous feature-based distillation strategy to achieve the knowledge transfer, expressed with respect to a convnet teacher network, into the training of a transformer student network.

Instead of directly matching the feature embeddings of the teacher and the student, we explore to transfer the structure relations captured with the feature embeddings from the teacher to the student with a relaxed contrastive loss. The relaxed contrastive loss is implemented by replacing the binary label of the original contrastive loss [7] with the pair-wise visual similarity in the feature embedding space of the teacher model. Specifically, the relaxed contrastive loss is formulated as:

$$L_{RCL} = \frac{1}{n} \sum_{i=1}^{n} \sum_{j=1}^{n} w_{ij}^t {d_{ij}^s}^2 + \frac{1}{n} \sum_{i=1}^{n} \sum_{j=1}^{n} \left(1 - w_{ij}^t\right) \left[\delta - d_{ij}^s\right]_+^2 \tag{1}$$

where $n$ is the number of samples in a batch, $\delta$ is the margin, $[\cdot]_+$ is the hinge function. $d_{ij}^s$ denotes the Euclidean distance between sample $x_i$ and $x_j$ in the feature embedding space of the student model. $w_{ij}^t$ is the visual similarity of sample $x_i$ and $x_j$ in the feature embedding space of the teacher model, which is implemented with a Gaussian kernel based on Euclidean distance, as shown in the formula Eq. (2):

$$w_{ij}^t = \exp\left(-\frac{\left\|\mathbf{z}_i^t - \mathbf{z}_j^t\right\|_2^2}{\sigma}\right) \tag{2}$$

where $\sigma$ is the kernel bandwidth and is set to 1 in the experiments, $\mathbf{z}_i^t = f^t(x_i)$ indicates the embedding vector of $x_i$ from teacher model $f^t$, and $\|\cdot\|_2$ represents $\ell_2$-norm of the embedding vector. The process of the heterogeneous distillation based on the relaxed contrastive loss is shown in Fig. 1.

The formula Eq. (2) indicates that the strength of aligning the structure relations is controlled by the prior visual similarity obtained with the teacher model. Minimizing it would force the student model to imitate the embedding space of the teacher model, which is beneficial to learn a better student model.

## 2.2 Quantized Heterogeneous Knowledge Distillation

Though the knowledge distillation strategy helps the student model to obtain compact representations of ensembles, the size of the student model also needs to be large enough for allowing learning to succeed. A too shallow or too narrow student model would hardly obtain satisfying performances. To learn a lightweight but powerful visual transformer model, we combine knowledge distillation and quantization.

To reduce the influence on accuracy, we follow [9] and apply the quantization-aware training strategy that training with simulated quantization, i.e., the model acts as if it were already quantized during the forward pass.

As illustrated in Fig. 2, the quantization-aware training strategy is to rely on projected gradient descent, where the loss and gradients are computed with respect to the quantized model, but the backward pass happens as normal, i.e., on the full-precision weights. This encourages the model to perform well during a quantized forward pass (which is what happens at inference time) while continuing to leverage the better representational power of longer-bit parameters and gradients.

Specifically, we use the uniform quantization function to quantify the student model. Then, the quantized student model $f^{s_q}$ is used to generate the embedding vector $\mathbf{z}_i^{s_q} = f^{s_q}(x_i)$ for the distillation loss, which is expressed as:

$$L_{RCL}^q = \frac{1}{n}\sum_{i=1}^{n}\sum_{j=1}^{n} w_{ij}^t d_{ij}^{s_q 2} + \frac{1}{n}\sum_{i=1}^{n}\sum_{j=1}^{n}\left(1 - w_{ij}^t\right)\left[\delta - d_{ij}^{s_q}\right]_+^2, \tag{3}$$

where $d_{ij}^{s_q}$ is the Euclidean distance between $\mathbf{z}_i^{s_q}$ and $\mathbf{z}_j^{s_q}$.

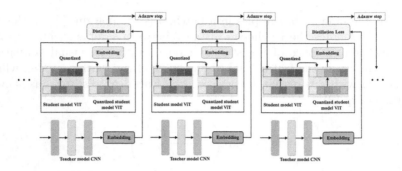

**Fig. 2.** Illustration of the quantization-aware training steps. Both the gradient and the embedding vector of the student model are obtained in the limited-precision network, and the gradient descent step is implemented in the full-precision network. Note that the accumulation over multiple steps of gradients in the unquantized model leads to a switch in quantization.

---

**Algorithm 1.** Quantized Heterogeneous Knowledge Distillation.

**Input:** Input batch data $(X, Y)$, teacher CNN model $f^t$, student ViT model $f^s$, quantization function $Q$, hyper-parameter $\lambda$, learning rate $\nu$.
**Output:** Quantitative student model $f^{s_q}$.
1: Let $\omega$ represents all the parameters that ViT needs to quantify.
2: **for** batch **do**
3:    $\omega^q \leftarrow Q(\omega)$;
4:    $\mathbf{Z}_{s_q} = f^{s_q}(X)$;
5:    $\mathbf{Z}_t = f^t(X)$;
6:    Run forward pass and compute objective $L^q_{RCL}$ in Eq. (3);
7:    Run backward pass and compute $\frac{\partial L^q_{RCL}(\omega^q)}{\partial \omega^q}$;
8:    Update original weights using Adamw in full precision $\omega = \omega - \nu \cdot \frac{\partial L^q_{RCL}(\omega^q)}{\partial \omega^q}$;
9: Finally quantize the weights before returning: $\omega^q \leftarrow Q(\omega)$.
10: **return** $f^{s_q}$.

---

Finally, we calculate the gradient of the quantized student model in the limited-precision network, and use the gradient descent step in the student model with full-precision. The optimisation details are summarised in Algorithm 1.

### 2.3   Distillation Heterogeneous Quantization for Multi-exit Networks

Deep neural networks generally require high computational resources and cause slow inference speed. A promising solution is dynamic inference strategy [8] that allows the deep models to modify their computation graph during inference. The popular method is multi-exit architecture [20,21] that inserts early exit branches after intermediate hidden layers of the backbone network and could provide early results. In this section, we explore the distillation heterogeneous quantization for the multi-exit architecture based on the quantized ViT in Sect. 2.2.

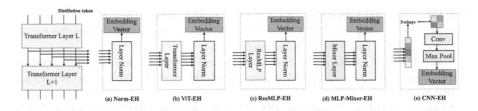

**Fig. 3.** Illustration of five exit heads explored in the paper.

Specifically, we apply the classifier-wise strategy [21] to train the multi-exit architecture. Once the quantized ViT in Sect. 2.2 is obtained, we freeze the backbone and only train the branches separately under the supervision of the teacher model. When training branch $b$, the distillation loss is used:

$$L_b^q = \frac{1}{n} \sum_{i=1}^{n} \sum_{j=1}^{n} w_{ij}^t d_{ij}^{b_q 2} + \frac{1}{n} \sum_{i=1}^{n} \sum_{j=1}^{n} \left(1 - w_{ij}^t\right) \left[\delta - d_{ij}^{b_q}\right]_+^2, \qquad (4)$$

where $d_{ij}^{b_q}$ is the Euclidean distance between $\mathbf{z}_i^{b_q}$ and $\mathbf{z}_j^{b_q}$, $\mathbf{z}_i^{b_q} = \phi_b\left(f_b^{s_q}(x_i)\right)$, $f_b^{s_q}$ is the frozen transformer block of the student network for branch $b$, $\phi_b$ is the exit head for branch $b$, which is introduced in the following.

As illustrated in Fig. 3, we explore five types of exit head in the section, including:

- Norm-EH directly adds a normalization layer to the token vectors of the intermediate layer;
- ViT-EH adds another transformer layer followed with a normalization layer;
- ResMLP-EH adds a ResMLP layer [24] followed with a normalization layer;
- MLP-Mixer-EH adds a MLP-Mixer layer [23] followed with a normalization layer;
- CNN-EH converts the sequence of token vectors in the intermediate layers of the ViT backbone to a 2D grid and further processes them using convolutional filters.

## 3 Experiments

In this section, we conduct experiments to evaluate the proposed models for image retrieval. We first describe the experimental settings and then provide comprehensive comparison results. Finally, we analyze the characteristics of five early head exits explored in this paper for the metric learning tasks based on ViT and the application of distillation quantization method in multi-exit architecture.

### 3.1 Experimental Setup

**Datasets.** We evaluate our models on four fine-grained datasets.

- **CUB-200–2011 (CUB)** [26] consists of 200 classes with 11,788 images in total. We split the first 100 classes for training (5,864 images) and the rest of the classes for evaluation (5,924 images).
- **Cars-196** [12] contains 16,185 images from 196 cars classes. We split the first 98 classes for training (8,054 images) and the rest 98 classes for evaluation (8,131 images).
- **Stanford Online Products (SOP)** [19] contains 120,053 images of 22,634 products collected from eBay.com. For the experiments, we split 59,551 images of 11,318 classes for training and 60,502 images of 11,316 classes for test.
- **In-Shop** contains 52,712 images of clothing items belonging to 7,986 categories, 3,997 of which used for training. The remaining 3,985 categories are split into 14,218 query and 12,612 gallery images for testing in [16].

**Model Architecture.** For a fair comparison, we select the variants of the ViT, DeiT_Small (DeiT_S) [25] and Swin_Tiny (Swin_T) [14] that are comparable to the widely adopted ResNet50 in terms of parameters count and FLOPS, as our primary student models. DeiT_S and Swin_T combine a contrastive loss with a differential entropy regularizer as the baseline of the experiment. Table 1 presents the neural networks used through this paper. They are all pre-trained on ImageNet1k [4]. The embedding vector

**Table 1.** Parameters count, FLOPS (G) and ImageNet Top-1 accuracy (%) of ResNet-50 (R50) and two ViT variants. † indicates the model pre-trained with distillation with a convnet trained on ImageNet1k.

| Model | #params | FLOPS(G) | Top-1 |
|---|---|---|---|
| R50 | 23M | 8.3 | 76.2 |
| DeiT_S | 22M | 8.4 | 79.8 |
| DeiT_S† | 22M | 8.5 | 81.1 |
| Swin_T | 29M | 9.0 | 81.3 |

dimensionalities of ResNet50 and the ViT variants are 512 and 384, respectively. We train ResNet50 with Proxy Anchor [10] as the teacher model.

**Implementation Details.** The ViT-based models and their pre-trained weights are from the public implementation of DeiT and Swin. All models are optimized using the AdamW optimizer [17] with learning rate $1e-5$, weight decay $1e-4$, and batch size of 64. For all experiments, the relaxed contrastive loss margin $\delta$ is set to 0.5. For DeiT_S and Swin_T, we use the class token as the embedding vector of the student model, and for DeiT_S†, we use the distillation token as the embedding vector. The details of distillation token is obtained by referring to [25].

We use standard data augmentation methods of resizing the image to 256×256 and then taking a random crop of size 224×224. Recall@K is used as the evaluation metric.

### 3.2 Comprehensive Comparison Results

Table 2 shows the comparison results of different models on four benchmarks. From the results, we have the following observations. First, the ViT models perform more competitively than the CNN counterparts that have similar parameter numbers. Taking the results of CUB as an example, SwinT and DeiT_S

**Table 2.** Comparison results (%) of different models on four benchmarks. ResNet-50 trained with Proxy Anchor [10] is taken as the baseline. Q represents the quantization operation in Sect. 2, the number represents quantization bit, and KD represents the distillation method in Sect. 2. KD_Q represents the distillation quantization method. The best results are marked in **bold**.

| Method | Size | CUB | | | SOP | | | Cars196 | | | In-Shop | | |
|---|---|---|---|---|---|---|---|---|---|---|---|---|---|
| | | R@1 | R@2 | R@4 | R@1 | R@10 | R@100 | R@1 | R@2 | R@4 | R@1 | R@10 | R@20 |
| ResNet50 [10] | 92.0 MB | 69.9 | 79.6 | 88.6 | 80.5 | 92.7 | 95.5 | 87.7 | 92.7 | 95.5 | 90.4 | 98.1 | 98.8 |
| SwinT | 116 MB | 75.0 | 85.4 | 90.3 | 83.8 | 93.6 | 97.2 | 87.8 | 93.0 | 95.6 | 91.3 | 98.3 | 99.1 |
| SwinT_Q16 | 55.7 MB | 76.2 | 85.5 | 90.5 | 83.6 | 93.0 | 96.4 | 88.2 | 93.2 | 96.1 | 91.1 | 98.2 | 98.8 |
| SwinT_Q8 | 27.6 MB | 76.1 | 85.2 | 90.3 | 83.3 | 93.0 | 96.8 | 88.0 | 92.8 | 95.9 | 91.2 | 98.2 | 98.9 |
| SwinT_Q4 | 13.3 MB | 75.3 | 84.5 | 90.1 | 81.0 | 92.0 | 95.8 | 85.8 | 91.5 | 95.2 | 90.9 | 98.1 | 98.7 |
| SwinT_KD | 116 MB | 78.0 | 85.6 | 90.6 | 84.0 | **93.7** | 97.3 | 88.6 | 93.1 | 95.9 | 94.9 | **99.1** | **99.4** |
| SwinT_KD_Q16 | 55.7MB | **78.1** | **85.9** | 91.1 | **84.1** | 93.6 | **97.4** | 88.7 | **94.0** | **96.5** | **95.2** | 99.0 | **99.4** |
| SwinT_KD_Q8 | 27.6MB | 77.9 | 85.6 | **91.2** | 83.5 | 93.2 | 97.1 | **88.8** | 93.7 | 96.5 | 95.1 | 98.9 | 99.2 |
| SwinT_KD_Q4 | 13.3MB | 75.6 | 84.5 | 89.5 | 81.7 | 92.4 | 96.2 | 87.6 | 92.6 | 95.5 | 95.0 | 98.9 | 99.1 |
| DeiT_S [6] | 88.0MB | 74.9 | 83.3 | 89.4 | 84.0 | 93.6 | 97.2 | 87.8 | 93.1 | 95.5 | 91.5 | 98.3 | 98.7 |
| DeiT_S_Q16 | 43.4MB | 75.9 | 85.0 | 90.3 | 84.1 | 93.0 | 96.4 | 87.7 | 93.2 | 96.2 | 91.6 | 98.2 | 98.8 |
| DeiT_S_Q8 | 21.5MB | 76.1 | 85.3 | 90.0 | 83.9 | 93.0 | 96.8 | 87.7 | 92.8 | 95.7 | 91.3 | 98.2 | 98.6 |
| DeiT_S_Q4 | 10.3MB | 75.4 | 84.4 | 90.3 | 81.1 | 92.2 | 96.1 | 85.8 | 91.6 | 95.1 | 90.7 | 98.0 | 98.5 |
| DeiT_S_KD | 88.0MB | 77.8 | 85.7 | 90.8 | 84.2 | **93.7** | 97.3 | 89.4 | 93.6 | 96.4 | 94.8 | 98.9 | 99.2 |
| DeiT_S_KD_Q16 | 43.4MB | 78.0 | 85.9 | 91.0 | **84.3** | 93.6 | **97.4** | **89.6** | 93.9 | **96.5** | 95.0 | 99.0 | 99.2 |
| DeiT_S_KD_Q8 | 21.5MB | **78.1** | **85.9** | **91.0** | 84.0 | 93.2 | 97.1 | 89.4 | 93.8 | 96.5 | 95.0 | 98.9 | **99.3** |
| DeiT_S_KD_Q4 | 10.3MB | 75.8 | 84.9 | 89.8 | 81.7 | 92.4 | 96.3 | 88.2 | 92.8 | 95.7 | 94.9 | **99.1** | **99.3** |
| DeiT_S† [6] | 88.0MB | 76.8 | 85.4 | 90.2 | 84.2 | 93.7 | 97.3 | 88.8 | 93.6 | 96.6 | 91.9 | 98.3 | 98.7 |
| DeiT_S†_Q16 | 44.1MB | 76.0 | 85.2 | 90.3 | 84.3 | 93.8 | 97.2 | 89.4 | 93.9 | 96.4 | 92.0 | 98.4 | 98.8 |
| DeiT_S†_Q8 | 21.9MB | 76.2 | 85.3 | 89.9 | 84.0 | 93.6 | 97.1 | 89.3 | 93.6 | 96.1 | 91.5 | 98.1 | 98.5 |
| DeiT_S†_Q4 | 10.5MB | 74.8 | 83.4 | 89.6 | 81.6 | 91.9 | 96.3 | 87.9 | 93.1 | 96.0 | 91.5 | 98.2 | 98.5 |
| DeiT_S†_KD | 88.0MB | 78.1 | 86.3 | 91.1 | 84.4 | **93.7** | 97.4 | 90.0 | 94.0 | 96.7 | 94.9 | 98.8 | 99.3 |
| DeiT_S†_KD_Q16 | 44.1MB | **78.5** | **86.7** | **91.3** | **84.5** | 93.6 | **97.4** | **90.3** | **94.1** | **96.9** | 95.0 | **99.2** | **99.5** |
| DeiT_S†_KD_Q8 | 21.9MB | 78.0 | 86.3 | 90.9 | 84.2 | 93.2 | 97.2 | 90.2 | 94.1 | 96.8 | **95.1** | 99.1 | 99.4 |
| DeiT_S†_KD_Q4 | 10.5MB | 76.1 | 85.0 | 90.5 | 82.0 | 92.5 | 96.4 | 89.7 | 94.0 | 96.7 | 94.9 | 99.0 | 99.4 |

respectively obtain 75% and 74.9% R@1, outperforming ResNet50 by about 5%. Second, the models with the knowledge distillation strategy significantly improve the counterparts without knowledge distillation strategy on four datasets. For example, SwinT_KD improves SwinT with 3.6% margin on In-Shop dataset. This indicates that the relaxed contrastive loss is more efficient than the original contrastive loss since SwinT, DeiT_S, and DeiT_S† are trained with contrastive loss. Third, the quantization strategy could significantly reduce the storage size while maintain a high performance when the quantization bit number is larger than 8. When the quantization bit number is 4, the performances of different models decrease on most of the datasets.Nevertheless, through the heterogeneous distillation quantization, we could compress the size of the model by 88% and still maintain the accuracy, enabling ViT-based models for resource-constrained environments. Taking the results of CUB as an example, DeiT_S_KD_Q16 and DeiT_S_Q16 respectively obtain 78.0% and 75.9% R@1, which shows that the combination of distillation and quantization is beneficial to the improvement

**Table 3.** Comparison results (%) with different teacher models on four datasets.

| Teacher | Student | CUB | | | SOP | | | Cars196 | | | In-Shop | | |
|---|---|---|---|---|---|---|---|---|---|---|---|---|---|
| | | R@1 | R@2 | R@4 | R@1 | R@10 | R@100 | R@1 | R@2 | R@4 | R@1 | R@10 | R@20 |
| Resnet50 | Resnet50 | 73.0 | 82.1 | 89.1 | 81.8 | 92.4 | 96.2 | 87.9 | 92.8 | 95.9 | 92.3 | 98.3 | 98.6 |
| Resnet50 | DeiT_S$^\dagger$ | **78.1** | **86.3** | **91.1** | **84.4** | **93.7** | **97.4** | **90.0** | **94.0** | **96.7** | **94.9** | **98.8** | 99.2 |
| DeiT_S$^\dagger$ | DeiT_S$^\dagger$ | 77.5 | 85.5 | 90.5 | 83.3 | 93.1 | 97.1 | 89.3 | 93.7 | **96.7** | 94.6 | 98.5 | **99.3** |
| Resnet50 | Resnet50_Q16 | 73.5 | 82.2 | 89.4 | 81.9 | 92.4 | 96.3 | 88.0 | 92.8 | 95.9 | 92.5 | 98.4 | 98.6 |
| Resnet50 | DeiT_S$^\dagger$_Q16 | **78.5** | **86.7** | **91.3** | **84.5** | **93.6** | **97.4** | **90.3** | **94.1** | **96.9** | **95.0** | **99.2** | **99.5** |
| DeiT_S$^\dagger$ | DeiT_S$^\dagger$_Q16 | 77.6 | 85.2 | 90.2 | 83.2 | 91.8 | 96.5 | 89.4 | 93.5 | 96.5 | 94.8 | 98.4 | 99.1 |
| Resnet50 | Resnet50_Q8 | 73.2 | 81.8 | 88.8 | 81.7 | 92.2 | 96.3 | 88.0 | 92.7 | 95.9 | 92.4 | 98.3 | 98.6 |
| Resnet50 | DeiT_S$^\dagger$_Q8 | **78.0** | **86.3** | **90.9** | **84.2** | **93.2** | **97.2** | **90.2** | **94.1** | **96.8** | **95.1** | **99.1** | **99.4** |
| DeiT_S$^\dagger$ | DeiT_S$^\dagger$_Q8 | 77.3 | 85.3 | 90.2 | 83.0 | 91.6 | 96.5 | 89.3 | 93.8 | 96.7 | 94.7 | 98.4 | 99.1 |

of performance. Besides, we observe that the DeiT_S$^\dagger$ and its variants perform more competitively than DeiT_S and its variants on most cases, which indicates that the distillation token is more suitable for feature embedding learning than the class token applied in [6].

**Heterogeneous V.S. Homogeneous.** Both convnets and transformers could serve as the teacher networks since the teacher network aims at providing the feature embeddings for calculating the pair-wise visual similarity. In this experiment, we evaluate the effects of different teacher models in Table 3. It is interesting to observe that the heterogeneous distillation (when using a convnet teacher to distill a transformer student) performs better than the homogeneous distillation (when using a transformer teacher to distill a transformer student) on four datasets, even though the performances of Resnet50 are inferior to those of DeiT_S$^\dagger$ on the four datasets. We speculate that the transformer student would inherit the inductive bias of the transformer teacher, which would be detrimental to the training of student to some extent.

### 3.3 Analysis of Distillation Quantization of Multi-exit Networks

To evaluate the performance of the heterogeneous distillation multi-exit architecture, we conduct experiments with DeiT_S$^\dagger$ on both CUB and InShop datasets. Specifically, DeiT_S$^\dagger$ consists of 12 layers and is divided into 9 early exits. The penultimate layer is taken as early exit 9 and the tenth layer is taken as early exit 8, and so on. From Table 4, we have the following several observations.

First, for most types of head exits, the performances are poor at the early positions. The reason may be that the early layers of the ViT capture the low-level features. Take Norm-EH as an example, it performs very poorly at the first three exit positions while gradually catching up at the later positions. Note that Norm-EH deals with the intermediate layers with a normalization layer, which is a practical choice since it is the most lightweight. Second, both CNN-EH and ViT-EH exits outperform other types in the first few positions. This is because

**Table 4.** R@1 results (%) of different exit heads with DeiT_S$^\dagger$ on both CUB and InShop datasets. The best results of different exits of different exit head types are marked in **bold**. The best results of different exit head types are marked in <u>underline</u>. The last row is the parameter quantity of each exit head of Norm-EH with 16 bits.

| Method | CUB | | | | | | | | | InShop | | | | | | | | |
|---|---|---|---|---|---|---|---|---|---|---|---|---|---|---|---|---|---|---|
| | E1 | E2 | E3 | E4 | E5 | E6 | E7 | E8 | E9 | E1 | E2 | E3 | E4 | E5 | E6 | E7 | E8 | E9 |
| Norm-EH | 14.4 | 19.0 | 28.8 | 69.2 | 74.7 | **78.1** | <u>**78.8**</u> | 77.7 | 77.7 | 49.7 | 55.2 | 66.0 | 81.1 | 87.7 | 91.0 | 91.9 | 93.3 | <u>94.7</u> |
| ResMLP-EH | 15.3 | 21.5 | 33.3 | 56.4 | 70.4 | 75.1 | <u>78.4</u> | **78.0** | 77.7 | 60.0 | 65.3 | 74.7 | 86.1 | 89.7 | 92.1 | 93.2 | 94.2 | <u>95.0</u> |
| MLP-Mixer-EH | 22.2 | 30.7 | 40.8 | 62.1 | 72.0 | 75.0 | <u>78.3</u> | 77.7 | 77.7 | 68.7 | 71.4 | 80.3 | 88.7 | 91.8 | 92.8 | 93.7 | 94.3 | <u>95.0</u> |
| ViT-EH | **51.4** | **58.2** | **63.0** | **69.8** | **75.1** | 76.8 | <u>78.5</u> | 77.9 | **77.9** | **85.0** | **87.2** | **90.3** | **92.0** | **93.4** | **94.0** | **94.5** | **94.8** | <u>95.0</u> |
| CNN-EH | 28.7 | 37.6 | 45.1 | 54.2 | 58.7 | 61.6 | 62.1 | <u>63.0</u> | 61.0 | 81.8 | 83.9 | 87.4 | 89.6 | 90.6 | 90.7 | 91.0 | <u>92.0</u> | 91.5 |
| Size_Q16(MB) | 11.0 | 14.5 | 18.0 | 21.5 | 25.0 | 28.5 | 32.0 | 35.5 | 39.0 | 11.0 | 14.5 | 18.0 | 21.5 | 25.0 | 28.5 | 32.0 | 35.5 | 39.0 |

both exit heads are better at extracting high-level information from the local features. However, CNN-EH fades away at the later locations perhaps due to that the later layers have already captured the high-level information, while ViT-EH holds the edge at the later locations due to that ViT-EH can capture multiple types of attention by using a multi-head attention layer in the Transformer encoder, outperforming ResMLP-EH and MLP-Mixer-EH processing without an attention mechanism. The multi-exit architecture further saves computational resources on the basis of quantization. Taking the results of CUB as an example in Table 4, the E7 of Norm-EH can achieve better results than subsequent exits. Therefore, we can deploy the E7 of Norm-EH to edge devices as the output result, saving more computational resources.

## 4 Conclusions

In this paper, we have combined quantization, knowledge distillation, and multi-exit strategies to train a lightweight ViT model for metric learning. From the extensive results on the four benchmarks, we have reached the following conclusions: (1) the heterogeneous knowledge distillation is empirically shown to perform better than the homogeneous knowledge distillation, (2) the combination of quantization and multi-exit strategies further reduce the model size, (3) the exit heads in the multi-exit architecture impact the performance significantly and the ViT-EH performs best in the early exits, (4) our method is still very competitive when reducing the model size more than 88%.

## References

1. Bhojanapalli, S., Chakrabarti, A., Glasner, D., Li, D., Unterthiner, T., Veit, A.: Understanding robustness of transformers for image classification. In: ICCV, pp. 10231–10241 (2021)
2. Caron, M., et al.: Emerging properties in self-supervised vision transformers. In: ICCV, pp. 9650–9660 (2021)
3. Chen, C.F.R., Fan, Q., Panda, R.: Crossvit: Cross-attention multi-scale vision transformer for image classification. In: ICCV, pp. 357–366 (2021)

4. Deng, J., Dong, W., Socher, R., Li, L.J., Li, K., Fei-Fei, L.: Imagenet: A large-scale hierarchical image database. In: CVPR, pp. 248–255 (2009)
5. Dosovitskiy, A., et al.: An image is worth 16x16 words: Transformers for image recognition at scale. ICLR (2021)
6. El-Nouby, A., Neverova, N., Laptev, I., Jégou, H.: Training vision transformers for image retrieval. arXiv preprint arXiv:2102.05644 (2021)
7. Hadsell, R., Chopra, S., LeCun, Y.: Dimensionality reduction by learning an invariant mapping. In: CVPR, pp. 1735–1742 (2006)
8. Han, Y., Huang, G., Song, S., Yang, L., Wang, H., Wang, Y.: Dynamic neural networks: A survey. arXiv preprint arXiv:2102.04906 (2021)
9. Jacob, B., et al.: Quantization and training of neural networks for efficient integer-arithmetic-only inference. In: CVPR, pp. 2704–2713 (2018)
10. Kim, S., Kim, D., Cho, M., Kwak, S.: Proxy anchor loss for deep metric learning. In: CVPR, pp. 3238–3247 (2020)
11. Kim, S., Kim, D., Cho, M., Kwak, S.: Embedding transfer with label relaxation for improved metric learning. In: CVPR, pp. 3967–3976 (2021)
12. Krause, J., Stark, M., Deng, J., Fei-Fei, L.: 3d object representations for fine-grained categorization. In: ICCV (2013)
13. Li, Z., Yang, T., Wang, P., Cheng, J.: Q-vit: Fully differentiable quantization for vision transformer. arXiv preprint arXiv:2201.07703 (2022)
14. Liu, Z., et al.: Swin transformer: Hierarchical vision transformer using shifted windows. ICCV, pp. 10012–10022 (2021)
15. Liu, Z., Wang, Y., Han, K., Ma, S., Gao, W.: Post-training quantization for vision transformer. NeurIPS (2021)
16. Liu, Z., Luo, P., Qiu, S., Wang, X., Tang, X.: Deepfashion: Powering robust clothes recognition and retrieval with rich annotations. In: CVPR, pp. 1096–1104 (2016)
17. Loshchilov, I., Hutter, F.: Decoupled weight decay regularization. ICLR (2017)
18. Mehta, S., Rastegari, M.: Mobilevit: light-weight, general-purpose, and mobile-friendly vision transformer. arXiv preprint arXiv:2110.02178 (2021)
19. Oh Song, H., Xiang, Y., Jegelka, S., Savarese, S.: Deep metric learning via lifted structured feature embedding. In: CVPR, pp. 4004–4012 (2016)
20. Sabet, A., Hare, J., Al-Hashimi, B., Merrett, G.V.: Temporal early exits for efficient video object detection. arXiv preprint arXiv:2106.11208 (2021)
21. Scardapane, S., Scarpiniti, M., Baccarelli, E., Uncini, A.: Why should we add early exits to neural networks? Cognitive Computation **12**(5), 954–966 (2020)
22. Strudel, R., Garcia, R., Laptev, I., Schmid, C.: Segmenter: Transformer for semantic segmentation. In: ICCV, pp. 7262–7272 (2021)
23. Tolstikhin, I., et al.: Mlp-mixer: An all-mlp architecture for vision. arXiv preprint arXiv:2105.01601 (2021)
24. Touvron, H., et al.: Resmlp: Feedforward networks for image classification with data-efficient training. arXiv preprint arXiv:2105.03404 (2021)
25. Touvron, H., Cord, M., Douze, M., Massa, F., Sablayrolles, A., Jégou, H.: Training data-efficient image transformers & distillation through attention. In: ICML (2021)
26. Wah, C., Branson, S., Welinder, P., Perona, P., Belongie, S.: The caltech-ucsd birds-200-2011 dataset. Tech. rep. (2011)
27. Yuan, L., et al.: Tokens-to-token vit: Training vision transformers from scratch on imagenet. In: ICCV, pp. 558–567 (2021)
28. Zhang, Z., Lu, X., Cao, G., Yang, Y., Jiao, L., Liu, F.: Vit-yolo: Transformer-based yolo for object detection. In: ICCV, pp. 2799–2808 (2021)
29. Zheng, S., et al.: Rethinking semantic segmentation from a sequence-to-sequence perspective with transformers. In: CVPR, pp. 6881–6890 (2021)

# Vision and Perception

# Segmented–Original Image Pairs to Facilitate Feature Extraction in Deep Learning Models

Yanqing Bi[ID], Dong Li, and Yu Luo[✉]

College of Computer, National University of Defense Technology, Changsha 410073, China
{Yanqing_bi,yuluo}@nudt.edu.cn

**Abstract.** Researchers in the field of computer vision have been working on improving the extraction of foreground features. We use Deeplab-V3plus to obtain 300,000 background-removed images (segmented images). However, a model trained on segmented images has a far lower recognition rate for original images, and vice versa. The visualization results of t-SNE further show that the features of the segmented and original images are very different. Because deep learning is based on the assumption that data are identically distributed, the recognition rate is low in these cases. In automatic speech recognition, pure data is readily available, and researchers add noise to the data to improve the robustness of the model. Inspired by this, we use segmented–original image pairs in which the images guide each other. According to our mathematical proof, the features learned by the model are controllable and located in the feature space between the segmented and original image. Experiments further verify our intuition that segmented–original image pairs facilitate feature extraction in deep learning models.

**Keywords:** Background-removed image · Feature extraction · Deep learning

## 1 Introduction

In the field of computer vision, clean data is challenging to obtain. Researchers have focused on reducing the influence exerted by the image's background on the model [1, 2]. The development of semantic segmentation technology [3–5] has made it possible to obtain a large number of images with the background removed. In our previous work, we used a semantic segmentation algorithm to create 300,000 background-removed images (segmented images) and build a dataset that includes pairs of segmented and original images. By constructing these segmented–original image pairs, both the original and segmented images can be indexed.

In our experiments, we found that a model trained on segmented images achieves a much lower recognition rate for original images than for segmented images; moreover, a model trained on original images has a much lower recognition rate for segmented images than original images. To humans, the segmented image conveys the same information as the original image. However, for deep learning models, the feature space of the segmented image is different from that of the original image. This runs counter to our intuition, as it indicates that models trained solely on segmented or original images do not learn

© The Author(s), under exclusive license to Springer Nature Switzerland AG 2022
S. Khanna et al. (Eds.): PRICAI 2022, LNCS 13631, pp. 253–266, 2022.
https://doi.org/10.1007/978-3-031-20868-3_19

the essential feature space of the image. This phenomenon is common in automatic speech recognition [6, 7], since datasets without noise are readily available. Models trained with clean data were found to be difficult to apply to noisy scenes. Therefore, the authors add noise to the data to increase the robustness of the model. For example, the wav2vec-Switch encodes noise robustness into contextualized representations of speech via contrastive learning, which feeds original–noisy speech pairs into the network simultaneously [8]. In addition, masked autoencoders (MAE) mask a high proportion of the input image, then reconstruct the original image from the latent representation and mask tokens [9], while Masked Feature Prediction (Mask-Feat) uses Histograms of Oriented Gradients (HOG) rather than pixels to reconstruct the original image [10]. These methods use some original features to guide the predicted feature closer to the real feature. Inspired by this approach, we propose that using segmented–original image pairs will enable the model to learn a robust feature that can express both the segmented image and original image. We accordingly use the segmented and original image to guide each other, forcing the network to close to consistent predictions for the original and segmented image. Specifically, if the model is robust to noise, the representation of an original image should also predict the target of its segmented image, and vice versa. This is equivalent to taking a feature space between the segmented image and the original image, and theoretically enables a robust feature space to be found. According to our mathematical proof, the features learned by the model are controllable and located in the feature space between the segmented image and the original image. Furthermore, our method does not add any complexity to the networks. Researchers can further optimize the model without changing the model structure. We validate our assumptions using ResNet [11], VGG [12], DesNet [13], GoogLeNet [14], and Autoencoder (AE) [15]. The datasets used are MS COCO [16], RLVS [17], and Hockey Fights [18]. The experimental results are consistent with our hypothesis. Our proposed method is accordingly of great value for image feature extraction in computer vision.

In summary, our contributions are as follows: we annotated 7,000 violent human poses and created a segmented image dataset that contains 300,000 pictures; moreover, we propose a new model training method that can adjust the feature space learned by the model.

## 2   Method

### 2.1   Datasets

**MS COCO Dataset.** We extract the original images and annotation files of cats, dogs, and people from the MS COCO dataset. We then combine the annotations and pictures to generate MASK images. The background pixel value of the Mask image is 0, and the foreground pixel value of the Mask image is 1. AND the Mask image and the original image to get the image with the background removed. Depending on the research needs, it is possible to create segmented–original image pairs on other semantic segmentation datasets using a similar process (Fig. 2).

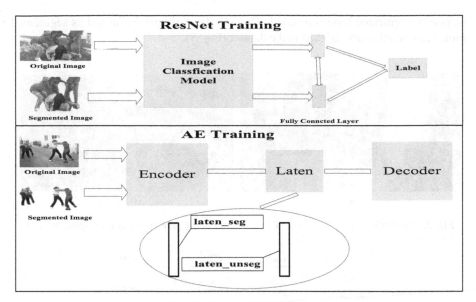

**Fig. 1.** Our model structure.

**Fig. 2.** The process of removing the background of MS COCO images.

**Violent Dataset.** The semantic recognition dataset is significantly different from Violent dataset. The semantic recognition dataset is significantly different from the violent behavior dataset. Specifically, semantic segmentation datasets use high-quality images, and the poses of the humans therein are normal (i.e., different from violent scenes). For example, the humans in the MS COCO dataset are positioned in staged poses, meaning that the dataset does not contain the poses found in violent scenes; moreover, the latest VSPW dataset represents the first large-scale dataset for video scene parsing in the wild, but more than 96% of its video frames are high-quality and lacking in violent behavior. However, violent behavior datasets tend to comprise low-quality videos captured by surveillance cameras or cellphones, and the body postures of the humans in the images are abnormal. Therefore, large segmentation errors will arise if a model trained on current semantic segmentation datasets is used to segment the violent behavior datasets. We therefore need a new dataset to train a semantic segmentation model suitable for violent scenes. To address this, we use Labelme to annotate video frames extracted from the RWF-2000, RLVS, and Hockey Fights datasets using the frame difference method. Our dataset includes 7,000 human poses (Fig. 3), which is sufficient to complete the training of the segmentation model when combined with the frames extracted from the MS COCO dataset. We use the trained model to segment the video frames and then delete the poorly segmented frames manually (Fig. 4). The original frame and its segmented frames can be mutually indexed in the dataset (Fig. 5).

(a)                                         (b)

**Fig. 3.** Annotation of video frames. The red curve is the annotation. (Color figure online)

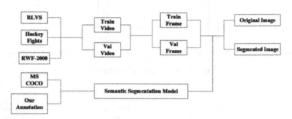

**Fig. 4.** The process of removing the background of the violent behavior dataset.

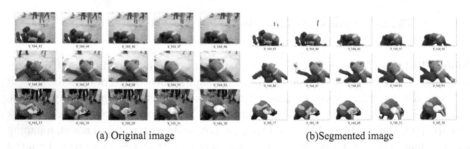

(a) Original image                    (b)Segmented image

**Fig. 5.** Our dataset.

## 2.2  Segmented–Original Image Pair Training Method

A deep learning model is a chain of simple, continuous geometric transformations that map one vector space to another. Deep learning models can only perform local generalization and adapt to new situations that are very close to past data; by contrast, human cognition is capable of performing extreme generalization, quickly adapting to radically novel situations, and planning for situations in the long-term future [19]. To humans, the segmented image conveys the same information as the original image; by contrast, for the deep learning model, the feature space of the segmented image is different from the original image, meaning that the vector mapped by the model is different. Suppose that the feature space learned by the model was between the segmented image and the original image, making it able to represent both images. In that case, the model is equivalent to having a certain degree of extreme generalization ability that the model generates consistent features from the segmented image and the original image. The wav2vec-Switch, MAE, and MaskFeat methods use some original image features to guide the predicted feature closer to the real feature. Inspired by these models, we place the segmented and original images in a pair and use them to guide each other, forcing the network to close to consistent predictions for the segmented and original image. This method is an extension of our other paper [20] with a wider range of applications. Proof for a special case is provided below. We define a loss function with the sum of squares due to error (SSE).

$A_{n \times m}$ is the perfect feature space of the segmented images. $B_{n \times m}$ is the perfect feature space of the original images. $n$ is the number of images, and $m$ is the dimension of the image feature vector. $a_i$ is the feature representation of $segment\_image_i$, while $b_i$ is the feature representation of $original\_image_i$. $l_i'$ is the model prediction feature of $segmented\_image_i$, and $l_i''$ is the model prediction feature of $original\_image_i$. $a_i, b_i, l_i'$ and $l_i''$ can denote the fully connected layer feature of the classification network or the hidden layer feature of the AE.

$$A_{n \times m} = [a_1, a_2, a_3 \cdots a_n]^T, B_{n \times m} = [b_1, b_2, b_3 \cdots b_n]^T, C_{n \times m} = [l_1', l_2', l_3' \cdots l_n']^T, D_{n \times m} = [l_1'', l_2'', l_3'' \cdots l_n'']^T$$

Let the SSE be the loss: $Loss = \sum_{i=1}^n k_i' |l_i' - a_i|^2 + k_i'' |l_i'' - b_i|^2, k_i' \geq 0, k_i'' \geq 0.$ The $k_i'$ and $k_i''$ are hyperparameters that can denote either the number of images or the loss factor.

When $\left[ \sum_{i=1}^n k_i' |l_i' - a_i|^2 + k_i'' |l_i'' - b_i|^2 \right]$ is the smallest, Loss is the smallest.

$$f\left(l_i', l_i''\right) = \sum_{i=1}^n k_i' |l_i' - a_i|^2 + k_i'' |l_i'' - b_i|^2 \tag{1}$$

Solve Eq. (1) to find the minimum point:

When $k_i' \neq 0, k_i'' \neq 0, l_i' = a_i, l_i'' = b_i$, Loss has a minimum. In this case, the segmented–original image pair is used for training. The model's predictions for the segmented image and the original image are inconsistent. $C_{n \times m} \nrightarrow A_{n \times m}, D_{n \times m} \nrightarrow B_{n \times m}$ indicates that the model has not learned a feature that can represent both the segmented and original images.

The segmented image is the foreground information of the original image; thus, in the ideal model, $l_i'$ and $l_i''$ would be close to each other. We then add Constraint (2):

$$l_i'' - l_i' = \Delta l_i, \Delta l_i = (\Delta_{i1}, \Delta_{i2}, \Delta_{i3}, \cdots \Delta_{im}) \tag{2}$$

$$g\left(l_i', l_i''\right) = l_i'' - l_i' - \Delta l_i \tag{3}$$

Use Lagrange multiplier to solve (1), (3) to get the minimum point: $l_i' = a_i + \frac{k_i''}{k_i' + k_i''}(b_i - a_i + \Delta l_i), l_i'' = l_i' + \Delta l_i.$

When the model converges, the distance between $l_i'$ and $l_i''$ tends towards 0. The model obtains a feature that can represent both the segmented image and original image:
$$l_i' = l_i'' = a_i + \frac{k_i''}{k_i'+k_i''}(b_i - a_i).$$

The feature space learned by the model is $E_{n \times m}$. When $k_i' \neq 0, k_i'' \neq 0$, the segmented–original image pair is used for training. The predictions of the model for the segmented image and the original image are consistent. The features predicted by the model are between $A_{n \times m}$ and $B_{n \times m}$, which is equivalent to $E_{n \times m} = A_{n \times m} + \frac{k_i''}{k_i'+k_i''}(B_{n \times m} - A_{n \times m})$.

We assume that a robust feature exists between $a_i$ and $b_i$. By controlling $\frac{k_i''}{k_i'+k_i''}$, the predicted features can be moved between $a_i$ and $b_i$. In this way, we can further optimize the model.

In ResNet, VGG, DesNet121, and GoogLeNet, $k_i'$ represents the number of $segmented\_image_i$, while $k_i''$ represents the number of $original\_image_i$ in the training set. The $\frac{k_i''}{k_i'+k_i''}$ affects the features learned by the model. During training, the loss between the segmented image and the prediction is reduced, the loss between the original image and the prediction is reduced (this is equivalent to finding the minimum value of formula (1)), and the distance between the segmented image's prediction and the original image's prediction is reduced (this is equivalent to finding the minimum value of formula (3)), because they are all close to the label. Due to the different number of segmented and original images in the dataset, the two images have different effects on the loss; thus, the feature space that the model can learn is between the segmented image's feature space and the original image's feature space. In addition, the foreground data in the training set is always larger than the background data, which is equivalent to adding an attention mechanism to the model through the data.

In ResNet, we also implement additional training methods. Specifically, during training, we let the features of the fully connected layers of the segmented and original images be close to each other, and further let the predictions of the two images be close to the label (because the perfect fully connected layer features of the segmented and original images are difficult to obtain). The loss consists of three parts ($Loss = k_1 * loss\_seg + k_2 * loss\_unseg + \beta * Distance$): the loss of the segmented image's prediction and label ($loss\_seg$), the loss of the original image' and label ($loss\_unseg$), and the distance between the fully connected layers of the two images ($Distance$). In training, the loss of the segmented–original image's prediction and labels is reduced, which is equivalent to finding the minimum value of formula (1). At the same time, the model's fully connected layer of the segmented–original image gradually approach, which is equivalent to reducing the value of $\Delta l_i$ in formula (2). $k_1, k_2, \beta$ affects how much the model pays attention to foreground information, thereby forcing the model to pay attention to the foreground information. Finally, the model learns a robust feature space that expresses both segmented and original image features.

In AE, the loss consists of three parts ($Loss = k_1 * recon\_loss\_seg + k_2 * recon\_loss\_unseg + \beta * Distance$): the reconstruction loss of the segmented image ($recon\_loss\_seg = |seg - recon\_seg|^2$), the reconstruction loss of the original image ($recon\_loss\_unseg = |unseg - recon\_unseg|^2$), and the distance between the hidden layers of the two images ($Distance = (laten\_seg - laten\_unseg)$). In training, *Loss* affects the features learned by the model. The model uses the backpropagation algorithm to reduce the loss equivalent to solving the minimum value of (1) and (3). $k_1$, $k_2$, $\beta$ affect how much the model pays attention to foreground information, thereby controlling the reconstruction effect. Although such a design increases the reconstruction loss, it also forces the model to pay attention to the foreground information, thereby decoupling the reconstruction from the background information. Our method can accordingly produce a better hidden layer feature that can represent both the segmented and original image.

## 3 Experiments

### 3.1 Segmentation Algorithm

In our experiments, we used a set of test videos, including surveillance videos and videos recorded on mobile devices (Fig. 6). We experimentally determined that KNN is suitable for scenes in which the camera is fixed, but cannot overcome the noise caused by the camera movement. Mediapipe is suitable for scenes where the camera is close to the target; however, features for distant targets will be lost. SegNet performs better in urban scenes but will lose features for near target segmentation. Deeplab-V3plus can adapt to segmentation tasks in multiple scenes, but the target will be lost in violent scenes. We accordingly combine the created dataset with the MS COCO dataset to train Deeplab-V3plus. The hyperparameter settings enable better adaptation to violent scenes (Table 1 [20]). The backbone network can choose "xception" and "mobilenet": the former has a better segmentation effect, while the latter has lower hardware requirements. A downsampling value of 8 for the model enables better capturing of small objects compared to a downsampling value of 16. The shape of the input image is selected according to the image quality. An input shape of $224 \times 224$ is suitable for RLVS, Hockey Fights, and CCTV. The model achieves performance of 89.51% and 87.70% on the training and test sets respectively.

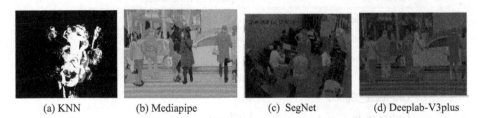

| (a) KNN | (b) Mediapipe | (c) SegNet | (d) Deeplab-V3plus |

**Fig. 6.** Comparison of four image segmentation algorithms.

### 3.2 Classification Tasks

We conducted experiments on six kinds of groups (Table 2 [20]). The No.1 group is used as a benchmark. Groups 1 and 2 evaluate the feature space learned on the original image. Groups 3 and 4 are used to evaluate the feature space learned on the segmented image. Finally, Groups 5 and 6 are used to evaluate the feature space learned on the segmented–original image pair.

As shown in Fig. 7, there is a significant difference in recognition rates between Groups 1 and 2; this indicates that the model trained on the original image has not learned the essential features, which is mainly due to the interference of background information. The recognition rate of Group 4 is much higher than that of Group 3 on the RLVS, HockeyFights and MS COCO datasets, indicating that the model trained by segmenting images has not learned the essential features; this is mainly due to the fact that the model trained on pure data is not robust. The mapping from inputs to outputs performed by deep nets quickly stops making sense if new inputs differ even slightly from what they observed at training time. We further demonstrate this conclusion by visualizing the original and segmented images using t-SNE dimensionality reduction. Specifically, we randomly select 4,000 original images and their corresponding segmented images from RLVS, Hockey Fights, and MS COCO, respectively. Figure 8 shows that the segmented image features differ significantly from those of the original image. Although the segmented image is the foreground information of the original image, the deep learning model perceives them as very different. Although the segmented image and the original image express similar meanings to humans, it is challenging for current deep learning models to learn robust features under these circumstances. We thus use segmented–original image pairs to force them to be close to each other in the feature space, enabling the model to learn a robust feature. As shown in Fig. 7, the No. 5 and No. 6 groups have high recognition rates for both original and segmented images, and performance is better on the violent behavior dataset than the MS COCO dataset. Therefore, our method can be seen to facilitate the feature extraction of deep learning models.

**Table 1.** Hyperparameters of DeeplabV3plus.

| Hyperparameter | |
| --- | --- |
| Backbone | Xception or mobilenet |
| downsample | 8 or 16 |
| input_shape | 224 × 224 |
| Freeze_Epoch | 10 |
| Freeze_lr | 5.00E−04 |
| UnFreeze_Epoch | 80 |
| Unfreeze_lr_ | 5.00E−05 |

To test the effect of $k_i'$ and $k_i''$ on deep learning networks, ResNet34 is trained on RLVS and tested on RLVS (Fig. 9 (a)), RWF-2000 (Fig. 9 (b)), Hockey Fights (Fig. 9 (c)).

①When $k_i'' = 0$, $\frac{k_i''}{k_i'+k_i''} = 0$. Segmented images are used for training, and the features predicted by the model are close to $a_i$. Figure 9 (a) shows that the recognition rates for

**Table 2.** Six experimental groups.

| No | Train dataset | Test dataset |
|----|---------------|--------------|
| 1 | Original image | Original image |
| 2 | Original image | Segmented image |
| 3 | Segmented image | Original image |
| 4 | Segmented image | Segmented image |
| 5 | Segmented + Original Image | Original image |
| 6 | Segmented + Original Image | Segmented image |

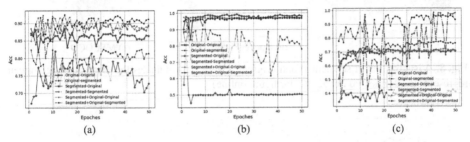

(a)                                      (b)                                      (c)

**Fig. 7.** (a) The recognition rate of DesNet121 on the RLVS dataset. (b) The recognition rate of GoogLeNet on the HockeyFights dataset. (c) The recognition rate of ResNet34 on the MS COCO dataset.

the original images are lower than those for the segmented images; this indicates that the model trained only with segmented images cannot adapt to complex scenes.

②When $k_i' = 0$, $\frac{k_i''}{k_i'+k_i''} = 1$. Original images are used for training, and the features predicted by the model are close to $b_i$. Figure 9 (a) shows that the recognition rates for the original images are higher than those for the segmented images. If the model has learned the essential features of the dataset, the recognition rates for the segmented images should be higher than those for the original images. This anomaly indicates that a model trained using only original images cannot learn essential features due to background interference.

③When $k_i' > 0$, $k_i'' > 0$, segmented–original image pairs are fed simultaneously into the model and the features predicted by the model are between $a_i$ and $b_i$. By controlling $k_i'$ against $k_i''$, the predicted features can be moved between $a_i$ and $b_i$. The model thereby learns a robust feature with higher recognition rates than the benchmark. In this way, we can further optimize the model. We evaluate the reasonableness of $\frac{k_i''}{k_i'+k_i''}$ based on the model's recognition rate. Experiments on the RLVS dataset show $\frac{k_i''}{k_i'+k_i''} = 0.63$ for images of violence and $\frac{k_i''}{k_i'+k_i''} = 0.44$ for images that do not contain violence (Fig. 9 (a)). Experiments on the Hockey Fights Dataset show $\frac{k_i''}{k_i'+k_i''} = 0.83$ for images of violence and

$\frac{k_i^{''}}{k_i^{'}+k_i^{''}} = 0.44$ for nonviolent images (Fig. 9 (b)). Experiments on the RWF-2000 dataset

show $\frac{k_i^{''}}{k_i^{'}+k_i^{''}} = 0.83$ for images of violence images and $\frac{k_i^{''}}{k_i^{'}+k_i^{''}} = 0.44$ for nonviolent

images (Fig. 9 (c)). This proves that our principle of adapting the model to complex

scenes by controlling $\frac{k_i^{''}}{k_i^{'}+k_i^{''}}$ is correct.

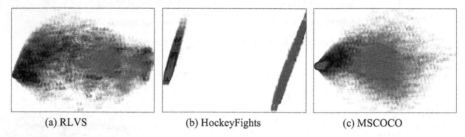

(a) RLVS          (b) HockeyFights          (c) MSCOCO

**Fig. 8.** Visualization of segmented and original images; red indicates the original image, green represents the segmented image. (Color figure online)

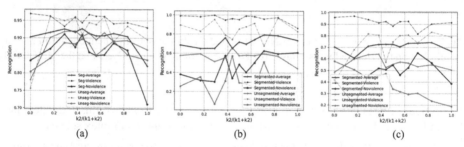

(a)          (b)          (c)

**Fig. 9.** (a) Training dataset: RLVS; testing dataset: RLVS. (b) Training dataset: RLVS; testing dataset: Hockey Fights. (c) Training dataset: RLVS; testing dataset: RWF-2000.

As Table 3 shows, our method can further optimize the model without the need to change the model structure. We conducted tests on different models (VGG19, ResNet34, DesNet121, and GoogLeNet). The datasets used were RLVS and MS COCO (Cat-Dog-Person). Experiments show that our method can effectively improve the model robustness.

**Table 3.** The effect of our method on different models

|  | RLVS | | MS COCO | |
|---|---|---|---|---|
|  | Original image | Segmented image | Original image | Segmented image |
| VGG19 | 85.70% | 70.79% | 62.27% | 52.20% |

*(continued)*

**Table 3.** (*continued*)

|  | RLVS | | MS COCO | |
|---|---|---|---|---|
|  | Original image | Segmented image | Original image | Segmented image |
| Ours (VGG19) | 88.34% | 89.34% | 62.53% | 96.87% |
| ResNet34 | 86.59% | 81.98% | 72.00% | 77.20% |
| Ours (ResNet34) | 92.56% | 91.81% | 73.06% | 96.46% |
| DesNet121 | 87.96% | 83.41% | 76.4% | 80.33% |
| Ours (DesNet121) | 93.01% | 92.34% | 76.33% | 98.73% |
| GoogLeNet | 90.49% | 84.42% | 76.26% | 76.40% |
| Ours (GoogLeNet) | 92.80% | 93.45% | 76.33% | 97.93% |

As shown in Table 4, our training method can make a simple model achieve the recognition rate of a complex model, which can reduce hardware requirements in practical applications. The experimental results further show that ResNet34 obtains a recognition rate far exceeding that of ResNet101 and DesNet21 on the RLVS dataset. However, our method does not get good results on the MS COCO dataset.

**Table 4.** Our method enables simple models to achieve higher recognition rates than complex models.

|  | RLVS | | MS COCO | |
|---|---|---|---|---|
|  | Original image | Segmented image | Original image | Segmented image |
| ResNet101 | 87.11% | 81.29% | 70.53% | 71.73% |
| DenseNet121 | 87.96% | 82.59% | 76.4% | 80.33% |
| ResNet34 | 86.59% | 81.98% | 72.00% | 77.20% |
| Ours (Resnet34) | 92.56% | 91.81% | 73.06 | 96.46% |

### 3.3 Unsupervised Learning Tasks

AE expects the training output to equal the input, which makes the latent representation valuable. The back-propagation algorithm allows the model to obtain parameters with a small reconstruction error, meaning that the background and foreground information have the same weight when calculating the reconstruction error. AE trained on original images has large loss when reconstructing segmented images (Fig. 10 (a) row 4), and vice versa (Fig. 10 (a) row 5), which indicates that the information in their hidden layers is different. The segmented and original images guide each other, making the model pay more attention to the foreground information (Fig. 10 (a) rows 7–10). Specifically, the reconstruction loss of the segmented and original image pair and the distance between the two hidden layers are used as the back-propagation loss, causing the vectors of the segmented and original image in the hidden layer to be close to each other. As shown in Fig. 10 (a) rows 7–10, the setting of the hyperparameter $k_1, k_2, k_3$ can adjust the feature space learned by the model. Moreover, as shown in Fig. 10 (b), the model back-propagated only the reconstruction loss in Epoche.1–30, and the model back-propagated the reconstruction loss and the hidden layer distance loss in Epoche.31–80. Reducing the distance of the segmented and original images does not cause a large change in the reconstruction loss, and enables more foreground information to be obtained at the same time. Our method makes the model pay more attention to the foreground information of the image and decouples the image's background and foreground. As a result, the hidden layer information of the AE network expresses more general features, which is very important for self-supervised tasks.

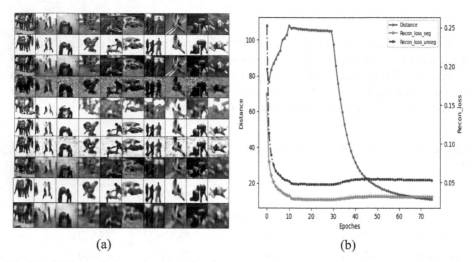

|                |                |
| :------------: | :------------: |
| (a)            | (b)            |

**Fig. 10.** (a) Rows 1–2 are the original and segmented images. Rows 3–4 and rows 5–6 are the reconstructions of the model trained on the original image and segmented image, respectively. Rows 5–6 and rows 7–8 are the reconstructions of the model trained by the segmented–original image pair with parameters $k1 = 3, k2 = 1, k3 = 0.001$ and $k1 = 5, k2 = 1, k3 = 0.01$, respectively. (b) Changes in loss in AE training. The parameters are $k1 = 3, k2 = 1, k3 = 0.001$.

## 4   Conclusion

We annotated 7,000 violent human poses to train the semantic segmentation model and obtained 300,000 pictures with backgrounds removed. We proposed a new training method that can facilitate feature extraction of the models by controlling the segment–original image pair without introducing additional components to neural networks. Experiments show that our method can effectively promote the model's learning of features. This has important implications for both classification tasks and unsupervised learning tasks.

# References

1. Nguyen, T.N., Meunier, J.: Anomaly detection in video sequence with appearance-motion correspondence. In: 17th IEEE/CVF International Conference on Computer Vision, Seoul Korea, pp. 1273–1283. IEEE (2019)
2. Cheng, Y., et al.: S3-net: a fast and lightweight video scene understanding network by single-shot segmentation. In: 21th IEEE/CVF Winter Conference on Applications of Computer Vision, Waikoloa USA, pp. 3329–3337. IEEE (2021)
3. Badrinarayanan, V., Kendall, A., Cipolla, R.: SegNet: a deep convolutional encoder-decoder architecture for image segmentation. IEEE Trans. Pattern Anal. Mach. Intell. **39**(12), 2481–2495 (2017)
4. Chen, L.-C., Zhu, Y., Papandreou, G., Schroff, F., Adam, H.: Encoder-decoder with atrous separable convolution for semantic image segmentation. In: Ferrari, V., Hebert, M., Sminchisescu, C., Weiss, Y. (eds.) ECCV 2018. LNCS, vol. 11211, pp. 833–851. Springer, Cham (2018). https://doi.org/10.1007/978-3-030-01234-2_49
5. Zheng, S., et al.: Rethinking semantic segmentation from a sequence-to-sequence perspective with transformers. In: 30th IEEE/CVF Conference on Computer Vision and Pattern Recognition, Nashville, USA, pp. 6881–6890. IEEE (2021)
6. Ravanelli, M., et al.: Multi-task self-supervised learning for robust speech recognition. In: 45th IEEE International Conference on Acoustics, Speech and Signal Processing, Barcelona, Spain, pp. 6989–6993. IEEE (2020)
7. Sadhu, S., et al.: Wav2vec-C: a self-supervised model for speech representation learning. arXiv preprint arXiv:2103.08393 (2021)
8. Wang, Y., Li, J., Wang, H., Qian, Y., Wang, C., Wu, Y.: Wav2vec-Switch: contrastive learning from original-noisy speech pairs for robust speech recognition. arXiv preprint arXiv:2110.04934 (2021)
9. He, K., et al.: Masked autoencoders are scalable vision learners. arXiv preprint arXiv:2111.06377 (2021)
10. Wei, C., et al.: Masked feature prediction for self-supervised visual pre-training. arXiv preprint arXiv:2112.09133 (2021)
11. He, K., et al.: Deep residual learning for image recognition. In: 25th IEEE Conference on Computer Vision and Pattern Recognition, Las Vegas, USA, pp. 770–778. IEEE (2016)
12. Simonyan, K., Zisserman, A.: Very deep convolutional networks for large-scale visual recognition. arXiv preprint arXiv:1409.1556 (2014)
13. Huang, G., et al.: Densely connected convolutional networks. In: 26th IEEE Conference on Computer Vision and Pattern Recognition, Honolulu, USA, pp. 4700–4708. IEEE (2017)
14. Szegedy, C., et al.: Going deeper with convolutions. In: 24th IEEE Conference on Computer Vision and Pattern Recognition, Boston, USA, pp. 1–9. IEEE (2015)
15. Kingma, D.P., Welling, M.: Auto-encoding variational bayes. arXiv preprint arXiv:1312.6114 (2013)
16. Lin, T.-Y., Maire, M., Belongie, S., Hays, J., Perona, P., Ramanan, D., Dollár, P., Zitnick, C.L.: Microsoft COCO: common objects in context. In: Fleet, D., Pajdla, T., Schiele, B., Tuytelaars, T. (eds.) ECCV 2014. LNCS, vol. 8693, pp. 740–755. Springer, Cham (2014). https://doi.org/10.1007/978-3-319-10602-1_48
17. Soliman, M.M., et al.: Violence recognition from videos using deep learning techniques. In: 9th International Conference on Intelligent Computing and Information Systems, Cairo, Egypt, pp. 80–85. IEEE (2019)

18. Bermejo Nievas, E., Deniz Suarez, O., Bueno García, G., Sukthankar, R.: Violence detection in video using computer vision techniques. In: Real, P., Diaz-Pernil, D., Molina-Abril, H., Berciano, A., Kropatsch, W. (eds.) CAIP 2011. LNCS, vol. 6855, pp. 332–339. Springer, Heidelberg (2011). https://doi.org/10.1007/978-3-642-23678-5_39
19. Chollet, F.: The limitations of deep learing. https://bg.keras.io/the-litions-of-deep-learning.html
20. Bi, Y., Li, D., Luo, Y.: Combining keyframes and image classification for violent behavior recognition. Appl. Sci. 12(16), 8014, (2022). MDPI

# FusionSeg: Motion Segmentation by Jointly Exploiting Frames and Events

Lin Wang[1], Zhe Liu[1], Yi Zhang[2], Shaowu Yang[1], Dianxi Shi[2],
and Yongjun Zhang[2](✉)

[1] College of Computer, National University of Defense Technology, Changsha, China
wanglin12@nudt.edu.cn
[2] Artificial Intelligence Research Center, National Innovation Institute of Defense
Technology, Beijing, China
yjzhang@nudt.edu.cn

**Abstract.** Segmentation of independently moving objects is an important stage in scene comprehension tasks like tracking and recognition. Frame-based cameras employed for dynamic scenes suffer from motion blur and exposure artifacts due to the sampling principle. In contrast, event-based cameras sample visual information based on scene dynamics and have the advantages of microsecond temporal resolution, high dynamic range, and more. Inspired by the complimentary of frame-based cameras and event-based cameras, we propose a cross-domain motion segmentation method, named FusionSeg, for fusing visual signals from frames and events to improve motion segmentation performance. To solve motion segmentation problem on the multi-objects scenario, we use the identification mechanism to embed multiple objects into the same feature space. In addition, to solve the feature matching and propagation problem, we design a long and short-term temporal-spatial attention. Our FusionSeg is evaluated on public datasets and outperforms the state-of-the-art by 4.7% in terms of detection rate. Experiments also demonstrate our method's robustness in situations with varying motion patterns and numbers of moving objects.

**Keywords:** Motion segmentation · Robot vision · Event camera

## 1 Introduction

Humans can easily perceive a complex scene as a set of distinct objects, a phenomenon known as perceptual grouping [23]. Robotic applications, such as autonomous driving and AR/VR, require the perception of dynamic scenes to interact effectively with the environment. In computer vision, perceptual grouping is closely related to the segmentation problem. That is, extracting objects with arbitrary shapes from a cluttered scene.

ⓒ The Author(s), under exclusive license to Springer Nature Switzerland AG 2022
S. Khanna et al. (Eds.): PRICAI 2022, LNCS 13631, pp. 267–280, 2022.
https://doi.org/10.1007/978-3-031-20868-3_20

Much of the work in the visual segmentation research field involves optical flow computing as the initial stage [2, 27]. However, precise optical flow calculation is difficult due to problems such as discontinuity and occlusion of moving objects. In the optimization field, various approaches use the idea of contrast maximization to accomplish the segmentation task [19]. In a multi-objects scenario, the motion-compensated images of each object need to be computed, which increases the computational cost. Feature point tracking allows for long-term estimation of pixel motion trajectories, which can resolve ambiguities in motion by analyzing pixel matches over larger time intervals. However, from a perceptual point of view, challenging visual effects (such as motion blur and underexposure/overexposure) make problem-solving with frame-based cameras more difficult. Therefore, inspired by biological visual motion processing mechanisms, neuromorphic engineers have developed a kind of sensor which is known as the event-based camera. It is not driven by a common clock because each pixel acts as an independent circuit, i.e., each pixel responds to motion independently and is therefore able to perceive dynamic changes in the scene efficiently and accurately. In addition, it can tolerate different lighting conditions and is sparsely encoded. The advantages in terms of temporal resolution, low latency ,and low bandwidth are enormous compared to frame-based cameras.

While event-based cameras have many benefits, they cannot measure absolute light intensity and difficult to capture slow motion and fine-grained texture information, which are important for high-performance segmentation. Frame-based cameras can just compensate for this. This unique complementarity leads us to propose a visual segmentation method based on the fusion of frames and events, called FusionSeg. In this paper, we use a simple and effective events aggregation method to discrete the time domain of asynchronous events. Thus it can be more easily processed based on CNN models. Another challenge is to efficiently obtain meaningful cues from the events domain and frames domain for different scenes. To this end, we introduce a new feature fusion method to efficiently fuse visual cues from both events and frames. The adaptive nature of our approach is maintained by a weighting scheme specifically designed to balance the contributions of both domains.

To make effective use of the motion information in the sequence, we propose a feature matching and propagation method. Firstly, we use an identification mechanism that assigns a unique recognition identity to each object and embeds multiple objects into the same feature space. The network can learn the association between all objects. The long and short-term temporal-spatial attention is then designed to implement feature matching and propagation. We demonstrate that our method outperforms other approaches on public datasets.

In summary, our contributions are:

(1) We introduce a feature fusion method that adaptively fuses visual cues from events and frames, and thus makes full use of both data for segmenting scene objects.
(2) We introduce feature matching and propagation methods to make effective use of motion information from time sequences. To our knowledge, this is

the first attempt to introduce Transformer into event-based motion segmentation.

(3) Our extensive experimental results show that our method has significant advantages over other state-of-the-art methods.

In the rest of the paper, we first review related work (Section II) and then explain our approach (Sections III). Finally, the model is validated (Section IV).

# 2 Related Work

## 2.1 Motion Segmentation

In the last decade, event-based motion segmentation has been solved for different scene complexities. For a moving event camera, events are triggered by static background and moving objects. The goal of motion segmentation is to infer the causal classification of each event. However, the amount of information carried by each event is small, and classifying each event is extremely challenging. Since moving objects produce different events trajectories in the image plane, event-based segmentation algorithms achieve the segmentation task primarily by inferring the trajectories of moving objects.

Assuming that the shape of the object to be segmented is known, Glover et al. [21]. Extracted the optical flow from the time window of the event stream based on the Hough transform, which in turn enables the segmentation and tracking of the ball. Later, they extended the method using particle filtering to improve tracking robustness, i.e.by dynamically selecting the duration of the observation window to accommodate sudden changes in object acceleration [4].

Some recent work has proposed the idea of using motion-compensated event images [3] to solve the problem of motion segmentation. Essentially, the technique associates events that produce sharp edges based on motion assumptions. The simplest assumption is a linear motion model, where the scene can be described as a collection of objects over a short period time, producing events that fit multiple linear motion models. Timo [20] et al. first fited a camera motion compensation model to the main events, then eliminated these events and finally greedily fited the remaining events to another linear model to produce motion compensated images with clear object contours. They later proposed an iterative clustering algorithm [19] that jointly estimated the motion parameters of the event-objects association and the objects that produced the sharpest motion-compensated event images. It allows a generic parametric motion model to describe each object and produces relatively good results. Immediately afterward, Anton et al. [10] segmented moving objects by fitting a motion-compensated model to events caused by the background and then detecting events that were inconsistent with the background, and they tested the method in challenging scenes (HDR, high speed) that are difficult to capture with frame-based cameras and published the dataset.

More and more machine learning methods have recently been used for motion segmentation tasks. Anton et al. [13] proposed a motion segmentation framework to jointly estimate optical flow, 3D motion and objects segmentation tasks and published the dataset for motion object segmentation. Later on, they used graph convolutional neural networks to segment the 3D events cloud [12], effectively improving problems such as occlusion and demonstrating that larger temporal slices can produce better results. In the same year Daniel et al. [7] proposed a visual motion network that predicts more accurate local visual motion and confidence levels as a way to achieve motion segmentation and camera pose estimation.

## 2.2  Visual Transformer

Through the attention mechanism, the Transformer architecture excels at modeling long-term relationships in input sequences. The Transformer module, like non-local neural networks, computes correlations with all input elements and aggregates their information using an attention mechanism. Transformer networks, when compared to RNNs, model global correlations in parallel, improving memory efficiency. They were originally used for language tasks but have since been applied to popular computer vision problems such as object segmentation [22] and object detection [1,9].

We use an attention mechanism in this work to match object features and pass segmentation masks from previous frames to the current frame. A long and short-term temporal-spatial attention is also designed to allow for efficient feature matching and propagation.

# 3  Methodology

## 3.1  Input Representation

From the perspective of perception principles, the frame-based camera records the intensity of all pixels by means of frames to capture the global scene. In contrast, the event-based camera asynchronously measures the light intensity changes in the scene. When the change in light intensity is greater than a threshold value, the pixel triggers an event independently. The polarity of the event reflects the direction of the change. As shown in Eq. 1, an event can be defined as

$$\varepsilon = \{e_k\}_{k=1}^N = \{[x_k, y_k, t_k, p_k]\}_{k=1}^N \tag{1}$$

where $e_k$ denotes an event. $(x_k, y_k)$ denotes the pixel location of the event. $t_k$ denotes the timestamp of the event. $p_k \in \{-1, +1\}$ is the polarity of the event, with a positive polarity indicating an increase in light intensity and a negative polarity indicating a decrease in light intensity.

Since the asynchronous events format is very different from synchronous frames, in order to accommodate the CNN input, previous approaches typically aggregate events into a frame-based representation. In this work we divide the event stream into successive time slices. Each time slice is projected onto a plane. The representation has three channels, two of which are accumulations of *positive* and *negative* events, and the third is a *temporal image* [26]. Compared to the 3D learning approach, the 2D input representation has the advantage of reducing the sparsity of the data, thus improving computational efficiency.

## 3.2    Network Architecture

The overall architecture of the FusionSeg is illustrated in Fig. 1. The first part of our approach is the feature fusion module, which is used to balance the advantages of two domain features. To accommodate multi-objects scenarios, we use an identification mechanism to associate multiple targets. In addition, based on the identification mechanism, we design a long and short-term temporal attention for feature matching and propagation. Finally, the prediction mask is output by the MLP layer and decoder.

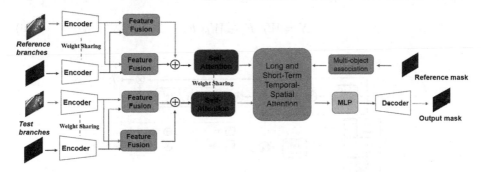

**Fig. 1.** An overview of our proposed Segmentation framework(FusionSeg) via collaboration of frames and events.

## 3.3    Feature Fusion Method

While frame-based cameras can easily capture rich textural and semantic cues, event-based cameras can easily capture edge information and have a high dynamic range. A feature fusion module is therefore designed to make effective use of both domain data. In the case of motion segmentation, objects are only detected when they are moving independently relative to the camera. Thus, previous work has attempted to compensate for camera motion. Instead of estimating the camera motion explicitly, we normalize the instances for each channel of each sample. Intuitively, the average activation tends to be controlled by motion in a large homogeneous region (usually the background). This normalization, combined with RELU, helps to separate background motion from foreground motion. As shown in the Fig. 2, the following feature enhancement scheme has been defined to generate enhanced features $\tilde{F}_e$ for events.

$$\hat{F}_e = \hat{F}_{e \to e} \oplus \hat{F}_{v \to e} \oplus F_e \tag{2}$$

$$\hat{F}_{e \to e} = \sigma \left( \psi_{3 \times 3} \left( F_e \right) \right) \otimes F_e \tag{3}$$

$$\hat{F}_{v \to e} = \sigma \left( \psi_{1 \times 1} \left[ \xi \left( \psi_{1 \times 1} \left( F_v \right) \right), \xi \left( \psi_{3 \times 3} \left( F_v \right) \right), \xi \left( \psi_{5 \times 5} \left( F_v \right) \right) \right] \right) \otimes F_e \tag{4}$$

$$W_{F_e} = \sigma \left( \psi_{1 \times 1} \left( \xi \left( \psi_{1 \times 1} \left( \mathcal{A} \left( \hat{F}_e \right) \right) \right) \right) \right) \tag{5}$$

where $[\cdot]$ indicates channel-wise concatenation. $\psi$ is convolutional layer. $\xi$ is the instance normalization followed by a ReLU activation function. $\hat{F}_{e \to e}$ indicates event-based self-reinforcing features. $\hat{F}_{v \to e}$ indicates frame-based cross-domain reinforced features designed to enhance event-based features. $W_{F_e}$ indicates the weight of event-enhanced features.

Inversely, the enhanced features of frames $\hat{F}_v$ and weight $W_{F_v}$ can be generated. To balance the contributions of frames and events, inspired by [28], we propose an adaptive weighting balancing scheme:

$$X = W_{F_e} \hat{F}_e \oplus W_{F_v} \hat{F}_v \tag{6}$$

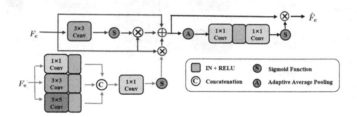

**Fig. 2.** The network structure of feature fusion network.

## 3.4   Multi-Object Association

The main challenge in propagating and decoding multi-objectes mask information in an end-to-end network is to use the network to accommodate different numbers of objects. To overcome this problem, inspired by [25], we use an identification mechanism consisting of **identity embedding** and **identity decoding**. For a multi-objects scenario, the identity embedding is constructed by assigning different identification vectors to different object regions. Specifically, we initialize a vector bank $D \in R^{M \times C}$. $M$ denotes the maximum number of objects. $Y \in \{0, 1\}$ is the mask of objects. Suppose there are $N \, (N < M)$ objects in the scenario. Then the identity embedding $E \in R^{THW \times C}$ can be expressed as

$$E = ID \left( Y, D \right) = YPD \tag{7}$$

where $P \in \{0, 1\}^{HW \times C}$ is the random permutation matrix. After ID assignment, different objects have different recognition embedding vectors.

Identity decoding: The convolution's decoding network is used to predict the probability of each identity in the identity bank before selecting the specified identity and calculating the probability. Common multi-classes segmentation losses, such an cross-entropy losses, are used during training to optimize multiple objects with respect to ground-truth labels. The identity bank is trainable and is randomly initialized at the start of training. We re-initialize the random permutation matrix at each sequence sample and optimization iteration to ensure that all identity vectors have the same chance of competing with each other.

## 3.5 Feature Matching and Propagation

Based on the identification mechanism, we elaborate the long and short-term temporal-spatial attention for feature matching and propagation. The network

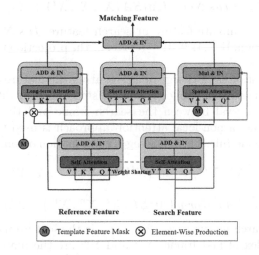

**Fig. 3.** The network structure of long and short-term temporal-spatial attention

starts with a self-attention layer that learns the correlation between objects in template frames and search frames, respectively. Then, long-term attention is introduced to aggregate features of template frames, short-term attention is introduced to learn memory frame features, and spatial attention is introduced to propagate memory frame object location information. Figure 3 illustrates the structure of our approach.

We define $Q \in R^{HW \times C}$, $K \in R^{HW \times C}$, $V \in R^{HW \times C}$ as the query embedding of the search frame, the key embedding of the template frame and the value embedding of the template frame, respectively. Where $T, H, W, C$ denote the time, height, width and channel dimensions, respectively. The following is the attention-based matching and propagation equation.

$$Att\,(Q, K, V) = Corr\,(Q, K)\,V = softmax\left(\frac{QK^T}{\tau}\right)V \qquad (8)$$

where $Corr(\cdot, \cdot)$ is the correlation function. $\tau$ is a temperature parameters controlling the softmax distribution, which is inspired by [5].

It is beneficial to propagate a representation of the objects when the camera changes dramatically in the scene. To suppress the background region, we multiply the template frame features by the mask recognition vector pixel by pixel, which propagates the template frame object features to the search frame.

$$V' = Att(Q, K, V \otimes ID(Y, D)) = Att(Q, K, V \otimes E) \tag{9}$$

where $\otimes$ is the pixel multiplication.

The self-attention operation is designed to enhance the features of the template frame and the search frame.

$$AttSA(X^t, X^t, X^t) = Att(X^t W^Q, X^t W^K, X^t W^V) \tag{10}$$

$$\hat{S}_{sa} = Ins.Norm(AttSA(X^t, X^t, X^t) + X^t) \tag{11}$$

where $X^t$ is the template feature or search feature. $Ins.Norm(\cdot)$ indicates instance normalization. $W^Q, W^K, W^V$ represent the projection matrix for matching and propagation.

Long-term attention is in charge of aggregating the features of the template frame objects to the current frame. Temporal smoothness is difficult to achieve because the time interval between the search frame and the template frame is variable. Therefore, a non-local attention approach is used to implement the long-term attention module. The following is the equation of long-term attention.

$$AttLT(X^t, X^m, Y^m) = Att(X^t W^Q, X^m W^K, X^m W^V \otimes E^m) \tag{12}$$

$$\hat{S}_{lt} = Ins.Norm(AttLT(X^t, X^m, X^m) + X^t) \tag{13}$$

where $X^t$ is the search feature. $t \in \{2, \ldots, T\}$ is the feature index of sequence. $m \in \{1\}$ is the index of first frame. $X^m$ and $Y^m$ are the template feature and masks, respectively.

Short-term attention is in charge of aggregating the memory frame's objects features to the current frame. Changes between successive time slices appear to be smooth and continuous. As a result, object matching and propagation can be limited to a small spatiotemporal domain, providing greater efficiency than non-local attention.

$$AttST(X^t, X^n, Y^n \mid p) = Att(X_p^t W^Q, X_{N(p)}^n W^K, X_{N(p)}^n W^V \otimes E_{N(p)}^n) \tag{14}$$

$$\hat{S}_{st} = Ins.Norm(AttST(X^t, X^n, Y^n \mid p) + X^t) \tag{15}$$

where $X_p^t$ is the search feature at location $p$. $N(p)$ is $15 \times 15$ spatial neighbourhood centered at location $p$. $n \in \{t-1\}$ is the memory feature index of sequence. $X_{N(p)}^n$ and $E_{N(p)}^n$ are the memory feature and masks of the spatial-temporal neighbourhood, respectively.

Spatial attention is in charge of aggregating the location information of memory frame objects to the current frame. The mutual attention establishes a pixel-to-pixel relationship between the two frames so that it supports object location propagation.

$$AttSP\left(X^t, X^n, E^n\right) = Att\left(X^t W^Q, X^n W^K, E^n W^V\right) \qquad (16)$$

$$\hat{S}_{sp} = Ins.Norm\left(AttSP\left(X^t, X^n, E^n\right) \otimes E^n\right) \qquad (17)$$

## 4    Experiment and Results

To explore the effectiveness of our proposed algorithm for the motion segmentation task, we validate it on two widely used and public datasets. Firstly, we present the implementation details. And then describe the use of the datasets. Finally, we show the performance of our method in both qualitative and quantitative terms.

### 4.1    Implementation Details

For feature extraction, we used MobileNet v3 [6] as the encoder and FPN [8] as the decoder to generate the objects' mask. The AdamW optimizer and a sequential training strategy [24] with a sequence length of 5 are used. The loss function is a combination of bootstrapped cross-entropy loss and soft Jaccard loss [15]. We used an exponential moving average (EMA) [17]. The initial learning rate was set to 0.0002. To reduce overfitting, the encoder's initial learning rate was reduced to 0.1 of the other network parts.

### 4.2    Overview of Datasets

The EV-IMO dataset [14] is a real dataset captured indoors with the DAVIS 346 camera that includes backgrounds like *box, floor, table,* and *wall* as well as multiple independently moving objects. It is one of the most challenging open-source datasets for segmenting independent motion objects. The authors provide dense segmentation masks of independently moving objects for quantitative evaluation. Two standard metrics are used in the quantitative evaluation, including detection rate and Intersection over Union (IoU). Details about the metrics can be found in [11,29].

The Extreme Event Dataset (EED) [11] is one of the first open-source datasets used for independent moving objects detection and tracking research. There are independent moving objects in addition to the camera's ego-motion. All sequences were captured in a laboratory setting to demonstrate the superior performance of event cameras in HDR scenes.

276    L. Wang et al.

**Table 1.** Segmentation performance on the EVIMO dataset, measured by IoU.

|  | EVDodgeNet [18] | MOMS [16] | EMSGC [29] | EV-IMO [14] | AOT [25] | **Ours** |
|---|---|---|---|---|---|---|
| EVIMO | 65.76 | 74.82 | 76.81 | 77.00 | 31.82 | **77.49** |

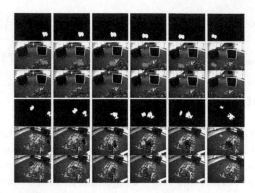

**Fig. 4.** Segmentation results on the EVIMO dataset, on sequences *Box*(rows 1–3) and *Table*(rows 4–6).Time runs from left to right. Our segmentation masks(rows 2 & 5) are shown on the frames. The masks from [29] (rows 3 & 6) are also shown on the frames. The first and fourth row are ground truth labels

### 4.3  Discussion of Results

As can be seen from the quantitative results in Table 1 , our method outperforms other state-of-the-art solutions. Moreover, due to the drastic changes in the scene recorded in the EVIMO dataset, the AOT [25] using only frames could not achieve satisfactory results, suggesting that exploiting the complementary of events and frames can improve the robustness of the model under degraded conditions.

**Table 2.** Segmentation performance on the EVIMO dataset, measured by detection rate.

| Algorithm | Mitrokhin [10] | MOMS [16] | **Ours** |
|---|---|---|---|
| Detection rate | 64.79 | 77.06 | **80.74** |

As shown in Table 2, our method outperforms other methods using the detection rate metric. Due to the lack of open source code, the numbers for the baseline method were obtained directly from the corresponding publications [16]. Figure 4 shows the example results of our method on EVIMO. In the *Box* sequence, The toy car moves from right to left on a highly textured carpet with multiple stationary interfering objects in the scene, and our model can still continuously detect it as a moving object. In the *Table* sequence, there are two Independent moving objects, which hit each other and meet in the middle. The toy plane moves slowly at the end of the sequence and [29] marks it as background. Even though they partially overlap, our method successfully segments out the independently moving plane.

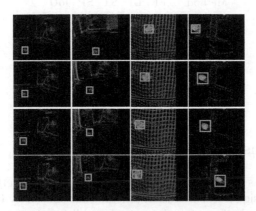

**Fig. 5.** Segmentation results on EED dataset. Time runs from top to bottom. The ground truth bounding boxes (in yellow) show the 2D location of the independent moving objects. column 1 and column 2 are recorded in low light conditions. column 3 and column 4 are recorded in the presence of obscuration. (Color figure online)

We ablate the main modules of our method. The key components of our method are feature fusion, long-term attention, short-term attention, and spatial attention. To verify their effectiveness, we modified the original model by removing each component and retrained the modified model, accordingly, we obtained four models. Table 3 reports the results of the four modified models. It shows that the feature fusion module is the key to our excellent results. The long and short-term spatio-temporal attention module does effectively match and propagate the target features and location information. This reflects the fact that our method can improve the model's segmentation ability by combining events and frames and using the attention mechanism to learn the motion information in the sequence, demonstrating that our method is robust to the shape, size, and the number of objects.

In addition to the quantitative results above, we also show example results from the EED dataset in Fig. 5. Note that it is sometimes difficult to detect the objects in the corresponding frames, which motivates us to combine frames and events and use motion cues for independent moving objects detection.

**Table 3.** Ablation studies on feature fusion(FF), long-term attention(LT), short-term attention(ST) and spatial-attention(SP).

| Method | FF | LT | ST | SP | IoU |
|--------|----|----|----|----|----|
| Ours-A | × | ✓ | ✓ | ✓ | 75.99 |
| Ours-B | ✓ | × | ✓ | ✓ | 74.97 |
| Ours-C | ✓ | ✓ | × | ✓ | 75.94 |
| Ours-D | ✓ | ✓ | ✓ | × | 76.94 |
| FusionSeg | ✓ | ✓ | ✓ | ✓ | **77.49** |

# 5  Conclusions and Future Work

This paper presents a multi-objects motion segmentation method using frames and events. We design a feature fusion scheme that effectively fuses the information obtained from the frames and events. In addition, we introduce the Transformer architecture to make full use of the motion cues for motion segmentation of multi-objects scenes.

Our method can address slow object motion and highly textured scenes through feature matching and propagation, demonstrating that exploiting the complementary of events and frames can improve the robustness of motion segmentation under degraded conditions. All these allow us to perform motion segmentation in challenging scenes, thus unlocking the remarkable capabilities of the event camera. In the future, we will investigate the feasibility of exploiting the high measurement rate of the event camera to increase the segmentation frequency.

**Acknowledgements.** This work was partially supported by the National Natural Science Foundation of China(No. 91948303).

# References

1. Carion, N., Massa, F., Synnaeve, G., Usunier, N., Kirillov, A., Zagoruyko, S.: End-to-end object detection with transformers. In: Vedaldi, A., Bischof, H., Brox, T., Frahm, J.-M. (eds.) ECCV 2020. LNCS, vol. 12346, pp. 213–229. Springer, Cham (2020). https://doi.org/10.1007/978-3-030-58452-8_13
2. Charig Yang, H.L., Lu, E., Zisserman, A., Xie, W.: Self-supervised video object segmentation by motion grouping (2021)
3. Gallego, G., Rebecq, H., Scaramuzza, D.: A unifying contrast maximization framework for event cameras, with applications to motion, depth, and optical flow estimation. In: Proceedings of the IEEE Conference on Computer Vision and Pattern Recognition, pp. 3867–3876 (2018)
4. Glover, A., Bartolozzi, C.: Robust visual tracking with a freely-moving event camera. In: 2017 IEEE/RSJ International Conference on Intelligent Robots and Systems (IROS), pp. 3769–3776. IEEE (2017)

5. Hinton, G., Vinyals, O., Dean, J., et al.: Distilling the knowledge in a neural network. arXiv preprint arXiv:1503.02531 2(7) (2015)
6. Howard, A., et al.: Searching for mobilenetv3. In: Proceedings of the IEEE/CVF International Conference on Computer Vision, pp. 1314–1324 (2019)
7. Kepple, D.R., Lee, D., Prepsius, C., Isler, V., Park, I.M., Lee, D.D.: Jointly learning visual motion and confidence from local patches in event cameras. In: Vedaldi, A., Bischof, H., Brox, T., Frahm, J.-M. (eds.) ECCV 2020. LNCS, vol. 12351, pp. 500–516. Springer, Cham (2020). https://doi.org/10.1007/978-3-030-58539-6_30
8. Lin, T.Y., Dollár, P., Girshick, R., He, K., Hariharan, B., Belongie, S.: Feature pyramid networks for object detection. In: Proceedings of the IEEE Conference on Computer Vision and Pattern Recognition, pp. 2117–2125 (2017)
9. Liu, L., Ouyang, W., Wang, X., Fieguth, P., Chen, J., Liu, X., Pietikäinen, M.: Deep learning for generic object detection: a survey. Int. J. Comput. Vis. 128(2), 261–318 (2020)
10. Mitrokhin, A., Fermüller, C., Parameshwara, C., Aloimonos, Y.: Event-based moving object detection and tracking. In: 2018 IEEE/RSJ International Conference on Intelligent Robots and Systems (IROS), pp. 1–9. IEEE (2018)
11. Mitrokhin, A., Fermüller, C., Parameshwara, C., Aloimonos, Y.: Event-based moving object detection and tracking. In: 2018 IEEE/RSJ International Conference on Intelligent Robots and Systems (IROS), pp. 1–9. IEEE (2018)
12. Mitrokhin, A., Hua, Z., Fermuller, C., Aloimonos, Y.: Learning visual motion segmentation using event surfaces. In: Proceedings of the IEEE/CVF Conference on Computer Vision and Pattern Recognition, pp. 14414–14423 (2020)
13. Mitrokhin, A., Ye, C., Fermüller, C., Aloimonos, Y., Delbruck, T.: Ev-imo: Motion segmentation dataset and learning pipeline for event cameras. In: 2019 IEEE/RSJ International Conference on Intelligent Robots and Systems (IROS), pp. 6105–6112. IEEE (2019)
14. Mitrokhin, A., Ye, C., Fermüller, C., Aloimonos, Y., Delbruck, T.: Ev-imo: Motion segmentation dataset and learning pipeline for event cameras. In: 2019 IEEE/RSJ International Conference on Intelligent Robots and Systems (IROS), pp. 6105–6112. IEEE (2019)
15. Nowozin, S.: Optimal decisions from probabilistic models: the intersection-over-union case. In: Proceedings of the IEEE Conference on Computer Vision and Pattern Recognition, pp. 548–555 (2014)
16. Parameshwara, C.M., Sanket, N.J., Gupta, A., Fermuller, C., Aloimonos, Y.: Moms with events: Multi-object motion segmentation with monocular event cameras. arXiv preprint arXiv:2006.06158 2(3), 5 (2020)
17. Polyak, B.T., Juditsky, A.B.: Acceleration of stochastic approximation by averaging. SIAM J. Contr. Optimization 30(4), 838–855 (1992)
18. Sanket, N.J., et al.: Evdodgenet: Deep dynamic obstacle dodging with event cameras. In: 2020 IEEE International Conference on Robotics and Automation (ICRA), pp. 10651–10657. IEEE (2020)
19. Stoffregen, T., Gallego, G., Drummond, T., Kleeman, L., Scaramuzza, D.: Event-based motion segmentation by motion compensation. In: Proceedings of the IEEE/CVF International Conference on Computer Vision, pp. 7244–7253 (2019)
20. Stoffregen, T., Kleeman, L.: Simultaneous optical flow and segmentation (sofas) using dynamic vision sensor. arXiv preprint arXiv:1805.12326 (2018)
21. Vasco, V., Glover, A., Mueggler, E., Scaramuzza, D., Natale, L., Bartolozzi, C.: Independent motion detection with event-driven cameras. In: 2017 18th International Conference on Advanced Robotics (ICAR), pp. 530–536. IEEE (2017)

22. Wang, Y., et al.: End-to-end video instance segmentation with transformers. In: Proceedings of the IEEE/CVF Conference on Computer Vision and Pattern Recognition, pp. 8741–8750 (2021)
23. Wertheimer, M.: Untersuchungen zur lehre von der gestalt. Psychologische forschung **1**(1), 47–58 (1922)
24. Yang, Z., Wei, Y., Yang, Y.: Collaborative video object segmentation by foreground-background integration. In: Vedaldi, A., Bischof, H., Brox, T., Frahm, J.-M. (eds.) ECCV 2020. LNCS, vol. 12350, pp. 332–348. Springer, Cham (2020). https://doi.org/10.1007/978-3-030-58558-7_20
25. Yang, Z., Wei, Y., Yang, Y.: Associating objects with transformers for video object segmentation. In: Advances in Neural Information Processing Systems, vol. 34 (2021)
26. Ye, C., Mitrokhin, A., Fermüller, C., Yorke, J.A., Aloimonos, Y.: Unsupervised learning of dense optical flow, depth and egomotion from sparse event data. arXiv preprint arXiv:1809.08625 (2018)
27. Zhang, J., Shi, F., Wang, J., Liu, Y.: 3D motion segmentation from straight-line optical flow. In: Sebe, N., Liu, Y., Zhuang, Y., Huang, T.S. (eds.) MCAM 2007. LNCS, vol. 4577, pp. 85–94. Springer, Heidelberg (2007). https://doi.org/10.1007/978-3-540-73417-8_15
28. Zhang, J., Yang, X., Fu, Y., Wei, X., Yin, B., Dong, B.: Object tracking by jointly exploiting frame and event domain. In: Proceedings of the IEEE/CVF International Conference on Computer Vision, pp. 13043–13052 (2021)
29. Zhou, Y., Gallego, G., Lu, X., Liu, S., Shen, S.: Event-based motion segmentation with spatio-temporal graph cuts. IEEE Transactions on Neural Networks and Learning Systems (2021)

# Weakly-Supervised Temporal Action Localization with Multi-Head Cross-Modal Attention

Hao Ren, Haoran Ren, Wu Ran, Hong Lu$^{(\boxtimes)}$, and Cheng Jin

Shanghai Key Lab of Intelligent Information Processing, School of Computer Science,
Fudan University, Shanghai, China
{hren17,hrren20,honglu,jc}@fudan.edu.cn, wran21@m.fudan.edu.cn

**Abstract.** Weakly-supervised temporal action localization seeks to localize temporal boundaries of actions while concurrently identifying their categories using only video-level category labels during training. Among the existing methods, the modal cooperation methods have achieved great success by providing pseudo supervision signals to RGB and Flow features. However, most of these methods ignore the cross-correlation between modal characteristics which can help them learn better features. By considering the cross-correlation, we propose a novel multi-head cross-modal attention mechanism to explicitly model the cross-correlation of modal features. The proposed method collaboratively enhances RGB and Flow features through a cross-correlation matrix. In this way, the enhanced features for each modality encode the inter-modal information, while preserving the exclusive and meaningful intra-modal characteristics. Experimental results on three recent methods demonstrate that the proposed Multi-head Cross-modal Attention (MCA) mechanism can significantly improve the performance of these methods, and even achieve state-of-the-art results on the THUMOS14 and ActivityNet1.2 datasets.

**Keywords:** Video analysis · Temporal action localization · Weakly-supervised learning · Attention

## 1 Introduction

The goal of temporal action localization is to discover the start and end times of relevant actions in untrimmed videos and categorize them. This task has a wide range of real-world applications, such as video retrieval [5] and intelligent visual question answering system [29], and it is becoming increasingly popular among researchers. Many fully-supervised approaches [3,17,25,33] have been presented in recent years to overcome this challenge, and they have demonstrated good localization accuracy on widely used public datasets (*e.g.*, THUMOS14 [9] and ActivityNet1.2&1.3 [1] datasets). However, they all require a considerable amount of frame-level labeled data, which is time-consuming and labor-intensive for large-scale dataset annotation, limiting the practical applicability of these methods. To address this issue, some research [6,18,21,26] has

S. Khanna et al. (Eds.): PRICAI 2022, LNCS 13631, pp. 281–295, 2022.
https://doi.org/10.1007/978-3-031-20868-3_21

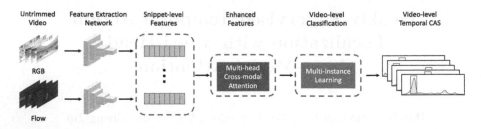

**Fig. 1.** The pipeline of a generic WTAL method that integrates our proposed MCA module. A pre-trained network is firstly applied to extract features from the untrimmed videos, and then our proposed MCA module is employed to enhance the features, finally, the enhanced features are fed into the MIL framework to train with the video-level labels. The more details of our proposed MCA are described in Sect. 3.3.

been conducted into Weakly-supervised Temporal Action Localization (WTAL) task. These methods no longer require a huge number of frame-level annotations, instead requiring only video-level category annotation, greatly reducing the effort of dataset annotation and improving the applicability of these methods.

The existing WTAL methods [6,8,14,31] basically follow the way of Multi-Instance Learning (MIL) [26] to solve this task. These methods treat the entire untrimmed video as a collection of positive and negative instances, *i.e.*, foreground action frames and background non-action frames. These methods first apply a pre-trained network (*e.g.*, I3D [2]) to extract the snippet-level features and then employ a classifier to obtain temporal Class Activation Sequences (CAS), finally, a top-$k$ mechanism is adopted to aggregate the video-level classification scores. Based on these classification scores, the typical binary cross entropy loss [7] is used to train the model. During the test phase, multiple thresholds are employed to filter the snippet-level CAS, after which the consecutive candidate snippets are grouped into a single proposal, and finally, Non-Maximum Suppression (NMS) is performed to obtain the action localization results.

These current WTAL approaches are primarily concerned with improving CAS or selecting more representative positive and negative snippets. For example, BaS-Net [14] introduces a suppression branch to help separating foreground (action snippets) and background (non-action snippets), allowing for more accurate CAS. RSKP [8] utilizes the Expectation-Maximization (EM) attention to learn the representative snippets, and alleviates the discrepancy with knowledge propagation. Most of these methods ignore the cross-correlation between modal characteristics. By considering the cross-correlation of RGB and Flow modalities, we propose a novel Multi-head Cross-modal Attention (MCA) mechanism to explicitly model the cross-correlation of these two modal features, and enhance the features to improve the localization performance implicitly. The proposed MCA is a plug-and-play module, and can be integrated with any existing WTAL methods. Figure 1 visually shows the pipeline of a generic WTAL method that integrates our proposed MCA module.

To sum up, our main contributions can be summarized as follows:

- We propose a novel multi-head cross-modal attention mechanism to explicitly model the cross-correlation of modal features, where the features are collaboratively learned for each modality under constraints from the other modality.
- Comprehensive weakly supervised temporal action localization experiments and ablation studies on THUMOS14 [9] and ActivityNet1.2 [1] datasets have been conducted. The experimental results demonstrate the superiority of the proposed method.

The rest of this paper is organized as follows. We first introduce the related work in Sect. 2, and then present the details of the proposed method in Sect. 3. The results of experimental evaluation are reported in Sect. 4, followed by the conclusion in Sect. 5.

## 2 Related Work

### 2.1 Fully-Supervised Temporal Action Localization (FTAL)

The temporal action localization task aims to locate the temporal duration of each action instance and identify its category. The fully-supervised temporal action localization requires the frame-level annotation during training. Some early work [25] uses sliding windows to process the input video frame by frame, then applies complex classifier to recognize the action categories one by one, resulting in a model with a very large calculation time. In the later work [33], some content related algorithms are introduced to generate candidate proposals, which helps to lessen the computational load. Recently, TAL-Net [3] applies the object detection algorithm to FTAL, and GTAN [17] introduces Gaussian kernels to dynamically optimize temporal scale of each action proposal, which improves the localization accuracy to a new level.

### 2.2 Weakly-Supervised Temporal Action Localization (WTAL)

The weakly-supervised temporal action localization task is proposed in order to address the problem of labor-intensive frame-level annotation in FTAL. Only video-level annotation is used by WTAL. UntrimNet [26] is the first to employ multi-instance learning to tackle this problem. On this basis, W-TALC [23] mines the similarity between video pairs and combine the co-activity similarity loss to improve localization accuracy even further. To better distinguish the foreground (action snippets) and background (non-action snippets), BaS-Net [14] suppresses the activation of the background by modeling it. CoLA [31] integrates contrast learning into WTAL and presents a hard snippet representation method to mine the hard samples.

## 2.3  Attention Mechanism

The majority of WTAL approaches focus on foreground-background separation or sample mining, and modal feature association is rarely used. On the other hand, some research towards feature enhancement has begun. Lee *et al.* [13] proposes a multi-stage cross-attention mechanism to fuse the audio and visual features progressively. HAM-Net [10] proposes a hybrid attention mechanism to capture the most discriminative frames by considering the frame relation. $CO_2$-Net [7] designs a cross-modal consensus module between RGB and Flow features to filter out the redundant information in current modal feature by the constraint from another modality. Inspired by ViT [4], ASM-Loc [6] presents intra-snippet and inter-snippet attention modules to capture the temporal structures within and across action snippets at the feature modeling stage. Different from these methods, we propose a multi-head attention module to model the cross-correlation between RGB and Flow features to encode the inter-modal information, while preserving the exclusive and meaningful intra-modal characteristics.

## 3  Proposed Method

In this section, we elaborate on the proposed Multi-head Cross-modal Attention (MCA) mechanism, which devotes to mining the correlation between different modals for WTAL. Specifically, fundamental notations and the problem definition for WTAL are depicted in Sect. 3.1. Then we revisit the pipeline of recent WTAL methods and introduce three latest methods on which we conduct our experiments, including HAM-Net [10], CoLA [31] and $CO_2$-Net [7]. In Sect. 3.3, we interpret the proposed MCA mechanism. Finally, we discuss the differences between the proposed MCA and existing methods.

### 3.1  Notations and Preliminaries

Suppose a set of $N$ untrimmed videos noted as $\mathcal{V} = \{V^{(n)}\}_{n=1}^N$ contain action instances from $C$ categories, where $V^{(n)}$ indicates the $n$-th video. For each video $V^{(n)}$, only the video-level label $\mathbf{y}^{(n)} \in \mathbb{R}^C$ is available, where $\mathbf{y}_i^{(n)} \in \{0, 1\}$ represents whether the instance of $i$-th action exists in $V^{(n)}$. Then WTAL aims to learn a model that simultaneously localizes and classifies all action instances temporally with the start time $t_s$, end time $t_e$, predicted category $c$, and the corresponding confidence score $q$, respectively.

### 3.2  WTAL Methods Pipeline Revisit

**Snippet-Level Feature Extraction.** Instead of directly feeding the untrimmed video $V$ into a neural network, recent WTAL methods [6–8,10,21,24,31] first divide $V$ into $L$ non-overlapping 16-frame snippets, and then employ a pre-trained network (*i.e.*, I3D [2]) to extract the features of appearance modality (RGB) and motion modality (Flow), respectively. We denote the RGB feature as $\mathbf{X}^R =$

$[\mathbf{x}_1^R, \mathbf{x}_2^R, \cdots, \mathbf{x}_L^R]^T \in \mathbb{R}^{L \times D}$ for video $V$, where $\mathbf{x}_j^R \in \mathbb{R}^D$ represents the $D$ dimensional feature vector of the $j$-th snippet. Analogously, $\mathbf{X}^F = [\mathbf{x}_1^F, \mathbf{x}_2^F, \cdots, \mathbf{x}_L^F]^T \in \mathbb{R}^{L \times D}$ means the Flow feature for the video $V$. In practice, WTAL utilizes the RGB feature $\mathbf{X}^R$ and the Flow feature $\mathbf{X}^F$ for the localization and classification of action instances.

**Snippet-Level Classification.** Given the extracted features from two modalities, there are two critical issues to address for WTAL to predict the categories of action instances in a video. The first is how to exploit the cross-modal information from the multi-modal features $\mathbf{X}^R$ and $\mathbf{X}^F$. Generally, let $\mathcal{G}(\mathbf{X}^R, \mathbf{X}^F)$ indicate the enhanced features containing cross-modal information. A simple way to process the multi-modal features is introduced in HAM-Net [10] and CoLA [31] by concatenating $\mathbf{X}^R$ and $\mathbf{X}^F$, where $\mathcal{G}(\mathbf{X}^R, \mathbf{X}^F) = [\mathbf{X}^R, \mathbf{X}^F]$. The simple concatenation of multi-modal features ignores the discrepancy between RGB and Flow modality. On the other hand, due to the inconsistency between action recognition and action localization, the multi-modal features extracted from I3D (trained on action recognition task) are not always appropriate for WTAL task. Therefore, $CO_2$-Net [7] introduces a feature re-calibration operation to remove the task-irrelevant information from one modality by using the global context information from another modality.

The second critical issue for the WTAL task is how to obtain the snippet-level classification score for a video with the enhanced features $\mathcal{G}(\mathbf{X}^R, \mathbf{X}^F)$. The enhanced features $\mathcal{G}(\mathbf{X}^R, \mathbf{X}^F)$ are first processed by an embedding module $f_{embed}$ to fully explore the temporal information. For instance, HAM-Net and CoLA implement the embedding module with temporal convolutions together with the ReLU activations. The embedded features $\tilde{\mathbf{X}} = f_{embed}(\mathcal{G}(\mathbf{X}^R, \mathbf{X}^F))$ are prepared for the action classification. Specifically, a classifier head $f_{cls}$ is employed to provide the category logits $Q = f_{cls}(\tilde{\mathbf{X}}) \in \mathbb{R}^{L \times C}$ for a specific video, where the logits $Q$ are commonly known as the temporal Class Activation Sequences (CAS).

**Video-Level Classification.** Since only the video-level label $\mathbf{y} \in \{0,1\}^C$ is accessible for the video $V$, WTAL methods then aggregate the snippet-level category logits $Q$ to offer a video-level prediction $\tilde{\mathbf{y}}$. Hence the embedding module and the classifier head can be supervised under a classification loss:

$$\mathcal{L}_{cls} = -\sum_{j=1}^C \mathbf{y}_j \log(\tilde{\mathbf{y}}_j). \tag{1}$$

In practice, the majority of the WTAL methods adopt a top-$k$ selection strategy to obtain the video-level logits $\mathbf{q} \in \mathbb{R}^C$ from $Q$ as mathematically formalized as

$$\mathbf{q}_j = \max_{l \subset \{1, \cdots, L\}} \frac{1}{k} \sum_{k \in l} Q_{k,j}, \quad s.t. \ |l| = k. \tag{2}$$

Then the video-level prediction $\tilde{\mathbf{y}} = Softmax(\mathbf{q})$. To suppress the contributions of *background* where no action occurs, some WTAL methods [7,8,10,21] impose

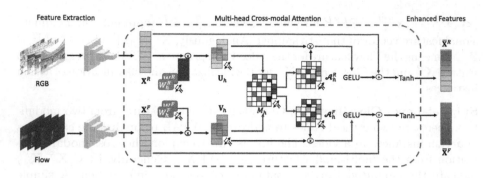

**Fig. 2.** The mechanism of Multi-head Cross-modal Attention (MCA). Firstly, the several projection heads are applied to convert the original features into multiple different hidden spaces to ensure diversity. Then the correlation matrix is introduced to mining the relations between RGB and Flow modalities in each head. After that, the normalized cross-attention weights are employed to re-calibrate the features. Finally, the re-calibrated features are aggregated to obtain the enhanced features.

an action-aware attention map $\mathcal{A}$ on the CAS, where $f_{att}$ represents a learnable attention module and $\mathcal{A} = f_{att}(\mathcal{G}(\mathbf{X}^R, \mathbf{X}^F))$. In addition, a specific attention loss $\mathcal{L}_{att}$ is utilized to guide the attention module focus on action-related snippets.

**Action Instances Localization.** The recent WTAL methods [7, 8, 10, 28] utilize an outer-inner contrastive strategy to localize the action instances in a video following Liu *et al.* [15]. Concretely, the video-level prediction $\tilde{\mathbf{y}}$ is firstly used to detect the existing actions with a specific threshold. Then for each existing action $c$, the CAS is utilized to localize the action instance by computing its start time $t_s$, end time $t_e$ and confidence score $q$.

### 3.3 Multi-Head Cross-Modal Attention Mechanism

As illustrated in Sect. 3.2, the localization and classification of action instances depend on the features from RGB and Flow extracted by a pre-trained I3D network. In this section, we detail the proposed Multi-head Cross-modal Attention (MCA) mechanism, which further exploits the cross-correlation between different modal characteristics and preserves the intra-modal characteristics in $\mathbf{X}^R$ and $\mathbf{X}^F$. This multi-head cross-modal attention results in the collaboratively enhanced features $\mathcal{G}(\mathbf{X}^R, \mathbf{X}^F)$, and thus can be incorporated into the pipelines of existing methods.

As presented in Fig. 2, we first utilize a set of matrices $\{W_h^R\}_{h=1}^H$ and $\{W_h^F\}_{h=1}^H$ to project $\mathbf{X}^R$ and $\mathbf{X}^F$ into a set of compact features $\{\mathbf{U}_h\}_{h=1}^H$ and $\{\mathbf{V}_h\}_{h=1}^H$, respectively. Each $\mathbf{U}_h = [\mathbf{u}_1^h, \mathbf{u}_2^h, \cdots, \mathbf{u}_L^h]^T$ represents the snippet-level RGB features for a specific video, where $\mathbf{u}_i^h \in \mathbb{R}^{\lfloor D/H \rfloor}$, $i = 1, \cdots, L$. While each $\mathbf{V}_h = [\mathbf{v}_1^h, \mathbf{v}_2^h, \cdots, \mathbf{v}_L^h]^T$ is the snippet-level Flow features. Therefore each pair of $\{\mathbf{U}_h, \mathbf{V}_h\}$ can be utilized to calculate the CAS for the WTAL task, and the total $h$ pairs $\{\mathbf{U}_h, \mathbf{V}_h\}$ form a *multi-head* input. Note that each input head corresponds to a head-specific response to the original features $\mathbf{X}^R$ and $\mathbf{X}^F$:

$$\mathbf{U}_h = \mathbf{X}^R W_h^R, \ \mathbf{V}_h = \mathbf{X}^F W_h^F$$
$$s.t. \ W_h^R \in \mathbb{R}^{D \times \lfloor D/H \rfloor}, \ W_h^F \in \mathbb{R}^{D \times \lfloor D/H \rfloor}, \ i = 1, 2, \cdots, H. \tag{3}$$

Inspired by Lee et al. [13], to further explore the cross-correlation of different modal characteristics, we employ a learnable weight matrix $M_h$ for each head and compute the correlation as formulated as

$$\mathcal{A}_h = \mathbf{U}_h M_h \mathbf{V}_h^T, \ M_h \in \mathbb{R}^{\lfloor D/H \rfloor \times \lfloor D/H \rfloor}, \tag{4}$$

where each row of $\mathbf{U}_h$ and $\mathbf{V}_h$ are $l_2$-normalized before computing Eq. (4), and $\mathcal{A}_h \in \mathbb{R}^{L \times L}$ indicates the correlation matrix for the $h$-th head between the RGB features $\mathbf{U_h}$ and the Flow features $\mathbf{V}_h$. Particularly, a high correlation value in $\mathcal{A}$ demonstrates that the corresponding RGB and Flow snippet features are closely correlated. In addition, the elements in the $i$-th row of $\mathcal{A}_h$ indicates the relevance of RGB feature vector $\mathbf{u}_i^h$ to all snippet-level Flow features $\mathbf{V}_h$. We then utilize the correlation matrix $\mathcal{A}_h$ to generate the cross-modal attention weights $\mathcal{A}_h^R$ and $\mathcal{A}_h^F$ by the row-wise *Softmax* operation of $\mathcal{A}_h$ and $\mathcal{A}_h^T$, respectively.

Note that in the correlation matrix $\mathcal{A}_h$, each RGB and Flow snippet feature vectors noted as $\mathbf{u}_i^h$ and $\mathbf{v}_j^h$, are correlated by the same matrix $M_h$. Hence, the normalized cross-attention weights $\mathcal{A}_h^R$ and $\mathcal{A}_h^F$ can be employed to re-calibrate the original RGB features $\mathbf{X}^R$ and Flow features $\mathbf{X}^F$. Specifically, we first re-weight the RGB features $\mathbf{U}_h$ and the Flow features $\mathbf{V}_h$ for all heads by

$$\tilde{\mathbf{U}}_h = \phi(\mathcal{A}_h^R \mathbf{U}_h), \ \tilde{\mathbf{V}}_h = \phi(\mathcal{A}_h^F \mathbf{V}_h), \ h = 1, 2, \cdots, H, \tag{5}$$

where $\phi(\cdot)$ is the GELU activation. Then the re-weighted RGB and Flow features from all $H$ heads are aggregated to re-calibrate the original RGB features $\mathbf{X}^R$ and Flow features $\mathbf{X}^F$ as defined below

$$\bar{\mathbf{X}}^R = \tanh\left(Concat([\tilde{\mathbf{U}}_1, \tilde{\mathbf{U}}_2, \cdots, \tilde{\mathbf{U}}_H]) + \mathbf{X}^R\right)$$
$$\bar{\mathbf{X}}^F = \tanh\left(Concat([\tilde{\mathbf{V}}_1, \tilde{\mathbf{V}}_2, \cdots, \tilde{\mathbf{V}}_H]) + \mathbf{X}^F\right), \tag{6}$$

where $Concat$ is the concatenation among all heads. Formally, $\mathcal{G}(\mathbf{X}^R, \mathbf{X}^F) = \{\bar{\mathbf{X}}^R, \bar{\mathbf{X}}^F\}$ denotes the collaboratively enhanced RGB and Flow snippet features. Hence the existing WTAL methods can directly utilize the collaboratively enhanced features $\mathcal{G}(\mathbf{X}^R, \mathbf{X}^F)$ for the subsequent localization and classification of action instances as elaborated in Sect. 2. In this paper, we have incorporated the proposed MCA on the latest three methods (HAM-Net [10], CoLA [31] and $CO_2$-Net [7]) to reveal the effectiveness of the introduced MCA.

## 3.4   Discussion

The cross-modal attention mechanism has also been introduced in $CO_2$-Net [7] and Lee et al. [13], and the differences are discussed as follows: (1) $CO_2$-Net aims to use the global context features from one modality to re-calibrate the snippet-level features from another modality. The global context features are obtained utilizing a temporal average pooling operation, which discards the temporal information. While the proposed MCA utilizes a weight matrix $M_h$ to calculate the cross-correlation of modal characteristics of different modalities. In addition, the extracted features are projected to generate a multi-head input, which increases the diversity of the collaboratively enhanced features $\mathcal{G}(\mathbf{X}^R, \mathbf{X}^F)$. (2) Lee *et al.* [13] introduces the cross-modal attention mechanism to better fuse features from the audio modality and visual modality. In addition, Lee *et al.* [13] develops the cross-modal attention in a multi-stage manner (in series), but the introduced MCA employs the multi-head attention (in parallel) to mine the cross-correlation between the features of the RGB and Flow modalities.

## 4    Experiments

In this section, we first introduce the datasets, followed by the implementation details of our method and the evaluation metrics. And then we compare our method with the state-of-the-art methods. Finally, extensive ablation studies are conducted to explore the effect about the number of heads in MCA.

### 4.1    Datasets

The proposed method is evaluated for temporal action localization on two popular datasets (THUMOS14 [9] and ActivityNet1.2 [1]) containing untrimmed videos with varying degree of activity duration.

The THUMOS14 dataset has temporal annotations for a subset of videos in the validation and testing sets for 20 classes. Following the previous work [7, 10,31], we use 200 videos in the validation set for training and 213 videos in the testing set for evaluation. This dataset is challenging for its finely annotated action instances. Each video contains 15.5 action clips on average. The length of action also varies significantly, from a few seconds to minutes.

The ActivityNet1.2 dataset has 100 activity classes consisting of 4819 videos for training, 2383 videos for validation, and 2480 videos for testing (whose labels are withheld). Each video contains 1.5 action instances on average. Following [7, 10,31], we use the training set to train our model and the validation set for evaluation.

### 4.2    Implementation Details

In this work, we employ the I3D network [2] pre-trained on Kinetics-400 [2] dataset for feature extraction. And TV-L1 algorithm [30] is used to extract optical flow features. To verify the effectiveness of our proposed method, we re-train the three recent models as baseline on our own machine by using the official implementations of HAM-Net, CoLA and $CO_2$-Net . The proposed MCA is integrated with these models and then trained with Adam [12] optimizer in the same experimental setting. The reason why we chose these three methods is that they provide open source code and a strong benchmark for our subsequent experiments. Our code is available on https://github.com/leftthomas/MCA, implemented with PyTorch [22] library and the experiments are conducted on NVIDIA Geforce GTX TITAN X GPU.

**Table 1.** Performance comparisons with state-of-the-art fully-supervised and weakly-supervised TAL methods on THUMOS14 testing set. AVG is the average mAP under the thresholds 0.1:0.1:0.7, while † means the use of additional information, such as action frequency or human pose, * indicates using I3D features, − means that corresponding results are not reported in the original papers, and (Rerun) represents the results are obtained by retraining the official code on our own machine. The best results for each baseline method are bold.

| Supervision | Method | mAP@IoU (%) | | | | | | | |
|---|---|---|---|---|---|---|---|---|---|
| | | 0.1 | 0.2 | 0.3 | 0.4 | 0.5 | 0.6 | 0.7 | AVG |
| Full | S-CNN [25], CVPR'16 | 47.7 | 43.5 | 36.3 | 28.7 | 19.0 | 10.3 | 5.3 | 27.3 |
| | SSN [33], ICCV'17 | 66.0 | 59.4 | 51.9 | 41.0 | 29.8 | − | − | − |
| | TAL-Net [3], CVPR'18 | 59.8 | 57.1 | 53.2 | 48.5 | 42.8 | 33.8 | 20.8 | 45.1 |
| | GTAN [17], CVPR'19 | 69.1 | 63.7 | 57.8 | 47.2 | 38.8 | − | − | − |
| Weak† | STAR* [27], AAAI'19 | 68.8 | 60.0 | 48.7 | 34.7 | 23.0 | − | − | − |
| | 3C-Net* [20], ICCV'19 | 59.1 | 53.5 | 44.2 | 34.1 | 26.6 | − | 8.1 | − |
| | SF-Net* [19], ECCV'20 | 71.0 | 63.4 | 53.2 | 40.7 | 29.3 | 18.4 | 9.6 | 40.8 |
| Weak | UntrimNet [26], CVPR'17 | 44.4 | 37.7 | 28.2 | 21.1 | 13.7 | − | − | − |
| | STPN* [21], CVPR'18 | 52.0 | 44.7 | 35.5 | 25.8 | 16.9 | 9.9 | 4.3 | 27.0 |
| | W-TALC* [23], ECCV'18 | 55.2 | 49.6 | 40.1 | 31.1 | 22.8 | − | 7.6 | − |
| | ASSG* [32], MM'19 | 65.6 | 59.4 | 50.4 | 38.7 | 25.4 | 15.0 | 6.6 | 37.3 |
| | BaS-Net* [14], AAAI'20 | 58.2 | 52.3 | 44.6 | 36.0 | 27.0 | 18.6 | 10.4 | 35.3 |
| | DGAM* [24], CVPR'20 | 60.0 | 56.0 | 46.6 | 37.5 | 26.8 | 17.6 | 9.0 | 37.0 |
| | EM-MIL* [18], ECCV'20 | 59.1 | 52.7 | 45.5 | 36.8 | 30.5 | 22.7 | 16.4 | 37.7 |
| | HAM-Net* [10], AAAI'21 | 65.9 | 59.6 | 52.2 | 43.1 | 32.6 | 21.9 | 12.5 | 41.1 |
| | CoLA* [31], CVPR'21 | 66.2 | 59.5 | 51.5 | 41.9 | 32.2 | 22.0 | 13.1 | 40.9 |
| | CO$_2$-Net* [7], MM'21 | 70.1 | 63.6 | 54.5 | 45.7 | 38.3 | 26.4 | 13.4 | 44.6 |
| | RSKP* [8], CVPR'22 | 71.3 | 65.3 | 55.8 | 47.5 | 38.2 | 25.4 | 12.5 | 45.1 |
| | ASM-Loc* [6], CVPR'22 | 71.2 | 65.5 | 57.1 | 46.8 | 36.6 | 25.2 | 13.4 | 45.1 |
| | HAM-Net* [10] (Rerun) | 65.9 | 59.4 | 51.0 | 41.2 | 31.1 | 20.4 | 10.9 | 40.0 |
| | HAM-Net* [10] with MCA | **66.8** | **60.9** | **52.2** | **42.9** | **33.4** | **22.7** | **12.2** | **41.6** |
| | CoLA* [31] (Rerun) | 64.9 | 59.0 | 50.9 | 41.8 | 32.2 | 22.5 | 12.5 | 40.6 |
| | CoLA* [31] with MCA | **67.5** | **60.6** | **51.9** | **43.2** | **34.2** | **24.2** | **13.9** | **42.2** |
| | CO$_2$-Net* [7] (Rerun) | 69.2 | 63.1 | 54.0 | 45.1 | 37.4 | 25.2 | 12.8 | 43.8 |
| | CO$_2$-Net* [7] with MCA | **70.8** | **64.7** | **55.7** | **46.8** | **39.8** | **26.5** | **13.8** | **45.4** |

### 4.3  Evaluation Metrics

Following the standard evaluation protocol [7,10,31], we evaluate the WTAL performance using mean average precision (mAP) values at different levels of IoU thresholds. Specifically, the IoU threshold sets are [0.1:0.1:0.7] and [0.5:0.05:0.95] for THUMOS14 and ActivityNet1.2 datasets, respectively. Higher mAP indicates better WTAL performance. For fair comparison, the results are calculated using the benchmark code provided by ActivityNet.

### 4.4  Comparison with State-of-the-Art Methods

We compare our method with state-of-the-art weakly-supervised methods on both THUMOS14 [9] and ActivityNet1.2 [1] datasets. The three recent models (HAM-Net [10], CoLA [31] and $CO_2$-Net [7]) are re-trained as baseline. It is worth noting that the performance of our re-train is slightly lower than the original papers, and the quantitative results are listed in Table 1 and Table 2.

**Table 2.** Performance comparisons with state-of-the-art fully-supervised and weakly-supervised TAL methods on ActivityNet1.2 validation set. AVG is the average mAP under the thresholds 0.5:0.05:0.95, while † means the use of action counts, * indicates using I3D features, – means that corresponding results are not reported in the original papers, and (Rerun) represents the results are obtained by retraining the official code on our own machine. The best results for each baseline method are bold.

| Supervision | Method | mAP@IoU (%) | | | |
|---|---|---|---|---|---|
| | | 0.5 | 0.75 | 0.95 | AVG |
| Full | SSN [33], ICCV'17 | 41.3 | 27.0 | 6.1 | 26.6 |
| Weak† | 3C-Net* [20], ICCV'19 | 37.2 | – | – | 21.7 |
| Weak | UntrimNet [26], CVPR'17 | 7.4 | 3.9 | 1.2 | 3.6 |
| | W-TALC* [23], ECCV'18 | 37.0 | 14.6 | – | 18.0 |
| | BaS-Net* [14], AAAI'20 | 38.5 | 24.2 | 5.6 | 24.3 |
| | DGAM* [24], CVPR'20 | 41.0 | 23.5 | 5.3 | 24.4 |
| | HAM-Net* [10], AAAI'21 | 41.0 | 24.8 | 5.3 | 25.1 |
| | ACSNet* [16], AAAI'21 | 40.1 | 26.1 | 6.8 | 26.0 |
| | CoLA* [31], CVPR'21 | 42.7 | 25.7 | 5.8 | 26.1 |
| | $CO_2$-Net* [7], MM'21 | 43.3 | 26.3 | 5.2 | 26.4 |
| | CSCL* [11], MM'21 | 43.8 | 26.9 | 5.6 | 26.9 |
| | HAM-Net* [10] (Rerun) | 41.1 | 24.6 | 5.0 | 24.5 |
| | HAM-Net* [10] with MCA | **41.3** | **25.2** | **5.5** | **25.4** |
| | CoLA* [31] (Rerun) | 40.7 | 26.9 | 2.8 | 26.0 |
| | CoLA* [31] with MCA | **41.0** | **27.5** | **4.2** | **26.4** |
| | $CO_2$-Net* [7] (Rerun) | 43.1 | 26.0 | 5.3 | 26.2 |
| | $CO_2$-Net* [7] with MCA | **44.4** | **27.0** | **5.4** | **27.1** |

We also keep the results of several fully-supervised methods for the sake of completeness. From the results we can see that when applying the proposed MCA on these three methods, the performances of these methods are significantly improved (1.6% on THUMOS14 dataset in terms of average mAP). Without bells and whistles, $CO_2$-Net [7] with MCA sets a new state-of-the-art performance, surpassing the previous best methods (45.4% *vs* 45.1% and 27.1% *vs* 26.9% on THUMOS14 and ActivityNet1.2 datasets in terms of average mAP, respectively). This demonstrates that the proposed MCA is a general method that can be well integrated with existing methods to boost performance even more. It also implies that our method is capable of extracting cross-correlation information between RGB and Flow modal characteristics and using it to improve the extracted features.

We present a visualization comparison in Fig. 3 between $CO_2$-Net [7] and $CO_2$-Net [7] with MCA on THUMOS14 dataset in order to more intuitively explain the benefits of our method. As we can see, two regions (indicated with yellow boxes) are mis-localized by $CO_2$-Net, however both are corrected with the assistance of MCA. Specifically, the correct segments should be the cliff diving action of two different persons (a man and a woman) in the area marked by the first yellow box, but $CO_2$-Net regards the two segments as the same continuous action, and with the help of our MCA, correctly identifies the two segments and gives the truncation. In the area marked by the second yellow box, $CO_2$-Net is confused by the complicated background information, and wrongly separates a continuous cliff diving action into two segments. Our method successfully identifies this continuous action despite the interference of the complicated background. Looking at all of the localization results, we can see that our method can effectively localize the easy segments as well as the difficult segments, indicating that our method implicitly enhances the extracted features to some extent, allowing it to better serve action localization and improve localization accuracy.

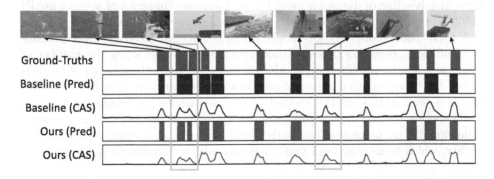

**Fig. 3.** Qualitative visualization results on an example of the *CliffDiving* action in the testing set of THUMOS14 dataset. The horizontal axis denotes the timestamps. The results of Ground-Truths, $CO_2$-Net (Baseline) and $CO_2$-Net with MCA (Ours) are shown in green, blue and red, respectively. "Pred" means the predicted action localization, and "CAS" means the corresponding activation sequence of *CliffDiving*. The yellow boxes include some difficult cases that $CO_2$-Net fails to detect but can be successfully localized by our method. (Color figure online)

**Table 3.** Ablation studies about the number of heads in MCA on THUMOS14 testing set and ActivityNet1.2 validation set. AVG is the average mAP under the thresholds 0.1:0.1:0.7 and 0.5:0.05:0.95 for THUMOS14 testing set and ActivityNet1.2 validation set, respectively. The best results for each baseline method are bold.

| Method | Heads | mAP@IoU (%) | | | | | | | | | | |
| | | THUMOS14 | | | | | | | | ActivityNet1.2 | | |
| | | 0.1 | 0.2 | 0.3 | 0.4 | 0.5 | 0.6 | 0.7 | AVG | 0.5 | 0.75 | 0.95 | AVG |
|---|---|---|---|---|---|---|---|---|---|---|---|---|---|
| HAM-Net [10] | 2 | **67.1** | **60.9** | 52.1 | 42.6 | 32.7 | 22.3 | **12.2** | 41.4 | 41.2 | 24.8 | 5.3 | 25.1 |
| | 4 | 66.8 | **60.9** | **52.2** | **42.9** | **33.4** | **22.7** | **12.2** | **41.6** | **41.3** | **25.2** | **5.5** | **25.4** |
| | 8 | 66.5 | 60.0 | 51.3 | 42.3 | 32.9 | 22.3 | 12.1 | 41.0 | 41.0 | 24.9 | 5.5 | 25.2 |
| CoLA [31] | 2 | 67.3 | **60.7** | 51.7 | **43.4** | **34.6** | 24.1 | 13.1 | 42.1 | 40.8 | 27.0 | 3.9 | 26.1 |
| | 4 | **67.5** | 60.6 | **51.9** | 43.2 | 34.2 | **24.2** | 13.9 | **42.2** | **41.0** | **27.5** | 4.2 | **26.4** |
| | 8 | 66.6 | 59.9 | 51.6 | 43.0 | 34.5 | 24.0 | **14.1** | 42.0 | 40.8 | 27.1 | **4.5** | 26.3 |
| CO₂-Net [7] | 2 | 70.4 | 64.0 | 54.9 | 46.0 | 38.8 | 26.3 | **14.1** | 44.9 | 43.7 | 26.3 | 5.1 | 26.5 |
| | 4 | **70.8** | **64.7** | **55.7** | 46.8 | **39.8** | **26.5** | 13.8 | **45.4** | **44.4** | **27.0** | **5.4** | **27.1** |
| | 8 | 70.4 | 64.1 | 55.2 | **47.0** | 39.1 | 25.8 | 13.7 | 45.0 | 44.3 | 26.9 | 5.3 | 27.0 |

## 4.5 Ablation Study

We can learn from the description of MCA in Sect. 3.3 that as the number of heads increases, the feature dimensions in each head decreases, implying that while diversity increases, the representation ability of a single head decreases. The resulting problem is how to make a trade-off between diversity and representation ability, that is, how to set the number of heads is a problem worth studying. As a result, we conduct ablation studies about the number of heads in MCA on both THUMOS14 [9] and ActivityNet1.2 [1] datasets with all the three baseline methods to determine the ideal value.

The quantitative results are shown in Table 3. The results show that no matter which baseline or dataset is used, the performance (in terms of average mAP) is highest when the number of heads is 4. Specifically, when the number of heads is 2, each head's representation capacity is sufficient, but MCA's overall diversity is insufficient, resulting in a performance inferior to that when the number of heads is 4. The overall diversity of MCA is sufficient when the number of heads is 8, but the representation ability of each head is considerably diminished, resulting in a performance inferior to that of the case where the number of heads is 4. Therefore, we can draw a conclusion that the head number of 4 is a reasonable equilibrium point that can both assure diversity and retain representation ability, which is also the head number finally adopted by our method.

## 5 Conclusion

In this paper, we propose a simple yet effective Multi-head Cross-modal Attention (MCA) mechanism to enhance the extracted RGB and Flow features and achieve state-of-the-art Weakly-supervised Temporal Action Localization

(WTAL) performance on THUMOS14 [9] and ActivityNet1.2 [1] datasets. By imposing the cross-correlation between RGB and Flow modalities explicitly, the proposed MCA module has shown better WTAL performance than both the baseline methods and recent state-of-the-art methods. This plug-and-play module is not only suitable for WTAL task, but also can be applied to more tasks, such as fully-supervised temporal action localization, action recognition and so on, to help enhancing the ability of extracting features.

**Acknowledgments.** This work was supported by National Natural Science Foundation of China under Grant No. 61732004.

# References

1. Caba Heilbron, F., Escorcia, V., Ghanem, B., Carlos Niebles, J.: ActivityNet: a large-scale video benchmark for human activity understanding. In: IEEE Conference on Computer Vision and Pattern Recognition, pp. 961–970 (2015)
2. Carreira, J., Zisserman, A.: Quo Vadis, action recognition? A new model and the kinetics dataset. In: IEEE Conference on Computer Vision and Pattern Recognition, pp. 6299–6308 (2017)
3. Chao, Y.W., Vijayanarasimhan, S., Seybold, B., Ross, D.A., Deng, J., Sukthankar, R.: Rethinking the faster R-CNN architecture for temporal action localization. In: IEEE Conference on Computer Vision and Pattern Recognition, pp. 1130–1139 (2018)
4. Dosovitskiy, A., et al.: An image is worth 16x16 words: transformers for image recognition at scale. In: International Conference on Learning Representations (2020)
5. Gabeur, V., Sun, C., Alahari, K., Schmid, C.: Multi-modal transformer for video retrieval. In: Vedaldi, A., Bischof, H., Brox, T., Frahm, J.-M. (eds.) ECCV 2020. LNCS, vol. 12349, pp. 214–229. Springer, Cham (2020). https://doi.org/10.1007/978-3-030-58548-8_13
6. He, B., Yang, X., Kang, L., Cheng, Z., Zhou, X., Shrivastava, A.: ASM-Loc: action-aware segment modeling for weakly-supervised temporal action localization. In: IEEE Conference on Computer Vision and Pattern Recognition (2022)
7. Hong, F.T., Feng, J.C., Xu, D., Shan, Y., Zheng, W.S.: Cross-modal consensus network for weakly supervised temporal action localization. In: ACM International Conference on Multimedia, pp. 1591–1599 (2021)
8. Huang, L., Wang, L., Li, H.: Weakly supervised temporal action localization via representative snippet knowledge propagation. In: IEEE Conference on Computer Vision and Pattern Recognition (2022)
9. Idrees, H., et al.: The Thumos challenge on action recognition for videos "in the wild.". Comput. Vis. Image Underst. **155**, 1–23 (2017)
10. Islam, A., Long, C., Radke, R.: A hybrid attention mechanism for weakly-supervised temporal action localization. In: AAAI Conference on Artificial Intelligence, vol. 35, pp. 1637–1645 (2021)
11. Ji, Y., Jia, X., Lu, H., Ruan, X.: Weakly-supervised temporal action localization via cross-stream collaborative learning. In: ACM International Conference on Multimedia, pp. 853–861 (2021)
12. Kingma, D.P., Ba, J.: Adam: a method for stochastic optimization. In: International Conference on Learning Representations (2015)

13. Lee, J.T., Jain, M., Park, H., Yun, S.: Cross-attentional audio-visual fusion for weakly-supervised action localization. In: International Conference on Learning Representations (2020)
14. Lee, P., Uh, Y., Byun, H.: Background suppression network for weakly-supervised temporal action localization. In: AAAI Conference on Artificial Intelligence, vol. 34, pp. 11320–11327 (2020)
15. Liu, D., Jiang, T., Wang, Y.: Completeness modeling and context separation for weakly supervised temporal action localization. In: IEEE Conference on Computer Vision and Pattern Recognition, pp. 1298–1307 (2019)
16. Liu, Z., et al.: ACSNet: action-context separation network for weakly supervised temporal action localization. In: AAAI Conference on Artificial Intelligence, vol. 35, pp. 2233–2241 (2021)
17. Long, F., Yao, T., Qiu, Z., Tian, X., Luo, J., Mei, T.: Gaussian temporal awareness networks for action localization. In: IEEE Conference on Computer Vision and Pattern Recognition, pp. 344–353 (2019)
18. Luo, Z., et al.: Weakly-supervised action localization with expectation-maximization multi-instance learning. In: Vedaldi, A., Bischof, H., Brox, T., Frahm, J.-M. (eds.) ECCV 2020. LNCS, vol. 12374, pp. 729–745. Springer, Cham (2020). https://doi.org/10.1007/978-3-030-58526-6_43
19. Ma, F., et al.: SF-Net: single-frame supervision for temporal action localization. In: Vedaldi, A., Bischof, H., Brox, T., Frahm, J.-M. (eds.) ECCV 2020. LNCS, vol. 12349, pp. 420–437. Springer, Cham (2020). https://doi.org/10.1007/978-3-030-58548-8_25
20. Narayan, S., Cholakkal, H., Khan, F.S., Shao, L.: 3C-Net: category count and center loss for weakly-supervised action localization. In: International Conference on Computer Vision, pp. 8679–8687 (2019)
21. Nguyen, P., Liu, T., Prasad, G., Han, B.: Weakly supervised action localization by sparse temporal pooling network. In: IEEE Conference on Computer Vision and Pattern Recognition, pp. 6752–6761 (2018)
22. Paszke, A., et al.: PyTorch: an imperative style, high-performance deep learning library. In: Annual Conference on Neural Information Processing Systems, pp. 8026–8037 (2019)
23. Paul, S., Roy, S., Roy-Chowdhury, A.K.: W-TALC: weakly-supervised temporal activity localization and classification. In: Ferrari, V., Hebert, M., Sminchisescu, C., Weiss, Y. (eds.) ECCV 2018. LNCS, vol. 11208, pp. 588–607. Springer, Cham (2018). https://doi.org/10.1007/978-3-030-01225-0_35
24. Shi, B., Dai, Q., Mu, Y., Wang, J.: Weakly-supervised action localization by generative attention modeling. In: IEEE Conference on Computer Vision and Pattern Recognition, pp. 1009–1019 (2020)
25. Shou, Z., Wang, D., Chang, S.F.: Temporal action localization in untrimmed videos via multi-stage CNNs. In: IEEE Conference on Computer Vision and Pattern Recognition, pp. 1049–1058 (2016)
26. Wang, L., Xiong, Y., Lin, D., Van Gool, L.: Untrimmednets for weakly supervised action recognition and detection. In: IEEE Conference on Computer Vision and Pattern Recognition, pp. 4325–4334 (2017)
27. Xu, Y., et al.: Segregated temporal assembly recurrent networks for weakly supervised multiple action detection. In: AAAI Conference on Artificial Intelligence, vol. 33, pp. 9070–9078 (2019)
28. Yang, W., Zhang, T., Yu, X., Qi, T., Zhang, Y., Wu, F.: Uncertainty guided collaborative training for weakly supervised temporal action detection. In: IEEE Conference on Computer Vision and Pattern Recognition, pp. 53–63 (2021)

29. Yu, Z., Yu, J., Cui, Y., Tao, D., Tian, Q.: Deep modular co-attention networks for visual question answering. In: IEEE Conference on Computer Vision and Pattern Recognition, pp. 6281–6290 (2019)
30. Zach, C., Pock, T., Bischof, H.: A duality based approach for realtime TV-L 1 optical flow. In: Joint Pattern Recognition Symposium, pp. 214–223 (2007)
31. Zhang, C., Cao, M., Yang, D., Chen, J., Zou, Y.: CoLA: weakly-supervised temporal action localization with snippet contrastive learning. In: IEEE Conference on Computer Vision and Pattern Recognition, pp. 16010–16019 (2021)
32. Zhang, C., et al.: Adversarial seeded sequence growing for weakly-supervised temporal action localization. In: ACM International Conference on Multimedia, pp. 738–746 (2019)
33. Zhao, Y., Xiong, Y., Wang, L., Wu, Z., Tang, X., Lin, D.: Temporal action detection with structured segment networks. In: International Conference on Computer Vision, pp. 2914–2923 (2017)

# CrGAN: Continuous Rendering of Image Style

Xiaoming Yu[✉] and Gan Zhou

National Computer System Engineering Research Institute of China, Beijing, China
xyuforart@gmail.com

**Abstract.** There are many continuous changes in nature, such as season, day and night, and face aging. These image processing tasks are interesting and somewhat challenging. Therefore, it is necessary to explore the intermediate domains of the transformation. We propose a new image-to-image translation model, named CrGAN, which aims to achieve continuous image translation. This continuous process is usually based on the interpolation of the latent code. CrGAN is different from that. First, images are encoded into content and style, and CrGAN extracts the content code of the source domain images and the style code of the target domain images. Then, we use a new functional instance normalization layer (NEWIN) to control the rendering degree of content and style. NEWIN is linked with the discriminator to form an interpolated adversarial loss to guide the generator to generate the image gradient process. Compared with state-of-the-art, CrGAN shows better performance in face changes, seasonal changes and other work.

**Keywords:** Generative Adversarial Networks (GAN) · Continuous image translation · NEWIN

## 1 Introduction

There have been a lot of studies on single-domain image translation [13,30,36] and multi-domain image translation [4,5,34], and have performed well. Many researchers have also explored image editing and image detail control [1,19,20]. Compared with end-to-end image translation, showing the intermediate translation process is a niche research direction and is full of huge challenges. It has relatively high requirements on image quality and translation smoothness. There have been many works focusing on the intermediate domains in image-to-image (I2I) translation. Disentanglement models such as DRIT [18] and MUNIT [12] encode images into content and style, and the interpolation of source and target domain style code can generate the translation process. Considering the input labels, [32] interpolates relative attributes to achieve continuous image translation. [31] generates continuous images based on model parameter interpolation.

To improve image quality and translation smoothness, we explore the intermediate domains from a new perspective.

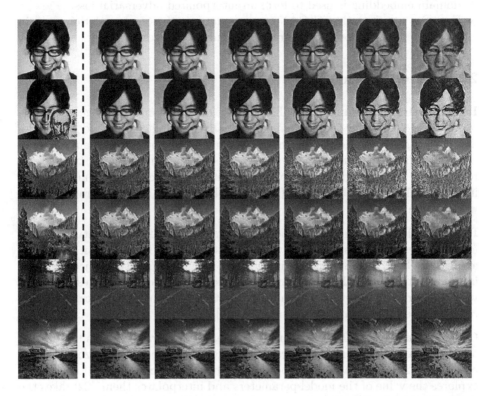

**Fig. 1.** The generated results. We show a continuous mapping of multiple tasks from the source domain to the target domain. The first row and the second row are the Photograph→Portrait task. The third row and the fourth row are the Summer →Winter task. The fifth row is fog image generation. The sixth row is the Van Gogh image generation. The style in the second and fourth rows is from the target domain image, and the rest is sampled from a Gaussian distribution.

Next, we introduce the proposed model CrGAN, which belongs to the disentanglement model, where images are disentangled into content space and style space. Different from the above methods, we do not interpolate the code nor the label, but control the display degree of content and style at the functional instance normalization layer. Therefore, we only need the content code of the source domain images and the style code of the target domain images. Figure 1 shows part of the experiment results. Given a source domain image, CrGAN can achieve continuous image translation by obtaining style from distribution sampling or encoding reference image. Our contributions are as follows:

- We introduce a new functional instance normalization layer NEWIN, which can control the combination degree of content code and style code, and realize continuous transformation across domains.

- We propose a new continuous image translation framework, the generator architecture is used to improve the image quality, and the discriminator with domain embedding is used to form an interpolated adversarial loss.
- Experiments show that CrGAN can complete continuous translation tasks in a variety of scenarios and generate high-quality images.

## 2   Related Works

**Image-to-Image Translation.** I2I translation is to convert images from the source domain to the target domain. Initially researchers focused on single-domain image translation, and it has been further improved from paired images [13,30] to unpaired images [36]. Based on single-domain image translation, researchers use a single generator to simultaneously complete multi-domain image translation with the help of extra labels [4,32,34] or multi-branched network structure [5,19].

**Disentanglement.** Disentanglement is to map different image features to different representation spaces, in which the same type features can be better expressed. [3,8,12,18,34] encode images into content and style, injecting style into content features. In image transformation, [33] encodes images into relevant and irrelevant factors. Domain information disentanglement can separate content code from domain representation [22].

**Continuous Image Translation.** Continuous image translation is the process of dynamically displaying image translation, which is generally realized by interpolation. [32] interpolates the label information representing the domain. [31] explores the value of the model parameters and interpolates them. [22] takes the domain code as a representation and interpolates the domain code. [29] interpolates the image depth features. There is also work [7] to interpolate the learned parameters at the functional instance normalization layer to enable continuous style transfer. [9] extracts the intermediate domains in a flow form. [24] uses the guidance of a physical model to achieve continuous image translation. Another class of methods [27,37] relies on the powerful capability of the StyleGAN pre-trained model [15,16] to interpolate latent code.

## 3   CrGAN

I2I translation, an end-to-end process, is the mapping of the source domain to the target domain. This mapping consists of multiple intermediate domains, but the data of the intermediate domains are often missing and cannot be trained end-to-end. CrGAN learns the combination of source domain image content and target domain image style from disentanglement, showing the intermediate process. We introduce the model overview in Sect. 3.1, the new functional instance normalization layer in Sect. 3.2, and the loss functions in Sect. 3.3.

## 3.1 Model Overview

In CrGAN, the source and target domain images share the content space, and we use the same content encoder to encode the images in both domains. Figure 2 shows the model structure, including the reconstruction process of the target domain image (left) and the translation process from the source domain to the target domain (right). The content encoder $E_c$ and the style encoder $E_s$ extract content code $c$ and style code $s$ from the target domain image $Y$. The two are fused in the generator $G$ to get the reconstructed image. $\ell_{rec}$ represents the image reconstruction loss. The content encoder extracts the content code from the source domain image $X$, and the style code is obtained by sampling from the standard Gaussian distribution $\mathcal{N}(0, I)$ or encoding the reference image. Then, NEWIN fuses content and style. We pass the generated image through the content encoder and the style encoder to get reconstructed content code and style code. With the help of the label $d$, the discriminator $D$ discriminates the authenticity of the intermediate domain images. $\ell_{KL}$ is the KL distance between the style code and the prior distribution, $\ell_c$ is the content reconstruction loss, $\ell_s$ is the style reconstruction loss and $\ell_{adv}$ is the adversarial loss.

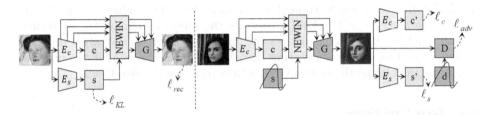

**Fig. 2.** The model structure. The left is the reconstruction of the target domain image, and the right is the translation of the source domain image to the target domain image. The key to the model is that NEWIN controls the fusion of content code and style code. Please refer to the main text for specific integration.

The skip connections of the content feature map can maintain the content structure of the generated images [2], we use the U-Net structure between the content encoder and the generator, and inject style code with NEWIN. Generated continuous images contain both the source and the target domain images. A single discriminator can only discriminate the authenticity of one domain images, and increasing the number of discriminator can increase the pressure of training. We use the basic structure of the discriminator in [34] and inject the label information representing the domain into the discriminator to discriminate the image authenticity from the three image dimensions of (256, 128, 64).

## 3.2    New Instance Normalization

Style transfer is the fusion of the style from one image to another. [28] uses Instance Normalization (IN) to incorporate one style:

$$IN(x) = \gamma \frac{x - \mu}{\sigma} + \beta, \tag{1}$$

where $x$ is the feature map, $\mu$ and $\sigma$ are the mean and standard deviation of the input feature map, $\gamma$ and $\beta$ are the parameters learned by the affine transformation. As an extension, the proposal of AdaIN [11] realizes the fusion of arbitrary style images and arbitrary content images. Besides, [35] proposes a new fusion method CBIN, which uses $tanh$ to handle style code and separates the content part and the style part. We rely on this advantage to propose NEWIN:

$$NEWIN(x, \phi) = (1 + \lambda)\frac{x - \mu}{\sigma} + (1 - \lambda)tanh(f(\phi)), \tag{2}$$

where $f(\cdot)$ is the affine transformation, and $\phi$ is the extra information injected into the feature map. In NEWIN, the first part represents the image content, and the second part represents the image style. $\lambda$ is used as a parameter to control the fusion degree of image content and image style. The value of $\lambda$ is $0 \sim 1$. In extreme cases, $\lambda = 1$, NEWIN controls the image to remain in the source domain, and $\lambda = 0$, NEWIN controls the image to convert to the target domain. When calculating the reconstruction loss, $\lambda = 0$ is held throughout the process, and when calculating the interpolated adversarial loss, $\lambda$ takes $0 \sim 1$.

## 3.3    Loss Functions

In addition to several losses shown in Fig. 2, we apply style loss and mode seeking loss in model training.

**Adversarial Loss.** Adversarial loss serves as the basic loss function of GAN. We use $\lambda$ in NEWIN to represent the interpolated adversarial loss. The computation of adversarial loss uses LSGAN [23]. $D_s$ means that the discriminator embeds the source domain label, $D_t$ means that the discriminator embeds the target domain label.

$$
\begin{aligned}
\ell_{adv}^D =& \lambda(\|D_s(X) - 1\|_2 + \|D_s(G(E_c(X), p(s))) - 0\|_2) \\
& + (1 - \lambda)(\|D_t(Y) - 1\|_2 + \|D_t(G(E_c(X), p(s))) - 0\|_2),
\end{aligned} \tag{3}
$$

$$\ell_{adv}^G = \lambda\|D_s(G(E_c(X), p(s))) - 1\|_2 + (1 - \lambda)\|D_t(G(E_c(X), p(s))) - 1\|_2. \tag{4}$$

**Image Reconstruction Loss.** The source domain and the target domain share the content space and have independent style space, therefore, we calculate the reconstruction loss of the target domain image. L1 norm is used to calculate the image reconstruction loss.

$$\ell_{rec} = \|G(E_c(Y), E_s(Y)) - Y\|_1. \tag{5}$$

**Style Reconstruction Loss.** For the generator to take full advantage of the style code, we compute the style reconstruction loss. One part is the sampled code $p(s)$ from the prior distribution, and the other part is the style code extracted by the style encoder from the generated image.

$$\ell_s = \|E_s(G(E_c(X), p(s))) - p(s)\|_1. \tag{6}$$

**Content Reconstruction Loss.** To keep the deep semantics of the generated image unchanged, we compute the content reconstruction loss of the generated image.

$$\ell_c = \|E_c(G(E_c(X), p(s))) - E_c(X)\|_1. \tag{7}$$

**Style Loss.** The generation tasks include two forms of reference image and latent code. The style transfer of the reference image is very difficult, and the style loss [14] encourage the generated image to inherit the style of the reference image. VGG19 is used as a pre-trained model to extract style features. The selection ratios of conv1_1, conv2_1, conv3_1, conv4_1, and conv5_1 outputs are 0.1, 0.2, 0.4, 0.8, and 1.6, respectively. The style features are represented by gram matrix.

$$\ell_{style} = \|Gram(VGG(G(E_c(X), E_s(Y)))) - Gram(VGG(Y))\|_1. \tag{8}$$

**KL Loss.** VAE [17] is used as the style encoder, and the KL distance is used to optimize the style code gradually close to the Gaussian prior distribution.

$$\ell_{KL} = KL(E_s(Y)\|p(s)). \tag{9}$$

**Mode Seeking Loss.** In order to solve the mode collapse and ensure the diversity of the generated images, we use mode seeking loss [21] to train the model.

$$\ell_{ms} = \frac{\|p_1(s) - p_2(s)\|_1}{\|G(E_c(X), p_1(s)) - G(E_c(X), p_2(s))\|_1}. \tag{10}$$

**Total Loss.** Through the above loss functions, we get the loss functions of the generation part and the discrimination part.

$$\ell_D = \ell_{adv}^D, \tag{11}$$

$$\ell_G = \ell_{adv}^G + \lambda_{rec}\ell_{rec} + \lambda_c\ell_c + \lambda_s\ell_s + \lambda_{style}\ell_{style} + \lambda_{KL}\ell_{KL} + \lambda_{ms}\ell_{ms}. \tag{12}$$

**Training Strategy.** The training tasks maintain a learning rate of 0.0001 and a batchsize of 2. The optimizer uses Adam with parameters set to (0.5, 0.999). The weights of the losses are $\lambda_{rec} = 10$, $\lambda_c = 1$, $\lambda_s = 10$, $\lambda_{style} = 1$, $\lambda_{KL} = 0.01$, $\lambda_{ms} = 1$. The image size is kept at 256256. Experiments are performed in NVIDIA RTX 3080.

## 4    Experiments

In this section, we demonstrate the continuous translation capability of CrGAN. First, we introduce the datasets and baselines. Next, a comparison of image quality and an ablation of structures are performed, followed by the generated results of some additional tasks.

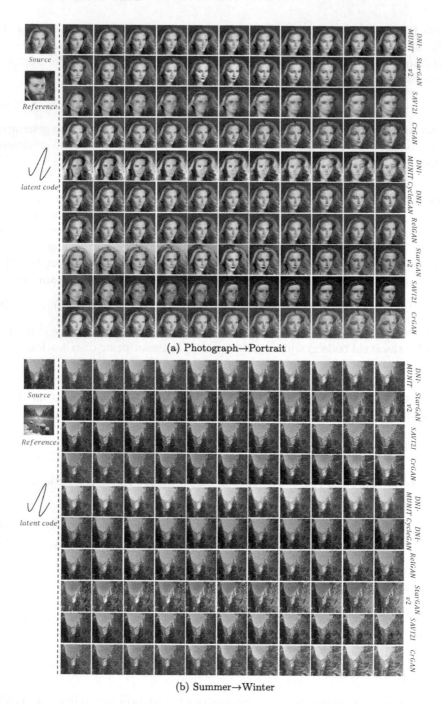

**Fig. 3.** Comparison of the results. In each subgraph, the style of the first four rows is from the reference image, and the style of the last six rows is the randomly sampled latent code.

## 4.1 Datasets

**Photograph→Portrait.** DRIT [18] provides a public dataset Portrait. The train set involves 6352 photograph and 1714 portrait. The number of both in the test set is 100.

**Summer→Winter.** The summer2winter_yosimite dataset is provided by Cycle-GAN [36]. The number of summer and winter images in the train set and test set is 1231/962 and 309/238.

**Additional Tasks.** The fog scene generation task uses the cityscapes dataset [6] and the computer-generated smoke dataset [25]. The dataset used for Van Gogh oil painting conversion is also provided by CycleGAN [36]. In addition, we pick cat and dog images in [5] to convert cat to dog.

## 4.2 Baselines

We use five continuous translation methods as baselines. DNI [31] interpolates model parameters and we combine it with MUNIT [12] and CycleGAN [36]. Rel-GAN [32] generates a continuous translation process through the interpolation of labels. StarGAN v2 [5] utilizes a multi-branch encoder for multi-domain image translation, and we interpolate source and target domain style code to generate a continuous process. SAVI2I [22] interpolates the domain code to generate continuous and diverse images.

## 4.3 Image Quality

**Visual Evaluation.** The output nodes of baselines are divided between 0 and 1 with an interval of 0.1. The output nodes of CrGAN are divided between 1 and 0 with an interval of 0.1. Figure 3 shows the generated results of CrGAN and baselines. In Fig. 3a, the style rendering degree in the images generated by DNI·MUNIT is insufficient, and the differences between the source domain images and the target domain images are minor. StarGAN v2 and SAVI2I generate realistic images, but intermediate domain images suffer from color distortion or artifacts, and the identity information of the source domain images cannot be preserved. The generation processes of DNI·CycleGAN and RelGAN are continuous, but for the target domain images, the rendering degree is not enough. CrGAN maintains the identity information of the original images and has smooth intermediate processes. In Fig. 3b, DNI·MUNIT cannot continuously transform the style of the reference image. DNI·CycleGAN and RelGAN cannot adequately transform the domain. StarGAN v2, SAVI2I and CrGAN can all generate a continuous transformation process, but in comparison, CrGAN generates the image style closest to the reference, and the images are the most realistic.

**Numerical Evaluation.** Frechet inception distance (FID) [10] evaluates the quality of the generated images by computing the similarity between the distribution of the generated images and the distribution of the target domain images.

The lower the value, the more similar the distributions are. Domain-invariant perceptual distance (DIPD) [12] is used to evaluate the content retention, the source domain images and the generated images are used as input, the lower the value, the more similar the content structure. Inception score (IS) [26] evaluates the diversity of the generated images, the higher the value, the richer the generated images. For multi-output models, DNI·MUNIT, StarGAN v2, SAVI2I, we choose the first 100 images of the test set, and at each output node, 10 images are randomly generated per input image. For single-output models, DNI·CycleGAN, RelGAN, we use all test set images for numerical comparison.

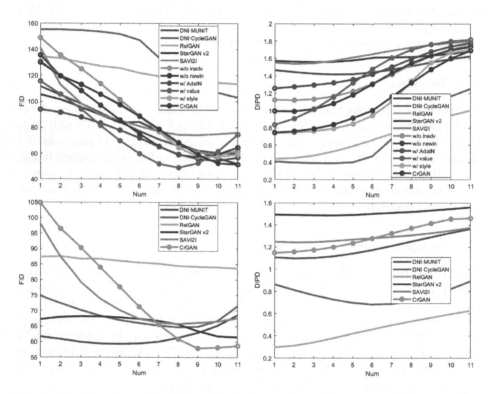

**Fig. 4.** Quality comparison. We evaluate the quality of the generated images using FID and content retention using DIPD. The first row is the comparison result of Photograph→Portrait. The second row is the comparison result of Summer→Winter.

Figure 4 shows the comparison results of FID and DIPD. In the two tasks of Photograph→Portrait and Summer→Winter, the FID of CrGAN has the best change effect, and the FID of the target domain images has reached the minimum, which are 51.47 and 58.76, respectively. In Photograph→Portrait, the DIPD of the single-output models is kept to a minimum. But compared to the multi-output models, the images generated by CrGAN maintain the best content structure throughout the transformation. In Summer→Winter, the DIPD

of CrGAN is not optimal, but from the perspective of FID, there is little difference between the source domain images and the target domain images generated
by DNI·MUNIT, DNI·CycleGAN and RelGAN, so the value of DIPD is always
kept low. We calculate the IS of each output node images and take the average
of 11 output nodes as the IS result for each model. As can be seen from Table 1,
CrGAN ranks second in both generation tasks, and the generated images are
relatively diverse.

**Table 1.** The results of IS in comparison experiments.

| Task | DNI·MUNIT | DNI·CycleGAN | RelGAN | StarGAN v2 | SAVI2I | CrGAN |
|------|-----------|--------------|--------|------------|--------|-------|
| Photograph→Portrait | 2.728 | 2.879 | 2.605 | 2.988 | 2.891 | 2.934 |
| Summer→Winter | 2.221 | 2.717 | 2.384 | 2.050 | 2.137 | 2.486 |

**Table 2.** The results of IS in ablation experiments.

| Task | w/o inadv | w/o newin | w/ AdaIN | w/ value | w/ style | CrGAN |
|------|-----------|-----------|----------|----------|----------|-------|
| Photograph→Portrait | 2.687 | 2.603 | 2.900 | 2.746 | 2.770 | 2.934 |

### 4.4  Ablation Study

To verify the effectiveness of the proposed model, we ablate NEWIN and interpolated adversarial loss (w/o inadv). We verify NEWIN from four aspects.
(1) w/o newin. When NEWIN is represented as $(1 + \lambda)\frac{x-\mu}{\sigma} + \lambda tanh(f(\phi))$,
$\lambda$ takes a continuous value from 0 to 1. As $\lambda$ increases, the style part and
the content part increase at the same time. (2) w/ AdaIN. Content part and
style part are not separated in AdaIN. We modify AdaIN to $AdaIN(x, \phi) =$
$(1 + \lambda)\sigma(\phi)\frac{x-\mu}{\sigma} + (1 - \lambda)\mu(\phi)$ and use it to fuse content and style. In the modified AdaIN, the first part approximates the content representation, and the sec-
ond part approximates the style representation. (3) w/ value. The value of $\lambda$ in
NEWIN is different from that of normal interpolation. According to the presence
or absence of style and content, its value ranges from −1 to 1. As $\lambda$ decreases,
the style part gradually increases, but the content part gradually disappears. We
add a set of experiments with $\lambda$ ranging from −0.2 to 1 to verify whether the
absence of content part can increase the image quality. (4) w/ style. Both the
content part and the style part in NEWIN keep changing. Next, we only control
one of the partial changes. When the representation is $\lambda\frac{x-\mu}{\sigma} + tanh(f(\phi))$, only
the content part changes. If $\lambda$ is 0, the content part disappears, which is unreasonable. Therefore, we only control for changes in the style part to verify the
effect of a single part change on the results $(NEWIN = \frac{x-\mu}{\sigma} + \lambda tanh(f(\phi)))$.

**Fig. 5.** Comparison results of ablation experiments.

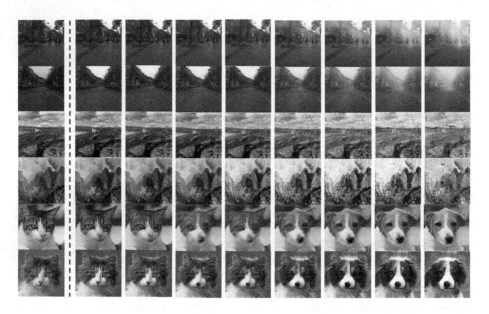

**Fig. 6.** Additional tasks. In addition to the above comparative experiments, we add several sets of generative experiments with different scenarios.

Figure 5 is the results of the ablation experiment. When the interpolated adversarial loss is missing, the source domain image cannot be preserved and there is color distortion. w/o newin means the changed NEWIN, when the style and content parts increase at the same time, the network cannot distinguish the difference between the two, resulting in the deviation of the identity information and the image artifacts. In modified AdaIN, the network also cannot distinguish the approximated style and content, and the generated images have serious artifacts. w/ value and w/ style are the closest to CrGAN, both generating a continuous change process. As can be seen from the ablation experiment part of Fig. 4, CrGAN maintains a smooth generation process and maintains optimal FID and DIPD. We can see from the w/ value curve that the FID first decreases and then increases. This means that when the content part is gradually missing, making the style part continue to overlap, which does not increase the image quality. The last three node FIDs in w/ style curve are basically no longer changed, and only changing the style part cannot show a better process. Table 2 includes the IS results of the ablation experiments, where CrGAN reaches the maximum and generates the most diverse images.

### 4.5   Additional Tasks

In portrait transformation and season transformation, the effectiveness of CrGAN has been verified. We conduct several additional experiments: fog image generation, Van Gogh image transformation, animal face transformation. Figure 6 is the generated results, the images are all continuously transformed cross domains.

## 5   Conclusion

We propose CrGAN, a new framework to demonstrate the continuous process of image translation. It only inputs the content of the source domain image and the style of the target domain image, a new functional instance normalization layer, named NEWIN, to control the fusion degree of style and content. With the control parameter in NEWIN, the discriminator can learn the state of intermediate domains and guide the generator to generate intermediate domain images. Through comparative experiments and ablation experiments, we prove that the proposed method can generate high-quality and continuously transformed images. The direction for further study is to extend and practice the model in several applications, such as video rendering, art painting and so on.

## References

1. Abdal, R., Zhu, P., Mitra, N.J., Wonka, P.: StyleFlow: attribute-conditioned exploration of styleGAN-generated images using conditional continuous normalizing flows. TOG **40**(3), 1–21 (2021)
2. Anokhin, I., et al.: High-resolution daytime translation without domain labels. In: CVPR, pp. 7488–7497 (2020)
3. Chang, H.-Y., Wang, Z., Chuang, Y.-Y.: Domain-specific mappings for generative adversarial style transfer. In: Vedaldi, A., Bischof, H., Brox, T., Frahm, J.-M. (eds.) ECCV 2020. LNCS, vol. 12353, pp. 573–589. Springer, Cham (2020). https://doi.org/10.1007/978-3-030-58598-3_34

4. Choi, Y., Choi, M., Kim, M., Ha, J.W., Kim, S., Choo, J.: StarGAN: unified generative adversarial networks for multi-domain image-to-image translation. In: CVPR, pp. 8789–8797 (2018)
5. Choi, Y., Uh, Y., Yoo, J., Ha, J.W.: StarGAN V2: diverse image synthesis for multiple domains. In: CVPR, pp. 8188–8197 (2020)
6. Cordts, M., et al.: The cityscapes dataset for semantic urban scene understanding. In: CVPR, pp. 3213–3223 (2016)
7. Dumoulin, V., Shlens, J., Kudlur, M.: A learned representation for artistic style. ICLR (2017)
8. Gabbay, A., Hoshen, Y.: Improving style-content disentanglement in image-to-image translation. arXiv preprint arXiv:2007.04964 (2020)
9. Gong, R., Li, W., Chen, Y., Gool, L.V.: DLOW: domain flow for adaptation and generalization. In: CVPR, pp. 2477–2486 (2019)
10. Heusel, M., Ramsauer, H., Unterthiner, T., Nessler, B., Hochreiter, S.: GANs trained by a two time-scale update rule converge to a local nash equilibrium. In: NeurIPS, vol. 30 (2017)
11. Huang, X., Belongie, S.: Arbitrary style transfer in real-time with adaptive instance normalization. In: ICCV, pp. 1501–1510 (2017)
12. Huang, X., Liu, M.-Y., Belongie, S., Kautz, J.: Multimodal unsupervised image-to-image translation. In: Ferrari, V., Hebert, M., Sminchisescu, C., Weiss, Y. (eds.) ECCV 2018. LNCS, vol. 11207, pp. 179–196. Springer, Cham (2018). https://doi.org/10.1007/978-3-030-01219-9_11
13. Isola, P., Zhu, J.Y., Zhou, T., Efros, A.A.: Image-to-image translation with conditional adversarial networks. In: CVPR, pp. 1125–1134 (2017)
14. Johnson, J., Alahi, A., Fei-Fei, L.: Perceptual losses for real-time style transfer and super-resolution. In: Leibe, B., Matas, J., Sebe, N., Welling, M. (eds.) ECCV 2016. LNCS, vol. 9906, pp. 694–711. Springer, Cham (2016). https://doi.org/10.1007/978-3-319-46475-6_43
15. Karras, T., Laine, S., Aila, T.: A style-based generator architecture for generative adversarial networks. In: CVPR, pp. 4401–4410 (2019)
16. Karras, T., Laine, S., Aittala, M., Hellsten, J., Lehtinen, J., Aila, T.: Analyzing and improving the image quality of styleGAN. In: CVPR, pp. 8110–8119 (2020)
17. Kingma, D.P., Welling, M.: Auto-encoding variational bayes. arXiv preprint arXiv:1312.6114 (2013)
18. Lee, H.-Y., Tseng, H.-Y., Huang, J.-B., Singh, M., Yang, M.-H.: Diverse image-to-image translation via disentangled representations. In: Ferrari, V., Hebert, M., Sminchisescu, C., Weiss, Y. (eds.) ECCV 2018. LNCS, vol. 11205, pp. 36–52. Springer, Cham (2018). https://doi.org/10.1007/978-3-030-01246-5_3
19. Li, X., et al.: Image-to-image translation via hierarchical style disentanglement. In: CVPR, pp. 8639–8648 (2021)
20. Lin, J., Zhang, R., Ganz, F., Han, S., Zhu, J.Y.: Anycost GANs for interactive image synthesis and editing. In: CVPR, pp. 14986–14996 (2021)
21. Mao, Q., Lee, H.Y., Tseng, H.Y., Ma, S., Yang, M.H.: Mode seeking generative adversarial networks for diverse image synthesis. In: CVPR, pp. 1429–1437 (2019)
22. Mao, Q., Tseng, H.Y., Lee, H.Y., Huang, J.B., Ma, S., Yang, M.H.: Continuous and diverse image-to-image translation via signed attribute vectors. IJCV **130**, 1–33 (2022)
23. Mao, X., Li, Q., Xie, H., Lau, R.Y., Wang, Z., Paul Smolley, S.: Least squares generative adversarial networks. In: ICCV, pp. 2794–2802 (2017)
24. Pizzati, F., Cerri, P., de Charette, R.: CoMoGAN: continuous model-guided image-to-image translation. In: CVPR, pp. 14288–14298 (2021)

25. Sakaridis, C., Dai, D., Van Gool, L.: Semantic foggy scene understanding with synthetic data. IJCV **126**(9), 973–992 (2018)
26. Salimans, T., Goodfellow, I., Zaremba, W., Cheung, V., Radford, A., Chen, X.: Improved techniques for training GANs. In: NeurIPS, vol. 29 (2016)
27. Shen, Y., Gu, J., Tang, X., Zhou, B.: Interpreting the latent space of GANs for semantic face editing. In: CVPR, pp. 9243–9252 (2020)
28. Ulyanov, D., Vedaldi, A., Lempitsky, V.: Improved texture networks: maximizing quality and diversity in feed-forward stylization and texture synthesis. In: CVPR, pp. 6924–6932 (2017)
29. Upchurch, P., et al.: Deep feature interpolation for image content changes. In: CVPR, pp. 7064–7073 (2017)
30. Wang, T.C., Liu, M.Y., Zhu, J.Y., Tao, A., Kautz, J., Catanzaro, B.: High-resolution image synthesis and semantic manipulation with conditional GANs. In: CVPR, pp. 8798–8807 (2018)
31. Wang, X., Yu, K., Dong, C., Tang, X., Loy, C.C.: Deep network interpolation for continuous imagery effect transition. In: CVPR, pp. 1692–1701 (2019)
32. Wu, P.W., Lin, Y.J., Chang, C.H., Chang, E.Y., Liao, S.W.: RelGAN: multi-domain image-to-image translation via relative attributes. In: ICCV, pp. 5914–5922 (2019)
33. Xiao, T., Hong, J., Ma, J.: DNA-GAN: learning disentangled representations from multi-attribute images. In: ICLR Workshops (2018)
34. Yu, X., Chen, Y., Liu, S., Li, T., Li, G.: Multi-mapping image-to-image translation via learning disentanglement. In: NeurIPS, vol. 32 (2019)
35. Yu, X., Ying, Z., Li, T., Liu, S., Li, G.: Multi-mapping image-to-image translation with central biasing normalization. arXiv preprint arXiv:1806.10050 (2018)
36. Zhu, J.Y., Park, T., Isola, P., Efros, A.A.: Unpaired image-to-image translation using cycle-consistent adversarial networks. In: ICCV, pp. 2223–2232 (2017)
37. Zhuang, P., Koyejo, O., Schwing, A.G.: Enjoy your editing: controllable GANs for image editing via latent space navigation. ICLR (2021)

# DPCN: Dual Path Convolutional Network for Single Image Deraining

Wenhao Zhang[1], Yue Zhou[1], Shukai Duan[1,2,3], and Xiaofang Hu[1,2,3](✉)

[1] College of Artificial Intelligence, Southwest University, Chongqing 400715, China
[2] Brain-inspired Computing & Intelligent Control of Chongqing Key Lab, Chongqing 400715, China
[3] Key Laboratory of Luminescence Analysis and Molecular Sensing (Southwest University), Ministry of Education, Chongqing, China
huxf@swu.edu.cn

**Abstract.** The visual effect of images captured on rainy days is severely degraded, even making some computer vision or multimedia tasks fail to work. Therefore, image rain removal is crucial for these visions and multimedia tasks. However, most existing works cannot strike a good balance between removing rain streaks and restoring the corresponding background detail. To address this problem, this paper proposes an effective dual path convolutional network (DPCN) for single image rain removal. Specifically, we complete the positioning, extraction and separation of rain streaks through multiple dual path units. Firstly, considering the irregularity of the size, density and shape distribution of rain streaks, a pixel-wise attention mechanism is applied to pinpoint the position of rain streaks. Simultaneously, for these rain streaks distributed across regions, we propose a multiscale aggregation method to extract and fuse features at different scales. Further, for some backgrounds with similar texture details as the rain streaks, we introduce a self-calibration operation that separates the rain streaks from these background details by adaptively constructing long-range spatial and internal channel dependencies at each spatial location. By cleverly combining multiple dual path units through a dual path topology, our network obtains rain removal results that are closer to the real background and largely remove rain streaks. The quantitative and qualitative results on synthetic and real datasets show that our proposed DPCN is superior to other state-of-the-art methods.

**Keywords:** Single image deraining · Dual path · Convolutional neural networks · Attention mechanisms

## 1 Introduction

The image processing task in computer vision requires clean background images as input, but the images collected in real-world scenarios are usually corrupted by rain, resulting in the reduction of image quality, which hurts the image processing results [4,30,35]. Hence, image deraining has become a critical preprocessing work in many tasks and applications, e.g., semantic segmentation and image restoration.

In the early period, the image rain removal problem is mainly solved by establishing a model based on the prior information of rain-free images or rain streaks. The most widely known model-based methods are as follows: image decomposition, low-rank model, spare coding, Gaussian mixture models [3,14,15,17,20]. While removing rain streaks, these prior-based methods often perform deraining operations in other rain-free areas, resulting in image smoothing in these regions. In addition, the limited generalization ability of these predefined models makes them perform poorly in recovering the image regions with similar texture details as rain streaks. Recently, deep learning based image deraining algorithms have been proposed one after another. They address the image deraining problem by building an end-to-end mapping between the rain images and the ground-truth. The well-known methods based on deep learning are as follows: deep convolutional neural networks, semi/unsupervised methods, and generative adversarial networks [6,11,30,34]. Although much progress has been made with these methods, there are still some shortcomings. It is mainly reflected in two aspects: First, they perform well on synthetic datasets but poorly on real-world datasets. Secondly, the rain-free background image cannot be recovered well while removing the rain streaks.

Considering these limitations of existing methods, we propose an effective dual path convolutional network for single image deraining, which is mainly composed of three modules: 1)Positioning Module, 2)Extraction Module, 3) Separation Module. Firstly, in order that rain streaks of different size, density and shape can be accurately positioned, we propose a Positioning Module, which uses Polarized Self-Attention that performs well in pixel-wise regression tasks. While maintaining high internal resolution in spatial and channel attention computation, this module directly fits the output distribution of typical fine-grained regression with non-linear function combination, which dramatically enhances the rain removal performance. Secondly, we design a Extraction Module that uses three different convolution kernels to obtain multi-scale information. Meanwhile, deep separable convolution is used in place of standard convolution to avoid generating too many parameters and calculations. Thirdly, to deal with the background with similar texture details as the rain streaks, we design a Separation Module that uses convolution operations performed in two different scale spaces to explicitly expand each layer's receptive field, which helps the network to generate more discriminative representations. By uniting the three modules in a dual path topology, the proposed method has better deraining performance that can be able to remove various rain streaks and preserve better details.

## 2   Related Works

**Traditional Methods.** Traditional methods exploit image priors to address the problem of single image deraining. Luo et al. [20] develop a discriminative sparse coding method that can accurately separate the rain and rain-free background layers. Kim et al. [15] first analyze the direction and the shape of the elliptical kernel to identify rain streak regions, and then remove the detected rain streaks by using the adaptive non-local means filter. Chang et al. [1] use the local and non-local sparsity of the image layer to analyze the relationship between the noisy and clean image. And they propose a method based on the composition directional total variational to solve the problem of image rain removal. Zhu et al. [36] analyze the local gradient information in rain images to determine the regions of rain streaks and then separate the rain streaks from the rain images according to the preset priors under the premise that rain streaks usually span a small area.

**Deep Learning Methods.** With the development of deep neural networks, deep learning methods are gradually replacing traditional methods. Zhang and Patel [33] propose a densely connected convolutional neural network to automatically estimate rain-density information and eliminate rain streaks using the predicted rain-density label. In [16], they present a deep recurrent neural network architecture that incorporates the squeeze-and-excitation block to allocate each alpha value to the rain streak according to intensity and transparency. Wang et al. [24] propose a semi-automatic method and design a spatial attentive network to solve the problem of single image rain removal in a local-to-global manner. In [27], they create a fractal band learning network that injects self-supervision, which is beneficial for removing rain streaks at different scales. Fu et al. [7] design a dual graph convolutional network to handle complex and spatially long rain streaks.

## 3   Proposed Network

This section details the proposed dual path convolutional network for single image rain removal, called DPCN. We use residual connections to realize the reuse of rain streak features. Meanwhile, in order to take full advantage of features at different levels, we use dense connections to connect multiple dual path units that consist of Positioning Module, Extraction Module, and Separation Module.

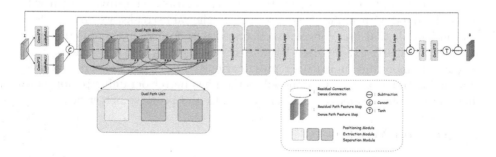

**Fig. 1.** Overview of our proposed DPCN for single image rain removal.

Specifically, given a rainy image $I$, we first input it into two convolutional layers to get the residual path feature map and the dense path feature map. Then, they are concatenated together and input into the dual path block to complete the positioning, extraction and separation of the rain streaks. To balance the number of channels and computational efficiency, we insert a transition layer after each dual path block. Finally, the corresponding rain-free background $B$ is obtained by subtracting pixel by pixel: $B = I - R$. As explained in Fig. 1, the overall structure of our proposed DPCN is given.

## 3.1 Positioning Module

In computer vision, attention mechanisms enhance convolution calculations by acting on the input tensor to highlight or suppress features. Most of the existing attention mechanisms [8,10,26] try to achieve the best compromise among multiple tasks, e.g., instance segmentation, object localization, image classification, etc. Still, they cannot estimate the highly non-linear pixel-wise semantics in fine-grained regression. Therefore, they perform poorly for image deraining problem in the pixel-wise regression. To avoid this problem, we introduce the Polarized Self-Attention [18] in the Positioning Module. The overall structure of the Polarized Self-Attention is described in Fig. 2.

Given an intermediate feature map $\mathbf{X} \in \mathbb{R}^{C \times H \times W}$ as input, the first step is to generate 1D channel features $\mathbf{M_c} \in \mathbb{R}^{C \times 1 \times 1}$ by the channel attention module that model the global relationships across channels in the feature map. As shown in the upper part of Fig. 2, the general formula for the channel attention module is:

$$\mathbf{M_c}(\mathbf{X}) = F_{SD}\Big[Conv_3\Big(\sigma_1\big(Conv_1(\mathbf{X})\big) \times \big(F_{SM}(\sigma_2(Conv_2(\mathbf{X})))\big)^T\Big)\Big], \quad (1)$$

where $Conv_1$, $Conv_2$ and $Conv_3$ are $1 \times 1$ convolution layers respectively, $\sigma_1$ and $\sigma_2$ represent two tensor reshape operators, $(\cdot)^T$ and " $\times$ " are matrix transpose and matrix dot-product operations. $F_{SM}(\cdot)$ and $F_{SD}(\cdot)$ represent SoftMax function and Sigmoid function, respectively. And then $\mathbf{M_c}$ is mapped to $\mathbf{X}$ to generate the channel attention feature map $\mathbf{X_{ch}} \in \mathbb{R}^{C \times H \times W}$. In the second step, the obtained $\mathbf{X_{ch}}$ is input into the spatial attention module to generate 2D spatial features $\mathbf{M_s} \in \mathbb{R}^{1 \times H \times W}$ to explore the global spatial relationships between pixels in the feature map. As shown in the lower part of Fig. 2, formulating the calculation of the spatial attention module can be expressed as:

$$\mathbf{M_s}(\mathbf{X}) = F_{SD}\Big[\sigma_3\big((\sigma_1(F_{GP}(Conv_1(\mathbf{X}))))^T \times F_{SM}(\sigma_2(Conv_2(\mathbf{X})))\big)\Big], \quad (2)$$

where $F_{GP}(\cdot)$ is a global pooling operator, here is the average pooling $F_{GP}(\mathbf{X}) = \frac{1}{H \times W} \sum_{i=1}^{H} \sum_{j=1}^{W} X(:,i,j)$. Then the final output $\mathbf{X_{out}} \in \mathbb{R}^{C \times H \times W}$ of the entire attention module is obtained by mapping $\mathbf{M_s}$ to $\mathbf{X_{ch}}$.

Both channel attention and spatial attention benefit from two critical designs of high-quality pixel-wise regression: 1) maintaining high internal resolution in the computation of spatial and channel attention while entirely collapsing input tensors along their counterpart dimension, 2) using a combination of non-linear functions composed of Sigmoid and SoftMax to directly fit the output distribution of typical fine-grained regression, which allows our Positioning Module to precisely localize irregularly distributed rain streaks, thus improving the rain removal performance of the network.

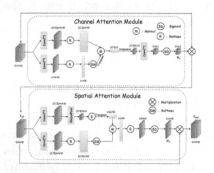

**Fig. 2.** Diagram of the Polarized Self-Attention.

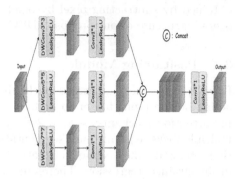

**Fig. 3.** Diagram of our proposed Extraction Module.

## 3.2   Extraction Module

Rational use of feature information at different scales is an effective means to improve network performance. Thus, we design an efficient Extraction Module that exploits the idea of multi-scale aggregation to extract rain streak details at different scales. Most of the existing scale aggregation algorithms utilize dilated convolutions [32], which employ different dilated factors to control the size of convolution kernels and use the difference in the size of the convolution kernel to extract multi-scale information. Although the dilated convolution operator can expand receptive fields without introducing additional parameters, there is a problem in the convolution process: not all rain streaks pixels are calculated. Such an approach leads to a loss of information continuity, which has a detrimental effect on the pixel-level rain removal task. To avoid this problem, we first perform feature extraction using convolutional kernels of sizes $3 \times 3$, $5 \times 5$ and $7 \times 7$, and then aggregate the feature information at different scales. In addition, in order to achieve a balance between parameters and efficiency, depthwise separable convolutions [9] are used instead of conventional convolutions. As shown in Sect. 4, the ablation study results in Table 3 verify the effectiveness of our proposed Extraction Module.

In Fig. 3, given the input feature map $\mathbf{X_{in}} \in \mathbb{R}^{C \times H \times W}$, it is subjected to depthwise convolutions with three convolution kernels of different sizes to complete feature extraction operations at different scales. Subsequently, the obtained feature maps are input to pointwise convolutions for feature fusion. This process can be formulated as:

$$\mathbf{X^i} = LReLU(Conv_1(LReLU(DWConv_i(\mathbf{X_{in}})))), \tag{3}$$

where $DWConv_{i \times i}(\cdot)$ represent depthwise convolutions with the convolution kernel size of $i \times i$, $LReLU(\cdot)$ is an activation function with the negative slope of 0.2, $Conv_{1 \times 1}$ represents $1 \times 1$ convolution, and $\mathbf{X^i}$ represents the feature map of different scales obtained from the convolution kernel of size $i \times i$. Finally, all features are aggregated together by $1 \times 1$ convolution get the final output $\mathbf{X_{out}} \in \mathbb{R}^{C \times H \times W}$ of the Extraction Module::

$$\mathbf{X_{out}} = LReLU(Conv_1(Concat[\mathbf{X^3}, \mathbf{X^5}, \mathbf{X^7}])). \tag{4}$$

where $Concat[\cdot]$ denotes the concatenation operation. Moreover, the stride of all the above convolution operations is 1.

### 3.3 Separation Module

In the process of locating and extracting the rain streaks, it is inevitable that the rain streaks and the background with similar texture details will be mixed together, which will lead to some loss of background details. Therefore, we propose a Separation Module to separate them, which utilizes self-calibration operation [19] and adopts different processing strategies according to the characteristics of different paths to enhance the feature transformation ability of the convolutional layers. The details are shown in Fig. 4.

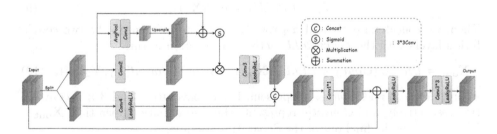

**Fig. 4.** Diagram of our designed Separation Module.

Given the input dual path feature map $\mathbf{X_{in}} \in \mathbb{R}^{C_{in} \times H \times W}$, according to the different paths, it is divided into two parts: a dense path feature map $\mathbf{X_1} \in \mathbb{R}^{C_d \times H \times W}$ in the upper branch and a residual path feature map $\mathbf{X_2} \in \mathbb{R}^{C_r \times H \times W}$ in the lower branch.

For the dense path feature map $\mathbf{X_1}$, we perform the self-calibration operation using three different $3 \times 3$ convolutions $\{Conv1, Conv2, Conv3\}$ to obtain $\mathbf{Y_1} \in \mathbb{R}^{C_d \times H \times W}$. This operation is performed in two spatial dimensions: an original scale and a small-scale space after down-sampling. For the given $\mathbf{X_1}$, average pooling is adopted to complete down-sampling:

$$\mathbf{T_1} = Avgpool_r(\mathbf{X_1}), \tag{5}$$

where $r$ represents the stride and down-sampling rate of the average pooling. Thanks to the down-sampling layer, the fields-of-view at each spatial location of $\mathbf{T_1}$ is significantly expanded. Then, the feature transformation of $\mathbf{T_1}$ is performed using the $Conv1$ operation:

$$\mathbf{X'_1} = Up(Conv1(\mathbf{T_1})), \tag{6}$$

where $Up(\cdot)$ represents a bilinear interpolation operation, which restores $\mathbf{T_1}$ to its original scale. After transformation, intermediate references are used to guide the feature transformation process in the original feature space to complete the calibration operation:

$$\mathbf{Y'_1} = Conv2(\mathbf{X_1}) \otimes F_{SM}(\mathbf{X_1} + \mathbf{X'_1}), \tag{7}$$

where $\otimes$ represents element-wise multiplication operation and $F_{SM}(\cdot)$ is the Sigmoid function. As shown in Eq. 7, we add $\mathbf{X'_1}$ as residuals to the dense path feature map $\mathbf{X_1}$, which is beneficial for calibration operation. The final output of the upper half calibration branch can be written as follows:

$$\mathbf{Y_1} = LReLU\big(Conv3(\mathbf{X_1})\big). \tag{8}$$

For the residual path feature map $\mathbf{X_2}$, the $Conv4(\cdot)$ is used to retain the original spatial context information to obtain $\mathbf{Y_2} \in \mathbb{R}^{C_r \times H \times W}$. The formula is as follows:

$$\mathbf{Y_2} = LReLU\big(Conv4(\mathbf{X_2})\big), \tag{9}$$

Then, we concatenate $\mathbf{Y_1}$ and $\mathbf{Y_2}$ together, and input them to the two convolution layers with the $LeakyReLU$ activation function in turn:

$$\mathbf{X_{out}} = LReLU\big(Conv_{3\times3}(LReLU(\mathbf{X_{in}} + Conv_{1\times1}(Concat[\mathbf{Y_1}, \mathbf{Y_2}])))\big), \tag{10}$$

where $Conv_{1\times1}$ and $Conv_{3\times3}$ represent $1 \times 1$ convolution and $3 \times 3$ convolution respectively, and $Concat[\cdot]$ represents the concatenation operation. $\mathbf{X_{out}} \in \mathbb{R}^{C_{out} \times H \times W}$ is the final out of the Separation Module.

### 3.4    Loss Function

The loss function of the most widely used training network in the single image rain removal problem is the mean square error ($MSE$). However, due to its $\mathcal{L}_2$ penalty, it usually results in blurred and over-smoothed results. We adopt the loss function combining $MSE$ with Structural Similarity ($SSIM$) to address this problem. The total loss can be defined as follows:

$$L_{total} = MSE(B,T) + \alpha[1 - SSIM(B,T)]. \tag{11}$$

where $\alpha$ is the hyper-parameter that balances the weights between the $MSE$ and $SSIM$, $B$ and $T$ are the derained image and the corresponding ground truth.

# 4 Experimental Results

In this section, we evaluate the proposed method on widely used two real-world datasets and four synthetic datasets. Meanwhile, to demonstrate the superiority of our proposed DPCN, we compare ten state-of-the-art image deraining algorithms published in the last four years. We first introduce the datasets and metrics, then describe the implementation details, and finally show the results compared with these image deraining algorithms.

## 4.1 Datasets and Metrics

**Datasets.** We experimentally demonstrate the effectiveness of DPCN on four synthetic datasets Rain200L [29], Rain200H [29], Rain800 [34] and Rain1200 [33], and two real-world datasets. Rain200L and Rain200H has 1,800 rainy/clean pairs of images for training and 200 testing ones. Rain200L has light rain streaks and Rain200H contains multiple heavy rain streaks. Rain800 includes 700 images for training and 100 images for testing. Rain1200 dataset has 12,000 images for training and 1,200 images for testing. The first real-word dataset is the SPA-Data [24], which contains 638,492 rainy/clean image pairs for training and 1,000 testing ones, and these images include a variety of real rain scenes. The second one is proposed by Yang et al. [29], which contains 15 rain images.

**Metrics.** We use PSNR [12] and SSIM [25] to compare the rain removal quality of different models on four synthetic datasets and SPA-Data [24]. As no corresponding ground-truth exists in another real-world dataset [29], it cannot be evaluated in the same way, so we perform the visual comparisons and local expansion of the recovered images. It is worth noting that the PSNR and SSIM are calculated in the RGB space for each dataset.

## 4.2 Implement Details

We initialize the channel numbers of the residual path and the densely connected path feature map to 32 and 8, respectively. We use the PyTorch framework and Adam optimizer with a mini-batch size of 16 to train our proposed network. The training images are randomly cropped into $64 \times 64$ patch sizes. The initial learning rate is $1 \times 10^{-3}$ and terminate training after 40 epochs. The learning rate is divided by 2 when reaching 10, 20, or 30 epochs. We train and test these networks based on an NVIDIA GeForce RTX 3070 with 8GB GPU memory.

## 4.3 Results on Synthetic Datasets

**Quantitative Evaluation.** As mentioned in Sect. 4, the proposed DPCN is evaluated on four synthetic datasets [29,33,34], and the performance is compared with other methods [2,5,13,16,21–24,28,31]. Table 1 shows the quantitative results evaluated on different methods. It can be clearly seen that DPCN achieves a remarkable improvement compared to other methods. The comprehensive experimental results of these four datasets demonstrate that our method effectively removes rain streaks with varying degrees of complexity while preserving the background details of the image.

**Qualitative Evaluation.** To further verify the feasibility of DPCN, we select two representative examples from Rain200H, and the visual comparison effects of our method with other methods are presented in Fig. 5. Since the antlers in Fig. 5a have similar texture details to the rain streaks, this causes most methods to remove them along with the rain streaks, e.g., SPANet [24] and JORDER-E [28]. Some other methods can only recover a little bit of the antler outline, and only our method restores the details of the antlers. Also, for the other example in Fig. 5b, it can be obviously seen that only our method is closest to the background sky in the ground truth. These two synthetic images simulate most of the real-world scenes, and the results of their visual comparisons show that the proposed DPCN can effectively eliminate the rain streaks while fully retaining the texture details of the ground-truth, ultimately obtaining the best visualization results.

**Table 1.** Comparison of the quantitative results of PSNR and SSIM on four synthetic datasets. The highest values are indicated in **boldface** and the second-highest values are indicated in underline

| Methods | Rain200L | | Rain200H | | Rain800 | | Rain1200 | |
|---|---|---|---|---|---|---|---|---|
| | PSNR | SSIM | PSNR | SSIM | PSNR | SSIM | PSNR | SSIM |
| RESCAN(ECCV'2018) [16] | 36.94 | 0.980 | 26.62 | 0.841 | 24.09 | 0.841 | 32.48 | 0.910 |
| SPANet(CVPR'2019) [24] | 35.60 | 0.974 | 26.32 | 0.858 | 24.37 | 0.861 | 32.38 | 0.913 |
| PReNet(CVPR'2019) [22] | 36.76 | 0.979 | 28.08 | 0.887 | 24.81 | 0.851 | 30.03 | 0.889 |
| JORDER-E(TPAMI'2019) [28] | 37.25 | 0.975 | 23.45 | 0.749 | 27.08 | 0.871 | 24.32 | 0.862 |
| ReHEN(ACMMM'2019) [31] | <u>38.57</u> | <u>0.983</u> | 27.48 | 0.863 | 26.96 | 0.854 | 32.64 | 0.914 |
| RCDNet(CVPR'2020) [23] | 35.28 | 0.971 | 28.83 | 0.886 | 24.59 | 0.821 | 29.81 | 0.859 |
| MSPFN(CVPR'2020) [13] | 37.12 | 0.981 | 26.97 | 0.835 | 25.52 | 0.830 | 30.34 | 0.881 |
| DRD-Net(CVPR'2020) [5] | 37.15 | **0.987** | 28.16 | <u>0.920</u> | 26.32 | **0.902** | – | – |
| RICNet(CVPR'2021) [21] | – | – | 28.84 | 0.893 | 27.11 | 0.869 | <u>32.67</u> | 0.892 |
| RLNet(CVPR'2021) [2] | – | – | <u>28.87</u> | 0.895 | <u>27.95</u> | 0.870 | 32.62 | <u>0.917</u> |
| DPCN | **39.40** | 0.987 | **30.38** | **0.923** | **28.14** | <u>0.873</u> | **33.23** | **0.927** |

## 4.4   Results on Real-World Datasets

To further validate the practicality of the proposed method in real scenarios, we conduct experiments on two real datasets [24, 29]. On the SPA-Data [24], because it contains ground truth, the rain removal performance of the network can be quantitatively evaluated, and the comparison results are shown in Table 2. As shown from Table 2, DPCN achieves the best performance and has a significant improvement over other methods.

**Table 2.** Comparison of the quantitative results of PSNR and SSIM on SPA-Data

| Methods | RESCAN [16] (ECCV'2018) | SPANet [24] (CVPR'2019) | PReNet [22] (CVPR'2019) | JORDER-E [28] (TPAMI'2019) | ReHEN [31] (ACMMM'2019) | RCDNet [23] (CVPR'2020) | MSPFN [13] (CVPR'2020) | RICNet [21] (CVPR'2021) | DPCN |
|---------|---------|---------|---------|---------|---------|---------|---------|---------|---------|
| PSNR | 36.94 | 38.53 | 40.16 | 40.78 | 38.65 | 41.47 | 37.87 | 37.98 | **44.38** |
| SSIM | 0.980 | 0.987 | 0.982 | 0.981 | 0.974 | 0.983 | 0.957 | 0.972 | **0.989** |

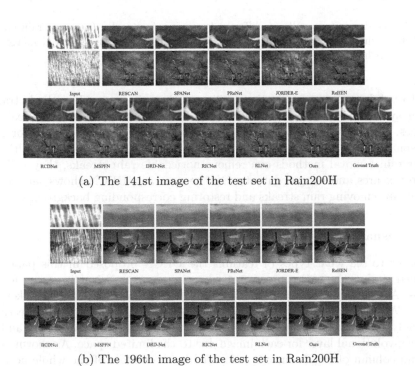

(a) The 141st image of the test set in Rain200H

(b) The 196th image of the test set in Rain200H

**Fig. 5.** Visual comparison of deraining results produced by different methods.

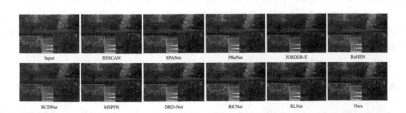

**Fig. 6.** Visual comparison on real-world data set [29]. Zoom to see the detail.

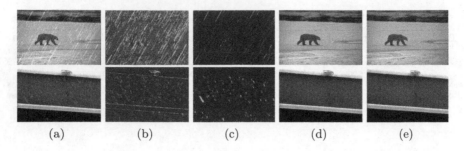

|  (a)  |  (b)  |  (c)  |  (d)  |  (e)  |

**Fig. 7.** The deraining results on different types of rain streaks. (a) Input rain images. (b) Intermediate feature maps. (c) Final feature maps. (d) Our restored images. (e) Ground truth.

To validate the generalization ability of the rain removal methods trained using synthetic datasets, qualitative experiments are performed on real rain images. All methods use only Rain200H during the training process for comparison purposes. As shown in Fig. 6, in the case of light rain streaks, although other rain removal methods can remove noticeable rain streaks, they will blur some textures and image contents. On the contrary, DPCN shows satisfactory results in removing rain streaks and restoring corresponding background details.

### 4.5  Visualization

In order to see what types of features the DPCN proposed in this paper has learned during the entire process of removing rain, we visualize some feature maps. Also, these features are visualized in heat maps to highlight the key features. We select an image from Rain200L [29] and SPA-Data [24], respectively. We only show a representative feature from the second dual path block and the last convolutional layer for each image due to the limited space. As shown in the second column of Fig. 7, since it is located in the middle of the whole network, the generated features retain the rain streak information and some obvious background features, i.e., animal's body and house beams, which can be seen as an indication that the network is progressively completing its mission. Besides, as shown in the third column of Fig. 7, the features generated by the last convolutional layer have more significant responses to different types of rain streaks. These two columns of visualization results show that our proposed DPCN accurately extracts the information of rain streaks, which significantly improves the rain removal performance of the network.

### 4.6  Ablation Studies

This section discusses the different convolution methods in the Extraction Module, the importance of different modules to prove the effectiveness of the structure and configuration in our proposed network. All the ablation experiments are conducted in the same environment using the Rain200L dataset.

**Ablation Study on Different Convolution Methods.** To demonstrate the effectiveness of the proposed Extraction Module, we compare the dilated convolutions commonly used in multi-scale aggregation with the depthwise separable convolutions used in this paper. We also list the number of network parameters and the FLOPs (floating point operations) for different convolution methods in Table 3. From the experimental results in Table 3, we can see that under the premise of using less than half of the parameters and FLOPs, our method has higher values on the PSNR and SSIM assessment metrics, indicating that it can better extract continuous rain streak information and thus enhance the rain removal performance of the network.

**Ablation Study on Different Modules.** Using the Extraction Module as the baseline unit, we investigate the impact of different modules on the rain removal performance of the network. The abbreviations of the different units are shown below:

**Table 3.** Parameter complexity, FLOPs, and average PSNR and SSIM comparison for different convolution methods

| Convolution Methods | Params | FLOPs | PSNR | SSIM |
| --- | --- | --- | --- | --- |
| Dilated Convolutions | 2.3M | 9.41G | 39.27 | 0.9870 |
| Depthwise Separable Convolutions | 1.1M | 4.41G | 39.40 | 0.9872 |

- $U_1$ : The Extraction Module as the baseline without Positioning Module and Separation Module.
- $U_2$ : Baseline with Positioning Module.
- $U_3$ : Baseline with Separation Module.
- $U_4$ : Baseline with Positioning Module and Separation Module, i.e., we proposed the dual path unit.

As can be seen in Table 4 that compared with the baseline unit, both the $U_2$ and $U_3$ show a significant improvement in the rain removal results, which verifies the effectiveness of the modules we have introduced. In addition, the dual path unit this paper proposed combines these three modules and achieves the best deraining results. These results can also draw several valuable conclusions: 1) the experimental results in the second column show that maintaining a high spatial resolution while exploring the correlation between channels is beneficial for the final rain removal performance; 2) the experimental results in the third column show that while multi-scale features are essential, the intrinsic correlation between different scales is worth exploring; 3) the combined effect of the three modules is beneficial to the removal of rain streaks because the absence of anyone module obviously reduces the rain removal performance of the model.

**Table 4.** Ablation study on different modules. The $\sqrt{}$ symbol indicates that the corresponding module is adopted

| Modules | $U_1$ | $U_2$ | $U_3$ | $U_4$ |
|---|---|---|---|---|
| Positioning Module | | $\sqrt{}$ | | $\sqrt{}$ |
| Extraction Module | $\sqrt{}$ | $\sqrt{}$ | $\sqrt{}$ | $\sqrt{}$ |
| Separation Module | | | $\sqrt{}$ | $\sqrt{}$ |
| PSNR | 38.48 | 39.15 | 39.00 | 39.40 |
| SSIM | 0.9852 | 0.9867 | 0.9863 | 0.9872 |

## 5   Conclusion

In this paper, we propose an effective dual path convolutional network (DPCN) for rain streak removal. The proposed network structure comprises three modules: Positioning Module, Extraction Module, and Separation Module. These three modules interact with each other and work together. First, Positioning Module is used to locate the position of rain streaks. Then, aggregating the rain streaks features at different scales by Extraction Module. Next, for those extracted background information with similar texture details as the rain streaks, we use the Separation Module to separate them from the rain streaks. Finally, we can get a clean rain-free background. In addition, the dual path topology runs throughout the network, providing support for the model to learn the rich feature representations. Comprehensive experimental evaluations on both real-world and synthetic datasets demonstrate that DPCN can effectively remove various types of rain streaks while restoring the texture details of the ground-truth. Experimental results also show that our method is superior to the state-of-the-art methods.

**Acknowledgments.** This work was supported by National Natural Science Foundation of China (Grant Nos. 61976246), Natural Science Foundation of Chongqing (Grant No. cstc2020jcyj-msxmX0385).

## References

1. Chang, Y., Yan, L., Zhong, S.: Transformed low-rank model for line pattern noise removal. In: IEEE ICCV, pp. 1735–1743 (2017)
2. Chen, C., Li, H.: Robust representation learning with feedback for single image deraining. In: IEEE CVPR, pp. 7738–7747 (2021)
3. Chen, Y.L., Hsu, C.T.: A generalized low-rank appearance model for spatio-temporally correlated rain streaks. In: IEEE ICCV, pp. 1968–1975 (2013)
4. Cui, X., Shang, W., Ren, D., Zhu, P., Gao, Y.: Semi-supervised Single Image Deraining with Discrete Wavelet Transform. PRICAI 2021: Trends in Artificial Intelligence, 18th Pacific Rim International Conference on Artificial Intelligence, PRICAI 2021, Hanoi, Vietnam, 8–12 November 2021, Proceedings, Part III (2021)

5. Deng, S., et al.: Detail-recovery image deraining via context aggregation networks. In: IEEE CVPR, pp. 14548–14557 (2020)
6. Fu, X., Huang, J., Ding, X., Liao, Y., Paisley, J.: Clearing the skies: a deep network architecture for single-image rain removal. IEEE TIP **26**(6), 2944–2956 (2017)
7. Fu, X., Qi, Q., Zha, Z.J., Zhu, Y., Ding, X.: Rain streak removal via dual graph convolutional network. In: Proceedings of the AAAI Conference on Artificial Intelligence, pp. 1–9 (2021)
8. Hou, Q., Zhou, D., Feng, J.: Coordinate attention for efficient mobile network design. In: IEEE CVPR, pp. 13708–13717 (2021)
9. Howard, A.G., et al.: Mobilenets: efficient convolutional neural networks for mobile vision applications. arXiv preprint arXiv:1704.04861 (2017)
10. Hu, J., Shen, L., Albanie, S., Sun, G., Wu, E.: Squeeze-and-excitation networks. IEEE TPAMI **42**(8), 2011–2023 (2020)
11. Huang, D.A., Kang, L.W., Yang, M.C., Lin, C.W., Wang, Y.C.F.: Context-aware single image rain removal. In: IEEE ICME, pp. 164–169 (2012)
12. Huynh-Thu, Q., Ghanbari, M.: Scope of validity of PSNR in image/video quality assessment. Electron. Lett. **44**(13), 800–801 (2008)
13. Jiang, K., et al.: Multi-scale progressive fusion network for single image deraining. In: IEEE CVPR, pp. 8343–8352 (2020)
14. Kang, L.W., Lin, C.W., Fu, Y.H.: Automatic single-image-based rain streaks removal via image decomposition. IEEE TIP **21**(4), 1742–1755 (2012)
15. Kim, J.H., Lee, C., Sim, J.Y., Kim, C.S.: Single-image deraining using an adaptive nonlocal means filter. In: IEEE ICIP, pp. 914–917 (2013)
16. Li, X., Wu, J., Lin, Z., Liu, H., Zha, H.: Recurrent squeeze-and-excitation context aggregation net for single image deraining. In: Ferrari, V., Hebert, M., Sminchisescu, C., Weiss, Y. (eds.) ECCV 2018. LNCS, vol. 11211, pp. 262–277. Springer, Cham (2018). https://doi.org/10.1007/978-3-030-01234-2_16
17. Li, Y., Tan, R.T., Guo, X., Lu, J., Brown, M.S.: Rain streak removal using layer priors. In: IEEE CVPR, pp. 2736–2744 (2016)
18. Liu, H., Liu, F., Fan, X., Huang, D.: Polarized self-attention: towards high-quality pixel-wise regression. arXiv preprint arXiv:2107.00782 (2021)
19. Liu, J.J., Hou, Q., Cheng, M.M., Wang, C., Feng, J.: Improving convolutional networks with self-calibrated convolutions. In: IEEE CVPR, pp. 10093–10102 (2020)
20. Luo, Y., Xu, Y., Ji, H.: Removing rain from a single image via discriminative sparse coding. In: IEEE ICCV, pp. 3397–3405 (2015)
21. Ni, S., Cao, X., Yue, T., Hu, X.: Controlling the rain: from removal to rendering. In: IEEE CVPR, pp. 6324–6333 (2021)
22. Ren, D., Zuo, W., Hu, Q., Zhu, P., Meng, D.: Progressive image deraining networks: a better and simpler baseline. In: IEEE CVPR, pp. 3932–3941 (2019)
23. Wang, H., Xie, Q., Zhao, Q., Meng, D.: A model-driven deep neural network for single image rain removal. In: IEEE CVPR, pp. 3100–3109 (2020)
24. Wang, T., et al.: Spatial attentive single-image deraining with a high quality real rain dataset. In: IEEE CVPR, pp. 12262–12271 (2019)
25. Wang, Z., Bovik, A., Sheikh, H., Simoncelli, E.: Image quality assessment: from error visibility to structural similarity. IEEE TIP **13**(4), 600–612 (2004)
26. Woo, S., Park, J., Lee, J.-Y., Kweon, I.S.: CBAM: convolutional block attention module. In: Ferrari, V., Hebert, M., Sminchisescu, C., Weiss, Y. (eds.) ECCV 2018. LNCS, vol. 11211, pp. 3–19. Springer, Cham (2018). https://doi.org/10.1007/978-3-030-01234-2_1

27. Yang, W., Wang, S., Xu, D., Wang, X., Liu, J.: Towards scale-free rain streak removal via self-supervised fractal band learning. Proc. AAAI Conf. Artif. Intell. **34**(7), 12629–12636 (2020)
28. Yang, W., Tan, R.T., Feng, J., Guo, Z., Yan, S., Liu, J.: Joint rain detection and removal from a single image with contextualized deep networks. IEEE TPAMI **42**(6), 1377–1393 (2020)
29. Yang, W., Tan, R.T., Feng, J., Liu, J., Guo, Z., Yan, S.: Deep joint rain detection and removal from a single image. In: IEEE CVPR, pp. 1685–1694 (2017)
30. Yang, W., Tan, R.T., Wang, S., Fang, Y., Liu, J.: Single image deraining: from model-based to data-driven and beyond. IEEE TPAMI **43**(11), 4059–4077 (2021)
31. Yang, Y., Lu, H.: Single image deraining via recurrent hierarchy enhancement network. In: ACM MM, pp. 1814–1822 (2019)
32. Yu, F., Koltun, V.: Multi-scale context aggregation by dilated convolutions. arXiv preprint arXiv:1511.07122 (2015)
33. Zhang, H., Patel, V.M.: Density-aware single image de-raining using a multi-stream dense network. In: IEEE CVPR, pp. 695–704 (2018)
34. Zhang, H., Sindagi, V., Patel, V.M.: Image de-raining using a conditional generative adversarial network. IEEE TCSVT **30**(11), 3943–3956 (2020)
35. Zhang, L., Zhou, Y., Hu, X., Sun, F., Duan, S.: MSL-MNN: image deraining based on multi-scale lightweight memristive neural network. Neural Comput. Appl. **34**(9), 7299–7309 (2022)
36. Zhu, L., Fu, C.W., Lischinski, D., Heng, P.A.: Joint bi-layer optimization for single-image rain streak removal. In: IEEE ICCV, pp. 2545–2553 (2017)

# All up to You: Controllable Video Captioning with a Masked Scene Graph

Zhen Yang[1,2(✉)] and Lin Shang[1,2]

[1] State Key Laboratory for Novel Software Technology, Nanjing University, Nanjing 210023, China
[2] Department of Computer Science and Technology, Nanjing University, Nanjing 210023, China
yangzhen@smail.nju.edu.cn, shanglin@nju.edu.cn

**Abstract.** Controllable video captioning is generating video descriptions following designated control signals. However, most controllable video captioning models focus exclusively on contents of interest or descriptive syntax. In this paper, we propose to guide the video caption generation with a Masked Scene Graph (MSG). Formally, given a video and a MSG, which not only contains semantic contents nodes, but also implies the syntactic form in the graph structure. The MSG can be constructed manually or be modified from the original scene graph of a sampled frame, due to the motion information is hard to be captured by the frame scene graph, so we mask the relationship node to obtain a MSG. From the MSG, we propose a MSG encoder and adopt a masked autoregressive decoding algorithm, which is able to recognize semantics and syntax information of the graph structure. Extensive experiments demonstrate that our framework can achieve better performance and controllability than several strong baselines on MSVD and MSR-VTT benchmarks.

**Keywords:** Video captioning · Controllable · Mask scene graph

## 1 Introduction

Video captioning is a task to generate natural language descriptions automatically for given video. It is one of the most important vision-language tasks which requires techniques both from computer vision and natural language processing. In recent years, template-based approaches [12,16] and deep learning models based on the encoder-decoder framework [29], have achieved remarkable advancements on this task. However, most conventional video captioning models focus only on understanding the general semantic content of the video so as to generate captions describing it, while a part of entities in the video, the syntactic structure and the diversity of captions are often ignored.

In order to generate specific sentences to describe the content what users are interested in, and to generate syntactic structure captions predefined by users, previous works have proposed to actively control video captioning process. The early works [9,13] for controllable captioning mainly focus on expressive styles of sentences such as factual, romantic, humorous style etc., but they are still difficult to control the generation process efficiently and precisely. To further improve the controllability, recent works gradually put a more emphasis on controlling the description content such as different object [18], part-of-speech tags [31], so that the model is able to describe the user interested contents or the user intended syntax. Thus, they can be classified into two categories: content controlled and structure-controlled.

However, all of above works can only handle a content-control or structure-control signal, which is hard to meet the user desired diverse control at all two sides, for example describing various objects they are interested in with different attributes as well as their relationships.

In this paper, we propose a new control signal, Mask Scene Graph(MSG), to meet both content-control and structure-control requirements simultaneously. The MSG is a directed graph consists of three types of nodes from the scene graph which is detected on the video, namely object, attribute and relationship, while the semantic tags of relationship nodes are masked. Therefore, such graph structure contains the semantic tag of objects what user is interested in as well as control the syntactic structure through the directed graph structure.

To generate sentences with respect to the MSG, we propose a MSG encoder, which embed the MSG to a representation from three aspects: node semantic tags, nodes types, and graph structure. In addition, for a controllable caption decoder, we propose a MSG-based masked autoregressive decoding algorithm, the words can be generated in parallel from the draft that is formed by the MSG, and then adopt the iterative refinement approach [10].

In summary, the contribution of our work are as follows:

- We propose a new control signal for controllable video captioning: Mask Scene Graph(MSG). As far as we know, MSG is the first control signal to consider both content-control and structure-control.
- Our model can learn the semantic and syntactic information from the graph structure, and the visualization examples demonstrate its reasonableness.
- We evaluate our approach on two datasets, our approach achieves competitive results with the state-of-the-art methods and generate diverse captions by using different MSGs.

## 2   Related Work

In the early stage, most methods for video captioning are based on specific templates [12,16], which first define a sentence template with grammar rules, and then align the subject, verb and object of the sentence template with the video content. These methods are highly dependent on templates, and the generated sentences are always fixed syntactic structures. With the rapid development of deep learning, Venugopalan et al. [29] propose an encoder-decoder framework based on sequence-to-sequence method, and following video captioning methods are mostly based on this architecture.

Recent video captioning works mainly focus on how to extract the multi modal features of videos and to encode them to generate accurate words. As commonly used, state of the art 2D-CNN and 3D-CNN pretrained on large dataset are leveraged to extract visual features [6,32]. In addition, diverse attention mechanism are designed to enhance the encoder. Yao et al. [35] propose a temporal attention mechanism to dynamically assign weight to the visual features of different frames. Chen and Jiang [4] further introduce a spatial attention mechanisms on different region of each frame. Detailed region features gained attention also. Bottom-up attention algorithm [1] exploits object detection to extract region features and achieves effective performance for image captioning significantly. This kind of encoders are also extended to video captioning, and prior video captioning methods [19,36,37] also detect the relationship between objects by attention mechanism or graph based methods such as GCN, they apply various graph structure to model the objects relationships and improve caption performance obviously. Benefiting from the success of Transformer, Transformer based decoder are also applied in video captioning [38].

Compared with conventional video caption, the controllable video captioning is a more challenging task. Recently, Wang et al. [31] propose to leverage the predicted Part-of-Speech (POS) tags to control the syntactic structure. Liu et al. [18] propose a object controlled model and non-autoregressive decoding algorithm for controllable decoding. Chen et at. [5] introduces the abstract scene graph to control the fine-grained caption generation. Inspired by above works, we propose a novel control signal MSG to express the content and syntactic structure requirements of users. On top of this, we adopt a mask non-autoregressive decoding algorithm to generate the target captions we want.

## 3 Method

The video captioning problem is regarded as a sequence to sequence task. Given a sequence of $T$ frames from Video $X = \{x_1, x_2, ..., x_T\}$, then we generate the caption $Y = \{y_1, y_2, ..., y_L\}$ to introduce the video, a control signal is added to input if we need to generate controllable caption. For flexible controllable video captioning, We first propose the Masked Scene Graph(MSG) as the control signal for generating captions with customized structure and content.

The overview of our proposed model architecture is illustrated in Fig. 1. Our model consists of 4 modules: (1) Visual Feature Encoder; (2) Masked Scene Graph Encoder; (3) Caption Length Decider; (4) Mask Language Decoder. We describe the details of each module in detail next.

### 3.1 Visual Feature Encoder

We feed the input video sequence $X$ into pretrained 2D-CNN & 3D-CNN to obtain visual features $V = \{v_t\}_{t=1}^{T}, v_t \in \mathbb{R}^{d_v}$, then apply a input embedding

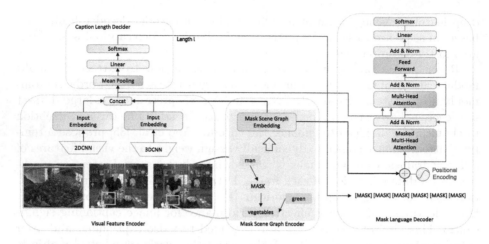

**Fig. 1.** The overview of our proposed model framework. It consists of a Visual Feature Encoder, a Masked Scene Graph Encoder, a Caption Length Decider and a Mask Language Decoder.

layer to encode them to intermediate representation $\hat{V} \in \mathbb{R}^{d_h}$. For the input embedding we adopt the shortcut connection in highway networks [24] as follows:

$$
\begin{aligned}
\hat{V} &= BN(\lambda \odot V_1 + (1 - \lambda) \odot V_2) \\
V_1 &= VW_1 \\
V_2 &= tanh(V_2 W_2) \\
\lambda &= \sigma(V_1 W_3)
\end{aligned}
\tag{1}
$$

where BN denotes batch normalization, $\odot$ is element wise product, $\sigma$ is sigmoid function, $W_1 \in \mathbb{R}^{d_v \times d_h}$, and $W_2, W_3 \in \mathbb{R}^{d_h \times d_h}$, $V_1, V_2$ are intermediate variables. After above input embedding, we obtain two embedded modality features $\hat{V}_a$ and $\hat{V}_m$.

### 3.2    Masked Scene Graph Encoder

**Construct MSG.** In order to meet the dual requirements of users for content and syntax, we construct a MSG as our control signal. For automatically constructing, we firstly extract scene graph from the sample frame of given video by the scene graph generation method [25]. The scene graph is formalized as $\mathcal{SG} = \{(o_x, attr_x)^P, (o_x, r_{xy}, o_y)^Q\}$, where $P$ denotes the attributes number of object $x$ and $Q$ denotes the relationship number between object $x$ and object $y$. On the one hand, we classify the nodes into three types: object node, attribute node and relationship node. Due to the dynamically changing nature of video, we replace the tag of relationship node with $< unk >$ to make the manual constructing easier for users. On the other hand, we build edges for $(attr_x, o_x)$, $(o_x, r_{xy})$ and $(r_{xy}, o_y)$ respectively. We hope to generate a caption which not only focus on describing the controllable subject and object, but also contains one or two attributes about them according to the requirements of users. Thus, MSG can effectively control the subject-object in the whole caption and the level of detail with which they are described, i.e., the content and syntax of caption. It is convenient to construct MSG manually. The users can add their interested entities, and can add a relationship node between entities if the user need to know. Besides, the user can specify the subject-object relationship by the directed edges. For the more details about the entity, the user can add one or more attribute node and assign directed edges to the entity node.

**MSG Embedding.** In the previous section we obtain a MSG automatically or manually, then we convert it to a adjacency matrix $G = (V, E)$ by the defined vertices and directed edges. To learn the node semantic information and graph structure information, we design a MSG embedding method as follow: For the $i$-th node in $G$, we firstly initialize it as its corresponding semantic tag $s_i$, then we enhance each node with type embedding and order embedding as follows:

$$X_i^{(0)} = W_s \cdot tag_i + W_t \cdot type_i + W_o \cdot pos_i,$$

$$type_i = \begin{cases} 0, & if \quad i \in objects \\ 1, & if \quad i \in attributes \\ 2, & if \quad i \in relationships \end{cases} \tag{2}$$

where $W_s, W_t, W_o \in \mathbb{R}^{d_w}$ is the embedding matrix, $d_w$ is the word size. $pos_i$ is a position embedding to distinguish the order of different nodes, e.g. the subject node is less than object node.

Since in the graph structure each vertex is not isolated, and we need to inference the mask node, so the context information from neighbor is also beneficial. In our MSG, the nodes have three types, the message pass from one type of node to another type is different too. Therefore, we follow the GAT [28] to calculate the attention value as different edges $e_{ij}$, then encode graph context in $G$ as follows:

$$e_{ij} = a(WX_i^{(n)}, WX_j^{(n)})$$

$$\alpha_{ij} = softmax(e_{ij}) = \frac{exp(e_{ij})}{\sum_{k \in \mathcal{N}_i} exp(e_{ik})} \tag{3}$$

$$X_i^{(n+1)} = \sigma(\sum_{k \in \mathcal{N}_i} \alpha_{ij} WX_i^{(n)})$$

where $\mathcal{N}_i$ denotes neighbors of $i$-th node, $\sigma$ is the ReLU activation function, $X_i^{(n)}$ denotes the features of $i$-th node in $n$-th GAT layer. We stack N layers to encode contexts from distant neighbors, then the outputs of the final $N$-th layer are employed as our final node embedding $\mathcal{X}$. We take an average of $\mathcal{X}$ to get a global encoded graph embedding $V_g \in \mathbb{R}^{d_h}$, then we concatenate $V_g$ with embedded visual features $\hat{V}_a, \hat{V}_m$ straightly, $V_{enc} = concat(\hat{V}_a, \hat{V}_m, V_g)$.

## 3.3 Deciding Caption Length

In the decoding process, non-autoregressive decoding needs to be known length in advance. So we add a auxiliary task which is deciding the caption length. Given the output $V_{enc}$ of visual feature encoder and MSG encoder and concatenate them, the length distribution is as follow [34]:

$$L = softmax(ReLU(MeanPool(V_{enc})W_{l1})W_{l2}) \tag{4}$$

where $W_{l1} \in \mathbb{R}^{d_h \times d_h}$, $W_{l2} \in \mathbb{R}^{d_h \times L_{max}}$, and $L_{max}$ is the preset maximum caption length. For the training, given a ground-truth length distribution $L^*$, whose $i$-th element indicates the percentage of sentences of length i in the training corpus for the video, then we define the loss function for deciding caption length as:

$$L_{len} = -\sum_{i=1}^{L_{max}} l_i^* \log \frac{l_i}{l_i^*} \tag{5}$$

i.e. Minimize the Kullback-Leibler (KL) divergence between $L$ and $L^*$.

## 3.4 Masked Language Decoder

Motivated by the BERT [8], we adopt a one-layer Transformer decoder as our non-autoregressive decoder. In order to fit our controllable decoding task, we modify some details. Specifically, we remove the original causal mask in the bottom self-attention layer, so that the decoder become bi-direction and the prediction of each token can use both left and right contexts. Besides, we enhance the decoder inputs by integrating the MSG information. We initial a fully masked sequence $X = (x_{m_1}, x_{m_2}, ..., x_{m_l})$ with the length $l$ by caption length decider, where the $x_{m_i}$ is the word embedding of $< mask >$ token. We repeat $V_g$ for $l$ times to $V_g = (g_1, g_2, ..., g_l) \in \mathbb{R}^{l \times d_h}$, then the MSG information $g_i$ and position embedding $e_i$ are added to $X$ as $x'_{m_i} = x_{m_i} + g_i + e_i$, then we obtain enhanced input $X'$ with MSG contexts. This is motivated by the masked language modeling objective in BERT. Therefore, the decoder takes $x'_{m_i}$ and representation $V_{enc}$ as inputs to predict the probability distribution over words, the cross entropy loss function is defined as follows:

$$L_{cap} = -\sum_{i=1}^{l} \log(p(y|V_{enc}, X')) \tag{6}$$

In order to take into account both semantic content and graph structure, we adopt a dedicated decoding algorithm Mask-Predict [10] to generate the captions we want. Specially, it consists of two steps and $t$-th iteration: Firstly, mask the lowest confidence token $m_t$; Secondly, base on the rest $N - m_t$ tokens to predict other masked tokens. We update the prediction results $Y^{(t)}$ and confidence $C^{(t)}$ for $t$ iterations.

$$y_n^{(t)}, c_n^{(t)} = \begin{cases} argmax_w p_\theta(y = w|V_{enc}, X') & if \quad n \in I_t \\ y_n^{(t-1)}, c_n^{(t-1)} & otherwise \end{cases} \tag{7}$$

where $I_t = \{n|y_n^{(t-1)} \notin Y_{cur}^{(t)}\}$ denotes the index set of masked tokens, The confidence $c_n^{(t)}$ is lowest means the token $y_n^{(t)}$ is not suitable compare with other tokens for the caption quality. Then the next iteration, $Y_{cur}^{(t+1)}$ is updated as:

$$Y_{cur}^{(t+1)} = \{Y_j^{(t)}|j \in topk(C), k = N - m_{t+1}\} \tag{8}$$

We use a linear decay ratio r to decide the reconsider number $m_t$:

$$r = \frac{T - t + 1}{T}, m_t = max(\lfloor N \cdot r \rfloor, 1) \tag{9}$$

After training, our model can generate controllable video captions given th vide and a designated MSG obtained manually or automatically.

## 4    Experiments

We conduct experiments on two popular benchmark datasets from the literature in video captioning: Microsoft Video Description Corpus (MSVD) [3], Microsoft Research-Video to Text (MSR-VTT) [33]. To verify the effectiveness of our proposed method, we report numbers on various standard evaluation metrics.

### 4.1    Datasets and Metrics

**MSVD.** The MSVD dataset [3] contains 1,970 YouTube short video clips. Each clip mainly describes a single activity of open domain and lasts 10–25 seconds. There are multilingual sentences as annotation, we only select the English captions so we get approximately 40 descriptions per video. Follow the prior practice [30], we split the dataset into 1,200 train, 100 validation and 670 test clips.

**MSR-VTT.** The MSR-VTT dataset [33] is another large-scale benchmark for video captioning which contains 10,000 video clips with 20 English annotations for each clip. The videos come from 20 categories, such as music, sport, cook, etc. Follow the previous works, we use the standard splits: 6,513 for training, 497 for validating, 2990 for testing.

**Evaluation Metrics.** In our experiments, we apply four widely used metrics in the field of video captioning, namely BLEU@4 [20], ROUGE-L [17], METEOR [2], and CIDEr [27]. These metrics are mainly based on n-gram to evaluate the quality of sentences from the perspective of recall and precision, CIDEr is specially designed for captioning task evaluation, BLEU and METEOR are from machine translation evaluation, ROUGE-L is from text summarization evaluation. Besides, we follow three evaluation metrics Novel, Unique and Vocab Usage from Dai, et al. [7] to evaluate the diversity of generated captions. Novel is the ratio of words in generated captions that do not appear in the training data. Unique is the ratio of generated unique words among the other all generated captions. Vocab Usage is the ratio of words which are used in caption generation in the vocabulary.

**Table 1.** Performance Comparison on MSVD and MSR-VTT benchmark. "-" means not available. The best results are shown in bold.

| Method | MSVD | | | | MSR-VTT | | | |
|---|---|---|---|---|---|---|---|---|
| | B@4 | M | R | C | B@4 | M | R | C |
| RecNet(2018) [32] | 52.3 | 34.1 | 69.8 | 80.3 | 39.1 | 26.6 | 59.3 | 42.7 |
| PickNet(2018) [6] | 52.3 | 33.3 | 69.6 | 76.5 | 41.3 | 27.7 | 59.8 | 44.1 |
| MARN(2019) [21] | 48.6 | 35.1 | 71.9 | 92.2 | 40.4 | 28.1 | 60.7 | 47.1 |
| MGSA(2019) [4] | 53.4 | 35.0 | – | 86.7 | 42.4 | 27.6 | – | 47.5 |
| POS-CG(2019) [31] | 52.5 | 34.1 | 71.3 | 88.7 | 42.0 | 28.2 | 61.6 | 48.7 |
| STG-KD(2020) [19] | 52.2 | 36.9 | 73.9 | 93.0 | 40.5 | 28.3 | 60.9 | 47.1 |
| SAAT(2020) [37] | 46.5 | 33.5 | 69.4 | 81.0 | 40.5 | 28.2 | 60.9 | 49.1 |
| ORG-TRL(2020) [36] | 54.3 | 36.4 | 73.9 | 95.2 | 43.6 | 28.8 | 62.1 | 50.9 |
| SGN(2021) [23] | 52.8 | 35.5 | 72.9 | 94.3 | 40.8 | 28.3 | 60.8 | 49.5 |
| O2NA(2021) [18] | 55.4 | 37.4 | 74.5 | 96.4 | 41.6 | 28.5 | 62.5 | 51.1 |
| ours | **55.6** | **37.7** | **74.6** | **96.6** | 41.6 | **28.9** | **62.8** | **51.2** |

## 4.2  Experiments Setup

**Data Preprocessing and Feature Extraction.**

*Corpus Preprocessing.* We follow the process of [34] for corpus preprocessing and feature extraction. For corpus preprocessing, we first convert the caption to lower case and remove punctuations, then we replace the words that appear less than 3 times in the training set with the $< unk >$ token, so we get a vocabulary of 10547 words for MSR-VTT and 9469 words for MSVD.

*Feature Extraction.* Follow Pei et al. [22], we uniformly sample 30 frames for each video. Specially, we utilize the ResNet-101 [15] pretrained on the ImageNet dataset to extract the 2048-D appearance features, utilize the ResNeXt-101 [14] pretrained on the Kinetics dataset to extract the 2048-D motion features, and we extract scene graph from each sampled frame by [26].

*Implementation Details.* For the training captions, the word embedding size is set to 300 without the use of any pre-trained embedding such as glove, and we apply the maximum sequence length with 26. For the transformer decoder, we apply 1 decoder layer, the model dimension is set to 512, hidden dimension is set to 2048, attention heads per layer is set to 8. For the MSG encoder, we apply 2 GAT layer, the maximum MSG node is set to 10. For the training, we set the batch size to 128, and adopt ADAM optimizer with an initial learning rate $8 \times 10^{-3}$, besides, we use 0.5 dropout and $8 \times 10^{-4} L_2$ weight decay. The beam size is set to 5 unless otherwise stated. For the non-autoregressive decoding, as machine translation usually does, we adopt the knowledge distillation [11] and teacher re-scoring technique [34], by this method, it generates several candidate sentences in parallel, then we select a best sentence with a max score.

**Table 2.** Diversity of generated captions on MSVD.

| method | Novel | Unique | Vocab Usage |
|--------|-------|--------|-------------|
| O2NA | 29.8 | 56.1 | 2.5 |
| baseline | 8.9 | 31.2 | 1.3 |
| ours | 35.1 | 60.3 | 3.3 |

## 4.3  Performance Evaluation

As shown in Table 1, we compare with some existed methods on the MSVD and MSR-VTT datasets to show the performance of our method. There are ten representative methods of recent years, and five are the state-of-the-art approaches, such as STG-KD [19], SAAT [37], ORG-TRL [36], SGN [23], O2NA [18]. The results illustrate that our model achieves the best performance on the MSVD and MSR-VTT datasets for all evaluation metrics, which demonstrates the effectiveness of our approach. In addition, to evaluate the diversity of the captions generated by our model, we compare with O2NA on the Novel, Unique and Vocab scores, and the results is shown as Table 2, the baseline is similar architecture with our proposed model, it excludes the MSG and adopt autoregressive decoding algorithm.

**Table 3.** Ablation study to demonstrate contributions from different proposed components.(MSG-enc denotes the masked scene graph encoder, MSG-NA denotes the autoregressive decoding algorithm with MSG enhanced input.)

| # | MSG-enc | MSG-NA | BLEU-4 | METEOR | ROUGE-L | CIDEr |
|---|---------|--------|--------|--------|---------|-------|
| 1 | | | 50.8 | 35.8 | 72.5 | 93.6 |
| 2 | √ | | 51.4 | 36.4 | 73.3 | 94.2 |
| 3 | | √ | 54.7 | 37.5 | 73.8 | 95.9 |
| 4 | √ | √ | 55.6 | 37.7 | 74.6 | 96.6 |

## 4.4  Ablation Study

Our model introduce the MSG encoder and the MSG-control mask language decoder. Therefore, we investigate the contribution of these two components and the results are shown in Table 3. As expected, both component are important for our model by exlicit enhancements on all metrics.

## 4.5  Qualitative Analysis

Finally, we show some qualitative results in Fig. 2 to show the controllability of our proposed MSG control signal intuitively. In the analysis, we illustrate a

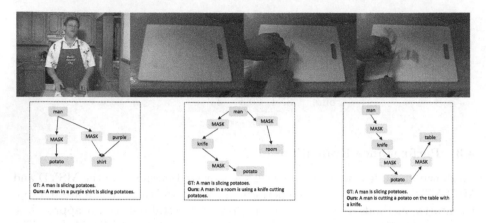

**Fig. 2.** Examples of captions generated by the automatically and manually created MSG using our method. The leftmost MSG is created automatically, the other two are created manually.

example video with different MSGs. It shows our approach is controllable and explainable.

## 5   Conclusion

In this paper, we argued that all existing controllable video captioning only handle a content-control or structure-control signal. For considering diverse user intentions to generate desired video descriptions, we propose a novel control signal called Masked Scene Graph(MSG), which is a directed graph with object nodes, attribute nodes and relationship nodes. Due to the dynamics of video and the convenience of manual construction, we mask the relationship nodes then obtain a MSG. An MSG encoder is then proposed with a mask language decoder specially for graphs to follow structures of the MSG. Our model can achieve better performance and controllability than several strong baselines on MSVD and MSR-VTT benchmarks.

**Acknowledgements.** This work is supported by the National Natural Science Foundation of China (No.51975294).

## References

1. Anderson, P., et al.: Bottom-up and top-down attention for image captioning and visual question answering. In: Proceedings of the IEEE Conference on Computer Vision and Pattern Recognition, pp. 6077–6086 (2018)
2. Banerjee, S., Lavie, A.: Meteor: an automatic metric for MT evaluation with improved correlation with human judgments. In: Proceedings of the Acl Workshop On Intrinsic and Extrinsic Evaluation Measures for Machine Translation and/or Summarization, pp. 65–72 (2005)

3. Chen, D.L., Dolan, W.B.: Collecting highly parallel data for paraphrase evaluation. In: Lin, D., Matsumoto, Y., Mihalcea, R. (eds.) The 49th Annual Meeting of the Association for Computational Linguistics: Human Language Technologies, Proceedings of the Conference, 19–24 June 2011, Portland, Oregon, USA, pp. 190–200. The Association for Computer Linguistics (2011)

4. Chen, S., Jiang, Y.G.: Motion guided spatial attention for video captioning. In: Proceedings of the AAAI Conference on Artificial Intelligence, vol. 33, pp. 8191–8198 (2019)

5. Chen, S., Jin, Q., Wang, P., Wu, Q.: Say as you wish: fine-grained control of image caption generation with abstract scene graphs. In: Proceedings of the IEEE/CVF Conference on Computer Vision and Pattern Recognition, pp. 9962–9971 (2020)

6. Chen, Y., Wang, S., Zhang, W., Huang, Q.: Less is more: picking informative frames for video captioning. In: Ferrari, V., Hebert, M., Sminchisescu, C., Weiss, Y. (eds.) ECCV 2018. LNCS, vol. 11217, pp. 367–384. Springer, Cham (2018). https://doi.org/10.1007/978-3-030-01261-8_22

7. Dai, B., Fidler, S., Lin, D.: A neural compositional paradigm for image captioning. In: Advances in Neural Information Processing Systems 31 (2018)

8. Devlin, J., Chang, M.W., Lee, K., Toutanova, K.: BERT: pre-training of deep bidirectional transformers for language understanding. arXiv preprint arXiv:1810.04805 (2018)

9. Gan, C., Gan, Z., He, X., Gao, J., Deng, L.: Stylenet: generating attractive visual captions with styles. In: Proceedings of the IEEE Conference on Computer Vision and Pattern Recognition, pp. 3137–3146 (2017)

10. Ghazvininejad, M., Levy, O., Liu, Y., Zettlemoyer, L.: Mask-predict: parallel decoding of conditional masked language models. arXiv preprint arXiv:1904.09324 (2019)

11. Gu, J., Bradbury, J., Xiong, C., Li, V.O.K., Socher, R.: Non-autoregressive neural machine translation. In: 6th International Conference on Learning Representations, ICLR 2018, Vancouver, BC, Canada, 30 April - 3 May 2018, Conference Track Proceedings. OpenReview.net (2018). https://openreview.net/forum?id=B1l8BtlCb

12. Guadarrama, S., et al.: Youtube2text: recognizing and describing arbitrary activities using semantic hierarchies and zero-shot recognition. In: Proceedings of the IEEE International Conference on Computer Vision, pp. 2712–2719 (2013)

13. Guo, L., Liu, J., Yao, P., Li, J., Lu, H.: MSCap: multi-style image captioning with unpaired stylized text. In: Proceedings of the IEEE/CVF Conference on Computer Vision and Pattern Recognition, pp. 4204–4213 (2019)

14. Hara, K., Kataoka, H., Satoh, Y.: Can spatiotemporal 3D CNNs retrace the history of 2D CNNs and imagenet? In: 2018 IEEE Conference on Computer Vision and Pattern Recognition, CVPR 2018, Salt Lake City, UT, USA, 18–22 June 2018, pp. 6546–6555. Computer Vision Foundation / IEEE Computer Society (2018). https://doi.org/10.1109/CVPR.2018.00685

15. He, K., Zhang, X., Ren, S., Sun, J.: Deep residual learning for image recognition. In: 2016 IEEE Conference on Computer Vision and Pattern Recognition, CVPR 2016, Las Vegas, NV, USA, 27–30 June 2016, pp. 770–778. IEEE Computer Society (2016). https://doi.org/10.1109/CVPR.2016.90

16. Kojima, A., Tamura, T., Fukunaga, K.: Natural language description of human activities from video images based on concept hierarchy of actions. Int. J. Comput. Vision 50(2), 171–184 (2002)

17. Lin, C.Y.: Rouge: A package for automatic evaluation of summaries. In: Text Summarization Branches Out, pp. 74–81 (2004)

18. Liu, F., Ren, X., Wu, X., Yang, B., Ge, S., Sun, X.: O2NA: an object-oriented non-autoregressive approach for controllable video captioning. In: Zong, C., Xia, F., Li, W., Navigli, R. (eds.) Findings of the Association for Computational Linguistics: ACL/IJCNLP 2021, Online Event, 1–6 August 2021. Findings of ACL, vol. ACL/IJCNLP 2021, pp. 281–292. Association for Computational Linguistics (2021). https://doi.org/10.18653/v1/2021.findings-acl.24

19. Pan, B., et al.: Spatio-temporal graph for video captioning with knowledge distillation. In: Proceedings of the IEEE/CVF Conference on Computer Vision and Pattern Recognition, pp. 10870–10879 (2020)

20. Papineni, K., Roukos, S., Ward, T., Zhu, W.: Bleu: a method for automatic evaluation of machine translation. In: Proceedings of the 40th Annual Meeting of the Association for Computational Linguistics, 6–12 July 2002, Philadelphia, PA, USA, pp. 311–318. ACL (2002)

21. Pei, W., Zhang, J., Wang, X., Ke, L., Shen, X., Tai, Y.W.: Memory-attended recurrent network for video captioning. In: Proceedings of the IEEE/CVF Conference on Computer Vision and Pattern Recognition, pp. 8347–8356 (2019)

22. Pei, W., Zhang, J., Wang, X., Ke, L., Shen, X., Tai, Y.: Memory-attended recurrent network for video captioning. In: IEEE Conference on Computer Vision and Pattern Recognition, CVPR 2019, Long Beach, CA, USA, 16–20 June 2019, pp. 8347–8356. Computer Vision Foundation/IEEE (2019). https://doi.org/10.1109/CVPR.2019.00854

23. Ryu, H., Kang, S., Kang, H., Yoo, C.D.: Semantic grouping network for video captioning. In: Proceedings of the AAAI Conference on Artificial Intelligence, vol. 35, pp. 2514–2522 (2021)

24. Srivastava, R.K., Greff, K., Schmidhuber, J.: Training very deep networks. In: Cortes, C., Lawrence, N.D., Lee, D.D., Sugiyama, M., Garnett, R. (eds.) Advances in Neural Information Processing Systems 28: Annual Conference on Neural Information Processing Systems 2015, 7–12 December 2015, Montreal, Quebec, Canada, pp. 2377–2385 (2015). https://proceedings.neurips.cc/paper/2015/hash/215a71a12769b056c3c32e7299f1c5ed-Abstract.html

25. Tang, K., Niu, Y., Huang, J., Shi, J., Zhang, H.: Unbiased scene graph generation from biased training. In: Proceedings of the IEEE/CVF Conference on Computer Vision and Pattern Recognition, pp. 3716–3725 (2020)

26. Tang, K., Niu, Y., Huang, J., Shi, J., Zhang, H.: Unbiased scene graph generation from biased training. In: 2020 IEEE/CVF Conference on Computer Vision and Pattern Recognition, CVPR 2020, Seattle, WA, USA, 13–19 June 2020, pp. 3713–3722. Computer Vision Foundation/IEEE (2020). https://doi.org/10.1109/CVPR42600.2020.00377

27. Vedantam, R., Lawrence Zitnick, C., Parikh, D.: Cider: Consensus-based image description evaluation. In: Proceedings of the IEEE Conference on Computer Vision and Pattern Recognition, pp. 4566–4575 (2015)

28. Veličković, P., Cucurull, G., Casanova, A., Romero, A., Lio, P., Bengio, Y.: Graph attention networks. arXiv preprint arXiv:1710.10903 (2017)

29. Venugopalan, S., Rohrbach, M., Donahue, J., Mooney, R., Darrell, T., Saenko, K.: Sequence to sequence-video to text. In: Proceedings of the IEEE International Conference on Computer Vision, pp. 4534–4542 (2015)

30. Venugopalan, S., Xu, H., Donahue, J., Rohrbach, M., Mooney, R.J., Saenko, K.: Translating videos to natural language using deep recurrent neural networks. In: Mihalcea, R., Chai, J.Y., Sarkar, A. (eds.) NAACL HLT 2015, The 2015 Conference of the North American Chapter of the Association for Computational Linguistics:

Human Language Technologies, Denver, Colorado, USA, 31 May - 5 June 2015, pp. 1494–1504. The Association for Computational Linguistics (2015)

31. Wang, B., Ma, L., Zhang, W., Jiang, W., Wang, J., Liu, W.: Controllable video captioning with POS sequence guidance based on gated fusion network. In: Proceedings of the IEEE/CVF International Conference on Computer Vision, pp. 2641–2650 (2019)

32. Wang, B., Ma, L., Zhang, W., Liu, W.: Reconstruction network for video captioning. In: Proceedings of the IEEE Conference on Computer Vision and Pattern Recognition, pp. 7622–7631 (2018)

33. Xu, J., Mei, T., Yao, T., Rui, Y.: MSR-VTT: a large video description dataset for bridging video and language. In: 2016 IEEE Conference on Computer Vision and Pattern Recognition, CVPR 2016, Las Vegas, NV, USA, 27–30 June 2016, pp. 5288–5296. IEEE Computer Society (2016)

34. Yang, B., Zou, Y., Liu, F., Zhang, C.: Non-autoregressive coarse-to-fine video captioning. arXiv preprint arXiv:1911.12018 (2019)

35. Yao, L., et al.: Describing videos by exploiting temporal structure. In: Proceedings of the IEEE International Conference on Computer Vision, pp. 4507–4515 (2015)

36. Zhang, Z., et al.: Object relational graph with teacher-recommended learning for video captioning. In: Proceedings of the IEEE/CVF Conference on Computer Vision and Pattern Recognition, pp. 13278–13288 (2020)

37. Zheng, Q., Wang, C., Tao, D.: Syntax-aware action targeting for video captioning. In: Proceedings of the IEEE/CVF Conference on Computer Vision and Pattern Recognition, pp. 13096–13105 (2020)

38. Zhou, L., Zhou, Y., Corso, J.J., Socher, R., Xiong, C.: End-to-end dense video captioning with masked transformer. In: Proceedings of the IEEE Conference on Computer Vision and Pattern Recognition, pp. 8739–8748 (2018)

# A Multi-Head Convolutional Neural Network with Multi-Path Attention Improves Image Denoising

Jiahong Zhang[1,2] (ORCID), Meijun Qu[3], Ye Wang[1,2], and Lihong Cao[1,2](✉)

[1] State Key Laboratory of Media Convergence and Communication, Communication University of China, Beijing, China
{zhangjh,yewang}@cuc.edu.cn
[2] Neuroscience and Intelligent Media Institute, Communication University of China, Beijing, China
lihong.cao@cuc.edu.cn
[3] School of Information and Communication Engineering, Communication University of China, Beijing, China
qumeijun@cuc.edu.cn

**Abstract.** Recently, convolutional neural networks (CNNs) and attention mechanisms have been widely used in image denoising and achieved satisfactory performance. However, the previous works mostly use a single head to receive the noisy image, limiting the richness of extracted features. Therefore, a novel CNN with multiple heads (MH) named MHCNN is proposed in this paper, whose heads will receive the input images rotated by different rotation angles. MH makes MHCNN simultaneously utilize features of rotated images to remove noise. To integrate these features effectively, we present a novel multi-path attention mechanism (MPA). Unlike previous attention mechanisms that handle pixel-level, channel-level, or patch-level features, MPA focuses on features at the image level. Experiments show MHCNN surpasses other state-of-the-art CNN models on additive white Gaussian noise (AWGN) denoising and real-world image denoising. Its peak signal-to-noise ratio (PSNR) results are higher than other networks, such as BRDNet, RIDNet, PAN-Net, and CSANN. The code is accessible at https://github.com/JiaHongZ/MHCNN.

**Keywords:** CNN · Image denoising · Deep learning

## 1 Introduction

Due to various problems in image acquisition equipment, the collected images often contain noise that can not be ignored. Image denoising aims to generate a clean image $x$ from a given noisy image $y$, modeled as $y = x + v$. Here $v$ denotes

S. Khanna et al. (Eds.): PRICAI 2022, LNCS 13631, pp. 338–351, 2022.
https://doi.org/10.1007/978-3-031-20868-3_25

the noise, and AWGN is commonly used. Recently, CNNs achieved remarkable results in this task. Compared to traditional denoising methods [5], CNNs can be trained end-to-end, which are easy to optimize and have better denoising results.

Zhang et al. [35] utilized residual learning and batch normalization to construct DnCNN for AWGN denoising, super-resolution, and JPEG deblocking. Then, [34] were proposed to deepen the network by residual connections and got better results than DnCNN. Some works such as BRDNet [29] and DHDN [24] showed that widening the network can also improve the denoising performance. However, these methods used more convolution layers, increasing the computational complexity. Therefore, it is essential to extract features effectively.

The attention mechanism is commonly used to increase the CNN's capacity and flexibility of extracting image features. This paper classifies the previous attention mechanisms into three types: pixel-level, channel-level, and patch-level. For pixel-level attention, the non-local operation is a classical method in image restoration. It makes full use of the information from adjacent pixels and achieves success in image restoration [20], image resolution [7] and image denoising [23,33]. Channel-level attention weights each feature channel and pays more attention to those important channels so that it improves denoising performance [2]. CSANN [31] and MRSNet [19] combined pixel-level attention with channel-level attention to get better denoising results than that of single attention. For patch-level attention, it can establish the relation between image patches and achieve good results in image enhancement [3].

Although these methods mentioned above achieved high performance, only one input head limits their abilities of extracting full features. This paper suggests that considering multiple rotation angles of the input image will get better results than one angle. It is different from the rotation pre-processing of data enhancement. Data enhancement can make CNNs learn the translated image features, but these features can not be simultaneously used because of the single input head limitation. We take a step to propose a multi-head convolutional neural network (MHCNN) with multi-path attention (MPA), which achieves state-of-the-art results. The different heads of MHCNN receive the input images rotated around the center to obtain rich features. MPA will integrate these features from different CNN heads to remove noise effectively, which is quite different from the previous attention mechanisms because MPA is image-level. The superiority of the proposed MHCNN is described in Sects. 4 and 5.

The main contributions of this paper are as follows:

(1) We propose a novel denoising network MHCNN. Its multiple heads (MH) will utilize features from multiple rotation angles of the input image.
(2) A novel attention module MPA is proposed to integrate the features from the different CNN heads. MPA focuses on image-level features rather than previous pixel-level, channel-level, and patch-level features.
(3) Ablation experiments show that the proposed MH with MPA mechanism is pluggable and can improve the denoising performance of the single head model.

(4) The proposed MHCNN can achieve state-of-the-art AWGN and real-world image denoising.

## 2    Related Work

Image denoising has received extensive attention for its indispensable role in many practical applications. This paper focuses on the CNN-based image denoising.

### 2.1    CNNs for Image Denoising

In [16], Jain et al. claimed that CNNs have similar or even better representation power than traditional denoising models. Then, Zhang et al. [35] achieved fast and stable training and good denoising performance by integrating the residual learning and batch normalization to CNN. Singh et al. [27] used ResNet blocks to construct the network and get better results than common convolution layers. In addition to deepening the network, widening the network is also an effective way. BRDNet [29] is two-path networks and get better results than the single-path networks. U-Net-based networks such as MWCNN [21] and DHDN [24] are three-path network architecture. They further improved the denoising performance. However, these methods only consider one angle of the input image, resulting in extracting insufficient features. The proposed MHCNN uses MH to receive image features of multiple rotation angles to solve this problem.

### 2.2    Attention Mechanisms for Image Denoising

Only MH is not enough because features from these heads need effective processing. Using attention mechanism is a popular method to increase this ability of CNNs. For pixel-level, non-local attention is commonly used, which restores the damaged pixel using its neighbors [20,33]. Some other pixel-level attention mechanisms use attention to guide the previous stage for image denoising. In ADNet [28], this guidance is achieved by convolution and multiplation operation. In PAN-Net [23], proportional-integral-derivative (PID) is used to get the guidance. Channel-level attention in RIDNet [2] utilized the relationship between the channel features to exploit and learn the critical content of the image. It achieves satisfying results both on AWGN and real-world image denoising. Patch-level attention is often used in vision transformer, which establishes the connection between image patches [3,8]. These attention methods also have the limitation of a single head. We propose a novel image-level MPA, which effectively integrate the features from the different heads of MHCNN.

## 3    The Proposed Method

### 3.1    Network Architecture

Figure 1 shows the proposed MHCNN. Given a noisy image, we firstly rotate it by 0°, 90°, and 180° to construct the inputs of the three heads. The main body of MHCNN consists of three parts as follows:

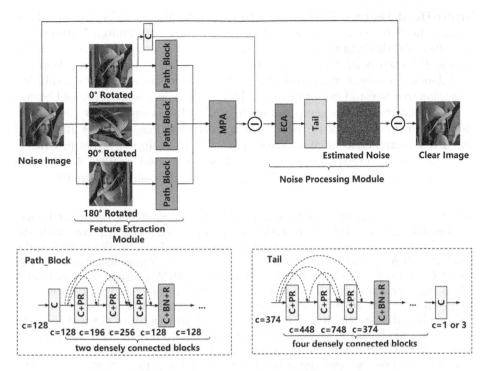

**Fig. 1.** The architecture of MHCNN. The feature extraction module consists of three heads to receive the input images with different rotation angles. Path_block is used to extract features from the different heads. MPA will integrate the features and get noise maps by the residual connection. At the end of MHCNN, noise processing module makes a further process to noise maps and genarates the estimated noise, where ECA is the effective channel attention layer [30]. Path_block and Tail are made up of densely connected blocks.

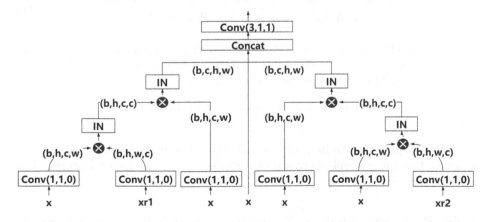

**Fig. 2.** The architecture of MPA module.

**Multi-Head Feature Extraction Module.** Traditional CNN denoisers have a single head to receive the noisy image, which extracts limited features. We introduce MH that utilizes the features from noisy images with different rotation angles. For each head, we use Path_block shown in Fig. 1 to extract features. Path_block is a variant of Densnet block [13]. We first execute a $1 \times 1$ convolution operation to generate 128 feature maps. These feature maps are processed by two densely connected blocks composed of three C+PR followed by one C+BN+R. Here C is convolution layer, BN is batch normalization [15], R is ReLU [18] and PR is parametric rectified linear unit [11]. Convolution layers in densely connected blocks are set kernel size $3 \times 3$, stride 1, and padding 1. Ablation experiments in Sect. 5 show that MH improves the denoising performance.

**MPA.** MH extracts features from multiple rotation angles of the input image. We assume that the rotated images contain many common features with the original one. In contrast, whether the image is rotated or not, the noise is independent. MPA module is designed to integrate the common features from different CNN heads, shown in Fig. 2. The input of MPA consists of $x$, $xr1$, $xr2$, which corresponds to the features of $0°$, $90°$, $180°$ rotated images, respectively. These three inputs have the same size $(b, c, h, w)$, where b is the batch size, c is the number of channels, h and w are the height and width of the features. We use $1 \times 1$ convolution to process the input so that it endows MPA the learning ability. After the convolution operations, there are three data flows, $xr1$, $x$, and $xr2$. For $xr1$ flow, we reshape $x$ to $(b, h, c, w)$ and $xr1$ to $(b, h, w, c)$, and then multiply them by matrix multiplication. This multiplication projects $x$ to space of $xr1$, which gets a fusion representation of the image and rotated image. Then, it is normalized by instance norm (IN) [14] and is reshaped to $(b, h, c, c)$. We subsequently project the $(b, h, c, c)$ fusion representation to the space of $x$ by multiplying it with another $(b, h, c, w)$ $x$. Normalization and resizing are used again, and we finally project the $xr1$ to $x$. According to Fig. 2, the projection $xr1\_p$ can be represented as follows:

$$xr1\_p = Reshape(IN(Reshape(IN(Reshape(Conv(x)) \\ \times Reshape(Conv(xr1)))) \times Reshape(Conv(x)))) \tag{1}$$

The projection from $xr2$ to $x$ denoted as $xr2\_p$ is similar to $xr1\_p$. For flow $x$, it remains the same. At the end of MPA, we concatenate these three data flows together. Thus the output of MPA is as follows:

$$MPA(xr1, xr2, x) = Conv(Concat(xr1\_p, xr2\_p, x)) \tag{2}$$

MPA projects the rotated images onto the original image through transformation. This image-level operation can effectively extract image features. The relevant analysis is in Sect. 5.2.

**Noise Processing Module.** The output of MPA is the integrated features containing $128 \times 3$ channels. We subtract these features from the $0°$ rotated

**Table 1.** PSNR (dB) results for different networks on Set12 with noise levels of 15, 25, 50.

| Methods | $\sigma = 15$ | $\sigma = 25$ | $\sigma = 50$ |
|---|---|---|---|
| BM3D [5] | 32.37 | 29.97 | 26.72 |
| DnCNN [35] | 32.86 | 30.43 | 27.18 |
| FFDNet [36] | 32.77 | 30.44 | 27.32 |
| ADNet [28] | 32.98 | 30.58 | 27.37 |
| BRDNet [29] | 33.03 | 30.61 | 27.45 |
| CSANN [31] | – | 30.72 | 27.64 |
| PAN-Net [23] | 33.14 | **30.90** | 27.58 |
| MHCNN | **33.21** | 30.84 | **27.70** |

image to obtain noise maps, which are used as the input of the noise processing module. Here we use a 1×1 convolution layer to get $128 \times 3$ features from the 0° rotated image. The effective channel attention (ECA) layer [30] is used to weigh the different channels, and the followed Tail block will further process the noise maps, which is shown in Fig. 1. Tail block consists of four densely connected blocks, and its output is the estimated noise with 1 channel for gray images or 3 channels for color images. After Tail, we subtract the estimated noise from the noisy image to generate the clear image.

Given an input, MHCNN can be represented as:

$$x = Path\_block(input)$$
$$xr1 = Path\_block(Rot90°(input))$$
$$xr2 = Path\_block(Rot180°(input)) \qquad (3)$$
$$noise = input - MPA(xr1, xr2, x)$$
$$output = input - Tail(ECA(noise))$$

We use l2 loss as the loss function of the proposed MHCNN, where $y_i$ is the real clear image, $output_i$ is the predicted clear image, and $N$ is the number of training samples:

$$L(\Theta) = \frac{1}{2N} \sum_n (y_i - output_i)^2, i \in [1, N] \qquad (4)$$

### 3.2  Training Setting

This model is implemented by python 3.5, PyTorch 1.5.1 with Cuda 9.2. The Adam [17] algorithm is adopted to optimize the trainable parameters. The initial learning rate is set as 0.0001 and decreases with the increment of training epochs. Before training, data augmentation is employed by randomly dividing the images into $80 \times 80$ patches and rotating them by 0°, 90°, 180°, and 270° randomly. The batch size is set as 128.

**Table 2.** Color image denoising results of different networks

| Datasets | Methods | $\sigma = 15$ | $\sigma = 25$ | $\sigma = 50$ |
|---|---|---|---|---|
| Kodak24 | *FFDNet* [36] | 34.69 | 32.16 | 29.00 |
| | *DnCNN* [35] | 34.55 | 32.07 | 28.86 |
| | *ADNet* [28] | 34.76 | 32.26 | 29.10 |
| | *BRDNet* [29] | 34.89 | 32.44 | 29.22 |
| | *PAN-Net* [23] | **35.41** | **32.89** | 29.37 |
| | *MHCNN* | 35.12 | 32.63 | **29.46** |
| MCMaster | *FFDNet* [36] | 34.71 | 32.37 | 29.20 |
| | *DnCNN* [35] | 33.46 | 31.55 | 28.61 |
| | *ADNet* [28] | 33.99 | 31.31 | 28.04 |
| | *BRDNet* [29] | 35.10 | 32.77 | 29.52 |
| | *PAN-Net* [23] | **35.61** | **33.08** | 29.67 |
| | *MHCNN* | 35.35 | 33.01 | **29.83** |

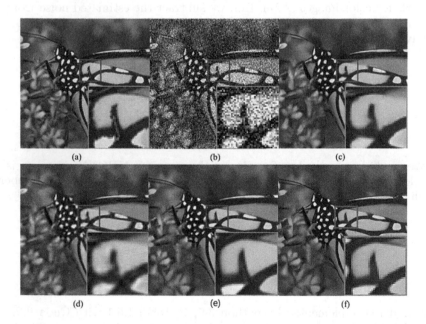

**Fig. 3.** Denoising results of the image Monarch from Set12 with noise level $\sigma = 50$: (a) original image, (b) noisy image/14.71 dB, (c) DnCNN [35]/26.78 dB, (d) BM3D [5]/25.82 dB, (e) BRDNet [29]/26.97 dB, and (f) MHCNN/27.12 dB.

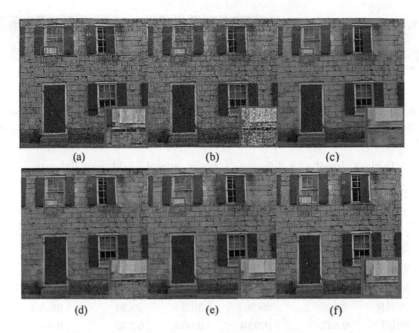

**Fig. 4.** Denoising results of the image from Kodak24 with noise level $\sigma = 50$: (a) original image, (b) noisy image, (c)DnCNN [35]/25.80 dB, (d) BRDNet [29]/26.33 dB, (e) FFDNet [36]/26.13 dB, and (f) MHCNN/26.52 dB.

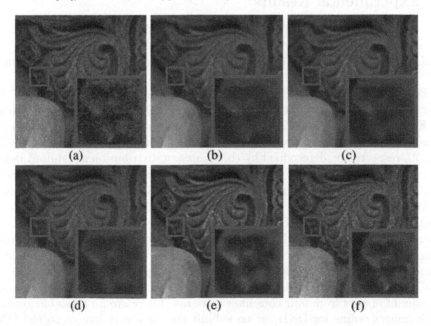

**Fig. 5.** Visual comparisons between MHCNN and other models. The test image was cropped from DND benchmark. (a) Input. (b) CBDNet [10]. (c) RIDNet [2]. (d) VDN [32]. (e) PAN-Net [23]. (f) MHCNN.

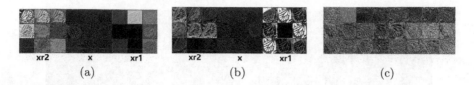

**Fig. 6.** Visualization of partial features of the Monarch. (a) is from three heads of MHCNN without MPA, (b) is from three heads MHCNN and (c) is the output of MPA.

**Table 3.** Results for different networks on real-world noise datasets.

| Test Data | SIDD validation | | | |
|---|---|---|---|---|
| Method | CBDNet [10] | RIDNet [2] | VDN [32] | MHCNN |
| PSNR | 38.68 | 38.71 | **39.28** | 39.06 |
| SSIM | 0.901 | **0.914** | 0.909 | **0.914** |
| Test Data | DND | | | | |
| Method | CBDNet [10] | RIDNet [2] | VDN [32] | PAN-Net [23] | MHCNN |
| PSNR | 38.06 | 39.26 | 39.38 | 39.44 | **39.52** |
| SSIM | 0.942 | **0.953** | 0.952 | 0.952 | 0.951 |

# 4    Experimental Results

## 4.1    Datasets

MHCNN is tested on the tasks of AWGN denoising and real-world image denoising.

For AWGN denoising, the training set includes 400 images from [4], 400 images from the validation set of ImageNet [6] and 4,744 images from the Waterloo Exploration Database [22]. The AWGN noise generation algorithm from [35] is used to generate the noisy images. We train MHCNN on noise levels 15, 25, and 50, respectively, determined by the Gaussian distribution's standard deviation $\sigma$. For each noise level, MHCNN is tested on the commonly used datasets Set12 [26] for gray images and MCMaster [37] and Kodak24 [9] for color images.

We use the training set from the Smartphone Image Denoising DATA set (SIDD) [1] to train MHCNN for real-world image denoising. It includes 160 different scene instances, and each scene instance has two pairs of high-resolution images. Each pair includes one noisy image and its corresponding ground-truth image. In total, there are 320 training image pairs. The testing sets are the SIDD validation and the Darmstadt Noise Data set (DND) [25]. DND includes 50 pairs of images from four consumer cameras. There are no available ground-truth images online for DND, so we submit the denoising images to the DND official website to get the results.

## 4.2   Comparison with Other Methods

**AWGN Denosing.** The peak signal-to-noise ratio (PSNR) [12] results are shown in Table 1 for gray images and Table 2 for color images. MHCNN performs better than other methods. At noise level $\sigma = 50$, MHCNN gets the best PSNR results on every dataset, which shows it is powerful for high-level noise.

We visualize the denoising results of MHCNN and other models. Figure 3 shows the denoising results of Monarch from Set12 at noise level $\sigma = 50$. MHCNN removes the noise well. For color images, the denoising results of the apartment wall from Kodak24 are shown in Fig. 4. The wall contains rich details information, which is very suitable for evaluating the model's performance. The denoised image of MHCNN preserves the most details and has the best visual effects.

**Real-World Image Denoising.** MHCNN has high performance on AWGN noise removing. We also do experiments on real-world images to ensure that MHCNN can be used in actual denoising tasks.

Table 3 lists the results of different methods on SIDD validation and DND. MHCNN has the best Structure Similarity Index Measure (SSIM) [38] on SIDD and the best PSNR on DND, demonstrating its superiority. Figure 5 shows the denoising result on DND, from which we observe that the noise has been removed successfully. Compared with other models, MHCNN does not smooth the local area of the noise too much and retains many details.

# 5   Results and Discussion

## 5.1   Ablation Experiments on MH

This section verifies the effectiveness of MH in MHCNN. Table 4 shows the PSNR results. We firstly study whether the number of heads affects denoising performance. According to Table 4, as the number of heads decreases, the denoising ability of MHCNN decreases. Of course, more heads will lead to more computation cost. We empirically choose three heads for a balance.

Different rotation angles of the input image are also studied. The results in Table 4 show that MHCNN ($0°$, $90°$, $270°$) and MHCNN ($0°$, $180°$, $270°$) have little impact on the performance. However, MHCNN ($0°$, $0°$, $0°$) leads to a performance degradation. This demonstrates that it is important to consider different rotation angles simultaneously.

## 5.2   Ablation Experiments on MPA

MPA achieves two crucial functions. One is integrating features from different heads of MHCNN. We visualized the features of the image Monarch extracted from each CNN head. As shown in Fig. 6 (b) and (c), the output features of MPA have the same angle as $x$, although the input angles are different. It illustrates that MPA projects the rotation images to the original image, achieving feature

**Table 4.** Results (PSNR) of ablation experiments on Set12.

| Methods | $\sigma = 15$ | $\sigma = 25$ | $\sigma = 50$ |
|---|---|---|---|
| MHCNN | 33.21 | **30.84** | **27.70** |
| MHCNN with 2 heads | 33.15 | 30.75 | 27.63 |
| MHCNN with 1 head | 33.10 | 30.71 | 27.58 |
| MHCNN $(0°, 0°, 0°)$ | 33.18 | 30.77 | 27.63 |
| MHCNN $(0°, 90°, 270°)$ | **33.22** | 30.83 | **27.70** |
| MHCNN $(0°, 180°, 270°)$ | 33.21 | 30.82 | 27.69 |
| MHCNN without MPA | 33.14 | 30.75 | 27.65 |

**Table 5.** Results (PSNR) of pluggable MH with MPA on Set12.

| Methods | $\sigma = 15$ | $\sigma = 25$ | $\sigma = 50$ |
|---|---|---|---|
| DnCNN [35] | 32.86 | 30.43 | 27.18 |
| Multi-head DnCNN | **32.97** | **30.56** | **27.32** |

integration. The other is that MPA helps to extract rich features. Figure 6 (a) and (b) show that MHCNN with MPA extracts richer images features, which have more details. For denoising performance, Table 4 shows MHCNN obtains higher PSNR results than that without MPA.

### 5.3 Pluggable MH with MPA

We indicate that the MH with MPA mechanism is also valuable for the other single-head CNN models such as DnCNN. We use it to replace the first 10 layers of DnCNN to keep the network depth unchanged for a fair comparison. The PSNR results are shown in Table 5, which demonstrates that adding MH with MPA significantly improves DnCNN.

## 6    Conclusion

This paper proposes a novel denoising network named MHCNN. It has the start-of-the-art results for AWGN denoising and real-world image denoising. The MH with MPA mechanism in MHCNN is proved effective by the ablation experiments. In addition, this mechanism can also be added to other models to improve performance. Although MH will cause many parameters and calculations, excellent parallelism can solve this problem. MHCNN adopts three CNN heads to obtain image features to balance computing costs. Furthermore, more CNN heads can be used to improve the denoising effect in practical applications. MH with MPA is a valuable attention mechanism, and we will exploit MH with MPA in image recognition and other visual tasks in the future.

**Acknowledgment.** This paper is supported by the National Natural Science Foundation of China (grant no. 62176241) and the National Key Research and Development Program of China (grant no. 2021ZD0200300) and the Open Project Program of the State Key Laboratory of Mathematical Engineering and Advanced Computing (grant no. 2020A09).

# References

1. Abdelhamed, A., Lin, S., Brown, M.S.: A high-quality denoising dataset for smartphone cameras. In: 2018 IEEE/CVF Conference on Computer Vision and Pattern Recognition, pp. 1692–1700 (2018)
2. Anwar, S., Barnes, N.: Real image denoising with feature attention. In: 2019 IEEE/CVF International Conference on Computer Vision (ICCV), pp. 3155–3164 (2019)
3. Chen, H., et al.: Pre-trained image processing transformer. In: Proceedings of the IEEE/CVF Conference on Computer Vision and Pattern Recognition, pp. 12299–12310 (2021)
4. Chen, Y., Pock, T.: Trainable nonlinear reaction diffusion: a flexible framework for fast and effective image restoration. IEEE Trans. Pattern Anal. Mach. Intell. **39**(6), 1256–1272 (2017)
5. Dabov, K., Foi, A., Katkovnik, V., Egiazarian, K.: Image denoising by sparse 3-D transform-domain collaborative filtering. IEEE Trans. Image Process. **16**(8), 2080–2095 (2007)
6. Deng, J., Russakovsky, O., Krause, J., Bernstein, M.S., Berg, A., Fei-Fei, L.: Scalable multi-label annotation. In: Proceedings of the SIGCHI Conference on Human Factors in Computing Systems, pp. 3099–3102 (2014)
7. Dian, R., Fang, L., Li, S.: Hyperspectral image super-resolution via non-local sparse tensor factorization. In: 2017 IEEE Conference on Computer Vision and Pattern Recognition (CVPR), pp. 3862–3871 (2017)
8. Dosovitskiy, A., et al.: An image is worth 16x16 words: transformers for image recognition at scale. arXiv preprint arXiv:2010.11929 (2020)
9. Franzen, R.: Kodak lossless true color image suite: Photocd pcd0992
10. Guo, S., Yan, Z., Zhang, K., Zuo, W., Zhang, L.: Toward convolutional blind denoising of real photographs. In: 2019 IEEE/CVF Conference on Computer Vision and Pattern Recognition (CVPR), pp. 1712–1722 (2019)
11. He, K., Zhang, X., Ren, S., Sun, J.: Delving deep into rectifiers: surpassing human-level performance on imagenet classification. In: 2015 IEEE International Conference on Computer Vision (ICCV), pp. 1026–1034 (2015)
12. Horé, A., Ziou, D.: Image quality metrics: PSNR vs. SSIM. In: 2010 20th International Conference on Pattern Recognition, pp. 2366–2369 (2010)
13. Huang, G., Liu, Z., Van Der Maaten, L., Weinberger, K.Q.: Densely connected convolutional networks. In: 2017 IEEE Conference on Computer Vision and Pattern Recognition (CVPR), pp. 2261–2269 (2017)
14. Huang, X., Belongie, S.: Arbitrary style transfer in real-time with adaptive instance normalization. In: Proceedings of the IEEE International Conference on Computer Vision, pp. 1501–1510 (2017)
15. Ioffe, S., Szegedy, C.: Batch normalization: accelerating deep network training by reducing internal covariate shift. In: International Conference on Machine Learning, pp. 448–456. PMLR (2015)

16. Jain, V., Seung, S.: Natural image denoising with convolutional networks. In: Koller, D., Schuurmans, D., Bengio, Y., Bottou, L. (eds.) Advances in Neural Information Processing Systems, vol. 21. Curran Associates, Inc. (2009)
17. Kingma, D.P., Ba, J.: Adam: a method for stochastic optimization. arXiv preprint arXiv:1412.6980 (2014)
18. Krizhevsky, A., Sutskever, I., Hinton, G.E.: ImageNet classification with deep convolutional neural networks. Adv. Neural. Inf. Process. Syst. **25**, 1097–1105 (2012)
19. Li, B., Wang, J., Zhang, J.: MRSNet: a spatial and channel attention integration network considering multi-resolution improves image denoising. In: 2021 7th International Conference on Computer and Communications (ICCC), pp. 719–724. IEEE (2021)
20. Liu, D., Wen, B., Fan, Y., Loy, C.C., Huang, T.S.: Non-local recurrent network for image restoration. In: Proceedings of the 32nd International Conference on Neural Information Processing Systems, pp. 1680–1689. NIPS2018, Curran Associates Inc., Red Hook, NY, USA (2018)
21. Liu, P., Zhang, H., Zhang, K., Lin, L., Zuo, W.: Multi-level wavelet-CNN for image restoration. In: 2018 IEEE/CVF Conference on Computer Vision and Pattern Recognition Workshops (CVPRW), pp. 886–88609 (2018)
22. Ma, K., et al.: Waterloo exploration database: new challenges for image quality assessment models. IEEE Trans. Image Process. **26**(2), 1004–1016 (2017)
23. Ma, R., Zhang, B., Zhou, Y., Li, Z., Lei, F.: PID controller-guided attention neural network learning for fast and effective real photographs denoising. IEEE Transactions on Neural Networks and Learning Systems, pp. 1–14 (2021)
24. Park, B., Yu, S., Jeong, J.: Densely connected hierarchical network for image denoising. In: 2019 IEEE/CVF Conference on Computer Vision and Pattern Recognition Workshops (CVPRW), pp. 2104–2113 (2019)
25. Plötz, T., Roth, S.: Benchmarking denoising algorithms with real photographs. In: 2017 IEEE Conference on Computer Vision and Pattern Recognition (CVPR), pp. 2750–2759 (2017)
26. Roth, S., Black, M.: Fields of experts: a framework for learning image priors. In: 2005 IEEE Computer Society Conference on Computer Vision and Pattern Recognition (CVPR2005), vol. 2, pp. 860–867 vol. 2 (2005)
27. Singh, G., Mittal, A., Aggarwal, N.: ResDNN: deep residual learning for natural image denoising. IET Image Proc. **14**(11), 2425–2434 (2020)
28. Tian, C., Xu, Y., Li, Z., Zuo, W., Fei, L., Liu, H.: Attention-guided CNN for image denoising. Neural Netw. **124**, 117–129 (2020)
29. Tian, C., Xu, Y., Zuo, W.: Image denoising using deep CNN with batch renormalization. Neural Netw. **121**, 461–473 (2020)
30. Wang, Q., Wu, B., Zhu, P., Li, P., Zuo, W., Hu, Q.: ECA-Net: efficient channel attention for deep convolutional neural networks, 2020 IEEE. In: CVF Conference on Computer Vision and Pattern Recognition (CVPR). IEEE (2020)
31. Wang, Y., Song, X., Chen, K.: Channel and space attention neural network for image denoising. IEEE Signal Process. Lett. **28**, 424–428 (2021)
32. Yue, Z., Yong, H., Zhao, Q., Zhang, L., Meng, D.: Variational denoising network: toward blind noise modeling and removal. arXiv preprint arXiv:1908.11314 (2019)
33. Zhang, J., Cao, L., Wang, T., Fu, W., Shen, W.: NHNet: a non-local hierarchical network for image denoising. IET Image Processing (2022)
34. Zhang, J., Zhu, Y., Li, W., Fu, W., Cao, L.: DRNet: a deep neural network with multi-layer residual blocks improves image denoising. IEEE Access **9**, 79936–79946 (2021)

35. Zhang, K., Zuo, W., Chen, Y., Meng, D., Zhang, L.: Beyond a gaussian denoiser: Residual learning of deep CNN for image denoising. IEEE Trans. Image Process. **26**(7), 3142–3155 (2017)
36. Zhang, K., Zuo, W., Zhang, L.: FFDNet: Toward a fast and flexible solution for CNN-based image denoising. IEEE Trans. Image Process. **27**(9), 4608–4622 (2018)
37. Zhang, L., Wu, X., Buades, A., Li, X.: Color demosaicking by local directional interpolation and nonlocal adaptive thresholding. J. Electron. Imaging **20**(2), 023016 (2011)
38. Zhou, W.: Image quality assessment: from error measurement to structural similarity. IEEE Trans. Image Process. **13**, 600–613 (2004)

# Learning Spatial Fusion and Matching for Visual Object Tracking

Wei Xiao and Zili Zhang[✉]

College of Computer and Information Science, Southwest University,
Chongqing 400715, China
zhangzl@swu.edu.cn

**Abstract.** Siamese network based trackers have achieved outstanding performance in visual object tracking, which in essence is the application of the efficient cross-correlation as the matching function. However, it is experimentally found that the cross-correlation based matching function is difficult to generate accurate tracking results in some challenging environments, such as background clutters and fast motion. Thus, a new Siamese-based tracker named SiamFAM is proposed. Specifically, from the perspective of feature fusion, a new matching function named Concatenation is introduced into our tracker, which can reduce the influence of background clutters by fine-grained matching with little computational overhead. Meanwhile, an adaptively spatial feature fusion (ASFF) module is proposed, which can take full use of multi-layer features and reduce poor prediction results during the prediction process. In addition, a refinement module is adopted to reduce the occurrence of tracking drift. Extensive experiments are conducted on six challenging benchmarks, including VOT2016, VOT2019, UAV123, NFS, OTB100, and LaSOT, demonstrating that our tracker is practical and can achieve a leading performance.

**Keywords:** Visual object tracking · Siamese network · Feature fusion

## 1 Introduction

Visual object tracking is an essential task in computer vision. After giving the state of the target in the first frame of the video, the tracker needs to track the target continuously in each subsequent video frame. Recently, visual object tracking has obtained widespread attention due to its expansive applications, such as human-machine interaction, intelligent surveillance and automatic driving, and has achieved considerable development. However, adaptive target tracking is still a big challenge due to the occlusion, background clutters, illumination variation, and fast motion.

© The Author(s), under exclusive license to Springer Nature Switzerland AG 2022
S. Khanna et al. (Eds.): PRICAI 2022, LNCS 13631, pp. 352–367, 2022.
https://doi.org/10.1007/978-3-031-20868-3_26

Current popular tracking methods [4,5,25,35,41] are basically based on the Siamese network architectures. Bertinetto [1] first used Siamese networks for visual object tracking, and then researchers significantly extended it and successively proposed excellent frameworks such as SiamRPN [20], SiamRPN++ [19], SiamBAN [4], and SiamRN [5]. By learning a generic matching map between the target template and the search region, Siamese-based trackers transform the challenge of visual object tracking into identifying the target from the search region by calculating the highest visual similarity. Therefore, the effect of the matching function is vital to the tracking results. In addition, as an intensive prediction task, whether the multi-layer features are effectively utilized will also affect the tracking. However, these two aspects have been ignored by many researchers. Most Siamese-based trackers still use the classical cross-correlation based matching function and simply perform matching and prediction on multi-layer features. The cross-correlation based matching function is fast, but the area of each matching operation is very large, which will make the matching results easily affected by background clutters. In addition, the separation prediction on different layers will break the advantages of different layer features, and the poor results produced in single-layer will also affect the final tracking accuracy.

In contrast, some individual researchers have begun to notice some matching functions that perform better than the cross-correlation based matching method and have started to take advantage of multi-layer features. SiamCAR [10] concatenates multi-layer features and performs one prediction on it. SOTS [39] applies various matching functions and uses binary channel manipulation to select the best matching functions for combination. In this work, a new tracker named SiamFAM is proposed to consider both the advantage of multi-layer features and the effect of the matching function. Specifically, an adaptively spatial feature fusion (ASFF) module is first introduced into visual object tracking, which can take full advantage of multi-layer features by fusing them. Meanwhile, a new matching function named Concatenation is used in our tracker, which can perform more intensive matching in a smaller area and significantly overcome the influence of background clutters. The visualized comparison results can be seen in Fig. 1.

The main contributions of our work are summarized in three aspects.

- A new Siamese-based tracking framework called SiamFAM is proposed for visual object tracking. This framework can be offline trained on well-annotated datasets.
- An adaptively spatial feature fusion (ASFF) module is firstly introduced into visual object tracking, which can fuse multi-layer features and reduce the poor results produced in a single layer. Benefiting from the ASFF, the prediction results of different layers become more stable.
- A method called Concatenation is used as our matching function. Concatenation can significantly retain the target information and reduce the influence of background clutters and similarity distractors through fine-grained matching. By combining ASFF and Concatenation matching method, our tracker achieves very competitive results on six benchmarks, including VOT2016 [17],

Fig. 1. The visualized comparisons of our tracker with other two trackers on three challenging sequences taken from OTB100 [33]. Our SiamFAM can get more robust and accurate results even when objects suffer from complex backgrounds and similar distractors. Observed from the visualization results, the SiamRN [5] results are much coarser, while Ocean [41] drifts to the background.

VOT2019 [18], NFS [16], OTB100 [33], LaSOT [8], and UAV123 [23], which indicates the effectiveness of our proposed tracker.

The organization of our paper is set as follows: Sect. 2 gives a related work on the visual object tracking. Section 3 introduces our proposed method in detail, followed by Sect. 4, which shows our experiments, and finally, Sect. 5 makes a conclusion of this paper.

## 2    Related Work

Visual object tracking is an active research subject in computer vision. In this paper, we focus on reviewing two aspects that are most relative to our work, one is matching function based tracking, and the other is Siamese network based tracking.

### 2.1    Matching Based Tracking

In recent visual object tracking, the process of predicting foreground probability is generally treated as a matching problem. SINT [29] identifies the search area locations matching with the initial target appearance by learning a matching function and simply defines the matching function as a *dot product operation*. GOTURE [13] directly regresses the concatenation feature of the template and searches images to predict the target location. ATOM [6] embeds the target information into the search area through the *Hadamard product*. Recently, cross-correlation has been recognized as the simplest and most effective matching method. On this basis, depth-wise cross-correlation and point-wise cross-correlation are further proposed. However, these methods have some drawbacks. Due to the large matching area, the depth-wise cross-correlation is easily affected by background clutters. Besides, in point-wise cross-correlation, the target information is not well used. To solve these problems, in this work, inspired by [28], we apply a new matching method to replace the classical matching method. Since our algorithm comes from Siamese-based trackers, we briefly review the evolution of Siamese network based tracking in the following.

## 2.2  Siamese Network Based Trackers

In recent years, the Siamese network based trackers have attracted extensive attention for their high tracking accuracy and efficiency [1,4,19,20,42]. SiamFC [1] uses the Siamese network to extract features and first adopts a cross-correlation module to generate a response map for classification and regression. Owing to its light structure, SiamFC is very efficient. CFNet [30] adopts a Correlation Filter layer for SiamFC to get more accurate tracking. However, these trackers need to perform a multi-scale search to deal with the scale change of the target, and the aspect ratio of the tracking frame cannot change adaptively. To solve this problem, SiamRPN [20] introduces a module named region proposal network into SiamFC, which can avoid the time-consuming step of extracting multi-scale feature maps. Though these above trackers improve the performance of SiamFC from different aspects, the main reason limiting the performance improvement is the tracker backbone AlexNet's weak feature extraction ability. SiamRPN++ [19] and SiamMask [32] solve the influence elements such as padding and use much deeper neural networks such as MobileNet [14], ResNeXt [34], and ResNet [12] as the tracker backbone, which further improves the performance of the tracker. Inspired by anchor-free object detection, SiamBAN [4] promotes the anchor-based tracker to anchor-free. Despite the current popular trackers using modern deep neural networks, the depth features are not well used, and some poor results are still produced in the prediction process. In this work, these above problems are solved by using an ASFF module and a Concatenation matching function. Compared with these above trackers, our tracker can reduce the influence of background clutters and can achieve more accurate and robust tracking.

## 3  Proposed Method

We now introduce the proposed Siamese network based tracker, and the framework of our tracker is shown in Fig. 2. Our tracker consists of four parts, includ-

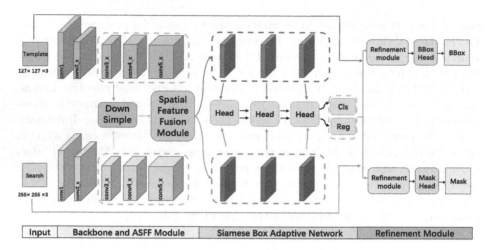

**Fig. 2.** The framework of the proposed SiamFAM network. It consists of a Siamese network backbone, an adaptively spatial feature fusion (ASFF) module, a Siamese box adaptive network, and a refinement module. The last three layer features of the backbone are extracted and fused by the ASFF module. The fused features generate two-stream and are fed into the Siamese box adaptive network to get a simple bounding box, and finally the simple box is refined by the refinement module.

ing a Siamese network backbone, an adaptively spatial feature fusion module, a Siamese box adaptive network, and a refinement module.

### 3.1   Siamese Network Backbone

Recently, new deep neural networks such as MobileNet [14], ResNeXt [34], and ResNet [12] have been widely used in Siamese-based trackers [19,40,41]. In this work, we take ResNet50 [12] as the tracker backbone. Although the application of the deep neural network ResNet50 will get more abstract features, the feature resolution will be reduced. However, detailed spatial information is crucial for Siamese-based trackers to perform dense predictions. To solve this problem, inspired by SiamBAN [4], we removed the down-sampling operations from the fourth and fifth convolution layers of the ResNet50 backbone. Meanwhile, an atrous convolution is added, which could improve the perceived field and improve the tracking effect of large-scale targets.

The Siamese network backbone consists of two branches. One is called the template branch, and the other is the search branch. The template branch takes the target template Z as input, while the search branch takes the search region X as input. These two branches share the same convolutional neural network parameters to ensure that the template and search regions are transformed in the same way. Meanwhile, to lighten the computational load, we reduce the feature channels from Conv3, Conv4, and Conv5 layers to 256 through 11 convolution.

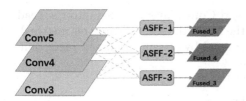 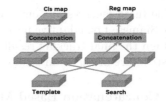

**Fig. 3.** Adaptively spatial feature fusion.    **Fig. 4.** The structure of the head.

## 3.2   Adaptively Spatial Feature Fusion Module

After utilizing the processed ResNet50, multi-level features can be used. Although the Conv3, Conv4, and Conv5 blocks of our backbone have the same spatial resolutions, the information captured is significantly different. As suggested by SiamBAN [4], low-level features contain more location and detail information, but due to less convolution, they have lower semantics and more noise. High-level features have more robust semantic information but a poor perception of detail. In other words, the information on each single-layer feature is not comprehensive. To reduce low-quality predictions due to incomplete feature information in the single layer, a spatial feature fusion module (ASFF) is proposed, which can enrich each single-layer feature details and semantic information by fusion.

As shown in Fig. 2, we use three ASFF modules to process the features of last three layers from our ResNet50 backbone. And the detailed operation can be seen in Fig. 3. For convenience, we use $x_{ij}^{n \to l}$ ($l, n \in \{3, 4, 5\}$) to represent the feature vector at the position (i, j) on the feature maps taken from layer n to layer $l$. Then the fusion operation at the corresponding layer $l$ can be denoted as follows:

$$y_{ij}^l = \alpha_{ij}^l \cdot x_{ij}^{3 \to l} + \beta_{ij}^l \cdot x_{ij}^{4 \to l} + \gamma_{ij}^l \cdot x_{ij}^{5 \to l}, \qquad (1)$$

where $y_{ij}^l$ implies the vector of the fused feature maps at the position (i, j) on the layer $l$. The $\alpha_{ij}^l, \beta_{ij}^l, \gamma_{ij}^l$ represents the spatial importance weights of the feature maps from three different layers to layer $l$, which can be adaptively learned by our network. Note that $\alpha^l, \beta^l$, and $\gamma^l$ are two-dimensional weight graph, which means that each position (i, j) on the feature maps of each layer has a spatial weight on it and share across all channels.

To get the spatial weights, we define

$$\alpha_{ij}^l = \frac{e^{\lambda_{\alpha_{ij}}^l}}{e^{\lambda_{\alpha_{ij}}^l} + e^{\lambda_{\beta_{ij}}^l} + e^{\lambda_{\gamma_{ij}}^l}}. \qquad (2)$$

The spatial weight $\alpha_{ij}^l, \beta_{ij}^l, \gamma_{ij}^l$ are defined by the softmax function with $\lambda_{\alpha_{ij}}^l, \lambda_{\beta_{ij}}^l, \lambda_{\gamma_{ij}}^l$ as the control parameters, respectively. And the weight scalar maps $\lambda_{\alpha_{ij}}^l, \lambda_{\beta_{ij}}^l, \lambda_{\gamma_{ij}}^l$ can be obtained from $x^3, x^4, x^5$ through $1 \times 1$ convolution. Inspired by [22], we force $\alpha_{ij}^l + \beta_{ij}^l + \gamma_{ij}^l = 1$ and $\alpha_{ij}^l, \beta_{ij}^l, \gamma_{ij}^l \in [0, 1]$.

The fused features of Conv3, Conv4, and Conv5 layers are fed into the head of the Siamese box adaptive network. In the head, the features are first matched, and then the final tracking results are obtained by classification and regression. The structure of the head is shown in Fig. 4.

### 3.3   Concatenation Based Matching

In current visual object tracking, depth-wise cross-correlation is widely used as a matching function for similarity matching. As shown in Fig. 5, the depth-wise cross-correlation takes the template feature as a convolution kernel to perform channel-by-channel convolution on the search area, which represents the matching operation. However, the resolution of the convolution kernel (template feature) is $15 \times 15$. In the $15 \times 15$ area of the search region, the target and a large number of background clutters will be included, which makes the matching results very susceptible to their influence. To solve this problem, inspired by [28], a fine-grained matching method is proposed.

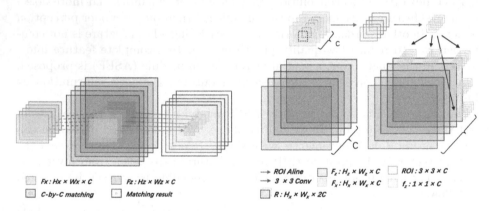

**Fig. 5.**   Depth-wise    cross-correlation matching method.

**Fig. 6.** Concatenation matching method.

As shown in Fig. 6, we define:

$$f_z^l = \varphi(F_z^l), \quad R^l = Conv([f_z^l, F_x^l]), \tag{3}$$

where $F_x^l \in \mathbb{R}^{H_z \times W_z \times C}$ and $F_z^l \in \mathbb{R}^{H_x \times W_x \times C}$ denote the feature maps of template Z and search X fused by the spatial feature fusion module at layer $l$. $\varphi(\cdot)$ represents the ROI_Align operation, which extracts ROI features from template $F_z^l$ through the template bounding box and adjusts the extracted features to $3 \times 3 \times C$ by bilinear interpolation. To reduce the matching area, the ROI features are fined to $1 \times 1 \times C$, and the result is recorded as $f_z^l$. To match the target, we first concatenate $f_z^l$ to the search region $F_x^l$ repetitively, making each position (i,j) have the information of the target. Then, we use $1 \times 1 \times 2C$ convolution to match the target at each position on the search region and generate the final matching result $R^l$.

## 3.4  Bounding Box Prediction

To get the target bounding box, we perform classification and regression on the response map $R_{w \times h \times c}$. The classification aims to identify which location is the tracking target, while the regression aims to predict the bounding box of the target. For the response map $R_{w \times h \times c}$, a classification feature map $P^{cls}_{w \times h \times 2}$ and a regression feature map $P^{reg}_{w \times h \times 4}$ can be obtained from the classification and regression, respectively, where $w$ and $h$ represent the width and height of the obtained feature map.

To improve the accuracy and robustness of the prediction, the prediction results from multi-layers are integrated by:

$$P^{cls-all}_{w \times h \times 2} = \sum_{l=3}^{5} \alpha_l P^{cls}_l, \quad P^{reg-all}_{w \times h \times 4} = \sum_{l=3}^{5} \beta_l P^{reg}_l, \tag{4}$$

where $\alpha_l$ and $\beta_l$ represent the weights of different layers, which can be trained together with the network. Note that after using the adaptively spatial feature fusion module, some poor single-layer predictions are reduced, which will make the final integration results more accurate. In addition, to reduce the occurrence of tracking drift, we fine-tune the tracking results with a pre-trained refinement module [36].

## 3.5  Training Loss

The cross-entropy loss and the IoU (Intersection over Union) loss are used for classification and regression, respectively. The total loss function is:

$$L = \lambda_1 L_{cls} + \lambda_2 L_{reg}, \tag{5}$$

where $L_{cls}$ denotes the cross-entropy loss and $L_{reg}$ denotes the IoU Loss. Especially, the IoU loss is defined as

$$L_{IoU} = 1 - IoU, \tag{6}$$

where $IoU \in (0,1]$ represents the intersection-over-union ratio of the predicted and the ground-truth bounding box. As for the two hyperparameters in Eq. 5, we set them to $\lambda_1 = \lambda_2 = 1$ as in our baseline [4].

## 4  Experiments

We conduct experiments on six benchmark datasets, including VOT2016 [17], NFS [16], OTB100 [33], UAV123 [23], VOT2019 [18], and LaSOT [8]. In the following, we first give an overview of the six tracking benchmarks, then we introduce our implementation in detail, followed by the comparison results with other trackers. Finally, an ablation study is provided to demonstrate the effectiveness of each proposed component.

## 4.1   Datasets

**VOT2016** [17] & **VOT2019** [18]. Both VOT2016 and VOT2019 are commonly used benchmarks for target tracking, and both of them have 60 sequences. Unlike VOT2016, VOT2019 has 30% more difficult tracking sequences, which means achieving a high score on VOT2019 will be more difficult. On VOT2016 and VOT2019, trackers are evaluated by using three metrics, including robustness (failure rate), accuracy (average overlap during successful tracking periods), and EAO (Expected Average Overlap). Note that the accuracy and robustness are combined in EAO. The higher the accuracy and the lower the robustness, the better result of the EAO.

**OTB100** [33]. OTB100 is a relatively common test dataset in target tracking, which contains 100 well-annotated sequences. It uses an area under curve (AUC) of success plot as the evaluation metric, which, at different thresholds, shows the percentage of successfully tracked frames.

**NFS** [16]. The NFS dataset includes 100 sequences of challenging objects captured from real-world surroundings. Same as OTB100, it uses area under curve (AUC) as the evaluation metric to measure trackers.

**UAV123** [23]. UAV123 is a new tracking benchmark, which contains 123 videos of small targets taken from the perspective of unmanned aerial vehicle. It reflects the ability of the evaluated tracker to track small target objects and also uses AUC as the evaluation metric.

**LaSOT** [8]. LaSOT is a large tracking dataset with 1400 training sequences and 280 test sequences. Compared to previous datasets, the sequences of LaSOT are longer, with an average of over 2500 frames in each, which can demonstrate the long-term performance of the evaluated trackers. LaSOT takes success plots, normalized precision plots, and precision plots in one-pass evaluation (OPE) as the evaluation metrics. The higher these three evaluation metrics are, the better the tracker tracking performance is.

## 4.2   Implementation Details

In this work, our tracker is trained with image pairs from COCO [21], GOT10k [15], YouTube-BB [26], ImageNet DET [27], LaSOT [8], and ImageNet VID [27]. For a fair comparison, same as $[1, 9, 10, 29, 35, 40]$, the input size is set to $127 \times 127$ for template patches and $255 \times 255$ for search patches.

Our backbone is initialized with modified ResNet50 pre-trained on ImageNET, and we use stochastic gradient descent (SGD) to train with a weight decay of $10^{-4}$ and a momentum of 0.9. The model is trained for 20 epochs with a minibatch of 32 pairs. Note that we set the learning rate exponentially decays from 0.001 to 0.005 in the first 5 epochs, and from $5 \times 10^{-3}$ to $5 \times 10^{-5}$ in the last 15 epochs.

The backbone parameters are frozen in the first ten epochs, while the last 3 blocks of the backbone are unfrozen in the last ten epochs for training at one-tenth of the current learning rate. Our approach is implemented in Python on a PC with Intel Xeon(R) E5-2620 2.10 GHz CPU, 64 GB RAM, Nvidia Titan XP.

**Table 1.** Detailed comparisons on VOT2016 and VOT2019, with EAO (expected average overlap), Accuracy and Robustness. The best three results are highlighted in red, blue and green fonts.

| Tracker | VOT2016 | | | VOT2019 | | |
|---|---|---|---|---|---|---|
| | Accuracy↑ | Robustness↓ | EAO↑ | Accuracy↑ | Robustness↓ | EAO↑ |
| ECO [7] | 0.55 | 0.20 | 0.375 | - | - | - |
| DaSiamRPN [42] | 0.61 | 0.22 | 0.411 | - | - | - |
| SPM [31] | 0.62 | 0.21 | 0.434 | 0.577 | 0.507 | 0.275 |
| SiamMask [32] | 0.67 | 0.23 | 0.442 | 0.594 | 0.461 | 0.287 |
| UpdateNet [38] | 0.61 | 0.21 | 0.481 | - | - | - |
| SiamRPN++ [19] | 0.64 | 0.20 | 0.464 | 0.599 | 0.482 | 0.285 |
| ATOM [6] | - | - | - | 0.603 | 0.441 | 0.292 |
| DiMP50 [2] | - | - | - | 0.582 | 0.371 | 0.321 |
| SiamBAN [4] | 0.632 | 0.149 | 0.505 | 0.602 | 0.396 | 0.327 |
| SiamAttn [37] | 0.679 | 0.150 | 0.525 | - | - | - |
| SiamRPN++ (ACM) [11] | 0.666 | 0.144 | 0.501 | 0.624 | 0.431 | 0.303 |
| Ocean [41] | - | - | - | 0.590 | 0.376 | 0.329 |
| SiamRN [5] | - | - | - | 0.593 | 0.306 | 0.341 |
| SiamRCR [25] | - | - | - | 0.602 | 0.386 | 0.336 |
| Ours | 0.652 | 0.121 | 0.540 | 0.617 | 0.381 | 0.342 |

## 4.3   Comparison with State-of-the-Art Trackers

**VOT2016** [17] & **VOT2019** [18]. Table 1 shows the comparation results on VOT2016 and VOT2019. On VOT2016, our tracker achieves 0.540 EAO, 0.121 robustness, and 0.652 accuracy, surpassing other state-of-the-art trackers under all metrics. Compared with recent SiamBAN and SiamRPN++(ACM), our tracker has significant improvements of 3.5% and 3.9% on EAO, respectively. Note that our tracker achieves a robustness of 0.121, which indicates that our tracker has the lowest tracking failure rate. On VOT2019, our method have a maximum EAO score while maintaining competitive accuracy and robustness with other compared trackers. SiamRN attains the best robustness, but the accuracy is only 0.593. Our method achieves a comparable accuracy of 0.617, which is 2.4% higher than SiamRN and our EAO is also slightly better than SiamRN. Notably, our tracker has much better tracking results than the baseline approach on both datasets. On VOT2016, our tracker improves by 3.5%, 3.0%, and 2.3%, and on VOT2019, our tracker improves by 1.5%, 1.5%, and 1.7% for the three evaluation metrics, respectively.

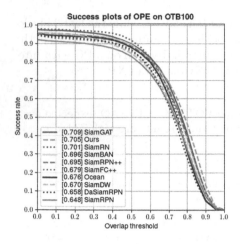

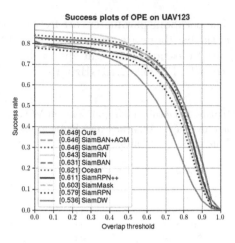

**Fig. 7.** Success plots on OTB100.     **Fig. 8.** Success plot on UAV123.

These comparison results show that our proposed method can improve tracking accuracy and effectiveness. Regarding tracking robustness, our tracker achieves the best result on VOT2016. While on VOT2019, although our tracking robustness is lower, we still improve the robustness by 1.5% over baseline, which also indicates the effectiveness of our proposed method.

**OTB100** [33]. Our tracker is compared with 9 other state-of-the-art trackers, including SiamGAT [9], SiamRN [5], SiamBAN [4], SiamRPN++ [19], Ocean [41], SiamMask [32], SiamRPN [20], and SiamDW [40]. The success plot of the OTB100 is shown in Fig. 7. Our tracker achieves the second AUC (area under curve) among all methods. Specifically, we achieve an AUC of 0.705, which is 0.9% higher than the classical method SiamBAN with traditional matching functions. And when compared with SiamFC++ [35], a classical anchor-free tracker, our tracker has a 2.5% improvement.

**UAV123** [23]. We compare our tracker with 9 other trackers, including SiamBAN(ACM) [11], SiamGAT [9], SiamRN [5], SiamBAN [4], Ocean [41], SiamRPN++ [19], SiamMask [32], SiamRPN [20], SiamDW [40], and Fig. 8 shows the success plots. As one can see our tracker ranks first in AUC (area under curve) in all trackers. And when compared with our baseline, our tracker has a 1.8% improvement with a small computational overhead.

**Table 2.** The detailed Comparison result on the NFS dataset.

|  | MDNet[24] | ECO [7] | SiamRPN++[19] | UPDT [3] | ATOM [6] | DiMP50[2] | SiamBAN[4] | Ours |
|---|---|---|---|---|---|---|---|---|
| AUC↑ | 42.2 | 46.6 | 50.2 | 53.7 | 58.4 | 62.0 | 59.4 | 59.0 |

**NFS** [16]. We compared our tracker with 7 other trackers in the NFS 30FPS videos, and the AUC (area under curve) scores are shown in Table 2. Our tracker achieves 59.0 in AUC, ranking third in all compared trackers, which indicates that our tracker is robust for tracking fast-moving objects and can reduce the effect of similarity distractors. Note that compared to the best tracker in the NFS paper, we have a significant improvement of 40.4%.

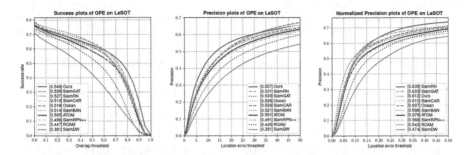

**Fig. 9.** Success, Precision and Normalized precision plot on LaSOT.

**LaSOT** [8]. Figure 9 shows the comparation results with 9 other progressive methods, including SiamGAT [9], SiamRN [5], SiamCAR [10], Ocean [41], SiamBAN [4], ATOM [6], SiamRPN++ [19], SiamDW [40], our tracker ranks first in success (AUC), precision, and third in normalized precision. Specifically, we achieve 0.549 in success (AUC), 0.557 in precision, and 0.612 in normalized precision. Compared with SiamGAT [9], our method has 2.7% and 1.0% improvements in precision and AUC, respectively. And when compared with our baseline, our method improves by 3.5%, 3.6% and 1.4% respectively for the three indicators, which means our tracker has a higher tracking success rate and tracking accuracy in long-term tracking.

## 4.4 Matching Function Evaluation and Ablation Study

To demonstrate the impact of the Concatenation matching function on Siamese tracking, we compared our concatenation-based tracker with our baseline depth-wise cross-correlation based tracker on OTB100. Table 3 shows the tracking performance. To display the details, we report eleven different aspect results. One can see the Concatenation matching function can achieve comparable results in many challenges. Specifically, our tracker gains a clear performance of 2.3%, 2.3%, and 2.0% in MB, FM, and OV. Besides, in IPR and OCC, Concatenation and depth-wise cross-correlation achieve similar effects. Finally, we obtain an overall precision of 0.705, which surpasses that of depth-wise cross-correlation by 0.9%. This comparison demonstrates that the classical depth-wise cross-correlation is not the best option for Siamese tracking, Concatenation matching function is more comprehensive.

**Table 3.** The tracking performance of two matching functions on OTB100. Scale Variation (SV), Motion Blur (MB), Occlusion (OCC), In-Plane Rotation (IPR), Fast Motion (FM), Low Resolution (LR), Out-of-View (OV), Deformation (DEF), Background Clutters (BC), Out-of-Plane Rotation (OPR), and Illumination Variation (IV) are 11 challenging attributes.

| Matching Function | Overall | SV | MB | FM | IPR | OV | IV | OCC | DEF | OPR | BC | LR |
|---|---|---|---|---|---|---|---|---|---|---|---|---|
| Depth-wise cross correlation | 0.696 | 0.693 | 0.698 | 0.687 | **0.717** | 0.640 | **0.724** | **0.648** | 0.662 | **0.687** | **0.680** | 0.719 |
| Concatenation | **0.705** | **0.705** | **0.721** | **0.710** | 0.716 | **0.660** | 0.714 | 0.646 | **0.667** | 0.676 | 0.669 | **0.737** |

**Table 4.** The Ablation study on LaSOT, and the baseline is SiamBAN.

| Method | NP↑ | P↑ | AUC↑ | ΔAUC |
|---|---|---|---|---|
| Baseline | 0.598 | 0.521 | 0.514 | - |
| Baseline+ASFF_Concatenation | 0.599 | 0.529 | 0.524 | +1.0% |
| Baseline+ASFF_Concatenation+Alpha-refine | 0.612 | 0.557 | 0.549 | +3.5% |

The ablation study on LaSOT can be seen in Table 4. Since the adaptively spatial feature fusion module (ASFF) is only an auxiliary module, we combine it with the Concatenation matching function in this discussion. As one can see, the combination of the adaptively spatial feature fusion module (ASFF) and Concatenation matching function achieves similar results on normalized precision while improving 0.8% on precision compared with our baseline. Finally, it brings a 1.0% AUC performance improvement. These results indicate that the center of our model prediction result has a smaller Euclidean distance from the center of the ground truth, demonstrating that our prediction results are more accurate. And alpha-refine can improve normalized precision and precision by 1.3% and 2.8%, respectively, and bring a 2.5% AUC performance improvement. These results indicate that compared with the adaptively spatial feature fusion module and Concatenation matching function, the alpha-refine module can further reduce the Euclidean distance between the center of prediction results and the ground truth in tracking and finally reduce the occurrence of tracking drift. Taken together, the combination of the adaptively spatial feature fusion module (ASFF) and the concatenation matching function can bring some performance improvement in tracking, while alpha-refine has a better tracking performance improvement.

## 5   Conclusions

In this work, a new Siamese network based tracker named SiamFAM is proposed for visual object tracking. Specifically, an adaptively spatial feature fusion module (ASFF) is introduced into our tracker, and a new matching method named Concatenation is used as the matching function. The spatial feature fusion module can take full use of multi-layer features to reduce poor prediction results during the prediction process. In contrast, the Concatenation matching method can reduce the influence of background clutters by taking a fine-grained matching. Finally, a refinement module named alpha-refine is used to solve the tracking drift problem. Extensive experiments are conducted on six visual tracking benchmarks, including VOT2016, VOT2019, UAV123, NFS, OTB100, and LaSOT, demonstrating that our tracker is efficient and can achieve a leading performance in both short-term and long-term tracking.

# References

1. Bertinetto, L., Valmadre, J., Henriques, J.F., Vedaldi, A., Torr, P.H.S.: Fully-convolutional Siamese networks for object tracking. In: Hua, G., Jégou, H. (eds.) ECCV 2016. LNCS, vol. 9914, pp. 850–865. Springer, Cham (2016). https://doi.org/10.1007/978-3-319-48881-3_56
2. Bhat, G., Danelljan, M., Gool, L.V., Timofte, R.: Learning discriminative model prediction for tracking. In: ICCV, pp. 6182–6191 (2019)
3. Bhat, G., Johnander, J., Danelljan, M., Khan, F.S., Felsberg, M.: Unveiling the power of deep tracking. In: Ferrari, V., Hebert, M., Sminchisescu, C., Weiss, Y. (eds.) ECCV 2018. LNCS, vol. 11206, pp. 493–509. Springer, Cham (2018). https://doi.org/10.1007/978-3-030-01216-8_30
4. Chen, Z., Zhong, B., Li, G., Zhang, S., Ji, R.: Siamese box adaptive network for visual tracking. In: CVPR, pp. 6668–6677 (2020)
5. Cheng, S., et al.: Learning to filter: Siamese relation network for robust tracking. In: CVPR, pp. 4421–4431 (2021)
6. Danelljan, M., Bhat, G., Khan, F.S., Felsberg, M.: Atom: accurate tracking by overlap maximization. In: CVPR, pp. 4660–4669 (2019)
7. Danelljan, M., Bhat, G., Shahbaz Khan, F., Felsberg, M.: Eco: efficient convolution operators for tracking. In: CVPR, pp. 6638–6646 (2017)
8. Fan, H., et al.: LaSOT: a high-quality benchmark for large-scale single object tracking. In: CVPR, pp. 5374–5383 (2019)
9. Guo, D., Shao, Y., Cui, Y., Wang, Z., Zhang, L., Shen, C.: Graph attention tracking. In: CVPR, pp. 9543–9552 (2021)
10. Guo, D., Wang, J., Cui, Y., Wang, Z., Chen, S.: SiamCAR: Siamese fully convolutional classification and regression for visual tracking. In: CVPR, pp. 6269–6277 (2020)
11. Han, W., Dong, X., Khan, F.S., Shao, L., Shen, J.: Learning to fuse asymmetric feature maps in Siamese trackers. In: CVPR, pp. 16570–16580 (2021)
12. He, K., Zhang, X., Ren, S., Sun, J.: Deep residual learning for image recognition. In: CVPR, pp. 770–778 (2016)
13. Held, D., Thrun, S., Savarese, S.: Learning to track at 100 fps with deep regression networks. In: Leibe, B., Matas, J., Sebe, N., Welling, M. (eds.) ECCV 2016. LNCS, vol. 9905, pp. 749–765. Springer, Cham (2016). https://doi.org/10.1007/978-3-319-46448-0_45
14. Howard, A.G., et al.: MobileNets: efficient convolutional neural networks for mobile vision applications. arXiv preprint arXiv:1704.04861 (2017)
15. Huang, L., Zhao, X., Huang, K.: GOT-10k: a large high-diversity benchmark for generic object tracking in the wild. IEEE Trans. Pattern Anal. Mach. Intell. **43**(5), 1562–1577 (2019)
16. Kiani Galoogahi, H., Fagg, A., Huang, C., Ramanan, D., Lucey, S.: Need for speed: a benchmark for higher frame rate object tracking. In: ICCV, pp. 1125–1134 (2017)

17. Kristan, M., et al.: The visual object tracking VOT2014 challenge results. In: Agapito, L., Bronstein, M.M., Rother, C. (eds.) ECCV 2014. LNCS, vol. 8926, pp. 191–217. Springer, Cham (2015). https://doi.org/10.1007/978-3-319-16181-5_14
18. Kristan, M., et al.: The seventh visual object tracking vot2019 challenge results. In: ICCV Workshops, pp. 2206–2241 (2019)
19. Li, B., Wu, W., Wang, Q., Zhang, F., Xing, J., Yan, J.: SiamRPN++: evolution of Siamese visual tracking with very deep networks. In: CVPR, pp. 4282–4291 (2019)
20. Li, B., Yan, J., Wu, W., Zhu, Z., Hu, X.: High performance visual tracking with Siamese region proposal network. In: CVPR, pp. 8971–8980 (2018)
21. Lin, T.-Y., et al.: Microsoft COCO: common objects in context. In: Fleet, D., Pajdla, T., Schiele, B., Tuytelaars, T. (eds.) ECCV 2014. LNCS, vol. 8693, pp. 740–755. Springer, Cham (2014). https://doi.org/10.1007/978-3-319-10602-1_48
22. Liu, S., Huang, D., Wang, Y.: Learning spatial fusion for single-shot object detection. arXiv preprint arXiv:1911.09516 (2019)
23. Mueller, M., Smith, N., Ghanem, B.: A benchmark and simulator for UAV tracking. In: Leibe, B., Matas, J., Sebe, N., Welling, M. (eds.) ECCV 2016. LNCS, vol. 9905, pp. 445–461. Springer, Cham (2016). https://doi.org/10.1007/978-3-319-46448-0_27
24. Nam, H., Han, B.: Learning multi-domain convolutional neural networks for visual tracking. In: CVPR, pp. 4293–4302 (2016)
25. Peng, J., et al.: SiamRCR: reciprocal classification and regression for visual object tracking. arXiv preprint arXiv:2105.11237 (2021)
26. Real, E., Shlens, J., Mazzocchi, S., Pan, X., Vanhoucke, V.: Youtube-boundingboxes: a large high-precision human-annotated data set for object detection in video. In: CVPR, pp. 5296–5305 (2017)
27. Russakovsky, O., et al.: ImageNet large scale visual recognition challenge. Int. J. Comput. Vision **115**(3), 211–252 (2015)
28. Sung, F., Yang, Y., Zhang, L., Xiang, T., Torr, P.H., Hospedales, T.M.: Learning to compare: relation network for few-shot learning. In: CVPR, pp. 1199–1208 (2018)
29. Tao, R., Gavves, E., Smeulders, A.W.: Siamese instance search for tracking. In: CVPR, pp. 1420–1429 (2016)
30. Valmadre, J., Bertinetto, L., Henriques, J., Vedaldi, A., Torr, P.H.: End-to-end representation learning for correlation filter based tracking. In: CVPR, pp. 2805–2813 (2017)
31. Wang, G., Luo, C., Xiong, Z., Zeng, W.: SPM-tracker: series-parallel matching for real-time visual object tracking. In: CVPR, pp. 3643–3652 (2019)
32. Wang, Q., Zhang, L., Bertinetto, L., Hu, W., Torr, P.H.: Fast online object tracking and segmentation: a unifying approach. In: CVPR, pp. 1328–1338 (2019)
33. Wu, Y., Lim, J., Yang, M.H.: Online object tracking: a benchmark. In: CVPR, pp. 2411–2418 (2013)
34. Xie, S., Girshick, R., Dollár, P., Tu, Z., He, K.: Aggregated residual transformations for deep neural networks. In: CVPR, pp. 1492–1500 (2017)
35. Xu, Y., Wang, Z., Li, Z., Yuan, Y., Yu, G.: SiamFC++: towards robust and accurate visual tracking with target estimation guidelines. In: Proceedings of the AAAI Conference on Artificial Intelligence, vol. 34, pp. 12549–12556 (2020)
36. Yan, B., Zhang, X., Wang, D., Lu, H., Yang, X.: Alpha-refine: boosting tracking performance by precise bounding box estimation. In: CVPR, pp. 5289–5298 (2021)
37. Yu, Y., Xiong, Y., Huang, W., Scott, M.R.: Deformable Siamese attention networks for visual object tracking. In: CVPR, pp. 6728–6737 (2020)
38. Zhang, L., Gonzalez-Garcia, A., van de Weijer, J., Danelljan, M., Khan, F.S.: Learning the model update for Siamese trackers. In: ICCV, pp. 4010–4019 (2019)

39. Zhang, Z., Liu, Y., Wang, X., Li, B., Hu, W.: Learn to match: automatic matching network design for visual tracking. In: ICCV, pp. 13339–13348 (2021)
40. Zhang, Z., Peng, H.: Deeper and wider Siamese networks for real-time visual tracking. In: CVPR, pp. 4591–4600 (2019)
41. Zhang, Z., Peng, H., Fu, J., Li, B., Hu, W.: Ocean: object-aware anchor-free tracking. In: Vedaldi, A., Bischof, H., Brox, T., Frahm, J.-M. (eds.) ECCV 2020. LNCS, vol. 12366, pp. 771–787. Springer, Cham (2020). https://doi.org/10.1007/978-3-030-58589-1_46
42. Zhu, Z., Wang, Q., Li, B., Wu, W., Yan, J., Hu, W.: Distractor-aware Siamese networks for visual object tracking. In: Ferrari, V., Hebert, M., Sminchisescu, C., Weiss, Y. (eds.) ECCV 2018. LNCS, vol. 11213, pp. 103–119. Springer, Cham (2018). https://doi.org/10.1007/978-3-030-01240-3_7

# Lightweight Wavelet-Based Transformer for Image Super-Resolution

Jinye Ran and Zili Zhang[✉]

College of Computer and Information Science, Southwest University,
Chongqing 400715, China
zhangzl@swu.edu.cn

**Abstract.** Suffering from the inefficiency of deeper and wider networks, most remarkable super-resolution algorithms cannot be easily applied to real-world scenarios, especially resource-constrained devices. In this paper, to concentrate on fewer parameters and faster inference, an end-to-end Wavelet-based Transformer for Image Super-resolution (WTSR) is proposed. Different from the existing approaches that directly map low-resolution (LR) images to high-resolution (HR) images, WTSR also implicitly mines the self-similarity of image patches by a lightweight Transformer on the wavelet domain, so as to balance the model performance and computational cost. More specifically, a two-dimensional stationary wavelet transform is designed for the mutual transformation between feature maps and wavelet coefficients, which reduces the difficulty of mining self-similarity. For the wavelet coefficients, a Lightweight Transformer Backbone (LTB) and a Wavelet Coefficient Enhancement Backbone (WECB) are proposed to capture and model the long-term dependency between image patches. Furthermore, a Similarity Matching Block (SMB) is investigated to combine global self-similarity and local self-similarity in LTB. Experimental results show that our proposed approach can achieve better super-resolution performance on the multiple public benchmarks with less computational complexity.

**Keywords:** Transformer · Lightweight network · Wavelet transform · Image super-resolution

## 1 Introduction

Single image super-resolution (SISR) aims to restore the high-resolution (HR) image corresponding to the low-resolution (LR) image. As a low-level computer vision task, SISR enjoys a wide range of applications in many fields, such as remote sense [36], surveillance [39], medical imaging [28], and security [16], amongst others. Essentially, SISR is an ill-posed problem since there are always

© The Author(s), under exclusive license to Springer Nature Switzerland AG 2022
S. Khanna et al. (Eds.): PRICAI 2022, LNCS 13631, pp. 368–382, 2022.
https://doi.org/10.1007/978-3-031-20868-3_27

infinite HR images degrading to the same LR image. To minimize the uncertainty, recently, extensive methods [2,8,15,32,33] based on deep neural networks have been proposed and have achieved remarkable performance on many public benchmarks. However, to improve the quality of super-resolution, most mainstream methods concentrate on developing a deeper and wider neural network and neglect the lightweight problem, which may limit the development of super-resolution networks in some resource-constrained devices, like edge computing devices.

**Fig. 1.** Self-similar information in the image (the same color bounding box region), which can reduce the difficulty of modeling the ill-posed problem. (Color figure online)

Although lightweight and performance are generally considered as a trade-off problem in SISR, there are still two feasible directions to address these issues. One is to build models with a parameter sharing strategy, such as recurrent learning [20,31] and recursive learning [30,33]. The other is to design some elaborate architectures, such as wide activation [37], group convolution [2], and information distillation [12]. However, the above two methods have disadvantages such as long inference time and complicated design of structures, which can not meet universal super-resolution application scenarios. Recently, [27] reported that mining the self-similar information in the images could greatly improve the super-resolution results. As shown in Fig. 1, the ill-posed problems in super-resolution would be greatly alleviated by referring to other similar image patches. Furthermore, we observed that the working principle (self-attention mechanism) of Transformer could effectively capture the self-similarity between the image patches, which encouraged us to build a lightweight super-resolution network by it. However, the existing Transformers cannot be directly used for pixel-level reconstruction tasks because they consume a lot of computing and memory resources, which are not conducive to constructing lightweight super-resolution networks.

To remedy this defect, we make a trade-off between the model performance and computational cost of the Transformer and propose a Wavelet-based Transformer for Image Super-Resolution (WTSR). As shown in Fig. 2, the proposed network is conducted on the wavelet domain because the wavelet transform

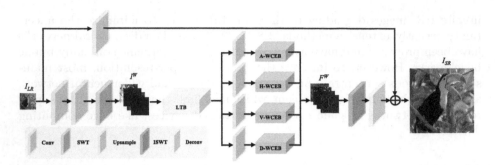

**Fig. 2.** The network of the proposed wavelet-based Transformer for super-resolution. The letters before WCEB denote different ABs for different wavelet coefficient.

can efficiently generate detailed information of images, which is beneficial for the mining of self-similarity in the images and the lightweight design of the model. Meanwhile, considering that the resolution of wavelet coefficients can significantly influence the difficulty of modeling, we finally decide to learn the mapping between LR and HR on the stationary wavelet domain. In addition, WTSR also includes a Lightweight Transformer Backbone (LTB) and a Wavelet Coefficient Enhancement Backbone (WCEB). For the LTB, inspired by [22] and considering lightweight, an Efficient Transformer (ET) encoder that adopts the design of wavelet coefficients partitioning and channel compression is proposed, which can significantly alleviate the requirements on hardware resources. Meanwhile, noting the effect of the partitioning method and partitioning size on self-similarity modeling, a Similarity Matching Block (SMB) is proposed to connect two ET encoders with different partitioning sizes. In other words, SMB combines global and local self-similarity to overcome the network receptive field constraints imposed by partitioning. For the WCEB, recovering each wavelet coefficient's structural information and channel redundancy is its main target. In particular, four WCEBs with different Asymmetric Blocks (ABs) are utilized to reconstruct corresponding wavelet coefficients, such as $1*3$ AB for the horizontal wavelet coefficient. For then, a coordinate attention layer [10] is used to balance the lightweight and performance. To make WTSR trainable end-to-end, the real stationary wavelet transform is realized by referring to the discrete wavelet transform based on the PyTorch Library.

The main contributions of this paper are summarized as follows:

- An end-to-end WTSR is proposed to solve the lightweight problem in the super-resolution. The competitive super-resolution results are achieved through a two-dimensional stationary wavelet transform and Transformer.
- A LTB is proposed to capture the long-term dependency between image patches in the images. Meanwhile, a SMB and an ET are designed to balance the performance of the model and the consumption of computing resources.

- Different WECBs are proposed to recover different wavelet coefficient's structural information and channel redundancy. Notably, four ABs for different wavelet coefficient characteristics are investigated.

The rest of the paper is organized as follow: Sect. 2 introduces the related work of this paper. Section 3 elaborates the details of our proposed approach. Section 4 presents the experimental particulars and results, along with the ablation experiments for each part of the method, and Sect. 5 concludes the paper.

## 2 Related Work

Our approach is closely related to wavelet transform for image super-resolution and Transformer in the computer vision. A brief introduction to these two aspects will be presented in this section.

### 2.1 Wavelet Transform for Image Super-Resolution

Wavelet transform has been widely employed for image super-resolution as an essential technology in traditional image processing [3,13]. With the arrival of the wave of neural networks, the wavelet transform, as a powerful content and texture representation tool, has been diffusely employed in many deep learning-based super-resolution networks. Kumar et al. [18] proposed a three-layer convolution neural network to map the wavelet coefficients of LR images to those of HR images. Inspired by encoder-decoder architecture and wavelet inverse transform, Liu et al. [21] focused on multi-level wavelet transform and proposed a multi-level wavelet convolution. By imposing constraints on the network in the wavelet domain, the performance of super-resolution reconstruction was greatly improved. Xue et al. [34] introduced the attention mechanism into the residual network based on wavelet transform and proposed a wavelet-based residual attention network. Significant performance was gained across multiple baselines with a well-designed multi-kernel network. Zhang et al. [38] and Xin et al. [33] designed recurrent and recursive structures in image super-resolution tasks. Through the parameter sharing mechanism and wavelet transform, the computational complexity of the model was remarkably reduced while maintaining the performance of the model. Above mentioned works, the resolution of the feature maps before and after the wavelet transform is different (the resolution of feature map is half after wavelet transform). For the image generation tasks, like super-resolution, generally, this means that the parameters of network will increase. To some extend, it is not conducive to lightweight.

### 2.2 Transformer in the Computer Vision

Transformer has become the most important technology in natural language processing due to its powerful model capability and efficient parallel capability. Recently, some high-level computer vision tasks have also tried to utilize the

Transformer as a backbone in the network to extract features, such as visual recognition [7, 29] and object detection [5, 24]. Carion et al. [5] proposed an end-to-end object detection with Transformer, which embedded images as sequential data and sent them to encoder and decoder, creating a precedent for Transformers in computer vision applications. Dosovitskiy et al. [7] proposed a Transformer for image recognition at scale, which greatly reduced the computational resource consumption of the Transformer by partitioning and serializing the image into a combination of some patches. Liu et al. [22] added the hierarchical structure to the Transformer and proposed Swin Transformer. As a new backbone in high-level computer vision tasks, it further reduced the computational complexity of the Transformer and could extract more useful feature information. Obviously, reducing the computation cost of Transformer is one of the most important problems in its computer vision applications. However, low-level computer vision tasks are generally more computation-intensive. In the field of super-resolution, Lu et al. [23] proposed an efficient Transformer for SISR by the lightweight design of the Transformer for image super-resolution. Meanwhile, they also designed a lightweight convolution backbone to reduce the need for a large amount of data for Transformer training. In other words, Transformer is still relatively underused on the super-resolution task due to the lightweight issue.

## 3   Proposed Method

### 3.1   Overall Network

As shown in Fig. 2, our WTSR mainly consists of six parts: shallow feature extractor, two-dimensional Stationary Wavelet Transform (SWT), LTB, WCEB, two-dimensional Inverse Stationary Wavelet Transform (ISWT) and reconstruction block. The input and output of WTSR are defined as $I_{LR}$ and $I_{SR}$. As a result, the shallow feature $F_0$ is extracted from $I_{LR}$ by two convolution layers:

$$F_0 = f_{1*1}(f_{3*3}(I_{LR}))  \quad (1)$$

where $f_{1*1}$ and $f_{3*3}$ denote a $1*1$ convolution layer and a $3*3$ convolution layer, respectively. Then, $F_0$ is fed to a two-dimensional SWT to obtain the stationary wavelet coefficients for each channel, which can be formulated as:

$$I^W = concat(SWT(F_0))  \quad (2)$$

$I^W$ represents the stationary wavelet coefficients after concatenation. All outputs of SWT are sent to LTB to capture and model the long-term dependency between the image patches:

$$F_L = \phi^5(\psi(\phi^8(f_{group}(I^W))))  \quad (3)$$

where $f_{group}$, $\phi$ and $\psi$ denote a group convolution, ET encoder and SMB. The superscript of $\phi$ indicates the partitioning size. The output of LTB is split by a split layer and then sent to WCEBs:

$$F_A, F_H, F_V, F_D = split(F_L)  \quad (4)$$

$$F^W = concat(\sigma_{A,H,V,D}(F_A, F_H, F_V, F_D)) \qquad (5)$$

where $\sigma_{A,H,V,D}$ denotes four different WCEBs, and $F^W$ stands for the wavelet coefficient after recovering the redundancy of channels and the structure information of different wavelet coefficients. Then, all outputs of WCEBs are concatenated and passed to two-dimensional ISWT:

$$F_D = ISWT(F^W) \qquad (6)$$

Finally, $F_D$ and $I_{LR}$ are sent into the reconstruction block simultaneously to get $I_{SR}$:

$$I_{SR} = f_{Deconv}(f_{3*3}(F_d)) + f_{up}(I_{LR}) \qquad (7)$$

where $f_{Deconv}$, $f_{3*3}$, and $f_{up}$ express a deconvolution layer, a $3*3$ convolution layer, and an upsample layer, respectively.

### 3.2    Lightweight Transformer Backbone

The LTB in Fig. 3 (a) consists of two ET encoders in Fig. 3 (b) with different partitioning size and a SMB. There are some modifications in ET encoder to make it more lightweight than the standard Transformer. Suppose the input wavelet coefficient $S_i$ has the shape of $B \times C \times H \times W$, where $B$, $C$, $H$, and $W$ denote batch size, channels, height, and width of wavelet coefficients. Firstly, a reduction layer is employed to reduce the number of channels by quarter ($B \times C_1 \times H \times W, C_1 = \frac{C}{4}$). Then, a partitioning layer with a partitioning size of $K$ is utilized to reduce the resolution of sub-bands ($(K * K * B) \times C_1 \times \frac{H}{K} \times \frac{W}{K}$). After that, a standard Transformer, including Normalization layer, Multi-Head Attention, and Multi-Layer Perceptrons, is used to capture and model the long-term dependencies. Finally, a reverse layer is designed to restore original resolution of wavelet coefficients ($B \times C_1 \times H \times W, C_1 = \frac{C}{4}$). Assume the output wavelet coefficients are $S_o$, and the output wavelet coefficients $S_o$ can be obtained by:

$$S_{m1} = f_{partitioning}(f_{reduction}(S_i)) \qquad (8)$$

$$S_{m2} = MHA(Norm(S_{m1})) + S_{m1} \qquad (9)$$

$$S_o = f_{reverse}(MLP(Norm(S_{m2})) + S_{m2}) \qquad (10)$$

where MHA($\cdot$), Norm($\cdot$), and MLP($\cdot$) represent Multi-Head Attention, Normalization layer, and Multi-Layer Perceptrons in the standard Transformer respectively. Meanwhile, $f_{partitioning}$, $f_{reduction}$ and $f_{reverse}$ denote a wavelet coefficients partitioning layer, a reduction layer and a wavelet coefficients reverse layer.

Although the ET encoder reduces a lot of computational resource consumption compared to the standard Transformer, the partitioning method and partitioning size have a great impact on the mining of self-similarity in the images. To deal with this issue, two ET encoders with different partitioning sizes are connected through a SMB, which can combine local self-similarity and global self-similarity. Notably, the reduction layer in the second ET encoder is dropped. For SMB, an unfold layer with both kernel size and stride size of M is adopted to unfold the output of the first ET encoder into multiple patches of shape $B \times M * M \times 1$. Then, the most similar patch except itself for each patch is found through the normalized inner product and a new wavelet coefficient is generated, which can be formulated as:

$$p_{i1c,j1c} = \arg \max_{p_{i2,j2}} \langle \frac{p_{i1,j1}}{\|p_{i1,j1}\|}, \frac{p_{i2,j2}}{\|p_{i2,j2}\|} \rangle \quad s.t. \quad |i1 - i2| + |j1 - j2| \neq 0 \quad (11)$$

where $p_{i1c,j1c}$ denotes the patch in the new wavelet coefficient, $p_{i1,j1}$ and $p_{i2,j2}$ represent the patch in the original wavelet coefficient. Finally, a concatenation layer and two convolution layers are applied to integrate and map the features.

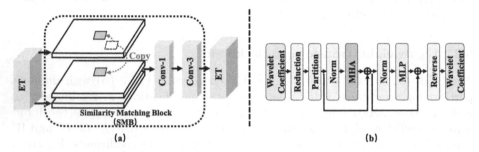

**Fig. 3.** (a) The structure of LTB in the WTSR. The dashed line area is SMB. (b) The structure of ET encoder in the LTB.

### 3.3   Stationary Wavelet Transform

The core of Transformer in computer vision applications is to model serialized image patches. From the perspective of super-resolution, it can implicitly mine self-similarity in the images. Meanwhile, there is no doubt that improving the embedding quality of images can effectively help the convergence of Transformer. As an efficient technique, wavelet transform depicts the contextual and textural information of an image without increasing parameters, which is beneficial for building a lightweight Transformer. For then, our experiments have shown that the resolution of wavelet coefficients also significantly influences the performance of lightweight Transformer, so WTSR learns the mapping between LR images and HR images on the stationary wavelet domain. Notably, stationary wavelet transform can also guarantee translation invariance on features and the stability of two-dimensional inverse stationary wavelet transformation (More details can be seen in the ablation study).

The process of stationary wavelet transform is shown in Fig. 4. $F_0$ extracted by the shallow extractor is filtered two times in different directions by a particular high-pass filter and a particular low-pass filter, yielding four distinct sets of wavelet coefficients, namely approximation (A), horizontal (H), vertical (V), diagonal (D), respectively. For the two-dimensional inverse stationary wavelet transform, by reversing the process and module of the two-dimensional stationary wavelet transform, almost the same data as before transformation can be obtained without changing any wavelet coefficients. In addition, the "Haar" kernel is employed to improve the efficiency of wavelet transform.

## 3.4  Wavelet Coefficient Enhance Backbone

The WCEB in Fig. 5 consists of two ABs, a $1*1$ convolution layer, and a coordinate attention layer [10]. For the AB, four particular convolution layers are designed to process wavelet coefficients with different characteristics. More specifically, approximation, horizontal, vertical, and diagonal coefficients are processed by a $3*3$ convolution layer, a $1*3$ asymmetric convolution layer, a $3*1$ asymmetric convolution layer, and an oblique asymmetric convolution layer. For the $1*1$ convolution layer, the channels of the wavelet coefficients after a concatenation layer are reduced by half. For the coordinate attention layer, it is an efficient and lightweight attention block that can improve the expressiveness of the model. For more details, suppose that one of the WCEBs has an input $M$ with a shape of $B \times C \times H \times W$. Firstly, an AB layer and a PRule layer are used to reconstruct a preliminary wavelet-specific structure without changing the number of channels and spatial resolution of the wavelet coefficients. Secondly, a concatenation layer is employed to contact the output and $M$, where the wavelet coefficients have a shape size of $B \times 2C \times H \times W$. Next, a $1*1$ convolution layer is utilized to compress the channel information, giving the wavelet coefficients the shape of $B \times C \times H \times W$. Then, a coordinate attention layer, a PRule layer, and an AB layer are used in turn for the more superior wavelet structure reconstruction. Finally, to constrain the WCEB modeling performance, the input M is added to the final output. The final output shape of the WCEB is $B \times C \times H \times W$.

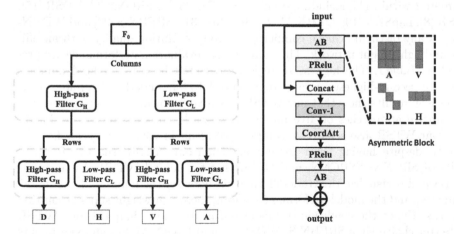

**Fig. 4.** Process of the two-dimensional stationary wavelet transform.

**Fig. 5.** The structure of WECB in the WTSR.

# 4 Experiments

## 4.1 Datasets and Metrics

To follow the previous literature [20], Flickr2K and DIV2K [1] are used as our training data. In our experiments, multiple data augmentations are adopted to make full use of training data, including image rotation, image flipping, and image scaling. For evaluation, five standard benchmark datasets: Set5 [4], Set14 [35], BSD100 [25], Urban100 [11], and Manga109 [26] are utilized. Meanwhile, Peak Signal-to-Noise Ratio (PSNR) and Structural Similarity (SSIM) are used to evaluate the performance of the reconstructed super-resolution images. Furthermore, the results are calculated on the Y channel of the YCbCr color space.

## 4.2 Implementation Details

All WTSRs in experiments are trained with a mini-batch size of 64 for 1000 epochs. To exploit self-similarity more in the images, a batch of RGB images are cropped to $80 \times 80$ patch size randomly and sent to the network in each step. Warmup [9] strategy is employed to increase the learning rate to $4 \times 10^{-3}$ after 10 iterations and decrease half for every 200 epochs. The network parameters are initialized according to [14] and optimized by Adam [17]. Meanwhile, L1 Loss is used as the loss function for our network training to avoid over-smoothing. Our experiments are run on the PyTorch platform with a single RTX3090 GPU.

## 4.3 Evaluation

Since our WTSR mainly focuses on implementing a lightweight and efficient super-resolution network, we compare it to other super-resolution methods with parameters within 1M, including Bicubic, SRCNN [32], FSRCNN [6], VDSR [15], DWSR [8], LapSRN [19], CARN-M [2], MemNet [31], SRFBN-S [20] and WDRN-S [33]. Many of them achieve competitive super-resolution quality with an efficient and lightweight network. The quantitative evaluation performance are presented in Table 1. The highest score is represented by a highlighted number, while the second-highest score is represented by an underlined number. The comparison results show that our WTSR has a very obvious advantage over the comparative approaches on five public benchmarks in ×4 scale factor. Meanwhile, our WTSR also achieves a competitive result in ×2 and ×3 scale factors. Notably, despite having fewer parameters than our WTSR, the PSNR/SSIM results of SRCNN, FSRCNN, and DWSR lag far behind WTSR. As shown in Fig. 6, we also visualize the trade-off analysis between the number of the model parameters and the model performance among these lightweight super-resolution networks. Under the condition of model parameters less than 1M, our WTSR is a better choice than SRFBN-S, WDSR-S, and CARN-M. So, all experiments fully give evidence that our WTSR achieves a better trade-off between model sizes and model performance.

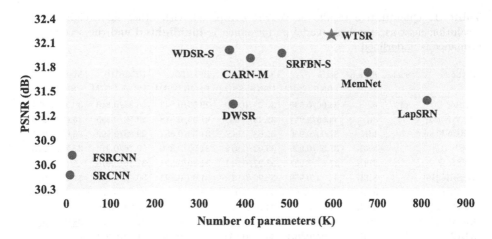

**Fig. 6.** The relationship between model sizes and model performance of different lightweight super-resolution networks on the Set5 with ×4 scale factor.

In Fig. 7, we provide a super-resolution visual comparison between WTSR and other lightweight super-resolution networks on the ×4 scale factor. Since WTSR can implicitly mine the self-similarity from the whole LR, the super-resolution results restored by our WTSR have more sophisticated particulars in some with multiple repeating structures, especially in the edges and lines.

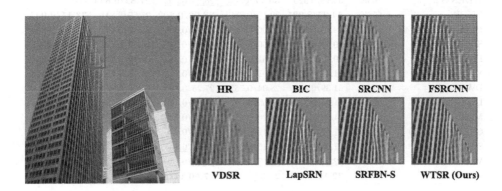

**Fig. 7.** Subjective visual quality compared with other super-resolution networks for ×4 scale factor on the pictures from BSD100.

### 4.4  Ablation Study

To explore the impact of embedding quality on Transformer, three versions of WTSR are trained. The first version (Version 1) is to use Discrete Wavelet Transform (DWT) to process the feature map, the second version (Version 2) is to

**Table 1.** Quantitative results of WTSR compared with other lightweight super-resolution network, the best model performance is **highlighted** and the second performance is underlined.

| Methods | Scales | Params | Set5 PSNR/SSIM | Set14 PSNR/SSIM | BSD100 PSNR/SSIM | Urban100 PSNR/SSIM | Manga109 PSNR/SSIM |
|---|---|---|---|---|---|---|---|
| Bicubic | x2 | - | 33.66/0.930 | 30.24/0.869 | 29.56/0.843 | 26.88/0.840 | 30.30/0.934 |
| SRCNN [32] | | 8K | 36.66/0.954 | 32.45/0.907 | 31.36/0.888 | 29.50/0.895 | 35.60/0.966 |
| FSRCNN [6] | | 13K | 37.00/0.956 | 32.63/0.909 | 31.53/0.892 | 29.88/0.902 | 36.67/0.971 |
| VDSR [15] | | 666K | 37.53/0.959 | 33.03/0.912 | 31.90/0.896 | 30.76/0.914 | 37.22/0.975 |
| DWSR [8] | | 374K | 37.43/0.957 | 33.07/0.911 | 31.80/0.894 | 31.46/0.916 | -/- |
| LapSRN [19] | | 813K | 37.52/0.959 | 32.99/0.912 | 31.80/0.895 | 30.41/0.910 | 37.27/0.974 |
| MemNet [31] | | 678K | 37.78/0.960 | 33.28/0.914 | 32.08/0.898 | 31.31/0.920 | 37.72/0.974 |
| CARN-M [2] | | 412K | 37.53/0.958 | 33.26/0.914 | 31.92/0.896 | 31.23/0.919 | -/- |
| SRFBN-S [20] | | 483K | 37.78/0.960 | 33.35/0.916 | 32.00/0.897 | 31.41/0.921 | 38.06/0.976 |
| WDRN-S [33] | | 344K | 37.93/**0.961** | 33.42/**0.916** | 32.08/**0.898** | 31.80/0.924 | -/- |
| WTSR | | 528K | **37.95**/0.961 | **33.51**/0.915 | **32.09**/0.893 | **31.91**/**0.928** | **38.42**/**0.976** |
| Bicubic | x3 | - | 30.39/0.868 | 27.55/0.774 | 27.21/0.739 | 24.46/0.735 | 26.95/0.856 |
| SRCNN [32] | | 8K | 32.75/0.909 | 29.30/0.822 | 28.41/0.786 | 26.24/0.799 | 30.48/0.912 |
| FSRCNN [6] | | 13K | 33.18/0.914 | 29.37/0.824 | 28.53/0.791 | 26.43/0.808 | 31.10/0.921 |
| VDSR [15] | | 666K | 33.66/0.921 | 29.77/0.831 | 28.82/0.798 | 27.14/0.828 | 32.01/0.934 |
| DWSR [8] | | 374K | 33.82/0.922 | 29.83/0.831 | -/- | -/- | -/- |
| LapSRN [19] | | 813K | 33.81/0.922 | 29.79/0.833 | 28.82/0.798 | 27.07/0.828 | 32.21/0.935 |
| MemNet [31] | | 678K | 34.09/0.925 | 30.00/0.835 | 28.96/0.800 | 27.56/0.838 | 32.51/0.937 |
| CARN-M [2] | | 412K | 33.99/0.924 | 30.08/0.837 | 28.91/0.800 | 27.55/0.839 | -/- |
| SRFBN-S [20] | | 483K | 34.20/0.926 | 30.10/**0.837** | 28.96/0.801 | 27.66/0.842 | 33.02/0.94 |
| WDRN-S [33] | | 366K | 34.18/0.925 | **30.17**/0.837 | 28.98/**0.802** | **27.82**/**0.844** | -/- |
| WTSR | | 558K | **34.27**/0.925 | 30.12/0.836 | **28.98**/**0.802** | 27.69/0.841 | **33.11**/**0.941** |
| Bicubic | x4 | - | 28.42/0.810 | 26.00/0.703 | 25.96/0.668 | 23.14/0.658 | 24.89/0.787 |
| SRCNN [32] | | 8K | 30.48/0.863 | 27.50/0.751 | 26.90/0.710 | 24.52/0.722 | 27.58/0.856 |
| FSRCNN [6] | | 13K | 30.72/0.866 | 27.61/0.755 | 26.98/0.715 | 24.62/0.728 | 27.90/0.861 |
| VDSR [15] | | 666K | 31.35/0.884 | 28.01/0.767 | 27.29/0.725 | 25.18/0.752 | 28.83/0.887 |
| DWSR [8] | | 374K | 31.39/0.883 | 28.04/0.767 | 27.25/0.724 | 25.26/0.755 | -/- |
| LapSRN [19] | | 813K | 31.54/0.885 | 28.09/0.770 | 27.32/0.728 | 25.21/0.756 | 29.09/0.890 |
| MemNet [31] | | 678K | 31.74/0.889 | 28.26/0.772 | 27.40/0.728 | 25.50/0.763 | 29.42/0.894 |
| CARN-M [2] | | 412K | 31.92/0.890 | 28.42/0.776 | 27.44/0.730 | 25.62/0.769 | -/- |
| SRFBN-S [20] | | 483K | 31.98/0.892 | 28.45/0.778 | 27.44/0.731 | 25.71/0.772 | 29.91/0.901 |
| WDRN-S [33] | | 366K | 32.02/0.890 | 28.47/0.774 | 27.47/0.730 | 25.82/0.776 | -/- |
| WTSR | | 593K | **32.16**/**0.895** | **28.57**/**0.781** | **27.56**/**0.735** | **26.03**/**0.784** | **30.44**/**0.908** |

employ SWT, and the last one (Version 3) does not utilize wavelet transform. The experimental results in Table 2 indicate that WTSR based on the SWT performs better than the other two in all benchmarks without any additional parameters. By comparing the experimental results of Version 2 and Version 3, it can be found that the feature map processed by wavelet transform at the same resolution is more conducive to the convergence of WTSR. Equally, wavelet transform is beneficial for Transformer to mine self-similarity in the images. By comparing the experimental results of Version 1 and Version 2, SWT has a noticeable promotion effect on the performance of super-resolution reconstruction, instead of DWT is harmful to the performance of super-resolution reconstruction. This is because the SWT does not change the resolution of the feature map, which guarantees translation invariance on the features and the stability of inverse wavelet transformation. Furthermore, SWT can greatly reduce the modeling difficulty of WTSR, which is beneficial for lightweight.

**Table 2.** Comparisons on PSNR/SSIM of WTSR with different wavelet transform. Best results are **highlighted**.

| Wavelet transform | Params | PSNR/SSIM | | | | |
|---|---|---|---|---|---|---|
| Type | | Set5 | Set14 | BSD100 | Urban100 | Manga109 |
| None | 593K | 32.01/0.893 | 27.47/0.781 | 27.51/0.734 | 25.84/0.777 | 20.22/0.905 |
| DWT | 593K | 27.56/0.790 | 25.51/0.682 | 25.54/0.647 | 22.69/0.635 | 24.19/0.767 |
| SWT | 593K | **32.16/0.895** | **28.57/0.781** | **27.56/0.735** | **26.03/0.784** | **30.44/0.908** |

To study the effect of different LTB structures on super-resolution reconstruction performance, another five experiments are designed by changing the partitioning size and arrangement order of the ET encoder. In Table 3, it can be found that using two ET encoders with different partitioning sizes can obtain better super-resolution reconstruction performance than using two ET encoders with the same partitioning size, and the SMB significantly improves the super-resolution reconstruction results. More details, in the case of two ET encoders with the same partitioning size, the impact of partitioning size on super-resolution reconstruction results is not apparent. On the contrary, in the case of two ET encoders with different partitioning sizes, the ET with a larger partitioning size is ranked first, which can obtain better super-resolution performance in all benchmarks.

**Table 3.** Comparisons on PSNR/SSIM of WTSR with different network of LTB. Best results are **highlighted**. The number after T indicates the partitioning size of ET encoder, S represents SMB, and the arrow denotes the direction of data flow.

| The network of LTB | Params | PSNR/SSIM | | | | |
|---|---|---|---|---|---|---|
| | | Set5 | Set14 | BSD100 | Urban100 | Manga109 |
| T5 → T5 | 567K | 31.92/0.892 | 27.43/0.779 | 27.46/0.734 | 25.78/0.777 | 30.06/0.904 |
| T8 → T8 | 569K | 31.96/0.892 | 28.46/0.779 | 27.48/0.733 | 25.79/0.776 | 30.09/0.904 |
| T5 → T8 | 568K | 31.97/0.893 | 28.44/0.779 | 27.48/0.733 | 25.79/0.776 | 30.04/0.903 |
| T8 → T5 | 568K | 32.00/0.893 | 28.47/0.779 | 27.50/0.733 | 25.87/0.778 | 30.11/0.904 |
| T8 → S → T5 | 593K | **32.16/0.895** | **28.57/0.781** | **27.56/0.735** | **26.03/0.784** | **30.44/0.908** |

To investigate the impact of different WCEB on super-resolution performance, we set the usage of WCEM on different wavelet coefficients and conduct five experiments in Table 4. By comparison, it demonstrates that using different WCEMs on different wavelet coefficients can significantly improve the super-resolution reconstruction quality of WTSR in all benchmarks.

**Table 4.** Study the effect of each WCEB on PSNR/SSIM, Best results are **highlighted**.

| WCEM type | Params | PSNR/SSIM | | | | |
|---|---|---|---|---|---|---|
| | | Set5 | Set14 | BSD100 | Urban100 | Manga109 |
| None | 416K | 31.91/0.892 | 28.44/0.778 | 27.47/0.732 | 25.75/0.7735 | 29.92/0.901 |
| A | 482K | 32.01/0.893 | 28.42/0.779 | 27.48/0.734 | 25.80/0.7782 | 29.99/0.924 |
| A + H | 519K | 32.06/0.894 | 28.54/0.780 | 27.52/0.733 | 25.91/0.7791 | 30.27/0.905 |
| A + H + V | 556K | 32.10/0.894 | 28.54/0.781 | 27.54/0.735 | 25.97/0.7823 | 30.31/0.907 |
| A + H + V + D | 593K | **32.16/0.895** | **28.57/0.781** | **27.56/0.735** | **26.03/0.784** | **30.44/0.908** |

## 5 Conclusion

In this article, a lightweight network called WTSR was proposed to extend the application scenarios of super-resolution algorithm. WTSR used SWT to enhance the representation of feature map, which was beneficial to the convergence and lightweight of the network. In the WTSR, a LTB was employed to capture and model the long-term dependency between similar image patches on the stationary wavelet domain. Then a set of WCEBs were utilized to recover the redundancy of the channels and the structure information of the wavelet coefficients. In the LTB, two ET encoders were investigated to mine local self-similarity while reducing the consumption of computing and memory resources. Meanwhile, a SMB was designed to combine global self-similarity and local self-similarity. In the WCEB, different ABs were designed according to the structural characteristics of different wavelet coefficients. Extensive experimental results in the public benchmarks showed that our WTSR achieved better trade-off between model performance and computation cost. However, WTSR still has some potential limitations, such as poor scalability of the network structure, difficulty in achieving better super-resolution reconstruction performance and higher super-resolution magnification by simple structure stacking. In the future, we will extend the proposed WTSR to specific mobile devices.

## References

1. Agustsson, E., Timofte, R.: Ntire 2017 challenge on single image super-resolution: dataset and study. In: CVPR Workshops, pp. 126–135 (2017)
2. Ahn, N., Kang, B., Sohn, K.-A.: Fast, accurate, and lightweight super-resolution with cascading residual network. In: Ferrari, V., Hebert, M., Sminchisescu, C., Weiss, Y. (eds.) ECCV 2018. LNCS, vol. 11214, pp. 256–272. Springer, Cham (2018). https://doi.org/10.1007/978-3-030-01249-6_16
3. Anbarjafari, G., Demirel, H.: Image super resolution based on interpolation of wavelet domain high frequency subbands and the spatial domain input image. ETRI J. **32**(3), 390–394 (2010)
4. Bevilacqua, M., Roumy, A., Guillemot, C., Alberi-Morel, M.: Low-complexity single-image super-resolution based on nonnegative neighbor embedding. In: BMVC, pp. 1–10. BMVA Press (2012)

5. Carion, N., Massa, F., Synnaeve, G., Usunier, N., Kirillov, A., Zagoruyko, S.: End-to-end object detection with transformers. In: Vedaldi, A., Bischof, H., Brox, T., Frahm, J.-M. (eds.) ECCV 2020. LNCS, vol. 12346, pp. 213–229. Springer, Cham (2020). https://doi.org/10.1007/978-3-030-58452-8_13

6. Dong, C., Loy, C.C., Tang, X.: Accelerating the super-resolution convolutional neural network. In: Leibe, B., Matas, J., Sebe, N., Welling, M. (eds.) ECCV 2016. LNCS, vol. 9906, pp. 391–407. Springer, Cham (2016). https://doi.org/10.1007/978-3-319-46475-6_25

7. Dosovitskiy, A., et al.: An image is worth 16x16 words: transformers for image recognition at scale. arXiv preprint arXiv:2010.11929 (2020)

8. Guo, T., Seyed Mousavi, H., Huu Vu, T., Monga, V.: Deep wavelet prediction for image super-resolution. In: CVPR Workshops, pp. 104–113 (2017)

9. He, K., Zhang, X., Ren, S., Sun, J.: Deep residual learning for image recognition. In: CVPR, pp. 770–778 (2016)

10. Hou, Q., Zhou, D., Feng, J.: Coordinate attention for efficient mobile network design. In: CVPR, pp. 13713–13722 (2021)

11. Huang, J.B., Singh, A., Ahuja, N.: Single image super-resolution from transformed self-exemplars. In: CVPR, pp. 5197–5206 (2015)

12. Hui, Z., Gao, X., Yang, Y., Wang, X.: Lightweight image super-resolution with information multi-distillation network. In: ACMM, pp. 2024–2032 (2019)

13. Ji, H., Fermüller, C.: Robust wavelet-based super-resolution reconstruction: theory and algorithm. IEEE Trans. Pattern Anal. Mach. Intell. **31**(4), 649–660 (2008)

14. K. He, X. Zhang, S. Ren, and J. Sun,: Delving deep into rectifiers: surpassing human-level performance on imagenet classification. In: ICCV, pp. 1026–1034. IEEE Computer Society (2015)

15. Kim, J., Lee, J.K., Lee, K.M.: Accurate image super-resolution using very deep convolutional networks. In: CVPR, pp. 1646–1654 (2016)

16. Kim, J., Li, G., Yun, I., Jung, C., Kim, J.: Edge and identity preserving network for face super-resolution. Neurocomputing **446**, 11–22 (2021)

17. Kingma, D.P., Ba, J.: Adam: a method for stochastic optimization. arXiv preprint arXiv:1412.6980 (2014)

18. Kumar, N., Verma, R., Sethi, A.: Convolutional neural networks for wavelet domain super resolution. Pattern Recogn. Lett. **90**, 65–71 (2017)

19. Lai, W.S., Huang, J.B., Ahuja, N., Yang, M.H.: Deep Laplacian pyramid networks for fast and accurate super-resolution. In: CVPR, pp. 624–632 (2017)

20. Li, Z., Yang, J., Liu, Z., Yang, X., Jeon, G., Wu, W.: Feedback network for image super-resolution. In: CVPR, pp. 3867–3876 (2019)

21. Liu, P., Zhang, H., Zhang, K., Lin, L., Zuo, W.: Multi-level wavelet-CNN for image restoration. In: CVPR, pp. 773–782 (2018)

22. Liu, Z., et al.: Swin transformer: hierarchical vision transformer using shifted windows. In: Proceedings of the IEEE/CVF International Conference on Computer Vision, pp. 10012–10022 (2021)

23. Lu, Z., Liu, H., Li, J., Zhang, L.: Efficient transformer for single image super-resolution. arXiv preprint arXiv:2108.11084 (2021)

24. Ma, T., et al.: Oriented object detection with transformer. arXiv preprint arXiv:2106.03146 (2021)

25. Martin, D., Fowlkes, C., Tal, D., Malik, J.: A database of human segmented natural images and its application to evaluating segmentation algorithms and measuring ecological statistics. In: ICCV, vol. 2, pp. 416–423. IEEE (2001)

26. Matsui, Y., et al.: Sketch-based manga retrieval using manga109 dataset. Multimedia Tools Appl. **76**(20), 21811–21838 (2017)

27. Mei, Y., Fan, Y., Zhou, Y., Huang, L., Huang, T.S., Shi, H.: Image super-resolution with cross-scale non-local attention and exhaustive self-exemplars mining. In: CVPR, pp. 5690–5699 (2020)
28. Oktay, O., et al.: Multi-input cardiac image super-resolution using convolutional neural networks. In: Ourselin, S., Joskowicz, L., Sabuncu, M.R., Unal, G., Wells, W. (eds.) MICCAI 2016. LNCS, vol. 9902, pp. 246–254. Springer, Cham (2016). https://doi.org/10.1007/978-3-319-46726-9_29
29. Srinivas, A., Lin, T.Y., Parmar, N., Shlens, J., Abbeel, P., Vaswani, A.: Bottleneck transformers for visual recognition. In: CVPR, pp. 16519–16529 (2021)
30. Tai, Y., Yang, J., Liu, X.: Image super-resolution via deep recursive residual network. In: CVPR, pp. 3147–3155 (2017)
31. Tai, Y., Yang, J., Liu, X., Xu, C.: MemNet: a persistent memory network for image restoration. In: ICCV, pp. 4539–4547 (2017)
32. Ward, C.M., Harguess, J., Crabb, B., Parameswaran, S.: Image quality assessment for determining efficacy and limitations of super-resolution convolutional neural network (SRCNN). In: Applications of Digital Image Processing XL, vol. 10396, p. 1039605. International Society for Optics and Photonics (2017)
33. Xin, J., Li, J., Jiang, X., Wang, N., Huang, H., Gao, X.: Wavelet-based dual recursive network for image super-resolution. IEEE Trans. Neural Netw. Learn. Syst. **33**(2), 707–720 (2022)
34. Xue, S., Qiu, W., Liu, F., Jin, X.: Wavelet-based residual attention network for image super-resolution. Neurocomputing **382**, 116–126 (2020)
35. Yang, J., Wright, J., Huang, T.S., Ma, Y.: Image super-resolution via sparse representation. IEEE Trans. Image Process. **19**(11), 2861–2873 (2010)
36. Yıldırım, D., Güngör, O.: A novel image fusion method using Ikonos satellite images. J. Geodesy Geoinf. **1**(1), 75–83 (2012)
37. Yu, J., et al.: Wide activation for efficient and accurate image super-resolution. arXiv preprint arXiv:1808.08718 (2018)
38. Zhang, H., Jin, Z., Tan, X., Li, X.: Towards lighter and faster: learning wavelets progressively for image super-resolution. In: ACMM, pp. 2113–2121 (2020)
39. Zou, W.W., Yuen, P.C.: Very low resolution face recognition problem. IEEE Trans. Image Process. **21**(1), 327–340 (2011)

# Efficient High-Resolution Human Pose Estimation

Xiaofei Qin[1], Lingfeng Qiu[1], Changxiang He[2], and Xuedian Zhang[1(✉)]

[1] School of Optical-Electrical and Computer Engineering,
University of Shanghai for Science and Technology,
516 Jungong Road, Yangpu, Shanghai 200093, China
`xiaofei.qin@usst.edu.cn, obmmdzxd@163.com`
[2] College of Science, University of Shanghai for Science and Technology,
516 Jungong Road, Yangpu, Shanghai 200093, China

**Abstract.** As a fundamental task of computer vision, human pose estimation (HPE) has achieved significant improvement with the rise of deep learning. However, many existing methods focus too much on model accuracy, leading to high complexity models, which are hard to be deployed especially in computation-limited devices. This paper proposes a lightweight HPE network named efficient high-resolution human pose estimation (EHR-HPE). EHR-HPE network first adopts the high-resolution pattern to acquire accurate heatmaps; then an efficient shuffle block is proposed to reduce the model complexity and boost model performance; finally, the efficient dense connections are designed to further improve model accuracy. Extensive experiment results on two benchmark datasets show that the proposed EHR-HPE network achieves a great tradeoff between accuracy and model complexity. EHR-HPE network can achieve 70.1 mean average precision scores on Common Objects in Context (COCO) test-dev dataset with only 1.7M parameters and 0.91 GFLOPs.

**Keywords:** Human pose estimation · Lightweight network · Efficient shuffle block · Dense connection

## 1 Introduction

Human pose estimation (HPE) task is to detect and localize body keypoints (elbows, wrists, knees, etc.) of the input person images. It is a fundamental yet challenging task in the field of computer vision and is widely adopted for action recognition, pose tracking, human-computer interaction, etc.

HPE can be divided into single-person pose estimation and multi-person pose estimation according to the number of human instances in the input image. This paper focuses on single-person pose estimation because it is the basis for related vision tasks, such as multi-person pose estimation, video-based pose estimation, and pose tracking. Significant progress has been made in the field of HPE due

S. Khanna et al. (Eds.): PRICAI 2022, LNCS 13631, pp. 383–396, 2022.
https://doi.org/10.1007/978-3-031-20868-3_28

to the widespread use of deep neural networks [3,7,16,21,22,24]. These state-of-the-art methods typically employ deep and wide networks with a large number of parameters and a huge amount of floating-point operations (FLOPs), which result in high memory requirements and serious latency. These complex models are hard to be deployed especially for computation-limited devices (such as smartphones and embedded devices). Therefore, it is necessary to develop lightweight yet capable HPE methods.

Instead of recovering the resolution of input representation through a low-to-high process, HRNet [21] has a branch that maintains the highest resolution of the input representation throughout the process, this pattern is called high-resolution pattern in HRNet. The high-resolution pattern and multi-level features fusion strategies make HRNet becomes an excellent backbone for several vision tasks. However, the complexity of HRNet is very high. Small HRNet[1] is a much lighter network by reducing the depth and width of the original HRNet, but its performance drops significantly. This paper designed an efficient shuffle block to replace the costly residual block in Small HRNet, further reducing model complexity but improving performance. Furthermore, we added some efficient dense connections between the adjacent modules in the same stage to encourage feature reuse, which can also improve the performance of the model. This paper follows the high-resolution pattern in HRNet and Small HRNet, and considering the use of efficient shuffle block and efficient dense connections in it, this paper is consequently named efficient high-resolution human pose estimation (EHR-HPE) which architecture is shown in Fig. 1.

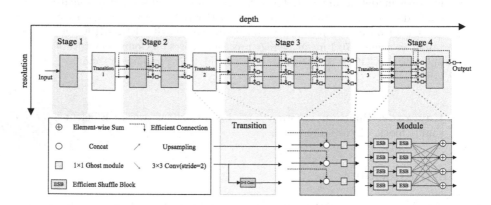

**Fig. 1.** The architecture of efficient high-resolution human pose estimation (EHR-HPE) network. The network consists of four stages, the deeper stage has more branches. Stages are connected by the transition layer that adds a new branch with lower resolution but more channel numbers through a $3 \times 3$ convolution. A stage has a sequence of modules, each module contains two efficient shuffle blocks for one branch and a multi-resolution fusing operation across the branches. The dashed lines indicate efficient dense connections between adjacent modules within a stage.

---

[1] Small HRNet: https://github.com/HRNet/HRNet-Semantic-Segmentation.

Experiments are conducted on two benchmark datasets to demonstrate the effectiveness and efficiency of the proposed EHR-HPE network. Experimental results show that the EHR-HPE network can achieve superior performance while maintaining a small model size and computation cost. The contributions of this paper can be summarized as follows:

1. The EHR-HPE network follows the high-resolution pattern of Small HRNet, and replaces the costly residual blocks with the newly designed efficient shuffle blocks. Efficient shuffle blocks adopt 1 × 1 Ghost modules [6] instead of costly pointwise convolutions to exchange information across channels. Additionally, an attention module is designed based on the GC block [2] to enhance the ability to model long-range dependencies and inter-channel relationships. Ablation studies have shown that the efficient shuffle block can achieve superior performance while halving computation cost and slightly reducing the number of parameters.
2. Efficient dense connections are added between the adjacent modules within the same stage, which inevitably widens the feature channels, so 1 × 1 Ghost modules are used to reduce the channel dimension. Efficient dense connections can strengthen feature reuse, facilitate convergence and promote network accuracy.

## 2    Related Works

In HPE tasks, the traditional methods adopt pictorial structure models [5, 18, 27] to infer the human pose. While these methods can perform efficient inference on simple images, they cannot handle complex scenarios such as occlusion. With the rise of deep learning, CNN-based methods [3, 7, 16, 17, 21, 23, 24, 26] have become the main solution for HPE.

CNN-based HPE methods can fall into two categories, i.e., regressing the position of keypoints directly and estimating the keypoints through heatmaps. Compared with the direct regression method, the method based on heatmap [16, 21, 24] can fully use of the spatial information in the image, and achieve better accuracy and robustness. CPM [24] utilizes a multi-stage network to gradually refine detection results and adopts intermediate supervision to alleviate the vanishing-gradient problem. Hourglass network [16] follows the multi-stage pattern of CPM, and designs a symmetric encoder and decoder structure with short connections between the downsampling and upsampling branches to integrate multi-scale features. HRNet [21] further exploits the benefits of multi-scale features fusion by connecting sub-networks of different resolutions in parallel, preserving high-resolution features while fusing multi-level semantics to gain more accurate and precise heatmap estimation. The results of extensive experiments demonstrate the excellent performance of HRNet for HPE tasks. The method proposed in this paper follows the high-resolution pattern of HRNet, but contrives to give a more lightweight version.

Lightweight networks have aroused pervasive enthusiasm in the HPE research community. Zhang et al. [30] proposed LPN, which applies depthwise convolution

and attention mechanism to SimpleBaseline [26]. Qin *et al.* designed a lightweight
HPE network named CVC-Net [19] based on pruned Hourglass, and many off-
the-shelf tricks are used to enhance model performance. Based on HRNet, Yu
*et al.* [28] proposed the conditional channel weighting unit to replace the costly
pointwise convolution, which can greatly improve the computational efficiency
at a slight decrease in accuracy.

Attention mechanism [11,12,25] can be regarded as a kind of conditional
weight generation. Cao *et al.* [2] designed GC block to capture long-range dependencies. This paper designed a channel global context block named CGC, and
combined CGC with GC block to form a more powerful attention module.

To capture more information across multiple scales, deep learning networks
are now designed to go deeper, but vanishing-gradient problem occurs as the network deepens. ResNets [8] and DenseNet [13] build short paths between layers to
alleviate vanishing-gradient, in which DenseNet realizes features reuse through
concatenating feature maps with all subsequent layers and achieves better performance on several public datasets with fewer parameters. To strengthen the
feature reuse of the HPE network, this paper follows the dense connection pattern of DenseNet to establish short paths between the adjacent modules within
the same stage of the high-resolution architecture.

## 3   Method

### 3.1   Efficient Shuffle Block

**Replacing Costly 1 × 1 Convolution.** Efficient shuffle block is designed based
on the shuffle block in ShuffleNet [15]. The shuffle block uses 1 × 1 convolutions
to exchange information across channels, which is very costly and dominates
the parameter and computational complexity of the shuffle block. As Fig. 2 (b)

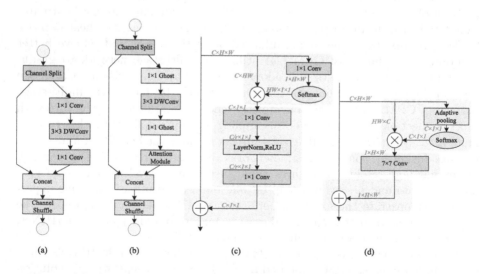

**Fig. 2.** (a) Shuffle block (b) efficient shuffle block (c) GC block (d) CGC block.

shows, this paper introduces the Ghost module proposed in GhostNet [6] to replace the costly pointwise ($1 \times 1$) convolutions in shuffle blocks, which can reduce the model complexity while improving the performance.

GhostNet asserts that a handful of intrinsic feature-maps contain most of the dominant information of the output, so as shown in Fig. 3, an ordinary convolution is divided into two parts, a primary convolution for generating intrinsic feature-maps and a cheap operation for generating the remaining feature-maps.

Specifically, given the input data $X \in \mathbb{R}^{c \times h \times w}$, the desired output feature-maps $Y \in \mathbb{R}^{h' \times w' \times n}$, where $c$ and $n$ represent the input and output channel numbers, and $h$, $w$ and $h'$, $w'$ represent the height and width of the input and output, respectively. A primary convolution is used to generate $l$ intrinsic feature-maps $Y' \in \mathbb{R}^{h' \times w' \times l}$:

$$Y' = X * f' \tag{1}$$

where $f' \in \mathbb{R}^{c \times k \times k \times l}$ is the convolution filter with $k \times k$ kernel size, and $l \leq n$.

Subsequently, a series of cheap operations are applied on each intrinsic feature-map in $Y'$ to obtain the other $n - l$ feature-maps according to the following function:

$$y_{i,j} = \Phi_{i,j}\left(y_i'\right), \quad \forall i = 1, \ldots, l, \quad j = 1, \ldots, r - 1 \tag{2}$$

where $y_i'$ is the $i$-th intrinsic feature-map in $Y'$, $\Phi_{i,j}$ is the $j$-th linear operation on $y_i'$ for generating the feature-map $y_{i,j}$. Concatenating the output feature-maps of primary convolution and cheap operation, the final output of a Ghost module $Y = [[y_1, \ldots, y_l], [y_{1,1}, y_{1,2}, \ldots, y_{l,r-1}]]$ can be obtained, where $n = l \times 1 + l \times (r - 1)$, $r$ represents the proportion of intrinsic feature-maps, and $l$ consequently equals to $\frac{n}{r}$.

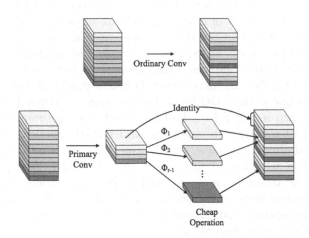

**Fig. 3.** The illustrations of a ordinary convolutional and a Ghost module.

In this paper, the kernel size of the Ghost module is set to 1 ($k = 1$), which results in a $1 \times 1$ Ghost module. In addition, $r$ is set to 2, and following Ghost-Net, $3 \times 3$ convolutions are used as the cheap operations. Consequently, after replacing the original $1 \times 1$ convolution with the $1 \times 1$ Ghost module, the theoretical compression ratio of parameters and speed-up ratio of computation can be calculated as:

$$R = \frac{c \cdot k \cdot k \cdot n}{c \cdot k \cdot k \cdot \frac{n}{r} + (r-1) \cdot \frac{n}{r} \cdot d \cdot d} = \frac{c \cdot 1 \cdot 1 \cdot c}{c \cdot 1 \cdot 1 \cdot \frac{c}{2} + (2-1) \cdot \frac{c}{2} \cdot 3 \cdot 3}$$
$$= \frac{2 \cdot c^2}{c^2 + 9 \cdot c} \approx 2 \tag{3}$$

As the above formulation shows, computation and parameters have been halved.

**Attention Module.** Capturing long-range dependencies is critical for HPE, but simply stacking ordinary convolution layers cannot effectively extract the global understanding of the visual scene. Cao *et al.* [2] proposed a global context network (GCNet), in which the global context (GC) block can effectively aggregate the global information. Consequently, this paper introduces GC block to strengthen the capture ability of long-range dependencies. Figure 2 (c) depicts the structure of the GC block, which can be abstracted into three procedures: (a) global attention pooling, which employs a $1 \times 1$ convolution and a softmax function to obtain the attention weights, and then use these attention weights to perform the attention pooling, which aggregates the features of all positions together to acquire the global context features; (b) feature transform, which adopts $1 \times 1$ convolution to capture channel-wise interdependencies; (c) Feature aggregation, which uses element-wise addition to merge the global context features into all positions.

Meanwhile, inspired by CBAM [25], this paper redesigns the GC block and proposes a new attention block named channel global context(CGC) block, which emphasizes the modeling of inter-channel relationships. The GC block can be regarded as a kind of first-spatial-then-channel attention, in contrast to the GC block, the CGC block firstly aggregates the features of all channels together to form a global channel descriptor; and then models the inter-spatial relationships to obtain the final global channel context. Different modeling order leads to different attention maps, the CGC block focuses more on dependencies between channels. As shown in Fig. 2 (d), the CGC block can be summarized as three procedures: (a) Channel attention pooling, which firstly applies average-pooling along the spatial dimension and a softmax function to obtain the channel attention weights, then attention pooling is performed by matrix multiplication, and the features of all channels are aggregated together to obtain channel context features; (b) Spatial features transform, which adopts a $7 \times 7$ convolution to capture the inter-spatial relationships; (c) Feature aggregation, which employs element-wise addition for feature fusion.

The CGC block can act as a complementary for the GC block to compensate for its insufficient modeling ability of inter-channel relationships. This paper combines GC and CGC blocks to enhance the modeling ability of both inter-channel and inter-spatial relationships. Experimental results show that the performance of GC-block-first combination form is slightly better than CGC-block-first form, so the attention module in the subsequent paper refers to the GC-block-first combination form.

## 3.2   Efficient Dense Connection

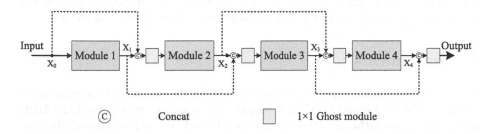

**Fig. 4.** The illustration of efficient dense connection.

DenseNet [13] proposed the concept of dense connection, which directly connects all layers with the same feature size to each other to ensure maximum information flow. Dense connections strengthen the feature propagation and reuse, alleviate vanishing-gradient problems, and make the network easy to train.

Inspired by DenseNet, this paper introduces dense connections between the different modules within the same stage and achieves feature reuse by concatenating operations. Existing studies [15] have shown that the connections between adjacent layers are much stronger than the others, therefore this paper only adds dense connections between the adjacent modules instead of all to achieve a better tradeoff between accuracy and speed.

Considering the $s$-th stage, there are $s$ parallel branches with different resolutions. Each stage contains $M$ modules, each of which implements a complex non-linear transformation $H_m(\cdot)$, where $m$ is the index of the module. As the Module in Fig. 1 shows, $H_m(\cdot)$ contains a sequence of two efficient shuffle blocks and one multi-resolution fusion. This paper denotes the output of the $m^{th}$ module as $\mathbf{x}_m$, the number of input channels as $\mathbf{c}_m$.

When the efficient dense connections are not added, the output of the $m^{th}$ module is fed into the $(m+1)^{th}$ module as input, which can be expressed as:

$$\mathbf{x}_m = H_m(\mathbf{x}_{m-1}) \tag{4}$$

Figure 4 illustrates the layout of efficient dense connections. The $m^{th}$ module receives the feature-maps of the preceding two modules (except $m = 1$), i.e., $\mathbf{x}_{m-2}$ and $\mathbf{x}_{m-1}$, as input:

$$\mathbf{x}_m = H_m(G_m([\mathbf{x}_{m-2}, \mathbf{x}_{m-1}])) \tag{5}$$

where $[\mathbf{x}_{m-2}, \mathbf{x}_{m-1}]$ is the concatenation of the feature-maps produced by modules $m-2$ and $m-1$. In addition, because the channel number has changed from $\mathbf{c}_m$ to $2\mathbf{c}_m$, this paper applies $1 \times 1$ Ghost module $G_m$ to recover the channel number to match the $m^{th}$ module. The $1 \times 1$ Ghost module adopts the same setting as Sect. 3.1.

This paper refers to the added connections as efficient dense connections because that, benefiting from the feature reuse of only adjacent modules and the efficiency of $1 \times 1$ Ghost module, these connections can facilitate convergence and promote network accuracy with a slight increase in model complexity.

## 4   Experiments

In this section, several experiments are conducted on two human pose estimation datasets, COCO [14] and MPII [1]. Comparative experiments between EHR-HPE and some state-of-the-art methods are conducted on both datasets, ablation studies are only carried out on MPII to demonstrate the effectiveness of each component.

### 4.1   Experimental Setup

**Datasets.** The COCO dataset [14] contains over 200K images and 250K person instances labeled with 17 keypoints. COCO is divided into train, validation, and test sets. This paper trains EHR-HPE on train2017 dataset, including 57K images and 150K person instances. Evaluations are carried out on val2017 set and test-dev2017 set, containing 5K images and 20K images, respectively. The MPII dataset [1] provides around 25K images containing over 40K labeled person instances, in which 12K instances are used for testing, and 28K are used for training.

**Training.** The network is implemented by PyTorch and random parameter initialization is used. Adam optimizer is adopted with a mini-batch of size 32 and 210 epochs are trained. The initial learning rate is set to $5e^{-4}$ and reduced by a factor of 10 at the 170th and 200th epoch. In data preprocessing, the human detection box is expanded to a fixed aspect ratio of 4: 3, and then crop the box from the images. The input images are resizeed to $384 \times 288$ for COCO dataset and $256 \times 256$ for MPII dataset. Data augmentation operations are performed on two datasets to strengthen models' robustness, including random rotation $([-30°, 30°])$, random scale $([0.75, 1.25])$, and random flipping, what's more, half body data augmentation is also used for COCO. All experiments are conducted on two NVIDIA 1080Ti GPUs.

**Testing.** For COCO, the two-stage top-down paradigm is used, i.e., firstly detect the person instance via a person detector provided by SimpleBaseline [26], and then predict keypoints. For MPII, the standard strategy (using the provided person boxes) is adopted to guarantee the fairness of the results. Following the common practice [28,30], heatmaps are computed via averaging the heatmaps of the original and flipped images.

**Evaluation Metrics.** For COCO, this paper uses the OKS-based mAP metric and reports standard average precision and recall scores. OKS (Object Keypoint Similarity) represents the similarity between human poses. $AP^{50}$ represents the AP scores at $OKS = 0.50$, $AP^{75}$ represents the AP scores at $OKS = 0.75$, AP represents the mean of AP scores at 10 positions, $OKS = 0.50$, 0.55, ..., 0.95. $AP^{M}$ represents AP for medium objects, $AP^{L}$ represents AP for large objects. For MPII, this paper uses the standard metric PCKh@0.5 (detected keypoint is considered correct if the distance between the predicted and ground-truth keypoints is less than 50% of the length of head bone link) to evaluate the performance.

## 4.2   Results

**Results on COCO Val.** Table 1 gives the results of EHR-HPE and other state-of-the-art methods. The proposed EHR-HPE achieves 71.2 AP score when the input size is $384 \times 288$, with only 1.7M parameters and 0.91 GFLOPs. EHR-HPE outperforms Small HRNet-16[2] over 15 AP points. Compared to ShuffleNetV2 and MobileNetV2, EHR-HPE achieves 7.6 and 3.9 points gain, respectively, while taking on much lower complexity. Compared to LPN, EHR-HPE improves AP by 2.1 points with lower complexity. Lite-HRNet is an effective lightweight pose network, and EHR-HPE achieves better accuracy than it with a slight increase in computation cost. Compared to FLPN whose accuracy is only 0.1 points higher than ours, our parameter size is only 16.8% of it, and the computation cost is also lower. In comparison with large models, EHR-HPE achieves a better AP score than CPN, Hourglass, and SimpleBaseline, with much less complexity.

Due to the effectiveness of our efficient shuffle blocks and the feature reuse of efficient dense connections, the proposed EHR-HPE achieves a great tradeoff between accuracy and model complexity.

**Results on COCO Test-Dev.** Table 2 reports the results of EHR-HPE and the existing state-of-the-art methods. The proposed EHR-HPE achieves 70.1 AP score, which outperforms all the small networks. Compared to Lite-HRNet, EHR-HPE achieves 0.4 points gain with a little increase in computation cost. In comparison with large models, EHR-HPE outperforms Mask-RCNN, G-RMI and Integral Pose Regression, achieves acceptable results, and is much more efficient in terms of model size (Params) and computation cost.

**Results on MPII Val.** This paper evaluates EHR-HPE on MPII to further compare it with other lightweight networks and the results is shown in Table 3.

---

[2] Available from https://github.com/HRNet/HRNet-Semantic-Segmentation.

**Table 1.** Comparison on the COCO val set.

| Model | Backbone | Input size | #Params | GFLOPs | AP | AP$^{50}$ | AP$^{75}$ | AP$^M$ | AP$^L$ | AR |
|---|---|---|---|---|---|---|---|---|---|---|
| *Large networks* | | | | | | | | | | |
| 8-stage Hourglass [16] | 8-stage Hourglass | 256 × 192 | 25.1M | 14.3 | 66.9 | - | - | - | - | - |
| CPN [3] | ResNet-50 | 256 × 192 | 27.0M | 6.20 | 68.6 | - | - | - | - | - |
| SimpleBaseline [26] | ResNet-50 | 256 × 192 | 34.0M | 8.90 | 70.4 | 88.6 | 78.3 | 67.1 | 77.2 | 76.3 |
| HRNetV1 [21] | HRNetV1-W32 | 256 × 192 | 28.5M | 7.10 | 73.4 | 89.5 | 80.7 | 70.2 | 80.1 | 78.9 |
| DARK [29] | HRNetV1-W48 | 128 × 96 | 63.6M | 3.6 | 71.9 | 89.1 | 79.6 | 69.2 | 78.0 | 77.9 |
| *Small networks* | | | | | | | | | | |
| Small HRNet | HRNet-W16 | 384 × 288 | 1.3M | 1.21 | 56.0 | 83.8 | 63.0 | 52.4 | 62.6 | 62.6 |
| ShuffleNetV2 1× [15] | ShuffleNetV2 | 384 × 288 | 7.6M | 2.87 | 63.6 | 86.5 | 70.5 | 59.5 | 70.7 | 69.7 |
| MobileNetV2 1× [10] | MobileNetV2 | 384 × 288 | 9.6M | 3.33 | 67.3 | 87.9 | 74.3 | 62.8 | 74.7 | 72.9 |
| LPN [30] | ResNet-50 | 256 × 192 | 2.9M | 1.0 | 69.1 | 88.1 | 76.6 | 65.9 | 75.7 | 74.9 |
| Lite-HRNet [28] | Lite-HRNet-30 | 384 × 288 | 1.8M | 0.70 | 70.4 | 88.7 | 77.7 | 67.5 | 76.3 | 76.2 |
| FLPN [20] | SResNet-50 | 256 × 192 | 10.0M | 1.10 | 71.3 | 91.6 | 79.0 | 68.8 | 75.3 | 74.5 |
| EHR-HPE | EHRNet | 384 × 288 | 1.7M | 0.91 | 71.2 | 89.1 | 78.8 | 69.0 | 76.8 | 75.3 |

The proposed EHR-HPE achieves 87.3 PCKh@0.5, outperforms Small HRNet-16, ShuffleNetV2, MobileNetV2, MobileNetV3 [9] and Lite-HRNet by 7.1, 4.5, 1.9, 3.0 and 0.3 points, respectively. Compared to FLPN, there is a little gap (0.5 points). However, the amount of the parameters and the computation cost of EHR-HPE are only 17% and 48% of FPLN, respectively.

**Table 2.** Comparision on the COCO test-dev set.

| Model | Backbone | Input size | #Params | GFLOPs | AP | AP$^{50}$ | AP$^{75}$ | AP$^M$ | AP$^L$ | AR |
|---|---|---|---|---|---|---|---|---|---|---|
| *Large networks* | | | | | | | | | | |
| Mask-RCNN [7] | ResNet-50-FPN | - | - | - | 63.1 | 87.3 | 68.7 | 57.8 | 71.4 | - |
| G-RMI [17] | ResNet-101 | 353 × 257 | 42.6M | 57.0 | 64.9 | 85.5 | 71.3 | 62.3 | 70.0 | 69.7 |
| Integral Pose Regression [22] | ResNet-101 | 256 × 256 | 45.0M | 11.0 | 67.8 | 88.2 | 74.8 | 63.9 | 74.0 | - |
| CPN [3] | ResNet-Inception | 384 × 288 | - | - | 72.1 | 91.4 | 80.0 | 68.7 | 77.2 | 78.5 |
| RMPE [4] | PyraNet | 320 × 256 | 28.1M | 26.7 | 72.3 | 89.2 | 79.1 | 68.0 | 78.6 | - |
| SimpleBaseline [26] | ResNet-152 | 384 × 288 | 68.6M | 35.6 | 73.7 | 91.9 | 81.1 | 70.3 | 80.0 | 79.0 |
| HRNetV1 [21] | HRNetV1-W32 | 384 × 288 | 28.5M | 16.0 | 74.9 | 92.5 | 82.8 | 71.3 | 80.9 | 80.1 |
| HRNetV1 [21] | HRNetV1-W48 | 384 × 288 | 63.6M | 32.9 | 75.5 | 92.5 | 83.3 | 71.9 | 81.5 | 80.5 |
| DARK [29] | HRNetV1-W48 | 384 × 288 | 63.6M | 32.9 | 76.2 | 92.5 | 83.6 | 72.5 | 82.4 | 81.1 |
| *Small networks* | | | | | | | | | | |
| Small HRNet | HRNet-W16 | 384 × 288 | 1.3M | 1.21 | 55.2 | 85.8 | 61.4 | 51.7 | 61.2 | 61.5 |
| ShuffleNetV2 1× [15] | ShuffleNetV2 | 384 × 288 | 7.6M | 2.87 | 62.9 | 88.5 | 69.4 | 58.9 | 69.3 | 68.9 |
| MobileNetV2 1× [10] | MobileNetV2 | 384 × 288 | 9.8M | 3.33 | 66.8 | 90.0 | 74.0 | 62.6 | 73.3 | 72.3 |
| LPN [30] | ResNet-50 | 256 × 192 | 2.9M | 1.0 | 68.7 | 90.2 | 76.9 | 65.9 | 74.3 | 74.5 |
| FLPN [20] | SResNet-50 | 256 × 192 | 10.0M | 1.10 | 68.7 | 90.6 | 77.2 | 65.9 | 74.0 | 74.5 |
| Lite-HRNet [28] | Lite-HRNet-30 | 384 × 288 | 1.8M | 0.70 | 69.7 | 90.7 | 77.5 | 66.9 | 75.0 | 75.4 |
| EHR-HPE | EHRNet | 384 × 288 | 1.7M | 0.91 | 70.1 | 91.2 | 77.9 | 66.7 | 75.6 | 75.2 |

## 4.3    Ablation Study

A series of ablation studies on MPII validation set have been conducted to analyze the effectiveness of each component proposed in this paper. Table 4 reports the results. Firstly, this paper combines shuffle blocks with Small HRNet as baseline, which achieves 86.38 points (PCKh@0.5) with 1.3 M parameters and 419 MFLOPs. To further improve the performance, two $1 \times 1$ Ghost modules ($r$ is set to 2) are introduced to replace the two $1 \times 1$ convolutions in shuffle blocks, thereby the number of parameters and the computation cost are reduced by 0.17M and 60 MFLOPs, respectively, whereas the performance is improved by 0.13 points.

**Table 3.** Comparisons on the MPII val set.

| Model | #Params | GFLOPs | PCKh@0.5 |
|---|---|---|---|
| Small HRNet | 1.3M | 0.74 | 80.2 |
| ShuffleNetV2 1× | 7.6M | 1.70 | 82.8 |
| MobileNetV3 1× | 8.7M | 1.82 | 84.3 |
| MobileNetV2 1× | 9.6M | 1.97 | 85.4 |
| Lite-HRNet-30 | 1.8M | 0.42 | 87.0 |
| FLPN | 10.0M | 1.10 | 87.8 |
| EHR-HPE | 1.7M | 0.53 | 87.3 |

**Table 4.** Ablation studies on the MPII val set.

| Model | #Params | MFLOPs | PCKh@0.5 |
|---|---|---|---|
| Small HRNet | 1.3M | 736 | 80.2 |
| Baseline | 1.3M | 419 | 86.38 |
| + $1 \times 1$ Ghost | 1.13M | 359 | 86.51 |
| + $1 \times 1$ Ghost + GC block | 1.24M | 361 | 86.63 |
| + $1 \times 1$ Ghost + CGC block | 1.13M | 365 | 86.58 |
| + $1 \times 1$ Ghost + attention module | 1.25M | 368 | 86.69 |
| EHR-HPE | 1.69M | 534 | 87.33 |

Subsequently, GC blocks are introduced into the shuffle blocks to strengthen the modeling ability on spatial long-range dependencies, and achieves 86.69 points. Based on GC block, CGC block is proposed to enhance the information exchange across channels, and achieves 86.63 points. This paper combines GC and CGC blocks as the attention module used in EHR-HPE to enhance the modeling ability of both inter-channel and inter-spatial relationships, performance has been improved by 0.18 points at the cost of 0.12M extra parameters and 9 extra MFLOPs.

Finally, efficient dense connections are proposed to facilitate convergence and promote network accuracy, resulting in the final EHR-HPE, which achieves 87.33 points with 1.69M parameters and 534 MFLOPs on MPII validation set.

## 5   Conclusion

Considering the deployment difficulty of large human pose estimation methods, this paper proposes an efficient and lightweight network named EHR-HPE. EHR-HPE network first follows the high-resolution pattern of Small HRNet to acquire accurate heatmaps; then an efficient shuffle block is designed to reduce the model complexity and boost model performance; finally, the efficient dense connections are added to further improve model accuracy. Extensive experiment results demonstrate that the proposed EHR-HPE network can achieve comparable results with those top-performing methods, while the model complexity is much lower, making it more suitable for resource-limited devices.

**Acknowledgements.** This work was funded by the Project Research on human-robot interactive sampling robots with safety, autonomy, and intelligent operations supported by NSFC (92048205).

## References

1. Andriluka, M., Pishchulin, L., Gehler, P., Schiele, B.: 2D human pose estimation: new benchmark and state of the art analysis. In: Proceedings of the IEEE Conference on computer Vision and Pattern Recognition, pp. 3686–3693 (2014)
2. Cao, Y., Xu, J., Lin, S., Wei, F., Hu, H.: GCNet: non-local networks meet squeeze-excitation networks and beyond. In: Proceedings of the IEEE/CVF International Conference on Computer Vision Workshops (2019)
3. Chen, Y., Wang, Z., Peng, Y., Zhang, Z., Yu, G., Sun, J.: Cascaded pyramid network for multi-person pose estimation. In: Proceedings of the IEEE Conference on Computer Vision and Pattern Recognition, pp. 7103–7112 (2018)
4. Fang, H.S., Xie, S., Tai, Y.W., Lu, C.: RMPE: regional multi-person pose estimation. In: Proceedings of the IEEE International Conference on Computer Vision, pp. 2334–2343 (2017)
5. Felzenszwalb, P.F., Huttenlocher, D.P.: Pictorial structures for object recognition. Int. J. Comput. Vision **61**(1), 55–79 (2005)
6. Han, K., Wang, Y., Tian, Q., Guo, J., Xu, C., Xu, C.: GhostNet: more features from cheap operations. In: Proceedings of the IEEE/CVF Conference on Computer Vision and Pattern Recognition, pp. 1580–1589 (2020)
7. He, K., Gkioxari, G., Dollár, P., Girshick, R.: Mask R-CNN. In: Proceedings of the IEEE International Conference on Computer Vision, pp. 2961–2969 (2017)
8. He, K., Zhang, X., Ren, S., Sun, J.: Deep residual learning for image recognition. In: Proceedings of the IEEE Conference on Computer Vision and Pattern Recognition, pp. 770–778 (2016)
9. Howard, A., et al.: Searching for mobilenetv3. In: Proceedings of the IEEE/CVF International Conference on Computer Vision, pp. 1314–1324 (2019)

10. Howard, A., Zhmoginov, A., Chen, L.C., Sandler, M., Zhu, M.: Inverted residuals and linear bottlenecks: mobile networks for classification, detection and segmentation (2018)

11. Hu, J., Shen, L., Albanie, S., Sun, G., Vedaldi, A.: Gather-excite: exploiting feature context in convolutional neural networks. In: Advances in Neural Information Processing Systems, vol. 31 (2018)

12. Hu, J., Shen, L., Sun, G.: Squeeze-and-excitation networks. In: Proceedings of the IEEE Conference on Computer Vision and Pattern Recognition, pp. 7132–7141 (2018)

13. Huang, G., Liu, Z., Van Der Maaten, L., Weinberger, K.Q.: Densely connected convolutional networks. In: Proceedings of the IEEE Conference on Computer Vision and Pattern Recognition, pp. 4700–4708 (2017)

14. Lin, T.-Y., et al.: Microsoft COCO: common objects in context. In: Fleet, D., Pajdla, T., Schiele, B., Tuytelaars, T. (eds.) ECCV 2014. LNCS, vol. 8693, pp. 740–755. Springer, Cham (2014). https://doi.org/10.1007/978-3-319-10602-1_48

15. Ma, N., Zhang, X., Zheng, H.-T., Sun, J.: ShuffleNet V2: practical guidelines for efficient CNN architecture design. In: Ferrari, V., Hebert, M., Sminchisescu, C., Weiss, Y. (eds.) Computer Vision – ECCV 2018. LNCS, vol. 11218, pp. 122–138. Springer, Cham (2018). https://doi.org/10.1007/978-3-030-01264-9_8

16. Newell, A., Yang, K., Deng, J.: Stacked hourglass networks for human pose estimation. In: Leibe, B., Matas, J., Sebe, N., Welling, M. (eds.) ECCV 2016. LNCS, vol. 9912, pp. 483–499. Springer, Cham (2016). https://doi.org/10.1007/978-3-319-46484-8_29

17. Papandreou, G., et al.: Towards accurate multi-person pose estimation in the wild. In: Proceedings of the IEEE Conference on Computer Vision and Pattern Recognition, pp. 4903–4911 (2017)

18. Pishchulin, L., Andriluka, M., Gehler, P., Schiele, B.: Poselet conditioned pictorial structures. In: Proceedings of the IEEE Conference on Computer Vision and Pattern Recognition, pp. 588–595 (2013)

19. Qin, X., Guo, H., He, C., Zhang, X.: Lightweight human pose estimation: CVC-Net. Multimedia Tools Appl. 81(13), 17615–17637 (2022)

20. Ren, H., Wang, W., Zhang, K., Wei, D., Gao, Y., Sun, Y.: Fast and lightweight human pose estimation. IEEE Access 9, 49576–49589 (2021)

21. Sun, K., Xiao, B., Liu, D., Wang, J.: Deep high-resolution representation learning for human pose estimation. In: Proceedings of the IEEE/CVF Conference on Computer Vision and Pattern Recognition, pp. 5693–5703 (2019)

22. Sun, X., Xiao, B., Wei, F., Liang, S., Wei, Y.: Integral human pose regression. In: Ferrari, V., Hebert, M., Sminchisescu, C., Weiss, Y. (eds.) ECCV 2018. LNCS, vol. 11210, pp. 536–553. Springer, Cham (2018). https://doi.org/10.1007/978-3-030-01231-1_33

23. Wang, X., Li, Z., Chen, Y., Jiang, P., Wang, F.: Stacked mixed-scale networks for human pose estimation. In: Nayak, A.C., Sharma, A. (eds.) PRICAI 2019. LNCS (LNAI), vol. 11670, pp. 217–229. Springer, Cham (2019). https://doi.org/10.1007/978-3-030-29908-8_18

24. Wei, S.E., Ramakrishna, V., Kanade, T., Sheikh, Y.: Convolutional pose machines. In: Proceedings of the IEEE Conference on Computer Vision and Pattern Recognition, pp. 4724–4732 (2016)

25. Woo, S., Park, J., Lee, J.-Y., Kweon, I.S.: CBAM: convolutional block attention module. In: Ferrari, V., Hebert, M., Sminchisescu, C., Weiss, Y. (eds.) ECCV 2018. LNCS, vol. 11211, pp. 3–19. Springer, Cham (2018). https://doi.org/10.1007/978-3-030-01234-2_1

26. Xiao, B., Wu, H., Wei, Y.: Simple baselines for human pose estimation and tracking. In: Ferrari, V., Hebert, M., Sminchisescu, C., Weiss, Y. (eds.) ECCV 2018. LNCS, vol. 11210, pp. 472–487. Springer, Cham (2018). https://doi.org/10.1007/978-3-030-01231-1_29
27. Yang, Y., Ramanan, D.: Articulated pose estimation with flexible mixtures-of-parts. In: CVPR 2011, pp. 1385–1392. IEEE (2011)
28. Yu, C., et al.: Lite-HRNET: a lightweight high-resolution network. In: Proceedings of the IEEE/CVF Conference on Computer Vision and Pattern Recognition, pp. 10440–10450 (2021)
29. Zhang, F., Zhu, X., Dai, H., Ye, M., Zhu, C.: Distribution-aware coordinate representation for human pose estimation. In: Proceedings of the IEEE/CVF Conference on Computer Vision and Pattern Recognition, pp. 7093–7102 (2020)
30. Zhang, Z., Tang, J., Wu, G.: Simple and lightweight human pose estimation. arXiv preprint arXiv:1911.10346 (2019)

# The Geometry Enhanced Deep Implicit Function Based 3D Reconstruction for Objects in a Real-Scene Image

Haiwei Mei[1] and Chenxing Wang[2][(✉)]

[1] Southeast University, Suzhou, China
meihaiwei@seu.edu.cn
[2] Southeast University, Nanjing, China
cxwang@seu.edu.cn

**Abstract.** For the 3D reconstruction of objects in a real scene, the state-of-the-art scheme is to detect and identify the target by a classic deep neural network and reconstruct the 3D object with deep implicit function (DIF) based methods. This scheme can be computationally and memory efficient, representing high-resolution geometry of arbitrary topology for reconstructing the 3D objects in a scene. However, geometry constraints are lacking in these procedures, which may lead to fatal mistaken identification or structural errors in the reconstruction results. In this paper, we propose to enhance the geometry constraint of the DIF-based 3D reconstruction. A geometry retainer module (GRM) ensures the detected target always retains the correct 2D geometry. The chamfer distance (CD) is introduced as a constraint on the 3D geometry for the DIF-based method. Correspondingly, a strategy to extract a point cloud from the signed distance field (SDF) is proposed to complete this 3D geometry constraint. Abundant experiments show that our method improves the quality of 3D reconstruction greatly.

**Keywords:** 3D reconstruction · Deep learning · Deep implicit function

## 1 Introduction

3D reconstruction from a single-view real-scene image is challenging because of an object's depth ambiguity and self-occlusion. A reliable scheme is to identify a target firstly and then reconstruct the 3D model of the target using prior templates [2–4]. As a real-scene image usually contains various targets, many works detect every target object firstly with 2D object detection networks, such as the faster region-based convolutional neural network (Faster RCNN) [5] or Single Shot MultiBox Detector (SSD) [7]. Generally, each target object is cropped according to the region of interest (ROI) output by the object detection networks to avoid interference from the background or other objects. The cropped image is usually resized to a fixed size and aspect ratio to be adapted to the requirements of CNN-based feature encoding blocks such as ResNet [8]. However, general resizing operations ignore retaining the reasonable 2D geometry of the target object, leading to distortion of the target after it is resized. The data with this type of

S. Khanna et al. (Eds.): PRICAI 2022, LNCS 13631, pp. 397–409, 2022.
https://doi.org/10.1007/978-3-031-20868-3_29

distortion may cause polluting interference to the network training and result in wrong object identification as well as large reconstruction errors. This is an easily ignored but important issue.

The way of representing an object is essential for 3D reconstruction. Traditional physical forms of expressing a 3D entity include point cloud, volume, and mesh. The implicit function is a popular parametric form in recent years, which has the advantages of small storage requirements, moderate computational cost, adaptability to different structures, and easily represented details. However, the implicit function based methods [6, 9] focus on the inside and outside distributions of the near-surface points in the SDF. The small errors estimated in such distributions can be serious topological errors in the solid 3D space due to the non-weighted evaluation for outliers. Moreover, since there is no entity in the training process for DIF-based methods, we can not design loss functions from the solid structure to supervise the 3D geometry.

Resolving the problems above, the contributions of this paper are listed below:

1) A GRM is proposed to resize a 2D image where the correct 2D geometry of the target object can be ensured.
2) The CD is introduced as a 3D geometry constraint to the network training of the DIF methods. Correspondingly, an approach of sampling a coarse point cloud is proposed to implement the 3D geometry constraint.

## 2 Related Work

3D reconstruction from RGB images has been researched for a long time [10]. Until recent years, deep neural networks have made it possible to implement a 3D reconstruction task from a single image. For this task, the image features preprocessing, the 3D representation, and the design of loss functions significantly affect the quality of 3D reconstruction.

### 2.1 Image Feature Preprocessing

The CNN-based encoding networks have a strong ability for feature extraction. Thus, they are widely applied in object detection [5], image classification [11], and image-based 3D structure extraction [1–3, 6, 9, 12, 13]. Most non-fully convolutional networks require that the input images have the same size to achieve efficient computation and keep the feature extraction in the same dimension for the downstream tasks. However, sometimes, the target in the image shows distortion in geometry after being resized. He et al. [14] have discussed the importance of this requirement and proposed a Spatial Pyramid Pooling (SPP) method that can adapt to feature maps with various dimensions and output a fixed-length feature map. However, the SPP cannot perform parallel processing in the early stage due to the inconsistent dimension of input feature maps. Moreover, this method is limited for small-size feature maps because of the max-pooling operation applied, but the cropped target image from a single-view real-scene image is usually small.

## 2.2   3D Representation

The general types of 3D representation usually include voxels, point clouds, depths maps, and implicit functions.

**Voxel.** Voxel-based methods [15–17] are usually conducted with 3D CNN, which can reconstruct objects with flexible topology. However, voxel-based methods require devices with strong computing power and large video memory. Although the octree method [18] can reduce the computation cost, the data amount is still extremely limited.

**Point.** PointOutNet [19] is the first network to output point clouds directly. It applies a fully connected neural network to each point and performs a global pooling operation to achieve permutation invariance. The point-based methods [19–22] do not need large storage and calculation as voxel-based methods, but they cannot utilize classic CNN directly and have to design new backbones because point sets are disordered.

**Depth Map.** A depth map represents the geometry of surfaces by projecting the depth information into an image. The depth-based methods [23–25] can only represent the visible shape of an object. Thus, calibration is necessary if an object's actual size is desired.

**Mesh.** Mesh is a general form representing a 3D structure [2–4, 12, 26]. Some methods, such as AtlasNet [1], represent a mesh by parameterized surface generation complexly. With a pre-defined mesh template, some methods [2–4, 12, 26] directly deform the template to get close to a mesh, which is effective and generalized. Among them, a network named Pixel2Mesh [26] uses a Graph Unpooling operation to generate more vertices to increase the resolution of meshes. However, this method can only increase to generate zero-genus meshes and cannot represent complex topology. A topology modification network (TMN) [2] and another mesh generation network (MGN) [3] both propose a redundant face-cutting strategy, which can output non-zero genus meshes by removing unwanted faces. However, their results sometimes appear hollow or have inadequate cutting problems in the output meshes. Moreover, the self-intersection or overlap may easily appear in mesh-based methods.

**Implicit Function.** Implicit function based methods [9, 27–30] have become popular recently. They can theoretically represent 3D structures without pre-defined templates and adapt to diverse structures. Furthermore, they need relatively small computation costs and have no resolution limitations. Occupancy networks (ONet) [29] are proposed to take 3D presentation as a binary classification problem, which outputs a distinct topology. However, it requires further fine-tuning to get a high-quality surface, leading that the method cannot be conducted end-to-end. A local DIF (LDIF) [9] based on structured implicit function (SIF) [30] is proposed to add multiple local depths maps to ensure more details are retained in the output result. However, obviously, this method is not suitable for single-view 3D reconstruction. To address this problem, C Zhang et al. [6] introduce the encoder from MGN [3] to replace the encoder of LDIF and build a local implicit embedding network (LIEN). LIEN achieves the best results in single-view reconstruction for real scenes. However, their reconstruction results sometimes appear as broken structures or isolated patches due to the lack of solid 3D geometry constraints. However, introducing the solid geometry to the DIF-based network training is not easy because the general extraction methods are not differentiable [31], such as Marching Cubes [32] and Dual Contouring [33]. Therefore, finding a way to match a zero iso-surfaces of implicit function to a correct local geometry is important, ensuring more accurate and complete reconstruction for overall topology 3D structures.

### 2.3 Loss Function for Geometry Structure

The loss function is usually applied to constrain some factors that can supervise the predictions of networks, and it must be designed according to the data presentations during the training process. For methods with solid outputs, such as point clouds, voxel, and mesh, the similarity of 3D structures is usually evaluated by calculating the spatial distance of sampling points on the ground truth and the output surface. Therefore, the L1 (or MAE) and L2 (or MSE) loss functions are often used. For voxel-based methods, another binary cross-entropy (BCE) is usually used to compare the occupancy of spatial cubes. Recently, the CD or earth moving distance [34] based on L1 and L2 are also widely used as loss functions in similarity evaluation for 3D structures.

For DIF-based methods [9, 29, 30], the signed distance value (SDV) of uniformly sampled points is used to supervise the overall 3D structure. However, since uniform sampling is generally random and not targeted to specified structures, the loss functions for DIF methods cannot purposely and accurately supervise structural skeleton integrity.

The DIF-based methods can flexibly reconstruct the 3D model for various objects and are less computational than other methods [15–17, 19]. However, this type of method processes the data in parameterization, which lacks the real geometry constraint and thus leads to some unexpected errors. We intend to introduce the geometry information to this parameterized method. At first, we propose a GRM to ensure the object segmented from a real-scene image can always maintain a correct 2D geometry. To introduce the constraint of 3D geometry to the DFF methods, we propose a method to reconstruct a coarse point cloud from the SDF and then introduce the CD as a loss. Experiments show that our geometry enhanced DIF method performs more accurately and robustly than other state-of-the-art methods.

## 3    Methodology

### 3.1    Network Architecture

Figure 1 shows the architecture of our network. The proposed GRM module ensures the object image is always resized with correct 2D geometry. The encoder (ResNet18 [8]) and MLP (3 Fully Connected Layers) modules are inspired by LIEN [6]. The decoder part is derived from LDIF [9], which performs well on single-object reconstruction. The Gaussian parameters describe the 3D geometry information of each Gaussian function, such as scale constant, center point, radius, and rotation angle. The DIF decoder obtains shape details from latent features that Gaussian elements cannot represent. Finally, these two parts are fused by multiplying and summing operations to get a full DIF representation. Furthermore, we introduce a loss function during parameter update via backpropagation for 3D geometry enhancement.

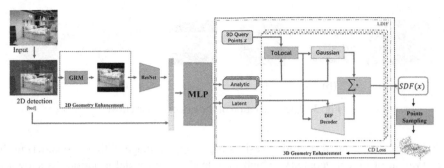

**Fig. 1.** The network architecture of our geometry enhanced DIF-based method: a cropped object image is resized by the proposed GRM that ensures the correct 2D geometry of objects; the features containing 2D geometry information are extracted by the ResNet and then sent to MLP modules to obtain the Analytic and Latent features; DIF decoders decode these features to predict the SDF; a coarse point cloud is sampled by our method from the SDF, and our CD loss is used to optimize the LDIF decoder to supervise the 3D structures.

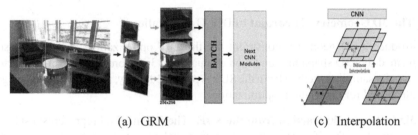

(a)  GRM                                    (c)  Interpolation

**Fig. 2.** The illustration of our GRM

### 3.2  The Geometry Retainer Module for 2D Constraint

Our GRM aims to reasonably resize the 2D image of a target object to a fixed size, as illustrated in Fig. 2(a). An image is firstly adjusted to a required aspect ratio by padding if needed, and the target object is set in the center of the image. Then, a grid is established according to the downstream required size. Finally, a four-point bilinear interpolation [35] is applied to calculate the pixel value of each grid point, as displayed in Fig. 2(b), and the interpolation is calculated as:

$$f(e) = \frac{1}{(x_d - x_a)(y_d - y_a)}\left[f(a)f(b)f(c)f(d)\right]\begin{bmatrix} x_d y_d & -y_d & -x_d & 1 \\ -x_d y_a & y_a & x_d & -1 \\ -x_a y_d & y_d & x_a & -1 \\ x_a y_a & -y_a & -x_a & 1 \end{bmatrix}\begin{bmatrix} 1 \\ x_e \\ y_e \\ x_e y_e \end{bmatrix} \quad (1)$$

where $f(e)$ denotes the pixel value of a point $e$, $x$ and $y$ are the horizontal and vertical coordinates, respectively, and $a, b, c, d$ denote the four points adjacent to $e$ separately.

The proposed GRM ensures that an image can be resized reasonably always. Figure 3 displays the effect of GRM in detail. A scene image is shown in Fig. 3(a), where a sofa is detected as a target object and marked by a bounding box. Then the target is cropped

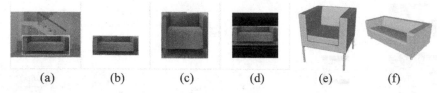

|   (a)   |   (b)   |   (c)   |   (d)   |   (e)   |   (f)   |

**Fig. 3.** The illustration of the effect of our GRM

as Fig. 3(b). The general operation resizes the cropped image without considering the preservation of object geometry, which may lead to object deformation, as shown in Fig. 3 (c). The proposed GRM can give a correct result in Fig. 3(d). According to the 2D geometry of the resized image, a corresponding 3D model is selected as the basis of 3D reconstruction. Therefore, the incorrect 2D geometry provided in Fig. 3(c) directly leads to a mistaken selection of the object in Fig. 3(e), but the result should be the one in Fig. 3(f). The solved issue of our GRM looks simple, but this module is significant for avoiding vital mistakes in practice.

### 3.3 The 3D Geometry Constraint in DIF Optimization

To introduce a 3D geometry constraint for the DIF optimization, the SDF must be transformed to a 3D shape first and then evaluate the 3D geometry by some measures. Thus, a point sampling method from the SDF is proposed firstly, and a CD loss is designed and introduced for the training optimization.

**The 3D Geometry Extraction from the SDF.** The DIF method represents a shape by the SDF, in which the SDV of each query point is calculated. Then, the zero iso-surface in the SDF should be found and processed further to reconstruct the shape [6, 30]. To obtain the zero iso-surface effectively, some interpolation operations are applied [32, 33]. However, these operations are not differentiable [31] and thus cannot be introduced directly to supervise the network training for the DIF methods. In fact, the shape can also be reconstructed roughly by some small SDVs close to and not exactly the zero iso-surfaces. Therefore, we propose to detect the close-zero iso-surface for ease. Figure 4 displays an example. In Fig. 4(a), a grid-point space is created according to the coordinates of corresponding query points corresponding to the SDF. After calculating the SDV of each intersection point in the grid-point space, the close-zero iso-surface is detected, and the corresponding points are marked black as in Fig. 4(b) and extracted as in Fig. 4(c). The extracted 3D geometry is consistent with the real shape in Fig. 4(d).

|      (a)      |      (b)      |      (c)      |      (d)      |

**Fig. 4.** The extraction of 3D geometry from SDF

The detection of close-zero iso-surface eases the 3D geometry extraction, and most importantly, it is differentiable and can be added to the network training directly. Note that the resolution of the grid-point space should be set moderately, considering better accuracy and less computational cost. Referring to [6], we set the resolution as $128^3$ for much finer presentation ability. Participating in the networking training, the grid points are further down-sampled randomly in every epoch for lighter processing, corresponding to which some smallest SDVs are roughly selected as the close-zero iso-surface. The number of down-sampled points and the number of SDVs selected as the close-zero iso-surface can be adjusted according to the dataset, introduced in detail in experiments.

**The Designed Chamfer Distance Loss.** In DIF-based methods, the loss functions of previous works mainly focus on the constraint of the sign [6, 9, 29, 30, 36] or the value [13, 37] of SDVs, where common L1 and L2 loss are usually used. These constraints work to supervise the network training in parameterized space all the time. However, the ambiguity of sign or distance computation may easily appear in the constraints of predicting the SDVs even if the loss in parameterized space changes satisfactorily. As the example below, Fig. 5(a) and (d) represent two different ground-truth surfaces, respectively. Due to the ambiguity of sign constraint or distance constraint to different iso-surfaces, some extra isolated patches are mistakenly assigned to the surface of a shape, as illustrated in Fig. 5(b), or some partial parts of a surface are mistakenly assigned not belonging to this surface, as in Fig. 5(e). After training iteratively, the final results appear large errors, as in Fig. 5(c) and (f).

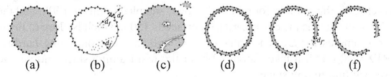

|     |     |     |     |     |     |
| (a) | (b) | (c) | (d) | (e) | (f) |

**Fig. 5.** The clarification of the problem

To solve the problem above, we design a loss function based on the CD to restrain the 3D geometry of the reconstructed shape. The CD loss is defined as

$$\mathcal{L}_{CD} = \frac{1}{P_f}\sum_{x\in P_f}\min_{y\in P_{f'}}||x - y||_2^2 + \frac{1}{P_{f'}}\sum_{y\in P_{f'}}\min_{x\in P_f}||y - x||_2^2 \qquad (2)$$

where $P_f$ is the point cloud near the ground-truth surface, and $P_{f'}$ is a corresponding point in the grid-point space obtained by our 3D geometry extraction method above, which has SDV as the close-zero iso-surface in the SDF. This loss is added to the overall loss function of the network like:

$$\mathcal{L}_{total} = \lambda_U\mathcal{L}_U + \lambda_S\mathcal{L}_S + \lambda_C\mathcal{L}_C + \lambda_{CD}\mathcal{L}_{CD} \qquad (3)$$

where $\lambda$ denotes the weight of each loss; $\mathcal{L}_U$, $\mathcal{L}_S$, and $\mathcal{L}_C$ are the loss functions of uniform sampling points, surface sampling points, and elements center, respectively, which can refer to [6] and [9]; $\mathcal{L}_{CD}$ is designed by Eq. (2). By introducing the 3D geometry constraint, the SDVs predicted by the network model tend to be more accurate.

# 4  Experiments

## 4.1  The Settings

**Dataset.** The Pix3D dataset is presented as a large-scale benchmark for 3D shape reconstruction, which provides nine categories of 395 furniture models and 10,069 images correspondingly. We keep the train/test split in line with [26], including 7556 images for training and 2513 images for testing. The mesh fusion method in ONet is used to get the watertight meshes for training, and we evaluate the post-processed mesh on original and watertight meshes.

**Metrics.** The widely used chamfer distance is selected as a primary metric to evaluate the shape similarity. For DIF-based methods, the marching cubes are used to extract entity triangle meshes from the SDF with a resolution of $256^3$, which is high to ensure quality and accuracy.

**Implementation.** Our GRM and CD loss are implemented based on LIEN [6], and the network is trained on the Pix3D dataset with watertight meshes. Most of our hyperparameters are the same as the original configuration in LIEN. Considering the training efficiency, our 3D geometry constraint, the CD loss, is only used as a fine-tuning for the network training. Therefore, we train the network in two stages. Firstly, the LIEN combined with our GRM is trained for 600 epochs, and then our CD loss is added and conducted a fine-tune for another 20 epochs of end-to-end training. The learning rate is 2e-5. In the introduction of our 3D geometry extraction, the resolution of the grid-point space is set $128^3$, the number for randomly down-sampled points is 150k, and the number of SDVs selected as the close-zero iso-surface is 1500, which is close to the number of uniform samples for $\mathcal{L}_S$. The value of $\lambda_{CD} = 0.55$. The computing hardware is a single RTX3090 GPU. It takes about 12 h for the first training stage and another 12 h for the second fine-tuning stage.

## 4.2  The Comparisons with the State-of-the-Arts

We compare our method with the state-of-the-art reconstruction methods [1–3, 6] on the Pix3D dataset. To make it fair, all networks are trained with images having category information. For AtlasNet [1] and TMN [2], we modified their code to concatenate the one-hot object category code with the appearance feature for these two methods. For the TMN network, the threshold is $\tau = 0.1$.

**Qualitative Comparison.** The visual results are compared in Fig. 6. The AtlasNet can restore the shape of 3D models better, but it cannot generate closed meshes, which thus appear to many overlaps. The redundant surface cutting operation of TMN and MGN can generate non-zero genus meshes, which perform well when the object structure is simple but appear under-cut or over-cut for complex structures. The LIEN can adapt to complex structures better, but some partial parts of the surfaces are lost, and some isolated patches result unreasonably. Our method overcomes these issues and outputs much more compact and complete 3D results.

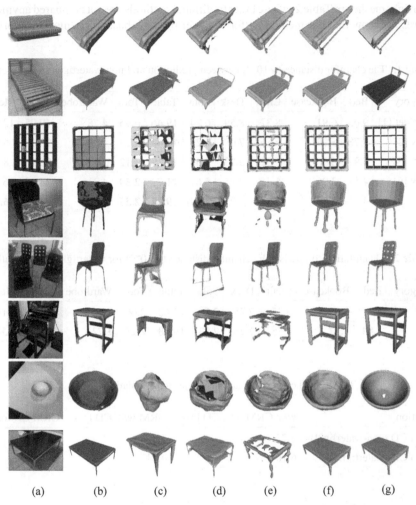

**Fig. 6.** Comparison of qualitative results. From left to right: (a) Input images; results of: (b) AtlasNet [1], (c)TMN [2], (d) MGN [3], (e) LIEN [6], (f) Ours, and (g) ground truth without watertight.

**Quantitative Comparison.** The widely used CD metric is adopted to evaluate the results quantitatively. We sample 10K points from the predicted mesh after aligning with the ground truth using ICP as in previous works [1–3, 6] to remove bias for different methods. Table 1 shows that our method outperforms the state-of-the-art methods in most categories, especially on the models with complex topology (e.g., chair and table).

The ground truth for traditional methods is a non-watertight mesh, while the DIF-based methods refer to a watertight one. However, the watertight process will fill the holes in the mesh but introduce some noise. So, we also compare the metrics with the watertight meshes in Table 2, where other traditional methods are not compared anymore. The results show that our method performs better than the baseline in most categories.

**Table 1.** The chamfer distance ($\times 10^{-3}$) between prediction and non-watertight ground truth.

| Category | Bed | Bookcase | Chair | Desk | Sofa | Table | Tool | Wardrobe | Misc | Mean |
|----------|-----|----------|-------|------|------|-------|------|----------|------|------|
| AtlasNet [1] | 9.03 | 6.91 | 8.37 | 8.59 | 6.24 | 19.46 | 6.95 | 4.78 | 40.05 | 12.26 |
| TMN [2] | 7.78 | 5.93 | 6.86 | 7.08 | 4.25 | 17.42 | 4.13 | 4.09 | 23.68 | 9.03 |
| MGN [3] | 5.99 | 6.56 | 5.32 | **5.93** | **3.36** | 14.19 | 3.12 | **3.83** | 26.93 | 8.36 |
| LIEN [6] | **4.11** | 3.96 | 5.45 | 7.85 | 5.61 | 11.73 | 2.39 | 4.31 | 24.65 | 6.72 |
| Ours | 4.12 | **3.85** | **5.05** | 7.95 | 5.29 | **9.64** | **2.35** | 3.85 | **21.95** | **6.07** |

**Table 2.** Quantitative comparison by chamfer distance ($\times 10^{-3}$) for watertight ground truth.

| Category | Bed | Bookcase | Chair | Desk | Sofa | Table | Tool | Wardrobe | Misc | Mean |
|----------|-----|----------|-------|------|------|-------|------|----------|------|------|
| LIEN [6] | 3.87 | 3.63 | 5.25 | 7.75 | **2.79** | 12.62 | 2.60 | 2.15 | 23.17 | 6.16 |
| Ours | **3.84** | **2.57** | **4.55** | **7.25** | 2.93 | **10.08** | **2.25** | **1.72** | **21.00** | **5.34** |

**Table 3.** The overall quantitative metric for ablation studies

| Ablation | w/o. GRM w/o. CD loss | GRM w/o. CD loss | GRM CD loss |
|----------|----------------------|------------------|-------------|
| Mean CD (non-watertight) | 6.72 | 5.67 | 6.07 |
| Mean CD (watertight) | 6.16 | 4.81 | 5.34 |

## 4.3  Ablation Studies

Figure 7 shows the ablation studies. Figure 7(a) is the input images. Figure 7(b) shows the results without our GRM and CD loss. Since the segmented object is resized deformedly with mistaken 2D geometry, the folding bed is mistakenly identified as a plank bed, so the final result is totally incorrect. Figure 7(c) shows the results of our GRM. Obviously, the result is correct, but the reconstruction result is dissatisfactory. In Fig. 7(d), the results are obtained by adding our CD loss further, which shows significant improvement compared with the ground truth in Fig. 7(e). Also shows the quantitative results correspondingly. Due to the influence of noisy parts generated, the overall evaluation results are not obvious, but the results in Fig. 7 and Fig. 6 still prove that our method is satisfactory.

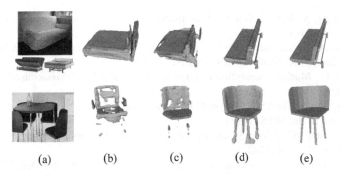

(a)          (b)          (c)          (d)          (e)

**Fig. 7.** Ablation studies

## 5 Conclusion

We propose introducing some geometry information for the DIF-based 3D reconstruction method to improve the accuracy. A GRM is proposed to ensure the 2D geometry, and a 3D geometry constraint based on CD is introduced for the DIF-based network training. The proposed method builds a bridge between DIF-based and traditional representation methods. The extensive quantitative or qualitative experiments show that our method significantly improves the 3D reconstruction results. However, some factors of our method are determined by experiments in this paper, such as the selection of sampling resolution. Moreover, our sampling method has high hardware requirements. However, the proportion of samples used in the final loss calculation is very small, and the calculation of many sampling points is unnecessary. How to filter out these unnecessary points in advance and reduce the calculation amount of sampling needs to be studied in our future work.

## References

1. Groueix, T., Fisher, M., Kim, V.G., Russell, B.C., Aubry, M.: AtlasNet: a papier-mâché approach to learning 3D surface generation. In: CVPR (2018)
2. Pan, J., Han, X., Chen, W., Tang, J., Jia, K.: Deep mesh reconstruction from single rgb images via topology modification networks, In: ICCV, pp. 9964–9973 (2019)
3. Nie, Y., Han, X., Guo, S., Zheng, Y., Chang, J., Zhang, J.J.: Total3DUnderstanding: joint layout, object pose and mesh reconstruction for indoor scenes from a single image. In: CVPR (2020)
4. Smith, E.J., Fujimoto, S., Romero, A., Meger, D.: GEOMetrics: exploiting geometric structure for graph-encoded objects. In: ICML, pp. 5866–5876 (2019)
5. Ren, S., He, K., Girshick, R., Sun, J.: Faster R-CNN: towards real-time object detection with region proposal networks, In: NIPS (2015)
6. Zhang, C., Cui, Z., Zhang, Y., Zeng, B., Pollefeys, M., Liu, S.: Holistic 3D scene understanding from a single image with implicit representation. In: CVPR, pp. 8833–8842 (2021)
7. Liu, W., et al.: SSD: single shot MultiBox detector. In: Leibe, B., Matas, J., Sebe, N., Welling, M. (eds.) ECCV 2016. LNCS, vol. 9905, pp. 21–37. Springer, Cham (2016). https://doi.org/10.1007/978-3-319-46448-0_2

8. He, K., Zhang, X., Ren, S., Sun, J.: Deep residual learning for image recognition. In: CVPR, pp. 770–778 (2016)
9. Genova, K., Cole, F., Sud, A., Sarna, A., Funkhouser, T.: Local deep implicit functions for 3d shape. In: CVPR, pp. 4857–4866 (2020)
10. Roberts, L.G.: Machine perception of three-dimensional solids, Massachusetts Institute of Technology (1963)
11. Krizhevsky, A., Sutskever, I., Hinton, G.E.: ImageNet classification with deep convolutional neural networks. In: NIPS.(2012)
12. Weng, Z., Yeung, S.: Holistic 3d human and scene mesh estimation from single view images. In: CVPR, pp. 334–343 (2021)
13. Park, J.J., Florence, P., Straub, J., Newcombe, R., and Lovegrove, S.: DeepSDF: learning continuous signed distance functions for shape representation. In: CVPR, pp. 165–174.(2019)
14. He, K., Zhang, X., Ren, S., Sun, J.: Spatial pyramid pooling in deep convolutional networks for visual recognition, pp. 1904–1916 (2015, 2015/09/10)
15. Choy, C.B., Xu, D., Gwak, J., Chen, K., Savarese, S.: 3D-R2N2: a unified approach for single and multi-view 3d object reconstruction. In: ECCV, pp. 628–644 (2016)
16. Wu, Z., et al.: 3D Shapenets: a deep representation for volumetric shapes. In: CVPR, pp. 1912–1920 (2015)
17. Liu, Z., Tang, H., Lin, Y., Han, S.: Point-voxel CNN for efficient 3D deep learning. In: NIPS, pp. 963–973 (2019)
18. Tatarchenko, M., Dosovitskiy, A., and Brox, T.: Octree generating networks: efficient convolutional architectures for high-resolution 3D outputs. In: ICCV (2017)
19. Fan, H., Su, H., Guibas, L.J.: A point set generation network for 3D object reconstruction from a single image. In: CVPR (2017)
20. Insafutdinov, E., Dosovitskiy, A.: Unsupervised learning of shape and pose with differentiable point clouds. In: NIPS (2018)
21. Huang, Z., Yu, Y., Xu, J., Ni, F., Le, X.: PF-Net: point fractal network for 3D point cloud completion, In: CVPR (2020)
22. Chen, R., Han, S., Xu, J., Su, H.: Point-based multi-view stereo network. In: ICCV (2019)
23. Eigen, D., Puhrsch, C., Fergus, R.: Depth map prediction from a single image using a multi-scale deep network. In: NIPS (2014)
24. Yin, Z., Shi, J.: GeoNet: unsupervised learning of dense depth, optical flow and camera pose. In: CVPR (2018)
25. Li, R., Wang, S., Long, Z., Gu, D.: UnDeepVO: monocular visual odometry through unsupervised deep learning, In: ICRA, pp. 7286–7291 (2018)
26. Wang, N., Zhang, Y., Li, Z., Fu, Y., Liu, W., Jiang, Y.-G.: Pixel2Mesh: generating 3D Mesh models from single RGB images. In: Ferrari, V., Hebert, M., Sminchisescu, C., Weiss, Y. (eds.) ECCV 2018. LNCS, vol. 11215, pp. 55–71. Springer, Cham (2018). https://doi.org/10.1007/978-3-030-01252-6_4
27. Remelli, E., et al.: MeshSDF: differentiable iso-surface extraction. In: NIPS, pp. 22468–22478 (2020)
28. Chen, Z., Zhang, H.: Learning implicit fields for generative shape modeling. In: CVPR, pp. 5939–5948 (2019)
29. Mescheder, L., Oechsle, M., Niemeyer, M., Nowozin, S., Geiger, A.: Occupancy networks: Learning 3d reconstruction in function space, In: CVPR, pp. 4460–4470 (2019)
30. Genova, K., Cole, F., Vlasic, D., Sarna, A., Freeman, W.T., and Funkhouser, T.: Learning Shape Templates With Structured Implicit Functions, In: ICCV.(2019)
31. Liao, Y., Donné, S., Geiger, A.: deep marching cubes: learning explicit surface representations. In: CVPR (2018)

32. Lorensen, W.E., Cline, H.E.: Marching cubes: a high resolution 3D surface construction algorithm. In: Proceedings of the 14th Annual Conference on Computer Graphics and Interactive Techniques, pp. 163–169 (1987)
33. Ju, T., Losasso, F., Schaefer, S., Warren, J.: Dual contouring of hermite data. In: Proceedings of the 29th Annual Conference on Computer Graphics and Interactive Techniques, pp. 339–169346.(2002)
34. Rubner, Y., Tomasi, C., Guibas, L.J.: The earth mover's distance as a metric for image retrieval, pp. 99–121 (2000)
35. Smith, P.R.: Bilinear interpolation of digital images, pp. 201–204 (1981)
36. Zheng, Z., Yu, T., Dai, Q., and Liu, Y.: Deep implicit templates for 3D shape representation. In: CVPR, pp. 1429–1439 (2021)
37. Venkatesh, R., Sharma, S., Ghosh, A., Jeni, L.A., Singh, M.: DUDE: deep unsigned distance embeddings for hi-fidelity representation of complex 3D surfaces (2020)

# Multi-view Stereo Network with Attention Thin Volume

Zihang Wan[1], Chao Xu[1,2(✉)], Jing Hu[1,2], Jian Xiao[1], Zhaopeng Meng[1,3], and Jitai Chen[4]

[1] College of Intelligence and Computing, Tianjin University, Tianjin 300350, China
xuchao@tju.edu.cn
[2] Higher Research Institute (Shenzhen), University of Electronic Science and Technology of China, Shenzhen 518063, China
[3] Tianjin University of Traditional Chinese Medicine, Tianjin 300193, China
[4] College of Computer Science and Technology, Jilin University, Changchun 130012, China

**Abstract.** We propose an efficient multi-view stereo (MVS) network for inferring depth value from multiple RGB images. Recent studies use the cost volume to encode the matching correspondence between different views, but this structure can still be optimized from the perspective of image features. First of all, to fully aggregate the dominant interrelationship from input images, we introduce a self-attention mechanism to our feature extractor, which can accurately model long-range dependencies between adjacent pixels. Secondly, to unify the extracted feature maps into the MVS problem, we further design an efficient feature-wise loss function, which constrains the corresponding feature vectors more spatially distinctive during training. The robustness and accuracy of the reconstructed point cloud are improved by enhancing the reliability of correspondence matches. Finally, to reduce the extra memory burden caused by the above methods, we follow the coarse to fine strategy. The group-wise correlation and uncertainty estimates are combined to construct a lightweight cost volume. This can improve the efficiency and generalization performance of the network while ensuring the reconstruction effect. We further combine the previous steps to get what we called attention thin volume. Quantitative and qualitative experiments are presented to demonstrate the performance of our model.

**Keywords:** Multi view stereo · Deep learning · Self attention

## 1 Introduction

Multi-view stereo is dedicated to recovering the depth value from overlapping photo sets, which has become a key issue in computer vision. In the past, many traditional methods adopt manually designed feature descriptors to determine the correspondence between pixels in different pictures. They often apply engineering regularization to recover three-dimensional point clouds. However, these methods have poor reconstruction effects in smooth areas such as weak textures and specular reflections. With the introduction of deep learning, the cost volume

S. Khanna et al. (Eds.): PRICAI 2022, LNCS 13631, pp. 410–423, 2022.
https://doi.org/10.1007/978-3-031-20868-3_30

is employed for simulation matching, and the quality of the reconstruction has been greatly improved.

Referring to the previous excellent learning-based MVS work, it is not difficult to find that using the cost volume to complete the correspondence matching is a crucial step. We focus on the construction of cost volume, start from image features, and propose an attention-thin volume structure to better solve the MVS problem.

For cost volume aggregating, the first step is to extract the feature maps from input images. In MVS task, the depth value of adjacent pixels changes either very drastically (at the edge of the object contour) or very smoothly (at the continuous surface of the object). This requires paying attention to the interrelationship between each pixel and its nearby pixels, that is, the long-range dependence in a single small context. CNN or global attention mechanisms [8] are not suitable enough, and the self-attention [24] has a lot of potential here.

At the same time, based on richer feature information, subsequent feature matching is also crucial to the construction result. Ideally, the feature vectors corresponding to the same pixel in different views should have sufficient similarity. In this way, robustness and accuracy can be ensured when using the cost volume to match the corresponding relationship. Therefore, we design a feature-wise loss function to strengthen this constraint, which can be shown to work well through experiments.

Besides, In the process of aggregating feature maps into cost volumes, previous works [4,12] have proved that direct variance aggregation will generate redundant information, and the redundancy of depth sampling will also lead to memory consumption. Therefore, we follow the coarse to fine strategy, specifically, combining group-wise correlation and uncertainty estimate. The similarity between feature map channels is calculated first and then aggregated into cost volumes, which reduces memory usage while improving information utilization efficiency. As for the coarse to fine framework, we use the uncertainty estimate strategy [4] to reduce the number of depth samples. These works make the similarity measurement of the corresponding regions of different pictures in the cost volume more accurate and efficient.

Our main contributions are as follows:

1. We design a multi-scale feature extractor with a self-attention mechanism to fully extract the interrelationship between adjacent pixels, so richer information can be provided for subsequent matching steps.
2. We design a novel feature-wise loss function to constrain the feature maps extracted by our feature extractor, which encourages the enhancement of features with spatial consistency. This improves the robustness and accuracy of matching correspondences.
3. We organically combine the group-wise correlation and uncertainty estimation strategies to complete the construction of the cost volume. The network is iteratively refined between different scales, reducing the memory burden of the framework, and optimizing the use of feature information.

4. We achieve good qualitative results on benchmark dataset. The complete performance is improved by 9.7% on the basis of the backbone, and the overall is improved by 3.8%.

## 2  Related Works

This chapter summarizes the related work of learning-based multi-view stereo methods and introduces several research directions that our work also covers.

### 2.1  Learned MVS

Recently, learning-based methods have shown remarkable performance on multi-view stereo. SurfaceNet [2] predicts voxel confidence to determine if the pixel is on the surface and reconstructs the 2D surface of the scene. The concept defined by DeepMVS [6] and MVSNet [3] is the basis of many similar works. Among them, the key idea is to perform plane sweep through homography, construct cost volume for correspondence matching based on variance, and use 3D CNN for depth map regression. RMVSNet [9] introduces a recurrent neural network and uses Gate Recurrent Unit (GRU) to replace the 3D CNN network, so it greatly optimizes the memory consumption. MVSCRF [15] introduces Conditional Random Field (CRF) for depth map prediction, and CRF is implemented in a cyclic neural network to facilitate end-to-end training. Point-MVSNet [14] proposes to use a smaller cost volume to first generate a rough depth map, and then use an iterative refinement network based on point clouds to further optimize the previously obtained depth map. PMVSNet [7] learns the patch-wise confidence from the reference image and the source images, and adaptively performs cost volume aggregation. PVA-MVSNet [13] introduces two novel adaptive view aggregations: pixel-level view aggregation and voxel-level view aggregation, which combine the cost variances in different views with small extra memory consumption.

### 2.2  Coarse to Fine

Cost volume requires a large number of depth hypotheses to cover potential depth range. Limited by the memory bottleneck, it is difficult to reconstruct a high-resolution depth map. The strategy of coarse to fine is introduced to solve this problem by iterative descaling depth sampling. CasMVSNet [12] proposes that by constructing cascade cost volume and reducing the number of depth hypothesis planes scale by scale, the network can more flexibly adapt to the needs of large-scale reconstruction scenarios. CVP-MVSNet [11] continuously improves the reconstruction accuracy between different scales by learning deep residuals. UCSNet [4] proposes to use uncertainty estimation to construct adaptive thin volumes (ATV), which can replace the previous plane sweep volume so that the hypothetical depth plane can become a curved continuous one. This strategy further improves the completeness and accuracy of the MVSNet framework.

## 2.3   Attention Mechanism

With the success of the attention mechanism in other fields of computer vision, this method has also been introduced to MVS by many researchers. Att-MVS [16] proposes enhanced matching confidence based on the attention mechanism, which combines the extracted pixel-level matching confidence with the context information of the local scene to improve matching robustness. At the same time, a regularization module guided by the attention mechanism was developed to aggregate and regularize the matching confidence to obtain a more accurate probability volume. PA-MVSNet [10] uses a multi-scale feature pyramid with an attention mechanism to capture larger receptive fields and richer information. The results of the pyramid attention modules of different scales are directly used for the next scale prediction. Compared with previous algorithms, the accuracy has been greatly improved. LA-Net [8] propose a remote attention network to selectively aggregate reference features to each location to capture the remote interdependence of the entire space.

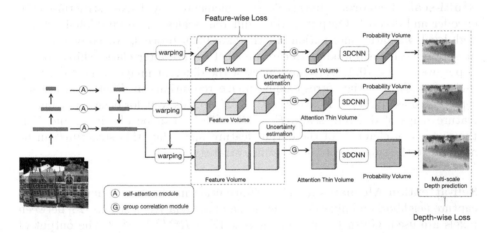

**Fig. 1.** Network architecture of our proposed network. The network is divided into three scales. As shown in the figure, we use the cost volume or the attention thin volume at different scales to express the correspondence of different perspectives.

# 3   Method

This section describes our process for depth inference. Given a reference image $I_0 \in R^{H \times W}$ and N source images $\{I_i\}_{i=1}^{N} \in R^{H \times W}$. The camera intrinsic, rotation matrix, and translation vector $\{K_i, R_i, t_i\}_{i=0}^{N}$ for each input view i are known. Our goal is to predict the depth map $D_0$ corresponding to reference image $I_0$.

The overall architecture is shown in Fig. 1. In Sect. 3.1, we introduce our designed feature extractor, feature maps can be extracted from images. And in Sect. 3.2, we show how we fuse the group-wise correlation into coarse-to-fine framework, specially how to aggregate the feature maps into attention thin volume. Section 3.3 introduces how to use the cost volume or attention thin volume to generate the probability volume and finally calculate the depth map, Sect. 3.4 introduces the our designed feature-wise loss function.

### 3.1   Multi-scale Feature Extractor with Self-attention Mechanism

Previous learning-based MVS methods mostly used multiple down-sampled convolutional layers or 2D UNet for feature extraction. For our consideration of neighborhood pixel association and information fusion between multi-scale images, we combine UNet [1] and self-attention mechanism [5,17,24] to design a multi-scale feature extractor with self-attention mechanism.

**Multi-scale Feature.** Multi-scale is implemented by U-Net structure with encoder and decoder. Output at three different scales, preserving low-level and high-level semantic information. In the skip-links process, we employ a self-attention mechanism module to capture local feature interrelationships. In this paper, we use $s \in (0, 1, \ldots, n)$ to represent the different image scales from original to rough, and the corresponding image resolutions in different scales are represented as $H_s, W_s = H \times 1/2^s, W \times 1/2^s$, In this way, for each input image, feature maps of different scales $F_i^s \in R^{H_s \times W_s \times C}$ can be obtained, and C is the number of channels of the output feature map, thus this structure can be adapted to the subsequent coarse to fine strategy.

**Self-attention Mechanism.** The self-attention mechanism is mainly used to capture neighborhood pixel dependencies, and the relative positions [23] between pixels are used. Given the network weight $W \in R^{k \times k \times d_{in} \times d_{out}}$, the output of each pixel position (i, j) after convolution is denoted as:

$$y_{i,j} = \sum_{a,b \in B} Softmax_{ab}(q_{ij}^T k_{ab} + q_{ij}^T r_{a-i,b-j}) v_{ab} \tag{1}$$

where B represents the image block, which size is as same as the kernel, $q_{ij} = W_q \times x_{ij}$, $k_{ab} = W_k \times x_{ab}$, $v_{ab} = W_v \times x_{ab}$ represent queries, keys and values respectively, $r_{a-i,b-j}$ indicates the offset of pixel rows and columns, W are the learned parameters of each component. The overall calculation of the formula is divided into four steps:

1. Determine the pixel position (i, j), the pixel area image block B(a, b) and the pixel relative offset $r_{a-i,b-j}$.

2. Calculate queries $q_{ij}$, keys $k_{ab}$, and values $v_{ab}$.
3. Use inner product to calculate the similar relationship between queries and keys and pixel offset, then map the result via softmax.
4. Perform the final calculation on the values and the similarity in step 3 to obtain the weight evaluation result of the pixel.

The output $y_{i,j}$ represents the similarity between query and the elements in image block B, and at the same time, it enjoys translation equivariance. At each scale s, given an input image $I_i$, a feature map $F_i^s \in R^{H_s \times W_s \times C}$ that aggregates long range dependencies can be obtained by our feature extractor.

## 3.2   Attention Thin Volume Generation

To perform a more efficient similarity measurement, we follow the framework of coarse to fine, and introduce group-wise correlation [22] based on uncertainty estimate [4], thereby constructing what we called attention thin volume, which reduced memory burden while minimizing information loss.

**Group-Wise Correlation.** At each scale, after obtaining the feature map, we warp source image feature maps to each hypothetical depth plane upon the reference camera frustum, and aggregate them to a cost volume by group-wise correlation. This can provide a wealth of similarity measurement, while reducing the memory burden. The calculation steps are as follows:

1. Homography is used to warp the feature maps of source images $F_1^s, F_2^s, \ldots, F_N^s$ to the depth hypothesis $d_i \in [d_{min}, d_{max}], i \in [0, D_s - 1]$ upon the reference camera frustum, where $D_s$ is different at each scales, $d_i$ is uniformly sampled within the range $[d_{min}, d_{max}]$. The homography between two feature maps can be expressed by the following formula:

$$H_i(d) = K_i T_i T_0^{-1} K_0^{-1} \tag{2}$$

where $\{K_i, T_i\}$ is the camera intrinsic and extrinsic corresponding to different images.

2. After homography transformation, at each depth hypothesis d, there corresponds to N+1 feature maps $F_{0,d}^s, F_{1,d}^s, \ldots, F_{N,d}^s \in R^{H_s \times W_s \times C}$. Divide each feature map into G groups according to the feature channel, and then use the inner product to calculate the similarity of different sub-feature maps in the same group $g \in [0, G - 1]$. The calculation formula is

$$M_{d,i}^{g,s} = \frac{1}{C/G} \langle F_{0,d}^{g,s}, F_{i,d}^{g,s} \rangle \tag{3}$$

where $\langle \Delta, \Delta \rangle$ represents the inner product, $F_{i,d}^{g,s}$ is the g-th group of sub-feature maps belong to the i-th feature map at depth d. $M_{d,i}^{g,s} \in R^{1 \times H_s \times W_s}$ are the similarity measurement of the corresponding two ones. After that, $M_{d,i}^{g,s}$ are aggregated in the order of group and depth, and the feature volume corresponding to the i-th source image can be obtained, denoted as $V_i^s = concat(M_{d,i}^{g,s}), V_i^s \in R^{G \times H_s \times W_s \times D_s}$.

3. Variance aggregation is performed on the feature volume corresponding to the feature maps of different views

$$C^s = \frac{1}{N} \sum_{i=1}^{N} (V_i^s - \overline{V_i^s})^2 \tag{4}$$

where, $\overline{V_i^s}$ is the mean volume of different feature volumes, the variance calculation can allow any number of input images.

It is worth noting that the group-wise correlation strategy will be applied at all scales, while at the last two scales with the higher resolution, the uncertainty estimate strategy will play an important role in determining the depth hypothesis.

**Uncertainty Estimate.** We follow the idea of uncertainty estimate [4] to dynamically adjust the depth hypothesis interval. So the uniformly defined sweep plane becomes a curved continuous variable one. Specifically, the depth assumption at the coarsest level $L_1(x)$is fixed based on the results of the sparse reconstruction. Then, on the basis of the probability volume $P_s$ generated at each scale, we calculate the variance of the probability distribution

$$U_s(x) = \sum_{d=1}^{D_s} P_{s,d}(x) \cdot (L_{s,d}(x) - D^s(x))^2 \tag{5}$$

and the corresponding standard deviation is $\widehat{\sigma(x)} = \sqrt{U_s(x)}$. So we set the depth prediction range of the next scale to

$$DR_{(s+1)}(x) = [D^s(x) - \lambda\widehat{\sigma(x)}, D^s(x) + \lambda\widehat{\sigma(x)}] \tag{6}$$

where, $\lambda$ is a scale parameter, which can adjust the range of the depth hypothesis range. Sampling a number of $D_{(s+1)}$ depth values uniformly on $DR_{(s+1)}(x)$ can obtain the corresponding $L_{(s+1)}(x)$. Thus, the cost of correspondence matching between the reference view and all source views under each depth hypothesis can been encoded into the attention thin volume. Our attention thin volume can integrate more crucial information by enhancing inter-channel connections and reduce memory burden.

### 3.3   Depth Map Regression

At each scale, after the aggregated cost volume(or attention thin volume) is obtained, a softmax-based regularization network is applied to get probability volume $P_s \in R^{H_s \times W_s \times D_s}$. It is treated as the weight of depth hypotheses. And we use formula

$$D^s(x) = \sum_{d=1}^{D_s} P_{s,d}(x) \cdot L_{s,d}(x) \tag{7}$$

to calculate the final depth prediction. $L_{s,d}(x)$ represents the value of each depth hypothesis, and $P_{s,d}(x)$ is the probability that the pixel x corresponds to the depth value $L_{s,d}(x)$.

## 3.4   Loss Function

We design a multi-metric loss function to constrain network training at different stages of the MVS task, which consists of feature-wise loss function and the traditional depth map loss function. The multi-metric loss function $L$ is the sum of the above two ones.

$$L = \sum (\beta_1 L_{fea} + \beta_2 L_{depth}) \tag{8}$$

**Feature-Wise Loss Function.** As an information source, the feature map will directly affect the matching relationship in the cost volume, ideally, feature vector of the same pixel at different views should have strong spatial invariance. When the camera intrinsic and extrinsic are known, it is easy to warp the feature vector of a special pixel in source images to the reference image view. To enhance the matching of corresponding pixels during cost volume aggregation, we use the **position term** to encourage degenerating the features with weak invariance. The formula is expressed as:

$$L_{pos} = \sum_{i,j \in V} \|F(T_i) - F(T_j)\|_2 \tag{9}$$

where, V is the valid area in the reference image, $T$ denotes an input tensor and $T_i, T_j$ the corresponding pixel feature vector pairs between two images, F represents the transform by our multi-scale feature extractor. At the same time, to reduce the degradation of reconstruction completeness due to the weakening of low-consistency features, we design a **neighbor balance loss** as a fault tolerance term to appropriately enhance feature similarity within the neighborhood. The formula is expressed as

$$L_{nei} = \sum_{i,j \in B} \|F(T_i) - F(T_j)\|_2 \tag{10}$$

where, B is the image block centered on i, j represents the other pixels in B. And we set the block size to 3*3 in our most experiments. The complete feature-wise loss is expressed as

$$L_{fea} = L_{pos} + \epsilon L_{nei} \tag{11}$$

$\epsilon$ is a scale parameter, which is set to 0.01 in our work.

**Depth Map Loss Function.** For the depth map predicted by the network, we follow the classic approach of the past and apply supervision to all outputs. The weighted sum of the l1 norm between the depth map prediction and the ground truth are used to construct the depth map loss function

$$L_{depth} = \sum_{s=1}^{s_{max}} (\Lambda^s \cdot \sum_{x \in \Omega} \|D^s(x) - D_{GT}^s(x)\|_1) \tag{12}$$

where, $\Lambda^s$ is the loss weight of scale s, $D_{GT}^s$ is the ground truth of the depth map adapted to the resolution of scale s, and $\Omega$ is all the valid pixels in the image.

# 4    Experiments

In this section, we evaluate our method on the benchmark dataset, which proves the effectiveness of our proposed network.

## 4.1    Datasets and Evaluation Metrics

The effect of our work is evaluated on two benchmark datasets, one is the indoor DTU dataset [18], the other is the outdoor Tank&Temples dataset [19].

**DTU dataset** contains 124 different indoor scenes, using an industrial robot arm equipped with a structured light scanner to scan structured light for different objects. Each scene contains 49 or 64 images which the viewpoints and lighting conditions are all deliberately designed. Camera pose parameters and point cloud ground truth have been provided.

**Tank&Temples dataset** contains two scene sets, namely intermediate and advanced. We use the intermediate set for evaluation. There are 8 different outdoor scenes. The dataset is very challenging, the reconstruction scene is very large, and there are many reflections and occlusion on the surface of the object.

**Evaluation Metrics.** Consistent with previous methods, the accuracy and completeness of the distance measurement are used for evaluation of the DTU dataset. The accuracy and completeness of the percentage measurement are used for the Tanks&Temples dataset. To obtain a summary measure of accuracy and completeness, the distance measure uses their mean value, and the percentage measure uses $F_1$ scores.

## 4.2    Implementation

**Post Processing.** We fuse all the predicted depth maps into a dense point cloud using the same post processing method [20] as our baseline [4], which consist three main steps: photo-metric filtering, geometric consistency filtering, and depth fusion.

**Training Details.** We train our proposed network on DTU training set. As same as previous works, we perform Poisson Surface Reconstruction [21] to get the ground truth depth map. For each reference image, we use 2 source images during training, which resolution are $H \times W = 640 \times 512$. The number of depth samples in the 3 scales are $D_1 = 32, D_2 = 16, D_3 = 8$, the init depth sampling range is [425 mm, 935mm] marked in the dataset. The scale parameter in the formula 6 is set to $\lambda = 1.5$. The ratio of the two loss functions in formula 8 is $\beta_1 = 1, \beta_2 = 1$. The weight of loss at different scales in formula 12 is $\Lambda_s = \{0.5, 1, 2\}$. The number of group is 8. We train the network for 16 epochs on a Tesla V100 GPU. We use the Adam optimizer at the same time, and set the initial learning rate to 0.0016.

**Table 1.** Performance comparison on DTU dataset (lower means better).

| method | Acc | Comp | Overall |
|---|---|---|---|
| Camp | 0.835 | 0.554 | 0.695 |
| Furu | 0.613 | 0.941 | 0.777 |
| Tola | 0.342 | 1.190 | 0.766 |
| Gipuma | **0.283** | 0.873 | 0.578 |
| MVSNet | 0.396 | 0.527 | 0.462 |
| R-MVSNet | 0.383 | 0.452 | 0.417 |
| Vis-MVSNet | 0.369 | 0.361 | 0.365 |
| Cas-MVSNet | 0.346 | 0.351 | 0.348 |
| CVP-MVSNet | 0.296 | 0.406 | 0.351 |
| UCSNet | 0.338 | 0.349 | 0.344 |
| Att-MVS | 0.383 | 0.329 | 0.356 |
| LANet | 0.320 | 0.349 | 0.335 |
| AACVP-MVSNet | 0.357 | 0.326 | 0.341 |
| ours | 0.347 | **0.315** | **0.331** |

**Table 2.** Quantitative results of F-scores (higher means better) on Tanks and Temples dataset.

| methods | Family | Francis | Horse | Lighthouse | M60 | Panther | Playground | Train | F-score |
|---|---|---|---|---|---|---|---|---|---|
| Colmap | 50.41 | 22.25 | 25.63 | 56.43 | 44.83 | 46.97 | 48.53 | 42.04 | 42.14 |
| MVSNet | 55.99 | 28.55 | 25.07 | 50.79 | 53.96 | 50.86 | 47.90 | 34.69 | 43.48 |
| R-MVSNet | 69.96 | 46.65 | 32.59 | 42.95 | 51.88 | 48.80 | 52.00 | 42.38 | 48.40 |
| CVP-MVSNet | **76.5** | 47.74 | 36.34 | 55.12 | **57.28** | 54.28 | 57.43 | 47.54 | 54.03 |
| Point-MVSNet | 61.79 | 41.15 | 34.20 | 50.79 | 51.97 | 50.85 | 52.38 | 43.06 | 48.27 |
| La-Net | 76.24 | 54.32 | **49.85** | 54.03 | 56.08 | 50.82 | 53.71 | 50.57 | 55.70 |
| Att-MVS | 73.90 | **62.58** | 44.08 | **64.88** | 56.08 | **59.39** | **63.42** | **56.06** | **60.05** |
| UCSNet | 76.09 | 53.16 | 43.03 | 54.00 | 55.60 | 51.49 | 57.38 | 47.89 | 54.83 |
| ours | 73.92 | <u>53.88</u> | <u>44.84</u> | 56.06 | <u>56.71</u> | 53.65 | <u>59.83</u> | 48.86 | <u>55.97</u> |

## 4.3 Benchmark Performance

**Overall Evaluation on DTU Dataset.** We evaluate our network on DTU testing set. For fair comparisons, we use the same view selection, image resolution and initial depth range as $N = 5, H \times W = 1600 \times 1184, d_{min} = 425mm, d_{max} = 933.8mm$.

The official Matlab evaluation scripts of DTU dataset is used to evaluate the accuracy and completeness of our results. It compares the distance between our produced point clouds and the ground-truth point clouds. Then we compare the results to state-of-the-art methods and show them in Table 1. It is not difficult to see that the traditional method Gipuma ranks first in accuracy metric, however, our approach performs better in **completeness** and **overall scores** (lower is better in both metrics). On the basis of quantitative analysis, we demonstrate the superiority of our method by visually comparing the reconstruction effects

(a) Ground-Truth     (b) UCSNet     (c) Ours     (d) Tank

**Fig. 2.** Qualitative analysis on DTU dataset and Tank&Temples dataset. **(a) to (c)**: **Top Row**: Reconstruction on scan75. **Bottom Row**: Reconstruction on scan13. **(d)** shows the reconstruction effect of our network on the Tank&Temples dataset.

**Table 3.** Ablation results on DTU testing set. "MFA" represents the multi-scale feature extractor with self-attention mechanism, "AG" is our attention thin volume aggregate process with the introduction of group-wise correlation. "AT" represents the combination of our feature extractor and our attention thin volume aggregate process.

| Method | MFA | AG | PL | NBL | DL | Acc | Comp | Overall | Memory |
|---|---|---|---|---|---|---|---|---|---|
| UCSNet | | | | | ✓ | **0.338** | 0.349 | 0.344 | 6226 Mb |
| UCSNet+MFA | ✓ | | | | ✓ | 0.350 | 0.327 | 0.338 | 7455 Mb |
| UCSNet+AG | | ✓ | | | ✓ | 0.363 | 0.316 | 0.340 | 5881 Mb |
| UCSNet+AT | ✓ | ✓ | | | ✓ | 0.357 | <u>0.312</u> | 0.335 | 6686 Mb |
| UCSNet+AT+PL | ✓ | ✓ | ✓ | | ✓ | 0.350 | 0.333 | 0.341 | |
| UCSNet+AT+NBL | ✓ | ✓ | | ✓ | ✓ | 0.355 | **0.311** | <u>0.333</u> | |
| UCSNet+AT+PL+NBL | ✓ | ✓ | ✓ | ✓ | ✓ | <u>0.347</u> | 0.315 | **0.331** | |

(see Fig. 2). Our method can obtain a more complete surface point cloud at some positions where the past methods is more disadvantageous.

**Overall Evaluation on Tank&Temples Dataset.** Now we show the generalization ability of our network. Without fine-tuning, we use the model trained on DTU dataset to test on Tank&Temples intermediate dataset. During testing, we set the number of input images and the image resolution to $N = 5, H = 1920, W = 1056$. The quantitative results are shown in the Table 2.

Our method performs better than the baseline(UCSNet [4]), achieving an average F-score (55.97), which is competitive in all public results. In addition, we have observed that in some difficult scenes, such as sand, cylindrical railings, etc., we can get a very complete point cloud, as shown in the Fig. 2.

## 4.4  Ablation Studies

In this section, ablation experiments are performed to evaluate the advantages of our work. The ablation experiments are performed and evaluated on the DTU dataset. We compare the baseline model UCSNet [4] with our approach on each component. This section will show the impact of each component. The results are in the Table 3.

**Benefits of Each Modules.** It is not difficult to find that both the self-attention module and attention thin volume aggregate module can improve the completeness. When the two components are superimposed, the improvement of the completeness score is the largest, while maintaining the high level of overall evaluation.

**Benefits of Multi-metric Loss Function.** As shown in Table 3, applying multi-metric loss function can significantly improve the effect of reconstruction. The position loss term (PL) can improve the accuracy, while the fault tolerance term (NBL) is beneficial to the completeness metric. In qualitative analysis, we found that the improvement in completeness bought by NBL is mainly concentrated on the local scale, which is consistent with our assumption. When the two are combined, we can achieve a balance of two metrics for the best overall score.

**Efficiency Discussion.** We also pay attention to the impact of each module on GPU memory. The details are shown in Table 3. We can see that the memory usage increases significantly when the self-attention module is applied, and as we expected, the group-wise correlation strategy can reduce the memory consumption, so that the overall network size is not excessively increased. The combination of two components can reduce the dependence on memory as around 10% under the premise of ensuring the reconstruction quality, which provides the possibility for large-scale scene reconstruction.

## 5  Conclusion

In this paper, around building an efficient and practical cost volume, we analyze the association of neighboring pixels in the MVS problem, introduce the self-attention mechanism to design a multi-scale feature extractor, and then employ feature-wise loss function to enhance the spatial similarity of the corresponding feature vectors. The entire network follows the coarse to fine framework, combining group-wise correlation and uncertainty estimation strategies to construct a lightweight attention thin volume. With this help, our network can better express the geometric correspondence. After extensive evaluation of two challenging benchmark datasets, the results show that our approach is very competitive compared with other methods. In the future, we hope to further improve our network and make the learning based MVS method more efficient and reliable.

**Acknowledgments.** The authors would like to thank all anonymous reviewers. This work was supported by the National Key Research and Development Program of China [grant number 2021YFF0901203].

# References

1. Ronneberger, O., Fischer, P., Brox, T.: U-Net: convolutional networks for biomedical image segmentation. In: Navab, N., Hornegger, J., Wells, W.M., Frangi, A.F. (eds.) MICCAI 2015. LNCS, vol. 9351, pp. 234–241. Springer, Cham (2015). https://doi.org/10.1007/978-3-319-24574-4_28
2. Ji, M., Gall, J., Zheng, H., Liu, Y., Fang, L.: Surfacenet: an end-to-end 3d neural network for multiview stereopsis. In: Proceedings of the IEEE International Conference on Computer Vision, pp. 2307–2315 (2017)
3. Yao, Y., Luo, Z., Li, S., Fang, T., Quan, L.: MVSNet: depth inference for unstructured multi-view stereo. In: Ferrari, V., Hebert, M., Sminchisescu, C., Weiss, Y. (eds.) ECCV 2018. LNCS, vol. 11212, pp. 785–801. Springer, Cham (2018). https://doi.org/10.1007/978-3-030-01237-3_47
4. Cheng, S., et al.: Deep stereo using adaptive thin volume representation with uncertainty awareness. In: Proceedings of the IEEE/CVF Conference on Computer Vision and Pattern Recognition, pp. 2524–2534 (2020)
5. Guo, C., Szemenyei, M., Yi, Y., Wang, W., Chen, B., Fan, C.: Sa-unet: spatial attention u-net for retinal vessel segmentation. In 2020 25th International Conference on Pattern Recognition (ICPR), pp. 1236–1242. IEEE, January 2021
6. Huang, P.H., Matzen, K., Kopf, J., Ahuja, N., Huang, J.B.: Deepmvs: learning multi-view stereopsis. In: Proceedings of the IEEE Conference on Computer Vision and Pattern Recognition, pp. 2821–2830 (2018)
7. Luo, K., Guan, T., Ju, L., Huang, H., Luo, Y.: P-mvsnet: learning patch-wise matching confidence aggregation for multi-view stereo. In: Proceedings of the IEEE/CVF International Conference on Computer Vision, pp. 10452–10461 (2019)
8. Zhang, X., Hu, Y., Wang, H., Cao, X., Zhang, B.: Long-range attention network for multi-view stereo. In: Proceedings of the IEEE/CVF Winter Conference on Applications of Computer Vision, pp. 3782–3791 (2021)
9. Yao, Y., Luo, Z., Li, S., Shen, T., Fang, T., Quan, L.: Recurrent mvsnet for high-resolution multi-view stereo depth inference. In: Proceedings of the IEEE/CVF Conference on Computer Vision and Pattern Recognition, pp. 5525–5534 (2019)
10. Zhang, K., Liu, M., Zhang, J., Dong, Z.: Pa-mvsnet: sparse-to-dense multi-view stereo with pyramid attention. IEEE Access **9**, 27908–27915 (2021)
11. Yang, J., Mao, W., Alvarez, J.M., Liu, M.: Cost volume pyramid based depth inference for multi-view stereo. In: Proceedings of the IEEE/CVF Conference on Computer Vision and Pattern Recognition, pp. 4877–4886 (2020)
12. Gu, X., Fan, Z., Zhu, S., Dai, Z., Tan, F., Tan, P.: Cascade cost volume for high-resolution multi-view stereo and stereo matching. In: Proceedings of the IEEE/CVF Conference on Computer Vision and Pattern Recognition, pp. 2495–2504 (2020)
13. Yi, Hongwei, Wei, Zizhuang, Ding, Mingyu, Zhang, Runze, Chen, Yisong, Wang, Guoping, Tai, Yu-Wing.: Pyramid multi-view stereo net with self-adaptive view aggregation. In: Vedaldi, Andrea, Bischof, Horst, Brox, Thomas, Frahm, Jan-Michael. (eds.) ECCV 2020. LNCS, vol. 12354, pp. 766–782. Springer, Cham (2020). https://doi.org/10.1007/978-3-030-58545-7_44
14. Chen, R., Han, S., Xu, J., Su, H.: Point-based multi-view stereo network. In: Proceedings of the IEEE/CVF International Conference on Computer Vision, pp. 1538–1547 (2019)
15. Xue, Y., et al.: Mvscrf: learning multi-view stereo with conditional random fields. In: Proceedings of the IEEE/CVF International Conference on Computer Vision, pp. 4312–4321 (2019)

16. Luo, K., Guan, T., Ju, L., Wang, Y., Chen, Z., Luo, Y.: Attention-aware multi-view stereo. In Proceedings of the IEEE/CVF Conference on Computer Vision and Pattern Recognition, pp. 1590–1599 (2020)
17. Yu, A., Guo, W., Liu, B., Chen, X., Wang, X., Cao, X., Jiang, B.: Attention aware cost volume pyramid based multi-view stereo network for 3d reconstruction. ISPRS J. Photogrammetry Remote Sens. **175**, 448–460 (2021)
18. Jensen, R., Dahl, A., Vogiatzis, G., Tola, E., Aanæs, H.: Large scale multi-view stereopsis evaluation. In: Proceedings of the IEEE Conference on Computer Vision and Pattern Recognition, pp. 406–413 (2014)
19. Knapitsch, A., Park, J., Zhou, Q.Y., Koltun, V.: Tanks and temples: benchmarking large-scale scene reconstruction. ACM Trans. Graph. (ToG) **36**(4), 1–13 (2017)
20. Galliani, S., Lasinger, K., Schindler, K.: Massively parallel multiview stereopsis by surface normal diffusion. In: Proceedings of the IEEE International Conference on Computer Vision, pp. 873–881 (2015)
21. Kazhdan, M., Bolitho, M., Hoppe, H.: Poisson surface reconstruction. In Proceedings of the Fourth Eurographics Symposium on Geometry Processing, vol. 7, June 2006
22. Guo, X., Yang, K., Yang, W., Wang, X., Li, H.: Group-wise correlation stereo network. In Proceedings of the IEEE/CVF Conference on Computer Vision and Pattern Recognition, pp. 3273–3282 (2019)
23. Shaw, P., Uszkoreit, J., Vaswani, A.: Self-attention with relative position representations. arXiv preprint arXiv:1803.02155 (2018)
24. Ramachandran, P., Parmar, N., Vaswani, A., Bello, I., Levskaya, A., Shlens, J.: Stand-alone self-attention in vision models. In: Advances in Neural Information Processing Systems, 32 (2019)

# 3D Point Cloud Segmentation Leveraging Global 2D-View Features

Martin Pellon Consunji and Yutong Liu[✉][iD]

Shanghai Jiao Tong University, Shanghai, China
{martinpellon,isabelleliu}@sjtu.edu.cn

**Abstract.** With the introduction of widely available depth cameras and the increasing demand for digitalizing our physical world, there is now more than ever a need for an automated segmentation system to process the 3D point cloud data. The latest developments in this field utilize graph neural networks (GNN), but do not take globally consistent features into account, which could aid in carrying out robust segmentation predictions across entire scenes.

In this paper, we propose a 3D point cloud segmentation method leveraging globally consistent features for improved performance. These global features are retrieved from a 2D fully convolutional network (U-Net) and then propagated to a 3D DGCNN together with raw point clouds for segmentation. Our segmentation based on globally coherent feature embedding space is novel and promising to perform classification and separation within entire scenes rather than in single blocks. Both quantitative and qualitative evaluations on widely known ScanNet and S3DIS datasets with a multitude of indoor RGBD scenes have proven the feasibility of considering global 2D-view features in 3D segmentation tasks with improved performance.

**Keywords:** Semantic segmentation · Instance segmentation · Point cloud analysis · Graph neural networks · Global features

## 1 Introduction

Due to the advent of commercial depth cameras such as Microsoft's Azure Kinect [1], the 3D depth data is widely collected for digitalizing and understanding our physical world [2]. As one of the important processing steps on 3D depth data, the automatic 3D point cloud segmentation can support object detection and instance separation in the view. It is useful in various daily scenarios, such as robot-assisted manufacturing [3], 3D computer-generated imagery (CGI) in entertainment industry [4], and retail maintenance [5]. For example, with a 3D point cloud segmentation technology, an automated shop camera can justify which product needs to be restocked, or a factory robotic arm can count the number of manufacturing pieces on the assembly line. However, to fulfill the requirements in the aforementioned application fields, the semantic and instance segmentation in this system must be highly accurate and reliable.

© The Author(s), under exclusive license to Springer Nature Switzerland AG 2022
S. Khanna et al. (Eds.): PRICAI 2022, LNCS 13631, pp. 424–437, 2022.
https://doi.org/10.1007/978-3-031-20868-3_31

| The input point cloud | Semantic segmentation | Instance segmentation |

**Fig. 1.** An example of semantic and instance segmentation.

Semantic segmentation classifies each point in the scene into a category, while instance segmentation separates different instances in the same category. For example, as shown in Fig. 1, semantic segmentation aims to distinguish between the table, chair, and board, and instance segmentation can separate different chairs and label them with different colors. In 2D images, multiple segmentation techniques have been extensively researched and the best-performing results generally come from deep learning-based methods. An example of a well-performing method for 2D images uses a fully convolutional network (U-Net) and data augmentation [6]. However, in the case of 3D point cloud analysis, new challenges arise due to the inherent nature of 3D point cloud data:

1. **Lack of structure:** The 3D point cloud data does not have limits in terms of point locations and relations. Every point is gathered independently and does not necessarily have fixed distances to other nearby points.
2. **Lack of order:** The 3D point cloud data does not have an order in scanning or generation. A point cloud will contain the same set of data no matter from which point to start.
3. **Lack of regularity:** The 3D point cloud data is not always equally sampled across the scanned area, leading to some areas having a higher density of points than others.

The intuitive approach to deal with these challenges is to transform the point cloud into more a structured, orderly, and regular form of data. However, this transformation will destroy the inherent construction of the 3D point cloud, resulting in varying and non-optimized results across generalized scenarios. Recent advances have been made on graph neural networks (GNNs) to directly process raw point cloud data to avoid such destruction [7]. We found that the segmentation based on global features is more robust across an entire scene, which is not considered in the latest methods. Therefore, the core design of our research is to carry out a more accurate and robust semantic and instance segmentation on 3D point clouds by leveraging globally consistent features.

In this paper, we propose a 3D point cloud segmentation system leveraging global 2D-view features. These global features are retrieved from multiple projected 2D views of the point cloud with a 2D U-Net. Together with raw point clouds, these global features are then propagated to a 3D DGCNN for final object segmentation. Our method is an advancement on the similarity group proposal network (SGPN) [8], where we remove its heuristic merging algorithm by using globally consistent features for learning. To the best of our knowledge, our method fills in the gap in 3D point cloud segmentation by considering globally consistent features across entire scenes.

Correspondingly, the main contributions of this paper are:

1. We have proposed a 3D point cloud segmentation method considering intrinsic structures of 3D point clouds through learning globally consistent features, thus can provide better segmentation performance for entire scenes.
2. We have further explored the capability of GNN on 3D segmentation. The updated 3D DGCNN as proposed in this paper takes both original point clouds and globally 2D features as inputs, which can avoid potential information loss as compared to the structured modification on 3D point clouds.
3. The proposed 3D point cloud segmentation method has been evaluated on widely known ScanNet and S3DIS datasets. Both qualitative and quantitative results have proven the feasibility and efficiency when considering global features in the segmentation of various practical indoor scenes.

## 2    Related Work

The segmentation methods of point clouds can be roughly categorized into structured and unstructured learning. The **structured learning** on point clouds aims to transform the original unstructured raw point cloud data into a more structured format, including three types: voxelated, multi-view, and high-dimension lattices. For *voxelated* methods, 3D point clouds are turned into $W \times H \times D$ voxels and convolved with $w \times h \times d$ 3D kernels having $\{w, h, d\} \leq \{W, H, D\}$ [9–11]. The *multi-view* approaches apply projection to 3D point clouds and input the projected results into extensively developed 2D CNNs [7,12–16]. Another structured learning method is based on *high-dimension lattices*, which convert point clouds into higher-dimension regular lattices [6,17,18].

In contrast to the previous methods which involve making changes to the point clouds that are used for learning, there are also **unstructured** methods that learn directly from the raw point cloud data. Deep learning methods which directly consume raw point cloud data begin with the effort of PointNet [19]. It applies a multi-layer perceptron (MLP) on 3D raw points to generate a 1024-dimensional space with shared parameters, and a max-pooling function is further adopted for segmentation. Considering that shapes are always formed by a collection of points, more methods were developed to deal with local correlations [20–22]. They consider the intrinsic structure of points in multiple aggregated regions like relative distances or positions among points. Other methods use a graph structure to represent point clouds [23].

To sum up, structured learning is based on globally consistent features, but they suffer from the loss of inherent information with the destruction of raw point clouds. On the contrary, unstructured learning can preserve the inherent construction of point clouds. It is expected to aggregate advantages from these two aspects. Thus in this paper, we tend to consider both global features and raw point clouds to conduct segmentation through entire scenes.

# 3 Problem Statement and Workflow

The point cloud $P$ is composed of $N$ unstructured points $p_i$ defined within a space through their $x, y$ and $z$ coordinates as well as per-point RGB values, so $P = \{p_i | i = 1, \ldots, N\} \in \mathbb{R}^F$. The 3D semantic segmentation is to achieve the assignation of per-point class labels in a point cloud. Mathematically, it is to minimize the loss function shown in Eq. 1, where $K$ is the total number of classes, $y_i$ represents the ground-truth label, and $y_{pred}$ denotes the predicted per-class scores. The loss function here is described as the per-point cross-entropy loss on multiple classes.

$$L(y_{pred}, y) = -\frac{1}{N} \sum_{i=1}^{N} \sum_{c=1}^{K} y_{i,c} \log y_{pred_{i,c}}. \tag{1}$$

Aside from carrying out the semantic segmentation previously mentioned, the instance segmentation distinguishes between individually separate instances of an object which belong to the same semantic class. This problem can also be mathematically denoted to minimize the loss function $L = L_{dist} - L_{var} + L_{reg}$, where $L_{dist}$ is the distance loss leads to separating points of different labels, $L_{var}$ is the variance loss leads to uniting points of the same instance label, and $L_{reg}$ is the regularization loss added to avoid overfitting. Typically, the L2 norm $S_{a,b}$ is used for evaluating the similarity of features $x_a$ and $x_b$ between pairs of points. Then we have

$$\begin{aligned} L_{dist} &= \sum_{c,c'=1, c \neq c'}^{C} \sum_{x_a \in S_c, x_b \in S_{c'}} [m_{dist} - S_{a,b}]_+, \\ L_{var} &= \sum_{c=1}^{C} \sum_{x_a, x_b \in S_c} S_{a,b}, \\ S_{a,b} &= \|x_a - x_b\|_2, \end{aligned} \tag{2}$$

where $[x]_+$ is the hinge representing $max(0, x)$ and $m_{dist}$ is a constant.

As surveyed in Sect. 2, the realization for 3D point cloud segmentation leveraging global 2D-view features can follow these steps: i) necessary 2D views generation from the point cloud; ii) global 2D features generation with a base network; iii) 3D segmentation with another neural network which takes both the output features from the previous base network and raw point clouds as its inputs. The overall workflow is shown in Fig. 2. The proposed method uses a U-Net on separated 2D projected views to generate globally consistent features. These features are then fed, alongside the raw point cloud data to, a dynamic graph convolutional neural network (DGCNN) for carrying out instance and semantic segmentation on entire 3D point cloud scenes. The point-wise features learnt from 2D-view images aim to help identify separate object instances on the 3D point cloud. This method offers a globally coherent feature embedding space, enabling clustering within an entire scene rather than single blocks.

This workflow allows globally consistent features as part of the inputs of the 3D DGCNN, so it does not solely rely on splitting the original point cloud into

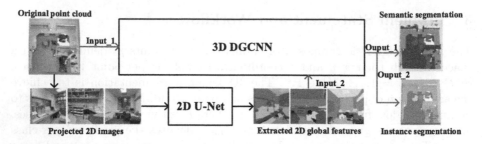

**Fig. 2.** The proposed workflow taking both original point cloud and global 2D features for 3D segmentation.

smaller chunks for processing. Also, the 2D U-Net portion of the workflow allows for learning from the entire scene by utilizing parallel sets of ordered data. By generating ordered data through projection from a disordered point cloud, this workflow is expected to mitigate challenges inherently encountered from solely processing unordered point clouds while carrying out segmentation tasks.

## 4    Detailed Designs

This section will explain in more detail the entire proposed system for 3D point cloud segmentation using the globally consistent features from 2D views.

### 4.1    3D Point Cloud to 2D Image Projection

The projection from the 3D point cloud to the 2D image is especially important, because 2D views will be primarily used to stay globally consistence across the entire point cloud in learning. A projection method is devised which projects the highest points of the point cloud and their respective RGB data to a plane to create 2D-view representations of the point cloud scene.

We first remove the depth component by placing all points and their RGB values at the same standardized height level. Points above a chosen threshold are removed to avoid unintended top-view blockers for the projection. Following this, we set a specific resolution of output images. For points that fall under the same pixel unit of that resolution grid, we choose only the point which has the highest height value and take its RGB value for that pixel on the grid.

**Fig. 3.** The visualization of separate projected viewpoints in a single scene from the ScanNet dataset prior to cropping.

For the projection portion, we generate 5 separate views, which are top, left, right, front, and back projections. As shown in Fig. 3, each view is generated by projecting points to the opposite side of the view. For example, for the left view, all points are projected to a grid on the right-most plane. In the case that there is more than one point ending up on the same cell of the grid, the point selected for that grid is the closest to the left side or farthest from the right-most plane. The final projection output is a 4-dimensional set of RGB-D values, where the depth D is the distance from the perspective plane to the point. Each projection view is generated and cropped prior to training and predicting. The corresponding output images will directly be input into the 2D U-Net and later for learning feature maps of object instances. A square room shown in Fig. 3 is a typical setup in most indoor scenes. For this type of scene, the 5-view projection is optimal on a trade-off between room coverage and computational cost. Note that other numbers and combinations of projection angles could be easily adjusted according to the shape of the scene in practice.

## 4.2   Global Feature Extraction from 2D Images

One key limitation of existing 2D image feature extraction methods [19–21] is the lack of globally consistent feature extraction across a point cloud scene, which makes them underperform when the density of objects in the scene increases or the resolution of point cloud data decreases.

The global feature extraction on the projected depth cloud in this paper is realized based on U-Net [24], which is a state-of-the-art (SOTA) attempt for understanding 3D scenes. In this research, we modify this model as the feature extraction backbone from the projected 2D scene projected-view images because it not only considers local point relations but also outputs globally consistent features. The U-Net is composed of top-down and bottom-up pathways with lateral connections, where the top-down pathway spatially upsamples feature maps from higher levels in the pyramid, and the upsampled features are extracted from the bottom-up pathway. For the U-Net used in this paper, we use a $3 \times 3$ kernel, batch normalization, and the ReLU activation function.

The projected images from the previous projection module are first pre-processed through data standardization and augmentation. The size and the resolution of projected images are standardized by cropping or adding a margin depending on the original size of each scene, so that input images are all to scale. Data augmentation is carried out by performing random changes in the image through scaling, flipping (on both X and Y-axis), and random rotating with multiples of ninety degrees.

The outputs of this U-Net are features learnt for instance and semantic segmentation respectively. The features for semantic segmentation are semantic scores defined by the cross-entropy loss. Moreover, the features for instance segmentation are represented by the loss function measuring similarities on pairs of pixels by the sum of the losses in relation to their distances and margins, therefore making sure that point-feature vectors from a singular object are homogeneous and feature space from separate instances are differentiating.

## 4.3    3D-Point Cloud Segmentation

Having completed the 2D projection and U-Net prediction part of the entire system, the segmented features gathered from the U-Net hold globally consistent predictions of segmentation across the scene. However, due to dimensionality reduction, there enters the possibility of some objects, having been hidden behind others and not having been considered during the 2D segmentation step. Thus, we design to take both global 2D features extracted from the previous module and the point cloud as inputs for 3D segmentation.

To deal with the disorder in point clouds, the structure of a graph is good for modeling the correlation between points explicitly as represented by the graph edges. DGCNN [25] proposes edge convolution where, within each edge convolution layer, there is a computation of each point applying a nonlinear function to nearing points as captured by the edge matrix. It can fully exploit the features across the entire scene where edges get updated after each edgeConv layer. Consequently, 3D DGCNN is used for carrying out 3D segmentation in this paper.

Thanks to the 2D U-Net we now have instance features for the points visible in each of the five view projections. Those predicted instance features are globally consistent and hence can be utilized for grouping. The starting point cloud features are concatenated with the learnt instance features from the 2D U-Net and their respective point indices which are used for mapping the instance features to the point cloud. During this process, all occluded points also have their instance features reset to zero. The 3D DGCNN specifically exploits local geometric structures by constructing a local neighborhood graph and running convolutions on the edges connecting neighboring pairs of points. These so-called edge convolutions have the advantage of having properties in-between nonlocality and translation invariance. The k-nearest neighbors of a point are dynamically morphing from each layer and computed similarly to those of embedding. There also exists a non-local diffusion of data due to the closeness in feature space not being the same as proximity in the input.

The 3D DGCNN serves for generating instance feature predictions based on the learnt features from the 2D U-Net and the original point cloud. The model architecture used for segmentation is separated as a top branch and a bottom branch respectively. The semantic segmentation branch calculates edge feature sets for each point and adds features in a set to calculate edge convolution responses for the related points. A 1D global descriptor for creating semantic segmentation scores for classes is created by using an aggregated output of features from the last layer. The output of the 3D DGCNN is much like that of the 2D U-Net, that is, two separate outputs with their own separate loss functions. Just as with the 2D U-Net, semantic segmentation loss is set to be the cross-entropy loss, and the instance segmentation loss is defined by its target instance features. Said target instance features are set as an average of all instance features which lie in the same ground truth instance. Hence, for points that are not captured by the 2D U-Net there is zero instance feature and during training will not be counted in the loss of the network.

# 5    Evaluation Results

In this section, the proposed 3D point cloud segmentation method using global 2D-view features is evaluated. In order to help with the evaluation, various SOTA datasets are used as benchmarks. The evaluation was conducted on a computer running with NVIDIA GeForce GTX 1060, Intel Core i7-7700HQ CPU, and a 16 GB DDR4 RAM.

## 5.1    Datasets

To evaluate the proposed method in this research, the input point cloud datasets should hold RGB as well as depth data and should already be annotated with preferably point-wise instance labels as well as semantic labels for each object instance in the scene. According to these requirements, the chosen datasets are the S3DIS [26] and the ScanNet v2 [27] datasets, as they present the most complete set of annotated scans, different types of scenes, and most past methods to compare against. The S3DIS dataset has RGB, and depth point cloud data is taken from six large indoor spaces and a total of 271 scenes or rooms, collected from three separate buildings. Hence, it has a wide arrange of different room setups as well as shapes and sizes as desired for the scope of this research. Moreover, it has 13 annotated semantic classes which are grouped by instances.

## 5.2    Training Setup

The resolutions of 5 cm and 3 cm per pixel were chosen for generating five projections on ScanNet and S3DIS databases respectively. A near-camera plane threshold is set at 20 cm for removing points that are too close to the sides prior to generating the projection, such as the ceilings or a wall. The data standardization and augmentation systems are added after generating projections. The standardized system aims to keep images within a standard size, by cutting or padding the output projections dependent on the room size. And the augmentation system involves random scaling, flipping, and rotation of the projections for each view before training. Besides, we set the learning rate as 0.001, batch size as 32, and epoch as 250 throughout the whole process of training.

For the 3D DGCNN, points are first divided into rooms and then into blocks. 1024 points are removed within a cylinder-shaped area of 1 m squared in diameter on the ground plane. The segmentation portion of the network is trained to predict the per point classes of each block with each point being represented by a 9-dimensional vector. Mentioned vector is composed of its normalized location, XYZ position, as well as its RGB values. During training, 4096 points in each block are randomly sampled, while all points are used during testing.

Semantic loss is weighted using the negative logarithm of class frequency and networks are trained using an Adam optimizer. For training and testing on the S3DIS dataset, which is composed of 13 classes from 271 rooms, we use a 6-fold cross-validation setup. For the ScanNet v2 dataset, which is composed of 20 classes from a wide array of different indoor spaces, we use 1100-, 363-, and 150-point clouds respectively for training, validating, and testing.

## 5.3   Evaluation Benchmarks

Due to the relative novelty of the 3D point cloud segmentation field, there are not yet any well-established evaluation benchmarks set as standards in the field. In our paper, the instance segmentation performance is evaluated with the comparison of benchmarks set in SGPN [8]. And for those experiments regarding semantic segmentation, results are compared against other benchmarks aside from SGPN, such as the ScanNet v2 benchmark.

In terms of benchmarks derived in SGPN, one of the important benchmarks is the intersection over union (IoU), an equation of which can be found below in Eq. 3. In said equation, $TP_{px}$ is a pixel-wise true positive result. $FP_{px}$ and $FN_{px}$ are pixel-wise false positives and false negatives.

$$IoU = \frac{TP_{px}}{TP_{px} + FP_{px} + FN_{px}}. \tag{3}$$

Another benchmark used in SGPN is average precision (AP). It is set as the per-category average over precision. For AP, predicted instances are associated with different categories in respect of a majority voting of the prediction semantic labels, and are judged on three separate levels of IOU thresholds: 0.25, 0.5, and 0.75. Any non-classified instances are not included in the counting of AP.

In terms of benchmarks not derived from the SGPN method, the ScanNet v2 benchmark measures the entire group of proposals given for each instance. Said proposals are assigned based on confidence scores, the chosen category of the object, and points belonging to it.

## 5.4   Experimental Results

This section offers both quantitative and qualitative comparisons against baselines across two tested databases.

**Segmentation Results on S3DIS Dataset.** Table 1 is a summary of the instance and semantic segmentation performance regarding AP using the S3DIS dataset. The DGCNN method here is a modification of the originally proposed SGPN using the improved DGCNN method as its base architecture instead of the PointNet. And the 3D segmentation part takes as same architecture as DGCNN. The difference between our proposed method and the compared DGCNN is that we take both global 2D features besides original point clouds into consideration.

It can be seen that nearly all results of our proposed method are better than those achieved by the original SGPN and SGPN using DGCNN. Specifically, a noticeable improvement across all APs and the mean accuracy (mAcc) values can be seen, with mean IoU (mIoU) being near-even to that of DGCNN. It proves the efficiency to consider global features in both instance and semantic segmentation.

**Table 1.** Comparison of instance and semantic segmentation results of proposed method, SGPN, and DGCNN using the S3DIS dataset.

| Methods | Instance | | | Semantic | |
|---|---|---|---|---|---|
| | AP 0.25 | AP 0.5 | AP 0.75 | mIoU | mAcc |
| SGPN | 62.47 | 42.91 | 23.89 | 48.27 | 71.07 |
| DGCNN | 70.73 | 58.56 | 39.73 | 59.29 | 80.71 |
| Proposed | **76.22** | **63.39** | **47.82** | 56.81 | **84.11** |

**Table 2.** Comparison of category specific AP 0.5 results of proposed method, SGPN, and DGCNN using the S3DIS dataset.

| Methods | Mean | Ceiling | Floor | Wall | Beam | Pillar |
|---|---|---|---|---|---|---|
| SGPN | 42.91 | 78.15 | 80.27 | 48.90 | 33.65 | 16.97 |
| DGCNN | 58.56 | **85.85** | 83.15 | 61.65 | **52.82** | 47.60 |
| Proposed | **63.39** | 70.98 | **92.68** | **71.29** | 46.39 | **59.83** |

| Window | Door | Table | Chair | Sofa | Shelf | Board |
|---|---|---|---|---|---|---|
| 49.63 | 44.48 | 30.33 | 52.22 | 23.12 | 28.50 | 28.62 |
| 55.12 | 62.22 | 34.97 | 66.02 | 42.50 | **55.93** | 54.85 |
| **63.31** | **64.40** | **59.93** | **72.43** | **48.65** | 54.45 | **56.38** |

**Category-Wise AP 0.5 on S3DIS Dataset.** Table 2 shows the category-wise scores for AP 0.5 using the S3DIS dataset. This table compares our method to the same two methods in the previous table which are capable of both semantic and instance segmentation. Most results are better than those of SGPN and SGPN using DGCNN.

In Table 2, it can be seen that our method outperforms SGPN and SGPN using DGCNN by its mean overlap using the S3DIS dataset. It also outperforms both previous methods in most categories. Some of the lower results in specific categories can be attributed to the projection views on a near-camera plane. These points near walls or ceilings are not able to be predicted as clearly as other learning objects that were placed within the room. Overall, the proposed method of this paper can reach highly competitive results.

Note that the results for SGPN and SGPN using DGCNN are not the same as those reported in their original papers. It is likely caused by slight differences in our implementations due to not having a full explanation of all implied methods that were used in gathering their results.

**Category-Wise AP 0.5 on ScanNet Dataset.** Table 3 shows the category-wise scores for AP 0.5 using the ScanNet dataset against solely SGPN. Most results are better than those achieved by the SGPN method. Alike on the S3DIS dataset, most categories are more accurately determined by using our method, with a few exceptions. Moreover, it should be noted that the SGPN method is

**Table 3.** Comparison of category specific AP 0.5 results of proposed method and SGPN using the ScanNet dataset.

| Methods | Mean | Wall | Floor | Cabinet | Bed | Chair | Desk | Curtain | Fridge |
|---|---|---|---|---|---|---|---|---|---|
| SGPN | 35.09 | 46.90 | 79.00 | **34.10** | 43.80 | 63.60 | 22.80 | **61.10** | 24.50 |
| Proposed | **52.49** | **65.32** | **94.59** | 28.60 | **67.88** | **69.26** | **29.33** | 60.26 | **57.56** |

| Sofa | Table | Door | Window | Book | Picture | Counter | Toilet | Sink | Bathtub |
|---|---|---|---|---|---|---|---|---|---|
| 36.80 | 40.70 | 0.00 | 0.00 | 22.40 | 0.00 | **26.90** | 60.50 | 35.80 | 46.20 |
| **63.48** | **64.90** | **29.54** | **36.04** | **54.58** | **15.49** | 17.87 | **63.69** | **48.67** | **74.92** |

**Table 4.** Results from ScanNet v2 benchmark challenge.

| Methods | AP | AP 0.25 | AP0.5 |
|---|---|---|---|
| PMRCNN | 2.1 | 22.7 | 5.3 |
| SGPN | 4.9 | 39.0 | 14.3 |
| Proposed | **13.6** | **48.6** | **27.9** |

not capable of labeling flat objects near walls in the ScanNet dataset such as doors, windows, and pictures, leading to 0.00 ratings on those.

**ScanNet V2 Benchmark Challenge.** Table 4 shows the mean average precision while overlapping 25% (AP 0.25), 50% (AP 0.5), and 50% to 95% with a stepping size of 0.05 (AP) on the ScanNet v2 benchmark challenge. These evaluations are compared against similar SOTA methods within the field, including PMRCNN [28] and SGPN [8]. As can be observed from the results, the proposed method beats them in chosen AP categories with its extraction on globally consistent features.

**Qualitative Results on S3DIS and ScanNet.** Our proposed method can differentiate multiple object classes and instances of said objects while using scenes from the S3DIS or ScanNet datasets as inputs.Examples can be visualized in Fig. 4. Said figure shows the RGBD input of the original point cloud in subfigures (a) and both semantic and instance segmentation ground truth in subfigures (b,d) and predictions in subfigures (c,e). Classes and instances are randomly colored to visually separate between instances.

In these qualitative evaluations, the segmentation results of our proposed method are relatively close to their ground truths. In some cases, flat objects such as parts of bookshelves placed near walls are left uncategorized in black. Moreover, a majority of points placed within the boundary of an object in the ground truths are placed on the correct semantic object group using the proposed method. This can be seen in subfigure (c) where part of the wall, likely due to a few points being at a different depth than the wall, is assigned a different classification in green. However, visually and qualitatively, across a variety of

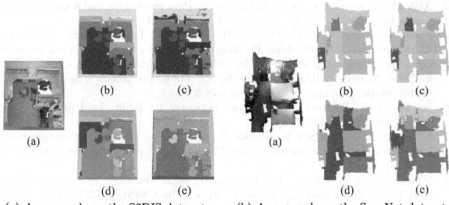

(a) An example on the S3DIS dataset.    (b) An example on the ScanNet dataset.

**Fig. 4.** Qualitative results of the proposed method with visualization.

scenes, the proposed method performs accurately for both semantic segmentation tasks and the more complex instance segmentation tasks.

## 6  Conclusion and Future Work

This paper proposes a novel 3D segmentation method which is composed of a 2D U-Net leveraging globally consistent 2D projections and a point feature propagating 3D DGCNN for making final segmentation. The main advantage of the proposed method in comparison to other SOTA approaches is the inclusion of globally consistent features which help to better identify separate object instances. It offers a globally coherent learnt feature embedding space and the ability to perform clustering within an entire scene rather than in single blocks.

According to observations in experiments, there could still be hidden objects which may not be shown from the chosen views even after optimization of the chosen angles, which could still hold significant data regarding globally consistent features within the point cloud. Hence, a new method for determining which view angles to project to depending on the room size, shape, or other properties of the point cloud could be looked at as a potential improvement for future work.

## References

1. Shotton, J., et al.: Real-time human pose recognition in parts from single depth images. In: CVPR, pp. 1297–1304. IEEE (2011)
2. Saiti, E., Danelakis, A., Theoharis, T.: Cross-time registration of 3d point clouds. Comput. Graph. **99**, 139–152 (2021)
3. Liu, Y., Kong, L., Wu, F., Chen, G.: Groupcoach: compressed sensing based group activity monitoring and correction. In: IEEE/ACM IWQoS, pp. 1–10 (2020)

4. Alahari, K., Seguin, G., Sivic, J., Laptev, I.: Pose estimation and segmentation of people in 3d movies. In: ICCV, pp. 2112–2119 (2013)
5. Paolanti, M., Pierdicca, R., Martini, M., Di Stefano, F., Morbidoni, C., Mancini, A., Malinverni, E.S., Frontoni, E., Zingaretti, P.: Semantic 3D object maps for everyday robotic retail inspection. In: Cristani, M., Prati, A., Lanz, O., Messelodi, S., Sebe, N. (eds.) ICIAP 2019. LNCS, vol. 11808, pp. 263–274. Springer, Cham (2019). https://doi.org/10.1007/978-3-030-30754-7_27
6. Su, H., et al.: Splatnet: sparse lattice networks for point cloud processing. In: CVPR, pp. 2530–2539 (2018)
7. Kanezaki, A., Matsushita, Y., Nishida, Y.: Rotationnet: joint object categorization and pose estimation using multiviews from unsupervised viewpoints. In: CVPR, pp. 5010–5019 (2018)
8. Wang, W., Yu, R., Huang, Q., Neumann, U.: Sgpn: similarity group proposal network for 3d point cloud instance segmentation. In: CVPR, pp. 2569–2578 (2018)
9. Wang, C., Cheng, M., Sohel, F., Bennamoun, M., Li, J.: Normalnet: a voxel-based cnn for 3d object classification and retrieval. Neurocomputing **323**, 139–147 (2019)
10. Wu, Z., et al.: 3d shapenets: a deep representation for volumetric shapes. In: CVPR, pp. 1912–1920 (2015)
11. Maturana, D., Scherer, S.: Voxnet: a 3d convolutional neural network for real-time object recognition. In: IROS, pp. 922–928. IEEE (2015)
12. Qi, C.R., et al.: Volumetric and multi-view cnns for object classification on 3d data. In: CVPR, pp. 5648–5656 (2016)
13. Bai, S., Bai, X., Zhou, Z., Zhang, Z., Jan Latecki, L.: Gift: a real-time and scalable 3d shape search engine. In: CVPR, pp. 5023–5032 (2016)
14. Kalogerakis, E., Averkiou, M., Maji, S., Chaudhuri, S.: 3d shape segmentation with projective convolutional networks. In: CVPR, pp. 3779–3788 (2017)
15. Cao, Z., Huang, Q., Karthik, R.: 3d object classification via spherical projections. In: 3DV, pp. 566–574. IEEE (2017)
16. Zhang, L., Sun, J., Zheng, Q.: 3d point cloud recognition based on a multi-view convolutional neural network. Sensors **18**(11), 3681 (2018)
17. Rao, Y., Lu, J., Zhou, J.: Spherical fractal convolutional neural networks for point cloud recognition. In: CVPR, pp. 452–460 (2019)
18. Rosu, R.A., Schütt, P., Quenzel, J., Behnke, S.: Latticenet: fast point cloud segmentation using permutohedral lattices, arXiv preprint arXiv:1912.05905
19. Qi, C.R., Su, H., Mo, K., Guibas, L.J.: Pointnet: deep learning on point sets for 3d classification and segmentation. In: CVPR, pp. 652–660 (2017)
20. Zhao, H., Jiang, L., Fu, C.-W., Jia, J.: Pointweb: enhancing local neighborhood features for point cloud processing. In: CVPR, pp. 5565–5573 (2019)
21. Wu, W., Qi, Z., Fuxin, L.: Pointconv: deep convolutional networks on 3d point clouds. In: CVPR, pp. 9621–9630 (2019)
22. Liu, J., Ni, B., Li, C., Yang, J., Tian, Q.: Dynamic points agglomeration for hierarchical point sets learning. In: ICCV, pp. 7546–7555 (2019)
23. Han, W., Wen, C., Wang, C., Li, X., Li, Q.: Point2node: correlation learning of dynamic-node for point cloud feature modeling. In: AAAI, vol. 34, 2020, pp. 10925–10932
24. Ronneberger, O., Fischer, P., Brox, T.: U-Net: convolutional networks for biomedical image segmentation. In: Navab, N., Hornegger, J., Wells, W.M., Frangi, A.F. (eds.) MICCAI 2015. LNCS, vol. 9351, pp. 234–241. Springer, Cham (2015). https://doi.org/10.1007/978-3-319-24574-4_28
25. Wang, L., Huang, Y., Hou, Y., Zhang, S., Shan, J.: Graph attention convolution for point cloud semantic segmentation. In: CVPR, pp. 10296–10305 (2019)

26. Armeni, I., et al.: 3d semantic parsing of large-scale indoor spaces. In: CVPR, pp. 1534–1543 (2016)
27. Dai, A., Chang, A.X., Savva, M., Halber, M., Funkhouser, T., Nießner, M.: Scannet: richly-annotated 3d reconstructions of indoor scenes. In: CVPR, pp. 5828–5839 (2017)
28. Scannet 3d semantic instance benchmark leader board (2018). http://www.kaldir. vc.in.tum.de/scannet_benchmark. Accessed 16 Nov 2018

# Self-supervised Indoor 360-Degree Depth Estimation via Structural Regularization

Weifeng Kong[1], Qiudan Zhang[1], You Yang[3], Tiesong Zhao[4], Wenhui Wu[2], and Xu Wang[1(✉)]

[1] College of Computer Science and Software Engineering, Shenzhen University, Shenzhen 518060, China
wangxu@szu.edu.cn
[2] College of Electronics and Information Engineering, Shenzhen University, Shenzhen 518060, China
[3] School of Electronic Information and Communications, Huangzhong University of Science and Technology, Wuhan 430074, China
[4] College of Physics and Information Engineering, Fuzhou University, Fuzhou 350108, China

**Abstract.** Estimating 360° depth information has attracted considerable attention due to the fast development of emerging 360° cameras. However, most researches only focus on dealing with the distortion of 360° images without considering the geometric information of 360° images, leading to poor performance. In this paper, we conduct to apply indoor structure regularities for self-supervised 360° image depth estimation. Specifically, we carefully design two geometric constraints for efficient model optimization including dominant direction normal constraint and planar consistency depth constraint. The dominant direction normal constraint enables to align the normal of indoor 360° images with the direction of vanishing points. The planar consistency depth constraint is utilized to fit the estimated depth of each pixel by its 3D plane. Hence, incorporating these two geometric constraints can further facilitate the generation of accurate depth results for 360° images. Extensive experiments illustrate that our designed method improves $\delta_1$ by an average of 4.82% compared to state-of-the-art methods on Matterport3D and Stanford2D3D datasets within 3D60.

**Keywords:** 360° image · Depth estimation · Self-supervised learning · Structure regularity

This work was supported in part by the National Natural Science Foundation of China (Grant 61871270, 62171134), in part by the Shenzhen Natural Science Foundation under Grants JCYJ20200109110410133 and 20200812110350001.

# 1   Introduction

With the rise of consumer spherical cameras, 360 image cameras are efficient and low-cost for indoor scene capture and reconstruction. 360° depth estimation is one of the fundamental tasks of indoor scene understanding and will be used as input for downstream applications such as autonomous navigation, augmented reality, and 3D reconstruction.

Currently, learning-based monocular depth estimation has been dramatically improved. However, most of the early methods are designed for perspective images with limited field-of-view (FoV). When the approach is directly applied to 360° images, it leads to sub-optimal performance without considering the distortion of panorama. Different from perspective image, although the whole scene can be perceived with a larger FoV, 360° image has serious distortion at both poles and slight distortion near the equator. To solve the distortion problem of panorama, Omnidepth [1] applied rectangular filters with various resolutions. Wang *et al.* [2] proposed a network to fuse the features from both equirectangular projection (ERP) and cubemap projection (CMP). However, most of these learning-based approaches rely on accurate depth ground truth which is labor-intensive and high-cost.

In addition, utilizing synthetic data and self-supervision are two ways to overcome the need of pixel-wise labeled data. Synthetic data can be generated cheaply, but the gap between synthetic and real domains needs to be bridged. Self-supervision refers to building a view synthesis task to indirectly estimate monocular depth from stereo pairs and monocular videos, which relies on a series of assumptions such as Lambertian reflectance and static scenes. Several works focus on self-supervised monocular spherical image depth estimation [3,4]. Their main goal is to overcome the distortion of 360° images. However, they ignore the rich structural information of the whole scene, resulting in poor performance of depth estimation. Since indoor depth estimation is a challenging task, full of textureless areas such as floors, walls and ceilings. Therefore, leveraging the structural information will help to train a robust model to estimate accurate depth information.

In this work, we propose to apply indoor structural regularities to self-supervised 360° depth estimation. Specifically, we design a dominant direction normal constraint and a planar consistency depth constraint for model training, where the dominant direction normal constraint aligns the surface normals with the dominant directions of the indoor scene, and the planar consistency depth constraint fits the estimated depth by its plane. During the training stage, the 360° image vanishing point detection scheme is employed to gain the dominant direction of the scene. Additionally, the geometric and raw color information are fused for panorama planar region detection. To verify the effectiveness of our proposed method, extensive experiments are conducted on Matterport3D [17] and Stanford2D3D [18] within 3D60 dataset [1]. Experimental results demonstrate that our proposed approach outperforms the state-of-the-art self-supervised 360° depth estimation methods. The main contributions of our proposed approach are summarized as follows:

- We propose a new training pipeline for self-supervised indoor 360° depth estimation via structural regularization and spherical view synthesis.
- We develop the dominant direction normal constraint derived from 360° image vanishing point detection and plane-consistent depth constraint as the structural regularity in the training procedure.
- Extensive experimental results demonstrate that our proposed approach outperforms the state-of-the-art methods and is capable of estimating depth maps with rich details and smooth planar regions.

## 2 Related Works

### 2.1 Learning-based 360° Indoor Scene Understanding

The ERP image is severely distorted at the poles and slightly distorted near the equator, which is not suitable to apply CNN directly. For instance, Monroy et al. [29] projected 360° images to cubemaps, and then utilized conventional CNN to extract features. Although the slight distortion, cubemaps still suffer from severe boundary discontinuity. Cube padding [20] was proposed to improve the connection of each cube face. In order to deal with 360° images directly, Khasanova et al. [30] proposed a way of graph construction based on the geometry of panoramas, in which their filters respond similarly to the same content on different positions. Subsequently, Tateno et al. [22] developed distortion-aware deformable convolution filters which adapt their shape according to the projection model of panoramas. Considering that ERP can revise the CMP discontinuity, while CMP is beneficial for the distortion of ERP, GLPanoDepth [36] proposed a two-branch network that fuses the features extracted from ERP and CMP. 360MonoDepth [37] projected a spherical image onto a set of tangent images and recombined the individual depth estimation.

### 2.2 360° Depth Estimation

Unlike the perspective image, 360° depth estimation focuses on solving the distortion of panorama and making good use of its larger FoV. For instance, OmniDepth [1] applied rectangular filters with various resolutions and developed an auto-encoder network to directly process panoramas. However, fully-supervised approaches rely on the pixel-wise depth ground truth, which is labor-intensive and expensive. Alternatively, Wang et al. [3] proposed a self-supervised learning network for 360° video depth estimation. Subsequently, Zioulis et al. [4] developed to learn a self-supervised network for monocular 360° depth estimation by investigating spherical view synthesis. However, these methods neglect the characteristics of panorama that can perceive the complete indoor scene.

In Manhattan-world Model [32], indoor scenes have strong structural regularities. Specifically, the indoor scene can be decomposed into multiple planes, where two of which are mutually parallel or orthogonal. In addition, normal vectors are naturally aligned with the dominant directions. Therefore, such structural regularities are widely studied in perspective image processing, e.g. indoor scene reconstruction [26] and visual-inertial odometry [33]. Since panoramas can perceive the whole indoor scene with a complete FoV, the structural regularities play an important role in 360-degree vision tasks. Based on this motivation, we propose to apply structural regularities for self-supervised 360° depth estimation. Concretely, we propose to utilize both dominate direction normal constraint deriving from 360° vanishing point detection and planar consistency depth constraint as structural regularities to estimate the depth for the 360° image. To mitigate the distortion, we use coordinate convolutions [28] which concatenate the input with two grid coordinates to learn the spatial context of panoramas. Besides, a spherically weighted attention matrix is designed for photometric loss and depth smooth loss.

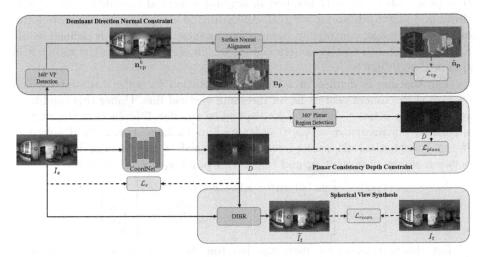

**Fig. 1.** The overall architecture of the proposed self-supervised indoor 360° depth estimation method.

## 3   The Proposed Method

The framework of our proposed self-supervised 360° depth estimation method is illustrated in Fig. 1. The overall training pipeline is comprised of four components, including depth estimation module, dominant direction normal constraint, planar consistency depth constraint and spherical view synthesis loss. During the inference stage, only the depth estimation module is implemented to produce the estimated depth map of the 360° image.

### 3.1   Depth Estimation Module

In this paper, the lightweight backbone named CoordNet [4] is employed as the depth estimation module, which utilizes ELU activations and coordinate

convolutions [28] to avoid the distortion of ERP. To learn the spatial context
of spherical image, the coordinate convolutions concatenate the feature map
with two grid coordinates. Given the input of source 360° image $I_s$, CoordNet
can produce the estimated depth map $D$. During the training stage, the model
parameters of CoordNet are optimized via the following structural constraints
and spherical view synthesis loss.

### 3.2  Spherical View Synthesis

**Spherical Disparity.** A spherical image is defined as ERP on 2D grids. The
local 3D coordinate system in Cartesian $\mathbf{v} = (x, y, z)$ and spherical $\rho = (r, \phi, \theta)$
are given in [4]. For an ERP image with resolution $W \times H$, its pixel coordinates
$\mathbf{p} = (u, v)$ can be directly mapped to angular spherical coordinates $\sigma = (\phi, \theta)$
through $\phi = 2\pi u/W$ and $\theta = \pi v/H$. According to the projection characteristics
of the ERP image, contrary to perspective images, 360° depth is defined as 3D
Euclidean distance to the camera center, which corresponds to the radius $r$ in
spherical coordinates.

The baseline is defined in a vertical orientation for spherical stereo which
ensures their camera centers lie on the same vertical line. Under this condition,
spherical disparities $\gamma = (\gamma_\phi, \gamma_\theta)$ correspond to angular differences in the angular
spherical coordinates $\sigma = (\phi, \theta)$ computed in radians. For vertical spherical
stereo, its spherical disparities $\gamma$ can be calculated by the baseline $\mathbf{b} = \mathbf{v_s} - \mathbf{v_t}$
between source viewpoint $\mathbf{v_s}$ and target viewpoint $\mathbf{v_t}$ according to the Eq. 1.

$$
\begin{bmatrix} \partial r \\ \partial \phi \\ \partial \theta \end{bmatrix} =
\begin{bmatrix}
\sin(\phi)\sin\theta & \cos(\theta) & \cos(\phi)\sin(\theta) \\
\frac{\cos(\phi)}{r\sin(\theta)} & 0 & \frac{-\sin(\phi)}{r\sin(\theta)} \\
\frac{\sin(\phi)\cos(\theta)}{r} & \frac{-\sin(\theta)}{r} & \frac{\cos(\phi)\cos(\theta)}{r}
\end{bmatrix}
\begin{bmatrix} \partial x \\ \partial y \\ \partial z \end{bmatrix}.
\tag{1}
$$

For the vertical stereo case, the baseline $\mathbf{b} = (dx, dy, dz)$ is defined as
$\mathbf{b}_y = (0, dy, 0)$, and the spherical disparities $\gamma = (\gamma_\phi, \gamma_\theta)$ is defined as $\gamma_{vert} =$
$d_y(\partial\phi/\partial y, \partial\theta/\partial y)$.

**Depth-Image-based Rendering (DIBR).** Traditionally, the source image is
synthesized by the target image through inverse wrapping and bilinear sampling for unsupervised learning. However, this approach fails to handle the
occluded regions or non-linear mappings. In order to apply the spherical stereo
for self-supervised learning, we utilize the soft local differentiable rendering approach [34], which comprises splattering the contributions of each pixel onto an
empty canvas and normalizing the rendered result $\tilde{I}_t$. Ultimately, the occlusion
and mapping problems are appropriately solved.

**Spherical View Synthesis Loss.** In spherical view synthesis task, the target
view $\tilde{I}_t$ is synthesized through the soft local differentiable rendering approach
(DIBR). The original photometric loss [12] is defined as:

$$
\mathcal{L}_{photo}(\mathbf{p}) = \alpha \frac{1 - SSIM(I_t(\mathbf{p}), \tilde{I}_t(\mathbf{p}))}{2}
+ (1 - \alpha)\left\| I_t(\mathbf{p}) - \tilde{I}_t(\mathbf{p})) \right\|,
\tag{2}
$$

where $\alpha$ is set to 0.85. Considering the distortion of the ERP image, we design a spherically weighted attention matrix $W$ as

$$W(\mathbf{p}) = \cos\left((v - \frac{H}{2} + \frac{1}{2})\frac{\pi}{H}\right). \tag{3}$$

Hence, the total spherical view synthesis loss $\mathcal{L}_{recon}$ is defined as the spherical weighted mean photometric error of all valid pixels:

$$\mathcal{L}_{recon} = \frac{1}{N} \sum_{\mathbf{p} \in \Omega} W(\mathbf{p}) \mathcal{L}_{photo}(\mathbf{p}), \tag{4}$$

where $\Omega$ denotes the pixels of valid ground truth.

In addition, we employ an L2 smoothness regularization $\mathcal{L}_s$ to smooth the estimated depth, and the formula is as follows,

$$\mathcal{L}_s = \frac{1}{N} \sum_{\mathbf{p}} \hat{W}(\mathbf{p}) e^{-\|\nabla I_s(\mathbf{p})\|_2} \sqrt{(\nabla_u \mathbf{v}(\mathbf{p}))^2 + (\nabla_v \mathbf{v}(\mathbf{p}))^2}, \tag{5}$$

where $\mathbf{v} = (x, y, z)$ denotes the back-projected Cartesian coordinates for each predicted pixel, and the weighted term $\hat{W}(\mathbf{p}) = 1 - W(\mathbf{p})$ is used to enhance the smoothness of the distorted region.

## 3.3 Dominant Direction Normal Constraint

Dominant direction refers to the normal direction of main faces (floors, walls and ceilings) of indoor scenes that satisfy the Manhattan world assumption. In this paper, the dominant direction is utilized as a supervised prior to align the predicted normal. Details are as follows.

360° **Vanishing Point Detection.** To obtain the dominant direction of the indoor scene, we first need to detect the 360° vanishing points. Since straight lines in the real world are projected as curves in the panorama, the conventional vanishing point detection method is not applicable. In the panorama, a straight line in the real world is projected as a circle on a sphere through the center of the camera, so we can represent each line with the normal of its corresponding 3D projective plane as in [7]. Specifically, we first perform Canny edge detection operation on the ERP image to obtain edge point groups. Subsequently, each edge is represented by the cross product of two randomly sampled points, which have been projected to unit spherical coordinates. Therefore, each edge is transformed as the normal of corresponding 3D projective plane. After computing the cross-product of each parallel line pair, all the possible vanishing points are acquired. The best vanishing point is calculated from all vanishing points through the RANSAC algorithm. Since the predicted surface normal may be in the inverse direction of vanishing points, the directions of vanishing point and their corresponding inverse directions, denoted as $\mathbf{n}_{vp}^k (k = 1, ..., 6)$ will be fed into the following surface normal alignment module.

**Surface Normal Alignment.** To predict the surface normal, we project the pixels back to 3D coordinates $\mathbf{P} \in \mathbb{R}^3$ according to the ERP image by

$$\mathbf{P} = D_{\mathbf{p}} K^{-1} \mathbf{p}, \tag{6}$$

where

$$K^{-1} = \begin{bmatrix} \cos(\phi)\cos(\theta) \\ \sin(\theta) \\ -\sin(\phi)\cos(\theta) \end{bmatrix} \tag{7}$$

denotes the back-projected ERP matrix and $D_p$ means the estimated depth. Then we compute the normal from 3D points. Moreover, the normal vector $\mathbf{n_p} \in \mathbb{R}^3$ of each pixel $\mathbf{p}$ is generated by calculating its $7 \times 7$ neighbourhood [8].

The aligned normal vector $\hat{\mathbf{n}}_\mathbf{p}$ of each pixel $\mathbf{p}$ is equal to the dominant direction with maximum cosine similarity to the predicted surface normal vector $\mathbf{n_p}$,

$$\hat{\mathbf{n}}_\mathbf{p} = \arg \max_{\mathbf{n}_{vp}^k} \cos(\mathbf{n_p}, \mathbf{n}_{vp}^k). \tag{8}$$

It is worth noting that we only align the surface normals whose maximum cosine similarity $\cos_\mathbf{p}^{max}$ exceeds a threshold $\epsilon$. Hence, the dominant direction mask $\mathbf{M_p}$ is devised as follows,

$$\mathbf{M_p} = \begin{cases} 1 & \cos_\mathbf{p}^{max} \geq \epsilon \\ 0 & \cos_\mathbf{p}^{max} < \epsilon \end{cases}. \tag{9}$$

Since the predicted normal may be noisy in the preliminary stage of model training, we design a small threshold that grows with the epoch number $N_{epoch}$ to help the model coverage. Same as in [9], we set the threshold as $\epsilon = \epsilon_1 \cdot N_{epoch} + \epsilon_2$, where $\epsilon_1$ and $\epsilon_2$ are set to $1.663e^{-3}$ and $0.9$, respectively.

**Dominant Direction Normal Loss.** Each predicted surface normal contained in the dominant direction mask is constrained by its aligned normal. We assign the aligned normal as a supervised signal and formulate the loss function $\mathcal{L}_{vp}$ as follows,

$$\mathcal{L}_{vp} = \frac{1}{N_v} \sum_\mathbf{p} \mathbf{M_p}(1 - \cos(\mathbf{n_p}, \hat{\mathbf{n}}_\mathbf{p})), \tag{10}$$

where $N_v$ denotes the number of pixels contained in dominant direction mask $\mathbf{M_p}$.

### 3.4 Planar Consistency Depth Constraint

Planar consistency depth constraint fits the 3D points with their 3D plane information. It is significant for depth estimation in textureless region which is hard to backpropagation in self-supervised mode. Moreover, it can overcome the limitation of dominant direction normal constraint which is not applicable for the inclined planar regions. The 3D planes are computed by detecting the 360° planar regions and back-projecting them to 3D space.

**Table 1.** Evaluation results of the proposed method and the state-of-the-art methods on Matterport3D [17] and Stanford2D3D [18] datasets. ($\downarrow$ represents the lower the better, $\uparrow$ represents the higher the better).

| Dataset | Method | Supervision | Abs Rel$\downarrow$ | Sq Rel$\downarrow$ | RMSE$\downarrow$ | RMSLE$\downarrow$ | $\delta_1 \uparrow$ | $\delta_2 \uparrow$ | $\delta_3 \uparrow$ |
|---|---|---|---|---|---|---|---|---|---|
| Matterport3D | Zioulis et al.'s method [4] | full-Sup. | 0.1004 | 0.0784 | 0.4495 | 0.1637 | 79.35% | 95.10% | 98.45% |
| | HoHoNet [31] | full-Sup. | 0.0556 | 0.0459 | 0.4141 | 0.1141 | 93.78% | 98.27% | 99.16% |
| | OmniFusion [35] | full-Sup. | 0.0888 | 0.0310 | 0.3107 | 0.1223 | 93.78% | 99.33% | 99.84% |
| | UniFuse [19] | full-Sup. | 0.0236 | 0.0098 | 0.1720 | 0.0540 | 97.84% | 99.31% | 99.58% |
| | P$^2$Net [11] | self-Sup. | 0.2312 | 0.2966 | 1.0593 | 0.3750 | 38.92% | 67.82% | 84.11% |
| | Structdepth [9] | self-Sup. | 0.2237 | 0.2742 | 1.0055 | 0.3541 | 42.34% | 70.43% | 85.88% |
| | Zioulis et al.'s method [4] | self-Sup. | 0.1360 | 0.1366 | 0.7756 | 0.2338 | 61.22% | 89.16% | 96.43% |
| | **Ours** | self-Sup. | **0.1178** | **0.0894** | **0.5062** | **0.1928** | **69.43%** | **93.31%** | **98.11%** |
| Stanford2D3D | Zioulis et al.'s method [4] | full-Sup. | 0.0760 | 0.0451 | 0.3681 | 0.1333 | 86.40% | 97.35% | 99.28% |
| | HoHoNet [31] | full-Sup. | 0.0496 | 0.0561 | 0.5400 | 0.1306 | 94.19% | 98.05% | 98.82% |
| | OmniFusion [35] | full-Sup. | 0.0721 | 0.0248 | 0.2854 | 0.1059 | 96.38% | 99.37% | 99.82% |
| | UniFuse [19] | full-Sup. | 0.0185 | 0.0086 | 0.1640 | 0.0510 | 97.88% | 98.98% | 99.24% |
| | P$^2$Net [11] | self-Sup. | 0.2071 | 0.2615 | 1.0052 | 0.3445 | 46.85% | 73.83% | 87.42% |
| | Structdepth [9] | self-Sup. | 0.2014 | 0.2462 | 0.8674 | 0.3296 | 49.63% | 76.01% | 88.68% |
| | Zioulis et al.'s method [4] | self-Sup. | 0.1309 | 0.1236 | 0.6943 | 0.2099 | 68.86% | 91.06% | 96.70% |
| | **Ours** | self-Sup. | **0.1211** | **0.0930** | **0.5090** | **0.1917** | **70.28%** | **93.14%** | **97.84%** |

360° **Planar Region Detection.** To detect the 360° planar regions, each pixel is first back-projected into 3D space with predicted depth. Geometry and color information are then fused to calculate the dissimilarity map as previous work [9]. The 360° planar regions are estimated from the obtained dissimilarity map by using the Felzenszwalb superpixel segmentation algorithm [10] and only keeping the planar regions larger than 200 pixels.

**Planar Consistency Loss.** After detecting the 360° planar regions, each plane in 3D is defined as [11]:

$$\mathbf{X}_i \mathbf{A}_i = \mathbf{Y}, \tag{11}$$

where $\mathbf{X}_i \in \mathbb{R}^{N_i \times 3}$ denotes the 3D points in the $i$-th planar region, $\mathbf{A}_i \in \mathbb{R}^{3 \times 1}$ means the planar parameters of each planar region, and $\mathbf{Y} = [1, 1, \cdots, 1]^\top$ is a column vector with $N$ dimension. The plane parameters $\mathbf{A}_i$ can be computed by solving the least squares problems, which is defined as

$$\mathbf{A}_i = (\mathbf{X}^\top \mathbf{X} + \epsilon \mathbf{E})^{-1} \mathbf{X})^\top \mathbf{Y}), \tag{12}$$

where $\epsilon \mathbf{E}$ is a scaled identity matrix for numerical stability. Afterwards, the planar depth $\hat{D}_\mathbf{p}$ can be calculated by its corresponding plane parameters $\mathbf{A}_i$ as:

$$\hat{D}_\mathbf{p} = 1/(\mathbf{A}_i^\top \mathbf{K}^{-1} \mathbf{p}). \tag{13}$$

Ultimately, the planar consistency loss is employed to calculate the difference between the predicted depth and the plane depth,

$$\mathcal{L}_{plane} = \frac{1}{N_{plane}} \sum_i \sum_{\mathbf{p} \in \mathbf{X}_i} |D_\mathbf{p} - \hat{D}_\mathbf{p}|, \tag{14}$$

where $N_{plane}$ is the total number of pixels belong to the planar regions.

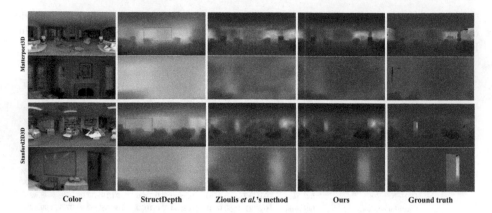

     Color         StructDepth     Zioulis *et al.*'s method     Ours        Ground truth

**Fig. 2.** Visual comparisons of our proposed method with two state-of-the-art depth estimation methods on the Matterport3D [17] and Stanford2D3D [18] datasets.

### 3.5 Overall Loss Function

The overall loss function is defined as

$$\mathcal{L}_{total} = \lambda_1 \mathcal{L}_{recon} + \lambda_2 \mathcal{L}_s + \lambda_3 \mathcal{L}_{vp} + \lambda_4 \mathcal{L}_{plane}, \tag{15}$$

where $\lambda_1$, $\lambda_2$, $\lambda_3$ and $\lambda_4$ are set to 0.95, 0.05, 0.05, 0.1, respectively.

## 4 Experiments

### 4.1 Datasets and Metrics

In the experiment, two indoor stereo 360° datasets named Matterport3D [17] and Stanford2D3D [18] within 3D60 [4] dataset are employed to optimize the model performance. 3D60 [4] dataset consists of 24934 panoramas rendered from large-scale realistic and synthetic 3D datasets (Matterport3D [17], Stanford2D3D [18] and SunCG [16]), in which horizontal and vertical stereo pairs, pixel-wise depth and normal ground truths are provided as well.

We follow the split of Matterport3D [17] dataset provided in [4], which contains 5811 vertical stereo images for training, 829 for validating and 1484 for testing. The split of Standford2D3D [18] dataset provided in [4] is also used in our experiment, which consists of 858 vertical stereo images for training, 77 for validating and 346 for testing. In addition, seven popular evaluation metrics are used to estimate the advantage of our proposed model, including absolute relative error (Abs Rel), squared relative error (Sq Rel), Root Mean Square Error (RMSE), Root Mean Squared Logarithmic Error (RMSLE) and the ratio $\delta$ between the estimated depth and ground truth depth is under threshold $(\delta_i < 1.25^i, i = 1, 2, 3)$ as [4].

## 4.2 Implementation Details

Our network is implemented in PyTorch [13] and the Xavier initialization [14] is used to initialize the model weights. We train the model on an Nvidia RTX 2080Ti GPU for 30 epochs by using a batch size of 16 and a fixed learning rate of $10^{-4}$. AdaBound [15] optimizer with a convergence speed of $2 \times 10^{-3}$ and a final target SGD learning rate of $10^{-3}$ are adopted in our experiment.

## 4.3 Overall Performance

To illustrate the advantage of our proposed method, a comprehensive comparison is provided between the proposed method and state-of-the-art self-supervised and fully-supervised methods on both Matterport3D [17] and Stanford2D3D [18] datasets.

**Results on Matterport3D Dataset.** The quantitative results of 360° depth estimation on Matterport3D dataset are reported in Table 1. The results show that our approach outperforms the state-of-the-art self-supervised methods. To be specific, our method outperforms Zioulis *et al.*'s method [4] by reducing Sq Rel from 0.1366 to 0.0894, RMSE from 0.7756 to 0.5062 and improving the accuracy metric of $\delta_1$ by 8.21%. We also provide the qualitative comparison of our method with these benchmark methods in Fig. 2. It is observed that the results of depth estimation by ours are closer to the ground truths than StructDepth [9] and Zioulis *et al.*'s method [4], especially in planar regions, such as floors, walls and ceilings. The results of StructDepth are obtained from their official training weights with our unified evaluation function as it fails to detect valid 360° vanishing points for training. From Fig. 2, we can see that ours achieves better results than StructDepth. It may be caused by the fact that StructDepth ignores panorama distortions and trains on perspective images with limited FoV. Furthermore, the results of Zioulis *et al.*'s method [4] are obtained by training their model using the same training set as ours. As shown in Fig. 2, we can observe that the results of Zioulis *et al.*'s method are still inferior to Ours. This may be due to their failure to address the problem of back-propagation of texture-less regions in self-supervised depth estimation. These illustrate that our proposed method can generate more accurate 360° depth information than existing methods.

**Results on Stanford2D3D Dataset.** We provide the comparison results of our method and the involved benchmark methods in Table 1. As shown in Table 1, our approach still outperforms all state-of-the-art methods. Concretely, the performance of our method is better than Zioulis *et al.*'s method [4] by reducing Sq Rel from 0.1236 to 0.0930 and RMSE from 0.6943 to 0.5090. We also report the visual comparisons in Fig. 2. From the results shown in Fig. 2, we can see that our method can estimate more details and smooth planar regions. It further demonstrates that our proposed two structure regularities are quite significant for predicting 360° depth information and can facilitate the model performance.

**Table 2.** The comparison results of methods involved in ablation studies on the Matterport3D [17] dataset.

| Method | Abs Rel↓ | Sq Rel↓ | RMSE↓ | RMSLE↓ | $\delta_1$ ↑ | $\delta_2$ ↑ | $\delta_3$ ↑ |
|---|---|---|---|---|---|---|---|
| $\mathcal{L}_{recon} + \mathcal{L}_s$ | 0.1295 | 0.1189 | 0.6457 | 0.2109 | 65.93% | 91.41% | 97.38% |
| $\mathcal{L}_{recon} + \mathcal{L}_s + \mathcal{L}_{plane}$ | 0.1219 | 0.1077 | 0.6631 | 0.2030 | 67.27% | 92.39% | 97.73% |
| $\mathcal{L}_{recon} + \mathcal{L}_s + \mathcal{L}_{vp}$ | 0.1214 | 0.1087 | 0.6216 | 0.2000 | 68.65% | 92.82% | 97.81% |
| $\mathcal{L}_{recon} + \mathcal{L}_s + \mathcal{L}_{vp} + \mathcal{L}_{plane}$ | **0.1178** | **0.0894** | **0.5062** | **0.1928** | **69.43%** | **93.31%** | **98.11%** |

**StructDepth**                                    **Ours**

**Fig. 3.** Example of 360° vanishing point detection over Matterport3D [17] dataset.

### 4.4 Ablation Study

Several ablation studies on Matterport3D dataset are performed to better illustrate the effectiveness of each component in our proposed full-version method. The comparison results are reported in Table 2. From this table, it can be clearly seen that both dominant direction normal loss and plane consistency loss are capable of facilitating the performance of the 360° depth estimation. Moreover, we compare the capability of StructDepth [9] and ours to detect 360° vanishing points. As shown in Fig. 3, StructDepth fails to detect valid vanishing points that only detect straight lines since straight lines in the real world are projected as curves in the panorama. The results shown in Fig. 3 illustrate that our proposed method can solve this problem well and accurately estimate 360° vanishing points.

## 5   Conclusion

In this work, we propose to apply indoor structural regularities for self-supervised 360° depth estimation, which embeds dominant direction normal constraint and planar consistency depth constraint to estimate 360° depth information. The qualitative and quantitative experimental results demonstrate that our proposed method achieves better performance than the existing state-of-the-art methods.

# References

1. Zioulis, N., Karakottas, A., Zarpalas, D., Daras, P.: OmniDepth: dense depth estimation for indoors spherical panoramas. In: Ferrari, V., Hebert, M., Sminchisescu, C., Weiss, Y. (eds.) ECCV 2018. LNCS, vol. 11210, pp. 453–471. Springer, Cham (2018). https://doi.org/10.1007/978-3-030-01231-1_28
2. Wang, F.-E., Yeh, Y.-H., Sun, M., Chiu, W.-C., Tsai, Y.-H.: Bifuse: monocular 360 depth estimation via bi-projection fusion. In: Proceedings CVPR, pp. 462–471 (2020)
3. Wang, F.-E., et al.: Self-supervised learning of depth and camera motion from 360° videos. In: Jawahar, C.V., Li, H., Mori, G., Schindler, K. (eds.) ACCV 2018. LNCS, vol. 11365, pp. 53–68. Springer, Cham (2019). https://doi.org/10.1007/978-3-030-20873-8_4
4. Zioulis, N., Karakottas, A., Zarpalas, D., Alvarez, F., Daras, P.: Spherical view synthesis for self-supervised 360 depth estimation. In: Proceedings 3DV, pp. 690–699. IEEE (2019)
5. Lai, Z., Chen, D., Su, K.: Olanet: self-supervised 360° depth estimation with effective distortion-aware view synthesis and l1 smooth regularization. In: Proceedings ICME, pp. 1–6. IEEE (2021)
6. Zhang, Y., Song, S., Tan, P., Xiao, J.: PanoContext: a whole-room 3D context model for panoramic scene understanding. In: Fleet, D., Pajdla, T., Schiele, B., Tuytelaars, T. (eds.) ECCV 2014. LNCS, vol. 8694, pp. 668–686. Springer, Cham (2014). https://doi.org/10.1007/978-3-319-10599-4_43
7. Fernandez-Labrador, C., Perez-Yus, A., Lopez-Nicolas, G., Guerrero, J.J.: Layouts from panoramic images with geometry and deep learning. IEEE Robot. Autom. Lett. 3(4), 3153–3160 (2018)
8. Yang, Z., Wang, P., Wang, Y., Xu, W., Nevatia, R.: Lego: learning edge with geometry all at once by watching videos. In: Proceedings CVPR, pp. 225–234 (2018)
9. Li, B., Huang, Y., Liu, Z., Zou, D., Yu, W.: StructDepth: Leveraging the structural regularities for self-supervised indoor depth estimation. In: Proceedings CVPR, pp. 663–673 (2021)
10. Felzenszwalb, P.F., Huttenlocher, D.P.: Efficient graph-based image segmentation. Int. J. Comput. Vis. 59(2), 167–181 (2004)
11. Yu, Z., Jin, L., Gao, S.: $P^2$Net: patch-match and plane-regularization for unsupervised indoor depth estimation. In: Vedaldi, A., Bischof, H., Brox, T., Frahm, J.-M. (eds.) ECCV 2020. LNCS, vol. 12369, pp. 206–222. Springer, Cham (2020). https://doi.org/10.1007/978-3-030-58586-0_13
12. Godard, C., Mac Aodha, O., Brostow, G.J.: Unsupervised monocular depth estimation with left-right consistency, In: Proceedings CVPR, pp. 270–279 (2017)
13. Paszke, A., et al.: Automatic differentiation in pytorch (2017)
14. Glorot, X., Bengio, Y.: Understanding the difficulty of training deep feedforward neural networks. In: Proceedings AISTATS, pp. 249–256. JMLR (2010)
15. Zhang, Y., et al.: ActiveStereoNet: end-to-end self-supervised learning for active stereo systems. In: Ferrari, V., Hebert, M., Sminchisescu, C., Weiss, Y. (eds.) ECCV 2018. LNCS, vol. 11212, pp. 802–819. Springer, Cham (2018). https://doi.org/10.1007/978-3-030-01237-3_48
16. Song, S., Yu, F., Zeng, A., Chang, A.X., Savva, M., Funkhouser, T.: Semantic scene completion from a single depth image. In: Proceedings CVPR, pp. 1746–1754 (2017)

17. Chang, A., et al.: Matterport3D: Learning from RGB-D data in indoor environments. In: Proceedings 3DV (2017)
18. Armeni, I., Sax, S., Zamir, A.R., Savarese, S.: Joint 2D–3D-semantic data for indoor scene understanding. arXiv preprint arXiv:1702.01105 (2017)
19. Jiang, H., Sheng, Z., Zhu, S., Dong, Z., Huang, R.: Unifuse: Unidirectional fusion for 360 panorama depth estimation. IEEE Robot. Autom. Lett. **6**(2), 1519–1526 (2021)
20. Cheng, H.-T., Chao, C.-H., Dong, J.-D., Wen, H.-K., Liu, T.-L., Sun, M.: Cube padding for weakly-supervised saliency prediction in 360 videos. In: Proceedings CVPR, pp. 1420–1429 (2018)
21. Su, Y.-C., Grauman, K.: Learning spherical convolution for fast features from 360 imagery. Adv. NIPS **30**, 529–539 (2017)
22. Tateno, K., Navab, N., Tombari, F.: Distortion-aware convolutional filters for dense prediction in panoramic images. In: Ferrari, V., Hebert, M., Sminchisescu, C., Weiss, Y. (eds.) ECCV 2018. LNCS, vol. 11220, pp. 732–750. Springer, Cham (2018). https://doi.org/10.1007/978-3-030-01270-0_43
23. Yang, S., Song, Y., Kaess, M., Scherer, S.: Pop-up slam: Semantic monocular plane slam for low-texture environments. In: Proceedings IROS, pp. 1222–1229. IEEE (2016)
24. Wang, R., Geraghty, D., Matzen, K., Szeliski, R., Frahm, J.-M.: VPLNet: deep single view normal estimation with vanishing points and lines. In: Proceedings CVPR, pp. 689–698 (2020)
25. Lu, X., Yaoy, J., Li, H., Liu, Y., Zhang, X.: 2-line exhaustive searching for real-time vanishing point estimation in manhattan world. In: Proceedings WACV, pp. 345–353. IEEE (2017)
26. Yu, Z., Zheng, J., Lian, D., Zhou, Z., Gao, S.: Single-image piece-wise planar 3D reconstruction via associative embedding. In: Proceedings CVPR, pp. 1029–1037 (2019)
27. Shah, A., Kadam, E., Shah, H., Shinde, S., Shingade, S.: Deep residual networks with exponential linear unit. In: Proceedings of the Third International Symposium on Computer Vision and the Internet, pp. 59–65 (2016)
28. Liu, R., et al.: An intriguing failing of convolutional neural networks and the coord-conv solution. In: Advances in Neural Information Processing Systems, vol. 31 (2018)
29. Monroy, R., Lutz, S., Chalasani, T., Smolic, A.: Salnet360: saliency maps for omnidirectional images with CNN. Sig. Process. Image Commun. **69**, 26–34 (2018)
30. Khasanova, R., Frossard, P.: Graph-based classification of omnidirectional images. In: Proceedings of the IEEE International Conference on Computer Vision Workshops, pp. 869–878 (2017)
31. Sun, C., Sun, M., Chen, H.-T.: HoHoNet: 360 indoor holistic understanding with latent horizontal features. In: Proceedings of the IEEE/CVF Conference on Computer Vision and Pattern Recognition, pp. 2573–2582 (2021)
32. Coughlan, J.M., Yuille, A.L.: Manhattan world: compass direction from a single image by bayesian inference. In: Proceedings of the seventh IEEE international conference on computer vision, vol. 2, pp. 941–947. IEEE (1999)
33. Zou, D., Wu, Y., Pei, L., Ling, H., Yu, W.: Structvio: visual-inertial odometry with structural regularity of man-made environments. IEEE Trans. Rob. **35**(4), 999–1013 (2019)

34. Tulsiani, S., Tucker, R., Snavely, N.: Layer-structured 3D scene inference via view synthesis. In: Ferrari, V., Hebert, M., Sminchisescu, C., Weiss, Y. (eds.) ECCV 2018. LNCS, vol. 11211, pp. 311–327. Springer, Cham (2018). https://doi.org/10.1007/978-3-030-01234-2_19
35. Li, Y., Guo, Y., Yan, Z., Huang, X., Duan, Y., Ren, L.: Omnifusion: 360 monocular depth estimation via geometry-aware fusion. In: Proceedings of the IEEE/CVF Conference on Computer Vision and Pattern Recognition, pp. 2801–2810 (2022)
36. Bai, J., Lai, S., Qin, H., Guo, J., Guo, Y.: GlpanoDepth: global-to-local panoramic depth estimation. arXiv preprint arXiv:2202.02796 (2022)
37. Area, M.R., Yuan, M., Richardt, C.: 360monodepth: high-resolution 360° monocular depth estimation. In: Conference on Computer Vision and Pattern Recognition (CVPR) (2022)

# Global Boundary Refinement for Semantic Segmentation via Optimal Transport

Feng Dai[1], Shuaibin Zhang[1], Hao Liu[2], Yike Ma[1], and Qiang Zhao[1]([✉])

[1] Institute of Computing Technology, Chinese Academy of Sciences, Beijing, China
{fdai,zhangshuaibin19s,ykma,zhaoqiang}@ict.ac.cn
[2] Artificial Intelligence on Electric Power System State Grid Corporation Joint Laboratory(State Grid Smart Grid Research Institute Co., Ltd.,), Beijing, China
liuhao2018@ict.ac.cn

**Abstract.** Semantic boundary prediction is an important but challenging problem in semantic segmentation. Previous methods usually regard the boundary prediction as a pure classification problem using binary cross-entropy loss, which does not consider the spatial distance between the predicted boundary and ground truth. To address this issue, we formulate semantic boundary prediction as the optimal transport problem where the minimum transport cost reflects the spatial distance. Specifically, the predicted boundary and the true boundary are formulated as source distribution and target distribution, respectively. Then, we calculate the spatial distance between source pixels and target pixels as the transport cost matrix. Finally, we solve the transport problem and obtain the minimum transport cost for effective boundary supervision. Additionally, our method does not explicitly fuse boundary and semantic feature, which only provides supervision for the predicted boundary during the training. And the boundary branch can be discarded during the inference, thus will not bring extra computations and parameters. Experiments show that our method can significantly and consistently improve the segmentation accuracy of various models on public segmentation benchmarks: Cityscapes and CamVid.

**Keywords:** Semantic segmentation · Optimal transport · Boundary refinement

## 1 Introduction

Semantic segmentation is a fundamental but challenging task in computer vision, which aims to assign every pixel with the category and plays an important role in autonomous driving, medical diagnosis, robotics, and other fields. Since the proposal of fully convolutional networks (FCNs) [21], various methods based on deep learning have become the mainstream of semantic segmentation. Existing researches mainly focus on contextual information [3,10,27,31,33] and high-resolution feature representation [16–18,23,26], which achieved significant improvements on semantic segmentation.

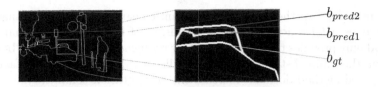

**Fig. 1.** The example demonstrates the problem of BCE supervision. $b_{gt}$, $b_{pred1}$ and $b_{pred2}$ represent the ground truth, the two predicted boundaries, respectively. $b_{pred1}$ is obviously superior to $b_{pred2}$, since $b_{pred1}$ is closer to ground truth in spatial domain. While BCE can not well distinguish the two boundary maps, since it calculates the pixel-by-pixel classification loss.

Recently, more and more researches focus on improving the accuracy of semantic boundary [8,15,24,30] [9], since inaccurate semantic segmentation is more likely to appear near the boundary and the thinner object can be significantly improved through the exact boundary. For example, Gated-SCNN [24] proposes a two-stream CNN architecture for semantic segmentation, then exploits Cross-Entropy(CE) with the dual-task regularizer term to supervise the predicted boundary. Additionally, DecoupleSegNet [15] proposes to decouple feature to body and edge, then utilizes Cross-Entropy and Binary Cross-Entropy(BCE) to supervise results of semantic segmentation and boundary. The BCE supervision regards boundary prediction as a pure pixel classification problem, which accumulates errors by pixel-by-pixel binary classification mode. Whereas, the criterion does not consider the spatial distance between misclassification pixels and the ground truth, which is another effective supervision for boundary prediction. As shown in Fig. 1, the first predicted boundary is obviously superior to the second one, since it's closer to ground truth in spatial domain. However, the criterion based on BCE can't distinguish them clearly, which calculates the pixel-by-pixel classification error, and thus leads to a sub-optimal solution.

To tackle the dilemma, we formulate semantic boundary prediction as the optimal transport problem and calculate the minimum transport cost to represent the spatial distance of two boundaries. And a novel boundary loss function is proposed based on optimal transport for effective boundary supervision. Specifically, the boundary extracted from the semantic label is formulated as the target distribution and the boundary predicted from the network is normalized to obtain the source distribution. Then we calculate the Euclidean distance between the source pixels and target ones as the transport cost. Finally, we solve the problem through Sinkhorn-Knopp methods [22] and conduct gradient back-propagation to supervise the predicted boundary.

By introducing boundary-distance criterion to pixel-by-pixel classification loss, the proposed method predicts the boundary region, and calculates the minimum transport cost to move the inaccurate boundary pixels to the target ones, which represents the distance between the predicted and target boundary. The proposed method can be used as a plug-in loss on any network structure and consistently improve the accuracy of semantic segmentation. Additionally, our method does not explicitly conduct the fusion of boundary and semantic feature, and only provides the global boundary refinement supervision for boundary branch in the training stage, which can be discarded in the inference stage. Thus the proposed method does not increase the computation complexity.

Our contribution can be summarized in three-fold:

- We are the first to introduce optimal transport theory to measure the spatial distance between the predicted boundary and ground truth, which can accurately predict the semantic boundary and then improve the performance of semantic segmentation.
- Our proposed method is agnostic to network structure with parameter-free and can be flexibly plugged in any network to improve semantic accuracy. Additionally, it is only utilized for supervision in the train stage, thus not increasing the inference computation and speed.
- The effectiveness of our method is validated in various models on Cityscapes and Camvid dataset.

## 2   Related Work

**Semantic Segmentation:** Deep learning methods have been the domain solution to semantic segmentation since the propose of full convolutional networks [21]. The subsequence approaches, e.g. [4,10,23] have achieved significant improvements in semantic accuracy.

The first key element to semantic segmentation is to enlarge receptive field and capture effective contextual information. To exploit multi-scale feature, PSP-Net [31] proposes the spatial pyramid pooling module in the final layer of network, which performs a sequence of pooling at several grid scales. Deeplab [3,4] methods employ multi-parallel atrous convolutions with different levels of dilation, thus creating a dense feature map compared to PSPNet. Additionally, several methods conduct feature augmentation by exploiting relational contextual feature, which aggregates the feature representations of the pixels with high similarity, DANet [10] exploit position attention to enhance the pixel feature, and OCRNet [29] considers the relation between pixel feature and category feature. APCNet [12] proposes to fuse the multi-scale and adaptive context by combining pyramid pooling and pixel similarity. Additionally, encoder-decoder network structure is widely used in semantic segmentation to increase the resolution of feature map and predictions [4,21]. And HRNet [23] proposes a parallel network structure and maintains high-resolution representations in the whole forward stage, since partial information may be lost during the down-sampling of the network.

**Boundary Segmentation.** Recently, there exist more researches focusing on improving the accuracy of boundary, since the semantic boundary region can not be accurately and exactly predicted. To tackle the dilemma, Gated-SCNN [24] proposes a two-stream architecture that the main stream is for semantic prediction using cross-entropy loss and the shape stream is designed for boundary prediction using binary cross-entropy with dual-task regularizer, respectively. The method fuses the information from the two branches to boost the performance on the thinner and smaller object. Additionally, DecoupleSegNet [15] proposes that image feature can be decomposed into boundary feature and body feature to be supervised separately. But both methods regard semantic boundary segmentation as a pure classification problem using a pixel-by-pixel loss, which ignores the spatial position of predicted result. As we show in Fig. 1, the binary cross-entropy can not distinguish the spatial distance between the different predicted results and truth boundary. The related experiment shows these methods can benefit from our proposed loss. Segfix [30] proposes a common post-processing network for boundary refinement, which considers the spatial distance. The method proposes to replace the boundary predicted result with the interior pixel. Specifically, the method firstly locates the boundary position and then learns the pixel-to-pixel offset toward the inner region. Different from the method, we utilize the optimal transport method to move the predicted boundary to target boundary and calculate the loss based on the spatial distance. Besides, the above methods conduct the fusion between edge feature and body feature or propose an edge post-processing module, which leads to more parameters and extra computations burden. Whereas, our proposed edge supervised loss can significantly and consistently improve the semantic accuracy without decreasing the speed in the inference stage.

**Optimal Transport Problem.** Optimal transport(OT) provides a framework to calculate cost for transporting one distribution to another and is widely used in machine learning. Nowadays, the method has attracted extensive attention in many computer vision tasks. Reference [25] formulates crowd counting as a distribution matching problem and utilizes optimal transport method to calculate the transportation cost. Reference [20] proposes to establish dense semantic correspondences through the optimal transport plan. And [11] considers a label assignment as an optimal transport problem and find the best optimal transport plan. Other applications include domain adaptation [6], generative model [2], and etc. According to our research, we are the first to introduce optimal transport to measure the distance in boundary segmentation.

## 3 Methods

In this section, we firstly review the preliminary knowledge of optimal transport theory and then describe how we formulate semantic boundary refinement as the optimal transport problem. At last, we introduce the framework of our method and the whole optimization function.

### 3.1 Optimal Transport

Optimal transport demonstrates the following problem: Let $\mu$ and $\nu$ be the source distribution and the target distribution, which are defined on spaces $X$ and $Y$, respectively. We assume $C : X \times Y \rightarrow [0, +\infty]$ are the cost matrix, where $c(x, y)$ represents the cost to transport one unit of mass from $x \in X$ to $y \in Y$. The goal of optimal transport is to find a optimal transport plan $\pi \in \mathcal{P}(X \times Y)$ to transport the source distribution to target distribution. The problem is formulated as follows:

$$M(\mu, \nu) = \min_{\pi \in U(\mu, \nu)} \langle \pi, C \rangle$$

where $U(\mu, \nu)$ stands for all the possible transport solution.

The dual formulation of optimal transport problem [25] is defined:

$$M(\mu, \nu) = \min_{\alpha, \beta \in \mathbb{R}^n} \langle \alpha, \mu \rangle + \langle \beta, \nu \rangle \tag{1}$$

Considering the discrete distributions situation, $\mu$ and $\nu$ can be written

$$\mu = \sum_{i=1}^{n_s} p_i \delta(x_i)$$

$$\nu = \sum_{i=1}^{n_t} q_i \delta(x_i) \tag{2}$$

where $\delta()$ representations the Dirac function, $n_s, n_t$ denotes the number of samples for source distribution and target distribution. $p_i$ and $q_i$ are the probability that the sample $i$ belongs to the two distributions. And the constraints situation can be written as follows:

$$\sum_{i=1}^{n_s} p_i^s = \sum_{i=1}^{n_t} q_i^t = 1$$

$$\pi 1_{n_t} = \mu$$

$$\pi^T 1_{n_s} = \nu$$

$$\pi_{ij} \geq 0$$

From the above formulation, optimal transport is actually a linear program that can be solved in polynomial time.

To supervise the predicted boundary via optimal transport, there exist three key issues to be solved. Firstly, How to formulate the predicted and target boundary as the distribution. Then how to calculate the transport cost matrix to represent the spatial distance between the predicted and target boundary. And finally how to solve the optimal transport problem and conduct gradient back-propagation.

Since the origin dataset only contains semantic label, we first need to extract boundary from ground truth. For every class, we calculate the distance map from other classes to this class, where the distance less than 2 pixels is defined as semantic boundary. Then, we formulate the extracted boundary as the target distribution through

$$\hat{b}_{target}(i, j) = \frac{b_{target}(i, j)}{\sum_{i,j} b_{target}(i, j)} \tag{3}$$

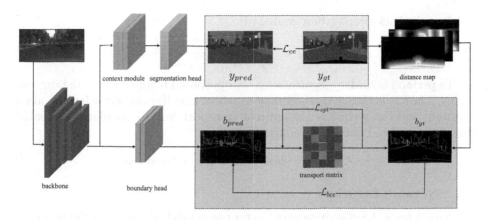

**Fig. 2.** The whole network of the proposed method. The image is input to the pre-trained backbone to extract feature, then passed into two branches. The above branch is utilized for semantic segmentation, which is consisted of object contextual module(e.g. ASPP [4], OCR [29]) and segmentation head. And the below is adopted for boundary segmentation. The supervision contains three parts, CE for semantic segmentation, BCE for boundary location and optimal transport loss for boundary refinement.

For the predicted boundaries $b_{pred} \in \mathbb{R}^{h_s \times w_s}$ from network, $b_{pred}(i,j) \in (0,1)$ represents the probability that every pixel $i,j$ belongs to the boundary. Then, the predicted boundary map is normalized to obtain the source distribution, thus

$$\hat{b}_{predict}(i,j) = \frac{b_{predict}(i,j)}{\sum_{i,j} b_{predict}(i,j)} \tag{4}$$

To measure the spatial distance between the two boundary maps, we calculate the Euclidean distance between the source pixels $p_s$ and the target pixels $p_t$ as the cost to move $p_s$ to $p_t$, and thus $C_{st} = (p_s - p_t)^2$. Since the cost matrix $C$ is calculated by the spatial distance, the total transport cost can evaluate the relative position between predicted boundary and ground truth, thus provide effective supervision for the predicted boundary.

Based on the aforementioned method, we formulate the boundary segmentation as the optimal transport problem, which can be solved by the solution to linear programming. Whereas solving the linear programming requires an extremely high complexity of $O(n^3)$. We introduce the entropy-regularized term in optimal transport to speed up the solution and solve the problem by Sinkhorn-Knopp method [7]. Finally, the object function of optimal transport problem is:

$$M(\mu, \nu) = \min_{\pi \in U(\mu,\nu)} \langle \pi, C \rangle - \frac{1}{w} h(\pi)$$

Based on the optimal transport solution, the boundary optimal transport loss is defined as follow:

$$\mathcal{L}_{opt} = \left\langle \alpha^*, \frac{b_{gt}}{\|b_{gt}\|_1} \right\rangle + \left\langle \beta^*, \frac{b_{pred}}{\|b_{pred}\|_1} \right\rangle \tag{5}$$

And the back-propagation gradient is

$$\nabla \mathcal{L}_{opt} = \frac{\beta^*}{\|b_{pred}\|_1} - \frac{\langle \beta^*, b_{pred} \rangle}{\|b_{pred}\|_1^2} \tag{6}$$

To perform boundary segmentation, our proposed boundary loss contains two terms. The one is binary cross-entropy to reflect classification error for boundary location, and the second is the optimal transport loss to calculate the spatial distance for global boundary refinement.

$$\mathcal{L}_b = \lambda_1 \mathcal{L}_{BCE}(b_{pred}, b_{gt}) + \lambda_2 \mathcal{L}_{opt}(b_{pred}, b_{gt}) \tag{7}$$

## 3.2   Network Structure

To demonstrate the effectiveness of the proposed method, we insert the proposed method in multiple public network architectures of semantic segmentation. The whole network is shown in Fig. 2. The semantic network structures generally consist of backbone(e.g. ResNet [13], HRNet [23]), context module(e.g. ASPP [3], OCR [29]) and segmentation head. Additionally, we add a new branch behind the backbone for boundary prediction. The branch is stacked by the convolution layer, BatchNorm layer, and activation function, and the last layer of boundary branch is sigmoid function to normalize the output to $(0, 1)$ range, representing the probability of pixels belonging to boundary. Then we formulate the predicted map and ground truth as the source distribution and target distribution. Besides, we construct the cost matrix by calculating the Euclidean distance from source pixels to target pixels. Finally, we solve the optimal transport problem by Sinkhorn-Knopp method and obtain the optimal transport matrix. And the minimum transport cost can be utilized to evaluate spatial distance between the predicted boundary and target ones. The proposed method obtains more accurate boundary region and semantic segmentation results can benefit from the exact boundary prediction.

Especially, we do not explicitly fuse the boundary feature and semantic feature, which only introduces the boundary branch with the proposed loss in the training stage. In this way, our method brings no extra computation burden, since the boundary branch is discarded in the inference stage.

## 3.3   Optimization

The whole objective function for the proposed method contains two part: a multi-class CE for semantic segmentation and a novel boundary loss for boundary prediction, where BCE reflects the boundary location loss and optimal transport loss reflects boundary refinement loss. The overall loss is:

$$\mathcal{L} = \mathcal{L}_{ce}(y_{pred}, y_{gt}) + \lambda_1 \mathcal{L}_{BCE}(b_{pred}, b_{gt}) + \lambda_2 \mathcal{L}_{opt}(b_{pred}, b_{gt}) \tag{8}$$

where $y_{pred}$, $y_{gt}$ is the semantic segmentation result and ground truth. $b_{pred}$, $b_{gt}$ represents the predicted boundary and target boundary, respectively. And $\lambda_1$ and $\lambda_2$ is utilized to control the balance of different loss. In our experiment, we set $\lambda_1 = 15, \lambda_2 = 0.1$ in Eq. 8.

# 4    Experiment

In this section, we firstly introduce some public dataset, evaluation metrics, and the implementation details, followed by ablation study to validate the effectiveness of the proposed method. At the end, we report more results on two public segmentation benchmarks: Cityscapes [5], and CamVid.

## 4.1    Experiment Setup

**Dataset.** We conduct the experiment on Cityscape and Camvid dataset.

**Cityscapes.** is collected to capture the complexity of real-world urban scenes, which contains 5000 finely annotated images and 20000 coarsely annotated labels from 50 cities. The finely annotated images are divided into 2,975 for training, 500 for validation, and 1,525 for testing. The collected images have a large resolution of 2048 × 1024, in which 30 categories are marked and only 19 of them are used for evaluation. We only utilize the finely annotated images for validating the effectiveness of our method. **Camvid** is another urban scene dataset for automatic driving. It is consisted of 367 training, 101 validation, 233 testing images, which have resolution of 960 × 720. The dataset contains 32 categories, which are grouped into 11 classes for evaluation.

**Evaluation.** We use two different metrics to validate the effectiveness of the proposed method. We firstly adopt the most widely used metrics of mean Intersection-over-Union (mIoU) to evaluate the performance of semantic segmentation. Additionally, the boundary F-score proposed in is utilized to measure the accuracy of semantic boundary, which calculates the F-score along the boundary of predicted mask with a small slack in distance. In our experiment, we set the thresholds to 0.00088, 0.0001875 and 0.00375. Corresponding to 3, 5, 9 pixel distance, respectively. Additionally, the model complexity is denoted by the number of parameters and the computations on a fixed input size.

**Implementation Details.** The proposed method is a plug-and-play module and can be inserted into any semantic segmentation structure. The same training policy is adopted for the baseline network and the proposed method. And the backbone is initialized by the pretrained model on ImageNet. We adopt mini-batch stochastic gradient descent (SGD) optimizer with momentum of 0.9 and weight decay of 0.005. The initialized learning rate is 0.01 and followed the polynomial decay. We utilize pytorch distribution framework to train the model with Synchronized BN on 4× NVIDIA 3090Ti, and the batch size is 4 in every GPU. Random scaling in the range of [0.5, 2], random flipping, random crop, and random brightness jittering are used as data augmentation.

**Table 1.** Comparison between the baseline model and the proposed method. The GFlops is calculated on the resolution $512 \times 1024$. The metric is evaluated on Cityscape Val split with ImageNet pretrained ResNet-50 backbone. $l_{ce}$ represents that the boundary branch is inserted into the baseline model with binary cross-entropy in the training stage. And $l_{opt}$ means the optimal transport criterion is introduced for boundary supervise.

| Method | $l_{bce}$ | $l_{opt}$ | mIoU(%) | Params | GFlops |
|--------|-----------|-----------|---------|--------|--------|
| DeeplabV3+ | | | 70.64 | 40.35 | 365.82 |
| | ✓ | | 71.49 | 40.35 | 365.82 |
| | ✓ | ✓ | **72.37** | 40.35 | 365.82 |

**Table 2.** The effect of our method for semantic boundary. The boundary F-score is calculated at different thresholds corresponding to different boundary distance.

| Method | th = 3px | th = 5px | th = 9px |
|--------|----------|----------|----------|
| DeeplabV3+ | 40.42 | 48.84 | 59.50 |
| DeeplabV3+ **w/bce** | 41.87 | 50.45 | 61.06 |
| DeeplabV3+ **w/ours** | **42.78** | **51.35** | **61.49** |

## 4.2 Ablation Study

We adopt DeeplabV3+ with backbone of resnet-50 as the baseline model to verify the effectiveness of the proposed method. The model is trained firstly using CE criterion with the auxiliary supervision, followed as [3]. Then, the boundary branch is inserted into the origin network structure with BCE criterion. Finally, we introduce the optimal transport loss to measure the spatial distance between the predicted boundary and the target for training.

We show the result of ablation study in Table 1. The 2nd row denotes the introduction of the boundary branch can improve the semantic segmentation accuracy. While the improvement is limited since BCE criterion is not exact and sufficient. And the proposed loss can refine the predicted boundary according to spatial distance and significantly improve semantic segmentation accuracy of 2.45%. More importantly, our method does not require extra parameters and computations, since the boundary branch is discarded in the inference stage.

Additionally, we demonstrate the effect of the proposed method in terms of F-score for boundary alignment in Table 2. Boundary F-scores are compared on three different thresholds. And the results show the proposed method can effectively refine the predicted boundary and improve the boundary accuracy.

Furthermore, we qualitatively compare the proposed method and the basline method on Cityscape dataset in Fig. 3. The results demonstrate our method can significantly correct the segmented errors, refine the boundary of semantic segmentation and improve the accuracy of the thinner objects.

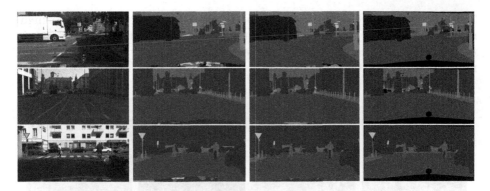

**Fig. 3.** Qualitative results on the Cityscape val set. From left to right, it represents the origin image, ground truth, the predicted results of baseline model, and the proposed method, respectively.

### 4.3   More Results on Camivd Dataset

To further verify the generalization of the proposed method, we insert the proposed method to OCRNet [29], which is the sota methods in semantic segmentation. Table 3 demonstrates DeeplabV3+ with backbone ResNet50 achieves 70.65% mIoU, and the proposed method can improve the accuracy of semantic segmentation by 2.52% without increasing the computations and inference time. OCRNet with the proposed method can achieve 75.24% mIoU, which is superior to other semantic segmentation methods.

**Table 3.** Experiments results on Camvid test split. All the results are test on single-scale input.

| Method | Pre-train | Backbone | mIoU |
|---|---|---|---|
| BiseNet [28] | ImageNet | ResNet50 | 69.1 |
| PSPNet [31] | ImageNet | ResNet50 | 69.1 |
| DenseDecoder [1] | ImageNet | ResNetXt101 | 70.9 |
| DeeplabV3+ [4] | ImageNet | ResNet50 | 70.65 |
| + our proposed loss | ImageNet | ResNet50 | **72.43** |
| OCR [29] | ImageNet | HRNet-W48 | 74.24 |
| + our proposed loss | ImageNet | HRNet-W48 | **75.27** |

### 4.4   More Results on Cityscape Dataset

Furthermore, we also compare our method with other soat methods on Cityscapes test split. Specifically, we insert the boundary branch into OCRNet structure [29] and utilize the proposed method for boundary supervision.

The HRNet-W48 is chosen as the backbone, since it has been proved that high-resolution feature representation is effective in semantic segmentation. We train the model on Cityscape train split and evaluate on the Cityscapes test utilizing multi-scale test with horizon flip.

**Fig. 4.** The results of the proposed method. Followed the order from left to right, it is the origin image, predicted semantic map, boundary map, and ground truth.

Table 4 denotes our methods can significantly improve the performance of OCRNet. Especially it does not increase the parameters and computations. Additionally, we denote the qualitative results on Cityscape in Fig. 4. It demonstrates our method can predict accurate results of boundary and semantic segmentation.

**Table 4.** Comparison of mIoU and per-class IoU with other state-of-the-art models on Cityscapes test set. All the methods are trained on the Cityscapes fine annotation and all the models utilize multi-scale inference to improve the accuracy.

| Model | mIoU | Road | Swalk | Build | Wall | Fence | Pole | tligh | tsign | Veg | terr | Sky | Pers | Rider | Car | Truck | Bus | Train | mcyc | bcyc |
|---|---|---|---|---|---|---|---|---|---|---|---|---|---|---|---|---|---|---|---|---|
| RefineNet [19] | 73.6 | 98.2 | 83.3 | 91.3 | 47.8 | 50.4 | 56.1 | 66.9 | 71.3 | 92.3 | 70.3 | 94.8 | 80.9 | 63.3 | 94.5 | 64.6 | 76.1 | 64.3 | 62.2 | 70.0 |
| PSPNet [31] | 78.4 | 98.6 | 86.2 | 92.9 | 50.8 | 58.8 | 64.0 | 75.6 | 79.0 | 93.4 | 72.3 | 95.4 | 86.5 | 71.3 | 95.9 | 68.2 | 79.5 | 73.8 | 69.5 | 77.2 |
| AAF [14] | 79.1 | 98.5 | 85.6 | 93.0 | 53.8 | 58.9 | 65.9 | 75.0 | 78.4 | 93.7 | 72.4 | 95.6 | 86.4 | 70.5 | 95.9 | 73.9 | 82.7 | 76.9 | 68.7 | 76.4 |
| PSANet [32] | 80.1 | – | – | – | – | – | – | – | – | – | – | – | – | – | – | – | – | – | – | – |
| DenseASPP [27] | 80.6 | **98.7** | 87.1 | 93.4 | **60.7** | 62.7 | 65.6 | 74.6 | 78.5 | 93.6 | 72.5 | 95.4 | 86.2 | 71.9 | 96.0 | **78.0** | **90.3** | 80.7 | 69.7 | 76.8 |
| BFP [8] | 81.4 | **98.7** | 87.0 | 93.5 | 59.8 | 63.4 | 68.9 | 76.8 | 80.9 | 93.7 | 72.8 | 95.5 | 87.0 | 72.1 | 96.0 | 77.6 | 89.0 | 86.9 | 69.2 | 77.6 |
| DANet [10] | **81.5** | 98.6 | 86.1 | 93.5 | 56.1 | 63.3 | 69.7 | 77.3 | 81.3 | 93.9 | **72.9** | 95.7 | 87.3 | 72.9 | 96.2 | 76.8 | 89.4 | **86.5** | **72.2** | 78.2 |
| OCR(our imp) [29] | 80.9 | **98.7** | **87.3** | 93.7 | 58.6 | 63.0 | 70.3 | 76.7 | 80.7 | 93.9 | 72.6 | 95.8 | 87.6 | 73.7 | 96.2 | 72.9 | 88.1 | 78.8 | 70.9 | 77.8 |
| OCR + the proposed method | **81.5** | **98.7** | 87.1 | **93.9** | 59.8 | **64.4** | **72.1** | **77.9** | **81.6** | **94.0** | 72.1 | **96.0** | 87.9 | 74.1 | **96.3** | 74.8 | 86.8 | 81.5 | 70.6 | **78.4** |

## 5   Conclusion

In this paper, we propose a novel boundary loss for semantic segmentation based on the optimal transport theory, which calculates the distance between the predicted boundary and the target boundary. The proposed loss can supervise the semantic boundary effectively, and the performance of semantic segmentation can benefit from the exact boundary. Additionally, the proposed method plays a plug-in module, and can be discarded in the inference stage. Thus our method does not increase extra computations and inference time.

**Acknowledgements.** This work is supported by National Natural Science Foundation of China (62072438, U1936110) and Hubei Science and Technology Plan Project (2020BAB099)

# References

1. Bilinski, P., Prisacariu, V.: Dense decoder shortcut connections for single-pass semantic segmentation. In: Proceedings of the IEEE Conference on Computer Vision and Pattern Recognition, pp. 6596–6605 (2018)
2. Bunne, C., Alvarez-Melis, D., Krause, A., Jegelka, S.: Learning generative models across incomparable spaces. In: International Conference on Machine Learning, pp. 851–861. PMLR (2019)
3. Chen, L.C., Papandreou, G., Schroff, F., Adam, H.: Rethinking atrous convolution for semantic image segmentation. arXiv preprint arXiv:1706.05587 (2017)
4. Chen, L.C., Zhu, Y., Papandreou, G., Schroff, F., Adam, H.: Encoder-decoder with atrous separable convolution for semantic image segmentation. In: Proceedings of the European conference on computer vision (ECCV), pp. 801–818 (2018)
5. Cordts, M., Omran, M., Ramos, S., Rehfeld, T., Enzweiler, M., Benenson, R., Franke, U., Roth, S., Schiele, B.: The cityscapes dataset for semantic urban scene understanding. In: Proceedings of the IEEE Conference on Computer Vision and Pattern Recognition, pp. 3213–3223 (2016)
6. Courty, N., Flamary, R., Tuia, D., Rakotomamonjy, A.: Optimal transport for domain adaptation. IEEE Trans. Pattern Anal. Mach. Intell. **39**(9), 1853–1865 (2016)
7. Cuturi, M.: Sinkhorn distances: Lightspeed computation of optimal transport. Advances in neural information processing systems 26 (2013)
8. Ding, H., Jiang, X., Liu, A.Q., Thalmann, N.M., Wang, G.: Boundary-aware feature propagation for scene segmentation. In: Proceedings of the IEEE/CVF International Conference on Computer Vision, pp. 6819–6829 (2019)
9. Ding, H., Jiang, X., Shuai, B., Liu, A.Q., Wang, G.: Semantic correlation promoted shape-variant context for segmentation. In: Proceedings of the IEEE/CVF Conference on Computer Vision and Pattern Recognition, pp. 8885–8894 (2019)
10. Fu, J., Liu, J., Tian, H., Li, Y., Bao, Y., Fang, Z., Lu, H.: Dual attention network for scene segmentation. In: Proceedings of the IEEE/CVF Conference on Computer Vision and Pattern Recognition, pp. 3146–3154 (2019)
11. Ge, Z., Liu, S., Li, Z., Yoshie, O., Sun, J.: Ota: optimal transport assignment for object detection. In: Proceedings of the IEEE/CVF Conference on Computer Vision and Pattern Recognition, pp. 303–312 (2021)
12. He, J., Deng, Z., Zhou, L., Wang, Y., Qiao, Y.: Adaptive pyramid context network for semantic segmentation. In: Proceedings of the IEEE/CVF Conference on Computer Vision and Pattern Recognition, pp. 7519–7528 (2019)
13. He, K., Zhang, X., Ren, S., Sun, J.: Deep residual learning for image recognition. In: Proceedings of the IEEE Conference on Computer Vision and Pattern Recognition, pp. 770–778 (2016)
14. Ke, T.W., Hwang, J.J., Liu, Z., Yu, S.X.: Adaptive affinity fields for semantic segmentation. In: Proceedings of the European Conference on Computer Vision (ECCV), pp. 587–602 (2018)
15. Li, X., Li, X., Zhang, L., Cheng, G., Shi, J., Lin, Z., Tan, S., Tong, Y.: Improving semantic segmentation via decoupled body and edge supervision. In: European Conference on Computer Vision, pp. 435–452. Springer (2020)

16. Li, X., You, A., Zhu, Z., Zhao, H., Yang, M., Yang, K., Tan, S., Tong, Y.: Semantic flow for fast and accurate scene parsing. In: European Conference on Computer Vision, pp. 775–793. Springer (2020)
17. Li, X., Zhao, H., Han, L., Tong, Y., Tan, S., Yang, K.: Gated fully fusion for semantic segmentation. In: Proceedings of the AAAI Conference on Artificial Intelligence, vol. 34, pp. 11418–11425 (2020)
18. Lin, G., Milan, A., Shen, C., Reid, I.: Refinenet: Multi-path refinement networks for high-resolution semantic segmentation. In: Proceedings of the IEEE Conference on Computer Vision and Pattern Recognition, pp. 1925–1934 (2017)
19. Lin, G., Milan, A., Shen, C., Reid, I.: Refinenet: multi-path refinement networks for high-resolution semantic segmentation. In: The IEEE Conference on Computer Vision and Pattern Recognition (CVPR) (2017)
20. Liu, Y., Zhu, L., Yamada, M., Yang, Y.: Semantic correspondence as an optimal transport problem. In: Proceedings of the IEEE/CVF Conference on Computer Vision and Pattern Recognition, pp. 4463–4472 (2020)
21. Long, J., Shelhamer, E., Darrell, T.: Fully convolutional networks for semantic segmentation. In: Proceedings of the IEEE Conference on Computer Vision and Pattern Recognition, pp. 3431–3440 (2015)
22. Sinkhorn, R.: Diagonal equivalence to matrices with prescribed row and column sums. Am. Math. Mon. **74**(4), 402–405 (1967)
23. Sun, K., Zhao, Y., Jiang, B., Cheng, T., Xiao, B., Liu, D., Mu, Y., Wang, X., Liu, W., Wang, J.: High-resolution representations for labeling pixels and regions. arXiv preprint arXiv:1904.04514 (2019)
24. Takikawa, T., Acuna, D., Jampani, V., Fidler, S.: Gated-SCNN: gated shape CNNS for semantic segmentation. In: Proceedings of the IEEE/CVF International Conference on Computer Vision, pp. 5229–5238 (2019)
25. Wang, B., Liu, H., Samaras, D., Nguyen, M.H.: Distribution matching for crowd counting. Adv. Neural Inf. Process. Syst. **33**, 1595–1607 (2020)
26. Xiao, T., Liu, Y., Zhou, B., Jiang, Y., Sun, J.: Unified perceptual parsing for scene understanding. In: Proceedings of the European Conference on Computer Vision (ECCV), pp. 418–434 (2018)
27. Yang, M., Yu, K., Zhang, C., Li, Z., Yang, K.: Denseaspp for semantic segmentation in street scenes. In: Proceedings of the IEEE Conference on Computer Vision and Pattern Recognition, pp. 3684–3692 (2018)
28. Yu, C., Wang, J., Peng, C., Gao, C., Yu, G., Sang, N.: Bisenet: Bilateral segmentation network for real-time semantic segmentation. In: Proceedings of the European Conference on Computer Vision (ECCV), pp. 325–341 (2018)
29. Yuan, Y., Chen, X., Wang, J.: Object-contextual representations for semantic segmentation. In: European Conference on Computer Vision, pp. 173–190. Springer (2020)
30. Yuan, Y., Xie, J., Chen, X., Wang, J.: Segfix: model-agnostic boundary refinement for segmentation. In: European Conference on Computer Vision, pp. 489–506. Springer (2020)
31. Zhao, H., Shi, J., Qi, X., Wang, X., Jia, J.: Pyramid scene parsing network. In: Proceedings of the IEEE Conference on Computer Vision and Pattern Recognition, pp. 2881–2890 (2017)
32. Zhao, H., Zhang, Y., Liu, S., Shi, J., Loy, C.C., Lin, D., Jia, J.: Psanet: Pointwise spatial attention network for scene parsing. In: Proceedings of the European Conference on Computer Vision (ECCV), pp. 267–283 (2018)

33. Zhu, Z., Xu, M., Bai, S., Huang, T., Bai, X.: Asymmetric non-local neural networks for semantic segmentation. In: Proceedings of the IEEE/CVF International Conference on Computer Vision, pp. 593–602 (2019)

# Optimization-based Predictive Approach for On-Demand Transportation

Keisuke Otaki[1]([✉]) [iD], Tomoki Nishi[1], Takahiro Shiga[1],
and Toshiki Kashiwakura[2]

[1] Toyota Central R&D Labs., Inc., Nagakute, Japan
{otaki,nishi,t-shiga}@mosk.tytlabs.co.jp
[2] Toyota Motor Corporation, Nagakute, Japan
kassy@mail.toyota.co.jp

**Abstract.** Optimizing the use of vehicles is an essential task for sustainable and effective mobility-on-demand services. In a service, a driver aims to accept maximum customers, while a customer wants to minimize his/her waiting time before getting notifications/served. A service platform always faces a trade-off between the two stakeholders and their key performance indicators (KPIs), i.e., the number of accepted customers and waiting times. This paper addresses the problem of maintaining the best possible KPIs by optimizing the use of facilities with solving Dial-a-Ride problems (DARP). We propose a new framework named FORE-SEAQER (FORecast Enhanced StepwisE Allocator with Quick answER), which predicts whether incoming customers can ride in assigned cars using both real and predicted future requests, and decides whether the platform accepts requests as soon as possible. We experimentally evaluate our framework on real-world service log data from Japan and confirm that the proposed framework reasonably works.

**Keywords:** Mobility-on-demand · Optimization · Routing

## 1 Introduction

Mobility-on-demand (MoD) services have been studied in various research fields [1,5,7,8,14,15]. Some studies focused on the matching between vehicles and customers [2,10,13,17,21]. Other studies focused platforms to build efficient and fair services [6,20]. Previous research (e.g., [2,17]) often assumed that the number of operating vehicles is large (e.g., $\geq 1000$ vehicles). In such cases, the platform can be optimized from a short-term perspective. However, in areas where small numbers of vehicles and customers are assumed (e.g., a start-up MoD service, in rural areas, or sharing limited vehicles), it is often necessary to pool requests and optimize routes of vehicles in order to make the service profitable.

Our targeting MoD service is operated in a selected area with a limited number of vehicles, where a basic reservation system is already installed. The difference between our system and existing studies is that we directly optimize vehicle

S. Khanna et al. (Eds.): PRICAI 2022, LNCS 13631, pp. 466–477, 2022.
https://doi.org/10.1007/978-3-031-20868-3_34

routes. Our service then adopts the classical *Dial-a-Ride* problems (DARP) [9], and sequentially solves DARP instances to manage vehicles. Note that sharing a vehicle by multiple customers is naturally considered by DARP in our setting[1]. The mechanism that decides whether or not a customer $c$ can travel by our service is called the *allocator* in our study.

Our motivation is from the low profitability of our MoD service. We try to improve the two key performance indicators (KPIs): the number of accepted customers and waiting times. To accept more customers, utilizing future information with optimization is promising. Recent methods also tried to estimate the values of future requests and utilize future information (e.g., [3,4,12,17]). Challenges behind these studies are from the fact that the long-term effects of current decisions are often uncertain. To our knowledge, there are no common frameworks concerning this approach for optimization-based MoD services with a small number of vehicles. Since some related work [7,18] adopted different formulations, directly applying their methods to our platform remains challenging.

Our research questions are follows: (1) how an optimization-based MoD service can be designed that balances between the current and future requests for sustainable services, and (2) how we improve existing platforms with limited resources. In this paper, we first organize two typical allocators (greedy and pooled) in Sect. 3. To solve issues of existing allocators, we develop FORE-SEAQER (FORecast Enhanced StepwisE Allocator with Quick answER) in Sect. 4; FORE-SEAQER predicts whether incoming customers could ride in assigned cars using synthetic requests and combinatorial optimization and decides whether the platform accepts these requests as soon as possible, without postponing any decisions for a long time. Note that FORE-SEAQER tries to minimize the waiting time while keeping the acceptance rate as high as possible, and it can be adopted in the current platform with a small modification. Last, we experimentally evaluate the three allocators using real data, and confirm both the advantages and disadvantages of FORE-SEAQER (Sect. 5).

## 2   Platform Overview

We explain how our platform works in a specific area on the day $day_0$.

- The service is managed according to the discrete time-step index $\mathbf{T}$, which is an ordered list $\langle s_{\mathbf{T}} = t_1, t_2, \ldots, e_{\mathbf{T}} = t_{|\mathbf{T}|} \rangle$.
- All pre-processing should be completed before $day_0$, labeled $day_{-1}$. We say that pre-processing optimizations are needed to be finished until $\text{OPTs}_0$ (e.g., the platform starts 7:30 a.m., then $\text{OPTs}_0$ should be earlier than 7:30).
- A customer has a request $r_i = (o_i, d_i, s_i, t_i)$. This means the customer tries to travel from $o_i \in V$ to $d_i \in V$ until $t_i \in \mathbf{T}$. The customer sends $r_i$ to the platform at $s_i \in \mathbf{T}$; this time is referred as the *search time*.

---

[1] For example, [2] considered such sharing in post-processing, and [10] did not consider sharing, both of which are different from ours.

- The set $\mathcal{R}$ of requests is partitioned into sets $\mathcal{R}_t$ for $t \in \mathbf{T}$ with the search time and are ordered as a list $\langle \mathcal{R}_{t_1}, \mathcal{R}_{t_2}, \ldots, \rangle$, where $\mathcal{R} = \sqcup_{t \in \mathbf{T}} \mathcal{R}_t$.
- A set $\mathcal{V}$ of vehicles is managed. Each vehicle in $\mathcal{V}$ includes the following information: the depot (initial location), capacity, and the operating time.
- For each $t \in \mathbf{T}$, an allocator $\mathcal{A}$ acts as follows. For each $r \in \mathcal{R}_t$, $\mathcal{A}$ makes a decision (whether $r$ can be served), denoted by $label_r = \mathcal{A}(r) \in \{\texttt{Accept}, \texttt{Reject}\}$ (or $\mathcal{A}(r) \in \{\texttt{Accept}, \texttt{Reject}, \texttt{Pending}\}$ if needed).

After running our platform, we have both the *decision label*$_r$ and the *decision notified time* $\hat{t}_r$ for $r \in \mathcal{R}$. Using these outputs, the KPIs are evaluated as follows.

**Definition 1 (Acceptance number/rate).** *The acceptance rate on day$_0$ by the specified allocator $\mathcal{A}$ is defined as* $accept_{\mathcal{A}} := |\{r \in \mathcal{R} \mid label_r = \texttt{Accept}\}| / |\mathcal{R}|$. *In some cases, the absolute number* $|\{r \in \mathcal{R} \mid label_r = \texttt{Accept}\}|$ *is also used.*

**Definition 2 (Waiting time).** *The waiting time (WT) on day$_0$ by the specified allocator $\mathcal{A}$ is defined as* $resp_{\mathcal{A}} := \sum_{r_c \in \mathcal{R}} |\hat{t}_r - s_c|$, *where the time difference is evaluated in minutes throughout this paper (e.g., 9:40–8:50 is 50 min.).*

## 3   Greedy and Pooled Allocators

We describe two allocators previously considered in our MoD platform. Our example is illustrated in Fig. 1, where $\mathbf{T} = \langle s_{\mathbf{T}} = t_1 = 8{:}00, t_2 = 9{:}00, t_3 = 9{:}20, t_4 = 10{:}00, e_{\mathbf{T}} = 12{:}00 \rangle$. The platform operates only one vehicle $V_1$ of capacity $Cap_{V_1} = 3$. We have six requests as $\mathcal{R}_{t_1} = \{r_1\}$, $\mathcal{R}_{t_3} = \{r_2\}$, $\mathcal{R}_{t_2} = \{r_3, r_4, r_5\}$, and $\mathcal{R}_{t_4} = \{r_6\}$. Here, we assume that $\mathcal{R}_{t_1}$ and $\mathcal{R}_{t_4}$ can be served; however, $\mathcal{R}_{t_2}$ and $\mathcal{R}_{t_3}$ cannot be served by $V_1$ simultaneously due to constraints.

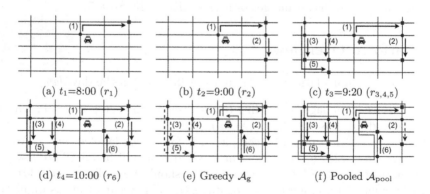

(a) $t_1=8{:}00$ $(r_1)$          (b) $t_2=9{:}00$ $(r_2)$          (c) $t_3=9{:}20$ $(r_{3,4,5})$

(d) $t_4=10{:}00$ $(r_6)$          (e) Greedy $\mathcal{A}_g$          (f) Pooled $\mathcal{A}_{\text{pool}}$

**Fig. 1.** 1a–1d illustrate six requests with $\mathbf{T} = \langle t_1, t_2, t_3, t_4 \rangle$. $(i)$ means $r_i$. Circles ($\circ$) are pick-up and rectangles ($\square$) are drop-off points. Blue arrows illustrate service routes. 1e by $\mathcal{A}_g$ shows the acceptance of $r_1, r_2, r_6$ and rejection of $r_3, r_4, r_5$. 1f by $\mathcal{A}_{\text{pool}}$ shows the rejection of $r_2$ instead of $r_3, r_4, r_5$ by optimization.

*Greedy Allocator.* The greedy allocator, denoted by $\mathcal{A}_g$, is an example of an allocator used in our MoD service. The allocator $\mathcal{A}_g$ greedily constructs routes for vehicles and customers, meaning that the WT of $\mathcal{A}_g$ is (ideally) zero and no pre-processing is required. Figure 1e illustrates an example. First, it decides $\mathcal{A}_g(r_1) =$ Accept because the platform has just started. Second, it receives $\mathcal{R}_{t_2}$ and again decides $\mathcal{A}_g(r_2) =$ Accept because this request can be served by $V_1$ after $t_1$. Unfortunately, $\mathcal{R}_{t_3}$ cannot be accepted as $\mathcal{R}_{t_2}$ is already in the queue for $V_1$; therefore, $\mathcal{A}_g(r) =$ Reject for $r \in \mathcal{R}_{t_3}$. Finally, the platform receives $\mathcal{R}_{t_4}$ and $\mathcal{A}_g(r_6) =$ Accept. We evaluate both the acceptance rate and the WT as the two KPIs after the platform halts for $day_0$ at $e_{\mathbf{T}} = 12 : 00$. For the acceptance rate, we compute the rate such that $accept_{\mathcal{A}_g} = \frac{3}{6} = 0.5$. For the WT, we have $resp_{\mathcal{A}_g} = 0$ according to its definition, i.e., for each $r \in \mathcal{R}_t, t \in \mathbf{T}, \hat{t}_r = t$ and Definition 2 leads to zero. The weakness of $\mathcal{A}_g$ is immediately revealed. If it rejects $\mathcal{R}_{t_2}$ and accepts $\mathcal{R}_{t_3}$, it could accept 5 customers. This is because the allocator $\mathcal{A}_g$ cannot incorporate the spatiotemporal information associated with $\mathcal{R}_{t'} (t' > t)$ at each $t, t' \in \mathbf{T}$, and makes its decisions based on only short-term information.

*Pooled Allocator.* We adopt optimization to estimate the (ideal) upper bound of acceptable customers. The *pooled allocator*, denoted by $\mathcal{A}_{pool}$, is designed to maximize $accept_{\mathcal{A}}$ by solving a DARP instance by optimization. The idea of $\mathcal{A}_{pool}$ is to collect $\mathcal{R} = \{r_1, r_2, r_3, r_4, r_5, r_6\}$ at $day_{-1}$ as *reservations*. This assumption indicates that the platform completely knows the future request information, and an optimal route can be used to operate the service at $day_0$. Due to the space limitation, we skip the details and implementation of DARP problems (see [9,11] for example). Figure 1f illustrates a DARP solution, where $accept_{\mathcal{A}_{pool}} = \frac{5}{6} \approx 0.833$. Since $\mathcal{A}_{pool}$ needs to collect $\mathcal{R}$ as reservations on $day_{-1}$, and to solve the DARP instance until the operating time $\text{OPTs}_0$ on $day_0$, the maximum waiting time for $r_c \subset \mathcal{R}$ is $|\text{OPTs}_0 - s_c|$, leading to a longer $resp_{\mathcal{A}_{pool}}$. Therefore, $\mathcal{A}_{pool}$ partially solves our low profitability problem by increasing the accepted customers, though it is difficult to design online MoD services.

## 4   FORE-SEAQER

FORE-SEAQER works like $\mathcal{A}_{pool}$, but it focuses on processing customers online. The key features of FORE-SEAQER are as follows. First, FORE-SEAQER *generates* multiple DARP instances with both *real* $\mathcal{R}_{real}$ and *synthetic* requests $\mathcal{R}_{syn}$, to consider the future information. Second, it estimates the acceptance probability $\hat{\mathbf{P}}(r)$ for $r \in \mathcal{R}$ using generated instances because we consider that displaying $\hat{\mathbf{P}}(r)$ is useful to customers to wait vehicles. Third, it generalizes the label $label_r$ for $r \in \mathcal{R}$ by introducing a new label Pending, which requires the customer $r$ to *wait* for the fixed decision (Accept or Reject), which is required to generalize the current reservation system. The following is an example of how FORE-SEAQER works, and Fig. 2 illustrates examples.

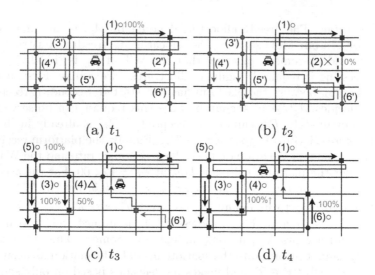

(a) $t_1$ (b) $t_2$ (c) $t_3$ (d) $t_4$

**Fig. 2.** FORE-SEAQER with $t_1, t_2, t_3, t_4$, using real (*black arrows*) and synthetic (*red arrows*) requests. Blue routes are obtained by solving DARP instances that consist of both real and synthetic requests. Using multiple instances, $\mathcal{A}_{FS}$ outputs the confidence $\hat{\mathbf{P}}(r)$. Some customers may wait for the decision (e.g., (4) in Fig. 2c with $\hat{\mathbf{P}}(r_4) = 50\%$, but at later time index $t_4$ in Fig. 2d, (4) would be accepted with higher probability 100% together with another request (6)).

($t_1$) In Fig. 2a, it has $\mathcal{R}_{\text{real}}(t_1) = \{r_1\}$ and generates $\mathcal{R}_{\text{syn}}(t_1) = \{r_2', r_3', r_4', r_5', r_6'\}$ (illustrated ($i'$)). After solving multiple instances on $\mathcal{R}_{\text{real}}(t_1) \cup \mathcal{R}_{\text{syn}}(t_1)$, $\mathcal{A}_{FS}$ decides $label_{r_1} = \texttt{Accept}$ (illustrated as ∘) with $\hat{\mathbf{P}}(r_1) = 100\%$.

($t_2$) In Fig. 2b, a new real request $r_2$ is received $\mathcal{R}_{\text{real}}(t_2) = \{r_1, r_2\}$, and then other synthetic requests $\mathcal{R}_{\text{syn}}(t_2) = \{r_3', r_4', r_5', r_6'\}$ are generated. $\mathcal{A}_{FS}$ decides to reject $r_2$ (illustrated as ×, $label_{r_2} = \texttt{Reject}$) with $\hat{\mathbf{P}}(r_2) = 0\%$.

($t_3$) In Fig. 2c, new real requests $r_3, r_4$, and $r_5$ are received. Since $r_2$ was rejected at $t_2$, $\mathcal{R}_{\text{real}}(t_3) = \{r_1, r_3, r_4, r_5\}$. Again $\mathcal{R}_{\text{syn}}(t_3) = \{r_6\}$ is generated and multiple instances are solved. $\mathcal{A}_{FS}$ estimates $\hat{\mathbf{P}}(r_3) = \hat{\mathbf{P}}(r_5) = 100\%$ but $\hat{\mathbf{P}}(r_4) = 50\%$, and sets $label_{r_4} = \texttt{Pending}$ (illustrated as △), but $label_{r_3} = label_{r_5} = \texttt{Accept}$; therefore $r_4$ needs to await its final fixed decision.

($t_4$) $\mathcal{A}_{FS}$ has $\mathcal{R}_{\text{real}}(t_4) = \{r_1, r_3, r_4, r_5, r_6\}$, where $r_2$ is already rejected. Similarly, $label_{r_6} = \texttt{Accept}$. Further, $label_{r_4} = \texttt{Accept}$, which was previously waiting as pending; therefore, $r_4$ waits $t_4 - t_3$[min].

After $\mathcal{A}_{FS}$ halts, we have $accept_{\mathcal{A}_{FS}} := \frac{5}{6}$, and $resp_{\mathcal{A}_{FS}}$ could be much smaller than $resp_{\mathcal{A}_{\text{pool}}}$. If we notify 100% of requests immediately, only the customer $r_4$ should wait because its acceptance is predicted at 50%, and the waiting time is $\hat{t}_{r_4} - t_3 = t_4 - t_3$. That is, FORE-SEAQER incorporated advantages of both $\mathcal{A}_g$ and $\mathcal{A}_{\text{pool}}$ using the generated synthetic future requests.

## 4.1   Components of FORE-SEAQER

FORE-SEAQER consists of a (1) DARP solver, (2) method to evaluate the probability $\hat{\mathbf{P}}(r)$, (3) mechanism to connect decisions, and (4) procedure to generate $\mathcal{R}_{\mathrm{syn}}(t)$ for each time $t$. We use the existing DARP solver for (1), and we explain the other components below. Algorithm 1 is a pseudo-code.

*(2) Prediction Method.* We expect that showing $\hat{\mathbf{P}}(r)$ for $r \in \mathcal{R}$ increases the usability for customers. We also use this value inside the platform. Requests having higher acceptance probabilities can be accepted sooner than those having lower probabilities. We evaluate the probability by generating *multiple instances* (i.e., $T$ times) and counting whether solutions include $r$, assuming that $r$ is included in the solution $n_r$ times out of $T$ trials. We then estimate $\hat{\mathbf{P}}(r) = \frac{n_r}{T}$.

*(3) Connection Mechanism.* Since FORE-SEAQER decides and notifies the results to customers at each $t$, it needs to incorporate previous decisions $\{label_r \mid r \in \mathcal{R}_{t'}, t' < t, t' \in \mathbf{T}\}$. Furthermore, FORE-SEAQER needs to consider any changes in the Accept, Pending, and Reject decisions for a better user experience. Note that Pending should be revised to either Accept or Reject until $day_0$ to fix final operational routes. We focus on the three cases below.

First, some requests (e.g., $r_2$ in Fig. 2b) have already been rejected and need to also be rejected at later time $t' > t, t' \in \mathbf{T}$.

Second, we need to design the method to deal with Pending (e.g., Fig. 2c). Here, FORE-SEAQER tries to decrease the number of changes between the decisions. FORE-SEAQER measures the first time that a decision is changed from Pending to either Accept or Reject to evaluate $\hat{t}_r$ when measuring $resp_{A_{\mathrm{FS}}}$.

Finally, we need to address the case in which Accept is changed to another decision because of the DARP solver, which may reject customers due to optimization. From the service perspective, such changes need to be compensated for by alternative methods (e.g., providing a taxi). In this paper, we measure the number of such changes and observe how we can minimize changes to reduce the total service cost. To connect each decision smoothly, we control penalties[2] $\{p_j\}$ for each location $j$ on $G$. For example, once $r_i$ is accepted before $t$, its origin $o_i$ and destination $d_i$ need to have higher penalties to make the DARP solver include them in the solutions. We call this connection a *penalty connection*.

We label the variations of FORE-SEAQER as follows. The naive FORE-SEAQER, labeled by FS, works without any connections. A variation, labeled by FS-P, runs with a penalty connection to preserve the Accept decisions by adjusting the penalty values. Another variation, labeled by FS-PR, which runs like FS-P, is an implementation of FS with both penalty and rejection connections.

*(4) Synthetic Request Generator.* We assume that synthetic requests can be generated. Without any prior service logs, possibly random or simple distributions that are proportional to the population in the area can be adopted. Once

---

[2] Default penalties are 1500[m]. Weights are implemented like $100 \times 1500$[m].

---

**Algorithm 1.** FORE-SEAQER $\mathcal{A}_{\mathrm{FS}}$

---

**Require:** $G, \mathcal{R} = \sqcup_{t \in \mathbf{T}} \mathcal{R}_t, \mathcal{V}, \mathbf{T}$, a method to generate synthetic requests, the maximal
number $T$ of trials, and parameters $\theta, \omega \in [0, 1]$
**Ensure:** Two KPIs $accept_{\mathcal{A}_{\mathrm{FS}}}$ and $resp_{\mathcal{A}_{\mathrm{FS}}}$
1: **for each** time index $t \in \mathbf{T}$ **do**                    ▷ offline simulation on $\mathbf{T}$
2:      Generate $T$ random DARP instances $\mathcal{R}_t^{(k)}, 1 \leq k \leq T$
3:      Solve $T$ random instances and obtain solutions $Sol^{(k)}, 1 \leq k \leq T$
4:      **for each** $r \in \mathcal{R}_t$ **do**
5:          $n_r = |\{r \in Sol^{(k)} \mid 1 \leq k \leq T\}|$ (count solutions that can accept $r$)
6:          **if** $n_r/T \geq \theta$ **then** notify `Accept`; $label_r =$ `Accept`
7:          **else if** $n_r/T < \omega$ **then** notify `Reject`; $label_r =$ `Reject`
8:          **else** notify `Pending`; $label_r =$ `Pending`
9:          Store information for $accept_{\mathcal{A}_{\mathrm{FS}}}$ and $resp_{\mathcal{A}_{\mathrm{FS}}}$ for later index $t' > t, t' \in \mathbf{T}$
10: Compute $accept_{\mathcal{A}_{\mathrm{FS}}}$ and $resp_{\mathcal{A}_{\mathrm{FS}}}$

---

a service is operated, we can store the pick-up and drop-off requests from real
requests $\mathcal{R}_{\mathrm{real}}$, and them empirical distributions can easily be prepared. Note
that any advanced ML-based model can be adopted for this purpose (e.g., [12]).

## 5   Computational Experiments

We experimentally evaluated the methods in this paper. We implemented all
scripts using Python 3.9 with Google OR-Tools (v8.1) [16][3]. All experiments
were run with an Intel Xeon W-2145 CPU at 3.70 GHz and 32 GB of memory.

*Data and Methods.* We collected log data from an MoD service operating in
Tokyo, Japan, from January 2020 to February 2020. Data are depicted in Fig. 3.
The number of customers over the service duration is shown in Fig. 3a. The
service prepared a set of possible pick-up and drop-off locations in Tokyo. All
the pairs and used pairs of distances between the locations are illustrated in
Fig. 3b. Figure 3c illustrates pick-up and drop-off locations, where the $x$ and $y$
values are normalized for anonymity.

For evaluations, we prepared three allocators; $\mathcal{A}_{\mathrm{g}}, \mathcal{A}_{\mathrm{pool}}$, and $\mathcal{A}_{\mathrm{FS}}$:

- $\mathcal{A}_{\mathrm{g}}$ re-implements the algorithm used in the real-world.
- $\mathcal{A}_{\mathrm{pool}}$ uses Google OR-tools (OPTs$_0$ is set to 0 a.m. at $day_0$).
- $\mathcal{A}_{\mathrm{FS}}$ includes three variants `FS`, `FS-P`, and `FS-PR` with fixed parameters $T = 10, \omega = 0.2$, and variable parameters $\theta \in \{0.8, 1.0\}$.

For simplicity, we use labels to display the results; $\mathcal{A}_{\mathrm{g}}$ (labeled `G`), $\mathcal{A}_{\mathrm{pool}}$
(labeled `P`), and FORE-SEAQER (labeled `FS`, `FS-P`, and `FS-PR`).

---

[3] Since many DARP instances cannot exactly solved in our experiments, the computational upper bound is set to time 600[s].

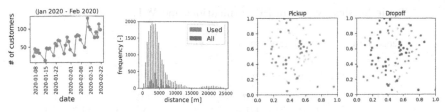

(a) # of customers    (b) Dist. histogram    (c) Pick-up and drop-off locations

**Fig. 3.** Data statistics of our targeting real MoD service logs (anonymized).

## 5.1   One-day Experiment

To confirm the performance and behaviors of the allocators, we sampled two days (Jan. 16, 2020, and Feb. 14, 2020), and tested the methods. We first evaluated the two KPIs: $accept_A$ for our service platform and $resp_A$ for the customers, and then focused the side effects by FORE-SEAQER, i.e., FP notifications.

**Table 1.** Mean values of accepted customers ($|\mathcal{V}| = 1, T = 10, \theta = 0.8, \omega = 0.2$).

| Date | $|\mathcal{R}|$ | G | P | FS | FS-P | FS-PR |
|------|-----|----|----|------|------|-------|
| Jan. 16, 2020 | 47 | 24 | **37** | **35.5** | **35.5** | 35.0 |
| Feb. 14, 2020 | 105 | 19 | 47 | 45.1 | 45.4 | **50.8** |

*KPI 1. $accept_A$* We measured the numbers of accepted customers. Table 1 summarizes the results. We confirm that the numbers of accepted customers by FSs are comparable to those accepted by P. In the best case (as on Feb. 14, 2020), FS-PR can accept more customers than P. We consider that this is because rejecting unacceptable customers benefits for the optimization problems. These results indicate that FSs are as promising as P in terms of KPI 1.

*KPI 2. $resp_A$* We evaluated the FSs in terms of the WTs and notification quality. As mentioned in Sect. 4, the decisions (i.e., notifications) from FORE-SEAQER are categorized in the following ways for the customer $c$.

1. $label_c = $ Accept is notified, and $c$ can be served on $day_0$.
2. $label_c = $ Accept is notified, but $c$ cannot be served.
3. $label_c = $ Reject is notified.

Points 1 and 3 are directly used to evaluate FS. However, Point 2 needs to be carefully evaluated because this notification does not coincide with final routes. We call the number of customers whose notifications are Point 2 *false positive (FP) notifications*. FP notifications arise because FS aggressively makes decisions before all requests are observed as reservations.

**Table 2.** Mean values of FP notifications and WTs on selected days.

| 2020-1-16 | | FS | FS-P | FS-PR | 2020-2-14 | | FS | FS-P | FS-PR |
|---|---|---|---|---|---|---|---|---|---|
| $\theta = 0.8$ | FP | 4.6 | 4.6 | 5.0 | $\theta = 0.8$ | FP | 22.7 | 22.5 | 26.5 |
| | WT | 47.4 | 47.4 | 33.1 | | WT | 55.8 | 56.2 | 48.4 |
| $\theta = 1.0$ | FP | 3.3 | 3.3 | 1.7 | $\theta = 1.0$ | FP | 5.1 | 5.1 | 9.3 |
| | WT | 173.1 | 173.1 | 177.2 | | WT | 161.4 | 161.7 | 156.0 |

We measured both WT and FP numbers. Table 2 shows the results when $T = 10, \theta = 0.8$ or 1.0, and $\omega = 0.2$. Figure 4 illustrates their histograms (the $x$-axes show WT and the $y$-axes correspond to the number of accepted customers), meaning that many customers have zero waiting times. We confirm that FORE-SEAQER achieves similar accepted numbers of customers with relatively small numbers of FP (particularly when $\theta = 1.0$); For example on Jan. 16, 2020, with $\theta = 1.0$, FORE-SEAQER accepts 35 customers with 1.7 FP notifications on average. Table 2 also indicates that there is a trade-off between FP and WT; A larger $\theta$ achieves a smaller FP notification with a longer WT. Therefore, tuning such parameters should be performed carefully according to service areas. If FP can be recovered by assigning additional vehicles (e.g., taxis), we could recover the FPs in a MoD service.

In summary, we confirm that utilizing future information by synthetic requests is effective to accept more customers than the current greedy allocator $\mathcal{A}_{\mathrm{g}}$, and they are comparable with optimization results by $\mathcal{A}_{\mathrm{pool}}$. Compared with $\mathcal{A}_{\mathrm{pool}}$, $\mathcal{A}_{\mathrm{FS}}$ achieves shorter WTs with a few additional FP notifications.

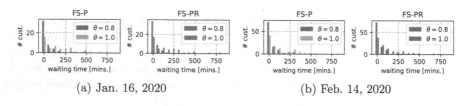

(a) Jan. 16, 2020          (b) Feb. 14, 2020

**Fig. 4.** Histograms of WTs ($x$-axes) ($T = 10, \omega = 0.2$, and two $\theta \in \{0.8, 1.0\}$)

## 5.2  One-month Experiments

To evaluate the average performance, we used two sets of logs on Jan. 2020 and Feb. 2020, and measured our two KPIs and FP notifications. Figure 5 illustrates results of numbers of accepted customers and WTs (the $x$-axes represent WTs and $y$-axes show numbers of accepted customers). Figure 6 shows relationships among numbers of accepted customers and FP notifications (the $y$-axes are now numbers of FP notifications though $x$-axes are the same of those in Fig. 5). We observed the assumed trade-off among two stakeholders (i.e., KPI 1 and KPI

2). Throughout experiments, we confirm that our FSs show an intermediary performance of G and P. We also observe that the larger $\theta$ value achieves better decisions, i.e., indicates smaller numbers of FP notifications. Variations of FORE-SEAQER seem to work similarly on average as shown in Fig. 6.

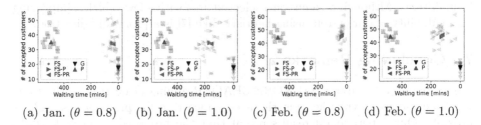

(a) Jan. $(\theta = 0.8)$    (b) Jan. $(\theta = 1.0)$    (c) Feb. $(\theta = 0.8)$    (d) Feb. $(\theta = 1.0)$

**Fig. 5.** Two KPIs: WT in $x$-axes and accepted numbers in $y$-axes in Jan. and Feb. 2020 with $\theta = 0.8$ and $\theta = 1.0$ (and $T = 10$ and $\omega = 0.2$). Thinner scatter plots represent individual days and thicker plots are mean values.

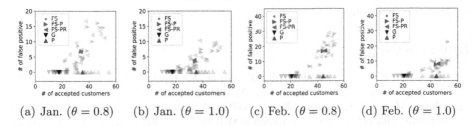

(a) Jan. $(\theta = 0.8)$    (b) Jan. $(\theta = 1.0)$    (c) Feb. $(\theta = 0.8)$    (d) Feb. $(\theta = 1.0)$

**Fig. 6.** Accepted customers in $x$-axes and FPs in $y$-axes in Jan. and Feb. 2020 with $\theta = 0.8$ and $\theta = 1.0$, with set values of $T = 10$ and $\omega = 0.2$.

In conclusion, we experimentally confirm that FORE-SEAQER operates at a level comparable to the pooled allocator in terms of the number of accepted customers. Sequentially solving DARP instances is promising to make decisions with our MoD service, given a small number of vehicles because we need to efficiently operate vehicles. Judging from the WT, as illustrated in Fig. 4, the WT for most customers is zero, which means that in our procedure, the confidence for accepting such customers is high. However, we found that our decisions sometimes return FP notifications (e.g., 10% of accepted customers). Thus, we need to deal with them in a real-world MoD service, for example, booking taxis as a possible alternative to serve customers and keep our service quality.

## 6    Related Work

MoD services have attracted much attention, but keeping the service sustainable is challenging, particularly in rural areas. As mentioned earlier, recent research (e.g., [2,17]) has mainly focused on some congested area. We believe that our study, focusing on a selected area with a small number of vehicles, is also critical to support sustainable MoD services. Though we focus on the two typical KPIs, other KPIs such as fairness can be taken into account (e.g., [19]). In terms of the scalability, a large scale experiment is done by [7] based on different formulations. Although we focus on a selected area with a few vehicles, improving the scalability of our system using heuristic like [7] is a promising direction.

## 7   Concluding Remarks

We proposed a new framework FORE-SEAQER aiming at decreasing the waiting time for users while keeping the acceptance rate for providers as high as possible. Our experimental results reveal that the proposed framework works reasonably well on real-world data. The accepted numbers of customers were comparable with those of the pooled allocator, the WT was much shorter, and service providing probabilities could be displayed to customers together with a few additional FP notifications. Our future work will include the development of faster response algorithms or more precise modules (e.g., reducing FP notifications) to build a sustainable MoD service with a small number of vehicles in a specified service area.

## References

1. Agatz, N., Erera, A., Savelsbergh, M., Wang, X.: Optimization for dynamic ride-sharing: a review. Eur. J. Oper. Res. **223**(2), 295–303 (2012)
2. Alonso-Mora, J., Samaranayake, S., Wallar, A., Frazzoli, E., Rus, D.: On-demand high-capacity ride-sharing via dynamic trip-vehicle assignment. Proc. Natl. Acad. Sci. **114**(3), 462–467 (2017)
3. Alonso-Mora, J., Wallar, A., Rus, D.: Predictive routing for autonomous mobility-on-demand systems with ride-sharing. In: Proceedings of IROS2017, pp. 3583–3590 (2017)
4. Asghari, M., Shahabi, C.: Adapt-pricing: a dynamic and predictive technique for pricing to maximize revenue in ridesharing platforms. In: Proceedings of SIGSPATIAL2018, pp. 189–198 (2018)
5. Atasoy, B., Ikeda, T., Ben-Akiva, M.E.: Optimizing a flexible mobility on demand system. Transp. Res. Rec. **2563**(1), 76–85 (2015)
6. Balasingam, A., Gopalakrishnan, K., Mittal, R., Arun, V., Saeed, A., Alizadeh, M., Balakrishnan, H., Balakrishnan, H.: Throughput-fairness tradeoffs in mobility platforms. In: Proceedings of MobiSys2021, pp. 363–375 (2021)
7. Bertsimas, D., Jaillet, P., Martin, S.: Online vehicle routing: The edge of optimization in large-scale applications. Oper. Res. **67**(1), 143–162 (2019)
8. Clewlow, R.R., Mishra, G.S.: Disruptive transportation: The adoption, utilization, and impacts of ride-hailing in the united states. Technical report, UC Davis (2017)
9. Cordeau, J.F., Laporte, G.: The dial-a-ride problem: models and algorithms. Ann. Oper. Res. **153**(1), 29–46 (2007)
10. Hikima, Y., Kohjima, M., Akagi, Y., Kurashima, T., Toda, H.: Price and time optimization for utility-aware taxi dispatching. In: Proceedings of PRICAI 2021, vol. 13031, pp. 370–381 (2021)

11. Ho, S.C., Szeto, W.Y., Kuo, Y.H., Leung, J.M., Petering, M., Tou, T.W.: A survey of dial-a-ride problems: literature review and recent developments. Transp. Res. Part B: Methodol. **111**, 395–421 (2018)
12. Lei, Z., Qian, X., Ukkusuri, S.V.: Efficient proactive vehicle relocation for on-demand mobility service with recurrent neural networks. Transp. Res. Part C: Emerg. Technol. **117**, 102678 (2020)
13. Liu, C., Sun, J., Jin, H., Ai, M., Li, Q., Zhang, C., Sheng, K., Wu, G., Qie, X., Wang, X.: Spatio-temporal hierarchical adaptive dispatching for ridesharing systems. In: Proceedings of SIGSPATIAL2020, pp. 227–238 (2020)
14. Lo, J., Morseman, S.: The perfect uberpool: a case study on trade-offs. In: Ethnographic Praxis in Industry Conference Proceedings, pp. 195–223. No. 1, Wiley Online Library (2018)
15. Peled, I., Lee, K., Jiang, Y., Dauwels, J., Pereira, F.C.: Preserving uncertainty in demand prediction for autonomous mobility services. In: Proceedings of IEEE ITSC2019, pp. 3043–3048 (2019)
16. Perron, L., Furnon, V.: Or-tools, https://developers.google.com/optimization/
17. Shah, S., Lowalekar, M., Varakantham, P.: Neural approximate dynamic programming for on-demand ride-pooling. In: Proceedings of AAAI2020, vol. 34(01), pp. 507–515 (2020)
18. Spieser, K., Treleaven, K., Zhang, R., Frazzoli, E., Morton, D., Pavone, M.: Toward a systematic approach to the design and evaluation of automated mobility-on-demand systems: a case study in Singapore. In: Road Vehicle Automation, pp. 229–245. Springer (2014)
19. Yan, A., Howe, B.: Fairness-aware demand prediction for new mobility. In: Proceedings of AAAI 2020, vol. 34 (01), pp. 1079–1087 (2020)
20. Yang, Y., Shi, Y., Wang, D., Chen, Q., Xu, L., Li, H., Fu, Z., Li, X., Zhang, H.: Improving the information disclosure in mobility-on-demand systems. In: Proceedings of KDD2021, pp. 3854–3864 (2021)
21. Zhao, B., Xu, P., Shi, Y., Tong, Y., Zhou, Z., Zeng, Y.: Preference-aware task assignment in on-demand taxi dispatching: an online stable matching approach. In: Proceedings of the AAAI 2019, vol. 33 (01), pp. 2245–2252 (2019)

# JointContrast: Skeleton-Based Mutual Action Recognition with Contrastive Learning

Xiangze Jia[1], Ji Zhang[2(✉)], Zhen Wang[3], Yonglong Luo[4], Fulong Chen[4], and Jing Xiao[5]

[1] Nanjing University of Aeronautics and Astronautics, Nanjing, China
`jiaxiangze@nuaa.edu.cn`
[2] University of Southern Queensland, Darling Heights, Australia
`Ji.Zhang@usq.edu.au`
[3] Zhejiang Lab, Hangzhou City, China
`wangzhen@zhejianglab.com`
[4] Anhui Normal University, Wuhu, China
`ylluo@ustc.edu.cn`
[5] South China Normal University, Guangzhou, China
`Chinaxiaojing@scnu.edu.cn`

**Abstract.** Skeleton-based action recognition relies on skeleton sequences to detect certain categories of human actions. In skeleton-based action recognition, it is observed that many scenes are mutual actions characterized by more than one subject, and the existing works deal with subjects independently or use the pooling layer for feature fusion leading to ineffective learning and fusion of different subjects. In this paper, we propose a novel framework, JointContrast, for Skeleton-based action recognition to deal with these challenges. Our JointContrast includes two innovative components. One is the pre-training process with a fine-grained contrastive loss that effectively enhances the representation ability of the model, and the other is an Interactive Graph (IG) representation for skeletal sequences that contributes to the fusion of features between subjects. We validate our JointContrast in the popular SBU and NTU RGB-D datasets, and experimental results show that our model outperforms other baseline methods in terms of recognition accuracy.

**Keywords:** Pre-training · Contrastive learning · Interactive graph · Action recognition

## 1 Introduction

Action recognition detects some pre-determined types of human actions through skeleton sequences, which enjoys a wide range of applications, including video surveillance, human-computer interaction and sports health, to name a few. Various types of data can be used for action recognition, such as pictures, depth maps

S. Khanna et al. (Eds.): PRICAI 2022, LNCS 13631, pp. 478–489, 2022.
https://doi.org/10.1007/978-3-031-20868-3_35

and skeleton data. Skeleton data record the trajectory of specific joints, making them robust against the change in appearance, background and viewpoint compared to other types of data [1, 2].

It is observed that many scenes in real-life scenarios and applications involve mutual actions, which are characterized by more than one subjects. This mutual action scenes may, for example, include one person pushing another person, one person taking pictures of another person, etc. In previous related works [3–5], the solutions to mutual action recognition can be divided into two categories: (1) Only the main subject of the skeleton sequence is used for action recognition; (2) all subjects of the skeleton sequence are used for action recognition, but each subject is treated independently. However, both categories of methods cannot obtain accurate feature representations of mutual action scene because (1) there are more than one key parties in mutual actions, using only one subject for action recognition will inevitably lead to feature loss; (2) processing each subject separately cannot effectively model or capture the interaction features among the subjects.

In addition, representation learning is one of the important methods used in deep learning for more an effective feature engineering, which is also playing an important part in modeling the features of human joints for action recognition. Pre-training a model on a rich training set can help improve the representation ability as well as the overall performance of the model. However, training from scratch is still the dominant approach in skeleton-based action recognition tasks, which limits their recognition performance. This work aims to advance action recognition through unsupervised pre-training. Unsupervised pre-training has achieved remarkable success in both natural language processing [6] and computer vision [7]. When the pre-training stage is unsupervised, it is possible to utilize train sets with a practically infinite size.

To solve the drawbacks of the existing work, we propose a new action recognition model called JointContrast. An Interactive Graph (IG), a new representation of skeleton data embedded with interactive information in the scene, is proposed for our model. Compared with the previous representation methods, the incorporation of interactive information makes the features more enriched. In JointContrast, we also introduce pretraining mechanism for our model. Specifically, we use NTU [8] as our pre-training source set, and ST-GCN [3] and GCN-LSTM [9] as the backbone networks. For the pre-training objective, we use a fine-grained contrastive loss, that is, the joint-level contrastive loss. We train the encoder of our model through contrastive objective, then carry out lightweight supervised fine-tuning in action recognition task.

The contributions of our proposed JointContrast model can be summarized as follows:

– We propose an innovative Interactive Graph (IG) that can, as a connected graph, effectively represent multiple subjects involved in the scenes. The Interactive Graph can help better model and capture the interactions of multiple subjects in the same and contributes to a better feature fusion for action recognition;

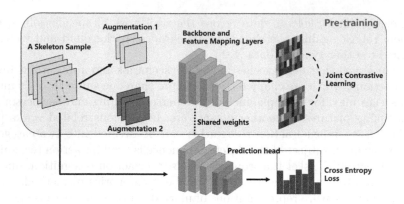

**Fig. 1.** JointContrast: The framework consists of two parts: pre-training and target tasks. In the pre-training process, two samples are generated from each raw data through data augmentation, then fed to the network to extract features, and a joint level contrastive loss is applied to the joint features. The pre-trained weights are used as the initialization and are further refined on the target downstream task, and a new prediction head replaces the feature mapping layer.

- we adopt a pretraining mechanism in the model with the use of the joint-level contrastive loss for improving the recognition effectiveness of the model, to the best of our knowledge, this paper is the first to study pre-training in the skeleton-based action recognition task;
- The IG representation and pre-training process are generic for a wide range of scenes and compatible with different models for improving their performance;
- We conduct experiments on three popular benchmark datasets including SUB, NTU60 and NTU120 datasets, and the experimental results show our framework achieves SOTA performance against several popular baseline methods.

The remainder of this paper is structured as follows. Section 2 discusses the related research works on skeleton-based action recognition and contrastive learning. The preparatory work and our model are presented in Sects. 3 and 4. In Sect. 5, we show the experimental evaluation of JointContrast on three datasets. The conclusion is presented in Sect. 6.

## 2   Related Work

### 2.1   Skeleton-Based Action Recognition

Unlike the grid structure of the images, the skeleton data have an irregular structure. Models based on CNN [2] project each frame of the skeleton data into a pseudo-image. However, it is necessary to design the joint permutation and renders the model to have permutation invariance. Models based on GCN abstract the human body in a skeleton graph in which joints are nodes and bones are edges. With the stacking of the layers, each vertex will have a larger receptive field and learn the dense feature representation. ST-GCN [3] uses a spatial-temporal graph to represent the skeleton sequence where the inner-subject and inter-frame edges connect the body joints and the same joints between consecutive frames. Li, M. et al. [4] find inconsistencies between potential dependencies between joints and physical connections and leverage a data-driven approach to build the skeleton graph, which indicates the action-specific potential dependencies. Attention-based models have been widely used, and they can learn more potential dependencies between joints with the original skeleton data. DEST-Net [10] introduces the attention blocks, allowing for modeling spatial-temporal dependencies between joints without the requirement of mutual connections.

## 2.2 Contrastive Learning

Contrastive learning [12] is becoming increasingly attractive due to its great potential in unsupervised tasks. The essence of contrastive learning is to maximize the similarity of representations between positive samples while encouraging the discrimination of negative samples [13]. Some recent works [14,15] have also utilized contrastive learning for self-supervised scene representation learning. Those representation learning methods can be easily transferred to skeleton-based tasks. However, much less attention has been devoted to representation learning that lies in the joints. We focus on the joints level contrastive learning in skeleton data, where our goal is to learn discriminative features representing the different joints.

## 3  Preliminaries: GCN

Graph Convolutional Network (GCN) is the generalization of CNN in the graph structure. We represent the skeleton graph as $G = (V, A)$, where $V = \{v_i\}_{i=1}^N$ represents the set of $N$ body joints, and $A$ is the adjacency matrix representing the adjacency relationship between joints. $A$ is defined according to the physical structure of the human body, and the input features are expressed as $X = \{x_1, x_2, \ldots, x_d\} \in \mathbb{R}^{N \times d}$, where $x_i$ indicates all joints' $i$-th feature channel. We use the three-dimensional coordinates of the joints and bones information as the input features and define $\Phi_k(A)$ as the polynomial of the adjacency matrix $A$.

$$[\Phi_k(A)]_{i,j} = \begin{cases} 1 & if \ dist(v_i, v_j) = k \\ 0 & else \end{cases} \tag{1}$$

We have $[\Phi_k(A)]_{i,j} = 1$ when the shortest distance between $v_i$ and $v_j$ is equal to $k$ and define $\Phi_0(A) = I$, which indicates the self-connection of the vertices. $\Phi_k(A)$ can be obtained from $A^k$ and $\Phi_j(A), j < k$. Slightly different from regular GCN.

$$Y_{gc}(X) = \frac{1}{K_1} \sum_{k=0}^{K_1-1} D_k^{-1} \Phi_k(A) X W_k \tag{2}$$

482     X. Jia et al.

**Fig. 2.** Interactive Graph: The joint edge (black) connects the joints in the same subject, and the subject edge (red) connects the same joints between different subjects. For brevity, only some subject edges are given in the figure. (Color figure online)

where $K_1$ is a hyper-parameter to determine the receptive field of the vertex. With the increase of $K_1$, more vertices are considered neighbors of the central vertex, which corresponds to the large kernel size in CNN. $D_k$ is the degree matrix of $\Phi_k(A)$, and its role is to normalize the features. $W_k \in \mathbb{R}^{d \times d'}$ is the learnable weights, and $Y_{gc} \in \mathbb{R}^{N \times d'}$ is the feature representation after GCN.

## 4  JointContrast

In this section, we introduce the Interactive Graph (IG) and the pre-training of our JointContrast. The Interactive Graph (IG), a new representation of skeleton data, is embedded with interactive information in the scene. Our JointContrast is a pre-training and fine-tuning framework for skeleton-based tasks.

### 4.1  Interactive Graph

As we mentioned earlier, the previous related works do not fully consider the interaction information between subjects. Given the limitations of existing works, we propose an interactive skeleton graph that has two types of edges, the joint edge and the subject edge. As shown in Fig. 2, the joint edge indicates that two joints in the same subject are adjacent, and the subject edge connects the same joints of different subjects who complete the action. Intuitively, the subject edge transforms multiple independent graphs into a connected graph used for feature fusion. Objectively, the subject edges to increase the receptive field of each vertex in GCN, which means that each vertex can learn the feature representations from the adjacent vertices and obtain helpful information from other subjects.

We introduce $\mathcal{A} \in \mathbb{R}^{MN \times MN}$ to represent the internal graph representation of each subject, i.e., joint edges, where $M$ is the number of subjects and $MN$ is the number of the joints of all subjects. $\mathcal{A} = diag(A, \ldots, A)$ is a diagonal matrix composed of $N$ independent $A$. We use the adjacency matrix $\mathcal{B} \in \mathbb{R}^{MN \times MN}$ to represent the subject edges. To fully extract features from Interactive Graph, we improve the Eq. 2 of GCN as

$$Y_{gc}(X) = \frac{1}{K_1} \sum_{k=0}^{K_1-1} D_k^{-1} \Phi_k(\mathcal{A}) X W_k + \frac{1}{K_2} \sum_{k'=1}^{K_2} D'_{k'} \Phi'_{k'}(\mathcal{B}) X W_{k'} \tag{3}$$

where $K_2$ is a hyper-parameter to determine the receptive field of the vertices on other subjects. $Y_{gc}$ consists of two parts, the first part is the feature fused from the subject's joints, and the second part is the interactive feature from other subjects. We define $\Phi'_{k'}(\mathcal{B})$ as

$$\Phi'_{k'}(\mathcal{B}) = \mathcal{B}\Phi_{k'-1}(\mathcal{A}) \quad k' > 0 \tag{4}$$

## 4.2   Pre-training with Contrastive Loss

A good pretext task for pre-training aims to learn parameters that are universally applicable and useful for target tasks. In Fig. 1, we summarize the pretext task framework explored in this work and name the framework JointContrast which contrasts two different joints. Specifically, given a skeleton data $x$, we generate two samples $x_1$ and $x_2$ aligned in the same world coordinate through common data augmentation including random horizontal flip, rotation, random translation, and scaling. Then we record the corresponding mapping $P$ of the same joints between these two samples, and a contrastive loss is defined over joints which minimizes the feature distance for matched joints and maximizes the distance of unmatched joints. This framework shares a similar pipeline with recent visual representation learning methods [12,16]. The critical difference is that most 2D works focus on instances/images, whereas contrastive learning is done at the joint level in our work.

InfoNCE [14] is widely used in unsupervised representation learning approaches for scene understanding, which is implemented with a Softmax loss and poses contrastive learning as a classification problem. It pulls corresponding joint features close together in embedding space and pushes non-corresponding ones farther away.

$$\mathcal{L} = - \sum_{(i,j)\in P} log \frac{exp(f^i \cdot f^j/r)}{\sum_{(\cdot,)\in P} exp(f^i \cdot f^k/r)} \tag{5}$$

where $r$ is a temperature hyper-parameter. $P$ is the set of all the positive matches, and we consider all non-matched joints as negatives. The joint feature $f_1^i$ serves as the query for a matched pair $(i,j) \in P$, and $f_2^j$ serves as the positive key. We use joint feature $f_2^k$ where $\exists(\cdot,k) \in P$ and $k \neq j$ as the set of negative keys. In addition, we use a GCN-based LSTM (GC-LSTM) network in this work. The GC-LSTM architecture is designed initially in [9] that achieved significant improvement over prior methods. The pre-trained weights are used for initialization and further refined on the target tasks. As shown in Fig. 1, we train the backbone and the feature mapping layers with the contrastive loss, after which we discard the feature mapping layers and fine-tune the pre-trained backbone with the newly added prediction head.

**Table 1.** The settings of hyperparameters in the JointContrast.

| Dataset | T | M | N | $K_1$ | $K_2$ |
|---------|-----|---|----|-------|-------|
| SBU | 40 | 2 | 15 | 2 | 1 |
| NTU60 & NTU120 | 300 | 2 | 25 | 2 | 1 |

# 5  Experimental Evaluation

## 5.1  Datasets and Performance Metrics

**SBU Dataset.** SBU dataset [17] is constructed by Kinect and contains the RGB-D sequence information of mutual actions. Seven participants in an experimental environment complete it. There are 282 sequence data, which are divided into eight categories. The skeleton sequences contain 15 joints, and three-dimensional coordinates represent each joint.

**NTU RGB-D Dataset.** NTU60 [18] has 56,880 action samples, divided into 60 classes and 11 mutual action categories. Three Kinect cameras simultaneously photograph each action sample from different perspectives. The advantages of this data set lie in the rich action categories, the vast number of video clips, and the diversity of camera perspectives. NTU120 [8] extends NTU60, adding 60 classes and another 57,600 video samples; NTU120 has 120 categories and 26 mutual action classes.

**Performance Metrics.** There are two ways to evaluate the recognition accuracy in NTU60 and NTU120, (1) Cross-Subject (CS) accuracy evaluation, where the action samples performed by different subjects are divided into the training set and test set; (2) Cross-View (CV) evaluation, where the action samples collected by different cameras are divided into the training set and test set.

## 5.2  Experimental Setup

We sample two subjects in every data and use the proposed Interactive Graph (IG) to represent the skeleton data. To fix the sequence length of the data, we divide a skeleton sequence into $T$ sub-sequences and randomly sample a frame in each sub-sequence. In addition, we convert the joint coordinates from the camera coordinate system to the body coordinate system based on the spine following previous works. We use the GC-LSTM as the backbone in this work, and Table 1 shows the settings of hyper-parameters where the temperature hyperparameter $r$ is set to a learnable weight. The feature mapping layers are implemented with MLP, and its role is to reduce the dimension of the features used for contrastive loss. The pre-trained weights of the backbone are used as the initialization and are further refined, and the feature mapping layers are discarded on the target task.

**Table 2.** The recognition accuracy of the SBU dataset, **acc** means recognition accuracy.

| Methods | acc |
|---|---|
| CFDM [19] | 89.4% |
| Co-occurrence LSTM [20] | 90.4% |
| ST-LSTM [1] | 93.3% |
| 2sGCA-LSTM [21] | 94.9% |
| VA-LSTM [22] | 97.2% |
| LSTM-IRN [23] | **98.2%** |
| SGCConv [24] | 94.0% |
| JointContrast | **98.2%** |

**Table 3.** The mutual actions recognition accuracy under the Cross-Subject (CS) and Cross-View (CV) accuracy evaluation on NTU60 and NTU120 datasets.

| Methods | NTU60 | | NTU120 | |
|---|---|---|---|---|
| | CS acc (%) | CV acc (%) | CS acc (%) | CV acc (%) |
| ST-LSTM [1] | 83.0 | 87.3 | 63.0 | 66.6 |
| LSTM-IRN [23] | 90.5 | 93.5 | 77.7 | 79.6 |
| AGC-LSTM [9] | 89.2 | 95.0 | 73.0 | 73.3 |
| SAN [25] | 88.2 | 93.5 | – | – |
| VACNN [26] | 88.9 | 94.7 | – | – |
| ST-GCN [3] | 83.3 | 88.7 | – | – |
| AS-GCN [27] | 87.6 | 95.2 | 82.9 | 83.7 |
| ST-TR [28] | 90.8 | 96.5 | 85.7 | 87.1 |
| 2sshift-GCN [29] | 90.3 | 96.0 | 86.1 | 86.7 |
| MS-G3D [30] | 91.7 | 96.1 | – | – |
| 2sKA-AGTN [11] | 90.4 | 96.1 | 86.7 | 88.2 |
| JointContrast | **94.1** | **96.8** | **88.2** | **88.9** |

## 5.3 Results

**SBU** The results are shown in Table 2, and we compare our JointContrast with several major existing models, including LSTM-IRN, VA-LSTM, and GCA-LSTM. Our JointContrast achieves similar accuracy as LSTM-IRM. Unlike LSTM-IRN using all inter-subject and intra-subject joint pairs as input., our JointContrast is more efficient, and the aggregation of joint features depends on the Interactive Graph which is a more straightforward feature fusion method (Table 3).

**NTU60 and NTU120.** Reproducing the previous works on our machine, we find that the recognition accuracy of mutual actions is similar to the average

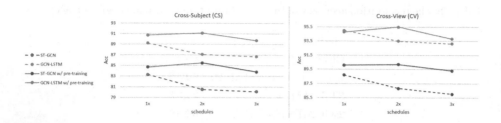

**Fig. 3.** Comparison in terms of accuracy of models w/ and w/o pre-training on the NTU60 dataset, **schedules** means the training epochs.

**Table 4.** Comparison in terms of recognition accuracy of the models w/ and w/o IG on the NTU60 dataset.

| Methods | CS acc (%) | CV acc (%) | IG | Parameters ($10^7$) |
|---------|-----------|-----------|------|---------------------|
| ST-GCN | 83.3 | 88.7 | w/o | 1.2 |
| ST-GCN | 88.5 | 92.1 | w/ | 1.3 |
| GC-LSTM | 89.2 | 95.0 | w/o | – |
| GC-LSTM | 93.7 | 96.1 | w/ | - |

accuracy of all actions. Although mutual actions have much more semantic information, most models do not fully use them. Most of the newer works are based on GCN or Attention which not only relies on manual data representation but explores the implicit dependencies between joints through data-driven. Moreover, our JointContrast learns the scene understanding and inter-subject information fusion. We report the recognition accuracy of mutual actions in Table 3 and classify these works as LSTM-based, CNN-based, GCN-based, and attention-based methods. Among the 11 categories involving mutual action, our model achieves 94.1% and 96.8% accuracy in CS and CV accuracy evaluation, respectively, which is the best among the methods we compare. As an extension of NTU60, the data form and distribution of NTU120 and NTU60 are similar. With the increase of classes and samples, the recognition accuracy of all models decreased compared with those in NTU60. However, our JointContrast is still the best in the CS and CV accuracy evaluation.

## 5.4   Ablation Study

**Pre-training with Contrastive Learning.** The finding that pre-training a network on a rich source set and fine-tuning on the target set can help boost performance has been key to the success of many applications. To evaluate how pre-training affects the performance of the models, we choose GC-LSTM and ST-GCN as the baseline for further experiments. As shown in Fig. 3, the model performances trained from scratch lag behind the pre-trained models, either ST-GCN or GC-LSTM. We also find that pre-trained models require more training epochs than the models trained from scratch to achieve optimal performance. A recent study suggests that simply training from scratch for more epochs might close the gap from pre-training. We conduct additional experiments to train the network from scratch with 2× and 3x schedules, and find that validation accuracy does not improve with more extended training. The results show that pre-training helps the model perform better in the downstream tasks.

**Interactive Graph.** We propose IG to enhance the feature fusion between subjects in the scene. To illustrate the applicability and effectiveness of our interactive skeleton graph, we still choose GCN-LSTM and ST-GCN as the baseline, and all of them are trained from scratch. As shown in Table 4, the accuracy of ST-GCN w/ IG improves by 5.2% compared to the ST-GCN w/o IG, and GC-LSTM w/ IG improved by 5.5%. Although the number of parameters has increased by 10%, we think the performance improvement is even more impressive. This result indicates that the interaction information between agents is essential in mutual actions involving multiple subjects. The results also show that IG can significantly improve the model's performance with few code modifications, and more importantly, it can be used by most models.

## 6    Conclusion

Considering the key limitations of the previous works in representation learning and mutual action modeling, we propose a novel JointContrast framework in this paper. In addition, we propose a novel representation of skeleton data, named Interactive Graph (IG), which can better capture and fuse features between subjects that are ignored by previous works. We also propose a joint-level unsupervised contrastive pretext task learning discriminative joint features to improve the model representation. Our future works will focus on (1) more flexible and efficient data representation methods in skeleton-based mutual action and (2) exploring better pretext tasks (supervised or unsupervised) for pre-training.

**Acknowledgment.** This research is partially supported by Zhejiang Lab (No. 2022PI0AC03 and No. 111010-AN2201) and National Natural Science Foundation of China (61972438).

## References

1. Liu, J., Shahroudy, A., Xu, D., Wang, G.: Spatio-temporal lstm with trust gates for 3d human action recognition. In: European Conference on Computer Vision, pp. 816–833. Springer, Cham (2016)
2. Ke, Q., Bennamoun, M., An, S., Sohel, F., Boussaid, F.: A new representation of skeleton sequences for 3d action recognition. In: Proceedings of The IEEE Conference on Computer Vision and Pattern Recognition, pp. 3288–3297. IEEE, Honolulu (2017)

3. Yan, S., Xiong, Y., Lin, D.: Spatial temporal graph convolutional networks for skeleton-based action recognition. In: Thirty-second AAAI Conference on Artificial Intelligence. AAAI, New Orleans (2018)
4. Li, M., Chen, S., Chen, X., Zhang, Y., Wang, Y., Tian, Q.: Actional-structural graph convolutional networks for skeleton-based action recognition. In: Proceedings of the IEEE/CVF Conference on Computer Vision and Pattern Recognition, pp. 3595–3603. IEEE, Long Beach (2019)
5. Shi, L., Zhang, Y., Cheng, J., Lu, H.: Skeleton-based action recognition with directed graph neural networks. In: Proceedings of the IEEE/CVF Conference on Computer Vision and Pattern Recognition, pp. 7912–7921. IEEE, Long Beach (2019)
6. Devlin, J., Chang, M. W., Lee, K., Toutanova, K.: Bert: pre-training of deep bidirectional transformers for language understanding. arXiv preprint, arXiv:1810.04805 (2018)
7. Bachman, P., Hjelm, R.D., Buchwalter, W.: Learning representations by maximizing mutual information across views. Advances in neural information processing systems, 32 (2019)
8. Liu, J., Shahroudy, A., Perez, M., Wang, G., Duan, L.Y., Kot, A.C.: Ntu rgb+ d 120: a large-scale benchmark for 3d human activity understanding. IEEE Trans. Pattern Anal. Mach. Intell. **42**(10), 2684–2701 (2019)
9. Si, C., Chen, W., Wang, W., Wang, L., Tan, T.: An attention enhanced graph convolutional lstm network for skeleton-based action recognition. In: Proceedings of the IEEE/CVF Conference on Computer Vision and Pattern Recognition, pp. 1227–1236. IEEE, Long Beach (2019)
10. Shi, L., Zhang, Y., Cheng, J., Lu, H.: Decoupled spatial-temporal attention network for skeleton-based action-gesture recognition. In: Proceedings of the Asian Conference on Computer Vision (2020)
11. Liu, Y., Zhang, H., Xu, D., He, K.: Graph transformer network with Temporal Kernel Attention for skeleton-based action recognition. Knowledge-Based Syst. **240**, 108146 (2022)
12. Chen, T., Kornblith, S., Norouzi, M., Hinton, G.: A simple framework for contrastive learning of visual representations. In: International Conference on Machine Learning, pp. 1597–1607. PMLR (2020)
13. Singh, A., Chakraborty, O., Varshney, A., Panda, R., Feris, R., Saenko, K., Das, A.: Semi-supervised action recognition with temporal contrastive learning. In: Proceedings of the IEEE/CVF Conference on Computer Vision and Pattern Recognition, pp. 10389–10399. IEEE (2021)
14. Van den Oord, A., Li, Y., Vinyals, O.: Representation learning with contrastive predictive coding. arXiv e-prints, arXiv-1807 (2018)
15. Radford, A., Kim, J. W., Hallacy, C., Ramesh, A., Goh, G., Agarwal, S., Sutskever, I.: Learning transferable visual models from natural language supervision. In: International Conference on Machine Learning, pp. 8748–8763. PMLR (2021)
16. He, K., Fan, H., Wu, Y., Xie, S., Girshick, R.: Momentum contrast for unsupervised visual representation learning. In: Proceedings of the IEEE/CVF Conference on Computer Vision and Pattern Recognition, pp. 9729–9738. IEEE (2020)
17. Yun, K., Honorio, J., Chattopadhyay, D., Berg, T. L., Samaras, D.: Two-person interaction detection using body-pose features and multiple instance learning. In: IEEE Computer Society Conference on Computer Vision and Pattern Recognition Workshops, pp. 28–35. IEEE (2012)

18. Shahroudy, A., Liu, J., Ng, T. T., Wang, G.: Ntu rgb+ d: A large scale dataset for 3d human activity analysis. In: Proceedings of the IEEE Conference on Computer Vision and Pattern Recognition, pp. 1010–1019. IEEE, Las Vegas (2016)

19. Ji, Y., Cheng, H., Zheng, Y., Li, H.: Learning contrastive feature distribution model for interaction recognition. J. Vis. Commun. Image Represent. **33**, 340–349 (2015)

20. Zhu, W., Lan, C., Xing, J., Zeng, W., Li, Y., Shen, L., Xie, X.: Co-occurrence feature learning for skeleton based action recognition using regularized deep LSTM networks. In: Proceedings of the AAAI Conference on Artificial Intelligence, vol. 30, No. 1. AAAI, Phoenix (2016)

21. Liu, J., Wang, G., Duan, L.Y., Abdiyeva, K., Kot, A.C.: Skeleton-based human action recognition with global context-aware attention LSTM networks. IEEE Trans. Image Process. **27**(4), 1586–1599 (2017)

22. Zhang, P., Lan, C., Xing, J., Zeng, W., Xue, J., Zheng, N.: View adaptive recurrent neural networks for high performance human action recognition from skeleton data. In: Proceedings of the IEEE International Conference on Computer Vision, pp. 2117–2126. IEEE, Honolulu (2017)

23. Perez, M., Liu, J., Kot, A.C.: Interaction relational network for mutual action recognition. IEEE Trans. Multimed. **24**, 366–376 (2021)

24. Wu, F., Souza, A., Zhang, T., Fifty, C., Yu, T., Weinberger, K.: Simplifying graph convolutional networks. In: International Conference on Machine Learning, pp. 6861–6871. PMLR. Long Beach (2019)

25. Cho, S., Maqbool, M., Liu, F., Foroosh, H.: Self-attention network for skeleton-based human action recognition. In: Proceedings of the IEEE/CVF Winter Conference on Applications of Computer Vision, pp. 635–644. IEEE, Snowmass Village (2020)

26. Zhang, P., Lan, C., Xing, J., Zeng, W., Xue, J., Zheng, N.: View adaptive neural networks for high performance skeleton-based human action recognition. IEEE Trans. Pattern Anal. Mach. Intell. **41**(8), 1963–1978 (2019)

27. Li, M., Chen, S., Chen, X., Zhang, Y., Wang, Y., Tian, Q.: Actional-structural graph convolutional networks for skeleton-based action recognition. In: Proceedings of the IEEE/CVF Conference on Computer Vision and Pattern Recognition, pp. 3595–3603. IEEE, Long Beach (2019)

28. Plizzari, C., Cannici, M., Matteucci, M.: Spatial temporal transformer network for skeleton-based action recognition. In International Conference on Pattern Recognition, pp. 694–701. Springer, Cham (2021)

29. Cheng, K., Zhang, Y., He, X., Chen, W., Cheng, J., Lu, H.: Skeleton-based action recognition with shift graph convolutional network. In: Proceedings of the IEEE/CVF Conference on Computer Vision and Pattern Recognition, pp. 183–192. IEEE (2020)

30. Liu, Z., Zhang, H., Chen, Z., Wang, Z., Ouyang, W.: Disentangling and unifying graph convolutions for skeleton-based action recognition. In: Proceedings of the IEEE/CVF Conference on Computer Vision and Pattern Recognition, pp. 143–152. IEEE (2020)

# Nested Multi-Axis Learning Network for Single Image Super-Resolution

Xianwei Xiao and Baojiang Zhong[✉]

School of Computer Science and Technology, Soochow University, Suzhou, China
bjzhong@suda.edu.cn

**Abstract.** Real-world images usually contain rich features at different granularity levels, such as illumination, edges, and textures. Performance of a deep-learning method for *single image super-resolution* (SISR) could be degraded if it fails to extract features over all granularity levels. To address this problem, a novel deep-learning network is proposed, which consists of a set of *nested multi-axis learning blocks* (NMLBs) and is thus termed the *nested multi-axis learning network* (NMLNet). Each NMLB has an outer multi-axis structure that contains 3 axes dedicated to extracting coarse-, medium-, and fine-grained features, respectively. With the concern that our human visual system is more sensitive to the medium-grained features (e.g., edges), the medium-grained axis further has an inner multi-axis structure, by which edge features are captured at a wide range of network depths. By transmitting image features via the nested multi-axis structure, efficient information propagation is achieved throughout our developed network. To boost the network performance, a two-tier attention block is also proposed, which adaptively rescales the extracted features in both channel and spatial domains to maximize the representation capacity of our network. Extensive experimental results show that the proposed NMLNet can deliver superior performance over a number of state-of-the-art SISR methods, especially with respect to the reconstruction quality of image edges.

**Keywords:** Single image super-resolution · Deep learning · Multi-axis learning · Feature extraction · Spatial attention · Channel attention

## 1 Introduction

Single image super resolution (SISR) pursues to recover a high-resolution (HR) image from a degraded low-resolution (LR) image, and has become a well-known image processing technique used in a variety of image-based tasks, such as medical imaging [30], security and surveillance imaging [1], face recognition [18] video super-resolution [5] and object detection [11], to name a few. However, the SISR is an ill-posed problem because a single LR image can be matched with multiple HR images. As a result, finding the best non-linear mapping between LR and its HR counterparts is a challenging problem. Over the years, a number

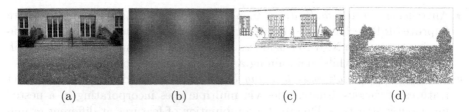

**Fig. 1.** Image features at different granularity levels. **a** The test image; **b** Coarse-grained features (e.g., color and illumination); **c** Medium-grained features (e.g., edges); **d** Fine-grained features (e.g., textures and spots).

of SISR methods based on deep convolutional neural networks (CNNs) (e.g., [14,16,17,21,26,29,34]) have been proposed.

For a typical deep-learning SISR method, image features are extracted from the input LR image through a set of network blocks first and then exploited to reconstruct the HR image. In general, the input image has features of different granularity levels, as demonstrated in Fig. 1. In this illustrative example, three feature granularities are specified: *coarse-grained features*, e.g., colors and illumination; *medium-grained features*, e.g., image edges; and *fine-grained features*, e.g., textures and spots. Note that there is no clear boundary between neighbouring feature granularities. For example, textures could be treated as small edges and thus belongs to the medium-grained level, especially when they are in a regular pattern.

The performance of a deep-learning SISR method could be degraded if it fails to extract features over all the granularity levels. To tackle this problem, a novel deep-learning network is proposed in the present paper. Our network consists of a set of *nested multi-axis learning blocks* (NMLBs) and is thus termed the *nested multi-axis learning network* (NMLNet). Each NMLB has an *outer* multi-axis structure, which contains three axes dedicated to extracting coarse-, medium-, and fine-grained features, respectively. Specifically, the first axis performs a global average pooling operation to extract coarse-grained features. The second axis extracts medium-grained features via a set of 7×7 depth-wise convolutions. The third axis delivers fine-grained features to the feature map at the next level through a skip connection. Moreover, with the concern that our human visual system has higher sensitivity to those medium-grained features (e.g., edges), the medium-grained axis further contains an *inner* multi-axis structure. This inner structure is stacked with four parallel axes and a few cross connections, and can capture rich medium-grained features of various depths. Then, by transmitting image features via the nested outer and inner multi-axis structure, efficient information propagation is achieved throughout our developed network. Finally, an efficient attention block, called the *two-tier attention block* (TAB), is proposed. By using the TAB, the vital features are highlighted and redundant features are suppressed on both the channel and spatial dimensions. In consequence, the discriminative representation ability of the network is improved. The main contributions of our work are summarized as follows:

- An efficient *nested multi-axis learning network* (NMLNet) is proposed to improve SISR performance via capturing rich image features at multiple granularity levels. The NMLNet achieves superior performance over the state-of-the-art methods while maintaining a relatively small model size.
- A novel *nested multi-axis learning block* (NMLB) is developed to extract features of various granularities via multiple axes incorporating in a nested inner-outer structure. Due to the combination of features at different granularity levels, our model has a powerful ability of feature representation.
- A *two-tier attention block* (TAB) is proposed to adaptively rescale both channel and spatial-wise features for further boosting the discriminative representation ability of the network.

## 2    Related Work

### 2.1    Deep Learning SISR Methods

Deep learning SISR methods have been extensively developed in recent years. As the first attempt, Dong et al. [8] developed a three-layer convolutional neural network for SISR, called the SRCNN. Residual learning strategies were then employed in the VDSR [16] and MemNet [31] to learn residual information. Later on, it was found that SISR performance can benefit to some extent from network depth and skip connections. Therefore, Lim et al. [20] built a deeper network (EDSR) structure by enhancing the residual block and expanding the network size, resulting in improved SISR performance. Zhang et al. [34] used a residual learning strategy to build a deep residual network (RCAN) with channel attention mechanism. Inspired by the attention mechanism as well, Dai et al. [6] proposed a second-order attention network (SAN) to enhance feature representation and correlation. Ahn et al. [3] used a cascade mechanism to construct a network (CARN) suitable for mobile scenes. Hui et al. [15] utilized information distillation to speed up network inference while achieving good performance. An information multi-distillation mechanism was used in IMDN [14] to extract hierarchical features. Luo et al. [26] proposed LatticeNet with lattice blocks to adaptively combine residual blocks.

### 2.2    Attention Mechanism

The attention mechanism in human visual system means that we always tend to focus on salient objects in real-world scenes. In recent years, many studies have been conducted on attention mechanisms in deep neural networks. Hu et al. [12] proposed SENet to exploit a channel attention mechanism for processing channel-wise features based on the weights of different channels. Woo et al. [32] designed CBAM to employs two serial attentions to deal with feature correlations in the spatial and channel dimensions. Liu et al. [22] developed a non-local neural network for SISR that incorporates non-local attention and captures long-range spatial dependencies. Lie et al. [23] proposed ESA that can pay more attention to the content of critical spaces. In this paper, an attention module will also also be developed and incorporated into our nested multi-axis learning block, by which salient features are enhanced while redundant features are suppressed.

## 3    The Proposed Method

### 3.1    Network Architecture

Our nested multi-axis learning network (NMLNet) consists of two stages: *feature extraction* (FE) and *high-quality image reconstruction* (HQR), as demonstrated in Fig. 2a. Denote the input LR and output SR images as $X$ and $Y$, respectively. At the beginning of the first stage, a set of shallow features, denoted as $F_0 \in \mathbb{R}^{H \times W \times C}$, are extracted from $X$:

$$F_0 = \text{Conv}_{3 \times 3}(X), \tag{1}$$

where $\text{Conv}_{3 \times 3}(\cdot)$ is a 3×3 convolution layer that performs a non-linear mapping from a low dimensional feature space to a high dimensional feature space.

A series of *hierarchical feature aggregation groups* (HFAGs) and *hierarchical learning connections* are then used to conduct feature extraction, followed by a 1×1 convolutional layer to control the number of output feature channels. Denote by $H_i(\cdot)$ the $i$-th HFAG, and $H_f(\cdot)$ a concatenation that fuses intermediate features $F_1, F_2, ..., F_K$. The output set of deep features, denoted as $F \in \mathbb{R}^{H \times W \times C}$, is formulated as follows:

$$F_i = H_i(F_{i-1}), \quad i = 1, 2, ..., M; \tag{2}$$

$$F = H_f(F_1, F_2, ..., F_M). \tag{3}$$

In more detail, the HFAG is stacked with $K$ *nested multi-axis learning blocks* (NMLBs) followed by a 1×1 convolutional layer, referring to Fig. 2b. Moreover, we use a 3×3 convolutional layer in the tail of HFAG to refine the feature maps. Denote by $F_i^{(0)}$ and $H_i^{(n)}$ the $i$-th HFAG input features and the $n$-th NMLB in the $i$-th HFAG, respectively. The intermediate feature sets $F_i^{(1)}, F_i^{(2)}, ..., F_i^{(K)}$ and the output feature set $F_i$ of the $i$-th HFAG are formulated as follows:

$$F_i^{(n)} = H_i^{(n)}\left(F_i^{(n-1)}\right); \quad n = 1, 2, ..., K; \tag{4}$$

$$F_i = \text{Conv}_{3 \times 3}\left(\text{Conv}_{1 \times 1}\left(F_i^{(K)}\right)\right). \tag{5}$$

The output of the feature extraction stage, $F$, is then fed into the second stage. In this image reconstruction stage, the *two-tier attention block* is exploited to perform a feature enhancement first. Then, a $3 \times 3$ convolutional layer is used to extract more spatial context information. After that, a global skip connection is executed to transfer shallow features $F_0$ into the image reconstruction process. Finally, an upsampling is conducted to produce the SR image $Y$. This stage can be formulated as:

$$Y = U(\text{Conv}_{3 \times 3}(T(F)) + F_0), \tag{6}$$

where $T(\cdot)$ denotes our developed TAB and $U(\cdot)$ is the upsampling module.

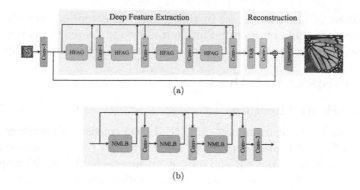

(a)

(b)

**Fig. 2.** Architecture of our developed *nested multi-axis learning network* (NMLNet). **a** Outline. **b** Details of the *hierarchical feature aggregation group* (HFAG).

## 3.2 Nested Multi-axis Learning Block

In this subsection, the details of our *nested multi-axis learning block* (NMLB) are presented and discussed. The NMLB has a nested multi-axis structure that aggregate features at different granularity levels, as demonstrated in Fig. 3. In particular, it is well-optimized for SISR and achieves a model size-performance trade-off. The outer multi-axis structure of our NMLB consists of three axes: the coarse-, medium- and fine-grained axes, described as follows, respectively.

**Coarse-Grained Axis.** This axis employs a *global average* pooling layer to extract features at a highly coarse granularity level, such as image colors and illumination. Note that at this granularity level, image spatial information related to edges, textures, and noise effects, can be strongly suppressed. To improve the representation of the extracted features while controlling the number of channels, an additional 1×1 convolutional layer is also added.

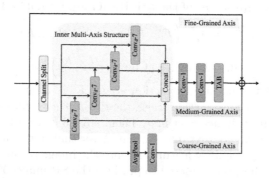

**Fig. 3.** The proposed *nested multi-axis learning block* (NMLB), where $Conv_d$-7 denotes a 7×7 depth-wise convolutional layer and TAB is the *two-tier attention block*.

**Medium-Grained Axis.** Our human visual system has a high sensitivity to medium-grained image features, e.g., edges. In fact, the quality of edges in a reconstructed HR image has a direct impact on the SISR performance visually. With this concern, the *medium-grained axis* has an *inner multi-axis structure*, by which informative edge features are captured over a wide range of network depths. Specifically, the inner multi-axis structure is stacked with four parallel axes and a few cross connections, referring to Fig. 3.

Recently, researchers revisited the use of large kernel size (say, lager than $5 \times 5$) and mentioned that stacking a set of large spatial convolutions could yield a powerful paradigm [7,10,24]. For example, Ding et al. [7] proved that a few large kernels can efficiently produce large effective receptive fields. Inspired by these previous works, the medium-grained axis is developed with $7 \times 7$ depthwise convolutions for achieving large receptive fields. To be specific, in each axis of the inner multi-axis structure, a depth-wise convolutional layer with a kernel size of $7 \times 7$ is used to extract features, followed by two $1 \times 1$ convolutions to add more nonlinearities and enhance the model's representational capacity.

The design of the inner multi-axis structure has multiple benefits. First, by splitting the input feature map equally into 4 groups with respect to the channel dimension, the number of channels in each group is only $1/4$ of the total channel number. Therefore, the enhancement of feature representation can be achieved without significantly increasing the number of parameters. Second, due to the parallel use of 4 axes, the inner multi-axis structure can produce different levels of medium-grained features over a wide range of network depths. Furthermore, the use of cross-connections allows the feature map of one axis to be fused with that of another axis, and thus enables information communication across channels. By aggregating the axes of different depths to share their weights, the network can obtain richer spatial information as well as better feature expression capability. Third, information of different levels can be efficiently propagated throughout the network via the parallel and cross-flow layout of this inner multi-axis structure. Finally, the TAB embedded in this medium-grained axis can further enhance salient features and suppress redundant ones.

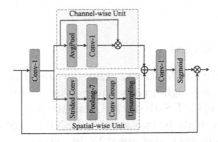

**Fig. 4.** The proposed *two-tier attention block* (TAB).

**Fine-Grained Axis.** This axis directly delivers the input feature map to the end of the current block through a skip connection. As a result, fine-grained features can be preserved in the current round of feature extraction and thus throughout the network. Moreover, the fine-grained axis effectively improves information conveying ability and benefits gradient propagation, thereby alleviating gradient disappearance and explosion issues during network training.

In closing, by transmitting features of different granularity levels via the nested outer-inner structure, an efficient flow of feature information throughout our developed network is achieved. Moreover, our proposed NMLB can aggregate coarse-, medium-, and fine-grained features, and then generate expressive and rich feature maps.

### 3.3    Two-Tier Attention Block

Liu et al. [23] introduced the *enhanced spatial attention* (ESA), which focuses on the region of interest in the spatial dimension and extracts more representative features by leveraging important spatial information. Although the ESA can improve SISR performance in terms of the PSNR value, it lacks feature correlations in the channel dimension and could produce redundant channel information. To overcome the difficulty, a *two-tier attention block* (TAB) is proposed and used is this paper. As depicted in Fig. 4, the TAB contains a channel-wise unit and a spatial-wise unit that can deal with feature correlations and highlight important information in both dimensions. In particular, a channel-wise unit in embedded into the initial ESA block to focus on important channel dimension features. The channel-wise unit consists of a global average pooling layer to capture global information from first-order statistics of features, followed by a 1×1 convolutional layer to enhance discriminative representations. Therefore, the network can emphasize meaningful channel features while suppressing redundant features with the help of the channel-wise unit. At the tail of TAB, the channel-wise and spatial-wise attentions are aggregated together to perform a feature enhancement in both the channel and spatial dimensions.

## 4    Experiments

### 4.1    Experimental Setups

**Datasets and Evaluation Metrics.**    Our developed network is trained with the DIV2K dataset [2] (800 high-quality images) and evaluated on five benchmark datasets: Set5 [4], Set14 [33], BSD100 [27], Urban100 [13], and Manga109 [28]. The SISR performance is evaluate by two metrics: PSNR and SSIM. Both metrics are computed on the Y channel of transformed YCbCr space.

**Implementation Details.** The LR images used in our experiments are created with the scaling factors $[\times 1/2, \times 1/3, \times 1/4]$ by exploiting the bicubic method in MATLAB R2017a. During the network training, $128 \times 128$ RGB image patches are fed into our model, and the mini-batch size is set to 32. The Adam optimizer [25] is adopted the optimization problem of training. The learning rate is initialized as $2 \times 10^{-4}$ and decreases to half every $2 \times 10^5$ steps. $L_1$ loss function is used to optimize the model. The PyTorch framework is applied to implement our model with NVIDIA TITAN Xp GPU (12G memory).

## 4.2 Comparison with State-of-the-Arts.

The proposed NMLNet is compared with 12 state-of-the-art methods: SRCNN [8], FSRCNN [9], VDSR [16], DRCN [17], LapSRN [19], NLRN [22], IDN [15], CARN [3], IMDN [14], B-GSCN10 [21], ARRFN [29], LatticeNet [26]. The SISR results with magnification factors $\times 2$, $\times 3$, and $\times 4$ are documented in Table 1. One can see that our NMLNet clearly outperforms the existing methods in most comparison cases. In particular, its performance gain is more prominent on Manga109 and Urban100. In fact, images in these two datasets have richer edges and regular-pattern textures, while our NMLNet has been designed to pay more attention to these medium-grained features with its inner multi-axis structure.

Subjective evaluation results obtained with three different test images are presented in Fig. 5. It is seen that the existing SISR methods frequently exhibit distinct ringing or blurring artifacts, especially around edges. In comparison, our method achieves much better performance, e.g., sharper edges and much less artifacts. These results consistently demonstrate the superiority of the proposed NMLNet in feature extraction and representation.

## 4.3 Ablation Studies

In what follows, three ablation studies are performed to investigate the impacts of the inner multi-axis structure, the two-tier attention block, and the nested multi-axis learning block, respectively.

**Table 1.** Comparison of different SISR methods in terms of average PSNR/SSIM for magnification factor ×2, ×3, and ×4. The best results are highlighted in boldface.

| Scale | Method | Params | Set5 | Set14 | BSD100 | Urban100 | Manga109 |
|---|---|---|---|---|---|---|---|
| ×2 | SRCNN [8] | 0.057M | 36.66/.9542 | 32.45/.9607 | 32.36/.8879 | 29.50/.8946 | 35.60/.9663 |
| | FSRCNN [9] | 0.012M | 37.00/.9558 | 32.63/.9088 | 32.53/.8920 | 29.88/.9020 | 36.67/.9710 |
| | VDSR [16] | 0.665M | 37.53/.9587 | 33.03/.9124 | 31.90/.8960 | 30.76/.9140 | 37.22/.9750 |
| | DRCN [17] | 1.774M | 37.63/.9588 | 33.04/.9118 | 31.85/.8942 | 30.75/.9133 | 37.55/.9732 |
| | LapSRN [19] | 0.813M | 37.52/.9591 | 33.08/.9130 | 31.80/.8950 | 30.41/.9101 | 37.27/.9740 |
| | IDN [15] | 0.579M | 37.85/.9598 | 33.58/.9178 | 32.11/.8989 | 31.95/.9266 | 38.23/.9758 |
| | NLRN [22] | 0.350M | 38.00/.9603 | 33.46/.9159 | 32.19/.8992 | 31.81/.9249 | -/- |
| | CARN [3] | 1.592M | 37.76/.9509 | 33.52/.9166 | 32.09/.8978 | 31.92/.9256 | 38.36/.9765 |
| | IMDN [14] | 0.694M | 38.00/.9605 | 33.63/.9177 | 32.19/.8996 | 32.17/.9283 | 38.88/.9774 |
| | B-GSCN10 [21] | 1.490M | 38.06/.9606 | 33.64/.9182 | 32.19/.8999 | 32.19/.9293 | 38.64/.9771 |
| | ARRFN [29] | 0.988M | 38.01/.9606 | 33.66/.9197 | 32.20/.8999 | 32.27/.9295 | -/- |
| | LatticeNet [26] | 0.756M | 38.15/.9610 | 33.78/**.9193** | 32.25/.9005 | 32.42/.9302 | -/- |
| | **NMLN (Ours)** | 0.916M | **38.17/.9612** | **33.81**/.9193 | **32.30/.9013** | **32.66/.9334** | **39.19/.9780** |
| ×3 | SRCNN [8] | 0.057M | 32.75/.9090 | 29.30/.8251 | 28.41/.7863 | 26.24/.7989 | 30.48/.9117 |
| | FSRCNN [9] | 0.012M | 33.18/.9140 | 29.37/.8240 | 28.53/.7910 | 26.43/.8080 | 31.10/.9210 |
| | VDSR [16] | 0.665M | 33.66/.9213 | 29.77/.8314 | 28.82/.7976 | 27.14/.8279 | 32.01/.9340 |
| | DRCN [17] | 1.774M | 33.82/.9226 | 29.76/.8311 | 28.80/.7963 | 27.51/.8276 | 32.24/.9340 |
| | IDN [15] | 0.588M | 34.24/.9260 | 30.27/.8408 | 29.03/.8038 | 27.99/.8489 | 33.30/.9421 |
| | NLRN [22] | 0.350M | 34.27/.9206 | 30.16/.8374 | 29.06/.8026 | 27.93/.8453 | -/- |
| | CARN [3] | 1.592M | 34.29/.9255 | 30.29/.8407 | 29.06/.8034 | 28.06/.8493 | 33.50/.9440 |
| | IMDN [14] | 0.703M | 34.36/.9270 | 30.32/.8417 | 29.09/.8046 | 28.17/.8519 | 33.61/.9445 |
| | B-GSCN10 [21] | 1.510M | 34.40/.9271 | 30.35/.8425 | 29.11/.8053 | 28.20/.8535 | 33.54/.9445 |
| | ARRFN [29] | 0.996M | 34.38/.9272 | 30.36/.8442 | 29.09/.8050 | 28.22/.8522 | -/- |
| | LatticeNet [26] | 0.765M | 34.52/.9281 | 30.39/.8424 | 29.15/.8059 | 28.33/.8538 | -/- |
| | **NMLN (Ours)** | 0.925M | **34.63/.9287** | **30.49/.8452** | **29.21/.8084** | **28.52/.8600** | **34.09/.9478** |
| ×4 | SRCNN [8] | 0.057M | 30.48/.8628 | 27.50/.7513 | 26.90/.7101 | 24.52/.7221 | 27.58/.8555 |
| | FSRCNN [9] | 0.012M | 30.72/.8660 | 27.61/.7550 | 26.98/.7150 | 24.62/.7280 | 27.90/.8610 |
| | VDSR [16] | 0.665M | 31.35/.8838 | 28.01/.7674 | 27.29/.7251 | 25.18/.7524 | 28.83/.8870 |
| | DRCNcite [17] | 1.774M | 31.53/.8854 | 28.02/.7670 | 27.23/.7233 | 25.14/.5710 | 28.93/.8854 |
| | LapSRN [19] | 0.813M | 31.54/.8850 | 28.19/.7720 | 27.32/.7270 | 25.21/.7560 | 29.09/.8900 |
| | IDN [15] | 0.677M | 31.99/.8928 | 28.52/.7794 | 27.52/.7339 | 25.92/.7801 | 30.22/.9032 |
| | NLRN [22] | 0.350M | 31.92/.8916 | 28.36/.7745 | 27.48/.7406 | 25.79/.7729 | -/- |
| | CARN [3] | 1.592M | 32.13/.8937 | 28.60/.7806 | 27.58/.7349 | 26.07/.7837 | 30.47/.9084 |
| | IMDN [14] | 0.715M | 32.21/.8948 | 28.58/.7811 | 27.56/.7353 | 26.04/.7838 | 30.45/.9075 |
| | B-GSCN10 [21] | 1.530M | 32.18/.8950 | 28.60/.7821 | 27.59/.7364 | 26.12/.7872 | 30.50/.9080 |
| | ARRFN [29] | 1.008M | 32.22/.8952 | 28.60/.7817 | 27.57/.7355 | 26.09/.7858 | -/- |
| | LatticeNet [26] | 0.777M | 32.30/.8962 | 28.68/.7830 | 27.62/.7367 | **26.25**/.7873 | -/- |
| | **NMLN (Ours)** | 0.936M | **32.41/.8978** | **28.70/.7839** | **27.63/.7383** | 26.24/**.7911** | **30.78/.9106** |

**The Inner Multi-axis Structure.** To investigate the impact of kernel size of the convolutional layers used in the inner multi-axis structure, four different cases are studied: 3×3, 5×5, 7×7, and 9×9. As shown in Table 2, when the kernel size increases from 3×3 to 7×7, the SISR performance can be progressively improved. To be specific, the inner multi-axis structure with kernel size 7×7 achieves the best results, at the expense of additional 18K parameters when compared to

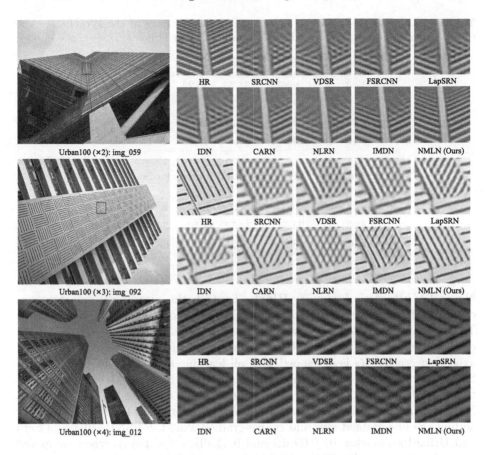

**Fig. 5.** SISR results of different methods.

the case of 5×5. On the other hand, as the kernel size further increases to 9×9, the PSNR values decrease. In consequence, the default size of the convolutional kernel is taken as 7×7.

**Two-Tier Attention Block.** To verify the effectiveness of our developed TAB, several alternative attention blocks proposed in the literature, as well as the TAB, are individually incorporated into the proposed network. The SISR results of different ablation cases are shown in Table 3, including a baseline case without using any attention block, and the cases using channel attention (CA) [12], CBAM [32], ESA [23] and our TAB, respectively. One can see that the NMLNet with CA achieves 34.54 dB on Set5 and 28.38 dB on Urban100, indicating a successful use of attention mechanism. However, the CBAM case yields a much lower PSNR value than that of the baseline and CA cases. In fact, for this case there is a loss of channel information related to textures and edges. The ESA case outperforms the CA due to its powerful spatial feature representations. In comparison, our TAB produces the best performance, and achieves PNSR gains over the ESA by 0.04 dB and 0.03 dB on Set5 and Urban100, respectively.

**Table 2.** Ablation study on the impact of different settings of the kernel size. The results are obtained on three benchmark datasets for ×3 SISR.

| Kernel Size | Params | Set5 | Set14 | BSD100 |
|---|---|---|---|---|
| 3×3 | 896K | 34.35 | 30.24 | 29.03 |
| 5×5 | 907K | 34.36 | 30.31 | 29.07 |
| 7×7 | 925K | **34.63** | **30.49** | **29.21** |
| 9×9 | 948K | 34.48 | 30.36 | 29.11 |

**Table 3.** Ablation study on the attention block of our NMLNet.

| Dataset | Baseline | CA | CBMA | ESA | TAB |
|---|---|---|---|---|---|
| Set5 (×3) | 34.51 | 34.54 | 34.50 | 34.59 | **34.63** |
| Urban100 (×3) | 28.34 | 28.38 | 28.30 | 28.49 | **28.52** |

**Nested Multi-Axis Learning Block.** To study the outer multi-axis structure of NMLB, four cases are developed, denoted as $R_a$, $R_b$, $R_c$, and $R_d$, respectively. To be specific, $R_a$ is developed with the medium-grained axis *only*. $R_b$ and $R_c$ are developed on $R_a$ by further adding the fine-grained axis and the coarse-grained axis, respectively. $R_d$ is developed with all learning axes, i.e., our used NMLB. SISR results are then obtained with the four cases on Set5 and Urban100, respectively, as documented in Table 4. One can see that the case $R_d$, i.e., our used NMLB, generates the best performance over the other cases. In more detail, after adding the fine-grained axis and coarse-grained axis, the PSNR values on Set5 and Urban100 increase by 0.09 dB and 0.24 dB, respectively, when compared to the baseline case $R_a$. This validates that the NMLB can fully utilize features at different granularity levels and enhance informative features to improve the quality of generated SR images.

## 4.4   Network Complexity

Fig. 6 depicts a comparison of different SISR methods in terms of PSNR and the number of network parameters. It is seen that our NMLNet delivers the highest PSNR over the existing state-of-the-arts with a medium-level model size. This indicates that our NMLNet has achieved a favorable trade-off between SISR performance and model complexity.

**Table 4.** Ablation study on the setting of granularity axes in our proposed NMLB.

| Name | $R_a$ | $R_b$ | $R_c$ | $R_d$ |
|---|---|---|---|---|
| Coarse-grained axis | | | ✓ | ✓ |
| Medium-grained axis | ✓ | ✓ | ✓ | ✓ |
| Fine-grained axis | | ✓ | | ✓ |
| Set5 (×3) | 34.54 | 34.55 | 34.58 | **34.63** |
| Urban100 (×3) | 28.28 | 28.30 | 28.31 | **28.52** |

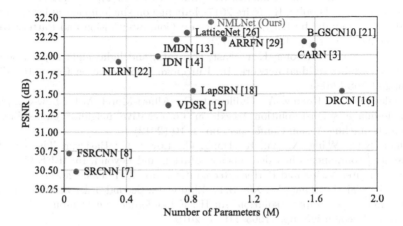

**Fig. 6.** A comparison of different SISR methods with respect to PSNR and the number of network parameters, where Set5 (×4) is experimented.

## 5   Conclusions

A novel deep-learning model for SISR that has a *nested inner-outer multi-axis* structure is proposed in this paper. Our network, termed NMLNet, can extract rich image features at multiple granularity levels, and thus significantly improve feature representation ability. Specifically, a *nested multi-axis learning block* (NMLB) is developed to extract coarse-, medium-, and fine-grained features with its outer multi-axis layout. The medium-grained axis further has an inner multi-axis structure for capturing edge features over a wide range of network depths. In consequence, image edges can be reconstructed with high quality, with which visually-pleasing SISR results are yielded. To maximize discriminative representations of the network, a *two-tier attention block* (TAB) is also developed to enhance salient features and suppress redundant ones in both the channel and spatial dimensions. Extensive experimental results obtained on benchmark datasets show that the proposed NMLNet delivers superior performance over a number of state-of-the-art SISR methods.

**Acknowledgement.** This work was supported in part by the Natural Science Foundation of the Jiangsu Higher Education Institutions of China under Grant 21KJA520007, in part by the National Natural Science Foundation of China under Grant 61572341, in part by the Priority Academic Program Development of Jiangsu Higher Education Institutions, in part by Collaborative Innovation Center of Novel Software Technology and Industrialization.

# References

1. Aakerberg, A., Nasrollahi, K., Moeslund, T.B.: Real-world super-resolution of face-images from surveillance cameras. IET Image Proc. **16**(2), 442–452 (2022)
2. Agustsson, E., Timofte, R.: Ntire 2017 challenge on single image super-resolution: dataset and study. In: IEEE Conference on Computer Vision and Pattern Recognition Workshops, pp. 126–135 (2017)
3. Ahn, N., Kang, B., Sohn, K.A.: Fast, accurate, and lightweight super-resolution with cascading residual network. In: European Conference on Computer Vision, pp. 252–268 (2018)
4. Bevilacqua, M., Roumy, A., Guillemot, C., Alberi-Morel, M.L.: Low-complexity single-image super-resolution based on nonnegative neighbor embedding. In: British Machine Vision Conference, pp. 1–10 (2012)
5. Chan, K.C., Wang, X., Yu, K., Dong, C., Loy, C.C.: Basicvsr: The search for essential components in video super-resolution and beyond. In: IEEE Conference on Computer Vision and Pattern Recognition, pp. 4947–4956 (2021)
6. Dai, T., Cai, J., Zhang, Y., Xia, S.T., Zhang, L.: Second-order attention network for single image super-resolution. In: IEEE Conference on Computer Vision and Pattern Recognition, pp. 11065–11074 (2019)
7. Ding, X., Zhang, X., Zhou, Y., Han, J., Ding, G., Sun, J.: Scaling up your kernels to 31x31: Revisiting large kernel design in CNNS. arXiv preprint arXiv:2203.06717 (2022)
8. Dong, C., Loy, C.C., He, K., Tang, X.: Learning a deep convolutional network for image super-resolution. In: European Conference on Computer Vision, pp. 184–199 (2014)
9. Dong, C., Loy, C.C., He, K., Tang, X.: Image super-resolution using deep convolutional networks. IEEE Trans. Pattern Anal. Mach. Intell. **38**(2), 295–307 (2015)
10. Han, Q., Fan, Z., Dai, Q., Sun, L., Cheng, M.M., Liu, J., Wang, J.: On the connection between local attention and dynamic depth-wise convolution. In: International Conference on Learning Representations (2021)
11. Haris, M., Shakhnarovich, G., Ukita, N.: Task-driven super resolution: object detection in low-resolution images. In: International Conference on Neural Information Processing, pp. 387–395 (2021)
12. Hu, J., Shen, L., Sun, G.: Squeeze-and-excitation networks. In: IEEE Conference on Computer Vision and Pattern Recognition, pp. 7132–7141 (2018)
13. Huang, J.B., Singh, A., Ahuja, N.: Single image super-resolution from transformed self-exemplars. In: IEEE Conference on Computer Vision and Pattern Recognition, pp. 5197–5206 (2015)
14. Hui, Z., Gao, X., Yang, Y., Wang, X.: Lightweight image super-resolution with information multi-distillation network. In: ACM International Conference on Multimedia, pp. 2024–2032 (2019)
15. Hui, Z., Wang, X., Gao, X.: Fast and accurate single image super-resolution via information distillation network. In: IEEE Conference on Computer Vision and Pattern Recognition, pp. 723–731 (2018)

16. Kim, J., Lee, J.K., Lee, K.M.: Accurate image super-resolution using very deep convolutional networks. In: IEEE Conference on Computer Vision and Pattern Recognition, pp. 1646–1654 (2016)
17. Kim, J., Lee, J.K., Lee, K.M.: Deeply-recursive convolutional network for image super-resolution. In: IEEE Conference on Computer Vision and Pattern Recognition, pp. 1637–1645 (2016)
18. Kim, J., Li, G., Yun, I., Jung, C., Kim, J.: Edge and identity preserving network for face super-resolution. Neurocomputing **446**, 11–22 (2021)
19. Lai, W.S., Huang, J.B., Ahuja, N., Yang, M.H.: Deep laplacian pyramid networks for fast and accurate super-resolution. In: IEEE Conference on Computer Vision and Pattern Recognition, pp. 624–632 (2017)
20. Lim, B., Son, S., Kim, H., Nah, S., Mu Lee, K.: Enhanced deep residual networks for single image super-resolution. In: IEEE Conference on Computer Vision and Pattern Recognition, pp. 136–144 (2017)
21. Liu, C., Lei, P.: An efficient group skip-connecting network for image super-resolution. Knowl.-Based Syst. **222**, 107017 (2021)
22. Liu, D., Wen, B., Fan, Y., Loy, C.C., Huang, T.S.: Non-local recurrent network for image restoration. Advances in Neural Information Processing Systems 31 (2018)
23. Liu, J., Zhang, W., Tang, Y., Tang, J., Wu, G.: Residual feature aggregation network for image super-resolution. In: IEEE Conference on Computer Vision and Pattern Recognition, pp. 2359–2368 (2020)
24. Liu, Z., Mao, H., Wu, C.Y., Feichtenhofer, C., Darrell, T., Xie, S.: A convnet for the 2020s. arXiv preprint arXiv:2201.03545 (2022)
25. Loshchilov, I., Hutter, F.: Decoupled weight decay regularization. arXiv preprint arXiv:1711.05101 (2017)
26. Luo, X., Xie, Y., Zhang, Y., Qu, Y., Li, C., Fu, Y.: Latticenet: towards lightweight image super-resolution with lattice block. In: European Conference on Computer Vision, pp. 272–289 (2020)
27. Martin, D., Fowlkes, C., Tal, D., Malik, J.: A database of human segmented natural images and its application to evaluating segmentation algorithms and measuring ecological statistics. In: IEEE International Conference on Computer Vision, pp. 416–423 (2001)
28. Matsui, Y., Ito, K., Aramaki, Y., Fujimoto, A., Ogawa, T., Yamasaki, T., Aizawa, K.: Sketch-based manga retrieval using manga109 dataset. Multimed. Tools Appl. **76**(20), 21811–21838 (2017)
29. Qin, J., Zhang, R.: Lightweight single image super-resolution with attentive residual refinement network. Neurocomputing **500**, 846–855 (2022)
30. Qiu, D., Zheng, L., Zhu, J., Huang, D.: Multiple improved residual networks for medical image super-resolution. Futur. Gener. Comput. Syst. **116**, 200–208 (2021)
31. Tai, Y., Yang, J., Liu, X., Xu, C.: Memnet: A persistent memory network for image restoration. In: IEEE International Conference on Computer Vision, pp. 4539–4547 (2017)
32. Woo, S., Park, J., Lee, J.Y., Kweon, I.S.: Cbam: Convolutional block attention module. In: European Conference on Computer Vision, pp. 3–19 (2018)
33. Zeyde, R., Elad, M., Protter, M.: On single image scale-up using sparse-representations. In: International Conference on Curves and Surfaces, pp. 711–730 (2010)
34. Zhang, Y., Li, K., Li, K., Wang, L., Zhong, B., Fu, Y.: Image super-resolution using very deep residual channel attention networks. In: European Conference on Computer Vision, pp. 286–301 (2018)

# Efficient Scale Divide and Conquer Network for Object Detection

Yangyang Liu[1], Yanyan Shi[1], Ziteng Qiao[2], Yi Zhang[2], Shaowu Yang[1],
and Dianxi Shi[1,2,3(✉)]

[1] College of Computer, National University of Defense Technology, Changsha, China
{liuyangyang,dxshi}@nudt.edu.cn
[2] Artificial Intelligence Research Center, Defense Innovation Institute, Beijing, China
[3] Tianjin Artificial Intelligence Innovation Center, Tianjin, China

**Abstract.** Multi-scale methods are often used to improve the accuracy of detection models. However, this approach is usually computationally expensive. In this paper, we introduce an efficient Scale Divide and Conquer Network (ScaleDCNet) based on the keypoint object detection framework, which accomplishes independent detection at each scale with minimal cost. To achieve this goal, we propose a new one-stage detection network, which consists of a scale feature selection module and a scale-aware keypoint matching approach. The scale feature selection module obtains features of various sizes through an attention mechanism to divide and conquer the scale problem. The scale-aware keypoint matching method is used to make independent predictions for the positions of objects of different sizes. With the above approaches, our ScaleNet improves the detection ability of objects of different sizes, reduces the probability of missing and false detection, and performs better in scale deformation and occlusion. We evaluate on the MS-COCO dataset and our model achieves high accuracy with low computational resources compared to baseline and other algorithms.

**Keywords:** Multi-scale detection · Anchor-free detection · Keypoint · Divide and conquer

## 1 Introduction

With the continuous exploration of convolutional neural networks, object detection has developed rapidly in recent years. However, object detection currently faces many challenges due to scale deformation and occlusion [5], making the multi-scale problem a critical one to be solved [17]. Notably, a major drawback of multi-scale detection algorithms is that they require more computational resources [18,23]. Due to the diversity of scales, both the multi-scale of the input features and the fusion of different features will require more computational resources. In addition, most of the existing object detection algorithms [7,15,25] use neural networks with deep layers or higher resolution image inputs to pursue higher accuracy, which inevitably brings high computational costs.

In this paper, we explore a more efficient scale divide-and-conquer object detection algorithm to achieve high-precision object detection with low computational resources. Attention maps of different sizes are obtained from low-resolution image inputs, which are used to propose the possible locations and approximate sizes of the targets. Feature regions of different scales are obtained by selective cropping on the original image, and the center point of the region is detected to obtain the object. This process can effectively reduce the number of pixels processed, making the training more efficient. As shown in Fig. 1, our algorithm performs better in detecting small-sized objects and dense objects.

|     (a)     |     (b)     |     (c)     |     (d)     |

**Fig. 1.** Qualitative examples: CornerNet-Saccade (ac) and our ScaleDCNet (bd). (ab) illustrates that our method has fewer missed detections and better detection of small objects (like the bird). (cd) illustrates that our method has fewer false detections and detects more correctly. The results show that our ScaleDCNet performs better in scale deformation and occlusion.

Considering the choice of the algorithmic framework, the traditional anchor-based object detection algorithm [3,9,20,21] will have many hyperparameters and the design of the anchor is mostly empirical. Its ability to locate objects with different geometric shapes is poor. In contrast, the anchor-free method can flexibly locate objects of any shape because it does not use anchor box candidates, so it has a better recall rate. Because of this, anchor-free object detection algorithm [6,14,15,28] has attracted much attention in recent years.

As an important representative of the anchor-free object detection algorithm, the keypoint object detection algorithm [6,15] is a method to obtain bounding boxes by extracting and matching feature points. The bottom-up algorithm in keypoint object detection groups multiple keypoints into one object. It first predicts all keypoints and then groups keypoints according to certain rules. This algorithm focuses on two processes: keypoint detection (how to generate keypoint feature maps) and keypoint grouping (how to achieve feature-to-object matching). We design a scale feature selection module and a scale-aware keypoint matching method for these two processes. Independent prediction of positions for objects of different sizes allows better control of the importance given to each position.

We summarize our contributions as follows: (1) We propose an effective divide-and-conquer strategy for scale, including a scale feature selection module and a scale-aware keypoint matching method. (2) Our approach uses selective cropping to focus on target regions, which saves more computational resources and makes training easier compared to other multi-scale algorithms. (3) We conduct extensive ablation experiments on the standard COCO benchmark to illustrate the effectiveness of our proposed components. Our method is more competitive in terms of accuracy compared to the popular one-stage detectors.

## 2   Related Works

**Multi-scale Detectors.** Multi-scale detection algorithms can be broadly classified into two approaches: image pyramids and feature pyramids. As a common method to improve the detection effect, the image pyramid mainly takes the multi-scale of the input image as the starting point. SNIP [23] and SNIPER [24] propose a scale normalization method that aims to perform multi-scale training more efficiently. Moreover, some general methods like multi-scale tests are widely used. The input of multi-scale images inevitably brings more computational power consumption and time cost. The memory and time overhead problems are becoming more and more prominent in practical applications. To solve this problem, some algorithms no longer take multiple images as input but use multi-scale features with different spatial resolutions to alleviate the scale variation. As a typical representative of feature pyramids, FPN [18] constructs semantically rich scale features by combining shallow and deep features [27]. FPN has also become an important component of object detection algorithms. Since then, a large number of feature fusion algorithms like PANet [19], NAS-FPN [7], Bi-FPN [26], etc. have emerged. To improve the detection performance of small objects, multi-scale feature fusion methods [29] have also been widely used in this field. This approach dominates in terms of speed, but it sacrifices the consistency of features at different scales. As confirmed by YOLOF [4], multi-scale feature fusion is not a critical role in FPN. The ability of FPN to effectively improve model accuracy stems from dividing and conquering the detection optimization problem, rather than simply fusing multi-scale features.

**Anchor-free Detectors.** CornerNet [15] starts the craze of keypoint-based object detection in the anchor-free framework. The CornerNet network model detects the bounding box as a pair of corner points (i.e., the top left and bottom right corners of the border). The authors of CornerNet then goes on to adapt their network architecture to design the more efficient CornerNet-Lite [16] algorithm. Based on the network architecture of CornetNet, a series of keypoint-based object detection algorithms with better accuracy emerged, such as ExtremeNet [30] and CenterNet [6]. Unlike CornerNet, the ExtremeNet algorithm detects objects by predicting extreme points and center points. CenterNet adds a central detection branch to the corner points and greatly improves the performance by verification of the center points. HoughNet [22] proposes a one-stage bottom-up object detection method based on a voting mechanism.

# 3   Method

## 3.1   Overview

We design an efficient scale divide and conquer algorithm based on the keypoint-based detector. In order to make independent predictions for the positions of objects of different sizes, we construct a scale feature selection module to obtain respective feature maps for small, medium and large objects. In the regression process, we use different matching strategies for keypoints of different sizes based on scale perception.

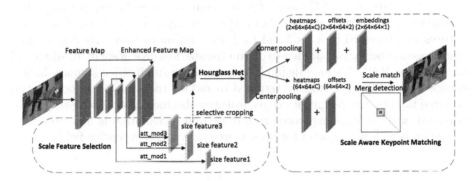

**Fig. 2.** An overview of our approach. It first predicts the size feature from low-resolution images and then selectively crops the objects of different sizes according to the size feature. The cropped images are input to the network to get the heatmap, offsets and embedding. Finally, the prediction is obtained by scale match and merge.

In this paper, we use CornerNet-Saccade [16] as the baseline. The overall network architecture is shown in Fig. 2. Like CornerNet-Saccade, we adopt Hourglass-54 as the backbone, which contains 3 hourglass modules with a depth of 54. Hourglass-54 uses residual modules [10] as the basic module for feature extraction. We use stride 2 instead of the max pooling to reduce the feature resolution. Each hourglass module reduces the feature resolution by 3 times and increases the number of feature channels (384, 384, 512). Different from CornerNet-Saccade corner detection, we use Hourglass to get 3 keypoints (top left, bottom right and center point). Therefore, the output of our network is $3\times$ C heatmaps, $3 \times 2$ offsets and $2 \times 1$ embeddings, where C denotes the category of the dataset. Heatmap denotes the location of keypoints in different categories and the possible confidence scores. Offset remaps the keypoints from the heatmap to the input image. The role of embedding is to help group pairs of corners belonging to the same object. A bounding box is generated if the distance of the embedding vectors is less than a threshold. The average scores of the corners are used as the detection scores.

## 3.2    Scale Feature Selection Module

The feature selection module in the existing Hourglass network obtains multi-scale features by fusing feature maps of different depths. However, it generates multi-level features thus sacrificing the consistency of features at different scales. In order to make different features deal with the target object of a specific size, the data label page used in training should be similar to the attention map, i.e., the center of the bounding box is set to 1 and the rest is set to 0. In the implementation process, the label is encoded into the form of the target and the network needs to generate the form of the attention feature. As shown in Fig. 3, the features obtained from the front layer of the Enhanced feature (feature1) after channel attention (SE layer) [12] are summed with the feature map after a jump connection (feature2) to obtain the back layer features. The back layer features are processed by a $3 \times 3$ and $1 \times 1$ convolution to obtain the size feature. This process is performed 3 times to obtain the size features of small, medium and large objects. With this module implementation, for small objects, more shallow feature information needs to be retained to reduce the impact of pooling, and for large targets, the weight of deeper features obtained after down-sampling is increased, while a large expansion rate of dilated convolution is used to obtain semantically rich higher-level features as well as a larger receptive field.

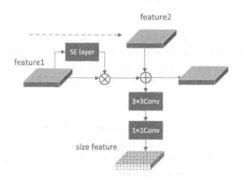

**Fig. 3.** Size feature selection module: for each Enhanced feature of the feature layer, the network prediction to get the attention feature form of size feature.

Independent prediction for different sizes of objects allows better control of the importance given to each size. Firstly, using low-resolution images as input, three size features are generated by the backbone network, corresponding to small, medium and large objects. The possible object locations are obtained based on the size feature. Then it uses the high-resolution input images and selects some of the regions extracted in the first step for accurate detection. After processing the downsized images, it is highly likely that some bounding boxes will be generated, but these boxes may not be very accurate due to the low resolution. Therefore, it needs to be evaluated in high resolution and get better bounding boxes. The position obtained from the bounding box prediction will provide more information about the object size. For the possible position and size information obtained from the size feature, different zoom sizes can be set for different sizes of objects. In brief, it is to selectively crop the input image according to the position and size information provided by the size feature, and then it uses the cropped result for more accurate object detection.

### 3.3   Scale Aware Keypoint Matching Method

Anchor-free methods tend to generate a large number of false-positive examples, so how to establish a close relationship between keypoints and objects becomes the main problem. After obtaining the heatmap of keypoints through corner pooling and center pooling, we first remove the bounding box based on simple geometric relationships and category information. The coordinates of the top left corner $(tl_x, tl_y)$ and the bottom right corner $(br_x, br_y)$ of bounding box j should satisfy $tl_x < br_x$ and $tl_y < br_y$. Then learning from the practice of CenterNet, we remove the unreasonable proposals by the geometric correspondence between corner points and center points. In this process, we find that the size of the center region in the bounding box affects the detection results. The key points of small-sized objects have a large impact on the whole when they are shifted, so a more relaxed matching strategy is needed, that is, the area of the center region should be larger. Correspondingly, the center region of large-size objects should be smaller. Different from CenterNet's dichotomy, we adopt different center matching regions for different objects of large, medium and small according to the border size. The center region is denoted as

$$R_c = \{(x, y) | ctl_x \le x \le cbr_x, ctl_y \le y \le cbr_y\} \tag{1}$$

Specifically, the relationship between the coordinates $(tl_x, tl_y), (br_x, br_y)$ of the bounding box j and the coordinates of its center region should be satisfied:

$$
\begin{cases}
ctl_x = \frac{tl_x + br_x}{2} - \frac{br_x - tl_x}{2n} \\
ctl_y = \frac{tl_y + br_y}{2} - \frac{br_y - tl_y}{2n} \\
cbr_x = \frac{tl_x + br_x}{2} + \frac{br_x - tl_x}{2n} \\
cbr_y = \frac{tl_y + br_y}{2} + \frac{br_y - tl_y}{2n}
\end{cases}
\begin{cases}
if \max(br_x - tl_x, br_y - tl_y) \le 32, n = 15 \\
elif \ 32 < \max(br_x - tl_x, br_y - tl_y) < 96, n = 20 \\
elif \max(br_x - tl_x, br_y - tl_y) \ge 96, n = 25
\end{cases}
\tag{2}
$$

According to Eq. 2, we can determine different center region for defferent size of objects.

### 3.4   Loss Function

In the design of the loss, we follow the basic design idea of CornerNet [15], and then add the attention loss for separate processing of the feature layer at multiple scales.

$$L = L_{\text{det}} + \alpha L_{\text{pull}} + \beta L_{\text{push}} + \gamma L_{\text{off}} + \theta L_{att} \tag{3}$$

The total loss function consists of regression loss $L_{\text{det}}$, grouping loss $L_{\text{pull}}$, $L_{\text{push}}$, offset loss $L_{\text{off}}$, and scale attention loss $L_{att}$. $L_{\text{det}}$ denote the focal loss and is used to train the network to detect corners and center keypoints. The grouping loss function consists of two parts, one is $L_{\text{pull}}$ that brings the keypoints of the same group closer together, and the other is $L_{\text{push}}$ that pushes the keypoints of different groups farther. The offset loss $L_{\text{off}}$ is designed to solve the accuracy loss problem when mapping the heat map to the input image, which uses SmoothL1Loss [8] in the training process. Attention loss $L_{att}$ is used to generate the size feature for different size objects. To weigh the impact of each loss function on the total loss function, it is controlled by $\alpha$, $\beta$, $\gamma$ and $\theta$. We set both $\alpha$ and $\beta$ to 0.1 and $\gamma$ to 1. Different from CornerNet, since our output is 3 keypoints, the loss associated with the center point is calculated when the regression and offset losses are calculated.

$$L_{\text{att}} = -\frac{1}{N} \sum_{c=1}^{C} \sum_{i=1}^{H} \sum_{j=1}^{W} \begin{cases} \left(1 - v_{c_{ij}}\right)^{\alpha} log\left(v_{c_{ij}}\right) & if\, y_{c_{ij}} = 1 \\ \left(1 - y_{c_{ij}}\right)^{\beta} \left(v_{c_{ij}}\right)^{\alpha} log\left(1 - v_{c_{ij}}\right) & otherwise \end{cases} \tag{4}$$

The multi-scale attention loss function is designed using a cross-entropy loss function, where $v_{cij}$ denotes the value of the predicted attention map at the (i, j) position of channel c and $y_{cij}$ denotes the ground truth at the corresponding position. In order to avoid the scale classification loss will have a large impact on the whole loss and avoid the regression loss being affected, we design a weight $\theta$ here, and this hyperparameter is set to 0.1 in the experiment.

## 4  Experiments

### 4.1  Experimental Setting

**Dataset.** We evaluate our model on the popular MS-COCO dataset. Consistent with other algorithms, we use the "trainval35k" setting [11]. That is, we use the 80K training images and the 35K validation images as training data. The remaining 5K images in the validation set are used for parameter tuning and ablation experiments. We finally evaluate it in the COCO Detection Challenge online test system (test-dev2017) for comparison with other algorithms.

**Training Efficiency.** We use fewer computational resources during training. We are able to train our module on only 4 Titan V GPUs with a total of 48GB GPU memory, while CornerNet, HoughNet, CenterNet and YOLOF require several times more GPU memory than our algorithm. These algorithms need to reduce the batchsize when they train with low computational resources, which affects the accuracy of the model. Moreover, unlike ExtremeNet and Hough-Net algorithms, our network is randomly initialized under the default setting of Pytorch with no pretraining on any external dataset.

**Table 1.** Computational resource allocation comparison.

| Method | GPU | Quantity | Total memory |
|---|---|---|---|
| CornerNet [15] | Titan X | 10 | 120 GB |
| HoughNet [22] | Tesla V100 | 4 | 128 GB |
| CenterNet [6] | Tesla V100 | 8 | 256 GB |
| YOLOF [4] | Tesla V100 | 8 | 256 GB |
| CornerNet-Saccade [16] | 1080Ti | 4 | 44 GB |
| ScaleDCNet(our) | Titan V | 4 | 48 GB |

**Training Details.** Consistent with CornerNet-Saccade, we set the input resolution to $255 \times 255$ and the output resolution to $64 \times 64$. We use a batch size of 38 and train the network on 4 Titan V GPUs (8 images on the master GPU, 10 images per GPU for the rest of the GPUs). The network is optimized with Adam [13]. The maximum number of iterations is 500K. We use a learning rate of $2.5 \times 10^{-4}$ for the first 450K iterations, then training 30K iterations with a rate of $2.5 \times 10^{-5}$ and a learning rate of $1 \times 10^{-5}$ for the last 20K iterations. To reduce overfitting, our data augmentation approach uses some general methods, including flipping, random scaling (scaling between 0.5 and 1.1), random cropping and random color jittering, image saturation and brightness adjustment, all of which act on the image and annotation information.

**Testing Details.** In the pre-processing stage, the long edges of the image are scaled to three scales, 192, 255 and 332, to predict the size feature. In the subsequent detection process, we use the cropped $255 \times 255$ input image. For each cropped input image, our network generates 3 c-channel heatmaps. We first process the predicted heatmap with softmax and $3 \times 3$ max pooling. Then we select the top 32 top-left, bottom-right and center points with the highest scores from the heatmap and we apply the scale-aware keypoint matching method (Section.3.3) to the selected points. For testing, we only process positions where scores are above a threshold t. In the experiment, it is set to 0.23. Finally, we merge the bounding boxes and suppress redundant detection by applying soft-nms [2]. The average inference time is 175ms per image on a Titan V GPU.

## 4.2 Results and Analysis

**Average Precision.** We compare our method with the baseline CornerNet-Saccade and other existing detectors. The AP reflects how many high-quality bounding boxes a method can predict. As shown in Table 2, our approach ScaleD-CNet with Hourglass-54 as the backbone network achieves an AP of 47.0% on MS-COCO test-dev. Compared with the baseline CornerNet-Saccade, the proposed ScaleDCNet achieves a remarkable improvement. We achieve an overall improvement of 3.8% in AP, with significant improvements in all metrics. We use fewer training resources in training and the size of the input images is much smaller than other algorithms. Compared with the one-stage algorithms, our model accuracy exceeds most of the algorithms, even though we use a backbone network with fewer layers. We achieve much higher accuracy than other one-stage algorithms for small and large size objects. Compared with the two-stage detectors, our model is competitive and its performance is close to 47.4%AP of PANet.

**Table 2.** Object detection performance comparison on MS-COCO test-dev.

| Method | Backbone | Input | AP | $AP_{50}$ | $AP_{75}$ | $AP_S$ | $AP_M$ | $AP_L$ |
|---|---|---|---|---|---|---|---|---|
| Two-stage: | | | | | | | | |
| Faster R-CNN [18] | ResNet-101 | 1000 × 600 | 36.2 | 59.1 | 39.0 | 18.2 | 39.0 | 48.2 |
| Mask R-CNN [9] | ResNet-101 | 1333 × 800 | 39.8 | 62.3 | 43.4 | 22.1 | 43.2 | 51.2 |
| D-RFCN+SNIP [23] | DPN-98 | 1333 × 800 | 45.7 | **67.3** | 51.1 | 29.3 | 48.8 | 57.1 |
| PANet [19] | ResNeXt-101 | 1000 × 600 | **47.4** | 67.2 | **51.8** | **30.1** | **51.7** | **60.0** |
| One-stage: | | | | | | | | |
| CornerNet (SS) [15] | Hourglass104 | 511 × 511 | 40.5 | 56.5 | 43.1 | 19.4 | 42.7 | 50.2 |
| CornerNet (MS) [15] | Hourglass104 | 511 × 511 | 42.1 | 57.8 | 45.3 | 20.8 | 44.8 | 56.7 |
| YOLOv4 [1] | Darknet-53 | 608 × 608 | 43.5 | **65.7** | 47.3 | 26.7 | 46.7 | 53.3 |
| HoughNet(SS) [22] | Hourglass104 | 512 × 512 | 43.1 | 62.2 | 46.8 | 24.6 | 47.0 | 54.4 |
| HoughNet(MS) [22] | Hourglass104 | 512 × 512 | 46.4 | 65.1 | 50.7 | 29.1 | 48.5 | 58.1 |
| CenterNet(SS) [6] | Hourglass104 | 511 × 511 | 44.9 | 62.4 | 48.1 | 25.6 | 47.4 | 57.4 |
| CenterNet(MS) [6] | Hourglass104 | 511 × 511 | 47.0 | 64.5 | 50.7 | 28.9 | **49.9** | 58.9 |
| CornerNet-Saccade [16] | Hourglass54 | 255 × 255 | 43.2 | - | - | 24.4 | 44.6 | 57.3 |
| ScaleDCNet(our) | Hourglass54 | 255 × 255 | **47.0** | 63.7 | **50.9** | **30.1** | 49.2 | **60.1** |

To further illustrate the effectiveness of our algorithm, we compare it with YOLOF, which is also a scale divide and conquer algorithm. As shown in Table 3, compared to YOLOF's most complex model, our method ScaleDCNet achieves an accuracy advantage of 0.1% on COCO val2017. In particular, we have better performance in the detection of large-size objects.

**Table 3.** Object detection performance comparison on COCO2017 validation set.

| Method | Backbone | Input | AP | $AP_{50}$ | $AP_{75}$ | $AP_S$ | $AP_M$ | $AP_L$ |
|---|---|---|---|---|---|---|---|---|
| CornerNet-Saccade [16] | Hourglass54 | 255 × 255 | 42.6 | - | - | 25.5 | 44.3 | 58.4 |
| YOLOF-X101(MS) [4] | RetNeXt-101 | 1333 × 800 | 47.1 | **66.4** | 51.2 | **31.8** | **50.9** | 60.6 |
| ScaleDCNet(our) | Hourglass54 | 255 × 255 | **47.2** | 63.9 | 51.2 | 31.5 | 49.7 | **62.2** |

**Average Recall.** AR reflects the ability of the model to detect the object in the dataset. As shown in Table 4, our method shows a significant improvement in the performance of AR. Our scale divide-and-conquer strategy allows for better representation of features at various scales, which we believe is an advantage of our method in terms of its ability to detect objects.

**Table 4.** Comparison of AR metric on MS-COCO test-dev.

| Method | $AR_1$ | $AR_{10}$ | $AR_{100}$ | $AR_S$ | $AR_M$ | $AR_L$ |
|---|---|---|---|---|---|---|
| CenterNet(SS) [6] | 36.1 | 58.4 | 63.3 | 41.3 | 67.1 | 80.2 |
| CenterNet(MS) [6] | **37.5** | 60.3 | 64.8 | 45.1 | 68.3 | 79.7 |
| ScaleDCNet(our) | 37.0 | **63.0** | **68.1** | **49.8** | **71.0** | **82.0** |

### 4.3  Ablation Study

**Scale Selecting.** To illustrate the important role of the scale feature selection module, we train the model without the scale feature selection module. The results in Table 5 show that our model has a 2.9% decrease in AP without scale selecting, which fully demonstrates the effectiveness of our divide and conquer algorithm.

**Keypoint Matching.** To verify the efficiency of the scale-aware keypoint matching method, we remove the center group and scale match respectively based on our model. The results in Table 5 show that both center group and scale match are important components of ScaleDCNet. Our model has a 1.9% decrease in accuracy with the missing center group and a 1.2% decrease in accuracy with the missing scale match.

**Table 5.** Comparison results of our ablation models.

| Method | AP | $AP_{50}$ | $AP_{75}$ | $AP_S$ | $AP_M$ | $AP_L$ |
|---|---|---|---|---|---|---|
| ScaleDCNet(our) | 47.2 | 63.9 | 51.2 | 31.5 | 49.7 | 62.2 |
| w/o Scale select | 44.3 | 60.6 | 47.8 | 27.4 | 46.7 | 60.4 |
| w/o Center group | 45.3 | 61.2 | 48.9 | 28.2 | 48.2 | 61.0 |
| w/o Scale match | 46.0 | 62.3 | 49.9 | 29.5 | 48.4 | 61.2 |

## 5  Conclusion

In this paper, we propose ScaleDCNet, which detects objects using a divide-and-conquer strategy. It starts with extracting keypoints using the scale feature selection module and composing them into object proposals using scale aware keypoint matching method. With the two approaches, both precision and recall of detection are significantly improved. We believe that our idea of the divide-and-conquer strategy can potentially be generalized to other existing object detection approaches and we take this as our future work.

**Acknowledgements.** This work was partially supported by the National Natural Science Foundation of China (No. 91948303).

# References

1. Bochkovskiy, A., Wang, C.Y., Liao, H.Y.M.: Yolov4: optimal speed and accuracy of object detection. arXiv preprint arXiv:2004.10934 (2020)
2. Bodla, N., Singh, B., Chellappa, R., Davis, L.S.: Soft-NMS-improving object detection with one line of code. In: Proceedings of the IEEE International Conference on Computer Vision, pp. 5561–5569 (2017)
3. Cai, Z., Vasconcelos, N.: Cascade r-CNN: Delving into high quality object detection. In: Proceedings of the IEEE Conference on Computer Vision and Pattern Recognition, pp. 6154–6162 (2018)
4. Chen, Q., Wang, Y., Yang, T., Zhang, X., Cheng, J., Sun, J.: You only look one-level feature. In: Proceedings of the IEEE/CVF Conference on Computer Vision and Pattern Recognition, pp. 13039–13048 (2021)
5. Dong, Z., Li, G., Liao, Y., Wang, F., Ren, P., Qian, C.: Centripetalnet: pursuing high-quality keypoint pairs for object detection. In: Proceedings of the IEEE/CVF Conference on Computer Vision and Pattern Recognition, pp. 10519–10528 (2020)
6. Duan, K., Bai, S., Xie, L., Qi, H., Huang, Q., Tian, Q.: Centernet: keypoint triplets for object detection. In: Proceedings of the IEEE/CVF International Conference on Computer Vision, pp. 6569–6578 (2019)
7. Ghiasi, G., Lin, T.Y., Le, Q.V.: Nas-fpn: Learning scalable feature pyramid architecture for object detection. In: Proceedings of the IEEE/CVF Conference on Computer Vision and Pattern Recognition, pp. 7036–7045 (2019)
8. Girshick, R.: Fast r-CNN. In: Proceedings of the IEEE International Conference on Computer Vision, pp. 1440–1448 (2015)
9. He, K., Gkioxari, G., Dollár, P., Girshick, R.: Mask r-CNN. In: Proceedings of the IEEE International Conference on Computer Vision, pp. 2961–2969 (2017)
10. He, K., Zhang, X., Ren, S., Sun, J.: Deep residual learning for image recognition. In: Proceedings of the IEEE Conference on Computer Vision and Pattern Recognition, pp. 770–778 (2016)
11. Hoiem, D., Chodpathumwan, Y., Dai, Q.: Diagnosing error in object detectors. In: European Conference on Computer Vision, pp. 340–353. Springer (2012)
12. Hu, J., Shen, L., Sun, G.: Squeeze-and-excitation networks. In: Proceedings of the IEEE Conference on Computer Vision and Pattern Recognition, pp. 7132–7141 (2018)
13. Kingma, D.P., Ba, J.: Adam: A method for stochastic optimization. arXiv preprint arXiv:1412.6980 (2014)
14. Kong, T., Sun, F., Liu, H., Jiang, Y., Li, L., Shi, J.: Foveabox: beyound anchor-based object detection. IEEE Trans. Image Process. **29**, 7389–7398 (2020)
15. Law, H., Deng, J.: Cornernet: detecting objects as paired keypoints. In: Proceedings of the European Conference on Computer Vision (ECCV), pp. 734–750 (2018)
16. Law, H., Teng, Y., Russakovsky, O., Deng, J.: Cornernet-lite: efficient keypoint based object detection. In: 31st British Machine Vision Conference 2020, pp. 1–15. BMVA Press (2020)
17. Li, Y., Chen, Y., Wang, N., Zhang, Z.: Scale-aware trident networks for object detection. In: Proceedings of the IEEE/CVF International Conference on Computer Vision, pp. 6054–6063 (2019)
18. Lin, T.Y., Dollár, P., Girshick, R., He, K., Hariharan, B., Belongie, S.: Feature pyramid networks for object detection. In: Proceedings of the IEEE Conference on Computer Vision and Pattern Recognition, pp. 2117–2125 (2017)

19. Liu, S., Qi, L., Qin, H., Shi, J., Jia, J.: Path aggregation network for instance segmentation. In: Proceedings of the IEEE Conference on Computer Vision and Pattern Recognition, pp. 8759–8768 (2018)
20. Liu, W., Anguelov, D., Erhan, D., Szegedy, C., Reed, S., Fu, C.Y., Berg, A.C.: Ssd: single shot multibox detector. In: European Conference on Computer Vision, pp. 21–37. Springer (2016)
21. Ren, S., He, K., Girshick, R., Sun, J.: Faster r-CNN: towards real-time object detection with region proposal networks. Advances in neural information processing systems 28 (2015)
22. Samet, N., Hicsonmez, S., Akbas, E.: Houghnet: integrating near and long-range evidence for bottom-up object detection. In: European Conference on Computer Vision, pp. 406–423. Springer (2020)
23. Singh, B., Davis, L.S.: An analysis of scale invariance in object detection snip. In: Proceedings of the IEEE Conference on Computer Vision and Pattern Recognition, pp. 3578–3587 (2018)
24. Singh, B., Najibi, M., Davis, L.S.: Sniper: Efficient multi-scale training. Advances in neural information processing systems 31 (2018)
25. Tan, M., Le, Q.: Efficientnet: rethinking model scaling for convolutional neural networks. In: International Conference on Machine Learning, pp. 6105–6114. PMLR (2019)
26. Tan, M., Pang, R., Le, Q.V.: Efficientdet: Scalable and efficient object detection. In: Proceedings of the IEEE/CVF Conference on Computer Vision and Pattern Recognition, pp. 10781–10790 (2020)
27. Tang, C., Liu, X., Zhu, X., Zhu, E., Sun, K., Wang, P., Wang, L., Zomaya, A.: $R^2$mrf: Defocus blur detection via recurrently refining multi-scale residual features. In: Proceedings of the AAAI Conference on Artificial Intelligence, vol. 34, pp. 12063–12070 (2020)
28. Tian, Z., Shen, C., Chen, H., He, T.: Fcos: fully convolutional one-stage object detection. In: Proceedings of the IEEE/CVF International Conference on Computer Vision, pp. 9627–9636 (2019)
29. Zeng, N., Wu, P., Wang, Z., Li, H., Liu, W., Liu, X.: A small-sized object detection oriented multi-scale feature fusion approach with application to defect detection. IEEE Trans. Instrum. Meas. **71**, 1–14 (2022)
30. Zhou, X., Zhuo, J., Krahenbuhl, P.: Bottom-up object detection by grouping extreme and center points. In: Proceedings of the IEEE/CVF Conference on Computer Vision and Pattern Recognition, pp. 850–859 (2019)

# Video-Based Emotion Recognition in the Wild for Online Education Systems

Genting Mai, Zijian Guo, Yicong She, Hongni Wang, and Yan Liang$^{(\boxtimes)}$

School of Software, South China Normal University, Guangzhou 510630, China
liangyan@m.scnu.edu.cn

**Abstract.** With the rapid development of the Internet, online learning has become one of the main ways of acquiring knowledge. In order to make teachers understand students' emotional states and adjust teaching programs on time, a new video-based model called the Wild Facial Spatiotemporal Network (WFSTN) is proposed in this paper for emotion recognition in online learning environments. The model consists of two modules: a pretrained DenseNet121 for extracting facial spatial features, and a Bidirectional Long-Short Term Memory (Bi-LSTM) network with self-attention for generating attentional hidden states. In addition, a dataset of student emotions in online learning environments (DSEOLE) is produced using a self-developed online educational aid system. The method is evaluated on the Acted Facial Expressions in the Wild (AFEW) and DSEOLE datasets, achieving 72.76% and 73.67% accuracy in three-class classification, respectively. The results show that the proposed method outperforms many existing works on emotion recognition for online education.

**Keywords:** Online learning · Emotion recognition · Facial spatiotemporal information · Bi-LSTM · Self-attention

## 1 Introduction

Online learning is becoming increasingly popular as it allows people to learn beyond the constraints of time and space [1]. However, it is difficult for teachers to be informed of students' emotional state promptly during online learning, which makes it difficult for them to understand students' level of mastery and adapt their teaching methods accordingly. Therefore, emotion recognition plays an important role in improving the quality of online education.

Research on human emotions based on visual perception is currently focused on facial expressions [2]. Most of the early studies on facial expression-based emotion recognition were for laboratory scenarios. However, these methods are difficult to be applied to practical applications [3]. Compared with the laboratory scene, the intra-class variations are larger in the natural scene due to illumination, pose, occlusion, race, etc. Moreover, the small amplitude and short duration of students' facial muscle movements further increase the difficulty of emotion recognition.

S. Khanna et al. (Eds.): PRICAI 2022, LNCS 13631, pp. 516–529, 2022.
https://doi.org/10.1007/978-3-031-20868-3_38

Emotion recognition methods can be divided into two categories, namely those based on traditional computer vision and those based on deep learning. The former mainly adopts manually extracted expression features, which are easily disturbed by unfavorable factors such as pose variation and illumination [4, 5]. With the significant improvement of computer processing ability, the emergence of well-performing neural network architectures, and the public availability of large expression databases, the focus of research in the field of emotion recognition has gradually shifted from traditional computer vision-based methods to deep learning-based methods [6–11]. Although great progress has been made, the accuracy of emotion recognition methods based on deep learning still cannot meet the needs of practical application. These methods often lack robustness to pose variations and occlusions. In addition, only a small number of studies have been done on online learning.

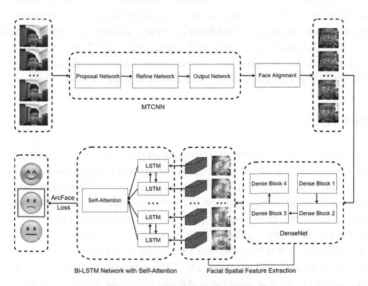

**Fig. 1.** Architecture of WFSTN

In this paper, we propose an emotion recognition method called Wild Facial Spatiotemporal Network (WFSTN), which is represented by a multi-stage image processing to extract features. The architecture of WFSTN is illustrated in Fig. 1. Firstly, facial regions are extracted and aligned by Multi-Task Convolutional Neural Network (MTCNN) [12]. Secondly, face spatial features are extracted by DenseNet [13] pretrained on the VGGFace2 dataset [14]. Thirdly, Bidirectional Long-Short Term Memory (Bi-LSTM) network [15] with self-attention is used to generate attentional hidden states from facial spatial features. Moreover, additive angular margin loss (ArcFace) [16] is used to reduce the intra-class distance and increase the inter-class distance to improve accuracy. In order to verify the application effect of the proposed method in online learning environments, we developed an online learning assistance system integrating emotion recognition. A dataset of student emotions in online learning environments (DSEOLE) was made by this system. We conducted experiments on the DSEOLE and the Acted

Facial Expressions in the Wild (AFEW) [17] datasets. The results show the effectiveness and robustness of the proposed method.

The contribution of our work can be summarized as follows:

(1) We propose a WFSTN model combining DenseNet and Bi-LSTM with self-attention to predict students' emotional states in online learning. Compared with existing models, WFSTN integrates spatiotemporal information of face. It fully considers the context of a sequence of facial frames, and pays more attention to the global and local features of face.

(2) Facial spatial features are extracted using the DenseNet model pretrained on the VGGFace2 dataset. Self-attention that considers both global and local features is suitable for our task and generates attentional hidden states together with Bi-LSTM, which can extract the emotional features of students' faces more accurately.

(3) We developed an online learning assistance system integrating emotion recognition, and used it to collect emotion data from 22 college students to establish the DSEOLE Dataset. In addition, a large in-the-wild dataset, i.e., AFEW, was used as the training and testing sets. We conducted experiments on these two datasets to evaluate the validity of the WFSTN model. The results show that the proposed method is feasible.

## 2    Related Work

Behavior-based approaches are one of the dominant methods for identifying emotions in online education scenarios. In these methods, behavioral features such as facial expressions, speech, and gestures are extracted to identify emotion. These methods are widely used because of their advantages of low invasiveness and easy deployment. However, considering that students spend most of their time in silent mode when they are learning online, the speech-based approaches are not suitable for emotion recognition in online learning. In addition, it has been shown that there is no one-to-one correspondence between a specific gesture and emotion [18]. Compared with other behavioral features, facial expressions have unique advantage and can represent more emotions [19]. Therefore, the algorithm based on facial expression has higher accuracy and robustness in online learning.

In traditional methods, facial features are extracted manually and then fed to a classifier or regressor to identify the emotion. Enadula et al. [4] extracted facial features based on the distance between 68 landmark points to identify emotion. In order to improve the effectiveness of emotion recognition, some researchers used machine learning algorithms such as support vector machines (SVM) to identify students' emotions. Sabri et al. [5] extracted facial features using gray-level co-occurrence matrix (GLCM), and then classified emotions by SVM and support vector regression (SVR). The features extracted by traditional methods are highly logical, but the performance of these methods relies on the validity of the features, especially in the wild.

With the development of deep learning, emotion recognition based on end-to-end methods has achieved good results and performance, which proves that some subtle combinations of facial features are more effective than some logical ones. Lasri et al. [7] proposed a CNN for student facial expression recognition and achieved an accuracy of

70% on FER2013. Chen et al. [8] first improved the deep residual network, ResNet18, and used it to extract global expression features of face images. A self-attention weighting module was then introduced to calculate the expression features of each face image. The method achieved 98.89% and 87.13% accuracy on CK+ and the Real-world Affective Faces Database (RAF-DB), respectively. Although these methods have achieved good performance, they are all aimed at static images.

In online learning, image-based emotion recognition only considers the information of a single frame and ignores the contextual information, which cannot accurately represent the emotional state of students at a certain period. Therefore, more and more work has been carried out on video-based recognition of students' emotions. Cai et al. [9] used VGG-Face16 to extract facial texture features in the spatial domain and Bidirectional Recurrent Neural Network (BRNN) to capture dynamic temporal domain emotion changes in the temporal domain. To further improve the effectiveness of emotion recognition, some scholars added an audio module to deep neural network [10] which enabled it to extract multimodal features. However, this method cannot extract the audio features of students since they are in a calm state most of the time in online learning. Meanwhile, although there are occasional expression changes, they are subtle and transient, which makes it difficult to extract more abstract spatiotemporal features of facial expressions using CNN-RNN models alone. With the proposal of Transformer [11], the attention mechanism is widely used in the fields of natural language processing and computer vision, which can pay attention to the important part of the sequence and ignore the irrelevant information. However, the attention mechanism is rarely used in the field of emotion recognition at present. It is a meaningful attempt to integrate the attention mechanism into CNN-RNN based methods.

## 3  Proposed Method

The architecture of the proposed method is shown in Fig. 1. First, a sequence of frames is extracted from each video. After face detection by MTCNN, the faces are aligned by image processing techniques such as rotation and stretching. Facial spatial features are then extracted from face images by DenseNet121, and attentional hidden states are further generated by Bi-LSTM with self-attention. After training, the method has a high recognition accuracy, so that it can be used in real online learning environments.

### 3.1  Facial Spatial Feature Extraction

In recent years, CNN has developed rapidly and has become one of the most important network structures in deep learning. DenseNet densely connects all the front layers with the back layers, and achieves feature reuse by connecting features on channels. These features allow DenseNet to achieve better performance with fewer parameters and computational cost. Therefore, DenseNet121 is used as the backbone architecture for feature extraction in our work, as shown in Fig. 2. In order to reduce the errors caused by the average-pooling rule and the max-pooling rule [20], DenseNet's pooling rules is changed to regional-weight-pooling (RWP) rules [21].

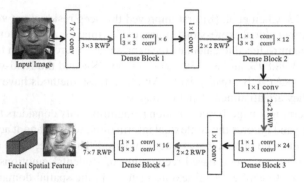

**Fig. 2.** Architecture of DenseNet121 (RWP is region-weight-pooling rule, conv is convolution operation)

Before training, MTCNN is used to crop the facial region, and every image is then resized to $224 \times 224$ to adapt to the training requirements of the model. In order to speed up the training and make the model have better generalization ability, we use the DenseNet121 model trained on VGGFace2 as a pre-training model. For each facial frame, a face is represented using 1024-dimensional features output by the last pooling layer of DenseNet121. In order to obtain a better facial spatial feature extraction model, we also tried to change the backbone architecture of feature extraction and the dataset of the pre-training model. Specific experiments are mentioned in the next section. The facial spatial feature sequence of the L-frame can be represented as:

$$V = \{v_1, v_2, \cdots, v_L\}, v_l \in \mathbb{R}^D \qquad (1)$$

where $v_l$ denotes the facial spatial feature of the l-th frame and D is the feature dimension. L is the number of frames sampled in each video. L should not be too small or too large, in case the samples lack sufficient time information or the model is difficult to converge. Therefore, we choose a compromise value, $L = 8$.

### 3.2 Bi-LSTM Network with Self-attention

Bi-LSTM is stronger than LSTM [22] in feature extraction because it can simultaneously use context information of the current location for training. For our task, we need to consider not only the facial spatial features, but also focus on some important facial frames to achieve a high recognition rate. Therefore, Bi-LSTM network and self-attention mechanism are adopted in this paper to extract temporal features of frames. The network structure is shown in Fig. 3.

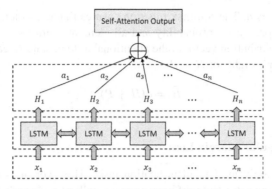

**Fig. 3.** Architecture of Bi-LSTM with self-attention

**Bi-lSTM Network.** Bi-LSTM network is a model composed of forward LSTM and backward LSTM. The hidden layer of the Bi-LSTM network consists of LSTM cells, which use input gates, output gates, and forget gates to control the input, output, and forgetting of past information respectively.

Bi-LSTM unit combines forward and backward LSTM data features, and its output vector can be denoted as follows:

$$H_t = [\overrightarrow{h_t}, \overleftarrow{h_t}] \tag{2}$$

where $\overrightarrow{h_t}$ and $\overleftarrow{h_t}$ are the output vectors of forward and backward LSTM units respectively. See literature [22] for detailed calculations. Then the set of hidden states $H = [H_1, H_2, \cdots, H_n]$ is obtained after the sequence training. The dimension of $H$ is $n \times 2u$ assuming that the number of hidden nodes of forward and backward LSTM is $u$. The model objective is to encode sequences of different lengths into fixed-length embedded representations by linear weighted summation of the $n$ hidden states of LSTM, while self-attention is needed for weight allocation.

**Self-attention.** Self-attention mechanism pays attention to the target that needs to be focused on, assigns more weights to obtain more details of the target and ignores unimportant information. Self-attention takes the hidden states set $H$ of Bi-LSTM as the input. Since self-attention mechanism does not record location information of the input sequence, which is required in facial expression recognition, positional encoding is used to record location information by self-attention. Positional encoding matrix $P \in \mathbb{R}^{n \times 2u}$ in which elements are calculated as follows:

$$P_{i,2j} = \sin\left(\frac{i}{10000^{j/u}}\right), \quad P_{i,2j+1} = \cos\left(\frac{i}{10000^{j/u}}\right) \tag{3}$$

Input $H + P$, and the output attention vector $a$ is:

$$a = softmax(W_2 tanh(W_1(H + P)^T)) \tag{4}$$

where $W_1$ is the weight matrix with dimension $D \times 2u$, and $W_2$ is a parameter vector with dimension D, both of which are trainable matrices or vectors. D is a hyperparameter and the dimension of $a$ is $n$. The Softmax function ensures that each element of the output attention vector represents a probability and all elements sum to 1. According to the attention weight distribution vector $a$, the attentional hidden state $\tilde{H}$ can be obtained by summing the linear weights of $H + P$:

$$\tilde{H} = a(H + P) \tag{5}$$

### 3.3  Additive Angular Margin Loss

Softmax loss is widely used in identification tasks. However, it is difficult to solve the problems of large intra-class differences and small inter-class differences in facial expression recognition caused by posture, illumination, age, etc.

In order to deal with this problem, we use additive angular margin loss (ArcFace) [16] instead of Softmax loss, which is calculated as follows:

$$L_{Arcface} = -\frac{1}{N} \sum_{i=1}^{N} log \frac{e^{s(\cos(\theta_{y_i}+m))}}{e^{s(\cos(\theta_{y_i}+m))} + \sum_{j=1, j \neq y_i}^{n} e^{s\cos\theta_j}} \tag{6}$$

where $\theta_j$ is the angle between $W_j$ and $\tilde{H}_i$, that is $W_j^T \tilde{H}_i = \|W_j\| \| \tilde{H}_i \| \cos\theta_j$. $\tilde{H}_i \in \mathbb{R}^{2u}$ represents the depth feature of the i-th sample, which belongs to class $y_i$, and $W_j \in \mathbb{R}^{2u}$ represents the j-th column of the weight $W \in \mathbb{R}^{2u \times n}$. According to the theory proposed by NormFace [23], $\|W_j\|$ is set to 1 and $\| \tilde{H}_i \|$ is scaled to $s$. In addition, an additive angular margin penalty $m$ is added between $\tilde{H}_i$ and $W_j$ to enhance intra-class tightness and inter-class variability. In order to normalize the weights and features, ArcFace sets the bias $b_j = 0$.

### 3.4  Ranger Optimizer

Traditional facial expression recognition generally adopts Stochastic Gradient Descent (SGD) optimizers [24]. However, SGD decreases slowly and updates parameters frequently, which make the cost function prone to severe oscillations and easy to converge to a local optimum. Ranger optimizer [25] is a collaborative combination of RAdam [26] and LookAhead [27]. RAdam can be customized according to actual datasets to ensure faster convergence in the early training stage. Nevertheless, RAdam has many hyperparameters. In contrast, LookAhead reduces the need to adjust most hyperparameters, while achieving faster convergence with minimal computational overhead. Ranger optimizer is simple to implement and efficient to calculate. Therefore, the Ranger algorithm is used in this paper to optimize the model, so that it can converge faster and obtain the global optimal solution more easily.

The LookAhead optimizer first copies the model parameters into two copies, Slow Weights $\phi$ and Fast Weights $\theta$. Then RAdam is used for normal training optimization of Fast Weights. See literature [26] for details of training optimization. Every $k$ training iterations, the algorithm uses linear interpolation to updates Slow Weights in the $\theta - \phi$ direction of the weight space:

$$\phi = \phi + \alpha_s(\theta - \phi) \tag{7}$$

where $\alpha_s$ is the learning rate of Slow Weights. $\alpha_s$ and $k$ are hyperparameters. Then, the updated Slow Weights are assigned to Fast Weights for the next $k$ training steps. After the training, Slow Weights are taken as the final model training output weight.

## 4 Experimental Evaluation

### 4.1 Experimental Setting

We conducted the experiments in PyTorch1.9 on a server with 16 GB RAM and NVIDIA RTX 3080 12 GB GPU. In our experiments, we first performed face detection, cropping, and alignment using MTCNN, and set the size of each facial frame to $3 \times 224 \times 224$. Then, data augmentation such as horizontal flip, random brightness, random contrast, and random saturation were used to avoid overfitting. We sampled 8 frames for each fragment as a single input, and each sample size was $8 \times 3 \times 224 \times 224$.

After adjustment, parameters of the network are set as follows. The input size of each unidirectional LSTM layer is 1024. The hidden size of LSTM cells is 512, and those cells share the same training parameters. The hidden layers number is 2. During the training stage, the total epoch number of training is 300. The batch size and the base learning rate are set as 48 and 0.001. Dropout which is used to avoid overfitting is set to 0.7.

### 4.2 Datasets

We evaluate our approach on the AFEW and DSEOLE datasets. AFEW [17] is the dataset of the Emotion Recognition in the Wild (EmotiW) challenge. It is one of the most challenging video datasets for facial expression recognition in the wild. This dataset consists of 1426 short movie clips of facial expressions in the wild containing seven basic expressions: anger, disgust, fear, happiness, sadness, surprise, and neutral. These movie clips capture the subjects' facial expressions, head posture movements, and occlusion. The subjects were across different ages, genders, and races, making AFEW closer to real-world environments and more challenging than other affective datasets. During online learning, teachers pay more attention to the emotions associated with the learning process rather than specific expressions [28]. Therefore, inspired by Pekrun et al. [29], we mapped the seven categories of expressions into three categories, namely positive, negative, and neutral, as shown in Table 1.

However, AFEW is not specifically established for emotion recognition in online learning. In order to verify the ability of the proposed method, we made a dataset and tested the proposed method on it. Firstly, we developed an online learning assistance system integrating emotion recognition, which can assist teachers to understand students' learning status and adjust teaching schedule in time. Secondly, 22 college students were invited to test it. The average age of these volunteers was about 21, and the ratio of male to female was 17:5. They used the system to take computer courses on MOOC and turned on the computer's internal or external cameras all the way. While they were studying, we used the system to collect segments of their emotional states in bright and dark environments, including positive, negative, and neutral. Each segment is about 3–6 s in length, and 132 emotional segments were collected to form the DSEOLE dataset. Finally, we divided AFEW into a training set and a test set in a ratio of 8:2. After training and evaluating on AFEW, we further evaluated the effectiveness and robustness of the proposed method on DSEOLE.

**Table 1.** Expression category mapping in AFEW

| Original category | Mapped category |
|---|---|
| Happiness | Positive |
| Surprise | |
| Anger | Negative |
| Disgust | |
| Fear | |
| Sadness | |
| Neutral | Neutral |

## 4.3   Results and Discussion

**Table 2.** Performance of different pretrained models on AFEW. The best result is highlighted in bold.

| Network | Pretrained dataset | Accuracy (%) |
|---|---|---|
| ResNet18 | VGGFace2 | 68.03 |
| | FER2013+ | 66.97 |
| ResNet50 | VGGFace2 | 69.69 |
| | FER2013+ | 67.21 |
| DenseNet121 | VGGFace2 | **72.76** |
| | FER2013+ | 68.32 |
| DenseNet169 | VGGFace2 | 72.54 |
| | FER2013+ | 68.91 |

**Ablation Study of Facial Spatial Feature Extraction.** Deep learning can automatically extract image features, but it requires a large amount of training data to make it per-form better. Although AFEW is a large dataset, it has only 1426 video clips, and the differences between frames of a video are subtle. Inspired by work related to facial expression recognition [30], we used a model pretrained on a facial dataset and ap-10 plied it to our task. In our experiments, we used the ResNet18, ResNet50 [31], DenseNet121, and DenseNet169 pretrained on VGGFace2 [14] and FER2013+ [32], respectively. The experimental results are shown in Table 2.

As can be seen from Table 2, the accuracy of the models pretrained on FER2013 + are all lower than 69%. The models pretrained on VGGFace2 perform better than those pretrained on FER2013 +, indicating that VGGFace2 is more suitable. Compared with ResNet, DenseNet performs better. It is worth noting that DenseNet121 is a little more accurate than DenseNet169, indicating that increasing the depth of DenseNet does not necessarily lead to better results. Therefore, DenseNet121 is selected as the CNN of the model.

**Ablation Study of Bi-LSTM Network with Self-attention.** Bi-LSTM is used as the RNN in this paper for the video-based student emotion recognition task. Attention mechanisms are used in order to better extract key information in video frames. There are three commonly used attention mechanisms, namely global attention, local attention, and self-attention. In order to select attention mechanism for our task, we did an experiment with model based on DenseNet121 and Bi-LSTM. The experimental results are shown in Table 3.

**Table 3.** Performance of different attentional mechanisms on AFEW. The best result is highlighted in bold.

| CNN + RNN | Attention | Accuracy (%) |
|---|---|---|
| DenseNet121 + Bi-LSTM | - | 68.34 |
| | Global attention | 69.93 |
| | Local attention | 68.78 |
| | Self-attention | 71.01 |
| | Self-attention + Position | **72.76** |

Table 3 shows the performance of different attention mechanisms on AFEW. It shows that the attention mechanisms can effectively improve the accuracy of emotion recognition. Global attention focuses on global information, while local attention focuses on local information, and self-attention focuses on both. For our task, it is necessary to pay attention to the global information to accurately recognize facial expression, and for a video, the hidden state of some frames can play a key role. Therefore, self-attention has the highest accuracy of the three attention mechanisms. However, self-attention does not consider the order of frames. In this paper, positional encoding is added to self-attention, and the results show that it can effectively improve the accuracy of emotion recognition. This demonstrates that the emotions of neighboring frames in video-based emotion recognition are correlated. Considering the location information of images in a frame sequence is beneficial for more accurate emotion recognition.

**Ablation Study of ArcFace.** In order to maximize ArcFace's ability to supervise the model to learn more separable features, we conduct experiments to test the effect of additional corner edge penalty m with different values on the model performance. We set the feature scale as 64 in accordance with [33], and selected five different groups of m for experiments. The results are shown in Table 4. It can be observed that when m = 0.5, the model achieved the best recognition accuracy. Therefore, we fixed m = 0.5 in other experiments.

**Table 4.** Performance of different *m* values on AFEW. The best result is highlighted in bold.

| *m* | 0.35 | 0.40 | 0.45 | 0.50 | 0.55 |
|---|---|---|---|---|---|
| Accuracy (%) | 72.35 | 72.72 | 72.46 | **72.76** | 72.53 |

**Comparison with Other Methods.** In order to illustrate the effectiveness of the proposed method, it was compared with other methods of student emotion recognition proposed in the last two years. Since the results of other methods are obtained for a seven-category task, whereas the proposed method is for a three-category task, the results of the three-category recognition in the relevant literature are obtained by reproducing code for fair comparison. The results are shown in Table 5. The training sets of all models are AFEW, and the test sets are AFEW and DSEOLE. It can be seen from Table 5 that the accuracy of WFSTN is higher than 72% on both datasets, which is higher than other methods. These methods for comparison are all CNN models and only consider the spatial features of frames. WFSTN integrates CNN, RNN, and attention mechanisms, which can effectively extract the temporal and spatial features of frames, and thus has higher accuracy. It is worth noting that WFSTN also has a high accuracy on DSEOLE, indicating that it is effective in online learning.

**Table 5.** Comparison with other methods (training set: AFEW, test set: AFEW, DSEOLE). The best result is highlighted in bold.

| Method | Accuracy (%) in AFEW | Accuracy (%) in DSEOLE |
|---|---|---|
| Shabrina et al. [34] | 66.26 | 63.62 |
| Nithiyasree et al. [35] | 67.79 | 65.88 |
| Li et al. [36] | 68.36 | 69.21 |
| Wang et al. [37] | 66.13 | 62.57 |
| WFSTN | **72.76** | **73.67** |

In order to further observe the performance of WFSTN on DSEOLE, we use the confusion matrix to describe the prediction of WFSTN on each category, as shown in Fig. 4. Among them, positive emotions containing Happiness and Surprise achieve 100% accuracy. In online learning, the majority of students' positive emotional states are Happiness. The facial features of Happiness have evident differences from other emotion, so the accuracy of positive emotion is the highest. However, the majority of students have little difference between negative emotions and neutral emotions. As shown in Fig. 5, WFSTN probably identifies negative emotion as neutral one, and a few neutral emotions are probably identified as positive and negative.

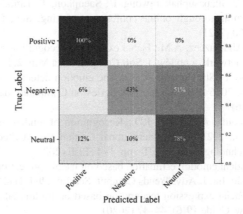

**Fig. 4.** Confusion matrix obtained by WFSTN prediction on the DSEOLE dataset

(a)    (b)

**Fig. 5.** Two consecutive sequences with different labels. (a) Negative (b) Neutral

## 5 Conclusion

In this paper, we propose a novel model for emotion recognition in online learning, namely the WFSTN model, which can fuse spatiotemporal feature of facial expressions. We generate facial spatial features from DenseNet121 pretrained on VGGFace2 according to Transfer Learning. It is shown that DenseNet121 have better performance even in the wild. The sequence of facial spatial features is then input to Bi-LSTM with self-attention, which generates attention hidden states that accurately represent the temporal feature. ArcFace is used as loss function to learn separable features and Ranger optimizer is used to optimize the training. Finally, we carry out experiments to verify the performance of our method, and the accuracy of WFSTN reaches 72.76% and 73.67% on

AFEW and DSEOLE, respectively. The results show that the proposed method outperforms many existing works in student emotion recognition. In future work, we will try to mix different datasets to get a larger dataset. Moreover, we'll try to use the Multi-headed self-attention to extract more abstract features to make it work more effectively.

# References

1. Panichkriangkrai, C., Silapasuphakornwong, P., Saenphon, T.: Emotion recognition of students during e-learning through online conference meeting. Sci., Eng. Health Stud. **15**, 21020010–21020010 (2021)
2. Abdullah, S.M.S., Abdulazeez, A.M.: Facial expression recognition based on deep learning convolution neural network: a review. J. Soft Comput. Data Min. **2**(1), 53–65 (2021)
3. Kollias, D., Tagaris, A., Stafylopatis, A.: On line emotion detection using retrainable deep neural networks. In: 2016 IEEE Symposium Series on Computational Intelligence (SSCI), pp. 1–8. IEEE (2016)
4. Enadula, S.M., Enadula, AS., Burri, RD.: Recognition of student emotions in an online education system. In: 2021 Fourth International Conference on Electrical, Computer and Communication Technologies (ICECCT), pp. 1–4 IEEE (2021))
5. Sabri, N., et al.: Student emotion estimation based on facial application in E-learning during COVID-19 pandemic. Int. J. Adv. Trends Comput. Sci. Eng, **9**(1.4) (2020)
6. Pi, B., Wang, Y.: Facial expression recognition based on traditional machine learning and deep learning. Softw. Guide **19**(6), 44–47 (2020)
7. Lasri, I., Solh, A.R., El Belkacemi, M.: Facial emotion recognition of students using convolutional neural network. In: 2019 third international conference on intelligent computing in data sciences (ICDS), pp. 1–6 IEEE (2019)
8. Chen, J., et al.: Research on facial expression recognition based on improved deep residual network model. J. Phys. Conf. Ser. **2010**(1), 012139 (2021). IOP Publishing
9. Cai, Y., Zheng, W., Zhang, T., Li, Q., Cui, Z., Ye, J.: Video based emotion recognition using CNN and BRNN. In: Tan, T., Li, X., Chen, X., Zhou, J., Yang, J., Cheng, H. (eds.) CCPR 2016. CCIS, vol. 663, pp. 679–691. Springer, Singapore (2016). https://doi.org/10.1007/978-981-10-3005-5_56
10. Kaya, H., Gürpınar, F., Salah, A.A.: Video-based emotion recognition in the wild using deep transfer learning and score fusion. Image Vis. Comput. **65**, 66–75 (2017)
11. Vaswani, A., et al.: Attention is all you need. Adv. Neural Inf. Process. Sys. **30** (2017)
12. Zhang, K., Zhang, Z., Li, Z., et al.: Joint face detection and alignment using multitask cascaded convolutional networks. IEEE Signal Process. Lett. **23**(10), 1499–1503 (2016)
13. Huang, G., et al.: Densely connected convolutional networks. In: Proceedings of the IEEE Conference on Computer Vision and Pattern Recognition, pp. 4700–4708 (2017)
14. Cao, Q., et al.: Vggface2: a dataset for recognising faces across pose and age. In: 2018 13th IEEE International Conference on Automatic Face & Gesture Recognition (FG 2018), pp. 67-74. IEEE (2018)
15. Schuster, M., Paliwal, K.K.: Bidirectional recurrent neural networks. IEEE Trans. Signal Process. **45**(11), 2673–2681 (1997)
16. Deng, J,, et al. Arcface: additive angular margin loss for deep face recognition. In: Proceedings of the IEEE/CVF Conference on Computer Vision and Pattern Recognition, pp. 4690–4699 (2019)
17. Dhall, A., et al.: Collecting large, richly annotated facial-expression databases from movies. IEEE Multim. **19**(03), 34–41 (2012)

18. Ekman, P., Friesen, W.V.: Detecting deception from the body or face. J. Pers. Soc. Psychol. **29**(3), 288 (1974)
19. Jain, A., Sah, H.R., Kothari, A.: Study for emotion recognition of different age groups students during online class. In: 2021 8th International Conference on Computing for Sustainable Global Development (INDIACom), pp. 621–625. IEEE (2021)
20. Szegedy, C,, et al.: Going deeper with convolutions. In: Proceedings of the IEEE Conference on Computer Vision and Pattern Recognition, pp. 1–9 (2015)
21. Mai, G., et al.: Calligraphy font recognition algorithm based on improved DenseNet network. Computer Syst. Appl.. **31**(2), 253–259 (2022)
22. Hochreiter, S., Schmidhuber, J.: Long short-term memory. Neural Comput. **9**(8), 1735–1780 (1997)
23. Wang, F., et al. Normface: L2 hypersphere embedding for face verification. In: Proceedings of the 25th ACM International Conference on Multimedia, pp. 1041–1049 (2017)
24. Robbins, H., Monro, S.: A stochastic approximation method. Ann. Math. Stat. **22**, 400–407 (1951)
25. Wright, L.: New deep learning optimizer, ranger: synergistic combination of radam+ lookahead for the best of both (2019). Github. https://github.com/lessw2020/Ranger-Deep-Learning-Optimizer
26. Liu L, Jiang H, He P, et al. On the variance of the adaptive learning rate and beyond[J]. arXiv preprint arXiv:1908.03265, 2019
27. Zhang, M., et al. Lookahead optimizer: k steps forward, 1 step back. Adv. Neural Inf. Process. Syst. **32** (2019)
28. Sarrafzadeh, A., et al.: "How do you know that I don't understand?" A look at the future of intelligent tutoring systems. Comput. Hum. Behav. **24**(4), 1342–1363 (2008)
29. Pekrun, R., et al.: Academic emotions in students' self-regulated learning and achievement: a program of qualitative and quantitative research. Educ. Psychol. **37**(2), 91–105 (2002)
30. Liao, J., Liang, Y., Pan, J.: Deep facial spatiotemporal network for engagement prediction in online learning. Appl. Intell. **51**(10), 6609–6621 (2021)
31. He,K., et al.: Deep residual learning for image recognition. In: Proceedings of the IEEE Conference on Computer Vision and Pattern Recognition, pp. 770–778 (2016)
32. Barsoum, E., et al.: Training deep networks for facial expression recognition with crowd-sourced label distribution. In: Proceedings of the 18th ACM International Conference on Multimodal Interaction, pp. 279–283 (2016)
33. Wang, H., et al. CosFace: large margin cosine loss for deep face recognition. In: Proceedings of the IEEE Conference on Computer Vision and Pattern Recognition, 5265–5274 (2018)
34. Shabrina, N.H., et al.: Emotion recognition using convolutional neural network in virtual meeting environment. Ultima Comput. Jurnal Sistem Komputer **13**(1), 30–38 (2021)
35. Nithiyasree, K.: Facial emotion recognition of students using deep convolutional neural network. Turk. J. Comput. Math. Educ. **12**(10), 1430–1434 (2021)
36. Li, Q., et al.: Real-time facial emotion recognition using lightweight convolution neural network. J. Phys. Conf. Ser. IOP Publish. **1827**(1), 012130 (2021)
37. Wang, W., et al.: Emotion recognition of students based on facial expressions in online education based on the perspective of computer simulatio. Complexity **2020** (2020)

# Real-world Underwater Image Enhancement via Degradation-aware Dynamic Network

Haotian Qian, Wentao Tong, Pan Mu$^{(\boxtimes)}$, Zheyuan Liu, and Hanning Xu

College of Computer Science and Technology, Zhejiang University of Technology,
Hangzhou, China
{201906062215,201906060619,panmu,202006010116,202006010425}@zjut.edu.cn

**Abstract.** Underwater degradations are various and sometimes scene-dependent such as different kinds of color distortion and different extent of fuzziness, attributed to complicated underwater environments. Recently methods produce promising restoration results, however, they are time-consuming and introduce suboptimal results when facing complicated scenes. Therefore, the two main challenges are how to maintain fast and generic processing when tackling complicated scenes. To address these problems, we develop a degradation-aware dynamic network named DD-Net by introducing the Koschmieder's light scattering model. Specifically, to handle various color distortions, we propose a scene-adaptive convolution, the basic element of which is no longer a float point number, but a function. The function outputs scene-adaptive parameters of the convolutions by taking the estimated scene factor of the underwater image as input, accordingly. In addition, to handle different extents of fuzziness degradation, we proposed a novel haze-adaptive regularization. The regularization uses medium transmission maps to guide the model to implicitly assign different attention to regions suffering from various degrees of degradation. By fully utilizing the global information (i.e., the global background light) and the local information (i.e., medium transmission map), our proposed method outperforms previous methods in terms of quantitative metrics. More importantly, our model is implemented in a lightweight manner, providing the possibility of real-time restoration.

**Keywords:** Uderwater image enhancement · Degradation-aware · Dynamic neural network

## 1 Introduction

Vision-based AUVs (Autonomous Underwater Vehicles) have been used in many underwater applications such as coral reef blenching monitoring [3], 3D reconstruction of the seabed [10], and underwater human-robot collaboration. However, underwater imaging always suffers from light absorption and scattering, the AUVs can hardly capture high-quality underwater images in such an environment

S. Khanna et al. (Eds.): PRICAI 2022, LNCS 13631, pp. 530–541, 2022.
https://doi.org/10.1007/978-3-031-20868-3_39

despite being equipped with a high-end camera, thus affecting the performance of vision-based tasks such as detection and tracking. Therefore, an effective and real-time solution for restoring degraded underwater images is urgently needed to help AUVs better explore the underwater world.

Typically, underwater images are captured with low contrast, low illumination, blur and color distortion due to the light absorption and scattering. In addition, the light scattering caused by suspending particles causes low contrast and blur in images.

In recent years, many traditional methods such as histogram equalization [14] and contrast stretching [23], and physical model-based methods such as [11] and [7] have been proposed to solve the underwater image restoration problem. However, those methods are mainly based on specific physical priors or direct pixel adjustments, such hand-crafted designs are limited in real-world applications. Alternatively, learning-based methods, which are implemented in a data-driven manner, can obtain promising results.

However, current deep-learning-based methods still face two challenges, generalizable ability and real-time inference. As shown in Figure 1(b), real-world underwater degradation is very complicated. Therefore, an effective network for real-world applications should be capable of handling various underwater scenes. Most current learning-based methods acquire fixed parameters after training to handle complicated and flexible degradations, thus achieving poor performance when facing challenging degradations. In addition, the network used on AUVs should be lightweight and can achieve real-time inference. However, many

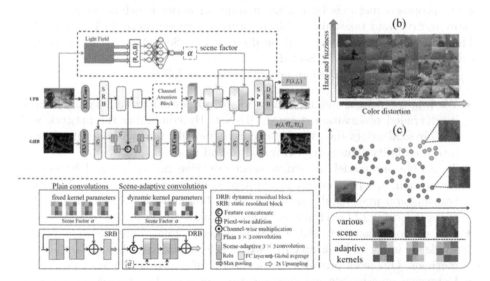

**Fig. 1.** Our model adopts U-shape encoding-decoding architecture. (a) shows the total framework of our proposed network. (b) shows variations of the underwater images. (c) presents the t-SNE distribution of some images of LUSI and UIEB datasets. of scene-adaptive convolutions

learning-based models have large amount of parameters and take long time to process a single image such as Ucolor [12].

To solve the above problems, we propose a degradation-aware dynamic network that can adaptively process degradations in various underwater scenes with approximately 1.97M parameters. Our method is based on the Koschmieders light scattering model [17,22], which describes underwater imaging with two parameters (i.e., the global background light and the medium transmission map). We propose two novel designs to fully utilize the global background light and the medium transmission map.

Specifically, inspired by [4,26,27,29], we design scene-adaptive convolutions. The smallest element of the scene-adaptive convolution is no longer a float-point weight, but a function of the parameter. The function takes scene factor as input and produces scene-adaptive parameters for forward inference. The scene factor is calculated based on the global background light in the Koschmieders light scattering model. Moreover, we propose a haze-aware regularization to implicitly guide the network to assign more attention to more seriously degraded regions by utilizing the medium transmission map. The above haze is similar to a mist of fog but specifically referred to the degradation due to the light scattering and absorption in water. Note that the haze-aware regularization is only used at the training stage, thus our proposed network is end-to-end and achieves a faster inference.

Our proposed network obtains strong generalization ability by fully utilizing global information (i.e., the global background light) and local information (i.e., the pixel-wise medium transmission map). Our proposed method outperforms many proposed methods by a large margin on many benchmarks in terms of many metrics and takes about 0.5s to process a single image in Desktop CPU. The implementation details will be discussed in Sect. 3, and the experiment results will be presented in Sect. 4.

Our main contributions can be summarized as follows:

- We propose a light weight framework to obtain a high-quality image from its degraded observation, termed DD-Net. By combining the network with the physical priors (i.e., the Koschmieder model), our method obtains more interpretability than many other end-to-end models.
- To enable our model to achieve scene-adaptive processing and haze-aware restoration, we propose scene-adaptive convolutions and a novel medium transmission map regularization. Such a Plug-and-Play design thereby furthers the study of faster and more generic underwater image restoration.
- Our proposed network with 1.97M parameters takes only 0.5s to process a single 4K image in Desktop CPU, which is 7 times faster than the suboptimal methods. Our work provides the possibility of real-time inference on AUVs.
- Extensive experiments and ablation study on many benchmarks demonstrate the effectiveness of our proposed method. Our model achieves state-of-the-art performance in terms of both full-reference and non-reference metrics.

# 2   Methods

## 2.1   The Overview of Our Method

As per Beer-Lamber law [25], light suffers from light attenuation when propagating due to suspending particles in the air, etc. Koschmieder [22] formulated the light scattering effect at a distance $d$ with the same attenuation factor based on the Beer-Lamber law. [17] then formulated the notion that the reflected light of the scene $J$ also gets attenuated by the factor $e^{-\beta d}$ and introduce the formulation of the degradation process due to the light scattering effect:

$$I(x) = J(x)e^{-\beta d(x)} + \left(1 - e^{-\beta d(x)}\right) A \qquad (1)$$

where $J$ denotes the high-quality uncorrupted radiance, $I$ denotes the corresponding degraded observation, $x$ denotes an image pixel of the captured image, and $d(x)$ denotes the associated scene depth at $x$. We extend (1) to the underwater image restoration, where $A$ denotes the global background light, and $t(x) = e^{-\beta d}$ denotes the underwater transmission map which indicates the percentage of the scene radiance reaching the camera. It is worth noting that $A$ is image-wise and $t(x)$ is pixel-wise. Especially, $t(x)$ is also channel-wise in underwater degradation due to the wavelength-dependent characteristics of the attenuation, thus different color channels need medium transmission maps with different beta. To some extent, the global background light and the medium transmission map represent the characteristics of underwater imaging. We then present the details of our proposed method to utilize two factors to achieve scene-aware and haze-aware restoration.

The whole architecture of our proposed network is presented in Figure 1(a). The proposed network applies a U-shape framework similar to the U-net [21]. The network consists of an encoder, a channel attention block, and a decoder. On the one hand, we know that the encoder is used to extract features from diverse degraded images, and the decoder is used to reconstruct these features to produce specific high-quality images. In other words, the decoder should be scene-adaptive, while the encoder that characterizes the representation for diverse underwater images of various degrees of degradation can be static. On the other hand, scene-adaptive convolution doubles the parameters compared to static convolutions (i.e., plain convolutions). Therefore, in order to achieve scene-adaptive and real-time inference simultaneously, only the decoder of our proposed network uses scene-adaptive convolution while the encoder and the channel attention block remain static.

Different from traditional methods which restore $J$ by (3) directly, we utilize $A$ and $t(x)$ as auxiliary information to restore underwater images in an end-to-end manner.

## 2.2   Scene-adaptive Convolution

For the input $I_f$ and output $O_f$ of a plain convolution layer, the layer process images directly with parameters, as presented below:

$$O_f = I_f * \theta \tag{2}$$

where $\theta$ and $*$ denotes the kernel paramters and convolution operation. $\theta$ is fixed once training finishes. This property of plain convolutions leads to poor representation ability to handle complicated real-world underwater degradations.

In this paper, we propose scene-adaptive convolutions to tackle the problem of poor generalization ability, whose parameters can adaptively change according to specific input. This is done by replacing fixed kernel parameters with a function $\mathcal{G}$. Specifically, we firstly get the global background light using an approach presented in [8]. After obtaining the global background light map, we do an average operation on it to get a scene factor $\alpha$. Then, the decoder of the network parameterizes the filters of the convolutions with a function that takes alpha as input and generates scene-adaptive parameters. To be simple enough, the function $\mathcal{G}$ is the linear function. The parameterization process is formulated as follows:

$$\mathcal{G}(\alpha, \theta_a, \theta_b) = \alpha\theta_a + (1 - \alpha)\theta_b \tag{3}$$

where $\mathcal{G}(\cdot)$ denotes the parameterization function used to generate parameters for various degrees of degradation, $\theta_a$ and $\theta_b$ are trainable kernel parameters. Scene-adaptive convolutions adaptively change parameters when facing degraded images with different global background light, thus obtaining a stronger representation ability than a single static convolution. The total computation cost increased by 0.0001%, as only a linear combination presented in (4) and the calculation of the global background light are added. To show the interpretability of proposed scene-adaptive convolution, we visualize kernels of the convolutions and plot t-SNE distributions in terms of some samples in the LUSI and UIEB datasets, presented in Figure 1(c). One easily can observe that the images with different extent of degradations are strictly seperated, and the kernels are different when facing different samples.

## 2.3   Haze-aware Regularization

The transmission map $t(x)$ is calculated in an approach proposed in [20], then, to be simple enough, the utilized reverse medium transimission map $\mathcal{R}$ is expressed as:

$$\mathcal{R} = 1 - t(x) \tag{4}$$

The $\mathcal{R}$ represents the extent of degradation that every pixel suffers. A higher $\mathcal{R}$ value means a more serious degradation at that pixel. However, the calculation of $\mathcal{R}$ is complicated and time-consuming. Besides, it is hard to design a module to explicitly integrate the obtained $\mathcal{R}$ into the end-to-end model. Therefore, we propose a haze-aware regularization to utilize the transimission map at the training stage to implicitly guide the model to assign more attention to the pixels with larger $\mathcal{R}$ values. The haze-aware regularization term is expressed as:

$$\mathcal{L}_H^c = \left\| \mathcal{R} \times (I^{GT} - I^r) \right\|_2 \tag{5}$$

where $c$ denotes the color channels (i.e., $r, g, b$), $I^{GT}$ denotes the ground-truth image, $I^r$ denotes the output of the network, and $\|\cdot\|_2$ denotes $\ell_2$-norm. This pixel-wise regularization fully utilizes the reverse transmission map, which indicates the degradation at the pixel level, constraining our proposed network to process regions that suffer from various degrees of degradation differently.

## 2.4   Loss Function

Our loss function consists of three parts, i.e., $\ell_2$-norm, perceptual loss, and the haze-aware regularization. Specifically, the perceptual loss is an $\ell_2$-norm, presented as follows:

$$\mathcal{L}_P(I^r, I^{GT}) = \|\phi_i(I^r) - \phi_i(I^{GT}))\|_1 \tag{6}$$

where $\phi_i(\cdot)$ denotes the output of the $i$-th layer of a pretrained VGG16 [24], and $\|\cdot\|_1$ denotes $\ell_1$-norm. The haze-aware regularization is presented in Subsect. 3.3. Thus,the final loss function can be expressed as:

$$\mathcal{L}(I^r, I^{GT}) = \beta\mathcal{L}_P(I^r, I^{GT}) + \gamma\mathcal{L}_H(I^r, I^{GT}) + \ell_2(I^r, I^{GT}) \tag{7}$$

where $\beta$, $\gamma$ are set to 0.01, 5, respectively.

## 3   Experiment

### 3.1   Experiment Settings

**Datasets.** We conduct experiments on many underwater image datasets including synthetic (i.e., EUVP [9]) and real-world (i.e., UIEB [13], LUSI [19], Test-C60 [13],SQUID [2] and RUIE [15]) datasets. EUVP contains 12K images which are synthesized using a CycleGAN-based model. UIEB and LUSI are two real-world datasets with reference images that are selected from the results generated by a fusion-based method [1]. Test-60 and SQUID have no reference images and are only being used when testing.

**Compared Methods.** We compare the proposed DD-Net with seven methods containing physical-priors-based methods (i.e., UDCP [5]), GAN-Based methods (FunIE-GAN [9], UGAN [6]), CNN-based method (i.e., WaterNet [13], Ucolor [12]) and unsupervised method (i.e., USUIR [8]). We conduct quantitative and qualitative comparisons on both synthetic and real-world datasets.

**Metrics.** Peak Signal-to-Noise Ratio (PSNR) and Structure Similarity Index (SSIM) are two widely-used metrics in image restoration tasks. We employ them to evaluate our proposed network objectively in this paper. Furthermore, since some datasets (e.g., RUIE) contain only raw images, we also use four no-reference metrics (i.e., UIQM [18], UCIQE [28], NIQE [16], and Perceptual scores (PS)).

**Training Details.** We implemented our proposed network with Pytorch. The batch size and the initial learning rate was set to 16 and 2e-4, respectively. The parameters were optimized with Adam optimizer. The network was trained for 100 epochs in NVIDIA A6000 GPU.

**Table 1.** Averaged PSNR, SSIM and MSE scores on synthesis (i.e., EUVP) and real-world underwater datasets (i.e., UIEB and LUSI).

| Methods | EUVP | | | UIEB | | | LUSI | | |
|---|---|---|---|---|---|---|---|---|---|
| | PSNR↑ | SSIM↑ | MSE↓ | PSNR↑ | SSIM↑ | MSE↓ | PSNR↑ | SSIM↑ | MSE↓ |
| UDCP | 16.38 | 0.64 | 1990 | 13.05 | 0.62 | 3779 | 12.66 | 0.62 | 4529 |
| Fusion | 15.36 | 0.62 | 2880 | 17.60 | 0.77 | 1331 | 14.48 | 0.79 | 3501 |
| Water-Net | 20.14 | 0.68 | 826 | 19.11 | 0.79 | 1220 | 17.73 | 0.82 | 1361 |
| UGAN | 23.67 | 0.67 | 359 | 20.17 | 0.82 | 874 | 19.79 | 0.78 | 883 |
| Funie-GAN | <u>26.78</u> | <u>0.86</u> | <u>209</u> | <u>20.68</u> | 0.72 | <u>752</u> | 19.37 | <u>0.84</u> | 946 |
| Ucolor | 21.89 | 0.79 | 505 | 20.63 | <u>0.84</u> | 770 | <u>21.56</u> | <u>0.84</u> | <u>563</u> |
| USUIR | 23.52 | 0.81 | 399 | 20.31 | <u>0.84</u> | 804 | 18.62 | 0.80 | 1025 |
| Ours | **27.25** | **0.86** | **269** | **22.06** | **0.89** | **521** | **24.14** | **0.88** | **377** |

## 3.2 Compared with SOTA Methods

**Quantitative Evaluation.** The quantitative evaluation is presented in Tables 1 and 2. The best result is highlighted in black bold. As can be seen, our proposed model outperforms all seven methods by a large margin in terms of the PSNR metric in the synthesized EUVP dataset. Physical-priors-based methods can not maintain stable and good performance in many datasets due to their dependence on the properties of priors. When facing real-world datasets, our network also achieves state-of-the-art performance. It is worth noting that even though Test-C60, SQUID, and RUIE are not used for training, our supervised model can still obtain the best results in all three datasets, thus demonstrating the strong generalization ability of our proposed network.

**Qualitative Evaluation.** We conduct qualitative comparisons on both synthetic and real-world underwater datasets. Figures 2 and 3 show the visual comparisons between our method (DD-Net) and the four methods (i.e., UGAN, Fuine-GAN, Ucolor, USUIR) which obtain relatively high PSNR and SSIM scores. One can observe that, our proposed method fully restores the red channel attenuation and the other four methods still introduce excessive blue and green tones. In addition, USUIR introduces obvious artifacts and FGAN introduces some noise in image. In contrary, our method introduce a more natural tone and the results looks like taken in air.

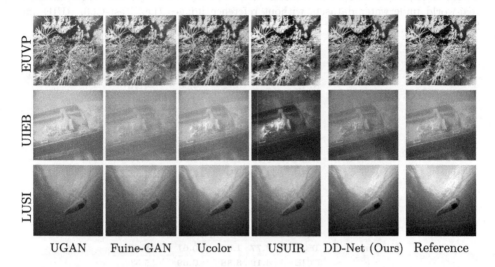

**Fig. 2.** Visual comparison with different underwater image enhancement methods on synthesis dataset (EUVP) and real-world datasets (UIEB and LUSI). Comparing with UGAN, Fuine-GAN, Ucolor and USUIR, our developed method (i.e., DD-Net) achieves an natural color and preserves more details. Our DD-Net performs the best visual quality obviously. (Color figure online)

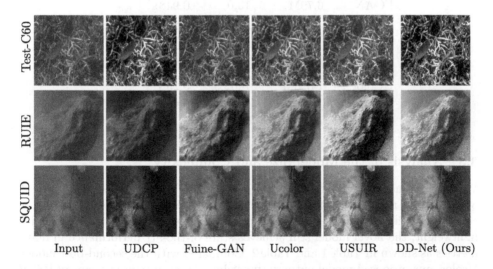

**Fig. 3.** Visual comparison with different underwater image enhancement methods on real-world UIEB dataset. Comparing with UDCP, FGAN, Ucolor and USUIR, our developed method (i.e., DD-Net) performs the best visual quality.

**Table 2.** Averaged unsupervised scores (i.e., PS, UIQM, UCIQE and NIQE) on three real-world underwater datasets without reference images (i.e., Test-C60, RUIE and SQUID).

| Methods | | PS↑ | UIQM↑ | UCIQE↑ | NIQE↓ |
|---|---|---|---|---|---|
| Fusion | Test-C60 | 2.11 | 1.22 | 0.60 | 4.94 |
| | RUIE | 2.96 | 3.72 | 0.66 | **4.26** |
| | SQUID | 2.93 | **1.30** | 0.62 | 5.01 |
| UDCP | Test-C60 | 2.01 | 0.85 | 0.53 | 5.94 |
| | RUIE | 3.03 | 2.09 | 0.51 | 5.13 |
| | SQUID | 2.57 | 1.13 | 0.51 | 4.47 |
| Funie-GAN | Test-C60 | 3.12 | 1.03 | 0.54 | 6.12 |
| | RUIE | 4.14 | 2.98 | 0.55 | 5.69 |
| | SQUID | 2.65 | 0.95 | 0.51 | 4.67 |
| Ucolor | Test-C60 | 3.74 | 0.88 | 0.53 | 6.21 |
| | RUIE | 3.95 | 3.49 | 0.66 | 6.21 |
| | SQUID | 2.82 | 0.82 | 0.51 | **4.29** |
| Ours | Test-C60 | **3.77** | **1.06** | **0.61** | **5.98** |
| | RUIE | **4.19** | **3.88** | **0.69** | 5.53 |
| | SQUID | **2.97** | 0.85 | **0.68** | 4.86 |

**Table 3.** Comparisons of model complexity and size, including model size, GFLOPs, and inference time

| Methods | Parameters | GFLOPs | Inference Time |
|---|---|---|---|
| USUIR | 0.22M | 14.7 | 0.78 s |
| FGAN | 6.79M | 15.0 | 0.948 s |
| UGAN | 44.4M | 21.4 | 3.23 s |
| Water-Net | 1.1M | 71.5 | 0.968 s |
| UWCNN | 40K | 5.0 | 0.58 s |
| UColor | 147.8M | 1402.9 | 3.23 s |
| Ours | 1.97M | 3.7 | 0.5 s |

### 3.3  Analysis of the Model Size and Complexity

We conduct model size and complexity analysis in Table 3. As shown in Table 3, our proposed model has 1.97M parameters and takes the shortest time to process a 4K underwater image on Desktop CPU. Although our proposed model is lightweight, the novel model still achieves state-of-the-art performance in many metrics as shown in Table 1 and Table 2. Compared with the second-best model, Ucolor, our proposed model outperforms it by a large margin in terms of PSNR metric while having a much smaller model size and less computation cost.

## 3.4   Ablation Study

As mentioned in Sect. 3, scene-adaptive convolution achieves better performance, but doubles the parameters of the plain convolution. Therefore, we conducted an ablation study to analyze the effectiveness of scene-adaptive convolution applied to different modules (i.e., the encoder, and the decoder), as shown in Table 4. In addition, to evaluate the effectiveness of the haze-aware regularization, we conducted another ablation study, as shown in Table 5. Both ablation studies are completed on UIEB real-world dataset.

As shown in the second and third rows of Table 4, the dynamic decoder brings much improvement to the network and the dynamic encoder brings slight improvement in terms of PSNR. Moreover, when the network applies scene-adaptive convolution to both, the performance drops compared to the network using the dynamic decoder. The results shows that more dynamic modules will not bring more performance improvement, but only more parameters to the network. Moreover, the results also demonstrate the description mentioned in Sect. 1, that the encoder can be static and the decoder should be dynamic. As shown in Table 5, the use of the haze-aware regularization significantly improves the performance, demonstrating the effectiveness of the haze-aware regularization.

**Table 4.** Effectiveness analysis of applying dynamic convolutions to different modules (i.e., the encoder and the decoder)

| Encoder | Decoder | PSNR↑ | SSIM↑ | UIQM↑ | Parameters |
|---------|---------|-------|-------|-------|------------|
| Dynamic | Dynamic | 21.40 | 0.87 | 2.56 | 2.71M |
| Dynamic | Static | 20.67 | 0.87 | 2.61 | 1.93M |
| Static | Static | 20.09 | 0.84 | 2.72 | 1.19M |
| Static | Dynamic | 22.06 | 0.89 | 2.88 | 1.97M |

**Table 5.** Effectiveness analysis of reverse medium transmission map regularization (i.e., Haze-aware regularization).

| $\ell 2$ | $\mathcal{L}_P$ | $\mathcal{L}_H$ | PSNR↑ | SSIM↑ | UIQM↑ | UCIQE↑ | NIQE↓ |
|------|------|------|-------|-------|-------|--------|-------|
| ✓ | ✗ | ✗ | 20.94 | 0.84 | 2.77 | 0.60 | 4.84 |
| ✓ | ✓ | ✗ | 21.01 | 0.84 | 3.01 | 0.61 | 4.93 |
| ✓ | ✗ | ✓ | 21.94 | 0.89 | 2.81 | 0.47 | 4.59 |
| ✓ | ✓ | ✓ | 22.06 | 0.89 | 2.88 | 0.44 | 4.41 |

# 4 Conclusion

In this paper, we review the Koschmieders light scattering model and propose a lightweight network for underwater image restoration, termed DD-Net. Our proposed method achieves scene-adaptive and pixel-wise restoration by using scene-adaptive convolution and the haze-aware regularization. Extensive experiments on many benchmarks demonstrate the superiority of our proposed method. Moreover, our proposed method furthers the study of light weight model design and real-time application in edge hardware platforms.

# References

1. Ancuti, C., Ancuti, C.O., Haber, T., Bekaert, P.: Enhancing underwater images and videos by fusion. In: 2012 IEEE Conference on Computer Vision and Pattern Recognition, pp. 81–88. IEEE (2012)
2. Berman, D., Levy, D., Avidan, S., Treibitz, T.: Underwater single image color restoration using haze-lines and a new quantitative dataset. IEEE Trans. Pattern Anal. Mach. Intell. **43**(8), 2822–2837 (2020)
3. Bryson, M., Johnson-Roberson, M., Pizarro, O., Williams, S.: Automated registration for multi-year robotic surveys of marine benthic habitats. In: 2013 IEEE/RSJ International Conference on Intelligent Robots and Systems, pp. 3344–3349. IEEE (2013)
4. Chen, Y., Dai, X., Liu, M., Chen, D., Yuan, L., Liu, Z.: Dynamic convolution: attention over convolution kernels. In: Proceedings of the IEEE/CVF Conference on Computer Vision and Pattern Recognition (CVPR) (June 2020)
5. Drews, P.L., Nascimento, E.R., Botelho, S.S., Montenegro Campos, M.F.: Underwater depth estimation and image restoration based on single images. IEEE Comput. Graphics Appl. **36**(2), 24–35 (2016). https://doi.org/10.1109/MCG.2016.26
6. Fabbri, C., Islam, M.J., Sattar, J.: Enhancing underwater imagery using generative adversarial networks. In: 2018 IEEE International Conference on Robotics and Automation (ICRA), pp. 7159–7165. IEEE (2018)
7. Fu, X., Zhuang, P., Huang, Y., Liao, Y., Zhang, X.P., Ding, X.: A retinex-based enhancing approach for single underwater image. In: 2014 IEEE International Conference on Image Processing (ICIP), pp. 4572–4576 (2014). https://doi.org/10.1109/ICIP.2014.7025927
8. Fu, Z., et al.: Unsupervised underwater image restoration: from a homology perspective (2022)
9. Islam, M.J., Xia, Y., Sattar, J.: Fast underwater image enhancement for improved visual perception. IEEE Robot. Autom. Lett. **5**(2), 3227–3234 (2020). https://doi.org/10.1109/LRA.2020.2974710
10. Johnson-Roberson, M., Bryson, M., Douillard, B., Pizarro, O., Williams, S.B.: Out-of-core efficient blending for underwater georeferenced textured D maps. In: 2013 Fourth International Conference on Computing for Geospatial Research and Application, pp. 8–15. IEEE (2013)
11. Li, C., Anwar, S., Hou, J., Cong, R., Guo, C., Ren, W.: Underwater image enhancement via medium transmission-guided multi-color space embedding. IEEE Trans. Image Process. **30**, 4985–5000 (2021)

12. Li, C., Anwar, S., Hou, J., Cong, R., Guo, C., Ren, W.: Underwater image enhancement via medium transmission-guided multi-color space embedding. IEEE Trans. Image Process. **30**, 4985–5000 (2021). https://doi.org/10.1109/TIP.2021.3076367
13. Li, C., et al.: An underwater image enhancement benchmark dataset and beyond. IEEE Trans. Image Process. **29**, 4376–4389 (2020). https://doi.org/10.1109/TIP. 2019.2955241
14. Li, C., Quo, J., Pang, Y., Chen, S., Wang, J.: Single underwater image restoration by blue-green channels dehazing and red channel correction. In: 2016 IEEE International Conference on Acoustics, Speech and Signal Processing (ICASSP), pp. 1731–1735. IEEE (2016)
15. Liu, R., Fan, X., Zhu, M., Hou, M., Luo, Z.: Real-world underwater enhancement: challenges, benchmarks, and solutions under natural light. IEEE Trans. Circuits Syst. Video Technol. **30**(12), 4861–4875 (2020)
16. Mittal, A., Soundararajan, R., Bovik, A.C.: Making a "completely blind" image quality analyzer. IEEE Signal Process. Lett. **20**(3), 209–212 (2012)
17. Narasimhan, S., Nayar, S.: Contrast restoration of weather degraded images. IEEE Trans. Pattern Anal. Mach. Intell. **25**(6), 713–724 (2003). https://doi.org/10.1109/ TPAMI.2003.1201821
18. Panetta, K., Gao, C., Agaian, S.: Human-visual-system-inspired underwater image quality measures. IEEE J. Oceanic Eng. **41**(3), 541–551 (2015)
19. Peng, L., Zhu, C., Bian, L.: U-shape transformer for underwater image enhancement. arXiv preprint arXiv:2111.11843 (2021)
20. Peng, Y.T., Cao, K., Cosman, P.C.: Generalization of the dark channel prior for single image restoration. IEEE Trans. Image Process. **27**(6), 2856–2868 (2018)
21. Ronneberger, O., Fischer, P., Brox, T.: U-Net: convolutional networks for biomedical image segmentation. In: Navab, N., Hornegger, J., Wells, W.M., Frangi, A.F. (eds.) MICCAI 2015. LNCS, vol. 9351, pp. 234–241. Springer, Cham (2015). https://doi.org/10.1007/978-3-319-24574-4_28
22. S., G.C.: Beiträge zur physik der freien atmosphäre. Nature 72 (1905). https://doi. org/10.1038/072053a0
23. Sahu, P., Gupta, N., Sharma, N.: A survey on underwater image enhancement techniques. Int. J. Comput. Appl. **87**(13) (2014)
24. Simonyan, K., Zisserman, A.: Very deep convolutional networks for large-scale image recognition. arXiv preprint arXiv:1409.1556 (2014)
25. Swinehart, D.F.: The beer-lambert law. J. Chem. Educ. **39**(7), 333 (1962)
26. Tian, Z., Shen, C., Chen, H.: Conditional convolutions for instance segmentation. In: Vedaldi, A., Bischof, H., Brox, T., Frahm, J.-M. (eds.) ECCV 2020. LNCS, vol. 12346, pp. 282–298. Springer, Cham (2020). https://doi.org/10.1007/978-3-030-58452-8_17
27. Yang, B., Bender, G., Le, Q.V., Ngiam, J.: Condconv: conditionally parameterized convolutions for efficient inference. In: Wallach, H., Larochelle, H., Beygelzimer, A., d'Alché-Buc, F., Fox, E., Garnett, R. (eds.) Advances in Neural Information Processing Systems, vol. 32. Curran Associates, Inc. (2019). https://proceedings. neurips.cc/paper/2019/file/f2201f5191c4e92cc5af043eebfd0946-Paper.pdf
28. Yang, M., Sowmya, A.: An underwater color image quality evaluation metric. IEEE Trans. Image Process. **24**(12), 6062–6071 (2015)
29. Zhang, Y., Zhang, J., Wang, Q., Zhong, Z.: DyNet: dynamic convolution for accelerating convolutional neural networks. arXiv preprint arXiv:2004.10694 (2020)

# Self-Supervised Vision Transformer Based Nearest Neighbor Classification for Multi-Source Open-Set Domain Adaptation

Jing Li⬤, Liu Yang$^{(\boxtimes)}$⬤, and Qinghua Hu⬤

College of Intelligence and Computing, Tianjin University, Tianjin, China
{jing_li,yangliuyl,huqinghua}@tju.edu.cn

**Abstract.** Domain adaptation alleviates the performance drop when models are deployed in a target domain. Models assuming a close-set world fail in realistic open-set scenarios where novel classes not present in the source domain exist. Moreover, there are likely to be multiple source domains sharing the same label set but having different data distributions. These real situations make multi-source open-set domain adaptation (MSOSDA) a practical problem but have not been fully explored. The difficulty of MSOSDA is learning a common discriminative feature space among all domains while maximizing the separation between source classes and target-private ones. In this work, we propose a self-supervised vision transformer (ViT) based nearest neighbor classifier for MSOSDA. Our critical insight is to exploit the strong nearest neighbor classification property of self-supervised ViT along with supervised contrastive learning. Straightforward strategies and an adaptive data-driven threshold are adopted to explicitly align among domains and recognize open-set classes in the target domain. Extensive experiments on three popular benchmarks demonstrate the effectiveness of our approach.

**Keywords:** Multi-source open-set domain adaptation · Vision transformer · Self-supervised

## 1 Introduction

To improve generalization performance and alleviate the dependency on substantial labeled data, researchers turn to domain adaptation [15] (DA), which trains a classifier with a label-rich source domain and transfers it to a label-scarce target domain. Traditional domain adaption has the close-set assumption that two domains possess the same set of categories. However, this assumption does not hold in practice. The classifier inevitably encounters unknown open-set classes that are not present in the source domain when deployed to the real world, which is the problem setting of open-set domain adaptation (OSDA) [23]. Moreover, it is likely that several source domains that share the same class set have different

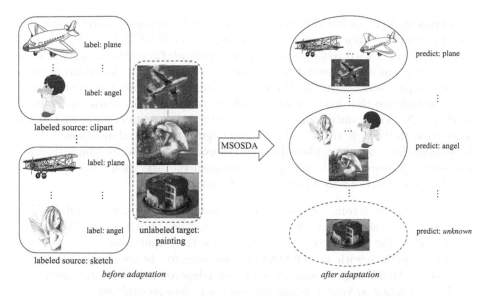

**Fig. 1.** Illustration of MSOSDA. Given multiple labeled source domains and an unlabeled target domain, source domains share an identical class set that is a subset of the class set of the target domain. Samples of the target domain should be classified as the classes shared with source domains or recognized as unknown. Example images are from benchmark DomainNet [18].

data distributions and are annotated asynchronously by separated agencies [19]. The model jointly trained with all the sources obtains better generalization performance than the model trained with a single source because generalization performance can be boosted by more training data [20]. Although it is practical, multi-source open-set domain adaptation (MSOSDA), presented in Fig. 1, is just considered in two recent works, MSOSDANET [19] and HyMOS [1].

Directly applying close-set DA methods to MSOSDA leads to negative transfer because close-set models misclassify open-set classes of the target as categories shared with the source. A straightforward solution to MSOSDA is that combine all the source domains into a single source domain and subsequently exploit any OSDA method. However, because of the different relatedness levels of the target with each of the source domains, samples belonging to the same semantic class from different source domains may be substantially different in appearance and style. Such a naive approach may fail to achieve optimal classification results for the target domain [19] because the domain shift among the source domains may hinder the learning process of discriminative features. The challenges of MSOSDA are aligning the shared classes among domains, including multiple source domains and the target one, and isolating unknown open-set classes from the known ones. Despite its features performing well with basic nearest neighbors classifiers, the potential of vision transformers (ViT) pretrained with DINO self-supervision (DINO-ViT) [3] has not been explored in MSOSDA.

In this work, we tackle MSOSDA through a self-supervised vision transformer-based nearest neighbor classifier. First, we exploit DINO-ViT [3] and supervised contrastive loss [13] to learn compact feature representations of semantic classes on a hyperspherical space. Second, we conduct nearest neighbor classification based on the compact representation. This avoids training a liner classification head with cross-entropy loss that leads to overconfident predictions and sensitivity to noisy labels [24, 26]. Third, data balanced mini-batch creating, conservative self-training together with the style transfer [12] in data augmentation, and an adaptive data-dependent threshold are exploited to align source domains, adapt source domains with the target domain, and reject open-set classes in the target domain, respectively. Our main contributions are summarized as follows:

– Leveraging the strong nearest neighbor classification property of DINO-ViT, we propose a simple but effective nearest neighbor classifier for MSOSDA.
– Instead of the cross-entropy loss, we adopt the supervised contrastive loss that synergizes with the DINO-ViT backbone to obtain compact category clusters. Well-designed strategies and an adaptive threshold are applied to the adaptation among domains and open-set class recognition.
– Extensive experiments on three popular benchmarks demonstrate that our approach is effective and outperforms the state-of-the-art in most cases.

The proposed model is NENO, which we interpret as a **ne**arest neighbor classifier based on **DINO**-ViT.

## 2    Related Work

Domain adaptation (DA) models are advocated to learn domain-invariant features over source and target domains [8, 15, 28]. Open-set domain adaptation (OSDA) [23] setting specifies that the target domain contains private categories. OSDA methods [2, 14, 16] are supposed to classify source classes correctly and recognize target-private classes as unknown. However, only two MSOSDA works [1, 19] are published previously. Based on the single-source OSDA method named OSBP [23], MSOSDANET [19] proposes a class-level alignment among multiple source domains through a clustering loss and designs an additional large margin loss to push unknown open-set classes away from the known ones. Instead of combining several losses and tuning hyperparameters, HyMOS [1] exploits a single supervised contrastive loss to learn features for discriminating known classes, conducts nearest neighbor classification in the target domain, and rejects open-set samples via a self-paced threshold. Although similar to HyMOS, NENO exploits the good nearest neighbor classification property of the self-supervised vision transformer. Moreover, NENO employs a gradual decay conservative multiplier when it includes potential known target samples in training.

Self-supervised pretraining contributes a lot to the success of Transformers in natural language processing [5] and shows their potential on images with convnets [10]. DINO [3] studies the impact of self-supervised pretraining on ViT

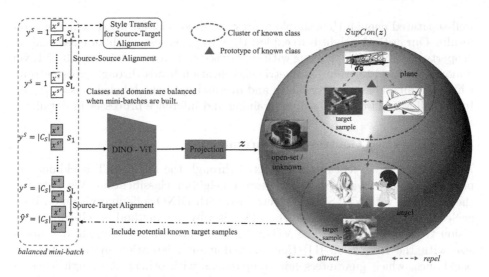

**Fig. 2.** Overview of NENO. Features $z$ of source samples $x^s$ are extracted and projected onto a hypersphere. For class-wise alignments among source domains $\mathcal{S}_1, \ldots, \mathcal{S}_L$, domain and class-balanced mini-batches are built. To learn domain-invariant features, NENO introduces target style transfer in transformations of data augmentation and includes potential known target samples $x^t$ in training. With the guidance of supervised contrastive loss $SupCon(z)$, clusters of known classes are compact and well-separated in the hyperspherical feature embedding, where unknown samples fall in the low-density margins between clusters.

features and identifies self-supervised ViT features perform well with an elemental nearest neighbors classifier. However, the application of ViT in DA is still very scarce. CDTrans [28] and SSRT [25] were transformer-based models designed for the close-set DA, while our proposed NENO exploits the self-supervised transformer encoder in the context of MSOSDA.

## 3 Method

### 3.1 Problem Setting and Notation

In MSOSDA, there are $L$ labeled source domains $\mathcal{S} = \{\mathcal{S}_1, \mathcal{S}_2, \ldots, \mathcal{S}_L\}$ where $\mathcal{S}_i = \{x_j^{s_i}, y_j^{s_i}\}_{j=1}^{N^{s_i}} \sim p_i$, one unlabeled target domain $\mathcal{T} = \{x_j^t\}_{j=1}^{N^t} \sim q$, and $p_i \neq q$, $p_i \neq p_j$ when $i \neq j$. The source domains share the same class set $\mathcal{C}_s$ which is a subset to that of the target domain $\mathcal{C}_t$, denoted as $\mathcal{C}_s \subset \mathcal{C}_t$. Open-set classes in $\mathcal{C}_{t \setminus s}$ are considered *unknown*. Given this setup, a model is supposed to classify each target sample as either one of the *known* $\mathcal{C}_s$ classes or *unknown*.

### 3.2 Model Overview

Our proposed NENO, illustrated in Fig. 2, concentrates on building a domain-aligned structured feature space where known class clusters are compact and well-separated enough that simple nearest neighbor classification achieves good results. Our critical insight is to exploit the strong nearest neighbor classification property of DINO-ViT [3] along with supervised contrastive learning [13]. NENO removes the need to train parametric classification heads through cross-entropy which is vulnerable to noisy labels and overfitting to the labeled classes [1,26]. In the following, we introduce the training and inference processes in detail.

### 3.3  Supervised Contrastive Learning

As shown in Fig. 2, features $z$ extracted through the DINO-ViT backbone are projected onto a hypersphere for nearest neighbor classification. We initialize the backbone with ViT-S/16 [6] pretrained with DINO self-supervision on ImageNet [4] without using any labels, which is why our method is self-supervised vision transformer based. The ViT-S/16 architecture has a comparable model size with the ResNet-50 [11] that most domain adaptation methods take as backbones, which guarantees fair comparisons with others. Although features extracted by DINO-ViT already perform well for nearest neighbors classification, they are further fine-tuned on the labeled source domains with supervised contrastive learning for a more tailored representation. For each source sample $\{x_i^s, y_i^s\}$ in a mini-batch, the supervised contrastive (SupCon) loss is written as

$$SupCon(z_i^s) = -\frac{1}{|\mathcal{N}(i)|} \sum_{q \in \mathcal{N}(i)} \log \frac{\exp\left(z_i^s \cdot z_q^s / \tau\right)}{\sum_n \mathbb{1}_{[n \neq i]} \exp\left(z_i^s \cdot z_n^s / \tau\right)}, \tag{1}$$

where $z_i^s = \phi(f(x_i^s))$ and $\mathbb{1}_{[n \neq i]}$ is an indicator function evaluating to 1 $iff$ $n \neq i$, and $\tau$ is a temperature value. $f$ is the DINO-ViT backbone, and $\phi$ is the multi-layer perceptron head projecting features onto the hypersphere, $\mathcal{N}(i)$ denotes the indices of other images having the same label as $x_i^s$ in one mini-batch. The total loss over the mini-batch is $\mathcal{L} = \sum_{i \in B} SupCon(z_i^s)$, where $B$ corresponds to the mini-batch. The intuition of supervised contrastive loss is that the distance between two samples of the same class is minimized, while the distance between two samples of different classes is maximized. It aims at learning a semantically meaningful feature space where class clusters are so compact and separated with large margins that unknown categories naturally fall in low-density regions. Projecting features to the hypersphere helps achieve this goal [1]. Some existing methods [2,14,22] combine several losses to alleviate the drawbacks of cross-entropy mentioned above. NENO only uses the supervised contrastive loss to nudge the backbone network towards a representation that is semantically related to the current classification task.

### 3.4  Alignment Among the Source Domains

Given the availability of labels for samples in the source domains, it is feasible to achieve a class-wise source-source alignment. Instead of using another loss, NENO adopts the domain and class-balanced strategy [19] to create each mini-batch, which is depicted in the left part of Fig. 2. Specifically, each mini-batch covers all the $|\mathcal{C}_s|$ classes, and each class is composed of an equal number of samples from all the $L$ source domains. Based on the balanced mini-batches, the DINO-ViT backbone and the supervised contrastive loss obtain a feature space where samples of the identical class are clustered in the same region despite the domain, while samples of different classes are repelled with each other.

## 3.5    Adaptation Between $\mathcal{S}$ and $\mathcal{T}$

The nonidentical appearance style visually reflects the gaps among domains. To obtain domain-invariant feature embedding between $\mathcal{S}$ and $\mathcal{T}$, NENO adds style transfer to the semantic-preserving transformations used in data augmentation. Specifically, an AdaIN [12] model, one of the state-of-the-art models for style transfer, is trained with both $\mathcal{S}$ and $\mathcal{T}$. Because AdaIN focuses on the style and disregards the semantic content, the entire $\mathcal{T}$, including the *unknown* categories, is used for training without the risk of negative transfer. Then the trained AdaIn model is applied randomly to transfer the target style to source samples as a kind of transformation for data augmentation. Standard transformations, such as grayscale, random crop, and color jittering, are applied if the style transfer is not applied. Within a mini-batch, the supervised contrastive learning explicitly compares original images with target-like ones, facilitating neglecting the style difference and learning a domain-agnostic representation.

Moreover, NENO conducts a class-wise alignment between $\mathcal{S}$ and $\mathcal{T}$ through self-training, which includes potential known samples of $\mathcal{T}$ into training at predefined iterations named breakpoints. As shown in Fig. 2, the potential known samples of $\mathcal{T}$ act as an additional source domain when building the mini-batch. These potential known samples of $\mathcal{T}$ are classified as one of the $|\mathcal{C}_s|$ known classes with a conservative strategy. The details of classification and conservative strategy are elaborated in the following subsection. For reliability of self-training, the breakpoints appear at least after one training epoch is over, ensuring the model trained with source data and style transfer becomes robust enough.

## 3.6    Classification on the Hypersphere

For nearest neighbor classification on the target domain, we should define the prototype of every source category $y^s \in \{1, \ldots, |\mathcal{C}_s|\}$ by computing the averaged feature of corresponding source samples $h_{y^s} = \frac{1}{N_{y^s}} \sum_{k=1}^{N_{y^s}} z_k^s$, where $z_k^s$ is a source sample labeled as class $y^s$, and $N_{y^s}$ is the number of the source samples in class $y^s$. For any target sample $z^t$, we compute its distance from any source class prototype $h_{y^s}$ as $d_{h_{y^s}}(z^t) = 1 - \sigma_{[0,1]}(z^t, h_{y^s})$, where $\sigma_{[0,1]}(z^t, h_{y^s})$ is the cosine similarity rescaled in $[0,1]$. In nearest neighbor classification, $z^t$ is assigned the same class as that of the nearest prototype, denoted as $\hat{y}^t = arg\,min_{y^s}(d_{h_{y^s}}(z^t))$.

However, there are *unknown* categories in the target domain. Any target sample $z^t$ should be decided if it is an *unknown* sample before the label assignment. A threshold on the minimum distance between $z^t$ and $h_{y^s}$ is required. Instead of manually tuning a value and keep it fixed during training, we adopt a adaptive threshold [1] computed online with the hyperspherical feature embedding. Our threshold $\alpha$ is defined by

$$\alpha = \gamma \cdot \left[ log \left( \frac{\beta}{2\gamma} \right) + 1 \right], \tag{2}$$

where $\beta$ is the average distance of two adjacent prototypes and $\gamma$ is the average radius of the class clusters. They are defined on the hypersphere as follows,

$$\gamma = \frac{1}{|C_s|} \sum_{y^s \in C_s} \left\{ \frac{1}{N_{y^s}} \sum_{k=1}^{N_{y^s}} d_{h_{y^s}}(z_k^s) \right\}, \tag{3}$$

$$\beta = \frac{1}{|C_s|} \sum_{y^s \in C_s} d_{h^*}(h_{y^s}), \tag{4}$$

where $h^*$ is the closest prototype to each $h_{y^s}$. In an ideal feature space where class clusters are well-separated, the ratio between the distance of two adjacent prototypes and the radii of the respective clusters is greater than one, denoted as $\frac{\beta}{2\gamma} > 1$, which results that $\alpha$ is greater than $\gamma$. The final label assignment for target sample $z^t$ during inference is defined as follows,

$$\hat{y}^t = \begin{cases} \arg\min_{y^s}(d_{h_{y^s}}(z^t)) & \text{if } \min_{y^s}(d_{h_{y^s}}(z^t)) < \alpha, \\ unknown & \text{if } \min_{y^s}(d_{h_{y^s}}(z^t)) \geq \alpha. \end{cases} \tag{5}$$

This label assignment strategy is also used to select potential known classes for self-training which was mentioned previously. However, to avoid selecting *unknown* samples as the known ones, NENO uses a conservative threshold $\alpha' = \epsilon \cdot \alpha$, where $\epsilon$ is the conservative multiplier whose value falls in $[0, 1]$. As the training goes on, $\gamma$ becomes larger because more training samples are employed, letting class clusters grow. Threshold $\alpha$ becomes larger as it is positively proportional with $\gamma$, so $\epsilon$ should decay gradually. The definition of $\epsilon$ is

$$\epsilon = \delta \cdot \frac{N_{breakpoints} - Index_{current}}{N_{breakpoints}}, \tag{6}$$

where $\delta$ is a task-specific hyperparameter in $[0, 1]$, $N_{breakpoints}$ is the number of breakpoints, and the $Index_{current}$ is the index of current breakpoint.

# 4   Experiment

## 4.1   Datasets and Settings

Three popular domain adaptation benchmarks are adopted for experiments. We follow the same setting in the previous works: one domain is considered the target domain in turn, while the rest are multiple source domains. **Office31** [21] is comprised of three domains: Webcam (W), Dslr (D) and Amazon (A). Each domain contains 31 categories. The first 20 classes in alphabetic order are set as known ones, while the remaining 11 are unknown. **Office-Home** [27] contains four domains: Art (Ar), Clipart (Cl), Product (Pr), RealWorld (Rw) with 65 classes. The first 45 categories in alphabetic order are known, and the rest acts as unknown. **DomainNet** [18] is a new and challenging benchmarks than the previous ones. It possesses six domains and 345 classes. Following previous works [19], we only use four domains of benchmark DomainNet, including Infograph (I), Painting (P), Sketch (S), and Clipart (C). We randomly select 50 samples per class or use all samples in case of lower cardinality. The first 100 classes in alphabetic order are treated as the known ones.

### 4.2  Evaluation Metrics

OS*, UNK, and OS [23] widely used in OSDA literature are adopted. OS* is the average recall over the known classes, whereas OS considers both OS* and UNK which is the recall of the *unknown*: $OS = \frac{|\mathcal{C}_s|}{|\mathcal{C}_s|+1} \times OS^* + \frac{1}{|\mathcal{C}_s|+1} \times UNK$. However, a large number of known classes make the role of UNK in OS negligible. We are more concerned with HOS which is the harmonic mean of OS* and UNK: $HOS = 2\frac{OS^* \times UNK}{OS^* + UNK}$ [2]. HOS is more reasonable than OS because it provides a high score only if both OS* and UNK are high.

### 4.3  Compared Methods

We compare NENO with **(1)** single-source OSDA methods: Inheritable [14], ROS [2], and PGL [16]; **(2)** MSOSDA methods: MOSDANET [19] and HyMOS [1]; **(3)** Universal domain adaptation (UniDA) methods: CMU [7] and DANCE [22]. UniDA [29] covers a wide range of scenarios, including the OSDA. UniDA approaches are supposed to tackle the adaptation task on common class space without prior knowledge about the relationship between the label sets of source and target domains. The *Source Combine* strategy [18] unifying all source domains as a single one is applied for methods only considering single-source scenarios.

### 4.4  Experimental Results and Ablation Study

The rounded results obtained on three benchmarks are listed in Table 1 ∼ 3, where the best results are **bold**.

For Office31 shown in Table 1, our model NENO achieves the best performance concerning UNK and HOS across all adaptation tasks except $W, D \rightarrow A$, where it still achieves a competing result. From those scores, it is easy to find that OS is dominated by OS*, which is decided by the definition of OS. Although the best two competitors, DANCE and MOSDANET, behave poorly for some tasks under the metric UNK, they obtain high scores concerning OS only because of the high OS* score. However, HOS treats OS* and UNK equally, making it more comprehensive than OS. NENO achieves the highest score in HOS averaged

**Table 1.** Results (%) averaged over three runs on the Office31 [21].

| | | Office31 | | | | | | | | | | | | | | |
|---|---|---|---|---|---|---|---|---|---|---|---|---|---|---|---|---|
| | | D,A → W | | | | W,A → D | | | | W,D → A | | | | Avg. | | | |
| | | OS | OS* | UNK | HOS | OS | OS* | UNK | HOS | OS | OS* | UNK | HOS | OS | OS* | UNK | HOS |
| Source Combine | Inheritable [14] | 69.0 | 68.1 | 87.6 | 76.6 | 74.7 | 74.1 | 85.6 | 79.5 | 63.7 | 62.9 | 78.9 | 70.0 | 69.1 | 68.4 | 84.0 | 75.4 |
| | ROS [2] | 82.2 | 82.3 | 81.5 | 81.8 | 95.3 | 96.5 | 68.7 | 80.1 | 53.8 | 52.2 | 84.9 | 64.7 | 77.1 | 77.0 | 78.4 | 75.5 |
| | CMU [7] | 96.1 | 98.7 | 44.6 | 61.4 | 96.2 | 98.7 | 47.3 | 64.0 | 73.1 | 74.5 | 45.4 | 56.4 | 88.5 | 90.6 | 45.8 | 60.6 |
| | DANCE [22] | 95.9 | **99.5** | 23.9 | 38.5 | **97.3** | **100.0** | 42.6 | 59.7 | 78.0 | 79.6 | 45.6 | 58.0 | 90.4 | 93.0 | 37.3 | 52.0 |
| | PGL [16] | 94.1 | 97.4 | 27.8 | 43.3 | 92.2 | 95.6 | 23.5 | 37.7 | 77.1 | 79.8 | 22.9 | 35.6 | 87.8 | 90.9 | 24.7 | 38.9 |
| Multi-Source | MOSDANET [19] | **97.7** | 99.4 | 43.5 | 60.5 | 97.0 | 99.0 | 55.9 | 71.5 | **80.9** | **81.5** | 67.6 | **73.9** | **91.9** | **93.3** | 55.7 | 68.6 |
| | HyMOS[1] | 96.1 | 96.6 | 84.6 | 90.2 | 96.7 | 97.3 | 83.6 | 89.9 | 49.6 | 48.0 | 83.1 | 60.8 | 80.8 | 80.6 | 83.8 | 80.3 |
| | **NENO** | 95.9 | 96.2 | **88.1** | **91.9** | 96.2 | 95.6 | **93.1** | **94.7** | 53.9 | 55.0 | **87.6** | 67.4 | 82.0 | 82.3 | **89.6** | **84.7** |

**Table 2.** Results (%) averaged over three runs on the Office-Home [27].

| | | Office-Home | | | | | | | | | | | | | | |
|---|---|---|---|---|---|---|---|---|---|---|---|---|---|---|---|---|---|
| | | Ar,Pr,Cl → Rw | | | | Ar,Pr,Rw → Cl | | | | Cl,Pr,Rw → Ar | | | | Cl,Ar,Rw → Pr | | | Avg. |
| | | OS | OS* | UNK | HOS | OS | OS* | UNK | HOS | OS | OS* | UNK | HOS | OS | OS* | UNK | HOS | OS | OS* | UNK | HOS |
| Source Combine | Inheritable [14] | 58.6 | 58.4 | 68.9 | 63.2 | 44.3 | 43.7 | 66.5 | 52.6 | 36.4 | 35.5 | 77.6 | 48.7 | 58.6 | 58.5 | 63.3 | 60.7 | 49.5 | 49.1 | 69.1 | 56.3 |
| | ROS [2] | 69.9 | 69.8 | 76.9 | **73.0** | 57.1 | 57.1 | 57.6 | 57.3 | 57.5 | 57.2 | 66.7 | 61.6 | 70.3 | 70.3 | 68.0 | 69.1 | 63.7 | 63.6 | 67.3 | 65.3 |
| | CMU [7] | 62.9 | 62.5 | **81.5** | 70.8 | 35.8 | 34.6 | **89.9** | 50.0 | 44.6 | 43.7 | **87.0** | 58.1 | 60.6 | 60.1 | **81.7** | 69.3 | 51.0 | 50.2 | **85.0** | 62.1 |
| | DANCE [22] | **83.9** | **85.6** | 4.5 | 12.4 | 66.8 | 68.0 | 9.2 | 16.1 | **72.7** | **74.1** | 10.7 | 18.6 | **85.1** | **86.7** | 13.4 | 22.9 | **77.1** | **78.6** | 9.4 | 17.5 |
| | PGL [16] | 83.4 | 84.6 | 26.2 | 40.0 | 62.0 | 63.0 | 21.0 | 31.5 | 69.5 | 70.6 | 20.5 | 31.8 | 82.6 | 83.8 | 28.2 | 42.2 | 74.4 | 75.5 | 24.0 | 36.4 |
| Multi-Source | MOSDANET [19] | 78.4 | 79.4 | 55.0 | 65.0 | **67.5** | **68.1** | 40.9 | 51.1 | 61.0 | 61.3 | 48.7 | 54.3 | 81.1 | 82.2 | 55.0 | 65.9 | 72.0 | 72.8 | 49.9 | 59.1 |
| | HyMOS[1] | 69.5 | 69.4 | 72.7 | 71.0 | 52.5 | 51.7 | 86.0 | 64.6 | 50.1 | 49.4 | 84.1 | 62.2 | 71.5 | 71.5 | 70.6 | 71.1 | 60.9 | 60.5 | 78.4 | 67.2 |
| | **NENO** | 71.3 | 71.3 | 74.1 | 72.6 | 59.5 | 59.2 | 74.1 | **65.8** | 55.1 | 54.6 | 75.9 | **63.5** | 68.2 | 68.1 | 75.7 | **71.6** | 63.5 | 63.3 | 75.0 | **68.4** |

**Table 3.** Results (%) averaged over three runs on the DomainNet [18].

| | | DomainNet | | | | | | | | | | | |
|---|---|---|---|---|---|---|---|---|---|---|---|---|---|
| | | I,P → S | | | | I,P → C | | | | Avg. | | | |
| | | OS | OS* | UNK | HOS | OS | OS* | UNK | HOS | OS | OS* | UNK | HOS |
| Source Combine | Inheritable [14] | 24.9 | 24.5 | 60.3 | 34.8 | 33.5 | 33.1 | 65.6 | 44.0 | 29.2 | 28.8 | 62.9 | 39.4 |
| | ROS [2] | 31.7 | 31.3 | 77.5 | 44.5 | 41.0 | 40.7 | 73.6 | 52.4 | 36.4 | 36.0 | 75.5 | 48.5 |
| | CMU [7] | 48.0 | 48.3 | 26.3 | 38.1 | 49.6 | 49.8 | 27.6 | 35.5 | 48.8 | 49.1 | 27.0 | 36.8 |
| | DANCE [22] | 45.6 | 45.8 | 22.3 | 30.0 | 54.4 | 54.7 | 28.7 | 37.6 | 50.0 | 50.3 | 25.5 | 33.8 |
| | PGL [16] | **54.9** | **55.3** | 11.1 | 18.5 | **59.6** | **60.1** | 11.6 | 19.0 | **57.3** | **57.7** | 11.4 | 19.0 |
| Multi-Source | MOSDANET [19] | 30.2 | 29.9 | 60.2 | 40.0 | 31.8 | 31.6 | 51.8 | 39.3 | 31.0 | 30.8 | 56.0 | 39.6 |
| | HyMOS[1] | 43.6 | 43.2 | **86.0** | 57.5 | 47.8 | 47.4 | **85.5** | 61.0 | 45.7 | 45.3 | **85.8** | 59.3 |
| | **NENO** | 49.4 | 49.1 | 73.0 | **58.7** | 57.0 | 56.8 | 73.2 | **64.0** | 53.2 | 53.0 | 73.1 | **61.4** |

across three tasks. A similar situation is observed in the results obtained with benchmarks Office-Home (Table 2) and DomainNet (Table 3). NENO achieves the best performance concerning HOS, while the best competitors only get high scores in OS* or UNK. Note that the results of compared methods are cited from the HyMOS paper.

NENO uses DINO-ViT as the backbone in the feature extraction and several strategies in the alignments among domains. To show their contributions to the performance, we conduct ablation studies with the task Ar,Pr,Cl → Rw in benchmark OfficeHome. The results are in Table 4. To demonstrate the importance of adopting DINO-ViT as the backbone, we replace DINO-ViT with the ImageNet pretrained ResNet50 in the variant denoted as *ResNet50 as Backbone*. As a result, performance drops in every metric, which shows the rationality of our

**Table 4.** Ablation study results (%) averaged over three runs.

| Method | Ar,Pr,Cl → Rw | | | |
|---|---|---|---|---|
| | OS | OS* | UNK | **HOS** |
| **NENO** | 71.3 | 71.3 | 74.1 | **72.6** |
| *ResNet50 as Backbone* | 69.6 | 69.5 | 72.8 | 71.1 |
| *w/o Source Balance* | 71.7 | **71.7** | 72.9 | 72.1 |
| *w/o Style Transfer* | 68.9 | 68.8 | **75.5** | 72.0 |
| *w/o Self-Training* | **71.8** | 71.7 | 73.0 | 72.3 |

crucial insight that exploits the strong nearest neighbor classification property of DINO-ViT. The bottom three rows show results of the variants that corresponding domain alignment strategies are ablated from NENO. Without the techniques for aligning domains, performance concerning HOS drops to varying degrees, which means the variants only outperform NENO in either OS* or UNK. Overall, every component of NENO works.

### 4.5 Visualization

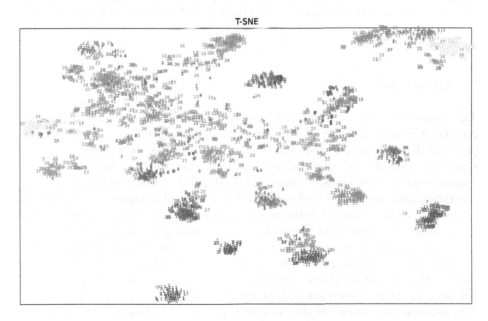

**Fig. 3.** Feature Space of Target Domain Amazon in Benchmark Office31 [21] (Best viewed in color and magnified). (Color figure online)

To show that NENO learns a compact and discriminative feature space, we visualize the feature space of target domain Amazon in Office31 through

552 J. Li et al.

t-SNE [17]. In Fig. 3, known classes in $\mathcal{C}_s$ are represented as colorful clusters, while unknown classes in $\mathcal{C}_{t\backslash s}$ are in gray. Note that different known classes clusters may have the same color. As it shows, known class clusters are compact and well-separated from each other, while unknown samples are far away from centroids of the clusters, scattered in the low-density regions among compact clusters.

Multi-head self-attention mechanism contributes a lot to the success of transformers [9], so we also visualize the overall attention maps. This visualization verifies that our model learns class-specific features that are key to classification.

**Fig. 4.** Attention Maps on Example Images from Domain Sketch of Benchmark DomainNet [18]. The first and the third column show original images, columns on their right demonstrate the attention maps (best viewed in color). (Color figure online)

## 5 Conclusion

This paper proposes a simple but effective nearest neighbor classifier named NENO. It exploits DINO-ViT and supervised contrastive loss to obtain a compact and discriminative feature space where class clusters are compact and well-separated. Domain and class-balanced mini-batches are built to align multiple source domains. Style transfer integrated as a kind of transformation in data augmentation and the inclusion of potential known target samples for self-training contribute to the alignment between source domains and the target one. Instead of manually setting a fixed threshold, NENO adopts an adaptive data-driven threshold to separate classes shared across all domains and target-private ones. Extensive experiments on three benchmarks show the advantage of our proposed model. The nearest neighbor classification bypasses the trouble of training a classification head. Nevertheless, with compact feature representation and suitable loss function instead of the cross-entropy one, classification heads can also achieve good results, which we leave for future work.

**Acknowledgements.** This work was supported in part by the National Natural Science Foundation of China (Grant No.61925602, 61732011, 62076179) and the Beijing Natural Science Foundation (Grant No.Z180006).

# References

1. Bucci, S., Borlino, F.C., Caputo, B., Tommasi, T.: Distance-based hyperspherical classification for multi-source open-set domain adaptation. In: Proceedings of the IEEE/CVF Winter Conference on Applications of Computer Vision, pp. 1119–1128 (2022)
2. Bucci, S., Loghmani, M.R., Tommasi, T.: On the effectiveness of image rotation for open set domain adaptation. In: Proceedings of the European Conference on Computer Vision, pp. 422–438. Springer, Berlin (2020)
3. Caron, M., Touvron, H., Misra, I., Jégou, H., Mairal, J., Bojanowski, P., Joulin, A.: Emerging properties in self-supervised vision transformers. In: Proceedings of the IEEE/CVF International Conference on Computer Vision, pp. 9650–9660 (2021)
4. Deng, J., Dong, W., Socher, R., Li, L.J., Li, K., Fei-Fei, L.: Imagenet: A large-scale hierarchical image database. In: 2009 IEEE Conference on Computer Vision and Pattern Recognition, pp. 248–255 (2009)
5. Devlin, J., Chang, M.W., Lee, K., Toutanova, K.: Bert: Pre-training of deep bidirectional transformers for language understanding. In: Proceedings of the 2019 Conference of the North American Chapter of the Association for Computational Linguistics: Human Language Technologies, vol. 1, pp. 4171–4186 (2019)
6. Dosovitskiy, A., Beyer, L., Kolesnikov, A., Weissenborn, D., Zhai, X., Unterthiner, T., Dehghani, M., Minderer, M., Heigold, G., Gelly, S., Uszkoreit, J., Houlsby, N.: An image is worth $16 \times 16$ words: transformers for image recognition at scale. In: International Conference on Learning Representations (2021)
7. Fu, B., Cao, Z., Long, M., Wang, J.: Learning to detect open classes for universal domain adaptation. In: European Conference on Computer Vision, pp. 567–583. Springer, Berlin (2020)
8. Ganin, Y., Ustinova, E., Ajakan, H., Germain, P., Larochelle, H., Laviolette, F., Marchand, M., Lempitsky, V.: Domain-adversarial training of neural networks. J. Mach. Learn. Res. **17**(1), 2030–2096 (2016)
9. He, J., Chen, J.N., Liu, S., Kortylewski, A., Yang, C., Bai, Y., Wang, C., Yuille, A.: Transfg: a transformer architecture for fine-grained recognition. In: Proceedings of the AAAI Conference on Artificial Intelligence (2022)
10. He, K., Fan, H., Wu, Y., Xie, S., Girshick, R.: Momentum contrast for unsupervised visual representation learning. In: Proceedings of the IEEE/CVF Conference on Computer Vision and Pattern Recognition, pp. 9729–9738 (2020)
11. He, K., Zhang, X., Ren, S., Sun, J.: Deep residual learning for image recognition. In: Proceedings of the IEEE Conference on Computer Vision and Pattern Recognition, pp. 770–778 (2016)
12. Huang, X., Belongie, S.: Arbitrary style transfer in real-time with adaptive instance normalization. In: Proceedings of the IEEE international Conference on Computer Vision, pp. 1501–1510 (2017)
13. Khosla, P., Teterwak, P., Wang, C., Sarna, A., Tian, Y., Isola, P., Maschinot, A., Liu, C., Krishnan, D.: Supervised contrastive learning. Adv. Neural. Inf. Process. Syst. **33**, 18661–18673 (2020)
14. Kundu, J.N., Venkat, N., Revanur, A., Babu, R.V., et al.: Towards inheritable models for open-set domain adaptation. In: Proceedings of the IEEE/CVF Conference on Computer Vision and Pattern Recognition, pp. 12376–12385 (2020)
15. Long, M., Cao, Y., Wang, J., Jordan, M.: Learning transferable features with deep adaptation networks. In: Proceedings of the 32nd International Conference on Machine Learning, pp. 97–105 (2015)

16. Luo, Y., Wang, Z., Huang, Z., Baktashmotlagh, M.: Progressive graph learning for open-set domain adaptation. In: International Conference on Machine Learning, pp. 6468–6478. PMLR (2020)
17. Van der Maaten, L., Hinton, G.: Visualizing data using t-SNE. J. Mach. Learn. Res. **9**(11) (2008)
18. Peng, X., Bai, Q., Xia, X., Huang, Z., Saenko, K., Wang, B.: Moment matching for multi-source domain adaptation. In: Proceedings of the IEEE/CVF International Conference on Computer Vision, pp. 1406–1415 (2019)
19. Rakshit, S., Tamboli, D., Meshram, P.S., Banerjee, B., Roig, G., Chaudhuri, S.: Multi-source open-set deep adversarial domain adaptation. In: European Conference on Computer Vision, pp. 735–750. Springer, Berlin (2020)
20. Ridnik, T., Ben-Baruch, E., Noy, A., Zelnik-Manor, L.: Imagenet-21k pretraining for the masses. In: Thirty-Fifth Conference on Neural Information Processing Systems Datasets and Benchmarks Track (Round 1) (2021)
21. Saenko, K., Kulis, B., Fritz, M., Darrell, T.: Adapting visual category models to new domains. In: Proceedings of the European Conference on Computer Vision, pp. 213–226. Springer, Berlin (2010)
22. Saito, K., Kim, D., Sclaroff, S., Saenko, K.: Universal domain adaptation through self supervision. Adv. Neural Inf. Process. Syst. **33**, 16282–16292 (2020)
23. Saito, K., Yamamoto, S., Ushiku, Y., Harada, T.: Open set domain adaptation by backpropagation. In: Proceedings of the European Conference on Computer Vision, pp. 153–168 (2018)
24. Sensoy, M., Kaplan, L., Kandemir, M.: Evidential deep learning to quantify classification uncertainty. Adv. Neural Inf. Process. Syst. **31** (2018)
25. Sun, T., Lu, C., Zhang, T., Ling, H.: Safe self-refinement for transformer-based domain adaptation. In: Proceedings of the IEEE/CVF Conference on Computer Vision and Pattern Recognition (2022)
26. Vaze, S., Han, K., Vedaldi, A., Zisserman, A.: Generalized category discovery. In: IEEE Conference on Computer Vision and Pattern Recognition (2022)
27. Venkateswara, H., Eusebio, J., Chakraborty, S., Panchanathan, S.: Deep hashing network for unsupervised domain adaptation. In: Proceedings of the IEEE Conference on Computer Vision and Pattern Recognition, pp. 5018–5027 (2017)
28. Xu, T., Chen, W., WANG, P., Wang, F., Li, H., Jin, R.: CDTrans: cross-domain transformer for unsupervised domain adaptation. In: International Conference on Learning Representations (2022)
29. You, K., Long, M., Cao, Z., Wang, J., Jordan, M.I.: Universal domain adaptation. In: Proceedings of the IEEE/CVF Conference on Computer Vision and Pattern Recognition, pp. 2720–2729 (2019)

# Lightweight Image Dehazing Neural Network Model Based on Estimating Medium Transmission Map by Intensity

Tian-Hu Jin[1], Yan-Yun Tao[1,2,3]($\boxtimes$), Jia-Ren Guo[1], Zi-Hao Huang[1], and Jian-Yin Zheng[1]

[1] School of Rail Transportation, Soochow University, Suzhou 215000, China
taoyanyun@suda.edu.cn
[2] Key Lab. of System Control and Information Processing, Ministry of Education, Shanghai Jiao Tong University, Shanghai 200240, China
[3] State Key Lab. for Novel Software Technology, Nanjing University, Nanjing, China

**Abstract.** Single image dehazing is a challenging ill-posed problem. The key to achieve haze removal is to estimate an accurate medium transmission map. By redefining the atmospheric scattering model, we obtain a new transmittance map scattering model, haze image and haze-free image, derive the medium transmission as a function of the scene intensity only, also deduce a priori condition that the intensity of hazy image is higher than that of haze-free image, and propose a lightweight image dehazing neural network (Intensity neural network, I-Net) based on estimating medium transmission map by intensity. I-Net uses a convolutional neural network (CNN) as the backbone, and takes the intensity of hazy image as the input, and outputs the intensity of haze-free image, the medium transmission map and the original haze-free image, also joints the priori condition derived previously to obtain a more accurate medium transmittance map. In this paper, the dehazing algorithm obtains the intensity of haze-free image through I-Net, derives the transmittance map using the functional relationship between transmittance and scene intensity, and finally recovers the original haze-free image through the transmittance map scattering model. The experimental results show that our dehazing results are clearer and more natural. The subjective and objective evaluations show that our image dehazing algorithm can achieve better dehazing results than traditional algorithms, and outperforms current advanced algorithms in terms of Peak Signal to Noise Rate (PSNR) and Structure Similarity Index Measurement (SSIM).

**Keywords:** Single image dehazing · Atmospheric scattering model · Medium transmission map · Deep CNN

## 1 Introduction

Due to the absorption and scattering of light in the hazy environment, the visibility is low. The images taken in the hazy environment usually have problems such as decreased contrast, loss of details, and saturation offset [19, 22]. This has a great negative impact on outdoor navigation [14, 21] video surveillance [29] and other visual systems. For advanced vision tasks such as scene understanding [5] and target detection [3], hazy images need to be dehazed. Therefore, Single image haze removal has attracted widespread attention. The purpose of the haze removal is to restore the clear image, reduce the image distortion caused by the environmental conditions of the haze, and the impact on various visual analysis tasks.

Estimating the clean image from a single hazy input is an ill-posed problem. Early methods [6, 12, 15–18, 20, 27] utilize priori assumptions to estimate the transmittance map and global atmospheric light values, and then recover a haze-free image by the atmospheric scattering model. However, these physical priors are not always reliable, which will lead to inaccurate transmission estimates and unsatisfied dehazing results.

With the availability of large-scale paired data and powerful CNNs, scholars have used convolutional neural network (CNN) to overcome the shortage of priori hypothetical conditions and proposed haze removal models based on convolutional neural networks [1, 4, 7–9, 25, 26, 28] and achieved better haze removal results. Unfortunately, due to the domain gap between synthetic and real data, dehazing models trained on synthetic images usually generalize poorly to real-world hazy images.

In this paper, we propose a model of single image haze removal which combines the atmospheric scattering model and the convolutional neural network: Lightweight image dehazing neural network (I-Net) based on estimating medium transmission map by scene intensity. The network outputs the intensity of the haze-free image, and then use the scene intensity function to obtain the medium transmission map. Finally, the transmittance map scattering model is used to restore the original haze-free images.

## 2  Related Work

### 2.1  Single Image Dehazing

Prior-based methods: In [18] Tan proposed a haze removal method by maximizing the local contrast of hazy images; Fattal [17] estimated the medium transmission map using the independent component analysis and Markov random field model [16]; He et al. [12] achieved impressive dehazing results using dark channel prior (DCP), which assumes that there exists at least one channel for every pixel whose value is close to zero, and refines the medium transmission map by using the soft matting algorithm or the guided filter [11]. Zhu et al. [11] performed image dehazing by using the color attenuation priori (CAP) hypothetical conditions. Berman et al. [6] proposed a dehazing algorithm (NLD) based on the assumption that colors of a haze-free image are well approximated by a few hundred distinct colors. Kim et al. [20] used the saturation and stretching functions of hazed images to estimate the saturation of clear images, and then used the functional relationship between saturation intensity and transmissibility to estimate the transmittance.

Learning-based methods: MSCNN [24] is one of the first studies to solve haze removal problem via CNN, where the network is trained to estimate transmission map of the hazy input in a coarse-to-fine manner. Cai et al. [1] proposed an end-to-end network to generate transmission estimates; Li et al. [4] designed a dehazing network (AOD-Net) based on reconstructing the physical scattering model to generate haze-free images; Zhang and Patel et al. [8] embedded the physical scattering model into the network, and the network could jointly estimate the transmittance map, atmospheric light and haze-free images with good dehazing effect, but the network structure was complex. The literature [26] proposed an effective iteration algorithm with deep CNNs to learn haze-relevant priors for image dehazing. The literature [25] proposed an end-to-end trainable Convolutional Neural Network (Gridnet). The network in [9] proposed a physics-based feature dehazing network for image dehazing. Dong et al. [7] incorporated an image enhancement strategy to gradually recover clear images. Chen et al. [28] proposed a synthetic to real dehazing framework (PSD), which established a new state-of-the-art performance for real-world dehazing, but it was susceptible to be influenced by the dehazing model and priori hypothetical conditions.

However, the essence of haze causes image degeneration is scene attenuation of hazy image caused by haze is related to the physical distance (that is, pixel depth). This is different from the general image degradation model. It can easily obtain the mapping relationship between the hazy images to the clear images through the atmospheric scattering model. The dehazing algorithms based on artificial verification assumptions or based on convolutional neural network deep learning did not consider the prior conditions derived from the atmospheric scattering model. In order to overcome this problem, we propose a lightweight image dehazing convolutional neural network (I-Net).

## 2.2 Transmittance Map Scattering Model

The scattering effect of particles in the atmosphere is the main cause of haze. Then there is a problem of contrast and decreased vision in the haze environment. Therefore, in order to describe the formation mechanism of hazy images. McCartney et al. [13] proposed the atmospheric scattering model in the 1980s firstly. Narasimhan and Nayar further developed and improved in [22, 23]. The image imaging process in the hazy weather is shown below:

$$H^C(x) = J^C(x)t(x) + A^c(1 - t(x)) \tag{1}$$

$H(x)$ is the hazy image; $J(x)$ is the haze-free image; $A$ is the global atmospheric light value; $t(x)$ is the medium transmission map, $c$ represents the RGB channels.

The expression for the medium transmission map is as follows:

$$t(x) = e^{-\beta d(x)} \tag{2}$$

Among them, $d(x)$ means the imaging distance; $\beta$ means the atmospheric scattering coefficient.

According to the formula (1), (2), when the distance of the imaging tends to be infinite, the medium transmission map is approaching 0, and a hazy image's pixel value is close to global atmospheric light value A.

$$A = H(x), t(x) = 0, \ if \ d(x) \to inf \tag{3}$$

By redefining the atmospheric scattering model, we obtain a new scattering model and a priority condition that the intensity of hazy image is higher than that of the clear image, derives the medium transmission map of the scene intensity function. It can be seen from the formula (1) that restoring the haze-free image needs to obtain the medium transmission map and the global atmospheric light value from the hazy image. As long as there is a certain ancestor knowledge, the transmission rate diagram and atmospheric light value can be estimated.

Assuming a global atmospheric light value, Eq. (1) can be redefined as follows:

$$\frac{H^c(x)}{A^c} = \frac{J^c(x)}{A^c}t(x) + (1 - t(x))$$ (4)

In this paper, $H_a^c(x) = \frac{H^c(x)}{A^c}$ was defined as a new hazy image, $J_a^c(x) = \frac{J^c(x)}{A^c}$ was defined as a new haze-free image. Equation (5) was defined as the scattering model of medium transmission map:

$$H_a^c(x) = J_a^c(x)t(x) + (1 - t(x))$$ (5)

Based on the conversion equation from the RGB color space to the hue, saturation and intensity (HSI) color space, the intensity $I_H(x)$ of the haze image and the intensity $I_J(x)$ of the haze-free image were defined as follows.

$$I_H(x) = \frac{H_a^r(x) + H_a^g(x) + H_a^b(x)}{3}$$

$$I_J(x) = \frac{J_a^r(x) + J_a^g(x) + J_a^b(x)}{3}$$ (6)

From Eq. (6), we can obtain a functional relationship between the hazy image and the haze-free image in RGB color space as follows:

$$H_a^r(x) = J_a^r(x)t(x) + (1 - t(x))$$
$$H_a^g(x) = J_a^g(x)t(x) + (1 - t(x))$$ (7)
$$H_a^b(x) = J_a^b(x)t(x) + (1 - t(x))$$

From Eq. (6) (7), it can be deduced that the functional relationship between the medium transmission map and the scene intensity is as follows:

$$t(x) = \frac{1 - I_H(x)}{1 - I_J(x)}$$ (8)

Therefore, the medium transmission map can be calculated from the intensity of hazy image and that of the haze-free image. In addition, Eq. (3) shows that the global atmospheric light value A is the pixel value of a hazy image with an infinite imaging distance. However, in the actual imaging process, the imaging distance cannot converge to infinity, so the global atmospheric light value A needs to be estimated from the hazy image. In most cases of low visibility, the atmospheric light A is assumed to be globally constant. According to Eq. (1), this global value of A can be obtained from the pixel points with the highest intensity in the hazy image [18]. Since there are no saturated pixels in the image, these pixels represent an object at an infinite distance.

In this study, the global atmospheric light value is taken as the highest intensity pixel value in the hazy image. Then hazy images and haze-free images take values ranging from 0 to 1. From the definition of t medium transmission map, the medium transmission map $t(x)$ also takes values from 0 to 1. Finally, from Eq. (9), it can be deduced that $1 - I_H(x) < 1 - I_J(x)$ and the intensity of the hazy image is higher than that of the haze-free image, which is $I_H(x)$ is higher than $I_J(x)$.

$$I_H(x) > I_J(x) \tag{9}$$

## 3  Image Dehazing Model

In this paper, we obtain a new transmittance map scattering model by redefining the atmospheric scattering model, deduce the medium transmission map function of the scene intensity parameter, and argue the priori condition that the scene intensity of the hazy image is higher than that of the free-haze image. Based on the transmittance map scattering model, we design a lightweight image dehazing neural network (I-Net).

The I-Net (Fig. 1), a lightweight image dehazing neural network based on medium transmission map estimation by intensity, consists of two main modules: the first is the intensity estimation module, which uses a 5-layer convolutional network as the backbone to estimate the $I_J(x)$ by $I_H(x)$. The other is the medium transmission map estimation module, which consists of an elemental multiplication layer and several elemental addition layers to recover the original haze-free image.

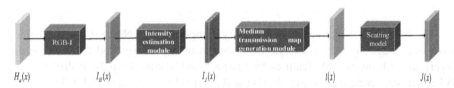

$H_a(x)$          $I_H(x)$          $I_J(x)$          $t(x)$          $J(x)$

**Fig. 1.**  I-Net dehazing model

### 3.1  Converting the Color Space RGB-I

The HSI model reflects the way in which the human visual system perceives color in terms of the three basic feature quantities of HSI. According to the mathematical relationship between the RGB color space and the HSI color space, $I_H(x)$ is calculated from the hazy image by Eq. (6).

$$I_H(x) = \frac{H_a^r(x) + H_a^g(x) + H_a^b(x)}{3}$$

## 3.2 Intensity Estimation Module

Most deep learning methods for image recovery enhancement employ end-to-end modelling: a model is trained and then a clear image is recovered directly from the corrupted image. The end-to-end depth dehazing models in [1, 4, 7, 9, 24–26] are complex in structure, have many layers and large number of parameters. However, the nature of image degradation in hazy environments is that the surface scene attenuation due to haze is related to the physical distance (pixel depth) between the camera and the object surface. This differs from the general image degradation model in that the mapping relationship from the hazy image to the haze-free image can be easily obtained through the atmospheric scattering model. Therefore, this paper designs an intensity estimation module (Fig. 2) based on the transmittance map scattering model and the priori condition that $I_H(x)$ is less than $I_J(x)$. The module is a lightweight convolutional neural network that takes $I_H(x)$ as input and $I_J(x)$ as output.

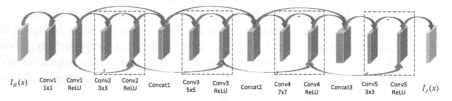

**Fig. 2.** The backbone and priori condition (dashed box) of intensity estimation module

The intensity estimation module is a key component of I-Net and is responsible for haze-free image intensity estimation. As shown in Fig. 2, we used five convolutional layers to form multi-scale features by fusing convolutional kernels of different sizes. What's more, our activation function is the Rectified Linear Unit (ReLU). The literature 24 connected coarse-scale network features with an intermediate layer of fine-scale networks; the literature 1 used parallel convolution with different convolution kernel sizes; the literature 4 connected different convolutional layers in parallel. Inspired by them, the "concat1" layer of I-Net connects the feature maps from the "conv1" and "conv2" layers. Similarly, "concat2" connects the layers from "concat1" and "conv3"; and so on. The training images are excerpted from the RESIDE dataset 2; see Sect. 4 for more details on the setup. " conv1", "conv2", "conv3", "conv4" and "conv5" each use a convolutional kernel of size $1 \times 1, 3 \times 3, 5 \times 5, 7 \times 7 and 3 \times 3$. This multi-scale design captures features at different scales. In addition, the I-Net incorporates the idea of residual learning 10 to satisfy the priori condition that $I_H(x)$ is higher than $I_J(x)$.

The input of the Rectified Linear Unit (ReLU) of each layer is the output of the previous layer minus the output of this convolutional layer to ensure that the output of each layer is not larger than the output of the previous layer (Fig. 2 dashed box). In addition, a Rectified Linear Unit (ReLU) layer is added to the last layer of the intensity estimation module, where the input of this layer is $I_H(x)$ minus the output of the last layer, strictly satisfying the priori condition that $I_J(x)$ is less than $I_H(x)$.

### 3.3    Medium Transmission Map Generation Module

The medium transmission map generation module introduces a medium transmission map estimation method based on scene intensity. Accurate estimation of the medium transmission map is the key to solving the image dehazing problem. In this paper, the medium transmission map of the scene intensity function is derived from the transmittance map scattering model. The intensity estimation module takes hazy image's intensity $I_H(x)$ as input and outputs haze-free image's intensity $I_J(x)$. The medium transmission map is obtained from $I_H(x)$ and $I_J(x)$ by Eq. (9), and finally the original haze-free image is recovered using the transmittance map scattering model.

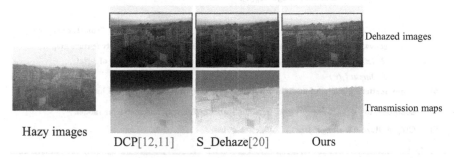

**Fig. 3.** Medium transmission map

As can be seen in Fig. 3, the DCP 1211 dehazing algorithm estimates the medium transmission map based on the dark channel priori conditions, but color distortion will occur in bright sky regions. The literature 20 proposed an image dehazing method (S_Dehaze) based on saturation and intensity image medium transmission map estimation, and the method obtained the intensity and saturation of haze-free image by a simple stretching function set manually. However, the artificially set stretching function is not suitable for diverse image dehazing. As can be seen from Fig. 3, our dehazing algorithm can get more accurate transmission, and the dehazing results of our algorithm is clearer, with less haze residue and no obvious color bias phenomenon.

### 3.4    Summary of Proposed Method

This paper derived the medium transmission map as a function of the scene intensity only. Then, a lightweight image dehazing neural network (I-Net) based on estimating medium transmission map by scene intensity is proposed in this paper. The intensity estimation module in this network outputs the intensity value of the haze-free image. The medium transmission map generation module estimates the medium transmission map. Table 1 lists the general flow of the proposed dehazing method in this paper.

**Table 1.** Overall dehazing algorithm

---

**Algorithm: I-Net Dehazing algorithm**

---

**Begin (Algorithm start)**

1)  **Input: Hazy image** $H(x)$

2)  **DO**

  1. Calculate $A$ // estimate global atmospheric light values from haze images $H(x)$ according to the formula $A^c = \max_c H^c(x)$.

  2. Calculate $H_a^c(x)$ // Calculate Hazy image $H_a^c(x)$ according to the formula $H_a^c(x) = \frac{H^c(x)}{A}$.

  3. Calculate $I_H(x)$ // Calculate haze image intensity according to the formula $I_H(x) = \frac{H_a^r(x)+H_a^g(x)+H_a^b(x)}{3}$ and hazy image $H_a^c(x)$.

3)  **Then**

  *1. I=Conv($I_H(x)$)* // Input intensity $I_H(x)$ of haze image is outputted by "conv1, conv2, conv3, conv4, conv5" convolutional neural network with intermediate intensity feature map *I*.

  *2. I_J(x)=Relu($I_H(x)$- I)* // Add a layer to the last network output layer of I-Net

  *3. Output I_J(x)*

4)  **Apply scattering model of medium transmission map** // restore the original haze-free image $J^c(x)$ according to $J^c(x) = \frac{A^c - J^c(x)}{t(x)} + A^c$, medium transmission map and scattering model.

5)  **Output: Haze-free image** $J^c(x)$

  *End*

---

# 4 Experimental Results

## 4.1 Training Parameter Settings

Dataset: The RESIDE dataset 2 contains synthetic hazy images in both indoor and outdoor scenarios. The Indoor Training Set (ITS) of RESIDE contains a total of 13990 hazy indoor images, generated from 1399 clear images with β ∈ [0.6, 1.8] and A ∈ [0.7, 1.0]. The Outdoor Training Set (OTS) of RESIDE contains a total of 296695 hazy outdoor images, generated from 8477 clear images with β ∈ [0.04, 0.2] and A ∈ [0.8, 1.0]. After data cleaning, 70000 pairs of haze and clear images composed of indoor and outdoor were selected to increase the robustness of the model. Our model is very small, so it is very convenient to train, and the speed of is very fast. The SOTS dataset is a test subset of the RESIDE dataset 2, which contains 500 synthetic indoor hazy images and 500 outdoor hazy images. For the purpose of comparison tests, all image dehazing methods were evaluated in the SOTS dataset.

Training method: The filter weights for each layer are initialized by randomly plotting a Gaussian distribution (mean μ = 0, standard deviation σ = 0.001) with the bias set to 0. Training is learned on a training set of clear images of haze selected from the RESIDE dataset 2 with learning rate t = 0.00001, batch size = 8, Epoch = 10. Based on the above parameters, I-Net was trained on a PC with an Nvidia GeForce RTX 1660Ti GPU.

The intensity estimation module belongs to supervised learning, which requires RGB values of both hazy and haze-free images, which uses the intensity $I_H(x)$ of the hazy image as input and the intensity $I_J(x)$ of the haze-free image as supervised information.

The output is minimized with the loss function of the supervised information. Therefore, we use the mean square error (MSE) as the loss function.

$$L(\theta) = \frac{1}{N} \sum_{x=1}^{N} ||F(I_H(x), \theta) - I_J(x)||^2 \tag{10}$$

## 4.2 Comparison Experiments

SWe compared the performance of the I-Net dehazing algorithm with several state-of-the-art dehazing methods. A series of experiments were conducted, including subjective evaluation and objective image quality evaluation.

Subjective evaluation: Evaluation of the image in terms of the human visual perception as a recovery. As shown in Fig. 4, DCP 12 is based on the dark channel priori assumption, which has a better dehazing effect in regions where the dark channel pixels are close to 0, but in regions with high intensity, such as the sky, there are phenomena such as color bias, oversaturation and overal. The dehazing effect is poor and the color distortion is severe. CAP 15 proposed a fast-dehazing algorithm based on color decay with better dehazing performance, but the method cannot fully remove the haze from the image and the sky region may produce color shift phenomena. NLD 6 could recover the details of the image well, but the method tends to overestimate the details of the image and has weaknesses in recovering uniform regions. S_Dehaze 20 estimated the saturation and transmittance map of a hazy image by setting the stretching function, but the fixed stretching function is not applicable to all hazed images. In contrast, the overall dehazing effect of the algorithm in this paper is ideal, with no color distortion, brighter sky areas and fuller, clearer colors.

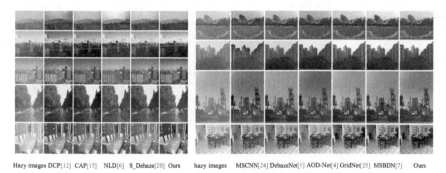

Hazy images  DCP[12]  CAP[15]  NLD[6]  S_Dehaze[20]  Ours        hazy images    MSCNN[24]  DehazeNet[1]  AOD-Net[4]  GridNet[25]  MSBDN[7]    Ours

**Fig. 4.** Performance comparison between this paper's dehazing algorithm and a priori hypothesis-based dehazing algorithm

From Fig. 4, it can be seen that the recovered images of MSCNN 24, DehazeNet 1, AOD-Net 4 are still a bit blurred, with more haze residue in the dehazed images and poor dehazing performance. Gridnet 25, MSBDN 7 and our image dehazing algorithm all have good dehazing performance, with better dehazing effect, more complete dehazing and clear and bright haze-free images. But the network structure of Gridnet 25, MSBDN 7 is complex, and the time and space complexity are higher.

Objective evaluation: The objective image evaluation criteria used in this paper are Peak Signal to Noise Rate (PSNR) and Structure Similarity Index Measurement (SSIM). Table 2 compares the dehazing performance of the SOTS dataset using PSNR and SSIM, showing the average scores of each algorithm for the two complete reference metrics. As can be seen from the Table 2, our algorithms is comparable to the current state-of-the-art dehazing algorithms in both PSNR and SSIM, two image quality evaluation metrics, for both outdoor and indoor images. The advantages of this algorithm are significant when considering the calculation time.

**Table 2.** Quantitative comparison of the dehazing performance of the SOTS image dataset dehazing algorithms

| Algorithms | Outdoor | | Indoor | |
|---|---|---|---|---|
| | PSNR | SSIM | PSNR | SSIM |
| DCP12 | 17.56 | 0.83 | 14.6 | 0.81 |
| CAP15 | 18.16 | 0.76 | 19.12 | 0.82 |
| NLD6 | 17.97 | 0.82 | 17.60 | 0.72 |
| S_Dehaze20 | 19.76 | 0.84 | 22.94 | 0.92 |
| MSCNN24 | 18.21 | 0.82 | | |
| DehazeNet1 | 22.61 | 0.86 | 22.34 | 0.85 |
| Aod-Net4 | 19.52 | 0.85 | 20.31 | 0.86 |
| GridNet25 | 30.86 | 0.98 | 31.12 | 0.98 |
| MSBDN7 | 32.52 | 0.98 | 31.92 | 0.97 |
| Ours | 25.56 | 0.91 | 23.36 | 0.86 |

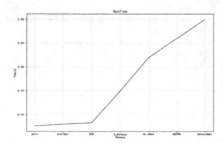

**Fig. 5.** Comparison of the running times of different dehazing methods

Runtime analysis: Our proposed I-Net dehazing algorithm, a lightweight convolutional neural network. Our unoptimized Python code was tested on a PC with a processor of Intel Core i5-9300 at 2.40 GHz with a CPU of 16 GB RAM and an Nvidia GeForce RTX 1660Ti GPU. The algorithm in this paper takes an average of 0.076 s to dehaze an image from a SOTS outdoor images. As can be seen in Fig. 5, the I-Net dehazing algorithm ranks among the top dehazing algorithms doing the comparison.

## 5 Summary

In this paper, we proposed a fast and effective single image dehazing method based on deep learning and estimating medium transmission map by intensity. The method designed a lightweight image dehazing network (I-Net) to obtain more accurate medium transmittance map, and then a clear dehazing image is obtained by atmospheric scattering model. We experimentally demonstrated its competitive performance in single-image dehazing. To overcome the limitations of the most advanced haze removal methods, a more rapid and effective dehazing method with wider applicability is needed. There are two main approaches: 1) dehazing methods based on strong prior conditions: the prior conditions must be proven to be true, effective and widely applicable. 2) Dehazing methods based on depth estimation of monocular images: clear haze-free images can be recovered by using the relationship between depth map and transmittance.

**Acknowledgment.** This work was supported by open fund project of Key Laboratory of System Control and Information Processing (Scip202105), open fund project of State Key Laboratory for Novel Software Technology (KFKT2021B40).

## References

1. Cai, B., Xu, X., Jia, K., Qing, C., Tao, D.: DehazeNet: an end-to-end system for single image haze removal. IEEE Trans. Image Process. **25**(11), 5187–5198 (2016)
2. Li, B., et al.: Benchmarking singleimage dehazing and beyond. IEEE Trans. Image Process. **28**(1):492–505, (2018)
3. Li, B., Peng, X., Wang, Z, Xu, Z., Feng, D.: End-to-end united video dehazing and detection. In Thirty-Second AAAI Conference on Artificial Intelligence, pp. 7016–7023 (2018)
4. Li, B., Peng, X., Wang, Z., Jizheng, X., Feng, D.: AOD-Net: all-in-one dehazing network. In: ICCV, pp. 4770–4778 (2017)
5. Sakaridis, C., Dai, D., Van Gool, L.: Semantic hazy scene understanding with synthetic data. Int. J. Comput. Vision **126**(9), 973–992 (2018)
6. Berman, D., Treibitz, T., Avidan, S.: Non-local image dehazing. In: IEEE Conference on Computer Vision and Pattern Recognition (CVPR), pp. 1674–1682 (2016)
7. Dong, H., et al.: Multi-scale boosted dehazing network with dense feature fusion. In: CVPR, pp. 2157–2167 (2020)
8. Zhang, H., Patel, V.M.: Densely connected pyramid dehazing network. In: CVPR, pp. 3194–3203 (2018)
9. Dong, J., Pan, J.: Physics-based feature dehazing networks. In: Vedaldi, A., Bischof, H., Brox, T., Frahm, J.-M. (eds.) ECCV 2020. LNCS, vol. 12375, pp. 188–204. Springer, Cham (2020). https://doi.org/10.1007/978-3-030-58577-8_12
10. He, K., Zhang, X., Ren, S., Sun, J.: Deep residual learning for image recognition. In: IEEE Conference on Computer Vision and Pattern Recognition (CVPR) (2016)
11. He, K., Sun, H., Tang, X.: Guided image filtering, IEEE Trans. Pattern Anal. Mach. Intell. **35**(6), 397–1409 (2013)

12. He, K., Sun, J., Tang, X.: Single image haze removal using dark channel prior, IEEE Trans. Pattern Analy. Mach. Intel. **33**, 2341–2353 (2009)
13. McCartney, E.J., et al. Optics of the atmosphere: scattering by molecules and particles. Phys Today **14**, 698 –699 (1977)
14. Shehata, M., et al.: Video-based automatic incident detection for smart roads: the outdoor environmental challenges regarding false alarms. IEEE Trans. Intell. Transp. Syst. **9**(2), 349–360 (2008)
15. Zhu, O., Mai, J., Shao, L.: A fast single image haze removal algorithm using color attenuation prior. IEEE Trans. Image Process. **24**(11), 3522–3533 (2015)
16. Fattal, R.: Dehazing using color-lines, ACM Trans. Graph. **34**(3), Art. no. 13 (2014)
17. Fattal, R.: Single image dehazing. ACM Trans. Graph. **27**(3), 1–9 (2008)
18. Robby, T.: Tan: visibility in bad weather from a single image. In: IEEE Conference on Computer Vision and Pattern Recognition, pp. 1–8 (2006)
19. Narasimhan, S.G., Nayar, S.K.: Contrast restoration of weather degraded images. IEEE Trans. Pattern Anal. Mach. Intell. **25**(6), 713–724 (2003)
20. Kim, S.E., Park, T.H., Eom II, Kyu: Fast single image dehazing using saturation based transmission map estimation. IEEE Trans. Image Process. **29**,1985-1998 (2020)
21. Bronte, S., Bergasa, L.M., Alcantarilla, P.F.: Haze detection system based on computer vision techniques. In: 2009 12th International IEEE Conference on Intelligent Transportation Systems, pp. 1–6 (2006)
22. Nayar, S., Narasimhan, S.: Vision in b ad weather, In: Proceedings of the Seventh IEEE International Conference on Computer Vision, pp. 820–827 (1997)
23. Narasimhan, S., Nayar, S.: Chromatic framework for vision in bad weather. In: Proceedings IEEE Conference on Computer Vision and Pattern Recognition. CVPR 2000 (Cat. No.PR00662), pp. 598–605 (2000)
24. Ren, W., Liu, S., Zhang, H., Pan, J., Cao, X., Yang, M.-H.: Single image dehazing via multi-scale convolutional neural networks. In: Leibe, B., Matas, J., Sebe, N., Welling, M. (eds.) ECCV 2016. LNCS, vol. 9906, pp. 154–169. Springer, Cham (2016). https://doi.org/10.1007/978-3-319-46475-6_10
25. Liu, X., Ma, Y., Shi, Z., Chen, J.: GridDehazeNet: attention-based multi-scale network for image dehazing IEEE/CVF International Conference on Computer Vision (ICCV), pp. 7313–7322 (2019)
26. Liu, Y., Pan, J., Ren, J., Su, Z.: Learning deep priors for image dehazing. In: ICCV, pp. 2492–2500 (2019)
27. Yueshu, X., Guo, X., Wang, H., Zhao, F., Peng, L.: Single image haze removal using light and dark channel prior. In: IEEE/CIC International Conference on Communications in China (ICCC), pp. 1–6 (2016)
28. Chen, Z., Wang, Y., Yang, Y., Liu, D.: PSD: Principled synthetic-to-real dehazing guided by physical priors. In: Proc eedings of the IEEE/CVF Conference on Computer Vision and Pattern Recognition (CVPR), pp. 7180–7189 (2021)
29. Jia, Z., et al.: A two-step approach to see-through bad weather for surveillance video quality enhancement. Mach. Vis. Appl. **23**(6): 1059–1082 (2012)

# CMNet: Cross-Aggregation Multi-branch Network for Salient Object Detection

Chenxing Xia[1], Yanguang Sun[1]($\boxtimes$), Xianjin Fang[1], Bin Ge[1], Xiuju Gao[2], and Jianhua Cui[3]

[1] College of Computer Science and Engineering, Anhui University of Science and Technology, Huainan, China
syg1513@163.com
[2] College of Electrical and Information Engineering, Anhui University of Science and Technology, Huainan, China
[3] Anyang Cigarette Factory, China Tobacco Henan Industrial Co., Ltd., Anyang, China

**Abstract.** Fully convolutional networks (FCNs) have shown extraordinary performance in salient object detection (SOD). However, when faced with complex and variable salient objects in terms of types and sizes, FCNs-based methods may still generate some under-segmentation saliency maps, such as inaccurate or incomplete object information, which is mainly caused by sub-optimal multi-scale context features and inadequate interaction of complementary information. In this paper, we devote to exploring an effective structure to capture contextual information and interact with complementary information for an accurate SOD task. Specifically, we first design a multi-source contextual cue extraction (MCCE) module to effectively capture context information with different receptive fields, and further aggregate the information to improve the expressive ability of the initial input features. Furthermore, we build a dual-residual adjacent feature interaction (DAFI) module to increase the exchange of high-level semantic and low-level space details information from multi-level features for better saliency prediction. Finally, extensive experimental results convincingly demonstrate that our method achieves more favorably against 15 state-of-the-art methods on five public SOD datasets.

**Keywords:** Fully convolutional networks · Salient object detection · Multi-scale context information

## 1 Introduction

Salient object detection (SOD) aims at locating and segmenting the most attractive objects or regions from an input image. With its the ability to quickly and efficiently process the image data, SOD has been widely used as a pre-processing step for other computer vision tasks, such as object detection [30], semantic

S. Khanna et al. (Eds.): PRICAI 2022, LNCS 13631, pp. 567–578, 2022.
https://doi.org/10.1007/978-3-031-20868-3_42

segmentation [29], image retrieval [8], scene classification [20], and visual tracking [33].

Currently, many effective SOD methods [6,11,14,21,22,34] are mainly based on fully convolutional networks (FCNs). Although these SOD methods have achieved great performance, it is still difficult to accurately detect salient objects with complicated structures, especially in some cluttered real scenes. Their limitations are mainly reflected in the following two aspects: 1) The limited receptive fields can only generate features by sequentially stacking single-scale convolution and max-pooling layers. To deal with such problem, some SOD methods try to introduce dilated convolutions with different filling rates to capture multi-receptive-field context information (e.g., multi-scale context-aware feature extraction module (MCFEM) in BDMPM [32], context module in CPD [26], and parallel dilated convolution (PDC) module in SUCA [11].) for saliency inference. However, the introduction of a filling rate will cause the problem of local information loss, which is fatal for the SOD task of dense prediction. 2) Many existing saliency detection models [18,25,36,37] improve prediction accuracy by widening or deepening the network, which would make the parameters and storage memory of the models too large. Therefore, these models have to face the problems of computational redundancy and training difficulties, which are not conducive to further applications.

For the above limitations, we propose a novel cross-aggregation multi-branch network (CMNet) for accurate SOD. Inspired by the ShuffleNet [35], we first design a multi-source contextual cue extraction (MCCE) module to capture better multi-scale contextual information. For each initial input feature, by stacking a series of group convolutions, channel shuffle operations and dilated depthwise separable convolutions with good lightweight, we obtain different receptive fields context features, which are then aggregated to improve the reasoning ability of salient objects. Furthermore, we put forward a dual-residual adjacent feature interaction (DAFI) module to adequately interact and aggregate complementary information (i.e., high-level semantic information and low-level spatial details information) from features of different levels. As a result, semantic information and boundary detail information are incorporated at different levels of features to restructure and generate powerful feature representations for accurate SOD.

In summary, the main contributions of this paper are summarized as follows: **(i)** A lightweight multi-source contextual cue extraction (MCCE) module is designed to capture and gather multi-receptive-field contextual information to optimize the performance of each initial feature. **(ii)** An effective dual-residual adjacent feature interaction (DAFI) module is constructed to aggregate different information from multi-level features for better salient object detection and segmentation.

## 2    Related Work

**MLP-Based Methods.** MLP-based methods usually capture deep features from each processing unit of an input image, such as generic object proposals and super-pixels/patches, to train an MLP-classifier for predicting saliency scores. For example, Zhang *et al.* [31] utilized a CNN model to produce a set of scoring bounding boxes and then selected an optimized compact subset of bounding boxes for different salient objects to detect salient objects. Wang *et al.* [23] extracted segment-level feature vectors from pixel-level deep features, which were used to predict saliency scores with the aid of an MLP. Although MLP-based methods have improved performance compared with traditional saliency detection methods, they still suffer from some shortcomings, such as, time-consuming and insufficient spatial structure information, limiting the performance of the predicted saliency maps.

**FCNs-Based Methods.** Inspired by the great achievement of fully convolutional networks (FCNs) in semantic segmentation [16], FCNs-based methods have been widely applied to SOD tasks. For instance, Zhang *et al.* [32] designed a multi-scale context-aware feature extraction module to extract abundant context information for initial input features to distinguish salient objects with different scales. Wu *et al.* [26] constructed a cascaded partial decoder with multiple convolutions and dilated convolutions for the ability to compress background noise to highlight the information of salient objects in features. Li *et al.* [11] introduced a parallel dilated convolution (PDC) module to capture the context-aware multi-scale multi-receptive-field features for efficient SOD. Although these methods have achieved excellent performance, they still have some limitations. For example, the strategy of improving model performance through broadening and deepening will increase the burden of parameters and model memory, which is not conducive to further applications. Besides, the introduction of filling rates may cause the problem of local information loss, which makes it difficult to predict precise saliency maps.

Unlike these methods, we focus more on the lightweight and accuracy of the module. In our method, we first propose a multi-source contextual cue extraction (MCCE) module with fewer parameters to efficiently capture multi-receptive-field contextual information from initial multi-level features for better inference and localization of salient objects. Besides, we design a dual-residual adjacent feature interaction (DAFI) module to adaptively aggregate complementary information to restructure internal information in multi-level features for SOD.

## 3 Method

### 3.1 Overview of Network Structure

In this paper, we propose a cross-aggregation multi-branch network (CMNet) for accurate SOD task. The proposed CMNet method mainly contains two modules: a multi-source contextual cue extraction (MCCE) module and a dual-residual adjacent feature interaction (DAFI) module. The complete structure of our CMNet network is depicted in Fig. 1. Specifically, the CMNet method adopts the FCN architecture [13] with the ResNet-50 network [9], where all the fully-connected layers and the last pooling layer are discarded, as a pre-trained

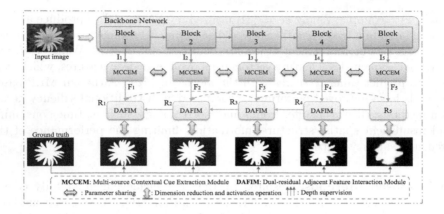

**Fig. 1.** The framework of the proposed CMNet method.

encoder to extract the five initial multi-level features $I = \{I_i | i = 1, 2, 3, 4, 5\}$. Then, we tactfully add an MCCE module after each initial multi-level feature to increase saliency information through aggregating multiple contexts with different receptive fields to generate discriminative features $F = \{F_i | i = 1, 2, 3, 4, 5\}$ for better salient objects inferring. To generate high-quality feature representations $R = \{R_i | i = 1, 2, 3, 4, 5\}$, we propose a DAFI module to adaptively interact with high-level semantic information and low-level spatial details information in a dual-residual structure. Finally, we apply a convolution operation with a $1 \times 1 \times 1$ kernel size and a sigmoid function on the features to produce saliency maps.

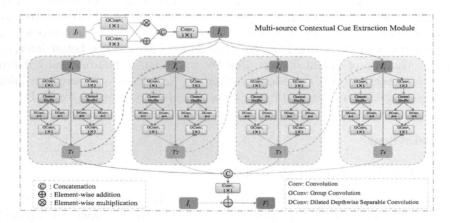

**Fig. 2.** Illustration internal structure of the proposed MCCE module.

## 3.2  Multi-source Contextual Cue Extraction (MCCE) Module

Multi-scale context information is quite important for understanding image content and localizing salient objects with diverse types. Some existing FCNs models [25,34] capture context information by staking multiple convolutions with different convolution kernel sizes. However, the increase of the convolution kernel will lead to too many parameters and too much computation, which is not conducive to the application of the model. Later, considering the above problems, other FCNs models [7,11,26,32] adopt dilated convolution operations with fewer parameters to capture multi-scale context information. Although the above methods achieve great results, the introduction of filling rates can cause the problem of local information loss, which is quite fatal for the dense saliency prediction. For that, how to design a lightweight and efficient context information extraction module is a key to an accurate SOD task.

Inspired by the ShuffleNet Unit [35], we propose a MCCE module and its complete architecture is shown in Fig. 2. Specifically, the MCCE module first takes the initial features $I$ as input. To obtain more effective saliency information from the initial features $I$, we use two group convolutions, where a grouping strategy is adopted to optimize and reduce feature channels, to get features $\widehat{I} = \{\widehat{I_i}|i = 1,2,3,4,5\}$. Here, referring to ShuffleNet Unit [35] setting, we set the group to 4. Formally, this process can be expressed as:

$$\widehat{I_i} = C_1(Cat(G_3(I_i) \oplus G_1(I_i),\ G_3(I_i) \otimes G_1(I_i)\,)),\ i = 1,2,3,4,5 \qquad (1)$$

where $C_1$ denotes a convolution layer with a kernel size $1 \times 1 \times 128$. $Cat$, $\oplus$, and $\otimes$ present concatenation, element-wise addition, and element-wise multiplication, respectively. $G_k$ is a group convolution with kernel sizes $k \times k \times 128$, where k $\in\{1,\ 3\}$. Then, $\widehat{I_i}$ is input into four branches in turn for multi-scale context information extraction. Unlike [35] only containing one residual connection and one set of the feature extraction operation, the proposed MCCE module of each branch, as depicted in Fig. 2, it consists of two group convolutions, channel shuffle operations, dilated depthwise separable convolutions and residual connections. In the MCCE module, we propose three strategies to be applied to each branch, that is, 1) We parallel add a set of new context extraction mechanisms to increase the captured context information. 2) We adopt the dilated depthwise separable convolution with fewer parameters instead of traditional dilated convolutions to capture context information efficiently and lightweight. 3) We hierarchically aggregate the contextual features with different receptive fields to enhance the correlation between contextual features. After this process, the four branches can extract the contextual features with different receptive fields. The whole process is as follows:

$$\begin{cases} T_{G3} = G_3(D_{2n-2}(\mathcal{B}|G_3(\widehat{I_i} \oplus T_{n-1})| \oplus D_{2n}(\mathcal{B}|G_3(\widehat{I_i} \oplus T_{n-1})|)) \\ T_{G1} = G_1(D_{2n-2}(\mathcal{B}|G_1(\widehat{I_i} \oplus T_{n-1})| \oplus D_{2n}(\mathcal{B}|G_1(\widehat{I_i} \oplus T_{n-1})|)) \\ T_n = T_{G1} \oplus T_{G3} \oplus \widehat{I_i} \oplus T_{n-1},\ n = 1,2,3,4 \end{cases} \qquad (2)$$

where $D_i$ denotes the dilated depthwise separable convolution with a kernel size $3 \times 3$ and the filling rates of $i$, $\mathcal{B}$ presents a channel shuffle operation.

$Cat$, $\oplus$, and $\otimes$ present concatenation, element-wise addition, and element-wise multiplication, respectively. $G_k$ is a group convolution with kernel sizes $k \times k \times 128$, where $k \in \{1, 3\}$. Note that $n - 1 \geq 1$ and the group is set to 4 empirically from ShuffleNet Unit [35]. Finally, all contextual information at different scales is aggregated by a concatenation with a residual connection to generate powerful features $F = \{F_i | i = 1, 2, 3, 4, 5\}$, namely,

$$F_i = \widehat{I}_i \oplus C_1(Cat(T_1, T_2, T_3, T_4)), \ i = 1, 2, 3, 4, 5 \tag{3}$$

where $C_1$ represents a dimension reduction operation that contains a convolution layer with a kernel size $1 \times 1 \times 128$, and $Cat$ denotes concatenation.

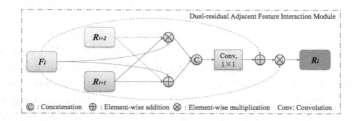

**Fig. 3.** Illustration internal structure of the proposed DAFI module.

### 3.3   Dual-Residual Adjacent Feature Interaction (DAFI) Module

Features of different levels represent diverse information, that is, high-level features contain a large amount of semantic information, which is beneficial to understanding image content for saliency inference, while low-level features have abundant boundary details, which is conducive to the refinement of edge structure. Considering that the high-quality saliency maps need not only precise position of salient objects but also contain rich edge structure information, some existing SOD methods [6,7,11,14,19] interact with high-level features and low-level features through a top-down pathway of the feature pyramid network (FPN) [13] structure and great results have been achieved. However, a single interactive manner, such as concatenation or element-wise addition, has a limited performance of the generated features. Moreover, with the deepening of the network depth from top to bottom, semantic information will gradually dilute, which is not conducive to guiding the positioning of salient objects for low-level features. To this end, we design a DAFI module to adaptively interact with complementary information by utilizing different interactive manners on the features $F$ to produce powerful feature representations $R = \{R_i | i = 1, 2, 3, 4, 5\}$.

The complete structure of DAFI module is shown in Fig. 3. The DAFI module aggregates complementary information in three interactive ways, *i.e.*, concatenation, element-wise addition, and element-wise multiplication. Besides, we introduce a guided connection in the top-down FPN structure [13] to alleviate the problem of semantic dilution by increasing the flow of semantic information. Specifically, the DAFI module receives features $F_i$, $R_{i+1}$, and $R_{i+2}$ as inputs from the upper-level DAFI module. Then, these features are aggregated through multiple interactions and we further use the same level of features to conduct residual guidance. Different from the traditional residual connection [9], our fusion method adopts element-wise addition and element-wise multiplication operations, which are then used to generate high-quality feature representations. Mathematically, we formulate feature $R_i$ as:

$$\begin{cases} R_i = F_i, \ i = 5 \\ R_i = (C_1(Cat((F_i \oplus R_{i+1}), (F_i \otimes R_{i+1}))) \oplus F_i) \otimes F_i, \ i = 4 \\ R_i = (C_1(Cat((F_i \oplus R_{i+1} \oplus R_{i+2}), (F_i \otimes R_{i+1} \otimes R_{i+2}))) \oplus F_i) \otimes F_i, \ i = 1, 2, 3 \end{cases} \quad (4)$$

where $Cat$ denotes concatenation operation, $\oplus$ and $\otimes$ represent element-wise addition and element-wise multiplication. $C_1$ represents a dimension reduction operation that contains a convolution layer with a kernel size $1 \times 1 \times 128$.

## 3.4   Loss Function

To obtain high-quality saliency maps, we train the CMNet network through a joint loss function, which is defined as:

$$\varsigma_{Joint} = \varsigma_{BCE} + \varsigma_{IoU}, \quad (5)$$

where $\varsigma_{BCE}$ and $\varsigma_{IoU}$ represent binary cross-entropy (BCE) loss function [4] and IoU loss function [17], respectively.

# 4   Experiments

## 4.1   Datasets and Experimental Details

We evaluate our CMNet method on five SOD datasets, including ECSSD [27], PASCAL-S [12], HKU-IS [10], DUT-OMRON [28], and DUTS-TE [24]. ECSSD [27] contains 1,000 challenging images with diverse complex scenes. PASCAL-S [12] consists of 850 images with the salient objects of complicated structures. HKU-IS [10] has 4,447 images with multiple salient objects. DUT-OMRON [28] comprises 5,168 images with salient objects of complicated structures and varying types. DUTS [24] is the largest saliency detection dataset, which contains 10,553 images for training and 5,019 images for testing.

We utilize the DUTS-TR [24] to train the proposed CMNet method. We implement the CMNet network with the PyTorch framework on a PC equipped with one NVIDIA 3090 GPU. In the training and testing process, each input image is resized to $320 \times 320$. In addition, we use the Adam optimizer with the momentum of 0.9 and the weight decay of 5e-4 to train our network. Besides, the initial learning rate is 5e-5, and the batch size is set to 10. Our network is trained 60 epochs and is an end-to-end progress without any post-processing operations.

**Table 1.** Quantitative results on five popular SOD datasets, the top three results are marked with red, green, and blue. The symbols "↑ / ↓" indicate that the larger the result, the better, and the smaller the result, the better.

| Method | Year, Pub | ECSSD(1000) | | | | PASCAL-S(850) | | | | HKU-IS(4447) | | | | DUT-OMRON(5168) | | | | DUTS-TE(5019) | | | |
|---|---|---|---|---|---|---|---|---|---|---|---|---|---|---|---|---|---|---|---|---|---|
| | | $MAE\downarrow$ | $AF_m\uparrow$ | $WF_m\uparrow$ | $E_m\uparrow$ | $MAE\downarrow$ | $AF_m\uparrow$ | $WF_m\uparrow$ | $E_m\uparrow$ | $MAE\downarrow$ | $AF_m\uparrow$ | $WF_m\uparrow$ | $E_m\uparrow$ | $MAE\downarrow$ | $AF_m\uparrow$ | $WF_m\uparrow$ | $E_m\uparrow$ | $MAE\downarrow$ | $AF_m\uparrow$ | $WF_m\uparrow$ | $E_m\uparrow$ |
| Amulet | 2017,CVPR | 0.059 | 0.868 | 0.840 | 0.912 | 0.100 | 0.757 | 0.728 | 0.827 | 0.051 | 0.841 | 0.817 | 0.914 | 0.098 | 0.647 | 0.626 | 0.784 | 0.085 | 0.678 | 0.658 | 0.803 |
| DGRL | 2018,CVPR | 0.046 | 0.893 | 0.871 | 0.935 | 0.077 | 0.794 | 0.772 | 0.869 | 0.041 | 0.875 | 0.851 | 0.943 | 0.066 | 0.711 | 0.688 | 0.847 | 0.054 | 0.755 | 0.748 | 0.873 |
| BDMPM | 2018,CVPR | 0.045 | 0.869 | 0.871 | 0.916 | 0.074 | 0.758 | 0.774 | 0.845 | 0.039 | 0.871 | 0.859 | 0.938 | 0.064 | 0.692 | 0.681 | 0.839 | 0.049 | 0.746 | 0.761 | 0.863 |
| PoolNet | 2019,CVPR | 0.039 | 0.915 | 0.896 | 0.945 | 0.075 | 0.815 | 0.793 | 0.876 | 0.032 | 0.900 | 0.883 | 0.955 | 0.056 | 0.739 | 0.721 | 0.864 | 0.040 | 0.809 | 0.807 | 0.904 |
| CPD | 2019,CVPR | 0.037 | 0.917 | 0.898 | 0.950 | 0.071 | 0.820 | 0.794 | 0.887 | 0.033 | 0.895 | 0.879 | 0.952 | 0.056 | 0.747 | 0.719 | 0.873 | 0.043 | 0.805 | 0.795 | 0.904 |
| AFNet | 2019,CVPR | 0.042 | 0.908 | 0.886 | 0.941 | 0.070 | 0.815 | 0.792 | 0.885 | 0.036 | 0.888 | 0.869 | 0.948 | 0.057 | 0.739 | 0.717 | 0.860 | 0.046 | 0.793 | 0.785 | 0.895 |
| EGNet | 2019,ICCV | 0.037 | 0.920 | 0.903 | 0.947 | 0.074 | 0.817 | 0.795 | 0.877 | 0.031 | 0.902 | 0.886 | 0.955 | | 0.756 | 0.738 | 0.874 | 0.039 | 0.815 | 0.816 | 0.907 |
| R2Net | 2020,TIP | 0.038 | 0.914 | 0.899 | 0.946 | 0.069 | 0.817 | 0.793 | 0.880 | 0.033 | 0.896 | 0.880 | 0.954 | 0.054 | 0.744 | 0.728 | 0.866 | 0.041 | 0.801 | 0.804 | 0.901 |
| RASNet | 2020,TIP | 0.036 | 0.916 | 0.905 | 0.941 | 0.068 | 0.820 | 0.804 | 0.883 | 0.030 | 0.906 | 0.892 | 0.956 | | | 0.745 | | 0.039 | 0.825 | 0.822 | 0.913 |
| GateNet | 2020,ECCV | 0.040 | 0.916 | 0.894 | 0.943 | 0.067 | 0.819 | 0.797 | 0.884 | 0.033 | 0.899 | 0.880 | 0.953 | 0.055 | 0.746 | 0.729 | 0.868 | 0.040 | 0.807 | 0.809 | 0.903 |
| ITSD | 2020,CVPR | 0.035 | 0.895 | | 0.932 | 0.066 | 0.785 | 0.812 | 0.863 | 0.031 | 0.899 | 0.894 | 0.953 | 0.061 | 0.756 | 0.750 | 0.867 | 0.041 | 0.804 | 0.824 | 0.898 |
| MINet | 2020,CVPR | 0.034 | 0.924 | | 0.953 | | | 0.809 | 0.898 | | | | | 0.056 | 0.756 | 0.738 | 0.873 | 0.037 | | 0.825 | |
| SUCA | 2021,TMM | 0.036 | 0.915 | 0.906 | 0.948 | 0.067 | 0.818 | 0.803 | 0.886 | 0.031 | 0.897 | 0.890 | 0.955 | - | - | - | - | 0.044 | 0.803 | 0.802 | 0.903 |
| CSF | 2021,TPAMI | | | | | 0.069 | 0.823 | 0.807 | 0.884 | - | - | - | - | 0.055 | 0.750 | 0.734 | 0.869 | | 0.823 | 0.823 | 0.914 |
| VST | 2021,ICCV | | 0.920 | 0.910 | 0.957 | 0.061 | | 0.816 | 0.902 | | 0.900 | | | 0.058 | 0.756 | | 0.872 | 0.037 | 0.818 | | 0.916 |
| Ours | - | 0.032 | 0.931 | 0.920 | 0.957 | 0.065 | 0.833 | | | 0.027 | 0.916 | 0.906 | 0.961 | 0.032 | 0.779 | 0.763 | 0.883 | 0.037 | 0.830 | 0.839 | 0.927 |

## 4.2 Evaluation Metrics

We evaluate the performance of the CMNet method as well as other state-of-the-art SOD methods utilizing four metrics: Mean Absolute Error ($MAE$), Average F-measure ($AF_m$), Weight F-measure ($WF_m$) and E-measure ($E_m$).

F-measure ($F_m$) : $F_m$ is computed by the weighted harmonic mean of precision and recall to balance the importance of precision and recall, that is, $F_m = \frac{(1+\beta^2) \times Precision \times Recall}{\beta^2 \times Precision \times Recall}$, where $\beta^2$ is set to 0.3 to emphasize the precision over recall [1]. $MAE$ can measures the average difference between the genereated saliency map $P$ and the ground truth $G$, $MAE = \frac{1}{W \times H} \sum_{x=1}^{W} \sum_{y=1}^{H} |P(x,y) - G(x,y)|$, where $H$ and $W$ are the height and width of input image, respectively. $P(x,y)$ is the saliency score of the pixel at $(x,y)$. $E_m$ [5] estimates the similarity between the predicted saliency map $P$ and the ground truth $G$ by computing local and global similarities and combining local pixel values with image-level averages, $E_m = \frac{1}{W \times H} \sum_{x=1}^{W} \sum_{y=1}^{H} \mathbb{Z}(m)$, where m is the alignment matrix, and $\mathbb{Z}(m)$ represents the enhanced alignment matrix.

## 4.3 Comparison with the State-of-the-Art

In this section, we compare the proposed CMNet method with 15 state-of-the-art SOD methods, including Amulet [34], DGRL [25], BDMPM [32], Pool-Net [14], CPD [26], AFNet [6], EGNet [36], RASNet [2], R2Net [7], GateNet [37], ITSD [38], MINet [18], SUCA [11], CSF [3] and VST [15]. Note that all the precicted saliency maps of the above saliency methods are generated by running source codes or provided by the authors. In addition, we use the same evaluation code for all evaluation results to ensure the fairness of the comparison.

**Quantitative Comparison.** Table 1 gives the quantitative comparison results of our CMNet and 15 state-of-the-art SOD methods on five public SOD datasets under four evaluation metrics. It can be seen that the proposed CMNet method has obvious advantages over the comparative SOD methods. Compared with

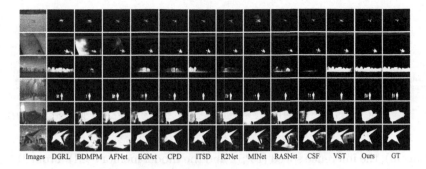

Images DGRL BDMPM AFNet EGNet CPD ITSD R2Net MINet RASNet CSF VST Ours GT

**Fig. 4.** Visual comparison of our CMNet with 11 state-of-the-art SOD methods.

**Table 2.** Efficiency comparison of the proposed CMNet method.

| Method | Input Size | #Param (M) | Inference Speed (FPS) | Model Memory (M) |
|---|---|---|---|---|
| Amulet | $320 \times 320$ | 33.15 | 8 | 132 |
| DGRL | $384 \times 384$ | 161.74 | 8 | 631 |
| EGNet | $256 \times 256$ | 111.64 | 9 | 437 |
| MINet | $320 \times 320$ | 162.38 | 25 | 635 |
| GateNet | $384 \times 384$ | 128.63 | 30 | 503 |
| **Ours** | $\mathbf{320 \times 320}$ | **27.08** | **22** | **107** |

the second-best SOD method under $MAE$ scores, our method improves the performance 3.13%, 7.41%, 1.92%, and 2.70% on the ECSSD, HKU-IS, DUT-OMRON, and DUTS-TE datasets, receptively. Besides, in terms of $AF_m$, the performance of our method is significantly improved by 1.96% and 2.66% on the DUT-OMRON and DUTS-TE datasets. Similarly, the proposed CMNet method has accomplished great performance under the evaluation metrics of $WF_m$ and $E_m$.

**Qualitative Comparison.** Figure 4 provides some predicted saliency maps of our CMNet as well as other 11 state-of-the-art SOD methods. These saliency maps are selected from five datasets for testing. It can be seen that the saliency maps generated by the proposed CMNet method are more similar to the ground truth in different challenging scenarios. For small salient objects (see the top 2 rows in Fig. 4), our CMNet method can efficiently detect salient objects with well-defined boundaries. Besides, the proposed CMNet method is also accurate and precise for images with multiple salient objects (as depicted in the 3 and 4 rows of Fig. 4) or similar and complicated semantic backgrounds (as shown in the 5 and 6 rows in Fig. 4).

**Efficiency Evaluation.** We also evaluate the efficiency and flexibility of our model and some existing SOD methods, including the model parameters

**Table 3.** Ablation analysis of the proposed CMNet method.

| Method | ECSSD(1000) | | | | PASCAL-S(850) | | | | HKU-IS(4447) | | | | DUT-OMRON(5168) | | | | DUTS-TE(5019) | | | |
|---|---|---|---|---|---|---|---|---|---|---|---|---|---|---|---|---|---|---|---|---|
| | $MAE\downarrow$ | $AF_m\uparrow$ | $WF_m\uparrow$ | $E_m\uparrow$ | $MAE\downarrow$ | $AF_m\uparrow$ | $WF_m\uparrow$ | $E_m\uparrow$ | $MAE\downarrow$ | $AF_m\uparrow$ | $WF_m\uparrow$ | $E_m\uparrow$ | $MAE\downarrow$ | $AF_m\uparrow$ | $WF_m\uparrow$ | $E_m\uparrow$ | $MAE\downarrow$ | $AF_m\uparrow$ | $WF_m\uparrow$ | $E_m\uparrow$ |
| ResNet50 | 0.054 | 0.881 | 0.854 | 0.923 | 0.082 | 0.790 | 0.754 | 0.874 | 0.043 | 0.865 | 0.843 | 0.936 | 0.069 | 0.694 | 0.657 | 0.840 | 0.053 | 0.770 | 0.744 | 0.893 |
| +FPN | 0.041 | 0.907 | 0.891 | 0.944 | 0.068 | 0.819 | 0.794 | 0.895 | 0.035 | 0.887 | 0.873 | 0.950 | 0.057 | 0.737 | 0.711 | 0.863 | 0.042 | 0.814 | 0.795 | 0.916 |
| +DAFI | 0.037 | 0.918 | 0.905 | 0.947 | 0.067 | 0.829 | 0.806 | 0.894 | 0.029 | 0.909 | 0.899 | 0.957 | 0.054 | 0.754 | 0.735 | 0.865 | 0.038 | 0.838 | 0.824 | 0.921 |
| +DAFI(add) | 0.039 | 0.914 | 0.900 | 0.947 | 0.067 | 0.820 | 0.798 | 0.895 | 0.033 | 0.894 | 0.881 | 0.948 | 0.055 | 0.744 | 0.720 | 0.855 | 0.041 | 0.823 | 0.805 | 0.914 |
| +DAFI(cat) | 0.037 | 0.918 | 0.905 | 0.947 | 0.066 | 0.827 | 0.801 | 0.896 | 0.030 | 0.905 | 0.893 | 0.956 | 0.056 | 0.750 | 0.722 | 0.868 | 0.040 | 0.831 | 0.813 | 0.919 |
| +DAFI(mul) | 0.038 | 0.915 | 0.902 | 0.948 | 0.068 | 0.823 | 0.799 | 0.895 | 0.031 | 0.901 | 0.891 | 0.954 | 0.055 | 0.747 | 0.727 | 0.866 | 0.040 | 0.825 | 0.814 | 0.917 |
| +MCCE | 0.035 | 0.924 | 0.912 | 0.953 | 0.066 | 0.832 | 0.810 | 0.898 | 0.028 | 0.915 | 0.903 | 0.959 | 0.055 | 0.769 | 0.750 | 0.877 | 0.037 | 0.847 | 0.834 | 0.927 |
| CMNet | 0.032 | 0.931 | 0.920 | 0.957 | 0.065 | 0.833 | 0.814 | 0.899 | 0.027 | 0.916 | 0.906 | 0.961 | 0.052 | 0.779 | 0.763 | 0.883 | 0.037 | 0.850 | 0.839 | 0.927 |

(#Param), the inference speed (FPS), and the model memory (M). From Table 2, we identify that the inference time of CMNet without any other post-processing achieves a speed of 22 FPS, which is very competitive compared with other saliency detection methods. Moreover, the model parameters and the size of model memory of the proposed CMNet are 27.08 and 107, respectively, which are much smaller than the other SOD methods.

### 4.4   Ablation Study

As shown in Table 3, we perform a series of ablation experiments to demonstrate the effectiveness of each module (*i.e.*, MCCE module and DAFI module). Note that all methods use the ResNet50 network [9] as the backbone network. Comparing the $2^{nd}$ and $7^{th}$ rows, it can be seen that the performance of the saliency maps predicted by the model is significantly improved after adding MCCE module. Besides, by comparing the quantitative comparison results of the $2^{nd}$ and $3^{rd}$ rows, it can be concluded that the proposed DAFI module is more favorable for the aggregation interaction of complementary information compared with the interactive manner of FPN structure [13]. Moreover, in order to prove the superiority of the proposed interactive way in DAFI module, we conduct ablation experiments in a single interactive manner (*i.e.*, element-wise addition, concatenation, and element-wise multiplication) in rows $4^{th}$ - $6^{th}$ of Table 3. Here, we use different interactive manner with the same input features. It can be seen that the performance of the DAFI module (as shown in row $3^{rd}$ of Table 3) with a hybrid interactive manner, is the most prominent than other three variants (rows $4^{th}$ - $6^{th}$).

## 5   Conclusion

In this paper, a novel cross-aggregation multi-branch network (CMNet) is proposed for accurate SOD, which consists of two modules: a MCCE module and a DAFI module. Benefiting from these two collaborative modules, abundant contextual information with different receptive fields can be efficiently captured to improve the understanding of image content for better localization of salient objects. At the same time, diverse complementary information is interacted adequately to restructure and optimize multi-level features for finer salient object segmentation. Extensive experimental results on five SOD datasets demonstrate that CMNet outperforms 15 SOTA saliency detection methods.

**Acknowledgements.** This work is supported by the National Science Foundation of China (62102003), Natural Science Research Project of Colleges and Universities in Anhui Province (KJ2020A0299), Anhui Provincial Natural Science Foundation (2108085QF258).

# References

1. Achanta, R., Hemami, S., Estrada, F., Susstrunk, S.: Frequency-tuned salient region detection. In: ICCV, pp. 1597–1604 (2009)
2. Chen, S., Tan, X., Wang, B., Lu, H., Hu, X., Fu, Y.: Reverse attention-based residual network for salient object detection. In TIP **29**, 3763–3776 (2020)
3. Cheng, M.M., Gao, S., Borji, A., Tan, Y.Q., Lin, Z., Wang, M.: A highly efficient model to study the semantics of salient object detection. In: TPAMI, pp. 1–1 (2021)
4. De Boer, P.T., Kroese, D.P., Mannor, S., Rubinstein, R.Y.: A tutorial on the cross-entropy method. Ann. Oper. Res. **134**(1), 19–67 (2005)
5. Fan, D.P., Gong, C., Cao, Y., Ren, B., Cheng, M.M., Borji, A.: Enhanced-alignment measure for binary foreground map evaluation. In: IJCAI, pp. 698–704 (2018)
6. Feng, M., Lu, H., Ding, E.: Attentive feedback network for boundary-aware salient object detection. In: CVPR, pp. 1623–1632 (2019)
7. Feng, M., Lu, H., Yu, Y.: Residual learning for salient object detection. In TIP **29**, 4696–4708 (2020)
8. Gao, Y., Wang, M., Zha, Z.J., Shen, J., Li, X., Wu, X.: Visual-textual joint relevance learning for tag-based social image search. In TIP **22**(1), 363 (2013)
9. He, K., Zhang, X., Ren, S., Sun, J.: Deep residual learning for image recognition. In: CVPR, pp. 770–778 (2016)
10. Li, G., Yu, Y.: Visual saliency based on multiscale deep features. In: CVPR, pp. 5455–5463 (2015)
11. Li, J., Pan, Z., Liu, Q., Wang, Z.: Stacked u-shape network with channel-wise attention for salient object detection. In TMM **23**, 1397–1409 (2021)
12. Li, Y., Hou, X., Koch, C., Rehg, J.M., Yuille, A.L.: The secrets of salient object segmentation. In: CVPR, pp. 280–287 (2014)
13. Lin, T.Y., Dollár, P., Girshick, R., He, K., Hariharan, B., Belongie, S.: Feature pyramid networks for object detection. In: CVPR, pp. 2117–2125 (2017)
14. Liu, J.J., Hou, Q., Cheng, M.M., Feng, J., Jiang, J.: A simple pooling-based design for real-time salient object detection. In: CVPR, pp. 3912–3921 (2019)
15. Liu, N., Zhang, N., Wan, K., Shao, L., Han, J.: Visual saliency transformer. In: ICCV, pp. 4722–4732 (2021)
16. Long, J., Shelhamer, E., Darrell, T.: Fully convolutional networks for semantic segmentation. In: CVPR, pp. 3431–3440 (2015)
17. Máttyus, G., Luo, W., Urtasun, R.: Deeproadmapper: extracting road topology from aerial images. In: ICCV, pp. 3438–3446 (2017)
18. Pang, Y., Zhao, X., Zhang, L., Lu, H.: Multi-scale interactive network for salient object detection. In: CVPR, pp. 9410–9419 (2020)
19. Ren, Q., Lu, S., Zhang, J., Hu, R.: Salient object detection by fusing local and global contexts. In TMM **23**, 1442–1453 (2021)
20. Ren, Z., Gao, S., Chia, L.T., Tsang, I.W.H.: Region-based saliency detection and its application in object recognition. In TCSVT **24**(5), 769–779 (2013)
21. Sun, H., Bian, Y., Liu, N., Zhou, H.: Multi-scale edge-based u-shape network for salient object detection. In: PRICAI, pp. 501–514 (2021)

22. Wang, L., Chen, R., Zhu, L., Xie, H., Li, X.: Deep sub-region network for salient object detection. In TCSVT **31**(2), 728–741 (2021)
23. Wang, L., Lu, H., Ruan, X., Yang, M.H.: Deep networks for saliency detection via local estimation and global search. In: CVPR, pp. 3183–3192 (2015)
24. Wang, L., et al.: Learning to detect salient objects with image-level supervision. In: CVPR, pp. 3796–3805 (2017)
25. Wang, T., et al.: Detect globally, refine locally: a novel approach to saliency detection. In: CVPR, pp. 3127–3135 (2018)
26. Wu, Z., Su, L., Huang, Q.: Cascaded partial decoder for fast and accurate salient object detection. In: CVPR, pp. 3902–3911 (2019)
27. Yan, Q., Xu, L., Shi, J., Jia, J.: Hierarchical saliency detection. In: CVPR, pp. 1155–1162 (2013)
28. Yang, C., Zhang, L., Lu, H., Ruan, X., Yang, M.H.: Saliency detection via graph-based manifold ranking. In: CVPR, pp. 3166–3173 (2013)
29. Zeng, Y., Zhuge, Y., Lu, H., Zhang, L.: Joint learning of saliency detection and weakly supervised semantic segmentation. In: ICCV, pp. 7223–7233 (2019)
30. Zhang, D., Han, J., Zhao, L., Meng, D.: Leveraging prior-knowledge for weakly supervised object detection under a collaborative self-paced curriculum learning framework. In IJCV **127**(4), 363–380 (2019)
31. Zhang, J., Sclaroff, S., Lin, Z., Shen, X., Price, B., Mech, R.: Unconstrained salient object detection via proposal subset optimization. In: CVPR, pp. 5733–5742 (2016)
32. Zhang, L., Dai, J., Lu, H., He, Y., Wang, G.: A bi-directional message passing model for salient object detection. In: CVPR, pp. 1741–1750 (2018)
33. Zhang, P., Zhuo, T., Huang, W., Chen, K., Kankanhalli, M.: Online object tracking based on cnn with spatial-temporal saliency guided sampling. Neurocomputing **257**, 115–127 (2017)
34. Zhang, P., Wang, D., Lu, H., Wang, H., Ruan, X.: Amulet: aggregating multi-level convolutional features for salient object detection. In: CVPR, pp. 202–211 (2017)
35. Zhang, X., Zhou, X., Lin, M., Sun, J.: Shufflenet: an extremely efficient convolutional neural network for mobile devices. In: CVPR, pp. 6848–6856 (2018)
36. Zhao, J.X., Liu, J.J., Fan, D.P., Cao, Y., Yang, J., Cheng, M.M.: Egnet: edge guidance network for salient object detection. In: ICCV, pp. 8779–8788 (2019)
37. Zhao, X., Pang, Y., Zhang, L., Lu, H., Zhang, L.: Suppress and balance: a simple gated network for salient object detection. In: ECCV, pp. 35–51 (2020). https://doi.org/10.1007/978-3-030-58536-5_3
38. Zhou, H., Xie, X., Lai, J.H., Chen, Z., Yang, L.: Interactive two-stream decoder for accurate and fast saliency detection. In: CVPR, pp. 9138–9147 (2020)

# More Than Accuracy: An Empirical Study of Consistency Between Performance and Interpretability

Yun Du[1], Dong Liang[1(✉)], Rong Quan[1], Songlin Du[2], and Yaping Yan[2]

[1] College of Computer Science and Technology, Nanjing University of Aeronautics
and Astronautics, MIIT Key Laboratory of Pattern Analysis and Machine
Intelligence, Nanjing, China
{muyun,liangdong,quanrong21}@nuaa.edu.cn
[2] Southeast University, Nanjing 210096, China
{sdu,yan}@seu.edu.cn

**Abstract.** Expected calibration error (ECE) is a popular metric to measure and calibrate the inconsistency between the classification performance and the probabilistic class confidence. However, ECE is inadequate to reveal why the deep model makes inconsistent predictions in specific samples. On the other hand, the class activation maps (CAMs) provide visual interpretability, highlighting focused regions of network attention. We discover that the quality of CAMs is also inconsistent with the model's final performance. In this paper, to further analyze this phenomenon, we propose a novel metric—VICE (Visual Consistency), to measure the consistency between performance and visual interpretability. Through extensive experiments with ECE and VICE, we disclose that the model architectures, the pre-training schemes, and the regularization manners influence VICE. These phenomena deserve our attention, and the community should focus more on a better trade-off in model performance and interpretability.

**Keywords:** Visual consistency · Expected calibration error · Model interpretability

## 1 Introduction

Besides pursuing superior performance via deep neural networks, its interpretability has increased attention in risk-sensitive real-world scenarios. In scenarios such as finance and medical care, where industry users are eager to know how the AI systems make decisions, deep neural networks still have a long way to yield complete interpretability. Trustworthy AI is less likely to be built by black-box models. It is thus a significant challenge to achieve an effective balance between performance and interpretability.

Expected calibration error (ECE) [22] is a metric to measure the inconsistency between the final classification performance and the probabilistic class confidence. Minimizing ECE could yield more accurate calibrated confidence.

S. Khanna et al. (Eds.): PRICAI 2022, LNCS 13631, pp. 579–590, 2022.
https://doi.org/10.1007/978-3-031-20868-3_43

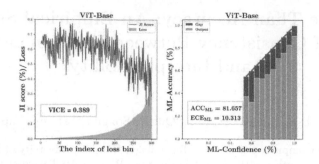

**Fig. 1.** The reliability diagrams on VOC2012Aug.

However, ECE and the calibrated confidence are inadequate to reveal why the deep model makes inconsistent predictions. As shown in the bottom right of Fig. 1, from the reliability diagrams of ECE, we can observe that the deep model is prone to over-confidence.

On the other hand, the class activation maps (CAMs) [34] is widely used to provide model's interpretable cues, providing consistent visual interpretability with human cognition. As shown in the bottom left of Fig. 1, the quality of CAMs is inconsistent with the sample loss. The average quality of the CAMs varied considerably between samples in neighbouring loss bins.

In this paper, we propose a novel metric—VICE, to measure the consistency between performance and visual interpretability. The top figure of Fig. 1 compares the differences between ECE and VICE, which are defined explicitly in Sect. 2 and Sect. 3, respectively. Our contribution can be summarized as follows,

(1) We propose VICE as a novel sample-wise fine-grained metric, to evaluate the consistency between model performance and visual interpretability in a new perspective.
(2) With case studies on five heterogeneous models, we found a series of inspiring conclusions involving the model capacity and architectures, the pre-training schemes, and the regularization mechanisms. Specifically, blindly increasing the model capacity may harm model interpretability; models with visual attention have better visual interpretability but worse consistency between model performance and visual interpretability; self-supervised pre-training and additional regularization learn more interpretable feature representation. These guide us to leverage more significant impact factors for trustworthy model design.

## 2   The ECE Metric

### 2.1   Revisiting the Expected Calibration Error

Expected calibration error (ECE) [22] is a popular tool to measure the distribution difference between the probabilistic confidence and the classification accuracy. More detailed, the samples are evenly partitioned into $M$ bins according to their confidence scores, measuring the differences between accuracy and confidence. ECE allows us to better judge the risk of the model's unexpected predictions.

## 2.2 Extend ECE for Multi-label Classification

Here, we first extend ECE to multi-label (ML) classification, which is a better approximation of realistic scenarios and more approaching to human cognition than single-label classification. Since multi-label classification assigns multiple labels to each sample, we define ML-accuracy (Eq. 1) and ML-confidence (Eq. 3) of samples in each bin, to enable ECE to realize evaluation under multi-label classification.

$$\text{acc}_{\text{ML}}(\text{B}_m) = \frac{1}{|B_m|} \, sum_{i \in B_m} \frac{|y_i \cap \hat{y}_i|}{|y_i \cup \hat{y}_i|} \tag{1}$$

In Eq. 1, $y_i$ is the true set of labels, $\hat{y}_i$ be the predicted set of labels. ML-accuracy is measured symmetrically how close $y_i$ is to $\hat{y}_i$ [9].

$$\text{conf}_{\text{ML}}^{i} = \begin{cases} \frac{1}{C} \sum_{c=1}^{C} \hat{p}_{i,c} \cdot \mathbf{1}(\hat{p}_{i,c} \geq t) \, , \exists \, \hat{p}_{i,c} \geq t \\ max(\hat{p}_{i,c}) \, , \forall \, \hat{p}_{i,c} < t \end{cases} \tag{2}$$

$$\text{conf}_{\text{ML}}(\text{B}_m) = \frac{1}{|B_m|} \sum_{i \in B_m} \text{conf}_{\text{ML}}^{i} \tag{3}$$

Equation 3 calculates the ML-confidence. If the confidence of a category $\hat{p}_{i,c}$ is greater than a threshold $t$ (usually be set as 0.5), the model believes that the category is present in the image. So the confidence for that sample is represented by the average of all the confidence above this threshold. If the model does not exceed the threshold for all categories, then the maximum posterior probability is taken as the confidence of the sample.

$$\text{ECE}_{\text{ML}} = \sum_{m=1}^{M} \frac{|B_m|}{n} \, |\text{acc}_{\text{ML}}(B_m) - \text{conf}_{\text{ML}}(B_m)| \tag{4}$$

Equation 4 extends ECE to $\text{ECE}_{\text{ML}}$ for multi-label classification.

# 3 The Proposed VICE Metric

## 3.1 Motivation

In many trials, we found an inconsistency between the performance of the deep learning models and their visual interpretability. Some samples with low loss have poor visual interpretability, with incomplete CAM coverage, while some other samples with relatively complete CAMs have biased predictions, as shown in Fig. 1. Such inconsistencies lead to restricted and unreliable applications. A model with good interpretability is not only consistent in confidence and accuracy (with lower ECE). In applications with a firm reliance on visual interpretability, we expect the good-performed models to be more interpretable and consistent with human perception. So we tend to introduce a sample-wise perspective to fine-grained measure the consistency of performance and visual interpretability, which is referred to as VICE (VIsual ConsistEncy). If a model has a good visual consistency, the visual interpretability output by the model will focus on the object itself for correctly predicted samples, and for incorrectly predicted samples we can find the reasons for poor performance in visual interpretability, such as label noise, background effects, etc.

In the following part of this section, we describe how to calculate the consistency of performance with visual interpretability. We first present two types of visual interpretability corresponding to CNN and Transformer architectures, then use a sample-wise loss to characterize the network performance on the corresponding samples, and finally calculate VICE to indicate the consistency.

### 3.2    The Visual Interpretability of CNNs and Transformers

Due to the different architectures of CNN and Transformer, the manner of generating CAMs is different. As for a CNN, we follow the setting from [34] to generate a CAM $M_{cnn}^c$ for class $c$, which is calculated as:

$$M_{cnn}^c = \sum_k w_k^c f_k \tag{5}$$

$M_{cnn}^c$ directly correlates with the importance of a particular spatial location for a specific class $c$ and thus functions as visual interpretability of the category predicted by the network.

The approach in [2] is adopted to generate CAMs for vision transformer. The layer's operation on two tensors $X$ and $Y$ is denoted by $L^{(n)}(X, Y)$. The two tensors are the input feature map and weights for layer $n$. Relevance propagation follows the generic Deep Taylor Decomposition [21].

### 3.3    The Quality for Visual Interpretability

The segmentation labels of CAMs are related to human cognition, and the quality of a CAM is the degree to which it conforms to human cognition. To evaluate the quality of visual interpretability (CAMs), we use the mean Jaccard index to measure the consistency of CAMs and segmentation labels. The definition is shown in Eq. 6.

$$JI(M_{cam}, M_{gt}) = \frac{1}{C} \sum_{i=0}^{C} \frac{|M_{cam} \cap M_{gt}|}{|M_{cam} \cup M_{gt}|} \tag{6}$$

A higher JI score means the model has higher quality CAMs with better visual interpretability.

## 3.4    The Sample-wise Performance

The sample-wise multi-label loss is used as an indicator of the model performance,

$$loss_{sw}(x, y) = -\frac{1}{C} \sum_c y_c \log[(1 + \exp(-x_c))^{-1}]$$

$$+ (1 - y_c) \log[\frac{\exp(-x_c)}{1 + \exp(-x_c)}] \tag{7}$$

As shown in Eq. 7, the error is measured by calculating the sigmoid cross-entropy between the output layer and the labels. Equivalently, the binary cross-entropy loss is calculated for each category.

## 3.5    The Final VICE

We quantitatively estimate the consistency between performance and interpretability by measuring the pearson correlation coefficient between sample-wise loss and the quality of CAMs. And the '−' of $loss_{sw}$ is to allow positive correlation.

$$VICE = \rho(loss, JI) = \frac{\sum_{i=1}^{n} (loss_i - \overline{loss}) (JI_i - \overline{JI})}{\sqrt{\sum_{i=1}^{n} (loss_i - \overline{loss})^2} \sqrt{\sum_{i=1}^{n} (JI_i - \overline{JI})^2}} \tag{8}$$

For samples with low loss, the model with a higher VICE score can give better visual interpretability than with a lower score. While for samples with high loss, we can also observe the reasons for their prediction errors via their CAMs. As shown in the top figure of Fig. 1, the VICE and $ECE_{ML}$ evaluate the consistency between performance and interpretability from different perspectives.

# 4    Empirical Evaluation

## 4.1    Experimental Setup

Our case study followed the standard multi-label classification setting. The metrics, model families, and datasets used are introduced next.

**Metrics for model performance:** mean average precision (mAP) over all categories and accuracy for multi-label (described in Eq. 1) is adopted for evaluating the performance of models. The larger the ACC and mAP, the better the model performance.

**Metrics for the consistency between the performance and interpretability:** $ECE_{ML}$ (described in Eq. 4) with 20 bins is to evaluate the consistency between accuracy and confidence. VICE (described in Eq. 8) is to measure the consistency between performance and visual interpretability. The smaller the $ECE_{ML}$ and VICE, the greater the consistency of model performance and interpretability.

**Model families**. We select recent and historic state-of-the-art classification models, including ResNet [14], Res2Net [8], EfficientNet [26], ResNeSt [31], ViT [7]. If not explicitly mentioned, all of them are pre-trained on ImageNet1k [5] with full supervision.

**Datasets**. We evaluate on PASCAL VOC 2012 dataset with 21 class annotations. The official dataset separation has 1464 images for training, 1449 for validation, and 1456 for testing. Following the common experimental protocol, we take additional annotations from SBD [12] to build an augmented training set with 10582 images, which is named as VOC2012Aug. It provides labels for semantic segmentation, which allows us to evaluate the quality of the CAMs (Eq. 6). All metrics reported were performed on the validation set.

### 4.2    Models with Different Capacity

**Table 1.** Models with Different Capacity. The VICE does not monotonically increase with increasing model capacity.

| Model | Params | mAP (%)↑/Acc (%) ↑ | $ECE_{ML}$ (%)↓ | VICE ↑ |
|---|---|---|---|---|
| ResNet-18 | 11.177 M | 83.917/72.188 | 14.897 | 0.185 |
| ResNet-34 | 21.285 M | 86.296/76.945 | 14.257 | **0.226** |
| ResNet-50 | 23.508 M | 87.470/78.617 | **13.401** | 0.215 |
| ResNeSt-14 | 8.563 M | 85.382/75.329 | 13.989 | 0.342 |
| ResNeSt-26 | 15.020 M | 87.395/79.170 | 13.248 | 0.311 |
| ResNeSt-50 | 25.434 M | 88.031/79.117 | 12.978 | **0.322** |
| ResNeSt-101 | 46.226 M | 88.856/80.415 | **12.735** | 0.272 |
| ViT-Small | 21.975 M | 90.253/81.172 | 10.361 | **0.393** |
| ViT-Base | 86.416 M | 91.238/81.657 | **10.313** | 0.389 |

Table 1 reports the model performance, $ECE_{ML}$, and VICE of the models with different capacities. As the model capacity increases, the mAP is increasing, and its $ECE_{ML}$ is decreasing, which is beneficial for practical tasks. But the VICE does not monotonically increase with increasing model capacity, which is confirmed in three architectures.

**Discussion.** Model capacity and representation capability have always been considered key to improving performance, but models are often over-parameterized. Increasing the model capacity would have a performance bottleneck and also increase the risk of overfitting. *Blindly increasing model capacity may harm visual interpretability and consistency*, which is unfavorable for scenarios highly dependent on visual interpretability.

### 4.3    Models with Various Architecture

To compare the impact of different model architectures fairly, we selected five models with similar model size and various feature extraction preferences. Figure 2 shows the $ECE_{ML}$ metrics for different models. From Eq. 3, if the confidence level of all classes is less than $t$, then the accuracy of this sample is equal

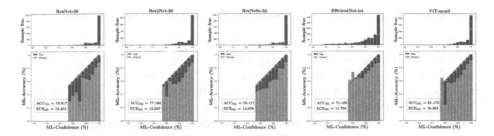

**Fig. 2.** We divided the samples into different bins according to the loss. The figure above shows the number of samples in each bin, and the figure below shows the accuracy and confidence in each bin. Regardless of the number of samples in each bin, the output prediction probabilities (light blue blocks) generally fall below the straight line y=x (dark blue blocks), which means that the deep model is prone to over-confidence. (Color figure oline)

**Table 2.** Models with Various Architecture. ResNeSt and ViT outperform ResNet in JI score, and their VICE fail to be better than that of ResNet.

| Model | Params | mAP (%)↑/Acc (%) ↑ | $ECE_{ML}$ (%)↓ | VICE ↑ |
|---|---|---|---|---|
| ResNet-50 | 23.508 M | 87.470/78.617 | 13.401 | 0.215 |
| Res2Net-50 | 23.238 M | 86.759/77.180 | 13.297 | 0.114 |
| ResNeSt-50 | 25.434 M | 88.031/79.117 | 12.978 | 0.322 |
| EfficientNet-b4 | 17.549 M | 83.690/71.180 | 11.765 | **0.449** |
| ViT-Small | 21.975 M | 90.253/81.172 | **10.361** | 0.393 |

to zero, which is the reason why the accuracy in the bins with confidence below 0.5 is zero. $ECE_{ML}$ is the calculation of the average discrepancy between the two statistical histograms. We find that the lower histogram shows that the output prediction probabilities (light blue parts) generally fall below the straight line $y = x$ (dark blue parts), which means that the deep model is prone to over-confidence. Moreover, according to Fig. 2, we can also conclude that the model calibration of the vision transformer is better than that of CNN. This inspires us to consider the potential of non-CNN models such as vision transformer, which not only unifies feature encoding architectures for multimodal tasks but also has better model calibration with lower $ECE_{ML}$. On the other hand, Table 2 shows the VICE score for different model architectures. ResNeSt and ViT outperform ResNet in terms of VICE score with comparable model sizes, suggesting that the CAMs of the models with integrated attention mechanisms are more complete. And EfficientNet-b4 has the highest VICE score, which hints at the potential of NAS-based architectures to achieve a better tradeoff between interpretability and performance.

**Discussion.** Models of different architectures have different consistency preferences, and the integration of multiple model architectures may improve interpretability for a given task.

## 4.4    Consistency Study with Self-supervised Pre-trained Models

**Motivation.** Recent approaches such as [1,3,4,10,13,18,28] show that the features extracted from networks training with a self-supervised learning paradigm can achieve better performance on downstream tasks that require more object semantics, such as object detection and semantic segmentation, which sparked the interest of many researchers. A large number of self-supervised learning algorithms focus on instance discrimination, considering a single image as a class, encouraging the model to bring the sample and its augmented image as close as possible on the feature space. MoCo [13] and SimCLR [3] with contrastive self-supervised learning even surpass the results of supervised learning. Reference [4] is the first work to apply self-supervision to Vision Transformer. DINO [1] explores the self-supervised approach so that ViT contains features related to semantic segmentation of images, which is useful for downstream tasks. Self-supervised models are more interpretable if they can explore target locations. Since the self-supervised learning paradigm is not constrained by category information, which allows the network to freely explore its suitable region of interest, rather than just focusing on the features about classification tasks. Therefore, we evaluate the performance of ResNet and ViT using different self-supervised schemes.

**Table 3.** Various Pre-train Setting with ResNet-50.

| Model | Pre-train Dataset | Pre-train Alg | Finetuning | mAP (%) ↑/Acc (%) ↑ | ECE$_{ML}$ (%) ↓ | VICE ↑ |
|---|---|---|---|---|---|---|
| ResNet-50 | ImageNet | Supervised | – | 87.470/78.617 | **13.401** | 0.215 |
| ResNet-50 | ImageNet | BYOL | – | 74.827/62.762 | 19.087 | 0.305 |
| ResNet-50 | ImageNet | DINO | – | 73.147/57.978 | 18.080 | 0.203 |
| ResNet-50 | ImageNet | MoCov3 | – | 76.200/64.114 | 18.212 | 0.324 |
| ResNet-50 | VOC2012Aug | MoCov3 | – | 39.701/21.731 | 28.483 | **0.348** |
| ResNet-50 | ImageNet | Supervised | fc | 84.492/74.028 | **12.510** | 0.260 |
| ResNet-50 | ImageNet | BYOL | fc | 59.351/27.029 | 24.452 | 0.369 |
| ResNet-50 | ImageNet | DINO | fc | 71.158/42.312 | 17.652 | 0.282 |
| ResNet-50 | ImageNet | MoCov3 | fc | 70.336/28.532 | 23.176 | 0.251 |
| ResNet-50 | VOC2012Aug | MoCov3 | fc | 38.105/19.587 | 29.203 | **0.401** |

**Table 4.** Various Pre-train Setting with ViT-Base.

| Model | Pre-train Dataset | Pre-train Alg | Finetuning | mAP (%) ↑/Acc (%) ↑ | ECE$_{ML}$ (%) ↓ | VICE ↑ |
|---|---|---|---|---|---|---|
| ViT-Base | ImageNet | Supervised | – | 91.238/81.657 | **10.313** | 0.389 |
| ViT-Base | ImageNet | DINO | – | 82.963/71.667 | 14.126 | 0.412 |
| ViT-Base | ImageNet | MoCov3 | – | 69.940/53.662 | 15.116 | **0.456** |
| ViT-Base | VOC2012Aug | MoCov3 | – | 50.173/27.923 | 25.317 | 0.331 |
| ViT-Base | ImageNet | Supervised | head | 88.329/80.267 | **11.300** | 0.430 |
| ViT-Base | ImageNet | DINO | head | 87.991/79.440 | 11.607 | 0.466 |
| ViT-Base | ImageNet | MoCov3 | head | 70.966/55.786 | 13.107 | **0.493** |
| ViT-Base | VOC2012Aug | MoCov3 | head | 52.738/33.101 | 23.105 | 0.404 |

Tables 3 and 4 reports the performance under different pre-training paradigms when using ResNet-50/ViT-Base for feature extraction. Performance and $ECE_{ML}$ of the models obtained by the supervised pre-training approach were superior to the self-supervised groups. However, in the experimental group loaded with the self-supervised pre-trained model, the VICE scores were generally better than those in the supervised group, which shows the potential of unsupervised pre-training in improving model interpretability.

For the evaluation protocol that fixes the backbone weights and learns only on the *fc* or *head* layer, the linear combination of only the features learned from pre-training stage can better exploit the advantages of different pre-training approaches. MoCov3 [4] obtains the highest VICE score in the unsupervised approach, which indicates that its learned features have strong visual interpretability. The absolute performance using the unsupervised pre-training approach is not very high, but they have a higher VICE score, indicating that their performance is more consistent with visual interpretability.

**Discussion.** Experimental exploration of model interpretability with various pre-training settings shows *the potential of self-supervised learning to improve the consistency between model performance and interpretability,* freeing us from the constraints of classification-based pre-training on ImageNet, allowing performance and interpretability to go hand in hand, and truly exploiting the potential of deep learning techniques. Compared to the supervised experimental group, the self-supervised schemes can achieve higher VICE score with the same settings.

### 4.5   How Regularization Enforces Interpretability Conformance?

**Motivation.** There is some recent work aimed to make classic Convnets like VGG [25] and ResNet [14] great again [6,23,30]. The performance of CNN is improved from the perspective of data and model[16,17], respectively. This indicates that the upper bound of deep neural networks has not been fully explored until now.

**Table 5.** The Impact of Regularization Techniques.

| Model | Regularization | mAP (%) ↑/Acc (%) ↑ | $ECE_{ML}$ (%) ↓ | VICE ↑ |
|---|---|---|---|---|
| ResNet-50 | – | 87.907/80.071 | 13.723 | 0.302 |
| ResNet-50 | Weight Decay | 87.470/78.617 | 14.401 | 0.315 |
| ResNet-50 | Random Erasing | 87.851/79.699 | **13.067** | **0.323** |
| ViT-Base | – | 90.968/82.724 | 9.368 | 0.379 |
| ViT-Base | Weight Decay | 91.238/81.657 | 10.313 | **0.389** |
| ViT-Base | Random Erasing | 90.765/83.190 | **8.201** | 0.384 |

Random erasing data augmentation [33] and weight decay are evaluated the performance in Table 5. Reference [19] is referred for the implementation of the weight decay regularization mechanism. We find that training with weight decay harms $ECE_{ML}$, but it improves the VICE metric. Weight decay seems to improve the quality of CAMs (JI Score) by constraining the model complexity and mitigating the model overfitting. Random erasing is a data augmentation method that constructs new samples by randomly erasing a region to prevent the model from overfitting the dataset. The random erasing data augmentation avoids over-confidence and effectively improves model consistency between interpretability and performance on the VICE metrics.

**Discussion.** As an essential tool to avoid overfitting, the regularization not only improves the generalization performance but also impacts the interpretability of the model. It encourages the model to achieve a trade-off between performance and interpretability through extra learning objectives.

## 5    Other Related Work

Predictions from deep neural networks frequently suffer from over-confidence, which leads to user distrust. Accurate estimation of prediction uncertainty (model calibration) is essential for the safe application of neural networks. [24] explore regularizing neural networks by penalizing low entropy output distributions as a strong regularizer. Extensive experiments have shown in [20] that structure is a major determinant of calibration characteristics.

Many strategies have been proposed to realize model calibration based on ECE, such as temperature scaling [11], predictions ensemble [15, 29]. It has been applied in model calibration for such as graph neural networks [27] and long-tailed recognition [32].

In contrast, the proposed consistency between model performance and visual interpretability VICE also deserves attention. The community should not only focus on model performance but also on achieving a better tradeoff in model performance and interpretability.

## 6    Conclusion

We proposed VICE as a novel sample-wise fine-grained metric to synergistically evaluate the consistency between model performance and visual interpretability from a different perspective. We selected five types of heterogeneous models for case studies using VICE and $ECE_{ML}$ from different perspectives, and we found a series of inspiring phenomena:

- Blindly increasing the model capacity may harm model interpretability.
- ResNeSt and ViT, designed upon the visual attention mechanism, have better visual interpretability and $ECE_{ML}$, but worse consistency between performance and visual interpretability.
- The self-supervised pre-training setting gets rid of the supervised objectives, and learns more interpretable feature representation, which shows the potential of the self-supervised learning paradigm.

– The learning objectives, introduced by different regularization, would also encourage the model to learn more interpretable features.

The proposed metrics and the found phenomena will guide us to focus on and leverage more significant impact factors for designing better performed and more interpretable models in future studies.

**Acknowledgements.** This work is partially supported by National Science Foundation of China (62272229), National Key Research and Development Program of China (No. 2021ZD0113200).

# References

1. Caron, M., Touvron, H., Misra, I., Jégou, H., Mairal, J., Bojanowski, P., Joulin, A.: Emerging properties in self-supervised vision transformers. In: ICCV (2021)
2. Chefer, H., Gur, S., Wolf, L.: Transformer interpretability beyond attention visualization. In: CVPR (2021)
3. Chen, T., Kornblith, S., Norouzi, M., Hinton, G.: A simple framework for contrastive learning of visual representations. In: ICML (2020)
4. Chen, X., Xie, S., He, K.: An empirical study of training self-supervised vision transformers. In: ICCV (2021)
5. Deng, J., Dong, W., Socher, R., Li, L.J., Li, K., Fei-Fei, L.: Imagenet: A large-scale hierarchical image database. In: CVPR (2009)
6. Ding, X., Zhang, X., Ma, N., Han, J., Ding, G., Sun, J.: Repvgg: Making vgg-style convnets great again. In: CVPR (2021)
7. Dosovitskiy, A., Beyer, L., Kolesnikov, A., Weissenborn, D., Zhai, X., Unterthiner, T., Dehghani, M., Minderer, M., Heigold, G., Gelly, S., et al.: An image is worth 16x16 words: Transformers for image recognition at scale. In: ICLR (2020)
8. Gao, S., Cheng, M.M., Zhao, K., Zhang, X.Y., Yang, M.H., Torr, P.H.: Res2net: a new multi-scale backbone architecture. IEEE Trans. Pattern Anal. Mach. Intell. **43**(2), 652–662 (2019)
9. Godbole, S., Sarawagi, S.: Discriminative methods for multi-labeled classification. In: PAKDD (2004)
10. Grill, J.B., Strub, F., Altché, F., Tallec, C., Richemond, P., Buchatskaya, E., Doersch, C., Pires, B., Guo, Z., Azar, M., et al.: Bootstrap your own latent: a new approach to self-supervised learning. In: NeurIPS (2020)
11. Guo, C., Pleiss, G., Sun, Y., Weinberger, K.Q.: On calibration of modern neural networks. In: ICML (2017)
12. Hariharan, B., Arbeláez, P., Bourdev, L., Maji, S., Malik, J.: Semantic contours from inverse detectors. In: ICCV (2011)
13. He, K., Fan, H., Wu, Y., Xie, S., Girshick, R.: Momentum contrast for unsupervised visual representation learning. In: CVPR (2020)
14. He, K., Zhang, X., Ren, S., Sun, J.: Deep residual learning for image recognition. In: CVPR (2016)
15. Lakshminarayanan, B., Pritzel, A., Blundell, C.: Simple and scalable predictive uncertainty estimation using deep ensembles. In: NeurIPS (2017)
16. Liang, D., Du, Y., Sun, H., Zhang, L., Liu, N., Wei, M.: Nlkd: using coarse annotations for semantic segmentation based on knowledge distillation. In: ICASSP (2021)

17. Liang, D., Geng, Q., Wei, Z., Vorontsov, D.A., Kim, E.L., Wei, M., Zhou, H.: Anchor retouching via model interaction for robust object detection in aerial images. IEEE Trans. Geosci. Remote Sens. **60**, 1–13 (2021)
18. Liang, D., Li, L., Wei, M., Yang, S., Zhang, L., Yang, W., Du, Y., Zhou, H.: Semantically contrastive learning for low-light image enhancement. In: AAAI (2022)
19. Loshchilov, I., Hutter, F.: Decoupled weight decay regularization. In: ICLR (2018)
20. Minderer, M., Djolonga, J., Romijnders, R., Hubis, F., Zhai, X., Houlsby, N., Tran, D., Lucic, M.: Revisiting the calibration of modern neural networks. In: NeurIPS (2021)
21. Montavon, G., Lapuschkin, S., Binder, A., Samek, W., Müller, K.R.: Explaining nonlinear classification decisions with deep Taylor decomposition. Pattern Recogn. **65**, 211–222 (2017)
22. Naeini, M.P., Cooper, G., Hauskrecht, M.: Obtaining well calibrated probabilities using Bayesian binning. In: AAAI (2015)
23. Paszke, A., Gross, S., Massa, F., Lerer, A., Bradbury, J., Chanan, G., Killeen, T., Lin, Z., Gimelshein, N., Antiga, L., et al.: Pytorch: an imperative style, high-performance deep learning library. In: NeurIPS (2019)
24. Pereyra, G., Tucker, G., Chorowski, J., Kaiser, Ł., Hinton, G.: Regularizing neural networks by penalizing confident output distributions. In: ICLR (2017)
25. Simonyan, K., Zisserman, A.: Very deep convolutional networks for large-scale image recognition (2014). arXiv:1409.1556
26. Tan, M., Le, Q.: Efficientnet: Rethinking model scaling for convolutional neural networks. In: ICML (2019)
27. Wang, X., Liu, H., Shi, C., Yang, C.: Be confident! towards trustworthy graph neural networks via confidence calibration. In: NeurIPS (2021)
28. Wang, X., Zhang, R., Shen, C., Kong, T., Li, L.: Dense contrastive learning for self-supervised visual pre-training. In: CVPR (2021)
29. Wen, Y., Tran, D., Ba, J.: Batchensemble: an alternative approach to efficient ensemble and lifelong learning. In: ICLR (2019)
30. Wightman, R., Touvron, H., Jégou, H.: Resnet strikes back: an improved training procedure in timm (2021). arXiv:2110.00476
31. Zhang, H., Wu, C., Zhang, Z., Zhu, Y., Lin, H., Zhang, Z., Sun, Y., He, T., Mueller, J., Manmatha, R., et al.: Resnest: split-attention networks (2020). arXiv:2004.08955
32. Zhong, Z., Cui, J., Liu, S., Jia, J.: Improving calibration for long-tailed recognition. In: CVPR (2021)
33. Zhong, Z., Zheng, L., Kang, G., Li, S., Yang, Y.: Random erasing data augmentation. In: AAAI (2020)
34. Zhou, B., Khosla, A., Lapedriza, A., Oliva, A., Torralba, A.: Learning deep features for discriminative localization. In: CVPR (2016)

# Object-Scale Adaptive Optical Flow Estimation Network

Mu Li[1], Bao jiang Zhong[1(✉)], and Kai-Kuang Ma[2]

[1] School of Computer Science and Technology, Soochow University, Suzhou, China
bjzhong@suda.edu.cn
[2] School of Electrical and Electronic Engineering, Nanyang Technological University,
Singapore, Singapore

**Abstract.** Current deep learning methods for optical flow estimation often use spatial feature pyramids to extract image features. To get the correlation between images, they directly compute the cost volume of the obtained image features. In this process, fine object details tend to be ignored. To solve this fundamental problem, an *object-scale adaptive optical flow estimation network* is proposed, in which multi-scale features are selectively extracted and exploited using our developed *feature selectable block* (FSB). As a result, we can obtain the multi-scale receptive fields of objects at different scales in the image. To consolidate all image features generated from all scales, a new cost volume generation scheme called *multi-scale cost volume generation block* (MCVGB) is further proposed to aggregate information from different scales. Extensive experiments conducted on the Sintel and KITTI2015 datasets show that our proposed method can capture fine details of different scale objects with high accuracy and thus deliver superior performance over a number of state-of-the-art methods.

**Keywords:** Optical flow estimation · Deep learning · Feature pyramids · Receptive fields · Multi-scale

## 1 Introduction

Optical flow estimation is the task of estimating per-pixel motion between video frames. It is a fundamental technique for a wide range of computer vision applications like motion segmentation [3,6,31], action recognition [13,27], and autonomous driving [26,33]. Optical flow estimation has traditionally been approached as a knowledge-driven techniques. Traditional approaches [1,2,17, 19,22] often construct optical flow as an energy function optimization problem that specifies various restrictions by taking into account existing knowledge. For many years, these techniques dominated the benchmark. However, optimizing such intricate functions typically takes too long and moves too slowly to be used in a real-time environment. On the other hand, hand-designing an optimization objective that is robust to a variety of corner cases is difficult.

S. Khanna et al. (Eds.): PRICAI 2022, LNCS 13631, pp. 591–605, 2022.
https://doi.org/10.1007/978-3-031-20868-3_44

(a) FlyingChairs          (b) FlyingThings          (c) Sintel          (d) KITTI2015

**Fig. 1.** Data sets often contain objects of different scales.

With the advancement of CNN in recent years, optical flow estimation has advanced remarkably. When compared to the knowledge-driven approach, the CNN-based approach offers a strong capacity for learning from large amounts of data. This makes these techniques data-driven strategies. For learning optical flow, many approaches use encoder-decoder or spatial pyramid architectures, e.g., referring to [4,11,23]. A pioneering work is the FlowNet proposed by Dosovitskiy et al. [4] in 2015, which puts forward two models, namely FlowNetS and FlowNetC. Ilg et al. [11] proposed the 'FlowNet 2.0' by stacking several diverse networks (FlowNetC, FlowNetS) into a large model and exploring different training schedules on multiple datasets. Although FlowNet and FlowNet2.0 may generate accurate and high-quality flow maps, their model size is too enormous for real-world applications.

In [18,23,25], many networks with smaller model sizes than encoder-decoder architecture are suggested as a solution to this problem. Spynet [18] introduce the feature pyramid module, which uses a spatial pyramid network that warps images at each level to break down large displacement into smaller displacement. As a result, just a little displacement needs to be calculated at each pyramidal level, drastically lowering the number of channels. Sun et al. [23] developed the PWC-Net, which uses a feature warping layer and iterative optimization. Teed and Deng [25] proposed the RAFT, in which a lightweight recurrent unit is coupled with a GRU cell as an update operator. Based on the RAFT, Jiang et al [14] developed a network that uses the sparse cost volume to replace the dense one used in [25].

In the above-mentioned networks, the receptive fields of artificial neurons in each layer are generally designed to be the same size during the process of feature extraction. Since they all use a single network structure, the cost volume is generated in a single way. However, the cost volume represents the similarity between two adjacent frames, and an accurate cost volume is the key to obtain accurate optical flow estimation. Unfortunately, this practice could result in a loss of fine details of various scale objects, leading to inferior estimation performance. Figure 1 shows some moving objects from different data sets. The existing optical flow estimation algorithms often can not well estimate the optical flow of objects of different scales.

To explore the effect of convolution kernels with different scales in each layer on the accuracy of optical flow estimation, we propose an *Object-scale adaptive optical flow estimation network* in this paper. Inspired by the work of Li et al. [15]

in image classification, a *feature selectable block* (FSB) is established and used. Our FSB is based on the fact that different sizes of kernels used in each layer can produce much richer information. To consolidate all image features generated from all scales, a new cost volume generation scheme, called the *multi-scale cost volume generation block* (MCVGB), is proposed to further increase the accuracy of optical flow estimation. To the best of our knowledge, our work is the first optical flow estimation network that focuses on objects at different scales in an image. Extensive simulation results have clearly justified that our proposed method indeed outperforms multiple comparable state-of-the-art methods.

The reminder of this paper is organized as follows. Related work is reviewed in Sect. 2. Details of our proposed method for conducting optical flow estimation are described in Sect. 3. Extensive experimental results are documented and discussed in Sect. 4. Finally, a conclusion is drawn in Sect. 5.

## 2 Related Work

**Enhanced Feature Extraction.** Since the popularity of convolutional networks, many improvements have been made in order to enhance the ability of feature extraction. The most commonly used is the dual-branch network. In the field of deep learning, this idea was first proposed in ResNet [7], where the branch path is the identity map. To combine more detailed and varied features, the InceptionNets [24] set each branch with unique kernel filters. In order to combine multi-scale feature information, the study [33] presents an atrous spatial pyramid pooling module. This module includes a global average pooling layer to collect global spatial contexts and numerous dilated convolutional layers with varying rates. The extracted features are then directly concatenated for the subsequent convolution. It should be noted that our multi-branch adaptive selection processes enable us to achieve the receptive field size of neurons without fixing the size of each branch, which is one of the main distinctions between our feature selectable block and the above work.

In addition to the dual-branch network, there are many ways to enhance feature extraction. Spatial Transform Networks [12] learn a parametric transformation to warp the feature map, which is considered difficult to train. In addition, group convolution, deep-wise convolution and dilated convolution are improved feature extraction methods. Some of them reduce the amount of convolution calculation, and some improve the feature extraction ability. Our work also uses dilated convolution combined with each feature selectable block.

**Cost Volume.** Stereo matching [8,20] literature first introduced the idea of cost volume. At each pixel coordinate, a cost volume holds the matching costs for various pixel displacement possibilities (also known as disparity in stereo). In stereo matching, it is therefore a 3D tensor ($H \times W \times D$), where D is the greatest disparity range. Strong optimization techniques can be used to filter outliers from the cost volume, which acts as a discriminative representation of the search space and typically produces accurate results. The optical flow community gains from

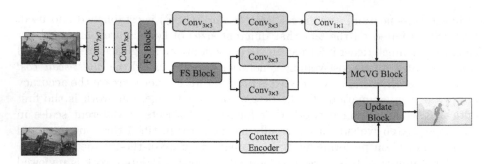

**Fig. 2.** Architecture of our network, where feature selectable and multi-scale cost volume generation are denoted as 'FS' and 'MCVG', respectively.

cost volume. But, the search space in optical flow is 2D as opposed to 1D disparity in stereo, this results in a 4D cost volume ($H \times W \times (2R + 1) \times (2R + 1))$) for the search radius R, which is computationally expensive for high displacements. A recent proposal by RAFT [25] is to compute all spatial correlations and then build a 4D cost volume ($H \times W \times H \times W$)). Recently, many scholars have made some efforts to further reduce the calculation amount of the cost volume, but it has brought a certain degree of performance degradation.

Jiang et al. [14] proposed a sparse cost volume representation, where only the top-k correlations for each pixel are stored in a sparse data structure defined by a key-value pair. Xu et al. [21] factorized the 2D search into two 1D substitutes in the vertical and horizontal directions, respectively, such that they could use 1D correlations to construct compact cost volume. These improvements to cost volume all lose the matching between image pairs on some images, resulting in inaccurate optical flow estimation.

In order to ensure more accurate optical flow estimation results, we consolidate all image features generated from all scales. A new multi-scale cost volume generation scheme is proposed to further increase the accuracy of optical flow estimation. Extensive simulation results have clearly justified that our proposed method indeed outperforms multiple comparable state-of-the-art methods.

## 3   The Proposed Method

### 3.1   Outline

For the feature extraction part of the optical flow estimation network, a siamese network is usually used to extract features from two adjacent frames of pictures at the same time, and then calculate the correlation between the features of the two frames to obtain the correlation volume. So how to extract richer features and how to calculate feature correlation are two key parts, and our network takes both factors into consideration. The RAFT [25] is followed to develop our network, with the intention of preserving richer image features and generating multi-scale cost volume in the optical flow estimation process.

As shown in Fig. 2, for a given image sequence, four convolution layers are exploited to extract image features at increasingly high levels, which are with kernel sizes of $7 \times 7$, $5 \times 5$, $3 \times 3$ and $3 \times 3$, respectively. Limited by figure length, we use an ellipsis to represent the middle $5 \times 5$ and $3 \times 3$ kernels. Then, our proposed method extracts multi-scale feature information from two adjacent frames using *feature selectable block* (FSB) and transfers to *multi-scale cost volume generation block* (MCVGB). After that, the context encoder [25] employs the first image as its input and outputs feature maps containing location information. Because the optical flow calculates the offset from the first frame to the second frame, the location information of the first frame is conducive to the network learning the initial point of the optical flow on the first frame. Finally, multi-scale cost volume and context encoder [25] will be promoted to the update operator [25] to iteratively calculate the optical flow estimation. Among them, FSB and MCVGB are the keys to improve the performance of optical flow estimation. More details of our developed FSB and MCVGB are described in the following sub-sections, respectively.

It is worth mentioning that the developed FSB serves as the last layers of the network, where the data are of the lowest resolution due to down-sampling. Also, we reduce the size of network parameters by controlling the number of channels. In addition, the MCVGB is only used to integrate multi-scale features, so it does not increase the size of the network.

## 3.2  Feature Selectable Block

By using the feature selectable block, our network can selectively employ the generated multi-scale features (fine scale and coarse scale). So it has the ability to capture objects of different sizes on the image. Figure 3 demonstrates the flowchart of this block, which mainly consists of three operators–*Split*, *Fuse*, and *Select*.

*Split*: Given an intermediate feature map $\mathbf{M} \in \mathbb{R}^{C \times H \times W}$ as input, the feature selectable block will produce two feature maps, $\widetilde{\mathbf{M}} \in \mathbb{R}^{C \times H' \times W'}$ and $\widehat{\mathbf{M}} \in \mathbb{R}^{C \times H' \times W'}$, as its output. This operation employs two convolutional layers with kernel sizes of 3 and 5, respectively. Among them, the conventional layer with a $5 \times 5$ kernel is replaced with the dilated convolution layer with a $3 \times 3$ kernel and a dilation size of 2 to improve efficiency. From this, we obtained image features of two different scales, and the follow-up work is how to make the two branches of the network adaptively selected.

*Fuse*: First, we fuse multi-scale information from above two different branches via element-wise summation. In this way, the features after the fusion of the two scales can be obtained:

$$\mathbf{M_{fuse}} = \widetilde{\mathbf{M}} + \widehat{\mathbf{M}} \tag{1}$$

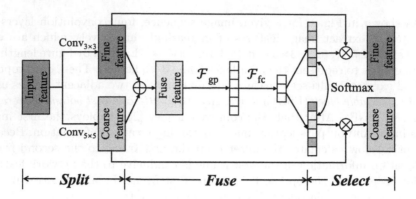

**Fig. 3.** The feature selectable block.

Then, we employ global average pooling on $\mathbf{M_{fuse}}$ to capture global information in the spatial dimension:

$$s_c = \mathcal{F}_{gp}(\mathbf{M_{fuse}}) = \frac{1}{H \times W} \sum_{i=1}^{H} \sum_{j=1}^{W} \mathbf{M_{fuse}}(i, j) \tag{2}$$

where $s \in \mathbb{R}^C$, $c \in C$, the c-th element of s is calculated by shrinking $\mathbf{M_{fuse}}$ through spatial dimensions $H \times W$. Further, the kernels are adaptively selected using a fully connected layer that learns the link between distinct scale features. A batch norm layer and a ReLU layer are added after the fully connected layer:

$$t = \mathcal{F}_{fc}(s) = \delta(\mathcal{B}(\mathbf{W}s)) \tag{3}$$

where $\delta$ is the ReLU function, $\mathcal{B}$ denotes the Batch Normalization, $\mathbf{W} \in \mathbb{R}^{d \times C}$ (after some trials, we set d = 32 in our experiments), so $t \in \mathbb{R}^{d \times 1}$.

**Select**: The feature matrix t guides the employment of soft attention across channels to adaptively select different spatial scales of information. Specifically, we need to expand the dimensionality of t, and a softmax operator is used as the channel-wise in particular:

$$\alpha_c = \frac{\exp(\mathbf{A}_c t)}{\exp(\mathbf{A}_c t) + \exp(\mathbf{B}_c t)}, \qquad \beta_c = \frac{\exp(\mathbf{B}_c t)}{\exp(\mathbf{A}_c t) + \exp(\mathbf{B}_c t)} \tag{4}$$

where $A, B \in \mathbb{R}^{C \times d}$, $\alpha, \beta$ are the obtained soft attention vectors on $\widetilde{\mathbf{M}}, \widehat{\mathbf{M}}$. $\alpha_c$ and $\beta_c$ have the relationship shown as follows:

$$\alpha_c + \beta_c = 1 \tag{5}$$

The attention weights on several kernels produce the final feature map $\mathbf{M_{fine}}$ and $\mathbf{M_{coarse}}$. That is to give the corresponding weight coefficient:

$$\mathbf{M_{fine}} = \sum_{c=1}^{C} \alpha_c . \widetilde{\mathbf{M}}_\mathbf{c}, \mathbf{M_{coarse}} = \sum_{c=1}^{C} \beta_c . \widehat{\mathbf{M}}_\mathbf{c} \tag{6}$$

The result is two feature maps with different scales after the network adaptively selects convolutional kernels for different sizes. As shown in Fig. 2, our network obtains multi-scale extracted features in three branches. We need to use FSB twice in the network, and the results of the three branches will be used for multi-scale cost volume generation.

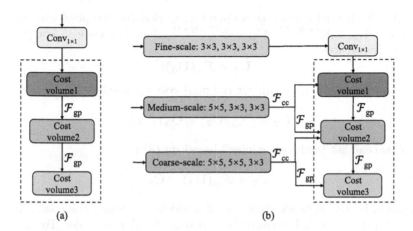

**Fig. 4.** A comparison of two multi-scale cost volume generation blocks: (a) block used in RAFT [25] and (b) our developed MCVG block.

### 3.3 Multi-scale Cost Volume Generation Block

In the RAFT [25], the cost volume generation process is achieved by simply using a set of global average pooling operators, which leads to a loss of fine details. Improvements in cost volume computation increase speed, but at the expense of optical flow estimation performance. In this paper, our proposed novel generation process, the multi-scale cost volume generation block (MCVGB), combines multi-scale extracted image feature sets (see Fig. 4), so the receptive field of each scale is taken into account.

In the multi-scale cost volume generation block, we make full use of feature information from different scales. Specifically, we denote above features as fine-scale features: $\mathbf{U_1} \in \mathbb{R}^{C \times H \times W}$, medium-scale features: $\mathbf{U_2} \in \mathbb{R}^{C \times H \times W}$, coarse-scale features: $\mathbf{U_3} \in \mathbb{R}^{C \times H/2 \times W/2}$. Firstly, we exploit one convolutional layer with kernel size 1 to extend fine-scale features dimension. Then, two global average pooling layers with stride 2 are employed for getting temporary multi-scale cost volume:

$$\mathbf{C_1} = \text{Conv}_{3 \times 3}(\mathbf{U_1}) \tag{7}$$

$$\mathbf{C_2} = \mathcal{F}_{gp}(\mathbf{C_1}), \mathbf{C_3} = \mathcal{F}_{gp}(\mathbf{C_2}) \tag{8}$$

where $\mathcal{F}_{gp}$ is global average pooling operator and $\mathbf{C_1} \in \mathbb{R}^{C' \times H \times W}$, $\mathbf{C_2} \in \mathbb{R}^{C' \times H/2 \times W/2}$, $\mathbf{C_3} \in \mathbb{R}^{C' \times H/4 \times W/4}$.

Then, we compress the dimension of medium-scale features and combine it with (7) to get the final cost volume1:

$$\widetilde{\mathbf{U}}_2 = \mathcal{F}_{cc}(\mathbf{U}_2) \tag{9}$$

$$\widetilde{\mathbf{C}}_1 = \widetilde{\mathbf{U}}_2 \otimes \mathbf{C}_1 \tag{10}$$

where $\mathcal{F}_{cc}$ is channel compression operator, $\otimes$ denotes the pixel-wise multiplication and $\widetilde{\mathbf{U}}_2 \in \mathbb{R}^{1 \times H \times W}$, $\widetilde{\mathbf{C}}_1 \in \mathbb{R}^{C' \times H \times W}$. Further, we also compress the coarse-scale features:

$$\widetilde{\mathbf{U}}_3 = \mathcal{F}_{cc}(\mathbf{U}_3) \tag{11}$$

Combining (8) (9) (11), we can get the final cost volume2:

$$\widetilde{\mathbf{C}}_2 = (\mathcal{F}_{gp}(\widetilde{\mathbf{U}}_2) + \widetilde{\mathbf{U}}_3) \otimes \mathbf{C}_2 \tag{12}$$

Finally, we can get final cost volume3 based on (8) (11):

$$\widetilde{\mathbf{C}}_3 = \mathcal{F}_{gp}(\widetilde{\mathbf{U}}_3) \otimes \mathbf{C}_3 \tag{13}$$

Limited by the network structure of a single structure, the cost volume of RAFT [25] does not fully utilize the features of different scales. By using our proposed FSB twice, the features of three branches are generated, and the performance of the cost volume is improved. The cost volume represents the correlation of two adjacent frames of images, and its improvement is beneficial to the optical flow network for better pixel matching, so it will achieve better optical flow estimation results.

## 4    Experiments

### 4.1    Datasets

Four datasets are used to train our network, including FlyingChairs [4], FlyingThings [16], Sintel [28], and KITTI2015 [5], described in detail as follows.

**FlyingChairs.** FlyingChairs is a synthetic dataset presented in [4], which consists of 22872 image pairs and corresponding flow fields. The images show renderings of 3D chair models moving in front of random backgrounds from Flickr. There are chairs of different sizes in the FlyingChairs dataset. This dataset is now used as a basic training dataset for supervised methods.

**FlyingThings.** The FlyingThings [16] dataset consists of about 25000 stereo frames. Frames show everyday objects flying along randomized 3D trajectories. It contains more different scale objects than FlyingChairs. After the network has been trained using the FlyingChairs dataset, this dataset is typically used to fine-tune the network.

**Sintel.** Sintel [28] is a dataset for the evaluation of optical flow derived from the open source 3D animated short film. It is a subset of the movie containing 1628 frames from 35 scenes. The Sintel dataset presents a significant challenge for current methods.

**KITTI2015.** KITTI2015 [5] is a real-world dataset with an autonomous driving scene that includes 200 image pairs for testing and 200 image pairs for training with sparse ground truth flow. Since it is collected by lidar, the sparse optical flow is not conducive to the stable convergence of the optical flow network.

**Table 1.** More training details about each dataset.

| Dataset | Epoch | Learning rate | Weight decay | Batch size | Crop size |
|---------|-------|---------------|--------------|------------|-----------|
| FlyingChairs [4] | 100 | 4e-4 | 1e-4 | 10 | 496 × 368 |
| FlyingThings [16] | 100 | 1.25e-4 | 1e-4 | 6 | 720 × 400 |
| Sintel [28] | 100 | 1.25e-4 | 1e-5 | 6 | 768 × 368 |
| KITTI2015 [5] | 50 | 1e-4 | 1e-5 | 6 | 960 × 288 |

### 4.2 Training Details

The pre-training and fine-tuning strategies adopted to train our network are specified in what follows.

**Pre-Training.** We use FlyingChairs [4] and FlyingThings [16] datasets to pre-train our network. Because the data of optical flow is difficult to obtain, using synthetic datasets to pre-train the network is conducive to accelerating the convergence speed. We first train 100 epochs at a learning rate of 4e-4 in FlyingChairs [4]. Then we train 100 epochs in the FlyingThings [16] dataset at a learning rate of 1.25e-4. We specifically employ a variety of data augmentation techniques, such as color jittering, random cropping, random scaling, and random flipping of the horizontal and vertical axes.

**Fine-Tuning.** We fine-tune the pre-trained model for Sintel [28] utilizing both final and clean passes. Follow other studies, KITTI2015 [5] is also used to fine-tune our model. We train our network using "AdamW" optimizer with $\beta_1 = 0.9$ and $\beta_2 = 0.999$. We use Leaky ReLUs with a slope of 0.1 for the entire network. More training details about each dataset are shown in Table 1.

## 4.3   Results

We compared our network with several state-of-the-art networks on the Sintel [28] and KITTI2015 [5] datasets. Like in previous work, we use EPE (End Point Error) as a measure of the performance of our method. EPE can be defined as:

$$EPE = \sum_{i=1}^{W} \sum_{j=1}^{H} \sqrt{(u_{i,j} - u'_{i,j})^2 - (v_{i,j} - v'_{i,j})^2} \qquad (14)$$

where $u_{i,j}$ and $v_{i,j}$ are the estimated optical flow with two directions, horizontal and vertical. $u'_{j,j}$ and $v'_{i,j}$ are the ground truth flow.

Table 2 presents quantitative outcomes of various neural network-based techniques on the Sintel [28] benchmark dataset. We can observe that our method performs well when compared to other models both before and after fine-tuning. Compared with the most advanced methods such as RAFT [25] and SCV [14], our method achieves better optical flow estimation results for objects with different scales. On the KITTI2015 [5], our method earns comparable EPE and F1 scores to other methods.

**Table 2.** Performance comparison of different optical flow estimation methods on Sintel [28] and KITTI2015 [5]. Where 'C+T' denotes the results trained with FlyingChairs (C) [4] and FlyingThings (T) [16] and tested on the training sets of Sintel [28] and KITTI2015 [5], and 'C+T+S/K' denotes the results trained with Sintel [28] and KITTI2015 [5] training sets after the training on FlyingChairs (C) [4] and FlyingThings (T) [16], and tested with the Sintel [28] and KITTI2015 [5] test sets.

| Training Data | Method | Sintel (train) | | Sintel (test) | | KITTI2015 (train) | |
|---|---|---|---|---|---|---|---|
| | | Clean | Final | Clean | Final | F1-epe | F1-all |
| | HD3 [30] | 3.84 | 8.77 | – | – | 13.17 | 24 |
| | LiteFlowNet [9] | 2.48 | 4.04 | – | – | 10.39 | 28.5 |
| | PWC-Net [23] | 2.55 | 3.93 | 3.88 | 5.69 | 10.35 | 33.7 |
| C+T | VCN [29] | 2.21 | 3.68 | – | – | 8.36 | 25.1 |
| | FlowNet2 [11] | 2.02 | 3.54 | 3.96 | 6.02 | 10.08 | 30 |
| | RAFT [25] | 1.43 | 2.71 | 2.46 | 3.75 | 5.04 | 17.40 |
| | Flow1D [21] | 1.98 | 3.27 | 2.43 | 3.62 | 6.69 | 22.95 |
| | SCV [14] | **1.36** | 2.95 | 2.40 | 3.69 | 6.80 | 19.30 |
| | Ours | 1.39 | **2.66** | **2.36** | **3.64** | **4.92** | **16.20** |
| | FlowNet2 [11] | 1.45 | 2.01 | 4.16 | 5.74 | 2.30 | 6.8 |
| | HD3 [30] | 1.87 | 1.17 | 4.79 | 4.67 | 1.31 | 4.1 |
| | IRR-PWC [10] | 1.92 | 2.51 | 3.84 | 4.58 | 1.63 | 5.3 |
| C+T+S/K | VCN [29] | 1.88 | 3.20 | 2.93 | 4.57 | 1.76 | 4.43 |
| | MaskFlowNet [32] | 1.76 | 3.14 | 2.68 | 4.26 | 1.22 | 3.95 |
| | RAFT [25] | 0.77 | 1.20 | 2.08 | 3.41 | 0.64 | 1.5 |
| | Flow1D [21] | 0.75 | 1.23 | 2.24 | 3.81 | – | – |
| | SCV [14] | 0.78 | 1.18 | 1.98 | 3.36 | 0.86 | 1.78 |
| | Ours | **0.69** | **1.14** | **1.88** | **3.31** | **0.62** | **1.48** |

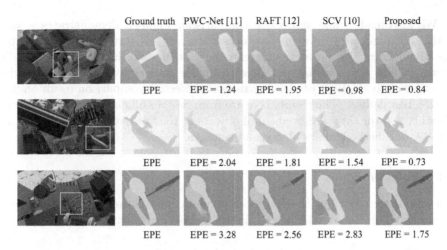

**Fig. 5.** Examples of predicted optical flow using different methods on images taken from the FlyingThings [16] dataset.

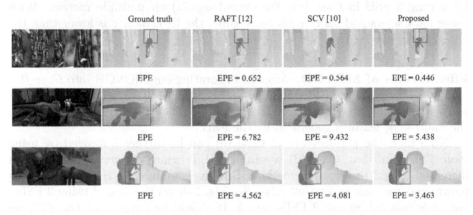

**Fig. 6.** Examples of predicted optical flow using different methods on images taken from the Sintel [28] Test dataset. We use HSV color space to represent the results of optical flow estimation, in which the direction is color coded and the length is saturation coded.

**Table 3.** An ablation study of four cases conducted on the dataset Sintel [28].

| Case | RAFT | FSB | Number | MCVGB | Params | Flops | Time | EPE |
|------|------|-----|--------|-------|--------|-------|------|-----|
| (a) | ✓ | – | – | – | 5.70M | 3.43G | 100ms | 1.200 |
| (b) | – | ✓ | 2 | – | 4.82M | 3.22G | 94ms | 1.186 |
| (c) | – | ✓ | 2 | ✓ | 5.20M | 3.34G | 96ms | 1.140 |
| (d) | – | ✓ | 3 | ✓ | 5.76M | 3.41G | 108ms | **1.124** |

We also made some subjective comparison. Figure 5 demonstrates a subjective comparison of different networks with a set of test images taken from the FlyingTings [16] dataset. One can see that our method can capture different scale objects and fine details with higher accuracy when compared with the other methods. Figure 6 demonstrates a subjective comparison result on Sintel [28] Test dataset. The results here are from Sintel's official evaluation system. Whether it is the overall movement of objects or the fine details of different scale objects, our method shows obvious advantages.

### 4.4  Ablation Study

To evaluate the contribution of each component of our method, an ablation study is conducted on the Sintel Clean(training) dataset, as shown in Table 3.

**Effectiveness of FSB.** Case (a) is on the study of the RAFT [25], it serves as a baseline in our comparison with the remaining cases. Case (b) is established by adding 2 FSB in Case (a). We exceed case(a) on multiple metrics. With fewer parameters and shorter inference time, the EPE metric is lower than the benchmark (1.20 → 1.186).

**Effectiveness of MCVGB.** After incorporating our MCVGB into Case (b), an 0.06 EPE decline is yielded in Case (c) (1.20 → 1.140). The MCVGB cannot be used alone because its multi-scale cost volume generation strategy comes from the multi-scale features generated by the FSB.

Note that, the performance of Case (c) can be further improved by using more FSBs. For that, Case (d) is established, in which the number of FSBs is increased from 2 to 3 for our method. But the computation time and network parameters may not be cost-effective. So, Fig. 2 shows the case of using 2 FSBs, and it is easy to expand 2 FSBs into 3. It should be noted that the EPE we calculate is the average EPE of each pixel in a image. We verify the effectiveness of our module on a relatively simple dataset Sintel Clean (training).

## 5  Conclusion

An object-scale adaptive optical flow estimation network has been proposed for optical flow estimation, in which multi-scale image features are extracted with feature selectable block and jointly used to produce multi-scale cost volume. Previous work focus on reducing the amount of calculation of the cost volume. Our network can enrich the ways to obtain the cost volume without increasing the amount of calculation. Specifically, our network uses feature maps of different scales generated by multiple paths to help cost volume learn, so we get more accurate pixel matching results. Then, the above blocks can produce more accurate optical flow estimation results. Experimental results obtained on benchmark datasets have clearly shown that our proposed method is able to capture fine details of various scale objects with high accuracy and thus deliver superior performance over many existing methods.

**Acknowledgements.** This work was supported in part by the Natural Science Foundation of the Jiangsu Higher Education Institutions of China under Grant 21KJA520007, in part by the National Natural Science Foundation of China under Grant 61572341, in part by the Priority Academic Program Development of Jiangsu Higher Education Institutions, in part by Collaborative Innovation Center of Novel Software Technology and Industrialization, and in part by the NTU-WASP Joint Project under Grants M4082184.

# References

1. Brox, T., Bruhn, A., Papenberg, N., Weickert, J.: High accuracy optical flow estimation based on a theory for warping. In: Pajdla, T., Matas, J. (eds.) ECCV 2004. LNCS, vol. 3024, pp. 25–36. Springer, Heidelberg (2004). https://doi.org/10.1007/978-3-540-24673-2_3
2. Brox, T., Malik, J.: Large displacement optical flow: descriptor matching in variational motion estimation. IEEE Trans. Pattern Anal. Mach. Intell. (TPAMI) **33**, 500-13 (2011)
3. C, Y., X, B., Y, F.: LightPIVNet: An effective convolutional neural network for particle image velocimetry. IEEE Trans. Instrum. Meas. **70**, 1–1 (2021)
4. Dosovitskiy, A., et al.: FlowNet: Learning optical flow with convolutional networks. In: International Conference on Computer Vision (ICCV), pp. 2758–2766 (2015)
5. Geiger, A., Lenz, P., Urtasun, R.: Are we ready for autonomous driving? the KITTI vision benchmark suite. In: IEEE Conference on Computer Vision and Pattern Recognition (CVPR), pp. 3354–3361 (2012)
6. Ghaywate, P., Vyas, F., Telang, S., Mangale, S.: A deep learning approach for motion segmentation using an optical flow technique. In: IEEE Conference on Computer Vision and Pattern Recognition (CVPR), pp. 1–6 (2019)
7. He, K., Zhang, X., Ren, S., Sun, J.: Deep residual learning for image recognition. In: IEEE Conference on Computer Vision and Pattern Recognition (CVPR), pp. 770–778 (2016)
8. Hosni, A., Rhemann, C.: Fast cost-volume filtering for visual correspondence and beyond. IEEE Trans. Pattern Anal. Mach. Intell. (TPAMI) **35**, 504–511 (2013)
9. Hui, T., Tang, X., Loy, C.C.: LiteFlowNet: A lightweight convolutional neural network for optical flow estimation. In: IEEE Conference on Computer Vision and Pattern Recognition (CVPR), pp. 8981–8989 (2018)
10. Hur, J., Roth, S.: Iterative residual refinement for joint optical flow and occlusion estimation. In: IEEE Conference on Computer Vision and Pattern Recognition (CVPR), pp. 5754–5763 (2019)
11. Ilg, E., Mayer, N., Saikia, T., Keuper, M., Dosovitskiy, A., Brox, T.: FlowNet 2.0: Evolution of optical flow estimation with deep networks. In: IEEE Conference on Computer Vision and Pattern Recognition (CVPR), pp. 1647–1655 (2017)
12. Jaderberg, M., Simonyan, K., Zisserman, A.: Spatial transformer networks. In: Advances in Neural Information Processing Systems. pp. 2017–2025 (2015)
13. Jayasundara, V., Roy, D., Fernando, B.: Flowcaps: Optical flow estimation with capsule networks for action recognition. In: IEEE Winter Conference on Applications of Computer Visio (WACV), pp. 3408–3417 (2021)

14. Jiang, S., Lu, Y., Li, H., Hartley, R.: Learning optical flow from a few matches. In: IEEE Conference on Computer Vision and Pattern Recognition (CVPR), pp. 16592–16600 (2021)
15. Li, X., Wang, W., Hu, X., Yang, J.: Selective kernel networks. In: IEEE Conference on Computer Vision and Pattern Recognition (CVPR), pp. 510–519 (2019)
16. Mayer, N., Ilg, E.: A large dataset to train convolutional networks for disparity, optical flow, and scene flow estimation. In: IEEE Conference on Computer Vision and Pattern Recognition (CVPR), pp. 4040–4048 (2016)
17. Papenberg, N., Bruhn, A., Brox, T., Didas, S., Weickert, J.: Highly accurate optic flow computation with theoretically justified warping. IEEE Int. J. Comput. Vision (IJCV) **67**, 141–158 (2006)
18. Ranjan, A., Black, M.J.: Optical flow estimation using a spatial pyramid network. In: IEEE Conference on Computer Vision and Pattern Recognition (CVPR), pp. 2720–2729 (2017)
19. Revaud, J., Weinzaepfel, P., Harchaoui, Z., Schmid, C.: Epicflow: Edge-preserving interpolation of correspondences for optical flow. In: IEEE Conference on Computer Vision and Pattern Recognition (CVPR), pp. 1164–1172 (2015)
20. Scharstein, D., Szeliski, R.: A taxonomy and evaluation of dense two-frame stereo correspondence algorithms. IEEE International J. Comput. Vis. (IJCV) **47**, 7–42 (2002)
21. Scharstein, D., Szeliski, R.: High-resolution optical flow from 1d attention and correlation. In: International Conference on Computer Vision (ICCV), pp. 10478–10487 (2021)
22. Sun, D., Roth, S., Black, M.J.: A quantitative analysis of current practices in optical flow estimation and the principles behind them. IEEE Int. J. Comput. Vis. (IJCV) **106**, 115–137 (2014)
23. Sun, D., Yang, X., Liu, M., Kautz, J.: PWC-Net: CNNs for optical flow using pyramid, warping, and cost volume. In: IEEE Conference on Computer Vision and Pattern Recognition (CVPR), pp. 8934–8943 (2018)
24. Szegedy, C., Liu, W., Jia, Y.: Going deeper with convolutions. In: IEEE Conference on Computer Vision and Pattern Recognition (CVPR), pp. 1–9 (2015)
25. Teed, Z., Deng, J.: RAFT: Recurrent all-pairs field transforms for optical flow. In: European Conference on Computer Vision (ECCV), pp. 402–419 (2020)
26. Wang, H., Cai, P., Fan, R., Sun, Y., Liu, M.: End-to-end interactive prediction and planning with optical flow distillation for autonomous driving. In: IEEE Conference on Computer Vision and Pattern Recognition (CVPR) Workshops, pp. 2229–2238 (2021)
27. Wang, L., Koniusz, P., Huynh, D.: Hallucinating IDT descriptors and I3D optical flow features for action recognition with CNNs. In: International Conference on Computer Vision (ICCV), pp. 8697–8707 (2019)
28. Wulff, J., Butler, D.J., Stanley, G.B., Black, M.J.: Lessons and insights from creating a synthetic optical flow benchmark. In: Fusiello, A., Murino, V., Cucchiara, R. (eds.) ECCV 2012. LNCS, vol. 7584, pp. 168–177. Springer, Heidelberg (2012). https://doi.org/10.1007/978-3-642-33868-7_17
29. Yang, G., Ramanan, D.: Volumetric correspondence networks for optical flow. In: Advances in Neural Information Processing Systems, pp. 793–803 (2019)
30. Yin, Z., Darrell, T., Yu, F.: Hierarchical discrete distribution decomposition for match density estimation. In: IEEE Conference on Computer Vision and Pattern Recognition (CVPR), pp. 6044–6053 (2019)

31. Zhao, C., Feng, C., Li, D., Li, S.: Optical flow-auxiliary multi-task regression network for direct quantitative measurement, segmentation and motion estimation. In: Association for the Advancement of Artificial Intelligence (AAAI), pp. 1218–1225 (2020)
32. Zhao, S., Sheng, Y., Dong, Y., Chang, E.I., Xu, Y.: MaskFlowNet: Asymmetric feature matching with learnable occlusion mask. In: IEEE Conference on Computer Vision and Pattern Recognition (CVPR), pp. 6277–6286 (2020)
33. Zuehlke, D., Posada, D.: Autonomous satellite detection and tracking using optical flow. CoRR abs/2204.07025 (2022)

# A Task-Aware Dual Similarity Network for Fine-Grained Few-Shot Learning

Yan Qi[1], Han Sun[1(✉)], Ningzhong Liu[1], and Huiyu Zhou[2]

[1] Nanjing University of Aeronautics and Astronautics, Jiangsu Nanjing, China
`sunhan@nuaa.edu.cn`
[2] School of Computing and Mathematical Sciences, University of Leicester, Leicester, UK

**Abstract.** The goal of fine-grained few-shot learning is to recognize sub-categories under the same super-category by learning few labeled samples. Most of the recent approaches adopt a single similarity measure, that is, global or local measure alone. However, for fine-grained images with high intra-class variance and low inter-class variance, exploring global invariant features and discriminative local details is quite essential. In this paper, we propose a Task-aware Dual Similarity Network (TDSNet), which applies global features and local patches to achieve better performance. Specifically, a local feature enhancement module is adopted to activate the features with strong discriminability. Besides, task-aware attention exploits the important patches among the entire task. Finally, both the class prototypes obtained by global features and discriminative local patches are employed for prediction. Extensive experiments on three fine-grained datasets demonstrate that the proposed TDSNet achieves competitive performance by comparing with other state-of-the-art algorithms.

**Keywords:** Fine-grained image classification · Few-shot learning · Feature enhancement

## 1 Introduction

As one of the most important problems in the field of artificial intelligence, fine-grained image classification [6,8] aims to identify objects of sub-categories under the same super-category. Different from the traditional image classification task [21,22], the images of sub-categories are similar to each other, which makes fine-grained recognition still a popular and challenging topic in computer vision.

Benefiting from the development of Convolution Neural Networks (CNNs), fine-grained image classification has made significant progress. Most approaches typically rely on supervision from a large number of labeled samples. In contrast, humans can identify new classes with only few labeled examples. Recently, some studies [25,31] focus on a more challenging setting, which aims to recognize fine-grained images from few samples, and is called fine-grained few-shot learning

© The Author(s), under exclusive license to Springer Nature Switzerland AG 2022
S. Khanna et al. (Eds.): PRICAI 2022, LNCS 13631, pp. 606–618, 2022.
https://doi.org/10.1007/978-3-031-20868-3_45

(FG-FSL). Learning from fine-grained images with few samples brings two challenges. On the one hand, images in the same category are quite different due to poses, illumination conditions, backgrounds, etc. So how to capture invariant features in limited samples is a particularly critical problem. On the other hand, it is complicated to distinguish subtle visual appearance clues on account of the small differences between categories. Therefore, we consider that the invariant global structure and the discriminative local details of objects are both crucial for fine-grained few-shot classification.

To effectively learn latent patterns from few labeled images, many approaches [7,33] have been proposed in recent years. These methods can be roughly divided into two branches: the meta-learning methods and the metric learning ones. Metric learning has attracted more and more attention due to its simplicity and effectiveness, and our work will focus on such methods. Traditional approaches such as matching network [29] and relation network [27] usually utilize global features for recognition. However, the distribution of these image-level global features cannot be accurately estimated because of the sparseness of the samples. In addition, discriminative clues may not be detected only by relying on global features. CovaMNet [15] and DN4 [16] introduce the deep local descriptors which are exploited to describe the distribution with each class feature. Furthermore, although these methods learn abundant features, they deal with each support class independently and cannot employ the contextual information of the whole task to generate task-specific features. In conclusion, the importance of different parts changes with different tasks.

In this paper, we propose a Task-aware Dual Similarity Network (TDSNet) for fine-grained few-shot learning, which makes full use of both global invariant features and discriminative local details of images. More specifically, first, a local feature enhancement module is employed to activate discriminative semantic parts by matching the predicted distribution between objects and parts. Second, in the dual similarity module, the proposed TDSNet calculates the class prototypes as global invariant features. Especially, in the local similarity branch, task-aware attention is adopted to select important image patches for the current task. By considering the context of the entire support set as a whole, the key patches in the task are selected and weighted without paying too much attention to the unimportant parts. Finally, both global and local similarities are employed for the final classification. We conduct comprehensive experiments on three popular fine-grained datasets to demonstrate the effectiveness of our proposed method. Especially, our method can also have good performance when there is only one training image.

## 2  Related Work

**Few Shot Learning.** Few-shot learning aims at recognizing unseen classes with only few samples. The recently popular literature on few-shot learning can be roughly divided into the following two categories: meta-learning based methods and metric-learning based methods.

Meta-learning based methods attempt to learn a good optimizer to update model parameters. MAML [9] is dedicated to learning a good parameter initialization so that the model can adapt to the new task after training on few samples. Ravi et al. [24] propose a meta-learner optimizer based on LSTM to optimize a classifier while also studying an initialization for the learner that contains task-aware knowledge.

Metric-learning based methods aim to measure the similarity by learning an appropriate metric that quantifies the relationship between the query images and support sets. Koch et al. [13] adopt a siamese convolutional neural network to learn generic image representations, which is performed as a binary classification network. Lifchitz et al. [18] directly predict classification for each local representation and calculates the loss. DN4 [16] employs k-nearest neighbors to construct an image-to-class search space that utilizes deep local representations. Unlike DN4, which is most relevant to our work, we argue that considering each support class independently may capture features shared among classes that are unimportant for classification. In this paper, task-aware local representations will be detected to explore richer information.

**Fine-grained Image Classification.** Because some early approaches [1,3] require a lot of bounding boxes or part annotations as supervision that needs a high cost of expert knowledge, more and more researchers are turning their attention to weakly supervised methods [20,23] that rely only on image-level annotations. Inspired by different convolutional feature channels corresponding to different types of visual modes, MC-Loss [5] proposes a mutual-channel loss that consists of a discriminality component and a diversity component to get the channels with locally discriminative regions for a specific class. TDSA-Loss [4] obtains multi-regional and multi-granularity features by constraining mid-level features with the attention generated by high-level features. Different from these methods, we consider that the discriminability of local features obtained only by the attention maps may not be guaranteed. In order to overcome this limitation, the proposed TDSNet activates the local representations with strong discriminability by matching the distribution between the global features and their sub-features, so that the discriminability of global features at fine-grained scales is improved.

## 3    Method

### 3.1    Problem Definition

In this paper, the proposed TDSNet also follows the common setup of other few-shot learning methods. Specifically, few-shot classification is usually formalized as N-way K-shot classification problems. Let $S$ denote a support set that contains $N$ distinct image classes, and each class contains $K$ labeled samples. Given a query set $Q$, the purpose of few-shot learning is classifying each unlabeled sample in $Q$ according to the support set $S$. However, limited samples in $S$ make it difficult to efficiently train a network. Therefore, auxiliary set $A$ is always introduced to learn transferable knowledge to improve classification performance. Note that $S$ and $A$ have their own distinct label spaces without intersections.

In order to learn transferable knowledge better, the episode training mechanism [29] is adopted in the training phase. Specifically, at each iteration, support set $AS$ and query set $AQ$ are randomly selected from auxiliary set $A$ to simulate a new few-shot classification task. In the training process, multiple episodes are constructed to train the model.

## 3.2 Overview

The overall framework of our method is shown in Fig. 1. First of all, images are fed into the feature extractor which is usually implemented by CNN or ResNet [11] to get image embeddings. In this stage, a LFE module is designed to explore local details with strong discriminability by the supervision of global features. Next, the features are used as inputs to the metric module. Our metric module adopts dual similarity that is composed of global and local metric branches, which can not only exploit the intra-class invariance of global features but also explore rich clues hidden in local details. Specially, in the local similarity branch, the discriminative patches are reweighted to eliminate noise, i.e., patches shared in the task, and enhance the significant regions. The proposed TDSNet focuses on the relationships among local patches rather than isolated individuals. Finally, the mean value of global and local classification scores is reported as the final result. LFE module is only used during training.

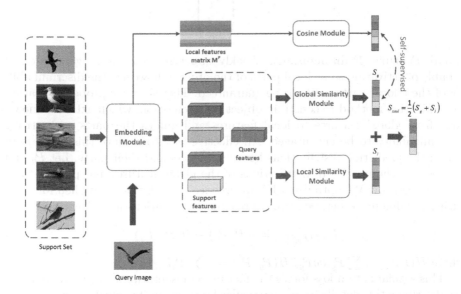

**Fig. 1.** Framework of the proposed TDSNet.

### 3.3   Local Feature Enhancement (LFE) Module

**Weakly Supervised Attention Generation.** Parts of the objects are predicted first. In this paper, we explore discriminative regions in a weakly supervised manner. Besides, instead of using a pre-trained convolutional neural network, we employ an attention generation strategy.

For the input image $X$, the feature $F \in R^{H \times W \times C}$ is explored through the feature embedding module $f_\varphi$, where $H$, $W$, and $C$ denote the height, width, and the number of channels of the feature respectively. Then, the attention maps $A^a \in R^{H \times W \times m}$ for each image can be determined by

$$A^a = f(F) = \bigcup_{k=1}^{m} A_k^a \tag{1}$$

$f(\cdot)$ represents a convolution operation and $A_k^a$ is the k-th local attention map. Similar to the bilinear pooling [10,28], element-wise multiplication between $A^a$ and $F$ is performed to produce the part feature map $f$, which can be expressed as

$$f_k = g(A_k^a \odot F), k = 1, 2, \ldots, m \tag{2}$$

$f_k$ is the k-th local feature, $\odot$ denotes element-wise multiplication, and $g(\cdot)$ is the global average pooling operation. Finally, we stack these part maps to obtain the final part feature matrix. It can be represented as

$$M^P = \begin{pmatrix} f_1 \\ f_2 \\ \ldots \\ f_m \end{pmatrix} \tag{3}$$

**Local Feature Enhancement.** Weakly supervised attention generation is capable of activating some local parts of the objects, however, the discriminability of these local parts may not be guaranteed. Therefore, we propose a feature regularization method to constrain object representation, which extracts knowledge from global features to local features and guides the parts with strong discriminability to be encouraged. An effective way to achieve this effect is to match the prediction distributions between objects and their parts. Let $P_g$ and $P_a$ describe the predicted distributions of the global features and part features $M^P$ respectively. We optimize a KL divergence loss[19] that is applied for measuring the difference between two probability distributions as follows,

$$L_{KL(P_g \| P_a)} = -H(P_g) + H(P_g, P_a) \tag{4}$$

where $H(P_g) = -\sum P_g log P_g$, $H(P_g, P_a) = -\sum P_g log P_a$

This regularization loss forces the feature representation learning to focus on the discriminative details from a particular local region, by which we can further filter out unnecessary and misleading information to improve the discriminability of global features at fine-grained scales. Only the one with global features is used for final target prediction.

### 3.4 Dual Similarity Module

**Global Similarity.** This branch adopts the global feature maps for classification, which employs the cosine distance as a metric function. The feature maps are fed into two convolution blocks ($h_{conv}$) to learn generic knowledge with global representations in the images, followed by a cosine similarity $cos(\cdot)$ to measure the similarity. For the query image $X_q$, the global similarity score corresponding to the support class $X_s$ is determined as follows,

$$S_g = cos(h_{conv}(\frac{1}{K}\sum_{s=1}^{K} f_\varphi(X_s)), h_{conv}(f_\varphi(X_q)))  \tag{5}$$

We take the mean value of feature mappings from each support class as the class prototype, which is used to calculate the global structure so that the invariant features within the class can be learned.

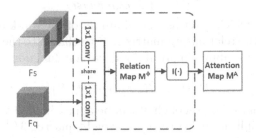

**Fig. 2.** The framework of task-aware attention.

**Task-aware Local Similarity.** Some recent works, such as DN4 and ConvM-Net, have shown that features based on local descriptors are richer than global. Specifically, local descriptors are able to capture local subtle information which is of greater benefit for fine-grained image recognition. For an image feature $F \in R^{H \times W \times C}$, it is regarded as a set of r(r = HW) C-dimensions local feature descriptors, which can be expressed as

$$f_\varphi(X) = [x_1, \ldots, x_r] \in R^{C \times r}  \tag{6}$$

where $x_i$ denotes the i-th depth local descriptor. These local descriptors correspond to spatial local patches in the raw image. Basically, for each query image $X_q$, we get HW local descriptors to estimate its distribution, denoted as $L^q = f_\varphi(X_q) \in R^{C \times HW}$. Similarly, for support set, all local descriptors of class prototypes will be employed together as $L^s = f_\varphi(X_s) \in R^{C \times NHW}$. Next, we calculate the similarity matrix $M$ between query image and support set by

$$M_{i,j} = cos(L_i^q, L_j^s)  \tag{7}$$

where $i \in 1, \ldots, HW$, $j \in 1, \ldots, NHW$, $cos(\cdot)$ represents cosine similarity. Each row in matrix $M$ represents the similarity of a specific query patch to all patches of the support set.

We then construct the task-aware attention map to reweight these parts. As shown in Fig. 2, we built another relation matrix $M^\phi$ for the next operation, which is obtained by a convolution layer and a cosine similarity layer. We consider that local descriptors shared by multiple classes in the task do not contribute to the classification. For instance, if the query image patch has a high level of similarity to multiple patches in the support set, it has a minuscule contribution to classification. Therefore, we distract attention to make local descriptors that are shared in the task get relatively small attention values. The attention matrix $M^A$ is defined as

$$M^A_{i,j} = \frac{I(M^\phi_{i,j})}{\sum_j I(M^\phi_{i,j})} \tag{8}$$

$$I(x) = \begin{cases} x, \text{ if } x > \beta \\ 0, \text{ otherwise.} \end{cases} \tag{9}$$

$\beta$ is the threshold, which is set as the minimum of the top-k elements obtained by k-NN [2] from the relationship matrix $M^\phi$ to eliminate the noises. Since $I(\cdot)$ is indifferentiable, we approximate it by a variant function of sigmoid with a hyperparameter t as

$$I^*(x) = x/(1 + exp^{-t(x-\beta)}) \tag{10}$$

Theoretically, when t is large enough, it can be approximated as $I(\cdot)$. We perform element-wise multiplication between the weight matrix $M^A$ and the relation matrix $M$. Finally, the local similarity score for n-th class between the query image $X_q$ and the support class $X_s$ can be calculated by applying the attention map to the similarity matrix $M$ as follows:

$$S_l = \frac{1}{HW} \sum_{i=1}^{HW} \sum_{j=1}^{HW} (M^A \odot M)_{i,j} \tag{11}$$

The total classification score is formulated as follows which is used to make a final prediction:

$$S_{total} = \frac{1}{2}(S_g + S_l) \tag{12}$$

In particular, our local similarity branch only introduces a small number of parameters and the overfitting problem in the few-shot learning can also be alleviated to some extent.

### 3.5   Loss Function

In the training phase, the purpose is to learn a task agnostic network for classification. We can obtain $y^g_q$ and $y^l_q$ as two predicted results by global and local branches respectively. Then, predicted values are compared with the ground-truth label $y_q$ to calculate two classification losses.

$$L^g_q = \sum_j^N (y^g_{q,j} - y_{q,j})^2, q = 1, \ldots, |Q| \tag{13}$$

$$L_q^l = \sum_j^N (y_{q,j}^l - y_{q,j})^2, q = 1, \ldots, |Q| \tag{14}$$

In the end, the whole loss function can be written as:

$$L_{total} = L_q^g + L_q^l + \lambda L_{KL} \tag{15}$$

where $\lambda$ is a trade-off parameter used to control the relative importance of the loss $L_{KL}$. Empirically, we set $\lambda = 0.4$.

## 4  Experiment

### 4.1  Datasets and Experimental Setting

We evaluate our method on three widely used fine-grained datasets, namely CUB-200-2011 [30], Stanford Dogs [12], and Stanford Cars [14]. We conduct experiments under the 5-way 1-shot and 5-way 5-shot settings. All images are resized to 84 × 84 before being fed into the feature extraction module. In the training process, episode training mechanism is used to train our model. For the three datasets, models are trained for 600 and 400 epochs corresponding to the 5-way 1-shot and 5-way 5-shot tasks, respectively. We use Adam optimizer to train the network with the initial learning rate of 0.001, decaying by half every 100,000 episodes. In the testing phase, the top-1 accuracy with 95% confidence interval will be reported by random sampling of 600 episodes from the test set.

**Table 1.** Comparison with typical FSL and FG-FSL methods on three fine-grained datasets. The best and the second best results are highlighted in red and green respectively.

| Dataset | CUB Birds | | Stanford Dogs | | Stanford Cars | |
|---|---|---|---|---|---|---|
| Setting | 1-shot | 5-shot | 1-shot | 5-shot | 1-shot | 5-shot |
| Matching Net [29] | 45.30±1.03 | 59.50±1.01 | 35.80±0.99 | 47.50±1.03 | 34.80±0.98 | 47.50±1.03 |
| Prototype Net [26] | 37.36±1.00 | 45.28±1.03 | 37.59±1.00 | 48.19±1.03 | 40.90±1.01 | 52.93±1.03 |
| Relation Net [27] | 59.58±0.94 | 77.62±0.67 | 43.05±0.86 | 63.42±0.76 | 45.48±0.88 | 60.26±0.85 |
| MAML [9] | 54.92±0.95 | 73.18±0.67 | 44.64±0.89 | 60.20±0.80 | 46.71±0.89 | 60.73±0.85 |
| PCM [32] | 42.10±1.96 | 62.48±1.21 | 28.78±2.33 | 46.92±2.00 | 29.63±2.38 | 52.28±1.46 |
| CovaMNet [15] | 52.42±0.76 | 63.76±0.64 | 49.10±0.76 | 63.04±0.65 | 56.65±0.86 | 71.33±0.63 |
| DN4 [16] | 46.84±0.81 | 74.92±0.64 | 45.41±0.76 | 63.51±0.62 | 59.84±0.80 | 88.65±0.44 |
| BSNet [17] | 65.89±1.00 | 78.48±0.65 | 51.68±0.95 | 67.93±0.75 | 54.39±0.92 | 73.37±0.77 |
| FOT [31] | 67.46±0.68 | 83.19±0.43 | 49.32±0.74 | 68.18±0.69 | 54.55±0.73 | 73.69±0.65 |
| ours | 69.34±0.89 | 80.34±0.59 | 54.48±0.87 | 69.45±0.69 | 62.14±0.91 | 75.64±0.72 |

## 4.2   Comparison with State-of-the-art Methods

To evaluate the validity of the proposed TDSNet, we conduct extensive experiments on three classic fine-grained datasets with 5-way 1-shot and 5-way 5-shot task settings and compare them with some SOTA methods.

As is demonstrated in Table 1, the results compared with four classical few-shot methods and five fine-grained few-shot methods illustrate that our method achieves good performance on all three datasets. Specifically, the proposed TDSNet performs better on the more challenging 1-shot task and shows high stability. The reason for this progress is that our approach focuses on the discriminative parts and gives them higher weights. Additionally, the changes in visual appearance may not affect our TDSNet because we also pay attention to invariant global structure.

## 4.3   Ablation Study

**Table 2.** Ablation study on the proposed components on CUB. LFE: local feature enhancement module, LS: local similarity module, att: task-aware attention.

| Method | 1-shot | 5-shot |
| --- | --- | --- |
| (a)Baseline | 63.33±1.01 | 77.64±0.67 |
| (b)Baseline+LFE | 65.20±0.99 | 78.77±0.67 |
| (c)Baseline+LFE+LS w/o att | 67.02±0.96 | 79.59±0.64 |
| (d)Baseline+LFE+LS w/ att | 69.34±0.89 | 80.34±0.59 |

**Effectiveness of Local Feature Enhancement Module.** We use the feature embedding module and the global similarity metric module of this paper as the baseline. Table. 2 shows that the addition of the local enhancement module makes the accuracy significantly improved by 1.87% and 1.13% respectively, which is mainly due to the activation of the features with strong discriminability. In this way, we can further filter out misleading information so as to improve the discrimination of features.

**Effectiveness of Dual-Similarity.** Compared with the results that only employ the global similarity measurement module, dual similarity demonstrates its superiority. It proves that only global features are hard to detect some detailed information that is suitable for fine-grained features, while only local features are sensitive to some intra-class changes.

**Effectiveness of Task-Aware Attention.** We verify the effectiveness of task-aware attention on CUB, with 2.32% and 0.75% improvements respectively. Task-aware attention makes the network pay more attention to the features that are most relevant to the current task and reweight the key parts so that the features shared between classes will obtain less attention.

## 4.4 Visualization

As can be seen from Fig. 3, our TDSNet has less activation in the background and is more concentrated on the discriminative regions of objects, which demonstrates that the features can be semantically enhanced by our approach. It highlights the local details on raw images that represent different semantic patches with strong discriminability, such as the head and wings of a bird.

**Fig. 3.** Visualization of the features under Relation Network, DN4, BSNet and the proposed TDSNet on CUB. The redder the region, the more discriminative it is.

## 4.5 Number of Trainable Parameters

As Table. 3 shows, compared to the BSNet, which is also a bi-similarity method on the global feature, we have only half the number of parameters of this approach. This illustrates that although we adopt additional architectures to improve the performance, the proposed TDSNet only introduces a small number of the trainable parameters.

**Table 3.** Comparison of the number of trainable parameters along on CUB.

| Model | Params | 5-way 5-shot |
|---|---|---|
| Prototype network | 0.113M | 45.28 |
| Relation network | 0.229M | 77.62 |
| DN4 | 0.113M | 74.92 |
| BSNet(R&C) | 0.226M | 78.84 |
| TDSNet(ours) | 0.114M | 80.34 |

## 5   Conclusion

In this paper, we propose a Task-aware Dual Similarity Network (TDSNet) for FG-FSL, which consists of two designed components, a local feature enhancement module and a measurement module that combines global and task-aware local similarity. Specifically, the former is designed to fully explore the discriminative details suitable for fine-grained classification, while the latter explores similarity by taking multiple perspectives, both global and local. Extensive experiments demonstrate that our proposed TDSNet achieves competitive results. In the future, we intend to reinforce the features of the foreground object and eliminate the negative effect of complicated backgrounds.

## References

1. Berg, T., Belhumeur, P.N.: Poof: part-based one-versus-one features for fine-grained categorization, face verification, and attribute estimation. In: Computer Vision & Pattern Recognition (2013)
2. Boiman, O., Shechtman, E., Irani, M.: In defense of nearest-neighbor based image classification. In: IEEE Conference on Computer Vision & Pattern Recognition (2008)
3. Branson, S., Horn, G.V., Belongie, S., Perona, P.: Bird species categorization using pose normalized deep convolutional nets. In: British Machine Vision Conference 2014 (2014)
4. Chang, D., Zheng, Y., Ma, Z., Du, R., Liang, K.: Fine-grained visual classification via simultaneously learning of multi-regional multi-grained features (2021). arXiv:abs/2102.00367
5. Chang, D., Ding, Y., Xie, J., Bhunia, A.K., Li, X., Ma, Z., et al.: The devil is in the channels: mutual-channel loss for fine-grained image classification. IEEE Trans. Image Process. **29**, 4683–4695 (2020)
6. Chang, D., Pang, K., Zheng, Y., Ma, Z., Song, Y.Z., Guo, J.: Your "flamingo" is my "bird": fine-grained, or not. In: 2021 IEEE/CVF Conference on Computer Vision and Pattern Recognition (CVPR), pp. 11471–11480 (2021)
7. Chen, H., Li, H., Li, Y., Chen, C.: Multi-scale adaptive task attention network for few-shot learning (2020). arXiv:abs/2011.14479
8. Ding, Y., Ma, Z., Wen, S., Xie, J., Chang, D., Si, Z., et al.: AP-CNN: weakly supervised attention pyramid convolutional neural network for fine-grained visual classification. IEEE Trans. Image Process. **30**, 2826–2836 (2021)
9. Finn, C., Abbeel, P., Levine, S.: Model-agnostic meta-learning for fast adaptation of deep networks. In: International Conference on Machine Learning (2017)
10. Fu, J., Zheng, H., Tao, M.: Look closer to see better: recurrent attention convolutional neural network for fine-grained image recognition. In: IEEE Conference on Computer Vision & Pattern Recognition (2017)
11. He, K., Zhang, X., Ren, S., Sun, J.: Deep residual learning for image recognition. In: 2016 IEEE Conference on Computer Vision and Pattern Recognition (CVPR) (2016)
12. Khosla, A., Jayadevaprakash, N., Yao, B., Li, F.: Novel dataset for fine-grained image categorization. In: CVPR Workshop on Fine-Grained Visual Categorization (2013)

13. Koch, G., Zemel, R., Salakhutdinov, R.: Siamese neural networks for one-shot image recognition. In International Conference on Machine Learning, vol. 37 (2015)

14. Krause, J., Stark, M., Deng, J., Li, F.F.: 3D object representations for fine-grained categorization. In: IEEE International Conference on Computer Vision Workshops (2014)

15. Li, W., Xu, J., Huo, J., Wang, L., Luo, J.: Distribution consistency based covariance metric networks for few-shot learning. In: Thirty-Third AAAI Conference on Artificial Intelligence (2019)

16. Li, W., Wang, L., Xu, J., Huo, J., Gao, Y., Luo, J.: Revisiting local descriptor based image-to-class measure for few-shot learning. In: IEEE Conference on Computer Vision and Pattern Recognition, pp. 7260–7268 (2019)

17. Li, X., Wu, J., Sun, Z., Ma, Z., Cao, J., Xue, J.H.: BSNet: Bi-similarity network for few-shot fine-grained image classification. IEEE Trans. Image Process. **30**, 1318–1331 (2021)

18. Lifchitz, Y., Avrithis, Y., Picard, S., Bursuc, A.: Dense classification and implanting for few-shot learning. In: 2019 IEEE/CVF Conference on Computer Vision and Pattern Recognition (CVPR) (2020)

19. Luo, W., Yang, X., Mo, X., Lu, Y., Davis, L., Li, J., Yang, J., Lim, S.N.: Cross-x learning for fine-grained visual categorization. In: 2019 IEEE/CVF International Conference on Computer Vision (ICCV), pp. 8241–8250 (2019)

20. Lz, A., Sh, B., Wei, L.A.: Learning sequentially diversified representations for fine-grained categorization. Pattern Recognit. **121**, 108219 (2021)

21. Ma, Z., Lai, Y., Kleijn, W.B., Song, Y.Z., Wang, L., Guo, J.: Variational Bayesian learning for Dirichlet process mixture of inverted Dirichlet distributions in non-gaussian image feature modeling. IEEE Trans. Neural Netw. Learn. Syst. **30**(2), 449–463 (2019)

22. Ma, Z., Xie, J., Lai, Y., Taghia, J., Xue, J.H., Guo, J.: Insights into multiple/single lower bound approximation for extended variational inference in non-gaussian structured data modeling. IEEE Trans. Neural Netw. Learn. Syst. **31**(7), 2240–2254 (2020)

23. Rao, Y., Chen, G., Lu, J., Zhou, J.: Counterfactual attention learning for fine-grained visual categorization and re-identification. In: IEEE/CVF International Conference on Computer Vision, pp. 1025–1034 (2021)

24. Ravi, S., Larochelle, H.: Optimization as a model for few-shot learning. In: International Conference on Learning Representations (2017)

25. Shermin, T., Teng, S.W., Sohel, F., Murshed, M., Lu, G.: Integrated generalized zero-shot learning for fine-grained classification. Pattern Recogn. **122**, 108246 (2022)

26. Snell, J., Swersky, K., Zemel, R.: Prototypical networks for few-shot learning. In: Advances in Neural Information Processing Systems, vol. 30 (2017)

27. Sung, F., Yang, Y., Zhang, L., Xiang, T., Torr, P., Hospedales, T.: Learning to compare: relation network for few-shot learning. In: 2018 IEEE/CVF Conference on Computer Vision and Pattern Recognition, pp. 1199–1208 (2018)

28. Tao, H., Qi, H.: See better before looking closer: weakly supervised data augmentation network for fine-grained visual classification (2019). arXiv:1901.09891

29. Vinyals, O., Blundell, C., Lillicrap, T., kavukcuoglu, k., Wierstra, D.: Matching networks for one shot learning. In: Advances in Neural Information Processing Systems, vol. 29 (2016)

30. Wah, C., Branson, S., Welinder, P., Perona, P., Belongie, S.: The caltech-ucsd birds-200-2011 dataset. In: California Institute of Technology (2011)

31. Wang, C., Song, S., Yang, Q., Li, X., Huang, G.: Fine-grained few shot learning with foreground object transformation. Neurocomputing **466**, 16–26 (2021)
32. Wei, X., Wang, P., Liu, L., Shen, C., Wu, J.: Piecewise classifier mappings: learning fine-grained learners for novel categories with few examples. IEEE Trans. Image Process. **28**(12), 6116–6125 (2019)
33. Wu, Y., Zhang, B., Yu, G., Zhang, W., Wang, B., Chen, T., Fan, J.: Object-aware long-short-range spatial alignment for few-shot fine-grained image classification, pp. 107–115 (2021)

# Rotating Target Detection Based on Lightweight Network

Yunxu Jiao[1,2] , Qingmeng Zhu[2] , Hao He[2(✉)] , Tianci Zhao[2] ,
and Haihui Wang[1]

[1] Wuhan Institute of Technology, Wuhan 430205, China
[2] Institute of Software, Chinese Academy of Sciences, Beijing 100190, China
{qingmeng,hehao21,zhaotianci}@iscas.ac.cn

**Abstract.** Current rotating object detection task achieves good results based on large models. In order to reduce the size of model, we propose a lightweight network SFC (ShuffleNet combines FPN with CSL) for rotating target detection. SFC first introduces circular smooth label (CSL) to detect target rotations, which transforms the traditional angle regression problem into classification problem. Then, the lightweight ShuffleNetV2 is utilized as the backbone to reduce the number of parameters. ShuffleNetV2 is used for feature extraction, and CSL is introduced to address the periodic problem of angles. Comparative experiments were carried out on DOTA 1.5 dataset. The experimental results show that the proposed method reduces the parameter by nearly 90% with a slight loss of accuracy, and increases the inferencing speed by 40% at the same time.

**Keywords:** Rotating object detection · Remote sensing images · Light-weight network

## 1 Introduction

Rotating object detection is an important task in traditional object detection, which faces the challenges to detect objects with arbitrary rotation angle. At present, the applications of rotating object detection algorithms include detecting the direction of objects in remote sensing images, and applying rotating object detection in the field of e-commerce to detect commodity labels on shelves.

Most networks for rotating object detection use different rotation detectors for angle prediction. Among the existing rotating object detectors, the region regression based approaches occupy the mainstream position. Although such detectors achieve good performance, these methods all face the problem of angle periodicity to some extent (in Fig. 1). To address the angle periodicity problem, the method based on regional regression could be transformed into a method of classification problem, which avoids the problem of angular periodicity.

Y. Jiao and Q. Zhu—Contributed equally to this work.
This work is partially supported by the National Natural Science Foundation of China (62101552) and by the Key R&D Program of the Chinese Academy of Sciences (ZDRW-XH-2021-3-03).

S. Khanna et al. (Eds.): PRICAI 2022, LNCS 13631, pp. 619–630, 2022.
https://doi.org/10.1007/978-3-031-20868-3_46

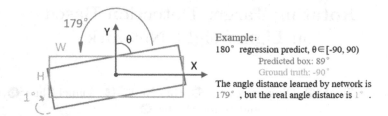

**Fig. 1.** The periodic (discontinuous boundary) problem in rotating object detectors.

Current classification based detectors working with One-Stage networks have achieved good performances, such as Yolov4 [1], RetinaNet [2]. However, since the scale of the remote sensing images are usually very large, the inference speed of such models are not satisfactory, and the parameters and weights will occupy a huge space, leading the model to be very heavy and difficult to run on the devices with power consumption and computational limitations.

To address the above problems, we try to explore whether a lightweight network can be used as the backbone network, and then combined with the rotation detector? The advantages of using a lightweight network as the backbone network are obvious, i.e., the model could have a faster inference speed, a small size of parameters. Therefore, such model could be expected to be deployed on the power and computation limited devices for real-time detection.

However, the existing lightweight models (such as SqueezeNet [3], MobileNet [4] and ShuffleNet [5] series, etc.) cannot detect rotating object. Among the current lightweight networks, ShuffleNetV2 hits a good trade-off between speed and accuracy. Under the same experimental environment, ShuffleNetV2 is more accurate than MobileNetV2. For the rotating object detector, we introduce the circular smooth label (CSL) [6], which is an efficient approach that transforms the angular regression problem into a classification problem to avoid beyond the boundary problems by using regression based method to predict angle.

Therefore, we propose a lightweight rotating object detection method, named SFC (ShuffleNet combines FPN with CSL). The overall structure of SFC is as follows: First, the ShuffleNetV2 network model is introduced as the backbone. Secondly, the neck part adopts the feature pyramid networks (FPN) [7] structure, and then SFC utilizes the CSL in the detector, and the labeling file format is the long-edge representation in rotational object detection. Further, an angular classification loss function is also introduced to learn the rotation information. Our main contributions are as follows:

(1) To the best of our knowledge, this is the first attempt to enable a lightweight network for rotating object detection based on the classification rotation detector (CSL).

(2) Compared with the conventional rotation detection method, our lightweight method has dropped about 90% parameters and weights, and the inference speed has increased to 28.0FPS compared to the 17.5FPS of the ResNet50+GWD [8] method, which is nearly 40%.

## 2    Related Works

In this section, we briefly review the related works about rotating object detection and lightweight networks, respectively.

### 2.1    Rotating Object Detection

Rotating object detection is mainly used in the detection of remote sensing images, which generally have the following characteristics: 1) complex background; 2) small detection objects; 3) objects in the aerial images with arbitrary rotation angles. Many works have been proposed in recent years, such as ROI Transformer [9], CAD Net [10], R3Det [11], CSL [6], FCOSR [12], DARDet [13], etc. The highest Mean Average Precision (mAP) on the dataset DOTA 1.0 [14] reaches about 70. Among them, the regression-based detection method is dominated, but such methods all face boundary problems i.e., predictions beyond the definition range. In order to solve the boundary problem, Xue Yang et al. designed Circular Smooth Label (CSL), an exploratory rotation detection method, which transforms the prediction of rotation angle from a regression problem to an angle classification problem, thus basically eliminating the problems caused by the boundary.

### 2.2    Lightweight Network

Many lightweight networks have been proposed in recent years. Some are classic lightweight network, such as SqueezeNet [3], MobileNet [4] and ShuffleNet [5] series, etc. SqueezeNet [3] series is one of the earliest studies focusing on lightweight networks, using the FIRE module for parameter compression. ShuffleNetV2 [5] proposes the channel split operation, which accelerates the network by reusing features. MobileNetV2 [4] proposes an innovative inverted residual with linear bottleneck unit.

However, among the existing lightweight models, there is no explicit lightweight rotating object detection method. Therefore, the motivation of this paper is to enable a lightweight network to do the rotating object detection.

## 3    Our Method

The overall architecture of SFC is shown in Fig. 2. First, the lightweight network ShuffleNetV2 is used as the backbone network, and the FPN structure is used to fuse features of different scales. Then, the rotating object detector is used for angle detection. After cutting and data augmentation of the training set, remote sensing images pass through the backbone network and the FPN structure, and finally the output is evaluated via the loss function. The detailed description of ShuffleNetV2 with FPN structure will be explained in Sect. 3.1. The CSL method and other loss functions will be explained in Sect. 3.2.

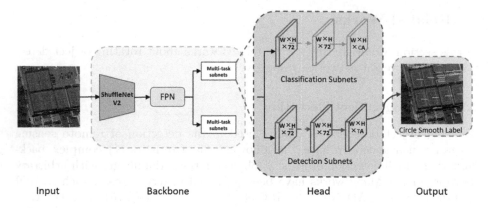

**Fig. 2.** SFC model architecture. "W" and "H" are the width and height respectively. "C" and "T" (red) represent the number of objects and angle categories respectively (Color figure online)

## 3.1 Lightweight Network Structure

ShuffleNetV2 modified the ShuffleNetV1 and proposed four guidelines for lightweight networks. The basic module unit of ShuffleNetV2 contains two modules, which are the basic module and the down-sampling module. We set the width hyper-parameter to 0.5 and set the output channels of each stage. Then an image (224*224) goes through a 3*3 convolution with a stride of 2 and a max-pooling layer with a pooling window size of 3. Then go through stage2, stage3, and stage4 respectively (Fig. 3). There are 4, 8, and 4 basic module units of ShuffleNetV2 in these three stages. The first module step is 2 in each basic module unit, and the rest steps are 1. After the ShuffleNetV2 network, the features extracted by stage3 and stage4 are input into the FPN layer for feature fusion.

The role of ShuffleNetV2 in our method is to perform feature extraction in remote sensing images. But the information of small object features in remote sensing images is dense and much information is lost after layers of down-sampling in the network. Therefore, we add the FPN [7] structure behind the backbone network to achieve multi-scale feature fusion. So that the network can extract the information of the deep network semantics, as well as the underlying fine-grained information, enhancing the detection accuracy of small objects.

The concept of FPN [7] mainly addresses the multi-scale problem in object detection and substantially improves the performance of small object detection without increasing the computation of the original model by changing the connections between each network layer. In the method we use, the channels output from the ShuffleNetV2 network are [−1, 24, 48, 96, 192], and then the input channels of the FPN structure are defined as [outchannels[−2]+outchannels[−1], outchannels[−1], outdepth], the number of channels is 288, 192, 72 respectively.

After the FPN layer, the feature maps output by stage3 and stage4 in the backbone network are fused with the up-sampled feature map.

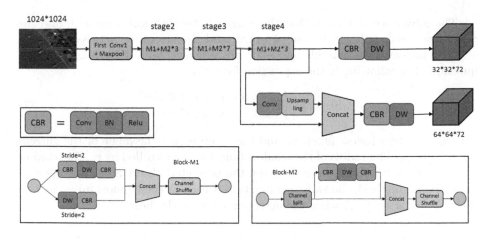

**Fig. 3.** Detailed structure diagram of the lightweight network.

## 3.2 Circular Smoothing Label for Classification

There are some problems in common angle regression methods, such as the periodicity of angular (PoA) problem shared by the OpenCV definition (90°-regression-based) and the long-edge definition (180°-regression-based), and the exchangeability of edges (EoE) problem of the OpenCV definition. These problems increase the difficulty of the model regression and the loss. The reason for the above problems is that the ideal prediction results are outside defined range, which leads to a boundary problem and generates a large loss value.

The Circular Smooth Label (CSL) method converts the angle prediction from a regression problem to a classification problem, which classifies one degree into one category, and use window function, as shown in the following Fig. 4.

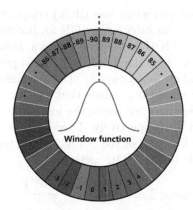

**Fig. 4.** The circular smooth label (CSL) for angle classification in SFC, adjacency of −90 to 89°, which avoids periodic problem and increases angular tolerance.

The advantage of CSL is that the range of classification is limited, and the prediction result will not be out of range, and the tolerance between adjacent angles is increased, so that $89°$ and $-90°$ are adjacent, solving the angle Periodic question. The following is the expression for CSL:

$$\text{CSL}(x) = \begin{cases} g(x), & \theta - r < x < \theta + r \\ 0, & \text{otherwise} \end{cases} \tag{1}$$

The $g(x)$ is the window function, and the $\theta$ represents the angle of the current bounding box. The radius of the window function is controlled by $r$. The window function measures the distance between the predicted object angle and the real angle. In our method, the Gaussian function is used as the window function, and the radius $r$ is set to 2, when the detection effect is the best.

### 3.3 Loss Function

There are five loss functions used in our method, namely bounding box border regression loss (lbox), class classification loss (lcls), confidence loss (lobj), theta angle classification loss (langle), and total loss (loss). We have added a new theta angle classification loss as well as a total loss to several commonly used loss functions.

The theta angle classification loss function is introduced to transform the theta angle regression problem into a classification problem. Then for the classification task, we add the classification loss function to the method by processing the theta dimensions within the label file for circular smoothing labeling, and then calculate the category loss of theta. The following is the formula for the expected loss of accuracy for the theta angle classification in the average case:

$$\text{E( loss )} = \int_a^b x * \frac{1}{b-a} dx = \int_0^{\frac{\omega}{2}} x * \frac{1}{\frac{\omega}{2} - 0} dx = \frac{\omega}{4} \tag{2}$$

The bounding box border regression loss (lbox) adopts the CIOU [15] method, which is originally suitable for calculating IOU for horizontal borders and is not applicable to calculation of IOU for rotated borders. However, because the CSL method converts the angle prediction from a regression problem to a classification problem, which is equivalent to decoupling the theta information in each image label from the border information, means that the loss function calculation of the rotation box is divided into two parts, the loss of the horizontal box and the angle loss of the rotated box, respectively. Therefore, we can still use the CIOU method to calculate the loss part of the bounding box regression. The following is the calculation formula of the CIOU method:

$$\mathcal{L}_{CIoU} = 1 - IoU + \frac{\rho^2 \left( b, b^{gt} \right)}{c^2} + \alpha v \tag{3}$$

The category classification loss function is calculated using the commonly used cross entropy loss function CrossEntropyLoss() [16], which combines nn.LogSoftmax() and nn.NLLLoss(). The Softmax operation is performed first, followed by the output after taking the log of the result with the corresponding position in the label to remove the negative sign, and finally the average is calculated. The following is the calculation formula of the CrossEntropyLoss() function:

$$\text{loss}(x, \text{ class }) = -x[\text{ class }] + \log \left( \sum_j \exp(x[j]) \right) \tag{4}$$

The lobj confidence loss uses the FocalLoss() function to control the weights of positive and negative samples. In our method, the weight coefficients of the confidence loss function are not chosen between the sizes of the edges of IOU, CIOU, DIOU [17], and GIOU [18], but the rotated IOU between the prediction frame and Ground Truth is used as the weight coefficient of the confidence loss function. Because the angular deviation of the rotating frame has a great impact on the rotating frame IOU, it is likely to have an impact on the final detection accuracy if the first approach is chosen. After the experiment, it is found that the error detection rate of the second scheme is lower than that of the first scheme, and both schemes have a certain leakage rate for small object detection. The following is the calculation formula of the FocalLoss() function:

$$\text{FL}(p_t) = -\alpha_t (1 - p_t)^\gamma \log(p_t) \tag{5}$$

Finally, the total loss function is the weighted sum of all the above loss functions. The size of the weight of each loss function in the total loss function is determined by the gradient change of the total loss function. The model training is complete when the total loss function converges to a stable minimal value. The following is the formula for the loss() function:

$$\text{Loss}(\lambda) = \lambda_1 * \text{lbox} + \lambda_2 * \text{lobj} + \lambda_3 * \text{lcls} + \lambda_4 * \text{langle} \tag{6}$$

After the calculation of the loss function is completed, the result will be back-propagated to solve the gradient and update the model parameters, and finally the saved model will be evaluated.

## 4  Experiment

### 4.1  Experimental Settings and Dataset

The experimental environment is under Linux system as follows: python version 3.8, using version 1.10.2 of the Pytorch framework on the Quadro RTX 5000 graphics server for experiments. In terms of experimental parameters, epoch is 200, initial learning rate is 0.001, the learning rate is adjusted in equal steps using the learning rate adjustment strategy, the default learning rate adjustment multiplier is 0.1, the learning rate is adjusted at 50 and 150steps, respectively, and the weight decay is set to 4e-5. We train on two GPU graphics cards with four images in each batch. The parameter settings in CSL are the same as in the original paper, and experiments are mainly performed on the dataset DOTA1.5 [19] to verify the feasibility of our method.

**Table 1.** Comparison of different backbones.

| Method | DOTA1.5 | | | | | |
|--------|---------|--------|--------|---------|--------|--------|
|        | Backbone | mAP | Params | Weights | FPS | FLOPs |
| CSL | Yolov5s | **61.97** | 7.77 M | 42.7 M | 21 fps | 18.5 G |
|     | ResNet50 | 58.55 | 30.6 M | 145 M | 24 fps | 8.2 G |
| SFC | ShuffleNetV2 | 51.39 | **3.13 M** | **6.34 M** | **28 fps** | **3.8 G** |

**Table 2.** Comparison of different rotating object detection methods.

| Method | DOTA1.5 | | | | | |
|--------|---------|--------|--------|---------|--------|--------|
|        | Backbone | mAP | Params | Weights | Speed | FLOPs |
| IoU-Smooth L1 [20] | ResNet50 | 59.15 | 25.98 M | 125 M | 15.6 fps | 7.6 G |
| RIDet [21] | ResNet50 | 58.91 | 25.38 M | 133 M | 15.3 fps | 6.9 G |
| RSDet [22] | ResNet50 | 61.42 | 26.06 M | 126 M | 13.4 fps | 7.3 G |
| RSDet++ [23] | ResNet50 | 62.18 | 26.83 M | 123 M | 19.3 fps | 7.1 G |
| GWD [8] | ResNet50 | **63.22** | 27.95 M | 130 M | 17.5 fps | 6.0 G |
| BCD | ResNet50 | 60.78 | 26.67 M | 122 M | 17.0 fps | 6.3 G |
| DCL [24] | ResNet50 | 59.38 | 31.8 M | 157 M | 23.0 fps | 9.3 G |
| CSL [6] | ResNet50 | 58.55 | 30.6 M | 145 M | 24.0 fps | 8.2 G |
| **SFC** | **ShuffleNetV2** | 51.39 | **3.13 M** | **6.34 M** | **28.0 fps** | **3.8 G** |

The experiments are carried on DOTA1.5 dataset, which includes 16 categories of images, totaling 2806 aerial images ranging from 800*800 to 4000*4000, with complete annotations. For the whole dataset, we use 60% as the training set, 20% as the validation set, and 20% as the test set. Due to the high resolution of remote sensing images, the dataset should be firstly cut and processed to reduce the resolution of the images before loading, then the cut images are predicted several times, and finally the prediction results are stitched together In our experiments, the cutting parameter gap is set to 50%, and if the resolution of the original image is smaller than the set subsize size, the original image will be filled directly. After we have finished the detection of the cut data set, the results should be merged to restore the position of the object in the original image. Above for image cutting and merging we directly use the existing toolkit DOTAdevkit.

The identification method of the labeled files in the experiments is the long-edge representation of the following form: classid, x, y, longside, shortside, theta. Where x and y are the center coordinates, theta is between $-90$ and $90°$, excluding $90°$. Since the purpose of proposed SFC is to improve the inference speed as well as reduce the number of parameters as much as possible while minimizing the loss of accuracy, in order to make the proposed method in this paper have a better detection effect, the data enhancement is to be performed on the finished cut data set, and the data enhancement is mainly done by random splicing using the Mosaic method to enhance the robustness of the model. The data are processed and input to the network for training.

## 4.2   Comparative Experiment

Since the aerial image dataset contains a large number of small targets and cluttered rotating objects, we use 20% of the DOTA1.5 dataset as the main test set. Our proposed method focuses on comparing the number of parameters, weight size, number of images processed per second, and computation volume in the model. For the comparison experiments, the same environment and parameters of CSL method and the 180° definition method was used. Table 1 shows the comparison of the metrics of different Backbone in the case of the same Circular Smooth Label method with rotating object detection head. Table 2 is an experimental table comparing our SFC method with other rotating object detection methods.

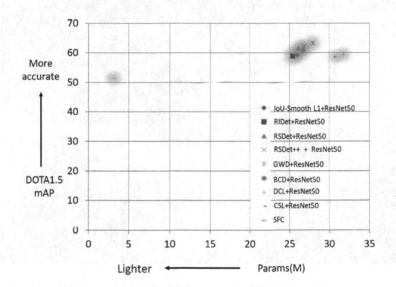

**Fig. 5.** Comparison chart of Params and mAP star point of each method.

After comparing the above two tables and the star point diagram, we found that the number of parameters and the weight size of our method (SFC) are reduced by nearly 90% compared with other methods, and the inference speed of remote sensing images is improved by 40%, and the accuracy rate is at least 81% of the original one. The reason for the decrease in accuracy may be that the backbone network loses part of the information when extracting features from remote sensing images, plus the fact that the lightweight network is already very difficult for small object detection, so it leads to the decrease in accuracy. As shown in Fig. 5, the star point comparison of all the methods in the above table shows that the number of parameters of our proposed SFC method is reduced by at least 22M compared with other methods, and the decrease in accuracy is within an acceptable range.

**Fig. 6.** Some examples of the detection results in DOTA1.5, with the detected categories and confidence levels marked on the detection box.

## 5   Conclusion

In this paper, we enable a lightweight network (SFC) to do the rotating object detection, and the advantages as well as drawbacks of the lightweight network for remote sensing image detection are verified through comparative experiments on a large remote sensing dataset DOTA1.5. We use ShuffleNetV2 as the backbone network, FPN structure for fusion of features, circular label smoothing (CSL) method for target angle detection. By introducing several different loss functions, this structure allows for lightweight compression with the least possible accuracy decreasing. Experiments on DOTA1.5 dataset yielded nearly 90% reduction in the number of parameters, weight and about 40% improvement in inference speed, thus demonstrating the effectiveness of the proposed SFC method.

# References

1. Bochkovskiy, A., Wang, C.-Y., Liao, H.-Y.M.: Yolov4: Optimal speed and accuracy of object detection. arXiv preprint arXiv:2004.10934 (2020)
2. Lin, T.-Y., Goyal, P., Girshick, R., He, K., Doll, P.: Focal loss for dense object detection. In: Proceedings of the IEEE International Conference on Computer Vision, pp. 2980-2988 (2017)
3. Iandola, F.N., et al.: Squeezenet: Alexnet-level accuracy with 50x fewer parameters andː 0.5 mb model size. arXiv preprint arXiv:1602.07360 (2016)
4. Howard, A.G., et al.: Mobilenets: Efficient convolutional neural networks for mobile vision applications. arXiv preprint arXiv:1704.04861 (2017)
5. Ma, N., Zhang, X., Zheng, H.-T., Sun, J.: ShuffleNet V2: practical guidelines for efficient CNN architecture design. In: Ferrari, V., Hebert, M., Sminchisescu, C., Weiss, Y. (eds.) Computer Vision – ECCV 2018. LNCS, vol. 11218, pp. 122–138. Springer, Cham (2018). https://doi.org/10.1007/978-3-030-01264-9_8
6. Yang, X., Yan, J.: Arbitrary-oriented object detection with circular smooth label. In: Vedaldi, A., Bischof, H., Brox, T., Frahm, J.-M. (eds.) ECCV 2020. LNCS, vol. 12353, pp. 677–694. Springer, Cham (2020). https://doi.org/10.1007/978-3-030-58598-3_40
7. Lin, T.-Y., Dollár, P., Girshick, R., He, K., Hariharan, B., Belongie, S.: Feature pyramid networks for object detection. In: Proceedings of the IEEE Conference on Computer Vision and Pattern Recognition (CVPR), pp. 2117–2125 (2017)
8. Yang, X., Yan, J., Ming, Q., Wang, W., Zhang, X., Tian, Q.: Rethinking rotated object detection with gaussian wasserstein distance loss. In: International Conference on Machine Learning (ICML), pp. 11830–11841. PMLR (2021)
9. Ding, J., Xue, N., Long, Y., Xia, G-.S., Lu, O.: Learning roi transformer for oriented object detection in aerial images. In: Proceedings of the IEEE/CVF Conference on Computer Vision and Pattern Recognition (CVPR), pp. 2849–2858 (2019)
10. Zhang, G., Shijian, L., Zhang, W.: Cad-net: a context-aware detection network for objects in remote sensing imagery. IEEE Trans. Geosci. Remote Sens. **57**(12), 10015–10024 (2019)
11. Yang, X., Yan, J., Feng, Z., He, T.: R3det: refined single-stage detector with feature refinement for rotating object. In Proc. AAAI Conf. Artif. Intell. **35**, 3163–3171 (2021)
12. Li, Z., Hou, B., Wu, Z., Jiao, L., Ren, B., Yang, C.: Fcosr: A simple anchor-free rotated detector for aerial object detection. arXiv preprint arXiv:2111.10780 (2021)
13. Zhang, F., Wang, X., Zhou, S., Wang, Y.: DARDet: A dense anchor-free rotated object detector in aerial images. IEEE Geosci. Remote Sensing Lett. **19** 1–5 (2021)
14. Ding, J., Xue, N., Long, Y., Xia, G.-S., Lu, Q.: Learning roi transformer for detecting oriented objects in aerial images. In: The IEEE Conference on Computer Vision and Pattern Recognition (CVPR) (2019)

15. Redmon, J., Farhadi, A.: Yolov3: An incremental improvement. arXiv preprint arXiv:1804.02767 (2018)
16. Zhang, Z., Sabuncu, M.: Generalized cross entropy loss for training deep neural networks with noisy labels. In: Advances in Neural Information Processing Systems (NeurIPS), vol. 31 (2018)
17. Zheng, Z., Wang, P., Liu, W., Li, J., Ye, R., Ren, D.: Distance-iou loss: faster and better learning for bounding box regression. In Proc. AAAI Conf. Artif. Intell. **34**, 12993–13000 (2020)
18. Rezatofighi, h., Tsoi, N., Gwak, J., Sadeghian, A., Reid, I., Savarese, S.: Generalized intersection over union: A metric and a loss for bounding box regression. In: Proceedings of the IEEE/CVF Conference on Computer Vision and Pattern Recognition (CVPR), pp .658–666 (2019)
19. Xia, G.-.S.: Dota: A large-scale dataset for object detection in aerial images. In: The IEEE Conference on Computer Vision and Pattern Recognition (CVPR) (2018)
20. Girshick, R.: Fast R-CNN. In: Proceedings of the IEEE International Conference on Computer Vision, pp. 1440–1448 (2015)
21. Ming, Q., Miao, L., Zhou, Z., Yang, X., Dong, Y.: Optimization for Arbitrary-Oriented Object Detection via Representation Invariance Loss. In: IEEE Geoscience and Remote Sensing Letters, pp. 1–5 (2021)
22. Qian, W., Yang, X., Peng, S., Yan, J., Guo, Y.: Learning modulated loss for rotated object detection In: Proceedings of the AAAI Conference on Artificial Intelligence, pp. 2458–2466 (2021)
23. Qian, W., Yang, X., Peng, S., Zhang, X., Yan, J.: RSDet++: Point-based modulated loss for more accurate rotated object detection. In: IEEE Transactions on Circuits and Systems for Video Technology (2022)
24. Yang, X., Hou, L., Zhou, Y., Wang, W., Yan, J.: Dense label encoding for boundary discontinuity free rotation detection. In: Proceedings of the IEEE/CVF Conference on Computer Vision and Pattern Recognition, pp. 15819–15829 (2021)

# Corner Detection Based on a Dynamic Measure of Cornerity

Yang Zhang, Baojiang Zhong[(✉)], and Xun Sun

School of Computer Science and Technology, Soochow University, Suzhou, China
bjzhong@suda.edu.cn

**Abstract.** Existing contour-based corner detectors generally identify corners from a contour curve by measuring the cornerity of each point (i.e., the confidence to be a corner) with a *fixed-radius* region of support (RoS), and thus could yield inferior performance due to low adaptivity to local structures of the input curve. To overcome the difficulty, a novel cornerity measure based on a *dynamic* RoS is proposed in this paper, with which an efficient corner detector is developed. For a given point on the curve, the dynamic RoS is constructed with two straight-line arms stretching towards both sides along the curve, under a pre-determined error tolerance imposed on the average perpendicular distance from the curve to each arm within its stretching range. Then, our cornerity model is established based on the lengths of the two arms and the angle between them, which is then exploited to evaluate whether the current point is a corner or not via a cornerity thresholding. Extensive experimental results show that the proposed corner detector can deliver superior performance and exhibit higher robustness over the existing state-of-the-arts.

**Keywords:** Feature extraction · Contour curve · Corner detection · Cornerity · Region of support · Dynamic measure

## 1 Introduction

As an important type of image features that delivers geometrical structure information of images, corners play a key role in solving many image-based tasks, such as 3D scene reconstruction [11], target tracking [5], image registration and understanding [12]. Existing corner detectors can be roughly divided into two categories: intensity-based and contour-based. Intensity-based methods extract corners by identifying significant intensity differences from the input image. Moravec *et al.* [13] defined corners as the points with large variations in all orientations. Xia *et al.* [22] established a junction detector based on the intensity variations of edge pixels (ACJ). Xue *et al.* [23] introduced an anisotropic-scale junction detector (ASJ). DeTone *et al.* [4] developed a point detector based on Self-supervised learning (SuperPoint). Zhang *et al.* [26] used the second-order generalized Gaussian directional derivative to extract corners (SOGGDD). Zhang&Sun [20] proposed a method which uses a multi-directional structure tensor with multiple

S. Khanna et al. (Eds.): PRICAI 2022, LNCS 13631, pp. 631–644, 2022.
https://doi.org/10.1007/978-3-031-20868-3_47

scales to detect corners. Kim *et al.* [10] developed a key-point method where corners are treated as one kind of key points. Wang *et al.* [21] constructed a specific type of filter that can enhance corners and suppress other edge points.

Compared to the intensity-based corner detectors, the contour-based corner detectors could obtain better performance when the image has rich edges. A typical method of this kind firstly extracts edge contours from the input image and then conducts an analysis of the contour shapes to identify corner points. Rattarangsi *et al.* [17] proposed a corner detector based on the curvature scale space (CSS) representation of contour shapes. Zhang *et al.* [28] developed a curvature measure, called the multi-scale curvature product (MSCP), to conduct corner detection. Zhong *et al.* [31] proposed the direct curvature scale space (DCSS) representation of planar curves and then developed a DCSS-based corner detector. He *et al.* [8,9] introduced a corner detector based on global and local curvatures. Awrangjeb *et al.* [1] proposed the chord-to-point distance accumulation (CPDA) for performing corner detection. Zhang *et al.* [30] proposed a corner detector based on evolution difference of scale pace. Zhang *et al.* [29] used the gradient correlation matrix to obtain corners. Teng *et al.* [19] introduced a corner detector using triangular theory and distance calculation (CTAR). Shui *et al.* [18] constructed a corner detector that uses anisotropic directional derivative representations (ANDD). Zhang *et al.* [25] proposed the weighted eigenvector-based angle estimator (WEAE) for corner detection. Zhang *et al.* [27] used discrete curvature representations of single and double corner models to detect corners (New-Curvature). Zhang *et al.* [24] developed a corner detector based on the multi-scale $k$-cosine angle (MSRJ).

To detect corners from an input curve, a key operation is to measure the *cornerity* (i.e., the confidence to be a corner) of each point on the curve. In the literature, this operation has been often referred to as the measure of discrete curvature. However, in mathematics 'curvature' is defined on an infinitesimal interval, while the identification of a corner point needs to be performed with a region of support (RoS) where local curve structures are taken into account. Therefore, in this paper the term 'cornerity' instead of 'curvature' is adopted. For the existing contour-based corner detectors, the cornerity is generally measured with a *fixed-radius* RoS that exhibits low adaptivity to local structures of the contour curve. In this paper, a novel cornerity measure exploiting a *dynamic* RoS is proposed. Compared to a fixed-radius RoS, our dynamic RoS can show significantly higher adaptivity to local contour structures. In consequence, the cornerity of each point can be measured with higher accuracy. By exploiting the new cornerity measure, an efficient corner detector is further developed. Extensive experiments will be conducted to show that our developed corner detector can clearly outperform the existing state-of-the-arts.

The remainder of this paper is organized as follows. In Sect. 2, our cornerity measure based on a dynamic ROS is proposed and investigated. In Sect. 3, the new corner detector is developed and discussed. In Sect. 4, experimental results are provided to verify the effectiveness of our developed corner detector. Finally, conclusions are drawn in Sect. 5.

## 2    The Proposed Cornerity Measure

In this section, a dynamic region of support (RoS) for corner identification is developed first, and then a novel cornerity measure based on this dynamic RoS is established.

### 2.1    Dynamic Region of Support

A contour curve extracted from the input image can be denoted as an ordered set of points:

$$\mathcal{C} = \{p_1, p_2, p_3, ..., p_N\},\tag{1}$$

where $p_i$ is the $i$'th point with coordinate $(x_i, y_i)$, and $N$ is the total number of points on the curve. For evaluating the confidence of $p_i$ to be a corner, a RoS is needed to take local contour structures into account. For existing contour-based corner detectors, the RoS generally has a fixed radius (in terms of the number of pixels) in the form that

$$\Omega(p_i) = \{p_{i-L}, ..., p_{i-1}, p_i, p_{i+1}, ..., p_{i+L}\}.\tag{2}$$

However, the selection of a proper radius of the RoS, i.e., the value of $L$ in (2), is rather challenging. A too large $L$ could incur many false negatives (i.e., miss-detections of true corners), while a too small $L$ might cause lots of false positives (i.e., incorrect detections). Furthermore, the fixed-radius RoS exhibits low adaptivity to local structures along the input curve. As a result, inferior corner detection performance could be yielded.

To address the above-mentioned problems, a dynamic RoS is proposed in this paper for measuring cornerity. Figure 1 depicts how the dynamic RoS is constructed at the point $p_i$. Subject to a pre-determined error tolerance $\tau_D$, two straight-line arms of $p_i$ stretch toward its both sides along the curve, denoted as $p_i p_{i-b}$ and $p_i p_{i+f}$, respectively. The stretching process of the forward arm $p_i p_{i+f}$ is described as follows. First, the initial value of $f$ is taken as 1. Then, the value of $f$ is increased in steps of 1 iteratively, and the average perpendicular distance from the points $\{p_{i+1}, p_{i+2}, \cdots, p_{i+f-1}\}$ to the arm $p_i p_{i+f}$ is calculated. Denote the perpendicular distance from the point $p_j$ to the arm $p_i p_{i+f}$ as $d_{i,j}^{(f)}$, for $j = i+1, i+2, \cdots, i+f-1$, respectively. The average perpendicular distance, denoted as $D_i^{(f)}$, is computed by:

$$D_i^{(f)} = \frac{\sum_{j=i+1}^{i+f-1} d_{i,j}^{(f)}}{f - 2}.\tag{3}$$

The stretching process continues if $D_i^{(f)} \leq \tau_D$, and finally we can get the longest possible forward arm $p_i p_{i+f}$ subject to this error tolerance $\tau_D$. In the same way, the longest possible backward arm $p_i p_{i-b}$ can also be obtained. As a result, the dynamic RoS of $p_i$ is constructed as follows:

$$\Omega(p_i) = \{p_{i-b}, ..., p_{i-1}, p_i, p_{i+1}, ..., p_{i+f}\}.\tag{4}$$

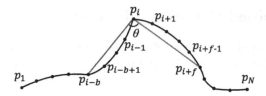

**Fig. 1.** The dynamic region of support proposed in this paper for corner identification.

Compared with the fixed-radius RoS as shown in (2) that has been used in previous studies (e.g., [1,17,19,24,31]), our dynamic RoS can exhibit much higher adaptivity to local structures of the input curve. On the other hand, it should be noted that in the literature there are some works related to an 'adaptive' or 'dynamic' RoS. For example, Guru et al. [7] developed an adaptive RoS based on the covariance matrix of a sequence of connected points; however, it is observed that their established RoS often has a small size and thus shows poor robustness to noise. Nasser et al. [16] used the *maximal blurred segment* to obtain a RoS that can adapt to the input curve; however, their RoS is used to produce a polygonal approximation of the curve and thus needs one arm along a single direction (clockwise or anti-clockwise) *only*. He and Yung [8] established a dynamic RoS, however, for round corner removal (a post-processing of corner detection) rather than corner identification.

## 2.2    Cornerity Measure Based on the Dynamic Region of Support

A pioneering work in corner detection [6] pointed out that the 'cornerity' of a point is proportional to the lengths of the discontinuity-free regions to either side as well as the severity of the discontinuity at this point. Following this insightful concept, a novel cornerity measure is defined in the present paper for conducting corner detection. For that, the dynamic RoS constructed in Sect. 2.1 is exploited to explore the 'discontinuity-free regions' to either side of the current point $p_i$. Moreover, let $\theta$ be the angle between the two arms of $p_i$, which measures the 'severity of the discontinuity' at this point, computed by

$$\theta = \arccos \frac{p_i p_{i-b} \cdot p_i p_{i+f}}{|p_i p_{i-b}| \, |p_i p_{i+f}|}. \tag{5}$$

Our cornerity measure is then defined on the determined RoS as follows:

$$c_i = \sqrt{\tanh(\mu \, |p_i p_{i+f}|) \cdot \tanh(\mu \, |p_i p_{i-b}|)} \cdot |\cos(\theta/2)|, \tag{6}$$

where $\mu$ is a constant parameter, and $\tanh(x)$ is the hyperbolic tangent function in the form that

$$\tanh(x) = \frac{\sinh(x)}{\cosh(x)} = \frac{\exp(x) - \exp(-x)}{\exp(x) + \exp(-x)}. \tag{7}$$

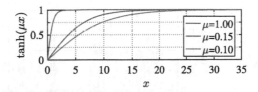

**Fig. 2.** An investigation of the normalization function $\tanh(\mu x)$ used in our cornerity measure model (6).

In our model (6), the function $\tanh(\mu x)$ is used to perform a normalization on the cornerity with respect to the arm lengths $|p_i p_{i+f}|$ and $|p_i p_{i-b}|$. To be specific, $\tanh(\mu x) \in [0, 1)$ for $x \in [0, \infty)$, as shown in Fig. 2. In consequence, extremely long arms will not lead to a very large cornerity. Accordingly, a merit of using this normalization function is that those corners with normal-length arms will be suppressed. As for the parameter $\mu$, it is easily seen from Fig. 2 that if $\mu = 1$, then short arms (say, with lengths of 3 pixels) can produce about the same cornerity as long arms *improperly*. Therefore, a less value of $\mu$ should be used to increase the efficiency of corner identification. In this work, the default value of this parameter is taken as $\mu = 0.1$.

It is worth pointing out that in our cornerity model (6), the radius of RoS is measured with Euclidean distance (i.e., the lengths of the forward and backward arms), while in most existing models (e.g., [6,9,17]) it is measured with the number of pixels. In consequence, our cornerity measure is more robust than the existing ones. For example, image rotation or noise could significantly change the number of pixels within a given local region, but cannot produce much impact on the Euclidean distance between the two endpoints of the region.

## 2.3 More Discussions

In the literature, no strict definition of a 'corner' has been established. In general, corners are identified as those points that have high 'curvatures'. As mentioned previously in Sect. 1, the term 'cornerity' is used instead in this paper for a more reasonable expression of the underlying idea of corner detection. In our developed model (6), the lengths of the two dynamic arms stretching from the current point and the angle between the two arms are integrated together to measure the confidence of this point to be a true corner. For demonstration, Fig. 3 depicts the measured cornerity of a test curve.

Intuitively, if the dynamic arms (i.e., $p_i p_{i+f}$ and $p_i p_{i-b}$) have long lengths, the point $p_i$ is more likely a corner and thus should have a high cornerity. For the angle between the two arms (i.e., $\theta$), if it has a small value in the interval $(0, \pi]$ or a large value in the interval $(\pi, 2\pi]$, then the point should have a high cornerity. These cues have been properly incorporated into our cornerity measure (6) by using two functions, i.e., $\tanh(\mu x)$ and $\cos(\theta/2)$. In particular, the measured cornerity $c_i \in [0, 1)$, which approaches 1 if the two arms both have very long

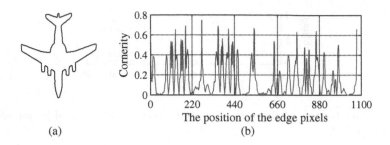

**Fig. 3.** A demonstration of the proposed cornerity measure: (a) the input curve; and (b) the measured cornerity.

lengths and the angle $\theta$ approaches 0. In general, the larger the $c_i$, the higher the confidence to take $p_i$ as a true corner.

## 3   The Developed Corner Detector

### 3.1   Algorithm

With our dynamic measure of cornerity proposed in the previous section, an efficient corner detector is developed, outlined as follows:

**Step 1.** *Edge extraction.* Produce an edge map of the input image by using the Canny method. The vector that specifies sensitivity thresholds for the Canny is taken as $[0, 0.35]$.

**Step 2.** *Contour curve tracing.* Trace each contour curve from the edge map, and represent it with a set of connected points, referring to Eq. (1).

**Step 3.** *Contour curve smoothing.* To remove quantization errors and trivial details, perform a smoothing of each contour curve by using the Gaussian filter with standard deviation $\sigma = 3$.

**Step 4.** *Dynamic RoS determination.* Determine the dynamic RoS for each point on the current curve with a pre-determined error tolerance $\tau_D$, referring to Eq. (4).

**Step 5.** *Cornerity measuring.* Measure the cornerity of the current point, referring to Eq. (6).

**Step 6.** *Local non-maximum suppression.* Perform a local non-maximum suppression with respect to the measured cornerity. The remaining points, i.e., local cornerity maximum points, are taken as corner candidates.

**Step 7.** *Cornerity thresholding.* With a predetermined cornerity threshold $t_c$, perform a cornerity thresholding on the corner candidates. That is, a corner candidate with its cornerity less than $t_c$ will be discarded as a false positive.

### 3.2   Parameter Setting

Our developed corner detector has three key parameters: the error tolerance $\tau_D$ used to determine the dynamic RoS (referring to Sect. 2.1); the parameter $\mu$

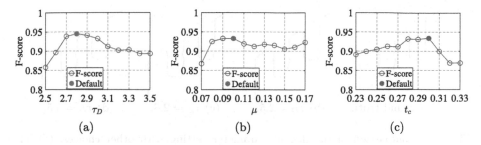

**Fig. 4.** Parameter tuning of (a) the error tolerance $\tau_D$ used to determine the dynamic RoS; (b) the parameter $\mu$ used in our cornerity model; and (c) the threshold $t_c$ used to perform cornerity thresholding.

used in the cornerity model (6); and the threshold $t_c$ used to perform cornerity thresholding (referring to Sect. 3.1). These parameters are first tuned on a set of test images (composed of 10 binary images and referred to as Dataset-1 in our experimental section), and then applied to all input images for evaluating our proposed approach.

Figure 4 depicts the results of parameter tuning, where the F-score averaged over the set of test images is plotted versus each of the three parameters. The default value of each parameter is then taken as the one where our corner detector can deliver its best performance in terms of F-score. To be specific, $\tau_D = 2.8$, $\mu = 0.1$, and $t_c = 0.3$, respectively. To show how this default parameter setting compares to other choices, Fig. 5 presents an illustrative example with respect to the parameter $\tau_D$. If a smaller $\tau_D$ is used (e.g., $\tau_D = 2.5$ as shown in Fig. 5 (b)), some false negatives (i.e., miss-detections) are yielded. On the other hand, if a lager $\tau_D$ is imposed (e.g., $\tau_D = 3.5$ as shown in Fig. 5 (d)), a few false positives (i.e., incorrect detections), as well as several false negatives, are produced. In comparison, the default setting of this parameter can generate the best result objectively and subjectively, as shown in Fig. 5 (c).

# 4    Experimental Results

## 4.1    Experimental Setup

Three image datasets are constructed and exploited to evaluate our proposed corner detector. The first and second datasets consist of 10 binary and 8 grayscale images, respectively; which have been commonly used in previous studies (e.g., [3,14,15,22]) to evaluate corner detection performance. The third dataset contains 21 color images that we collected from several image sets of city buildings. Note that *no* ground truths of actual corners from these datasets have been provided in the literature. For that, 'true' corners are manually labelled by us with great care (which will be released for public access online), as shown in Fig. 6. For convenience, these three datasets are referred to as 'Dataset-1', 'Dataset-2' and 'Dataset-3', respectively.

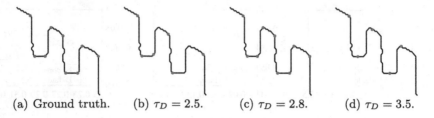

(a) Ground truth.     (b) $\tau_D = 2.5$.     (c) $\tau_D = 2.8$.     (d) $\tau_D = 3.5$.

**Fig. 5.** A comparison of the default parameter setting with other choices. (a) The ground-truth corner points on a test curve, and detection results with (b) a smaller $\tau_D$; (c) the default $\tau_D$; and (d) a larger $\tau_D$, respectively.

Furthermore, to evaluate the robustness of our corner detector under various circumstances, each test image is degraded by five types of image-quality attacks individually as follows. As a result, 39 original test images and $16,497$ degraded images will be used in our evaluation.

**Noise.** Zero-mean Gaussian white noise was added to each image. The variance of the Gaussian is chosen in $[0.005, 0.05]$ at $0.005$ apart.

**Rotation.** Each image was rotated with different angles in $[-90°, 90°]$ at $10°$ apart (excluding $0°$, as it corresponds to the original image).

**Scaling.** Each image was scaled (uniformly and non-uniformly) with the scaling factors $s_x$ and $s_y$ chosen in $[0.5, 2]$ at $0.1$ apart, independently and respectively (excluding the case $s_x = s_y = 1$).

**Combined transformation.** Combined transformations (by rotation and scaling) were applied to each image with rotation angles sampled in $[-30°, 30°]$ at $10°$ apart excluding $0°$, and scaling factors $\{s_x, s_y\}$ sampled in $[0.8, 1.2]$ at $0.1$ apart excluding $s_x = s_y$, independently and respectively.

**Lossy compression.** Each image was compressed by using JPEG lossy compression with the quality factor sampled in $[5, 100]$ at $5$ apart.

Fourteen existing state-of-the-art corner detectors are compared, including: MSCP [28], CPDA [1], He&Yung [9], Fast-CPDA [2], DOG [30], GCM [29], ANDD [18], WEAE [25], SuperPoint [4], ASJ [23], New-Curvature [27], SOG-GDD [26], MSRJ [24] and Zhang&Sun [20]. For most of these methods, the original codes with default parameters released by their respective authors are used. The MSCP [28] and MSRJ [24] have no publicly available resources online. Thus, we coded these two methods and included them for comparison with their default parameter settings suggested in the respective references.

### 4.2 Objective Evaluation

In our objective evaluation, four frequently-used metrics are adopted, including the *precision, recall, APR* (i.e., the arithmetic mean of precision and recall), and *F-score*. First, objective evaluation is performed on the three datasets with original test images, and the results are documented in Table 1. It is seen that

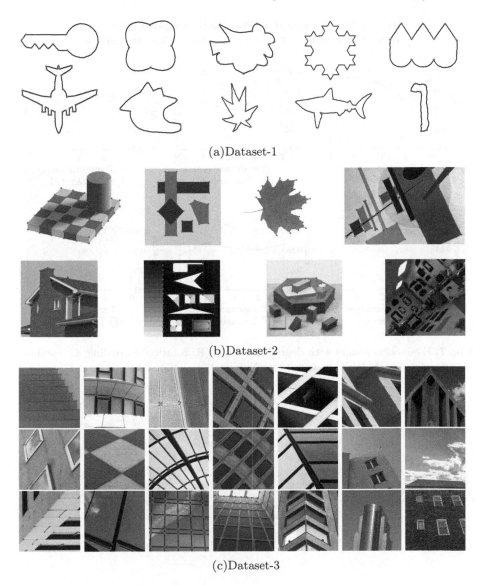

(a)Dataset-1

(b)Dataset-2

(c)Dataset-3

**Fig. 6.** Image datasets constructed and used to conduct our evaluation, where the ground-truth corners are manually labelled by us and marked with dots.

our proposed corner detector generates competitive performance with respect to the precision and recall metrics. In particular, it delivers the best precision on Dataset-1 and Dataset-3. Actually, there exists a trade-off between the precision and the recall for each corner detector. For example, although the SOGGDD [26] can generate a higher recall, it yields a much lower precision than that of ours. In

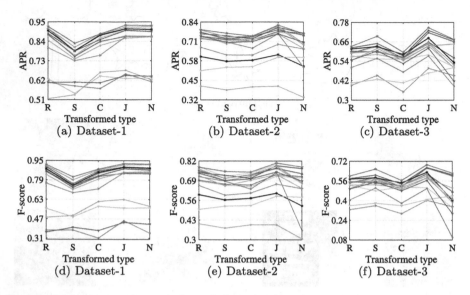

Fig. 7. Evaluation results with degraded images (R: rotation; S: scaling; C: combined transformations; J: JPEG compression; N: noise).

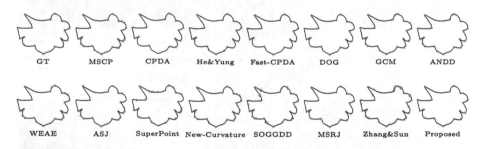

Fig. 8. Subjective evaluation results on a binary image.

comparison, our developed corner detector produces the best performance with respect to both the APR and F-score on every dataset.

Then, the robustness of each corner detector is evaluated by using the three datasets with degraded test images. The evaluation results are presented in Fig. 7, where the APRs and F-scores of the compared methods have been plotted versus attack types on each used dataset, respectively. One can see that our developed corner detector consistently delivers superior performance over the existing methods in most comparison cases.

**Table 1.** Evaluation results in terms of Precision/Recall (1st entry) and APR/F-score (2nd entry). The highest average with respect to each used metric achieved on each image dataset is highlighted in boldface.

| Detector | Dataset-1 [15, 22] | Dataset-2 [3, 14, 15] | Dataset-3 (Newly developed) |
|---|---|---|---|
| MSCP [28] | 0.8224/0.9517 | 0.8271/0.7450 | 0.7256/0.5918 |
|  | 0.8870/0.8661 | 0.7860/0.7692 | 0.6587/0.6098 |
| CPDA [1] | 0.9368/0.8198 | 0.9355/0.6028 | 0.8154/0.6143 |
|  | 0.8783/0.8595 | 0.7691/0.7203 | 0.7186/0.7008 |
| He&Yung [9] | 0.9132/0.9170 | 0.8165/**0.8302** | 0.4408/**0.7392** |
|  | 0.9151/0.9104 | 0.8234/0.8132 | 0.5900/0.5173 |
| Fast-CPDA [2] | 0.9350/0.8006 | 0.9403/0.6095 | 0.8198/0.6183 |
|  | 0.8678/0.8440 | 0.7749/0.7292 | 0.7187/0.7042 |
| DOG [30] | 0.8493/0.8687 | 0.8665/0.6462 | 0.7356/0.5809 |
|  | 0.8590/0.8557 | 0.7563/0.7279 | 0.6583/0.6033 |
| GCM [29] | 0.8744/0.9472 | 0.8405/0.7246 | 0.7115/0.6091 |
|  | 0.9108/0.8974 | 0.7825/0.7633 | 0.6603/0.6189 |
| ANDD [18] | 0.8181/0.9436 | 0.6568/0.7304 | 0.3963/0.5927 |
|  | 0.8809/0.8667 | 0.6936/0.6753 | 0.4945/0.4020 |
| WEAE [25] | 0.8703/0.9694 | 0.8566/0.7910 | 0.7234/0.6921 |
|  | 0.9199/0.9049 | 0.8238/0.8114 | 0.7078/0.6516 |
| ASJ [23] | 0.5849/0.7289 | 0.4207/0.8132 | 0.6646/0.6411 |
|  | 0.6569/0.6206 | 0.6169/0.5392 | 0.6528/0.6123 |
| SuperPoint [4] | 0.4622/0.7142 | 0.6526/0.5191 | 0.4808/0.4086 |
|  | 0.5882/0.5282 | 0.5858/0.5704 | 0.4447/0.3945 |
| New-Curvature [27] | 0.8409/0.9694 | 0.8806/0.7451 | 0.8218/0.6614 |
|  | 0.9052/0.8872 | 0.8128/0.7987 | 0.7416/0.6784 |
| SOGGDD [26] | 0.4267/**0.9895** | 0.8403/0.7416 | 0.5260/0.6305 |
|  | 0.7081/0.5625 | 0.7910/0.7776 | 0.5782/0.5159 |
| MSRJ [24] | 0.9426/0.9006 | **0.9372**/0.7045 | 0.7428/0.6051 |
|  | 0.9216/0.9146 | 0.8208/0.7922 | 0.6740/0.6300 |
| Zhang&Sun [20] | 0.3196/0.9725 | 0.8221/0.7161 | 0.6941/0.5817 |
|  | 0.6461/0.4385 | 0.7691/0.7562 | 0.6379/0.5833 |
| Proposed | **0.9587**/0.9381 | 0.8723/0.7904 | **0.8195**/0.7102 |
|  | **0.9484/0.9447** | **0.8313/0.8176** | **0.7649/0.7119** |

## 4.3  Subjective Evaluation

One binary image and two grayscale images taken from the used datasets are exploited to conduct subjective evaluation, and the results are shown in Figs. 8 and 9, respectively. It is seen that the contour-based corner detectors generally outperform the intensity-based ones (e.g., SOGGDD [26] and Zhang&Sun [20]), especially on the binary image. In comparison, our proposed corner detector

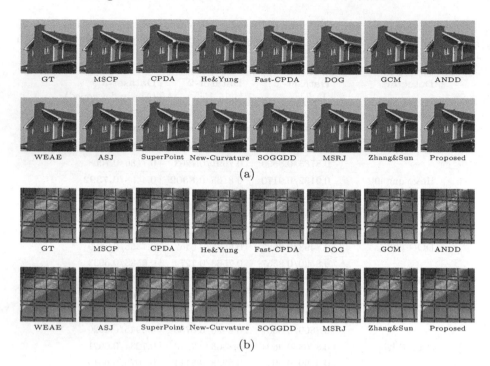

**Fig. 9.** Subjective evaluation results on grayscale images.

achieves the best performance as it produces the least numbers of false positives and false negatives.

## 5    Conclusions

A novel cornerity measure is proposed by using our established dynamic region of support (RoS). Compared to existing measures using *fixed-radius* RoSs, our proposed model shows higher adaptivity to local structures of the input curve, and thus can be used to evaluate the confidence of the current point being a corner with higher accuracy. An efficient contour-based corner detector is then developed with the new cornerity measure. Extensive experimental results show that our corner detector can deliver superior performance and exhibit higher robustness over the existing state-of-the-arts.

**Acknowledgements.** This work was supported in part by the Natural Science Foundation of the Jiangsu Higher Education Institutions of China under Grant 21KJA520007, in part by the National Natural Science Foundation of China under Grant 61572341, in part by the Priority Academic Program Development of Jiangsu Higher Education Institutions, in part by Collaborative Innovation Center of Novel Software Technology and Industrialization.

# References

1. Awrangjeb, M., Lu, G.: Robust image corner detection based on the chord-to-point distance accumulation technique. IEEE Trans. Multimed. **10**(6), 1059–1072 (2008)
2. Awrangjeb, M., Lu, G., Fraser, C.S., Ravanbakhsh, M.: A fast corner detector based on the chord-to-point distance accumulation technique. In: Digital Image Computing: Techniques and Applications, pp. 519–525. IEEE (2009)
3. Beus, H.L., Tiu, S.S.: An improved corner detection algorithm based on chain-coded plane curves. Pattern Recogn. **20**(3), 291–296 (1987)
4. DeTone, D., Malisiewicz, T., Rabinovich, A.: SuperPoint: self-supervised interest point detection and description. In: IEEE Conference on Computer Vision and Pattern Recognition, pp. 224–236 (2018)
5. Elliott, J., Khandare, S., Butt, A.A., Smallcomb, M., Vidt, M.E., Simon, J.C.: Automated tissue strain calculations using Harris corner detection. Ann. Biomed. Eng. **50**(5), 564–574 (2022)
6. Freeman, H., Davis, L.S.: A corner-finding algorithm for chain-coded curves. IEEE Trans. Comput. **26**(03), 297–303 (1977)
7. Guru, D., Dinesh, R.: Non-parametric adaptive region of support useful for corner detection: a novel approach. Pattern Recogn. **37**(1), 165–168 (2004)
8. He, X.C., Yung, N.H.: Curvature scale space corner detector with adaptive threshold and dynamic region of support. In: IEEE Conference on Pattern Recognition, vol. 2, pp. 791–794 (2004)
9. He, X., Yung, N.H.C.: Corner detector based on global and local curvature properties. Opt. Eng. **47**(5), 057008 (2008)
10. Kim, S., Jeong, M., Ko, B.C.: Self-supervised keypoint detection based on multi-layer random forest regressor. IEEE Access **9**, 40850–40859 (2021)
11. Luo, Z., et al.: ASLFeat: learning local features of accurate shape and localization. In: Proceedings of the IEEE/CVF Conference on Computer Vision and Pattern Recognition, pp. 6589–6598 (2020)
12. Ma, J., Jiang, J., Zhou, H., Zhao, J., Guo, X.: Guided locality preserving feature matching for remote sensing image registration. IEEE Trans. Geosci. Remote Sens. **56**(8), 4435–4447 (2018)
13. McAndrew, A.: A Computational Introduction to Digital Image Processing, vol. 2. CRC Press, Boca Raton (2016)
14. Medioni, G., Yasumoto, Y.: Corner detection and curve representation using cubic b-splines. Comput. Vis. Graph. Image Process. **39**(3), 267–278 (1987)
15. Mokhtarian, F., Suomela, R.: Robust image corner detection through curvature scale space. IEEE Trans. Pattern Anal. Mach. Intell. **20**(12), 1376–1381 (1998). Dec
16. Nasser, H., Ngo, P., Debled-Rennesson, I.: Dominant point detection based on discrete curve structure and applications. J. Comput. Syst. Sci. **95**, 177–192 (2018)
17. Rattarangsi, A., Chin, R.T.: Scale-based detection of corners of planar curves. In: IEEE International Conference on Pattern Recognition, vol. 1, pp. 923–930 (1990)
18. Shui, P.L., Zhang, W.C.: Corner detection and classification using anisotropic directional derivative representations. IEEE Trans. Image Process. **22**(8), 3204–3218 (2013)
19. Teng, S.W., Sadat, R.M.N., Lu, G.: Effective and efficient contour-based corner detectors. Pattern Recogn. **48**(7), 2185–2197 (2015)
20. Zhang, W., Sun, C.: Corner detection using multi-directional structure tensor with multiple scales. Int. J. Comput. Vis. **128**(2), 438–459 (2020)

21. Wang, M., Sun, C., Sowmya, A.: Efficient corner detection based on corner enhancement filters. Digit. Signal Process. **122**, 103364 (2022)
22. Xia, G.S., Delon, J., Gousseau, Y.: Accurate junction detection and characterization in natural images. Int. J. Comput. Vis. **106**(1), 31–56 (2014)
23. Xue, N., Xia, G.S., Bai, X., Zhang, L., Shen, W.: Anisotropic-scale junction detection and matching for indoor images. IEEE Trans. Image Process. **27**(1), 78–91 (2017)
24. Zhang, S., Li, B., Zhang, Z., Ma, J., Li, P., Wang, H.: Robust corner finding based on multi-scale k-cosine angle detection. IEEE Access **8**, 66741–66748 (2020)
25. Zhang, S., Yang, D., Huang, S., Zhang, X., Tu, L., Ren, Z.: Robust corner detection using the eigenvector-based angle estimator. J. Vis. Commun. Image Represent. **45**, 181–193 (2017)
26. Zhang, W., Sun, C.: Corner detection using second-order generalized gaussian directional derivative representations. IEEE Trans. Pattern Anal. Mach. Intell. **43**(4), 1213–1224 (2019)
27. Zhang, W., Sun, C., Breckon, T., Alshammari, N.: Discrete curvature representations for noise robust image corner detection. IEEE Trans. Image Process. **28**(9), 4444–4459 (2019)
28. Zhang, X., Lei, M., Yang, D., Wang, Y., Ma, L.: Multi-scale curvature product for robust image corner detection in curvature scale space. Pattern Recogn. Lett. **28**(5), 545–554 (2007)
29. Zhang, X., Wang, H., Smith, A.W., Ling, X., Lovell, B.C., Yang, D.: Corner detection based on gradient correlation matrices of planar curves. Pattern Recogn. **43**(4), 1207–1223 (2010)
30. Zhang, X., Wang, H., Hong, M., Xu, L., Yang, D., Lovell, B.C.: Robust image corner detection based on scale evolution difference of planar curves. Pattern Recogn. Lett. **30**(4), 449–455 (2009)
31. Zhong, B., Liao, W.: Direct curvature scale space: theory and corner detection. IEEE Trans. Pattern Anal. Mach. Intell. **29**(3), 508–512 (2007)

# Author Index

Printed in the United States
by Baker & Taylor Publisher Services

Printed in the United States
by Baker & Taylor Publisher Services